MULTIDISCIPLINARY ECONOMICS

To Stephen with many thanks for the great effort he shows to come to a fruitful cooperation between the Utrecht School of Economics and Binghamton University.

Binghamton 19 January 2007

Multidisciplinary Economics

The Birth of a New Economics Faculty in the Netherlands

Edited by

PETER DE GIJSEL

Utrecht School of Economics, The Netherlands and
Osnabrück University, Germany

and

HANS SCHENK

Utrecht School of Economics,
The Netherlands

Springer

A C.I.P. Catalogue record for this book is available from the Library of Congress.

ISBN-10 0-387-26258-X (HB)
ISBN-13 978-0-387-26258-1 (HB)
ISBN-10 0-387-26259-8 (e-book)
ISBN-13 978-0-387-26259-8 (e-book)

Published by Springer,
P.O. Box 17, 3300 AA Dordrecht, The Netherlands.

www.springeronline.com

Printed on acid-free paper

Printed in the Netherlands.

PREFACE

On the occasion of the opening of the Utrecht School of Economics (USE) and the Tjalling C. Koopmans Research Institute an inaugural conference, called a 'nullustrum' in Dutch, was organised at Utrecht University on October 21st -23rd, 2003.

Organising a 'nullustrum' is quite unusual in the Netherlands, as it is customary to celebrate the first lustrum only after five years. However, because of the history of multidisciplinary economics at Utrecht University, going back to the 17th century, and the fact that the new economics faculty did not have to be built up from scratch, the celebration of a 'nullustrum' made sense. It allowed the opening of USE and its research institute to be seen as a milestone in the development of multidisciplinary economics at Utrecht University. At the same time the 'nullustrum' created an opportunity to introduce five newly appointed full professors, a unique event in the long history of Utrecht University.

During the research 'nullustrum', six seminars were organised where guest speakers presented papers that were related to subjects in the domain of multidisciplinary economics. These seminars covered issues in the fields of international economics, public economics, organisational economics, finance & financial markets, labour economics and applied econometrics. Five of the six seminars were organised by the newly appointed USE professors, who delivered their inaugural lectures during the 'nullustrum'.

Besides the opening addresses, this volume includes a selection of papers that were presented during the 'nullustrum', or that have been published elsewhere by the guest speakers, and the inaugural addresses delivered by the newly appointed USE professors. The contributions of the guest speakers and the USE staff members convey the research perspectives of USE in a very natural way by focusing on themes that are open to multidisciplinary economics research and that are fostered by eminent scholars from the economics discipline. They also make clear how USE is already embedded in an international network of research activities that forms a solid basis for a new economics faculty to develop as an internationally recognised research institution promoting high standing multidisciplinary economics research with a special focus on the Institutional, Historical and Spatial dimensions (IHS-dimensions) of economic problems.

As editors we have the pleasure of acknowledging the very helpful assistance of Brooke Hansen and Dirk Smits for reading the final manuscript, Mariska van Dort for her help with the references and Janet Sartorius who provided considerable secretarial assistance and editorial support. We particularly admire the way in which Janet managed the tedious production of the manuscript patiently and skilfully and how she handled two editors who constantly struggled with the deadlines during the gestation period. Our thanks go, too, to the editorial staff of the Wiarda Institute for their invaluable help in giving the manuscript its final layout.

The editors

CONTENTS

CONTRIBUTORS

EDITORS

Peter de Gijsel
Professor de Gijsel took his PhD at the university of Dortmund in 1980. He taught economics at the universities of Dortmund, Regensburg and Maastricht and was professor of economics at the University of Osnabrück from 1994 to 1998. From 2000 onwards he was the driving force behind the setting up of the new Faculty of Economics of Utrecht University. He was appointed the first Dean of the faculty in 2004. De Gijsel´s special fields of interest are micro-, labour market and monetary economics.
www.econ.uu.nl

Hans Schenk
After studying economics and business administration at the universities of Nyenrode, Amsterdam, Oregon and Leuven, professor Schenk took his PhD at the university of Nice-Sophia Antipolis in France. He taught economics and business at various universities in the Netherlands (e.g. in Groningen and Rotterdam) and abroad (e.g. in Beijing and Strasbourg), and was professor of Industrial Policy and Corporate Strategy at Tilburg University before coming to Utrecht as professor of Organisational Economics in 2002. A year later, he became director of the Tjalling Koopmans Research Institute. Schenk has advised numerous firms and governments and specialises in mergers and acquisitions and competitiveness policy.
http://go.to/hans.schenk

AUTHORS

Marius Brülhart
Before taking his PhD at the University of Dublin in 1996, professor Brülhart worked as an economist for the Union Bank of Switzerland (1991–1992). He taught economics at the Universities of Dublin (1995-1997), Manchester (1998-1999), and Lausanne (1999-2002). At present he is professor of economics, Département d'Économétrie et Économie Politique (DEEP), University of Lausanne.
http://www.unil.ch

Willem Buiter

Professor Buiter took his PhD at Yale University in 1975. Apart from academic appointments at Princeton, Bristol, the London School of Economics, Yale and Cambridge, he has worked as a consultant and adviser to the International Monetary Fund, The World Bank, The Inter-American Development Bank and the European Communities. From 1997 to 2000 he was an External Member of the Monetary Policy Committee of the Bank of England. He has published widely on monetary and exchange rate theory, fiscal policy, social security, economic development and transition economies. Since 2000, Buiter has held the position of Chief Economist and Special Adviser to the President of the European Bank for Reconstruction and Development.
www.nber.org/wbuiter/

Anne Koopmans Frankel

Dr. Frankel, daughter of Tjalling C. Koopmans, was born in Geneva, Switzerland, in 1940, and soon after emigrated with her parents to the U.S. She graduated from Swarthmore College with a BA in Biology (1962) and from the University of Iowa with a PhD in Zoology-genetics (1969). For the past 26 years, she has worked as an academic adviser specialising in the natural and health sciences. Simultaneously, she raised two children, Rebecca and Martin, who are working in information technology.

Michele Fratianni

Professor Fratianni received his PhD in economics at Ohio State University in 1971. He has taught at various universities in Belgium, Italy and Germany and has been economic adviser to various governments, international organisations and private-sector firms. Fratianni is the founder and managing editor of the *Open Economies Review* and a member of the review board of several economics journals. Currently he is the W. George Pinnell Professor and holds the Chair of Business Economics and Public Policy at the Kelley School of Business of Indiana University in Bloomington, Indiana (USA).
www.kelley.indiana.edu/fratiann/

Bruno S. Frey

Professor Frey studied economics at the University of Basel where he took his PhD in 1965. He was professor of economics at the University of Constance (1970-1977), and at the University of Zurich (1977-...) and has been the managing editor of Kyklos since 1969. Frey has received honorary doctorates from the University of Göteborg and the University of St. Gallen. He is research director at the Center for Research in Economics, Management and the Arts.
www.iew.unizh.ch/home/frey

Willem Hendrik Gispen

Professor Gispen studied biology at Utrecht University and received his PhD in neuroscience in 1970. After post-doctoral research positions in the USA, Italy and Sweden he became head of the Department of Molecular Neurobiology in Utrecht. In 1980 he became professor and in 1988 research manager of the Rudolf Magnus Institute for Neurosciences. For his research on neuroplasticity he received honorary doctorates in the USA, Italy, Russia and Moldova. He is a member of the Royal Netherlands Academy of Arts and Sciences and the Academia Europaea, and was president of the Federation of European Neuroscience Societies. He is editor of the European Journal of Pharmacology. Gispen was appointed Rector Magnificus of Utrecht University in 2001.

Charles Goodhart
Professor Goodhart CBE, FBA took his PhD in economics at Harvard University. He held the Norman Sosnow Chair of Banking and Finance at LSE from 1985 until his retirement in 2002 and before that worked at the Bank of England for seventeen years as a monetary adviser. From 1997-2000 he was one of the outside independent members of the Bank of England's new Monetary Policy Committee. He is still a member, having been Deputy Director, 1986-2004, of the Financial Markets Group at the London School of Economics, which he helped found in 1986. Goodhart is an acknowledged authority on monetary theory and monetary policy.
http://fmg.lse.ac.uk/people/peopledetail.php?peopleid=433

Nikolai Hovanov
Professor Hovanov earned a PhD in physics and mathematics from the St. Petersburg State University (SpbSU) in 1972 and a doctorate of science in physics and mathematics (DSci) from the Russian Academy of Sciences in 1991. He has worked at the St. Petersburg State University since 1972, first as professor of Mathematical Statistics and Reliability Theory and then, from 1995, as professor of Economic Cybernetics at the Faculty of Economics. Over the periods 1983-1994 and 2001-2003, Hovanov was the scientific supervisor on six government projects, which were developed by SPbSU. He is the author of several monographs and textbooks and has published widely on mathematical models and methods of multicriteria decision-making under uncertainty.

Michael Hurd
Dr. Hurd received a master's in statistics and a PhD in economics from the University of California, Berkeley. His current work includes the effects of pensions on retirement, the use of subjective information to explain economic decisions such as saving and retirement, bracketing and anchoring effects in the elicitation of economic information, and the relationship between socioeconomic status and mortality. He served on many panels among which expert panels of the Social Security Advisory Council, the World Bank, and the National Research Council. He is the Director of the RAND Center for the Study of Aging and a Research Associate at the National Bureau of Economic Research.
www.nber.org/vitae/vita274.htm

Arie Kapteyn
Professor Kapteyn received his PhD from Leiden University in 1977. He held several positions, among others at the universities of Bristol, Princeton and Southern California, and has been a professor of econometrics at Tilburg University in the Netherlands

since 1982. He was Dean of the Faculty of Economics and Business Administration at Tilburg University (1989-1992) as well as director of CentER, the faculty´s research institute (1992-2000). In 1994 he was elected a fellow of the Econometric Society. Kapteyn has been working as a senior economist with RAND from 2001 to the present where he is director of the Population Research Center. His expertise lies in demographics, savings, wealth and retirement.
http://center.uvt.nl/staff/kapteyn/

John Kay
Professor Kay studied economics at the University of Edinburgh and at Nuffield College, Oxford. At the age of 21 he was elected a fellow of St John's College, a position that he still holds. He was research director and director of the Institute for Fiscal Studies and professor of economics at the London Business School and at Oxford University. In 1986, Kay founded the independent economic consultancy, London Economics, of which he was executive chairman until 1996. He then became the first director of Oxford University's Said Business School. After resigning his position at Oxford in 1999 and selling his interest in London Economics, he devoted his time principally to writing. He is an authority on the analysis of changes in industrial structure and the competitive advantage of individual firms.
www.johnkay.com

James Kolari
Professor Kolari has taught financial markets and institutions since earning his PhD at the Arizona State University in 1980. Previously a Visiting Scholar at the Federal Reserve Bank of Chicago in 1982 and a Fullbright Scholar at the University of Helsinki and Bank of Finland, he has been a consultant to the U.S. Small Business Administration, American Bankers Association, Independent Bankers Association of America, U.S. Information Agency and numerous banks and other organisations. In recent years he has taught at Hanken Swedish School of Economics and Business Administration in Finland, as well as St. Petersburg State University and St. Petersburg Technical University in Russia. Kolari has published numerous articles and monographs and has co-authored several books. He is at present the Chase Professor of Finance at Texas A&M University in the U.S.

Ron Martin
Professor Martin took his PhD at Cambridge University. Martin is, or has been, editor of various journals on economics and geography and edits the Regional Development and Public Policy book series (Routledge). He was awarded the British Academy's Special Thanksgiving to Britain Senior Research Fellowship in 1997-1998. Martin is currently professor of Economic Geography (1974-....) at the University of Cambridge, a Fellow of St Catharine's College and the Cambridge-MIT Institute. His interests lie in Economic geography: regional development theory, economic theory and economic geography, labour market geography, regional political economy of state intervention, geography and public policy and the geography of money and finance.
www.geog.cam.ac.uk/people/martin/

Bart Nooteboom

Professor Nooteboom received a PhD in Econometrics from Erasmus University Rotterdam. After working for Shell for a short while, he was at the Research Institute for Small Business before accepting the professorship of Industrial Marketing and, later, Industrial Organisation and the directorship of the research school of the University of Groningen's Faculty of Management and Organisation. He has served on various committees advising the Dutch government. In 1999, Nooteboom became professor of Organisational Dynamics at the Rotterdam School of Management. He was elected a member of the Royal Dutch Academy of Sciences (KNAW) a year later and in 2004 was appointed professor of Innovation Policy at Tilburg University. He has published many articles and books on entrepreneurship, innovation and diffusion, technology and innovation policy, interfirm collaboration and networks, organisational learning, and trust.
http://www.tilburguniversity.nl/faculties/few/organizationandstrategy/members/nooteboom/

Luigi Orsenigo

After receiving his PhD from the Science Policy Research Unit, University of Sussex, in 1989, professor Orsenigo was affiliated with Bocconi University and the University of Brescia. He has held positions as visiting professor or visiting scholar at various universities in Europe and the USA. In addition to being the editor of the *Journal of Evolutionary Economics*, he has acted as adviser on matters of innovation and industrial policy to several Italian and international institutions, including the European Commission. At present he is Professor of Industrial Organisation at the University of Brescia and Deputy Director of CESPRI (Center on the Processes of Internationalisation and Innovation), Bocconi University, Milan, Italy. His work mainly concerns the economics of innovation, industrial dynamics and the biopharmaceutical industry.
http://www.lem.sssup.it/cv/cv_luigi_orsenigo.pdf

John Pattison

Dr. Pattison is Senior Vice-President Compliance at Canadian Imperial Bank of Commerce, where he has previously held positions as Managing Director, CIBC Limited (London, England) and Vice-President, Finance. He is currently a member of the Steering Committee on the reform of deposit insurance under the auspices of the Deputy Minister of Finance. He is a former faculty member of the School of Business Administration, University of Western Ontario and was an economist at the OECD in Paris, France. Dr. Pattison's activities involve managing compliance risk on a global basis in order to ensure adherence to laws, regulations and the by-laws of self-regulatory bodies such as stock exchanges, in order to promote sound corporate governance of CIBC.
http://www.iedm.org/library/palda8 en.html

Janneke Plantega

Professor Plantenga works at the Utrecht School of Economics and the University of Groningen. She received her PhD in Economics from the University of Groningen in

1993. Her research interest focuses on labour market flexibilisation, the reconciliation of work and family, and (European) social policy. She is the Dutch member and co-ordinator of the European Experts Group on Gender, Social Inclusion and Employment. She has written widely on (the redistribution of) unpaid work, changing working time patterns, child care issues and modernising social security.
www.econ.uu.nl

Rick van der Ploeg
Professor Van der Ploeg studied applied sciences at the University of Sussex and did his PhD at King's College, Cambridge. He has worked in the UK (Cambridge Growth Project and London School of Economics) and in the Netherlands at CentER (Tilburg University) and the Tinbergen Institute (1985-1991) and the University of Amsterdam (1991-1998). Van der Ploeg was State Secretary for Culture, Heritage and Media in the Dutch cabinet for the period 1998-2002. Currently, he is professor of economics at the Robert Schuman Centre and the Department of Economics of the European University Institute, Florence, professor of Political Economy at the University of Amsterdam and Research Fellow of CESifo, Munich University and CEPR.
www.iue.it/Personal/RickvanderPloeg/

Helen Koopmans Sandoz
Mrs. Sandoz was born in Chicago, Illinois in 1945 as the third child of Mr. and Mrs Tjalling Koopmans and grew up there and in the New Haven area of Connecticut. She studied Russian at Yale and Brown Universities. Since leaving university, Mrs Sandoz has run several different small businesses, currently a bicycle store. She also develops and sells computer programmes tailored to running such businesses as well as programming for the Palm Pilot. Concurrently, she has brought up two sons, Jason and Brian Weinert, and three stepchildren, Katherine, Edouard and Jesse Sandoz.

Günther Schmid
Professor Schmid studied political science, sociology and history at the University of Freiburg and received his PhD from the Free University of Berlin. He has worked for the Social Science Research Centre Berlin (WZB) since 1974, and was appointed professor of Economic Theories in Politics at the Free University of Berlin and director of the WZB research unit Labour Market Policy and Employment in 1989, a position that he has held since. Schmid has worked as a consultant for the OECD, was a member of the Hartz commission on Modern Services for the Labour Market in 2002 and has been a member of the European Employment Task force set up by the European Commission since 2003. He also takes an active interest in the comparative studies of political systems and the philosophy of science.
http://www.wz-berlin.de/ars/ab/staff/schmid.en.htm

William G. Shepherd
Professor Shepherd studied at Amherst College and Yale University where he obtained his PhD in 1963. His book *The Economics of Industrial Organization* has had multiple editions and is a standard text at many universities. He was the editor of the *Review of*

Industrial Organization from 1990-2001. He was the first economist to severely criticise the theory of contestable markets, and established himself after the 1950s as a critical observer of many new trends in the field. He was the Special Economic Assistant of the Antitrust Division of the U.S. Dept. of Justice from 1967-1968 and has advised many governments and authorities on issues of competition and antitrust. Though retired from the Department of Economics at Massachusetts now, Shepherd is still actively engaged in public and academic debate and is in the throes of writing a new volume on the pioneering innovators in the modern field of industrial economics. www.umass.edu/economics/Staff/shepherd.html

Luc Soete

Professor Soete completed his first degrees in economics and development economics at the University of Ghent, Belgium, before obtaining his PhD in economics at the University of Sussex. He worked at the University of Antwerp (UFSIA), the University of Sussex, and Stanford University before moving to Maastricht in 1986. Since 1988 he has been founding director of MERIT, the Maastricht University economics research institute in the area of innovation studies and the socioeconomic analysis of technological change. He joined the Dutch Council for Science and Technology (AWT) in 2004. Soete's research interests cover a broad range of theoretical and empirical studies of the impact of technological change, in particular new information and communication technologies, on employment, economic growth, and international trade and investment, as well as the related policy and measurement issues.
www.soete.nl

Mikhail V. Sokolov

Dr. Sokolov graduated from the Department of Economics at the St. Petersburg State University in 2001 and earned his PhD in economics at the same university in 2004. His fields of scientific interest include applications of mathematics in economics, theory of economic indices, utility theory, and measurement theory. Sokolov has written about 20 scientific publications.

Rolf Traeger

Mr. Traeger obtained his MSE at the University of Lausanne (Switzerland) and his BA in economics at the Getúlio Vargas Foundation in São Paulo (Brazil). Since 1991 he has been working as an economist for the United Nations, first at the United Nations Conference on Trade and Development (UNCTAD) and later at the Economic Commission for Europe (UNECE). His publications include 'An account of geographic concentration patterns in Europe' (with Marius Brülhart), *HWWA Discussion Paper* 226 (Hamburg) and several contributions to the UNECE *Economic Survey of Europe* from 1999 to 2004. His main research interest areas are economic geography, international trade, trade policy, industry and technology.

Jan G.F. Veldhuis

Drs. Veldhuis (1938) graduated in history, with a focus on economics and constitutional law, from Utrecht University. He was a Fullbright fellow in political history and political economy at the University of Minnesota, USA. He started his working career at the European Co-operation Department of the Ministry of Foreign Affairs in The Hague after which he moved to Leiden University where he later became secretary to the board. In 1974 he joined the Ministry of Education and Science where he became director-general and senior chief inspector of education in the Netherlands in 1979. In 1986 he was appointed president of his alma mater, Utrecht University. He held this position until he retired in November 2003. Veldhuis has held, or still holds, positions in management or supervisory boards of numerous educational and/or scientific research organisations, such as QANU (Quality Assurance Netherlands Universities) and TNO (Netherlands Organisation for Applied Scientific Research). Abroad, he has been active, mostly as chairman, in the NGIZ (Dutch Organisation for International Affairs), in the Fullbright Commission and in the Fondation Descartes. Veldhuis holds an honorary doctorate of the University of Florida, USA.

AUTHORS INAUGURAL LECTURES USE

Rob Alessie

Professor Alessie worked for a number of scientific institutions such as CentER at Tilburg University, University College London, CREST-INSEE in Paris, ICER in Turin and the European University Institute in Florence. Between 1989 and 1994, he was a member of the monitoring mission of the INAS-project, the purpose of which was to improve the national accounts statistics of Pakistan. He took his PhD in econometrics at CentER, Tilburg University, in 1994 and taught economics and econometrics at various universities in the Netherlands. He was editor of the 2002 'Preadviezen' (Reports) made to the Dutch Royal Economic Society (KVS), a position that was held also by two other USE professors (Schenk in 2001 and Garretsen in 2003). Alessie is currently professor of econometrics at the Utrecht School of Economics.
www.econ.uu.nl

Harry Garretsen

Professor Garretsen took his PhD at the University of Groningen in 1991. From 1993-1996 he worked for the department of monetary and economic policy of the Central Bank of the Netherlands as a senior policy maker, after which he joined the University of Nijmegen (now Radboud University) as professor of economic theory and economic policy. He is a research fellow of SOM of the University of Groningen, of CESifo of the University of München and of NAKE. Garretsen has recently been appointed a crown representative of the Social and Economic Council of the Netherlands (SER). At present he is professor of international economics at the Utrecht School of Economics and director of the Graduate School.
www.econ.uu.nl

Clemens Kool

After receiving his PhD in economics at Erasmus University Rotterdam in 1989, professor Kool taught at the universities of Rotterdam and Maastricht, and worked for

a short while for the research department of the Central Bank of the Netherlands. He was appointed professor of Money, Credit and Banking and Jean Monnet professor of European Financial Markets at the University of Maastricht in 1996. Kool has been a visiting professor at the Federal Reserve Bank of St. Louis and the Kelley School of Business of Indiana University. He is especially interested in the functioning of international financial markets, monetary policy, banking and European financial integration. Kool is currently professor of Finance and Financial Markets at the Utrecht School of Economics and director of the Undergraduate School.
www.econ.uu.nl

Hans Schenk
See above.

Brigitte Unger
Professor Unger studied music and French before earning a PhD in economics at the Vienna University of Economics and Business Administration (Wirtschaftsuniversität Wien) in 1987. For her interdisciplinary approach, the World Economic Forum in Davos nominated her as Global Leader for Tomorrow in 1993. She worked at various universities in Austria and the US, and was professor of economics at the Wirtschaftsuniversität Wien from 1998-2002. Her fields of interest are Public Sector Economics and Finance, Institutional Economics, Economic Policy and International Monetary Economics. Unger was appointed professor of Public Economics at the Utrecht School of Economics in 2002.
www.econ.uu.nl

I
MULTIDISCIPLINARY ECONOMICS: THE BIRTH OF A NEW ECONOMICS FACULTY IN THE NETHERLANDS

P.P. DE GIJSEL

OPENING ADDRESS

Ladies and Gentlemen,

I have the great honour today of introducing you to USE, the Utrecht School of Economics. It is fair to say that USE is the joint product of a very large group of people from Utrecht University who have intensively cooperated in the past in setting up the youngest economics faculty in the Netherlands. I want to mention in particular the staff members and students of USE, the deans and colleagues from the faculties of law, geography, social sciences and humanities and last but not least the University Board and the staff members of the University Strategic Programme. I am very happy to see that so many of my companions have come here today to celebrate the opening of USE and I would like to give you all a warm welcome. It is also a great pleasure to welcome our guests from outside the university, in particular Tjalling C. Koopmans' relatives and our guest speakers.

Setting up a new economics curriculum and a new centre of economics education and research was challenging. When I was asked for this job I was fascinated by the idea that Utrecht University could have an economics faculty in the near future where new routes in economics would be explored systematically and be encouraged in an organisational setting that created the right incentives for economists to engage in promising but risky research and teaching projects.

Whether economists like risky projects is far from certain. I bet that if you were to grant a research project on tax evasion to an average economist and ask him to choose between hiring an economist or a psychologist or a sociologist to help him he would probably hire an economist. The reason is that he would feel more secure with an economist if he were unfamiliar with the other two disciplines. Mechanisms of stereotyping and risk aversion are at work here. One of the important reasons for the economist's risk aversion is simply that in most economics curricula today students are not motivated to cross the border of the economics discipline and to have a look at whether other disciplines can contribute to solving the problem they are investigating. Using insights gained in their own disciplines, psychologists or sociologists could seriously qualify the economist's call for increasing monetary fines as an efficient solution of the tax evasion problem.

Education in economics that does not stimulate students to look beyond their own discipline runs the risk of missing efficient solutions of economic problems that can be found by a multidisciplinary approach. And it neglects the increasing demand for

P. de Gijsel and H. Schenk (eds.), Multidisciplinary Economics, 3–5.

graduates who are able to communicate and co-operate with graduates from other fields.

Starting from these observations, USE recognised that relevant economic problems have institutional, historical and spatial dimensions showing the way to other disciplines. USE is convinced that students will benefit from an economics curriculum that explicitly pays attention to these dimensions in the economics core programme and allows them to combine economics with law, geography, history or social sciences.

USE launched her bachelor's programmes in 2002 and I am very proud to report that they have already proved to be successful. I refer here to the results of a survey published quite recently in a special edition of Elsevier on the best studies in the Netherlands in 2003. USE was awarded third place when compared to five other economic programmes. If you consider that the students ranked the programmes of the internationally respected economics faculties of Tilburg, Groningen, Rotterdam and Amsterdam lower than the USE bachelor's programmes, this is certainly a great success even if one has to accept that the difference between these faculties and USE are statistically not significant. At least USE does not score significantly lower than these outstanding faculties.

USE has focused heavily on the development of an innovative economics curriculum during the past few years. But this in no way means that economics research has been neglected. The Utrecht University Board accepted an economics research master plan in 2001, which included the establishment of six new economics chairs and the creation of new assistant- and associate professor positions. Our economics research capacity has increased steadily since then. The Tjalling C.Koopmans Research Institute that will be opened today by the rector magnificus, professor Willem Hendrik Gispen, is designed to co-ordinate and organise the research activities of USE.

With the opening of the Tjalling C. Koopmans Institute the scientific 'nullustrum' will start. It is the purpose of this 'nullustrum' to give you an overview of the research topics that will rank high on the research agenda of the Tjalling C. Koopmans Institute in the years to come. I hope that after a three days' academic debate on important economic issues and the inaugural lectures of our newly appointed full professors of economics, you will share my view that USE offers interesting research perspectives.

Ladies and gentlemen,

Both the success of our economics education programme and the research perspectives of USE are promising and encouraging. They confirm the view that setting up a new academic faculty of economics can only be successful if the University Board was ready to invest in curriculum innovation and innovative research as she has done with economics in Utrecht. I have defended this view from the very beginning when I was appointed programme director and interim dean of USE.

I have successfully resisted looking back today on the role of economics at Utrecht University and answering the interesting question why it has taken such a long time for Utrecht University to get its own faculty of economics. I consider it a privilege of the president of the university, Jan Veldhuis, to express his view on this issue. I am very happy to welcome Jan Veldhuis who has played such an important role in establishing the youngest economics faculty in the Netherlands. Jan, the floor is yours.

J.G.F. VELDHUIS

HISTORICAL MISTAKES RECTIFIED

The first of September 2000 saw the launch of a full degree programme in economics in Utrecht. In my speech of the thirtieth of August 1999, here in the Dom Church, on the occasion of the opening of the 1999-2000 academic year, I spoke about the protracted gestation period and the lengthy preparation process needed for establishing a full economics degree programme at Utrecht and pointed out the necessity and the desirability of doing so. In my short speech today I will repeat some of these points and give more specific background information that – after more than five years – is not so sensitive or confidential anymore.

In order to establish a full degree programme in economics, we needed to gain support, co-operation and/or even approval from the national government and from departments and people within Utrecht University.

We needed the government's approval to include the programme in the CROHO, the Central Register of Higher Education Programmes. The road to this approval was long and full of obstacles. Government policy ensures the macroefficiency of degree provision in order to avoid a proliferation of degrees.

Therefore, a full economics degree programme at Utrecht was a thorny issue: there were already six full degree programmes in the Netherlands: Groningen, Rotterdam, two in Amsterdam, Tilburg and Maastricht. We expected that the national government would not fully support the idea of a seventh full economics degree programme! And our sister institutions with a faculty of economics were not likely to be too happy either! After all, the battle for students has been going on for years.

But we were lucky. The government was keen to reshape the overall university-level provision in the Netherlands and even keener to rationalise provision. Under the *Government Higher Education and Scientific Research Plan* (Hoop-96), the minister and the universities agreed to simplify provision and to enhance its transparency. Their main task was to reduce the number of degree programmes in order to create greater clarity for prospective students and their parents, and for employers.

The Association of Universities in the Netherlands, the VSNU, took it upon itself to develop proposals for this reshaping process. It appointed a committee: the 'Simplification and Clarification of University-Level Provision 1996' committee. The president of Utrecht University became the chairman. Utrecht had some special stakes in the process, the most prominent of which was economics.

From the early 90's Utrecht had four partial programmes in economics. These programmes were not classified in the economics sector of the CROHO register, except

P. de Gijsel and H. Schenk (eds.), Multidisciplinary Economics, 7–10.

for one partial programme: 'International economics and economic geography', which was included by accident or on purpose, that remains a mystery to this very day. But the creators of this programme deserve praise.

The composition of the committee reflected the importance of the issue: the other universities, especially the younger ones, deployed heavyweight representatives. The committee meetings and the drafting process went as expected: in the successive drafts, the other universities, notably Tilburg and Maastricht, moved the Utrecht-based partial programme from the economics sector to the social sciences sector, division human geography. Utrecht, referring to vested rights, moved it back to its original classification. In this process, my role as chairperson offered me strong strategic advantages. The classification of the partial economics programme of Utrecht – economics or social sciences sector – was ping-ponged back and forth in the various drafts at least four or five times.

The committee's definitive document of 1997 recommended that the total number of degree programmes should be halved: from 272 to 131. The four partial Utrecht programmes were to be clustered into one full degree programme, and classified in the ... economics sector! And this is how the partial programmes became a single, full degree programme. The ministry was left with little choice but to adopt the proposals in their entirety. It was extremely pleased that the number of degree programmes was to be halved and it did not want to jeopardize this feat by taking issue with some of the other recommendations. So, the CROHO was adjusted, and Utrecht University had a full economics degree programme.[1]

We also had to muster support within the university. Of the general, classical universities only Utrecht (and Leiden) *had never combined* the well-respected political economy programme – in their law faculties! – with business economics in a single, full economics degree. *The reasons* have become the subject of ongoing historical research. In my speech of the thirtieth of August 1999 I ventured one or two hypotheses myself, in my capacity as pseudo-historian. I summarise them below.

In 1997, the deans and the board of the university commissioned a programme board to formulate proposals to start an economic programme. The proposal development process was ponderous. Understandably, there were serious doubts, especially among the providers of the more established, successful partial programmes: the Law Faculty, with its long-standing, well-established political economy programme, and Human Geography, which ran a good quality programme that had had a hugely positive impact on the faculty's enrolment rates for years. And all these successes were achieved by committed, hard working staff, who had thus firmly secured their positions. All these doubts were very understandable indeed.

For this reason the board of the university engaged in intensive discussions with the programme board, which consisted of four deans. It is undeniably true that the board of the university exerted great pressure. In fact, the plans were pushed through, especially after the issue had come up of a recognised economics programme that was

1 Utrecht also got Public Administration Science – Bestuurskunde – and Communication and Information Sciences.

to be included in the CROHO. A unique opportunity. The board of the university is greatly indebted to the four deans who were involved in this process, and to its central administration staff, in particular Erwin Vermeulen and Eline den Boer. And also to the many employees that gave their loyal support during this lengthy process.

Economics in Utrecht. A programme we needed. A programme we wanted. For at least four, partially interdependent reasons.

1. Economics is a fully-fledged academic discipline.
In the 19th century, handelswetenschappen, commercial science, was not considered an academic subject. This was a mistake. When handelswetenschappen emancipated into business economics, separate academic institutions were established in which the subject was studied. But there was as yet no university that offered this course of study: the class-based attitudes that prevailed in the 19th and 20th centuries resisted this. Another mistake. And this is why in 1913 the *Nederlandse Handelshogeschool* was set up in Rotterdam, and why in 1927 a Roman Catholic Handelshogeschool was established in Tilburg.

But progressive universities soon followed suit: the municipal University of Amsterdam (1922), and after World War II Groningen and the *Vrije Universiteit* in Amsterdam (both of them in 1948). Utrecht and Leiden did not: too conservative, too aristocratic? Perhaps, but it was another mistake. The new university in Maastricht (1976) also established a faculty of economics. So wasn't it time, high time, Utrecht University set up an economics programme? After more than a century of mistakes, especially here in Utrecht, we finally corrected this particular mistake in 2000.

2. Economics is a respectable academic discipline.
Economics is also an essential discipline, especially for a general, classical university, because of the discipline itself and because of its relation to other disciplines. Utrecht is a broad-based university that offers a wide array of programmes in humanities, natural sciences, life sciences (biomedical sciences), behavioural, and social sciences. Economics is particularly essential for the Social Sciences Cluster. Therefore economics belongs in Utrecht.

3. The influence of the practical application of economics has expanded considerably.
In the last century, the science of economics has had a great impact on our affluence and our well-being, and thus on the quality of our society. In 1969, a Nobel Prize for Economics was established, and deservedly so. One of the two first laureates was a Dutchman: Jan Tinbergen, who graduated in physics from Leiden. Tjalling Koopmans, who also completed a physics degree here in Utrecht, received the Nobel Prize for Economics in 1975.

4. Over the past decades, economists and economics graduates have entered the industry sector as well as the public sector. Increasingly they are taking over administrative and policy-making positions as well. Traditionally, in the Netherlands, these positions were held almost exclusively by law graduates – a phenomenon that has to do with the

class structure of society and with the nature of the law degree programme. It is important for a university to have graduates hold these prominent, indeed powerful positions. It brings respect and prestige to a university and serves as an 'insurance policy' in difficult times. You may call this a narrow-minded, defensive or even plain opportunistic viewpoint, but we should be realistic and acknowledge that this is indeed important for a university.

So there are plenty of reasons for us to be happy and proud today. And grateful!

Grateful to all the pioneers, the ones I mentioned and the ones I did not, for their efforts through to the year 2000, particularly where they were able to put aside their own interests. Grateful to those people who since 2000 have put in a lot of time and work under the leadership of the energetic Dean Peter de Gijsel and his pioneering staff.

Grateful to all those people willing to come to Utrecht to embark on the educational adventure that is called the Utrecht School of Economics. Grateful to everyone for their hard work and dedication to the task of securing a respectable place for the school within the university and of finding the right niche in the market.

Ladies and gentlemen, the Utrecht School of Economics offers a good-quality, innovative programme. It has already been ranked third in the country by the Elsevier magazine in its October issue. There are competent staff, five of whom are newly-appointed professors. This week, they will deliver their inaugural lectures.

Thanks, many thanks. And I wish you every success and an enriching experience.

W.H. GISPEN

TJALLING C. KOOPMANS: AN INSPIRING EXAMPLE

Ladies and Gentlemen, and in particular the two daughters of Prof. Koopmans, Mrs. Anne Frankel and Mrs. Helen Sandoz:

It gives me great pleasure to address you today at the start of the inaugural conference of the Utrecht School of Economics. You will hear more than once during this conference that Economics in Utrecht is something out of the ordinary. Utrecht has chosen not monodisciplinary economics, but economics that is interwoven with other disciplines. Economics that crosses the borders between disciplines in teaching and in research.

It is extremely fitting that the name of Tjalling Koopmans was chosen for the research institute of the economics faculty in Utrecht. He crossed borders both literally and figuratively speaking. He was born in 's-Graveland and emigrated to the US. He studied mathematics and physics in Utrecht, and obtained his Ph D in Economics in Leiden. He worked as lecturer and researcher at the universities of Princeton, New York, Chicago, Yale and Harvard. There are not many people who can boast of connections with such a long row of famous universities. He was the president of the American Economic Association. And lastly, his name would probably not mean quite so much to us if he had not received the Nobel prize for Economics (together with his Russian colleague Kantorovich) in 1975 for his contributions to the theory of the optimum allocation of resources.

An impressive career. But inspiring above all. Not only because of his proficiency and his ability to master several disciplines and link them to each other. He was fond of scientific debates and took part in them with complete commitment. He succeeded in linking developments in research with their practical use in society, characteristics that inspire universities and other educational institutions greatly.

The interaction between disciplines and the possibility of choosing, within limits, from among the programmes offered by the different disciplines are the foundation stones of the bachelor/master education model that we are at present introducing at our university. More than other universities in the Netherlands, we are moving towards the Anglo-Saxon style of university teaching because we believe that students should be given the opportunity to learn to base their thinking and work on the integration of disciplines. Our efforts to reform our teaching style are moving forward step by step, thanks to all the work our staff put in. And we seem to be succeeding, as the early results show. In this work, which is taking effect in and outside Utrecht, we follow the example of the pioneers who preceded us, such as Tjalling Koopmans.

P. de Gijsel and H. Schenk (eds.), Multidisciplinary Economics, 11–12.

I am very glad that the faculty of economics has taken the initiative to name its research institute after a Utrecht scholar who crossed borders both in his life and in his work. I wish the institute, its staff and its students every success. I hereby declare that the institute has been opened.

Tjalling Koopmans in 1954[1]

Tjalling on the Maine coast, 1983[2]

1 Reprinted from the Tjalling Koopmans family collection.
2 Idem.

A.W.K. FRANKEL AND H.J.K. SANDOZ[1]

STYLES OF RESEARCH IN ECONOMICS AT COWLES

Dames en Heren, Ladies and Gentlemen:

We, Helen and I, are grateful for the opportunity to be part of the formal opening of the Tjalling C. Koopmans Research Institute – part of your consolidation and reorganisation of the Utrecht School of Economics.

Tjalling (Charles) Koopmans – as you know – started his university studies here in Utrecht in 1927. He studied mathematics, emphasising analysis and geometry, and earned a B.A. in 1930. This happened just after he completed his secondary school education in a gymnasium in Hilversum, commuting perhaps 12 km from home. His father sent him here to this university, because Utrecht is also not very far from the small village of 's-Graveland where Tjalling was born and raised. His early education had been in one of the town's schools, the 'School of the Bible' (Protestant) where his father was the headmaster.

The last time I was in 's-Graveland in 1987, the little community looked just about as Tjalling described it in 1976 for his Nobel autobiography. My brother, Henry, tells me that it has expanded since, though many of the original elements remain.

In 1930, Tjalling changed the emphasis of his studies from mathematics to theoretical physics, continuing to study here in Utrecht with Professor Hans Kramers. He completed a master's degree here in 1933 in theoretical physics, finishing two papers in the process. We were told in 1975 that one of them was then still cited frequently in textbooks on theoretical physics.

But 1933 was a time of considerable economic upheaval, and my father felt that his mathematical and statistical approaches to physics might have more social relevance and be more effective, if he transferred them to the study of economics. For this reason, Tjalling arranged to be introduced to Jan Tinbergen, who lectured once a week at the Municipal University of Amsterdam. His association with Professor Tinbergen, plus studies abroad with Professor Ragnar Frisch (in Oslo) and a briefer visit with Professor Ronald A. Fisher (in England) prepared him for completion of his Ph D, sponsored jointly by Professors Kramers and Tinbergen (1936, University of Leiden, where

1 Both daughters of Tjalling C. Koopmans. The address was given by Mrs. Frankel.

P. de Gijsel and H. Schenk (eds.), Multidisciplinary Economics, 13–18.

Professor Kramers was then newly relocated). The topic was the 'Linear Regression Analysis of Economic Time Series' and it was published as a book a year later.

Natal family – Sjoerd and Wijtske Koopmans and three sons, 1914 or 1915. Tjalling was the youngest.

These years, many of them at this university, were the formative years for Tjalling's development as a scholar. My family would like to acknowledge and celebrate the role that the Utrecht University has had in forming the man that you are honouring today by naming, for him, your research institute.

The next fifteen years brought Tjalling into several situations where problems of shipping and successful distribution of goods led him to collaborative studies at the British Shipping Mission in Washington D.C. and more fully at the Cowles Commission in the development of a general 'activity analysis' model for production. The simplex method developed by Professor George Dantzig provided the computational mode for handling this form of econometric planning and model building. Linear programming, for which Tjalling Koopmans and Leonid Kantorovitch received the Nobel Prize in 1975, is a special case within the general area of activity analysis (Scarf, 1995). There were two additional substantial areas of economics that were to interest

Tjalling during his professional life after 1955. The first one was the 'theory of economic growth', in which he examined 'optimality and efficiency in dynamic models of production' (Scarf, 1995). Thereafter, Tjalling turned to some practical applications of econometric theory. In the first, he led a collaborative and interdisciplinary study dealing with renewable resources such as those involved in energy production (for the National Science Foundation). A later project dealt with nonrenewable resources, in particular examining the use and impending scarcity of copper (among other attributes as a carrier of electric current). Professor William Nordhaus and Tjalling worked on economic modelling of decision making with diminishing resources while two Yale geologists contributed their geological understanding (Scarf, 1995). But, I'm not an economist, so what you are getting from me is a layperson's idea of the breadth of Tjalling's interests.

Tjalling Koopmans, passport photo of about 1934.

Now I want to shift my emphasis. As a child, ages 7-12, and then as a teenager, I watched my father function as a young professional and a leader of the research, initially in the Cowles Commission at the University of Chicago and later in the Cowles Foundation at Yale University. In Chicago, Tjalling's study was my bedroom and I learned to fall asleep with the light on. His pattern was often to read from reprints, journals, and books, and write at home before lunch, eat a small meal, and then, after a short nap, leave for his office. He returned for a relatively late evening meal by US standards; then, in the evening he continued to use his study. Probably twice a week and maybe more frequently, the Cowles Commission economists met in the afternoons for often free-ranging discussion of their joint research – sometimes, it was difficult to say later who had an initial idea. I believe that this social pattern had already been established within the Cowles group by its earlier leader, Professor Jacob Marshak, even before Tjalling was invited to join Cowles in 1944 when his war work in Washington DC in the British Merchant Shipping Mission ended. Although sometimes difficult to keep functioning smoothly (as I learned later from Tjalling in a personal communication, ca. 1968), he continued this open and collegial form for advancing research when he became director of research in Chicago in 1948. This type of open collaboration is clearly shown in this series of photos all taken on the same day in 1945, '46, or '47 during one group discussion at the Cowles Commission (Figures 3-5).

He later returned to this style of research in his applied work.

Herman Rubin.

Jacob Marschak.

Tjalling Koopmans.

Because the deterioration of the adjacent urban community made it difficult to hire quality researchers, the Cowles Commission moved out of Chicago in the summer of 1955. About half (6) of the Cowles research group joined with others from Yale University and elsewhere to form anew as the Cowles Foundation under the initial leadership of Professor James Tobin (a Yale recruit). Suddenly, the style of doing research was different, in part because the needs of advances to econometrics had changed. Researchers each did their own projects with less open discussion during the formation of ideas, which were instead shared at a later stage in their development. When Tjalling resumed the directorship in 1961, I was no longer on the scene. But I do gather from a long discussion with Tjalling, from reviewing private letters, and from Professor Herbert Scarf's 1995 memoir that the new pattern had been set and didn't change significantly. It is interesting that in both of his later collaborative studies, Tjalling returned to the first method of research, i.e. the Cowles Commission pattern of discussion and development of ideas. I got my own Ph D in a different field using mostly the second method of doing research – it's lonely to work in this way!

Both styles do work and well. Cowles has fostered very fine economists, among them a number of Nobel Prize winning scholars from both the University of Chicago and Yale University periods. But now you have a special opportunity as you add five research chairs to the new Tjalling C. Koopmans Research Institute. I am suggesting here that you consider carefully among yourselves what type of learning styles you want to develop to foster good quality research from your students and within your community of scholars.

REFERENCES

Family owned photos: Cowles Commission (ca. 1945-'47) and others.

Frankel, Anne W. K. (1968 or 1971). *A conversation with Tjalling C. Koopmans on 'The role of the leader in keeping group projects working smoothly and motivating others to do their part in a timely manner so that the whole group is energized'.*

Scarf, Herbert E. (1995). Tjalling Charles Koopmans (August 28, 1910 – February 26, 1985). In *Biographical Memoirs, Volume 67* (pp. 263-291). Washington DC: National Academy Press.

II
MULTIDISCIPLINARY ECONOMICS AT UTRECHT UNIVERSITY

P.P. DE GIJSEL

ORIGINS AND DEVELOPMENT OF MULTIDISCIPLINARY ECONOMICS AT UTRECHT UNIVERSITY

On 1st January 2004, the Utrecht School of Economics (USE), the youngest economics faculty in the Netherlands, came into being. Considering the fact that expenditure on academic teaching and research in the Netherlands had been economised on for years and that the Netherlands already had a number of outstanding economics faculties, the birth of the new faculty was remarkable. Understandably, questions were asked about the reasons why the new economics faculty had come into being and whether its existence was justifiable.

The answer to these questions must be sought in the history of one of the oldest universities in the Netherlands. From this perspective, the establishment of USE is a milestone in the development of multidisciplinary economics at Utrecht University. It is therefore not surprising that its founders, at least, do not see the new faculty as a duplication of the large number of Dutch sister economics faculties. Rather, they consider the establishment of USE as a serious attempt to explore new paths in the field of academic economics teaching and research.

In both teaching and research USE accentuates the study of the Institutional, Historical and Spatial dimensions (IHS dimensions) of economic problems, interpreting multidisciplinary economics, which has a long, unique tradition at Utrecht University, in a special way. Originally, this tradition came into being at the Faculty of Law, where it was stimulated.

What the Faculty of Law has meant for the study of economics at Utrecht University is made quite clear by the history of the university. It so happened that in 1636, when both Utrecht University and the Faculty of Law were founded, the first PhD thesis on a subject to do with economics was submitted to the newly founded faculty. This occurrence is considered as the start of the study of economics in Utrecht (Nieuwenburg, 2003).[1] From 1720 onwards, students studying Cameralism, a subject belonging to the science of public administration sui generis, were taught economics at the Faculty of Law. In 1815 this faculty established its first chair in economics, the Chair of Political Economy and Statistics.

1 The thesis discussed the economic function of pawnshop owners who, at the time, had a very bad reputation among the poor because they charged exorbitant interest rates and received stolen goods.

P. de Gijsel and H. Schenk (eds.), Multidisciplinary Economics, 21–24.

Since then, the number of economists attached to Utrecht University has grown steadily. What is remarkable is that in the past these economists were members of different faculties. The most important reason for this was that there was no policy at Utrecht University aiming to concentrate economics expertise in an economics faculty. For a long time, the Board of the University and the economics professors attached to the faculties of Law and the Social Sciences did not see the need of stimulating the establishment of an economics faculty (cf. Nieuwenburg, 2003). As a result it was left to the faculties to take on economists or hire their services from other faculties when necessary for teaching or research. In actual fact, this policy created the substrate at Utrecht University on which multidisciplinary economics was able to develop. Economists who were taken on by the different faculties were selected in the first place to meet the requirements of other disciplines that needed economists. With their economics expertise, they were able to contribute to the teaching and research of the discipline where economic problems played a role. Those economists were first considered for the job who were prepared to look further than the borders of their own discipline and who saw the added value of multidisciplinary co-operation with representatives of other disciplines.

Over the years, the policy described above led to the fact that the largest group of economists was to be found in the economics department of the faculty of Law, followed by the faculties of Social Sciences and Geography and the department of History. In 1991/2 economics combination courses were developed in these faculties by economists, lawyers, historians, social scientists and geographers, where students were able to combine their main discipline with economics as a minor. These economists have made an important contribution to the further development of multidisciplinary economics at Utrecht University (see for example Siegers, 1992). At the same time, the University Board gradually came to realise that economics was of strategic importance for Utrecht University.

In 1996 the Minister of Education, Culture and Science decided to reduce the number of university studies. This decision created the opportunity for the Utrecht University board to combine the four economics combination courses into a single four-year doctoral economics study, which started officially in 2000. Because of the change-over to the bachelor-master system in 2002, this four-year doctoral study has been replaced by a bachelor of economics study, after which economics students can go on to do one of the five master of economics programmes, starting in 2005.

The development of a new fully-fledged economics programme has had far-reaching financial and organisational consequences for economics teaching and research at Utrecht University. Considering that the share of economics in the economics combinations courses was about 30% of the total study load, it was necessary to increase the share in the new economics curriculum drastically in order to compete with existing economics studies. Because the number of students taking part in the new economics study in 2000 was considerably larger than the number of students doing the old economics combination studies, the demand for economics staff increased. For competitive reasons it also became necessary to hire more researchers. This was why the University Board agreed to a staff plan for Economics in 2001 that took into account the existing economics staff at the different faculties and provided for new economics staff. At the same time, bearing in mind the administrative renewal taking place at the university, the University Board decided to set up the Utrecht School of Economics (USE) as a (sub) faculty of economics and to transfer a major part of the economics staff still employed by the faculties of Law and Social Sciences in 2002 to the new school. The developments of the past four years make clear why, in fact, a faculty of some size came into existence when the Utrecht School of Economics was founded.

From 1st January 2004, the sub faculty of economics and the two sub faculties of law and governance together form the cluster faculty of Law, Economics and Governance (**R**echtsgeleerdheid, **E**conomie en **B**estuurs- & **O**rganisatiewetenschap). The establishment of the new faculty is one of the results of the administrative renewal that has taken place at Utrecht University during the past few years and that has given rise to the formation of seven cluster faculties.

For the study of economics at Utrecht University, its establishment as a (sub)faculty means more than an organisational embedding in a new administrative structure. By combining three independent disciplines organisationally in one cluster faculty, a framework has been created within which co-operation among different disciplines will be stimulated and furthered in the future, a framework that will contribute to a clearer profile for multidisciplinary economics in Utrecht.

The history of economics at Utrecht University is largely responsible for an interpretation of multidisciplinary economics that can rightly be termed unique. During their study, economics students learn to look across the borders of the economics discipline systematically and to recognise that economic problems have institutional, historical and spatial dimensions pointing the way to other scientific disciplines that examine economic problems from a different perspective using different methods.

Multidisciplinary economics deliberately uses the insights and approaches of other disciplines and examines what consequences their contributions have for existing economic methods, theories and solutions to economic problems. Multidisciplinary economists should be at home in their own discipline and meet the high international standards of economic teaching and research that the discipline has developed. At the same time they should be able to recognise the limits of economics and be willing to open up new horizons by following new, discipline-transcending paths on which new insights into the analysis and solutions of economic problems can be found in collaboration with representatives of other disciplines. As a result of this search, economic methods and theories may have to be adjusted in such a way that they take insights from other disciplines into account. They may even have to be replaced by methods and theories that have been developed by other disciplines.

It is the ambition of the Utrecht School of Economics to develop eventually into an internationally recognised scientific institution that promotes multidisciplinary teaching and research in the field of economics. Teaching and research at the Utrecht School of Economics will be developed according to the IHS dimensions of economic problems. The multidisciplinary orientation of the Utrecht School of Economics implies that not only will co-operation between economists and noneconomists be encouraged, but also cooperation between business economics and general economics as two sub-disciplines of the science of economics.

Considering the ambition of the Utrecht School of Economics, the success of the new economics faculty in the years to come will depend to a great extent on the further development of multidisciplinary economics research. Unlike economics teaching, which has received extensive attention during the past nine years, the proliferation of multidisciplinary research has started quite recently. Only four years ago, the University Board made decisions, indicative of the direction the faculty was to take, about the financing of economics research. This made it possible to appoint five new professors and other academic staff all at once in 2002, an occurrence that was not only unique for Utrecht University but also for other economics faculties in the Netherlands. Since then USE's research capacity has increased steadily. Up until 2002 economists at Utrecht University, who have since moved to USE, were concerned mainly with problems in the fields of labour economics, economics and law and institutional and social economics. Considering the research interests of the new staff that has been appointed since 2002, problems to do with international economics, public economics, organisation, finance & financial markets and quantitative methods will be within the scope of multidisciplinary economics.

In the past nine years the Utrecht University board has invested heavily in multidisciplinary economics. The results are impressive. On 1st January 2004 an economics faculty came into existence with eighty eight staff members and an annual budget of € 6.2 million. The faculty employs 9 full professors, 3 extraordinary professors and 56 lecturers, assistant and associate professors who teach economics to more than 850 students.

Though the start of the Utrecht School of Economics can be seen as promising, a lot remains to be done in order to make its ambitions true, i.e. to become an internationally recognised centre of multidisciplinary economic research. In the years to come USE will face the challenge of developing a research programme that stimulates research projects in the field of multidisciplinary economics.

REFERENCES

Nieuwenburg, C.F.K. (2003). *Staathuishoudkunde en Statistiek aan de universiteit Utrecht van 1636 tot 2000 - van scholastiek naar domeingericht:* farewell speech, Utrecht University.

Siegers, J.J. (1992). Interdisciplinary Economics. *The Economist, 140 (2),* 531-544.

H. SCHENK

MULTIDISCIPLINARY ECONOMIC RESEARCH AT UTRECHT UNIVERSITY

Setting up a new faculty of economics in a country that has already got six full-blown and another two small economics departments is likely to evoke the question why this should be necessary. Behind such a question there is an implicit assumption that economies of scale are both relevant and important in higher education. The enthusiasm with which mergers in industry are often surrounded, indeed, acts like a signal to politicians and educators – and, for that matter, to hospital and building society executives too – that their organisations would also benefit from large scale. Several papers in this volume demonstrate, however, that economies of scale presumptions are rather unjustified. Instead, mergers in industry are often undertaken without any clear view on the economic benefits of the venture – and indeed in the majority of cases turn out to have none at all. At universities, moreover, what really counts is discovering the truth and developing unexplored avenues. Beyond a certain, rather low, critical threshold, size does not appear to be related to discovery and innovation. Instead, as has been convincingly argued by such diverse minds as Joseph Schumpeter and Thomas Kuhn, innovations are likely to arise as new combinations are made, especially cross-disciplinary combinations, in business as well as in science.

USE and its Tjalling C. Koopmans Research Institute aim at fostering such boundary-crossing research work. Both have been set up with the explicit idea of increasing diversity in order to be better able to provide new answers to unsolved, or incompletely solved, problems. In other words, what we are trying to do is to prevent our graduates, as well as our discipline more generally, from falling prey to what Schumpeter called the 'Ricardian vice', that is, drawing conclusions, especially policy conclusions, from models that deal with only part of an economic problem (Schumpeter, 1954).

Consequently, USE and the Koopmans Institute have set out to expand the room for multidisciplinary economics, as has already been noted in De Gijsel's earlier introduction. The directions for this expansion are rather obvious. Looking back at the development of economics over the last fifty years, both abroad and in the Netherlands, one can observe in various places a growing focus on rigour rather than relevance. While, according to some, economics may have gained in terms of academic reputation, it may have lost in terms of usefulness. The underlying processes are difficult to catch. Certainly, part of this development has been the unintended result of economists seriously searching for increases in the scientific basis for the understanding of daily practice. Partly also, however, theory development was not meant to have any relationship to the

P. de Gijsel and H. Schenk (eds.), Multidisciplinary Economics, 25–27.

real world at all. For example, Debreu, when asked about the relevance of his work to economic policy, with some pride said it had none. For another part, as especially France's so-called postautistic economics movement in the early years of this century has demonstrated, it has been the result of the expulsion of pluralism from the major institutes (see Fullbrook, 2003).

Whichever way you look at this, it may be hard to see how economics can be fully helpful when its models are dependent on first principles like utility-maximising by consumers and profit-maximising by firms, or far-sighted individual rationality and beliefs in equilibrium. Yet, by the late 20th century, 'these principles formed the core of economists' vision of reality, in the sense that all economic models were built on (them), or around variations of these principles like assumptions of bounded rationality or imperfect information' (Colander, 2001: 175).

However, it is not just a matter of the way in which theory developed. For example, McCloskey and Ziliak (1996) found that statistical inference was incorrectly used in a large majority of articles that had been published in one of the field's premier journals, the *American Economic Review*. Besides, economists pride themselves on being able to apply the newest econometric gadgetry even though the data collected are below any standard. Indeed, the very tedious and laborious way of collecting data from rather inadequate sources stands in sharp contrast to the low esteem that such work gets in the economics profession.

Thus, the founders of USE and the Koopmans Institute were led to ask whether they could do a better job? The answer was not a resounding 'yes'. Rather it was a 'no' to which was added, though, that a change in direction might contribute to making economics more adequate. In practice, this change in direction entailed first not separating business studies and economics, as is the case in most other (Dutch) departments. The idea is that strategic management and organisational structuring and restructuring concepts – elements whose treatment is normally left to business schools – determine the behaviour of firms at least as much as technology determines the optimal way of combining resources. Especially the dramatic growth of firms during the last fifty years has created too much behavioural freedom to be left untouched. Studying this discretionary part of firm behaviour at the same time requires studying its setting, i.e. the ways in which it in turn is determined by psychological factors, by history (e.g. in terms of path dependence), by location and, in a more general sense, by institutions. Similarly, financial markets are considered not just as parts of the economic fabric, but also as tools in the strategies of firms.

Secondly, we think that realising a multidisciplinary approach to economics involves confronting economic concepts and ideas with a special line-up of other social sciences. Naturally, this is easier said than done. While many researchers will find it difficult, for example, to depart from general equilibrium theory to include bits and pieces of evolutionary theory, or to insert regret assumptions when goal-directed behavioural models are simulated, or to introduce irrational exuberance when the development of financial markets is on the agenda, we intend to support such initiatives by fostering plurality.

Thus, as the inaugural addresses in this volume demonstrate: when we study competition policy, we combine economics with law; when we study the impact of mergers on firms, we also study the macroeconomic effects; when we study the multinational firm, we combine the economics of trade with the geography of locational decisions; when we study the development of financial markets, we study both the implications of the efficient market hypothesis and those of behavioural finance; when we study optimal tax regimes, we combine economics and political science.

In the end, we may be only vaguely right. But we think that such is preferable to being exactly wrong.

REFERENCES

Colander D. (2001). *The Lost Art of Economics*. Cheltenham: Edward Elgar.

Fullbrook E., ed. (2003). *The Crisis in Economics*. London: Routledge.

Mayer T. (1993). *Truth versus Precision in Economics*. Cheltenham: Edward Elgar.

McCloskey D. & Ziliak S.T. (1996). The Standard Error of Regressions, *Journal of Economic Literature* XXXIV (March): 97-114.

Schumpeter J. (1954). *History of Economic Analysis*. New York: Oxford University Press.

III
SPANNING MULTIDISCIPLINARY ECONOMICS: THE INSTITUTIONAL, HISTORICAL AND SPATIAL DIMENSIONS OF ECONOMICS

RESTRUCTURING THE WELFARE STATE

J. PLANTENGA AND P.P. DE GIJSEL

INTRODUCTION

An important element of the European social model is a rather extensive safety net, providing income and employment security as part of a comprehensive welfare state. The importance of a social safety net is generally accepted, despite the fact that the current design of most European welfare states is under pressure due to economic, demographic and financial reasons. An illustration of the commitment to combine economic efficiency with social justice is the newly designed European Employment Strategy (EES), which focuses on three overarching objectives, namely full employment, improving quality and productivity at work, and strengthening social cohesion and inclusion. The aim is to create a viable and feasible economic community, not by eliminating social rules and practices, but rather by redefining the rules and practices so that they will support economic efficiency. Yet, despite the overall support, the challenges are enormous. Education no longer guarantees stable employment and the family has turned from a risk absorbing into a risk generating institute. New – manufactured – risks demand a proper place in the social security framework and create a change in perspective. Indeed the question is who shall be responsible for taking over the (financial) consequences of critical events during the life course.

Some of the analyses and debates accompanying this striving towards new European welfare states are summarised in the following articles. Schmid's contribution focuses most explicitly on the European agenda. The ultimate aim is to present an alternative to the social liberal model and to sketch the contours of a risk sharing society, where the state empowers individuals, enterprises and other collective actors to take their responsibility, but at the same time ensures solidarity in case of risks that are beyond individual control. Plantenga summarises the Dutch debate on modernising the social security system by introducing the life course as a frame of reference. Although hailed as a policy of 'all benefits, no costs', the life course policy has become a divisive element in the once praised Dutch polder model. Both articles illustrate the complexities of a shift towards a proactive, tailor-made, flexible, yet solidaristic welfare state regime. At a more conceptual level, Nooteboom analyses the process of trust building as a process of learning, by combining framing theory and decision heuristics. In the context of social security, trust refers to mutual dependency, reciprocity and identification. The development of trust may also be an important issue when construct-

P. de Gijsel and H. Schenk (eds.), Multidisciplinary Economics, 31–32.

ing new, stable relationships between the state and the citizen and/or the employer and the employee.

Together, these articles illustrate a growing research agenda within USE, which combines modern labour and welfare economics with a sound knowledge of social trends and institutional detail. Intensive forms of co-operation, especially with lawyers and sociologists stimulate a multidisciplinary approach of welfare state restructuring. The labour market group and/or theoretical microeconomics group of USE participate in the multidisciplinary research programmes 'Labour, Market and Social Policy' and 'Market and Competition in Europe' of the Wiarda Institute of the subfaculty of law. They are also involved in the High-Potential project 'Dynamics of Co-operation, Networks and Institutions'. They supervise multidisciplinary PhD dissertation projects and participate in a number of projects funded by the Netherlands Organisation for Scientific Research (NWO), among them 'New organisational structures and employees of the future' (Nieuwe organisatievormen en werknemers van de toekomst), 'Time competition. Disturbed balances and new options in work and care' and 'Solidarity at work' (Solidariteit in het werk).

Long standing relationships exist between the research groups and the Interuniversity Centre for Social Science Theory and Methodology (ICS) and the Netherlands Interdisciplinary Demographic Institute (Nederlands Interdisciplinair Demografisch Instituut, NIDI).

On an international level members of the research groups participate in the EU Expert Group on Gender, Social Inclusion and Employment and in TLM-NET and the European Institute of Social Security and co-operate with the Social Science Centre Berlin (WZB).

G. SCHMID

TOWARDS A EUROPEAN SOCIAL MODEL:

Managing Social Risks Through Transitional Labour Markets

INTRODUCTION

The 'European social model' provokes different reactions. Most people probably associate with it generous social security, moderate inequalities in income, and corporate governance; some may even add full employment. While many want to maintain or regain these features, others see them just as the problem for a sustainable European welfare state and recommend the workfare model of the United States. Between these extremes appears a kind of social-liberal model, often sold as 'asset welfare capitalism', 'social investment state' or the 'third way' between workfare and welfare (Giddens, 1998, 2001).

Although the 'third way' has sympathetic features, it misses one important point in the hidden agenda of the 'old' European social model: the solidarity with people who do not succeed in the market despite provisions of equal opportunity and severe struggling in the competitive game. In the following essay, therefore, an alternative to the 'social-liberal' model is presented. The argument is that the 'old' social welfare state could evolve into a *risk-sharing state* where the state *empowers* individuals, enterprises and other collective actors to take over more responsibilities to manage social risks but *ensures* solidarity when individuals cannot be made responsible for external circumstances or lack the capabilities to take over risks. This thesis is developed by addressing three questions:

- First, what is the changing nature of social risks? After providing some evidence about the development of risks in the labour market, it is argued that the new emerging risks require a substantial adjustment of the established insurance institutions and a shift from state social policy to joint managing of social risks.
- Second, what is the 'social' in the European social model? It is argued that the concept of 'shared responsibilities' and 'equality of resources' lies at the root of the European social model. This concept is derived from the ethical theory of justice and stands in contrast to the tradition of utility theory emphasising 'equality of welfare'.
- Third, how should the European social model respond to the employment crisis in Europe? It is argued that the traditional unemployment insurance system could be extended to a work-life insurance based on four pillars and the institutionalisation of 'transitional labour markets' ensuring security in critical transitions over the life

P. de Gijsel and H. Schenk (eds.), Multidisciplinary Economics, 33–51.

course. The capacity to manage new social risks through transitional labour markets is demonstrated for income risks related to flexible working time regimes.

1. THE EMERGENCE OF NEW SOCIAL RISKS: FROM SOCIAL POLICY TO MANAGING SOCIAL RISKS

The distinction between class risks, life course risks and (inter-)generational risks (Esping-Andersen, 1999) is a useful typology to start with when identifying new risks, since it relates the nature of risks to the problem of allocating the responsibilities for coping with old and new risks.

1.1 Class Risks

'*Class risks*' are social risks mainly related to employment and work organisation and affecting or accruing to specific groups (or social strata). Familiar examples are miners who are more prone to occupational injury than are university professors; unskilled blue collar workers who are particularly vulnerable to technological change, low earnings and unemployment; women who often have lower wages than men, and single mothers who run higher risks of poverty than married women. Social (health, occupational, pension and unemployment) insurance and employment protection, especially for the 'male breadwinners', were the traditional responses of the welfare state.

On the demand side, the decline of manufacturing, especially of industrial mass production, the rise of service industries and the information technology are changing the nature of these risks; on the supply side, the ageing work force, rising female labour force participation and increasing educational levels have to be taken into account. This is not the place to deliberate extensively on these changes. Two main and interrelated changes, however, challenge the traditional responses of the welfare state to class risks: first, the erosion of internal labour markets, and second, the erosion of the standard employment relationship.

Internal labour markets can be considered as a risk sharing device between employer and employee, with the state in the background ensuring contract compliance (e.g. employment protection legislation) and additional support (e.g. short-time compensation to overcome cyclical demand fluctuations). Employers and employees enter into an implicit contract in which the employer guarantees stable and increasing wages and permanent employment throughout the life course in exchange for subordination, loyalty, and hard work. Employable young entrants receive wages higher than their productivity (as an incentive to stay and to invest heavily in firm specific human capital), in their middle years, they are paid below their productivity so that they will get seniority wages above their productivity during the end-phase of their work career. Thus, internal labour markets functioned like work-life insurance for the employees. However, increasing competition, new forms of work organisation (from intra-firm mass production to inter-firm project production), the larger availability of a highly educated young work force, the transferability of formerly firm specific skills through information technology etc. have lead to the erosion of this institution[1] with at least the following consequences:

- First, employment risks are run by people who have so far not been affected, namely medium or high skilled (male) senior people. As a consequence, *risks of income maintenance* through unemployment are shifting even to senior people who were formerly protected by permanent contracts and employment protection.
- Second, the *risk of income volatility* during the life course spreads over more and more people due to increasing performance and result-oriented payment or wage elements in form of capital or equity shares.
- Third, the new information technology devalues traditional skills in a much more radical way than the classical 'new' technologies of mechanics and engineering. For many trained adult people, the new technologies require a qualitative jump from practical skills to abstract and communicative skills (including foreign languages), and continuous learning even for older employees. Thus, the *risk of losing income capacity* (employability) is not only increasing but also spreading through all classes of workers.
- Fourth, wage formation based on seniority rules establishes a considerable mobility barrier for job mobility due to high reservation wages. Although we do not have historical data on the income consequences of job mobility, it is reasonable to assume that the necessary move from industrial (internal labour market) jobs to service jobs is accompanied by considerable income losses especially for elderly wage earners.
- Fifth, with the break of the natural coalition between low and high skilled workforce in the internal labour market, cross-subsidisation of wages from high skill to low skill people is no longer working, implying an outpricing of the low skilled from market entries as long as their wages or non-wage costs are not following the 'market rules'. In addition, the number of entry ports for lower skilled people is also reduced due to the decline of employment in industries prone to internal labour markets.

Closely related to the erosion of internal labour markets, but also an independent trend is the complementation of the so-called standard employment relationship by new types of work relationships, reflected especially in the increasing number of temp agencies, fixed-term contracts, self-employed contracting work (free lancers) and other 'artists' in the labour market.[2] Such new employment relationships and contingent work tend

1 For comparative evidence of changing work organisations and employment relationships see among others Auer and Cazes 2002, Cappelli et al. 1997, Marsden 1999, Supiot 2001. Gautié (2003) provides an excellent overview of the reasons and the different consequences of eroding internal labour markets plus additional references. Two caveats have to be kept in mind: First, the thesis of 'erosion' does not mean that internal labour markets are disappearing at all; second, 'occupational labour markets' follow a different 'insurance logic' and still play a large role in some countries (especially in Germany); Marsden sees or recommends even a revitalisation of occupation labour markets.

2 For an extended discussion plus references to related literature see Schmid 2002a: 152-174; especially from a labour law and gender perspective see Supiot 2001. Informative case studies on contingent work for the UK, Sweden, Spain, Germany, USA and the Netherlands are provided by Bergström and Storrie

to raise the *income security risks* throughout the individual life course for specified groups on the labour market.

Summing up the consequences of the changing nature of class risks, one can see a clear shift of the income and employment risks from unskilled male workers from external labour markets to low skilled young and female workers trying to enter or re-enter the labour market, and to skilled elderly displaced (male) workers. Traditional social insurance institutions are not well adapted to these new social risks. On the one hand, the erosion of the work-life insurance through internal labour markets has shifted the burden to the welfare state leading to an overload especially through the extension of unemployment benefits (without giving the unemployed corresponding incentives to find new employment), early retirement or disability benefits. On the other hand, many of the new risks related to atypical work remain uncovered in the traditional system, thus shifting the burden to the individuals concerned, especially to the low skilled young, the women returning to the labour market and the increasing number of self-employed.

1.2 Life course Risks

'Life course risks' are social risks depending on critical events during the life course. Originally, the family was the locus of pooling life course risks. The traditional welfare state has taken over these risks more and more often at the two 'passive' tail ends of life: children (via family allowances) and old age (pensions). Unemployment insurance, especially the Bismarckian type, was also oriented towards a stable and continuous work career, possibly only interrupted through cyclical downturns and industrial restructuring.

Changes in the family structure (from male bread-winner to two-earner families), increasing risks related to household dissolution (DiPrete, 2002), widespread (youth) unemployment or insecure careers concentrate *life course risks* more and more around the youth and prime age groups (Esping-Andersen, 1999). One indicator is the increasing number of children in families depending on social assistance because of long-term unemployment and precarious jobs.[3]

The most important change is the sustained aspiration of women to gainful employment, higher education and economic independence from the men. This does not only call for radical equal opportunity policies on the labour market in terms of affirmative action or child care infrastructure, but also for a fundamental shift in perspective. Risks are increasingly the result of human intervention in social life and in nature. In fact, they are becoming '*manufactured risks*' (Giddens, 1996: 4) more and more often, thereby producing a mix of risks difficult to disentangle, caused by external circumstances

2003; an illuminating overview about nonstandard work in developed economies is given by Houseman and Osawa (2003).

3 In Germany, the number of elderly over 65 depending on social assistance decreased to a level of 1.3 %. The number of children under 18 living in households depending on social assistance increased in West-Germany from 2.1 % (1980) to 7.2 % (1997), in East-Germany from 2.8 % (1991) to 5.0 % (1997) (Hauser and Becker, 2001: 294).

and individual or collective choices. For example, as soon as both men and women decide to share the caring functions in the family, the event of child bearing and rearing becomes a social risk requiring *income support* due to reduced earning capacities during child care. The same applies for the care for the elderly or the disabled at home. Regional job mobility required from one working partner automatically induces a risk for the other working partner: the risk of whether she or he will get a new job, if possible at the same or an even better level. Involuntary unemployment, thus, becomes not only related to technological or economic change, but also, increasingly, to household or family change, a phenomenon not yet reflected in most of the unemployment insurance schemes. Neither premium nor benefit regulation has been adjusted to the fact that more and more people (and, in future, not only women) have to take part-time jobs 'involuntarily' or even have to interrupt employment completely due to compelling family or care obligations. At present, not allowing for the adjustment of employment insurance premiums to the household situation is a strong form of 'institutionally prescribed' gender discrimination.[4]

We also observe that in almost all countries there is an increasing risk of physical and psychic disabilities highly correlated with age. This poses the challenge of managing *income replacement risks* through intelligent measures 'activating' older people, which means stimulating labour market participation instead of applying the still widespread praxis of early retirement or disability insurance. Age, in the traditional welfare state however, was more or less a biological risk not closely related to the labour market. Only a few health and occupational risks (for instance for miners) were covered by special insurances. Today and in the future (including the 'future future'), age seems to become more and more of a labour market risk. It becomes increasingly uncertain whether an occupation for which one has received training can be maintained over the entire work-life course, even if this kind of job is in further demand in the economy. Some jobs can still be fulfilled at the age of 70 or even 80, many jobs are out of range today at the age of 40, 50 or 60. Implicit and explicit hiring rules or physical or (even more) psychical conditions exclude more and more elderly from certain jobs.

However, the risk of work disability is not only related to age but more and more often to changing working conditions, often interacting with family problems. In personal services, for instance, we observe more and more burnout syndromes eventually requiring a change in job or in the location of the workplace or even both. The consequence is more stress or mobility pressure for the workers, requiring *income security* measures or, in case of (increasing frictional or transitional unemployment), *income maintenance* measures. This is especially true for young women who are challenged to make five formative choices in early adulthood within a short period of time: choices on education, job, career, partner, and having the first child. Earlier generations in the

4 This is also true for the unemployment insurance system in the United States where it is to the advantage of the employers, due to experience rating of their contributions, that non-working related resignations (even for good causes for instance due to compelling family obligations) are not attributed to their payroll budget. A study shows that women quitting their job for a good reason receive considerably less benefits than men. The authors propose, among others, unemployment benefits for (involuntary) part-timers (Smith et al, 2003).

20th century had an average of 12 to 15 years to make the same choices, and the parameters of their choices were often limited. The present generation has about 5 years in which to make the same choices, with fewer limitations (women 4.5 years and men 6 years). Educational expansion and the accompanying credential inflation are the primary causes of this development. The striking feature is that most of the young women entering disability insurance early for mental or psychological reasons did not make the formative life course decisions or at least did not make them very successfully. Their job and career choices have taken an unfortunate turn. They have often not yet found or chosen a partner. And the choice of having or not having a first child has rarely been made. The *compressed career path,* thus, turns out to be extremely stressful, and many young women especially drop out and become psychically disabled. The number of young women entering disability insurance has risen dramatically during the last decade (de Bruijn, de Vries and ten Cate, 2003).

1.3 (Inter-)Generational Risks

'(Inter-)Generational risks' are social risks associated with the generational status (age or so-called 'cohort'), ethnic background and/or regional environment. These risks are, in distinction to 'class risks', inherited and carried through the generation. Old risks were, for instance, belonging to a baby boom generation, to an ethnic (and discriminated) minority, or living in a depressed or underdeveloped area. Even in the case of migration (induced by local risks), employment careers are usually contingent for a long time on the former regional background where people come from. Although logically independent from market mechanisms, inheritance and markets are usually mutually reinforcing.

New *(inter-)generational risks* are, first, evidently emerging with the ageing of the work force. Due to the changing relationship between the 'active' and the 'passive' population, the demand for a new generational contract related to social security (especially pension insurance) is at stake. More and more often, managing pension systems means managing active ageing.

Second, although inherited poverty has declined, the information society might create new inherited risks related to new educational, communicative and intellectual skills. For *Germany* in particular, the so-called PISA shock was not so much finding the country at the end of the ranking scores in various ability tests. The real shock was the high correlation of inequalities in employability or *income capacities* with the socioeconomic status of the parents.

Third, to be born in a generation means also to be born in a certain location and regional environment. It is evident that geography has a tremendous impact on employment and income chances. This is certainly nothing new. What is new is, however, that internationalisation, especially European integration reinforced by the common Euro-currency, and last but not least the coming accession of ten new member states, will intensify and change the character of competition. Whereas the eastern European countries will have to speed up the change from agriculture to industry or even to jump immediately to services, the western European countries will have to adjust even further to diversified high quality production and services with low chances for unskilled people, with higher pressure on wage moderation and mobility. Thus, these new social risks will be sources of new ethnic, local or regional inequalities calling for adjustment of social policies and established institutions of risk management. Unemployment insurance has either not yet developed far in many European countries, or is lacking incentives for status, income and regional mobility. Since the causes of (inter-)generational risks become more and more interrelated internationally, the new measures probably require more international co-ordination or even new transnational institutions.

Welfare state regimes responded to these new risks more or less with their established social policy instruments, albeit quite differently: liberal regimes responded with minimal intervention, social-democratic regimes with maximal intervention, conservative regimes somewhere in between (Scharpf and Schmidt, 2000). Disappointing results, however, lead them to change direction. Although the reactions were quite different (with different measures, intensity and speed), one common underlying pattern appears: a shift from public to public-private forms of managing social risks.

The intrusion of 'risk management' into the public discourse, however, has to be registered with care. In fact, the term implies taking over more individual responsibility as a social norm without showing clearly the conditions under which such a paradigm change promises higher adaptability to structural change without seriously demolishing the life-chances of people protected so far by traditional social policy. Thus, we should not allow risk management to be only cheap and metaphorical talk. The necessity of shifting from old-fashioned social policy to 'risk management' requires careful normative, analytical, empirical and methodological underpinning which is still underdeveloped (Esping-Andersen, 1999).[5] In the following, only the normative dimension is attacked and a possible solution suggested.

2. THE RISK-SHARING SOCIETY: FROM 'EQUALITY OF WELFARE' TO 'EQUALITY OF RESOURCES'

'Life guarantees a chance but no just distribution' (Anonymous). This quotation from an anonymous writer reflects a widespread opinion that a 'just distribution' is a utopia. The paradox, however, is that the discussion on the guarantee of just distribution is exactly what is on the hidden agenda of discourses such as those about the European social model. It deals with the question of how gratuitous social and economic inequality can be avoided, that is, inequality that cannot be justified on rational grounds in terms of differences in effort or talent. As we have discussed above, risk management promises a direction that might bring us nearer to the utopia in the sense of a world without unjustified inequalities. The task, now, is to clear up two related questions:

5 From an historical point of view see the illuminating book by Bernstein (1996); for a lucid presentation of analytical problems related to social risk management see Gigerenzer (2003); for a stimulating and even provocative discussion of how risk management techniques of the financial sector can be adapted or adopted by the social policy sector see Shiller (2003); for the economic 'classics' see Arrow (1974) and Stiglitz (1983).

First, what is an unjustified inequality? Second, how are individual and collective responsibilities to be reallocated in the shaping of a new 'European social model'?

2.1 The 'Social' in the European Social Model

'Equality of welfare' and 'equality of resources' are the two mainstream theories of social justice. *'Equality of welfare'* stems from utilitarian theory. It aims at maximising average welfare under the condition that nobody will be worse off. Utilitarian theory, however, is ethically insensitive. It makes no distinction between whether the distribution of income or life chances results from individual choice (and efforts) or circumstances. *Equality of resources* aims at maximising equal opportunity. With respect to distribution of outcomes, it sets explicit criteria either from a social contract or from an ethical point of view. The most prominent representative of contract theory is John Rawls (1990), whom Ronald Dworkin (2000) opposes from an ethical point of view. Although highly abstract and inconclusive in institutional details, Dworkin's theory seems to be promising in solving some of the ambivalences and weaknesses of Rawls' theory of justice.

Rawls and Dworkin are united in their criticism against the utilitarian theory of justice. The main problem with welfare economics is the lack of any explicit social criteria for distributing welfare. Rawls offers a solution for such a criterion by suggesting a thought experiment that became famous: What kind of contract regarding welfare distribution would people conclude under the 'veil of ignorance'? They would vote, he concludes, for the difference principle:[6] no inequality in 'primary goods' is justified unless it improves the position of the economically worst-off group.[7]

However, there are severe problems in applying this principle to managing social risks. First, the difference principle offers no advice where the ceiling defining the worst-off class should be drawn. Second, it legitimises any inequality as long as the situation of the worst-off improves only a tiny margin.[8] Third, it does not appeal to the majority of people. It draws attention only to the position of those who have the fewest

6 It is important to note that the 'difference principle' is the third priority in the catalogue within the 'two principles of justice'; note also, that Rawls, reacting to critics, made only 'stylistic' changes of the second principle of justice (Rawls, 2001: 42 f).

7 A little calculation shows the difference between the average utility justice and Rawls maximin social contract justice: Let the average income be 1,000, the lowest quintile having 200 and the upper quintile 2000 (relation 1:10). The increase of average income to 1,500 leaving the lowest quintile at 200 and the upper at 3000 (relation 1:15) would fit with the utility approach (nobody is worse off), but not with Rawls. His 'maximin strategy' on the basis of the difference principle would, for instance, prefer an increase to 1,200 at 300 for the lowest quintile and 2,000 for the highest (relation 1:7), thus leading to a lower average income per capita.

8 This objection might be contested depending on how Rawls' first principle of justice, equality in primary goods, is interpreted. If 'having a decent job' were subsumed under primary goods, then the requirement of redistribution would be much higher than in case of not including labour market participation under 'primary goods'. In his restatement, Rawls seems to give, for instance, equal opportunity for education the status of 'basic liberty'; he also acknowledges that the state has to ensure that 'excessive concentration of property and wealth' has to be prevented (Rawls, 2001: 43 f). For an illuminating discussion of the theory of justice see also Standing 1999, Vandenbroucke 2001.

primary goods. Those who are better off but nevertheless have to struggle to secure a decent living for their families are neglected. The difference principle seems, therefore, most appropriate in times of rising general expectations. But in times of dramatic social and economic change, the likelihood is great that the middle class will be affected most. It is not surprising that these losers (or people in danger) feel great resentment when part of their hard-earned wage is taken in taxes and paid to those who do not work at all.

Dworkin's main objection, however, is that Rawls' difference principle is ethically insensitive. It is not based on the basic distinction between the causal effects of (external) circumstances and individual choices. It neglects individual responsibility for outcomes under given circumstances such as differences in talent or differences in the exposure to economic change. Responsibility for the consequences of individual choice, however, is a crucial and widely accepted ethical principle. It also underlies the notion of risk management, which assumes an active participation of individuals in responding to external challenges. Taking over responsibility for the consequences of individual choice, however, is fair only under the condition of equality of resources.

The other side of the coin of *'responsibility for the consequences of individual choice'* is reflected in Amartya Sen's concept of '*capabilities*'. Social justice in terms of responsible 'equality of resources' also means equality of opportunities in the sense of having a choice between alternative sets of resources. Even if one has to acknowledge the advance Rawls made by extending the concept of income as well-being to the notion of 'primary goods' (rights, liberties and the social bases of self-respect), the equality of these resources does not yet ensure the individual capability to choose a life one has reason to value. If the object is to concentrate on the individual's real opportunity to pursue her objectives (as Rawls explicitly recommends), then one has to take into account not only the primary goods that people respectively hold, but also the relevant personal characteristics that govern the conversion of primary goods into the person's ability to promote her ends. An essential element of this ability is the freedom of choice. *'A person's "capability" refers to the alternative combinations of functionings that are feasible for her to achieve. Capability is thus a kind of freedom: the substantive freedom to achieve alternative functioning combinations (or less formally put, the freedom to achieve various lifestyles)'* (Sen, 2001: 75).

Dworkin offers the *hypothetical insurance scheme* to solve the twin problem of consequences related to choices and to circumstances. He starts with the following ideal-type assumptions: wealth and other opportunities are fairly distributed. Everyone is aware of global competition, technological instability, increasing average age, and all the other factors that contribute to our contemporary economic insecurity. Everyone is offered the opportunity to buy insurance providing a stipulated income replacement in case of unemployment or income volatility. The insurance is offered at community rates, that is, at the same premium for the same package of benefits for everyone, because everyone assumes that each person, including him or herself, is equally likely to lose his/her job or to be affected by the erosion of human capital or income capacity. People make their individual insurance decisions prudently; that is, they decide whether to insure against low income, and what income to insure against not earning in a way appropriate to their dominant hopes, tastes, and values.

2.2 The Risk-Sharing State: A New Balance between Individual and Collective Responsibilities

What kind of insurance will come out of this hypothetical situation? Dworkin concludes that neither a severe policy (which means cutting benefits at some point and enforcing workfare) nor a generous policy (with no restriction beyond the provision that the claimant must seek and accept employment) would be chosen if reasonable people were put in the hypothetical insurance situation. They would rather chose, what he calls, the '*mandatory interventionist policy*'. According to this model, which Dworkin does not develop in detail, the state would obligate people to buy a minimum insurance (and also guarantee the solvability) topped up by optional insurance according to their preferences. The aim of minimum insurance would be to ensure equality of resources rather than finding ways of equalizing welfare. Since human capital is the most essential resource to surviving in the labour market, one obvious solution would be that the unemployed claimant pursues job training at the expense of the insurer and takes any suitable job, while the insurer must provide training and use its best efforts to support the finding of jobs.

Dworkin deliberates only on the design of unemployment insurance in the narrower sense. He makes only indirect reference to the broader set of income risks during the life course by emphasising the need of periodic redistribution, for instance, through inheritance tax and progressive income taxation. His framework for responsible equality of resources, however, can easily be adapted to the growing complexity of the labour market. Four ideal-type forms of risk management can be distinguished according to whether risks arise from choices or circumstances, and depending on who should be made accountable to manage the risks.

Case I, *individual responsibility*, comprises cases where the risks arise from individual choices and could be managed completely through private insurance, including implicit or explicit contracts between employers and employees or agreements by collective bargaining. Examples are private unemployment insurance schemes, implicit insurance through seniority wages, and employment insurance through concession bargaining, co-financing of apprenticeship and training.

Case II, *equal opportunity through civil rights*, refers to the redistribution of resources to promote equality in opportunities. Although risks are the result of individual choices, this kind of redistribution gets its justification by compassion or civil rights status. Some consequences of individual choices are so crucial and the ensuing vulnerability so overwhelming that we want to correct these effects anyway.[9] In this case, the state has to ensure – by own provision or by entrusting non-profit organisations – that the damages from such risks are compensated or at least relieved. Examples are basic income guarantees, drawing rights or vouchers, targeted measures for the losers of structural change.

9 For example, intensive care units admitting two critically wounded drivers will not ask themselves which of the two violated the traffic regulations and which one did not. The same applies to a great number of decisions where the question 'How did you get into such dire straits?' is simply not asked (Vandenbroucke, 2002: XV).

Case III, *measures stimulating labour market participation*, refers to risks arising from (external) circumstances that are out of the range of individual influence. Individuals, households or firms would be able to do much to prepare against such risks, to prevent or alleviate them to some extent or to adjust quickly to the new circumstances through active job search, retraining or temporary acceptance of lower wages. Individual learning accounts, mobility accounts or time saving would be other examples serving as an individual insurance buffer against external risks. The state would share the risks through providing the necessary infrastructure, the regulatory framework or tax incentives for private insurance arrangements.

Case IV, *redistribution of resources*, refers to pure external risks (circumstances) completely out of the range of individual choices (for instance economic recessions, structural change through new technologies or globalisation) whose damage can only be compensated through the (ensuring) state either by public provision of corresponding services, goods and cash, or by delegating the task and by close supervision of implementation (regulated self-organisation). Classical unemployment insurance (UI) is the typical example. The idea of 'inequality insurance' (Shiller, 2003: 149 ff) also belongs to this category; it proposes reframing the tax system in such a way that a certain (politically chosen) level of inequality is maintained, compensating thereby the consequences of an economy constantly buffeted by changing technology for which individual people cannot be held responsible.

In practice, of course, we will always find mixes of these ideal types. The typology, however, might help to find reasons for failures of existing social policy arrangements or to find hints for their reform or even for social innovation. Dworkin's emphasis on the need of (periodic) redistribution in favour of the equality of resources fits well with the concept of transitional labour markets (see next section). The changes in the labour market require a continuous shift of resources from old to new risks. Equality of resources is a precondition for the freedom of (employment) choices during the life course. High minimum income guarantees, subsidised individual development accounts and drawing rights (e.g. one year sabbatical during a life course) would be elements of a corresponding employment strategy.

In addition, the 'equality of resources' approach clearly advises on the proper strategy for financing social risk management: the main resources for redistribution are income taxes, especially high inheritance taxes, since low taxed inheritance would give children of rich parents an unfairly better start than children of poor parents. Active labour market policies with an impact on redistribution would also be financed through progressive income taxes and not through payroll taxes (social security contributions) or consumption taxes. It can be argued that, for redistribution, it is fairer to rely on overall income than on wages only, since taxes on income cover a much broader base of resources (wages, assets, interest).

What kind of employment or labour market policy follows from this conceptual framework? The following section will try to provide at least a partial answer.

3. MANAGING SOCIAL RISKS THROUGH TRANSITIONAL LABOUR MARKETS: FROM UNEMPLOYMENT INSURANCE TO WORK-LIFE INSURANCE

The concept of transitional labour markets (TLM) offers a conceptual guideline for managing employment related social risks during the life course (Schmid and Gazier, 2002). As an *analytical concept*, TLM refer to the observation that the borderlines between gainful employment and other productive activities are becoming increasingly blurred. The 'standard labour contract' is eroding. People transit more and more between different employment statuses: between part-time and full-time, dependent and self-employment, unemployment and employment, education or training and work, unpaid family and gainful labour market work, work and retirement. Thus, as an analytical concept, TLM emphasise the dynamics of labour markets by focusing the analysis on flows rather than purely on stocks, and they apply methodologies that detect, compare and explain patterns in the myriad of individual transitions. Some of these transitions are critical in the sense that they may lead to downward spirals of job careers ending in recurrent unemployment or (finally) in long-term unemployment, poverty, discouraged inactivity or violent protest. In line with the concept of risk management, the TLM approach measures probabilities or frequencies of social risks during the life course, for instance the risk of becoming unemployed, of getting stuck in fixed-term contracts or of moving downward as regards one's career after shifting from full-time to part-time work.

As a *normative concept*, TLM therefore envisage new kinds of arrangements to prevent those transitions from becoming gates to social exclusion and to transform them into gates to a wider range of opportunities or capabilities for the employed as well as for inactive or unemployed people. TLM aim at '*making transitions pay*' through institutional arrangements that enhance employability and flexibility both for the unemployed (*integrative transitions*) as well as for the employed (*maintenance transitions*) through a differentiated set of negotiated mobility options, entitlements and income insurance not only in case of unemployment but also in case of income variations related to risky transitions. TLM focus therefore on preventative measures to avoid open unemployment or '*exclusionary transitions*'. They support the development of career paths, allowing the combination of paid and unpaid activities (including, especially, education and training), facilitating job re-entry or two-way mobility and gradual retirement. In brief: TLM aim at providing institutional arrangements, which mutually support flexibility and security ('flexicurity'), and stepping stones to help people move from precarious to stable jobs, or establishing bridges to overcome discontinuities during the life course.

3.1 Principles of Transitional Labour Markets

'*Making transitions pay*' requires institutions that realise in one way or the other the following principles:

- An organisation of work that enables people to combine wages with other income sources such as transfers, equity shares or savings.

- *Entitlements, or social rights,* which allow choices between different employment statuses according to shifting preferences and circumstances during the life course.
- *Policy provisions* which support multiple usages of insurance funds, especially the (preventive) usage of work-life insurance for financing measures that enhance employability.
- *Public and/or private employment services* which focus not only on the unemployed but also on the employed who run the risk of unemployment or who are in need of or desire risky transitions during their life course.

In dealing with social risks, it is important to identify the actors, their interests and ability to adjust or possibly to resist to changes in social risks. The typology of social risks that we have used in section 1 is suitable for answering the related structural questions: Which persons are affected by social risks (social space)? When are they affected (social time)? How are they affected relative to others (social justice)? This 'structural' typology, however, is incomplete since it does not characterise the type of income risk related to the life course events considered as 'risky'. A combination of the 'structural' with a 'functional' perspective is required in order to get hints about which type of policy might be suitable. Since we are primarily interested in employment and income related risks, we also have to ask which specific kinds of income resources or employability capacities are affected during the life course.

For this kind of question, the TLM framework delivers a logical structure according to the five main critical events during a life course:

- First, developing, maintaining and enhancing the *income capacity* (known also as 'employability') for successful transitions between education and employment and during transitions between (continuous) training and employment.
- Second, guaranteeing *income security* during critical transitions between various employment relationships, especially between part-time and full-time work, between dependent employment and self-employment, and – increasingly important – between high and low wage jobs.
- Third, providing *income support* during phases in the life course in which the income capacity is reduced due to social obligations such as the care for children or other dependent persons.
- Fourth, securing *income maintenance* during transitions between employment and unemployment.
- Fifth, providing *income replacement* in case of disability or retirement, i.e. in phases in which employability is severely reduced or lacking completely.

In the following, the capacity of TLM to manage new social risks will be demonstrated only in the case of income security risks related to changes of the employment status that might for various reasons occur during the life course.[10]

10 For an extensive presentation of TLM and for more details on specific measures see de Koning/Mosley 2001, Gazier 2003, O'Reilly et al 2000, Schmid/Gazier 2002 (especially chapter 12), Schmid 2002c, Schömann/O'Connell 2002; with particular reference to the Netherlands and including some creative extensions of the original concept of TLM see Wilthagen 2002, and in the spirit of TLM also Sarfati 2002.

3.2 Managing Transitions between Different Employment Statuses

How can *income security* related to risky transitions between different employment statuses be managed? One strategy is *pooling precarious jobs and virtually 'normal' full-time jobs*. For instance, we find in France or Italy that multiple employment relationships are treated as one regular employment, and, especially in the Netherlands, we find more and more multiple part-time jobs or combinations of part-time self-employment and part-time dependent employment. In Germany, provisions have been developed to maintain full unemployment insurance benefits for some time in case of failed attempts to develop self-employment, and since 1983 artists as well as journalists are protected through a special social insurance in which the state co-operates by sharing 20% of the contributions (Haak and Schmid, 2001).

Another strategy is *enhancing internal flexibility*. An example is 'concession bargaining', which means exchanging wage flexibility for employment protection. Intermittent working time reduction without (full) wage compensation complemented by publicly subsidised training is another example of bridging employment risks without open unemployment. Work sharing arrangements that pool preferences of (intermittent) worktime reductions and unemployment risks are still underdeveloped, but good practices are available (Schmid, 2002b: 406). With the 5,000 x 5,000 agreement, Volkswagen recently provided another model of (flexible) performance-oriented wages combined with training measures and cost sharing of training to enhance sustainable employability.

A new trend is some kind of *mobility insurance*, or – in other words – the transition from passive to active employment protection. The recently (January 2003) changed severance pay law in Austria ('Abfertigungsrecht'), initiated by the social partners (!), is an interesting example. Guided by the principle of 'flexicurity', it refers explicitly to the increasing mobility and instability of jobs. In case of dismissal, each employee receives a severance allowance, which she can save if she wishes, even if she has only a brief employment record or resigns of her own accord. The size of the severance allowance increases with the number of years employed. For three years, e.g., one is entitled to two months' salary, 12 months' salary for 25 years. This is financed out of the employers' contributions of 1.53 % of the salary. Payment of severance is excluded as long as contributions do not exceed three years in the case of dismissal for personal failure or voluntary resignation. However, also in these cases, the entitlement remains virtually on account for as long as necessary until there is a legitimate claim for payment. A special 'Employee Accounting Office' (Mitarbeiterversorgung, MV-Kasse) administrates the fund. The claim, therefore, is directed to the MV-account and not to the individual employer! The employees have the choice of cash payment or of additional premium to the pension fund.

The Netherlands also has sector-specific severance funds ('Wachtgeld') financed by employers and incorporated in its unemployment insurance system (from contributions of 0.07 % of wages in the insurance economy to 2.78 % in cultural services). The Danish employment protection system combining a low level of dismissal protection with a high level of transfer payments in case of unemployment (at least for low and medium income earners) is a *functional equivalent to such mobility insurance*. About 40 per cent of the unemployed return to the same employer.

Finally, new risk management technologies or the adoption of techniques already established by financial markets open up the possibility of *private insurance schemes* reducing risks of income volatility or supporting mobility.[11] The analogy is as follows: a company that uses oil as an input in production can, for example, buy an option to purchase it at a predetermined price and thus eliminate the risk that the oil will get too expensive. Or a European firm that has a cash inflow denominated in American dollars can, with the help of an investment bank, sign a swap contract that exchanges this dollar income for Euros at a predetermined exchange rate, thereby eliminating currency risk. Similarly, in the United States at least, one finds venture capital firms that help young start-up companies by insuring salaries thereby protecting employees from the great income volatility connected with such companies and at the same time stimulating them to take over such risks and, eventually, to take advantage of the potential rewards of such risky business.

In addition, by analogy to financial markets, individuals may be able to buy financial swaps of average incomes in their region (as measured by a regional income index), thereby reducing the risk of falling wages through foreign competition. It will also be possible to create home equity insurance contracts that protect them against a decline in the market value of their homes, thus reducing regional mobility barriers. In this vein it would also be possible to create contracts for individuals that provide incentives for them to advance their own individual careers. An individual may then develop a highly risky personal career, acquiring specialised skills that might turn out to be extremely important but also run the risk of becoming useless. Such individual contracts could stimulate the economic dynamics, if they free people from career risks and allow them to be more adventurous in all aspects of their careers. Career insurances combined with career services might set free enormous energies of individual creativity and diversity.

3.3 The European Social Model: Towards a Work-Life Insurance in Europe

The answers to the three questions of how the European social model could become meaningful or even start off in a new direction can now be summarised. The main suggestion is to consider the social dimension as a problem of 'risk management' and to look especially for institutional arrangements that cope with the risks related to critical events during the work-life course. We have identified five types of such critical events: the transition from school to work or between employment and education, the transition between various employment statuses or the combination of different employment statuses, the transition between unpaid (usually family) work and labour market work, the transitions between unemployment and employment, and finally the transitions from employment to retirement or between (partial) work disability and full employment.

11 The following examples are inspired by Shiller 2003.

Managing social risks through transitional labour markets suggests extending the time-honoured unemployment insurance to work-life insurance. If such a system were to be established in a systematic way and co-ordinated properly with the other social protection or social security systems, it would be an effective functional equivalent for rigid employment protection systems. The shift from unemployment insurance towards multifunctional work-life insurance would not necessarily imply more public expenditure. In many cases, legal entitlements to negotiate collectively or individually on various transitional arrangements would suffice. It could even reduce the tremendous costs of conventional unemployment benefits through activating transfer entitlements to job or employability investments. However, as it became quite clear, the concept of 'activation' based on the philosophy of balancing 'individual rights and responsibilities' cannot completely substitute for the need to redistribute means and ends in favour of those people who become the losers of structural change due to bad luck or circumstances for which they cannot be held responsible. And even if people might indeed be responsible, they can run into dire situations that require immediate help. 'Managing social risks through transitional labour markets' would redistribute resources periodically in favour of enlarging the opportunity set for all people, independent of their talent and fortune, out of compassion and solidarity.

It was therefore suggested that the concept of 'equality of resources' – developed by Ronald Dworkin and complemented by Armatya Sen's concept of 'capabilities' – should be followed instead of the utilitarian concept of 'equality of welfare.' Following the typology of risk management derived from this framework, work-life insurance would consist of four pillars:

- First, the conventional unemployment insurance pillar would be reduced to the core function of covering income risks of involuntary unemployment through pure circumstances. Since the income portfolio, especially of middle or high wage earners, is broadening, the financing basis of such schemes would have to include a redistribution element through extending the contribution base, for example including non-wage income from equity shares or other profits, and through abolishing wage income ceilings. The corresponding reduction or exemption of payroll taxes for low-wage earners would help to create jobs in the low-wage sector and increase the work incentive through reduced tax wedges. In addition, an overall income inequality insurance would help to overcome income volatilities due to technological and economic change thereby encouraging overall risk taking and enhancing productivity.[12]
- The second pillar would consist of various individualised social security, employability or mobility accounts. The current unemployment insurance contributions could be divided into two parts, one covering the costs of the first pillar, the classical unemployment insurance (unconditional solidarity), and the other covering the costs of the second pillar, the individualised mobility accounts, either legally mandated or collectively bargained (negotiated solidarity).

12 For the productivity enhancing effects of unemployment (and respectively income inequality) insurance probably exceeding the related moral hazard effects see Acemoglu and Shimer 1999 and Gangl 2003.

- The third pillar, equality of opportunity transfers or funds would be financed through general taxes. Selective active labour market policies, and state subsidised mobility accounts could be used to establish drawing rights or vouchers to 'insure' the income risks related to various kinds of transitions during the life course. Vouchers would enable and empower workers legally and financially to engage in transitions and to manage their own transitions adequately. Another strategy of equalizing resources through ex ante redistribution would be some kind of basic income guarantee independent from the work-life course, especially basic pensions. Discontinuity of income streams during the life course, caused by a mix of individual choices, cultural inheritance or just by 'accidents', would thereby not be punished but even encouraged. Labour market policy would no longer only stimulate people (so far mostly men) to take regular jobs, but also stimulate people (from now on especially men) to take on unpaid family work or other kinds of civil work.
- The fourth pillar would consist of various private insurance schemes, individually or collectively negotiated between employers and employees. Since established (implicit) private insurances are eroding, such as seniority wages (especially in internal labour markets) and status related wages (especially related to formal educational levels and to family status), new forms of insurances based on individual responsibility will have to be developed. We found that new techniques of risk management and the adoption of management techniques from financial markets might enormously extend the possibility of insuring against labour market risks privately.

European integration created a fundamental asymmetry between policies promoting market efficiency at the European level and those promoting social protection and equality still basically at the national level. The debate on the European social model, therefore, is a debate on Europeanising social policy (Scharpf, 2002). In reality medium-term social policy in Europe will be shaped differently according to the different welfare traditions and to the different stages of economic development. However, the open method of co-ordination – understood not only as a cognitive but also as a normative process – might help to shape something like a 'European social model' in the long run (Rodrigues, 2002: 22-23).

The proposal of an encompassing work-life insurance based on the concept of TLM contributes to this debate. It could serve as a regulatory idea for social justice over the life course as well as for work-life balance endorsing overall gender equality on the labour market and increasing freedom of choice. The social-liberal vision of 'asset equality' or of the 'social investment state' cannot substitute for the need of continuous redistribution during the life course in favour of people hit by old and especially new risks. Supporting the work force alone does not suffice since bad luck can get all people into desperate situations despite their talents and individual efforts. Thus, the modern welfare state has also to ensure solidarity – out of sheer compassion and out of the desire to avoid gratuitous inequality – through the periodic redistribution of resources and through re-establishing the ability of individuals to manage their own life. The concept of 'Managing social risks through transitional labour markets' provides a modern and realistic strategy for an equality and efficiency enhancing strategy, emphasising both individual as well as collective responsibility in sharing social risks. Needless to say, it requires further rigorous empirical and analytical research.

REFERENCES

Acemoglu, D., & Shimer, R. (2000). Productivity gains from unemployment insurance. *European Economic Review, 44,* 1195-1224.

Arrow, K. J. (1974). *Essays in the theory of risk-bearing, Amsterdam and Oxford.* New York: North-Holland Publishing Company, American Elsevier Publishing Company.

Auer, P., & Cazes, S. (Eds.).(2002). *Employment stability in an age of flexibility.* Geneva: International Institute for Labour Studies.

Bergström, O., & Storrie, D. (Eds.). (2003). *Contingent employment in Europe and in the United States.* Cheltenham, UK and Northampton, MA, USA: Edward Elgar.

Bernstein, P. L. (1996). *Against the gods. The remarkable story of risk.* New York: John Wileys & Sons.

Bruijn, J. de, Vries, G. de, & Cate, H. ten,. (2003). *The burden of late modernity: work-related disability among women in the Netherlands.* Unpublished manuscript.

Cappelli, P., Bassie, L., Katz, H., Knoke, D., Osterman, P., & Useem, M. (1997). *Change in work.* New York and Oxford: Oxford University Press.

DiPrete, T. (2002). Life course risks, mobility regimes and mobility consequences: a comparison of Sweden, Germany, and the United States. *American Journal of Sociology, 108,* 267-309.

Dworkin, R. (2000). *Sovereign virtue. The theory and practice of equality.* Cambridge, Mass., and London: Harvard University Press.

Esping-Andersen, G. (1999). *Social foundations of postindustrial economies.* Oxford: Oxford University Press.

Gangl, M. (2003). *Unemployment dynamics in the United States and West Germany: economic restructuring, institutions, and labor market processes.* Heidelberg and New York: Springer.

Gautié, J. (2003). *From internal to transitional labour markets.* Unpublished manuscript (University of Reims and Centre d'Etudes de l'Emploi).

Gazier, B. (2003). *Tous 'Sublimes'. Vers un nouveau plein-emploi.* Paris: Flammarion.

Giddens, A. (1996). *Beyond left and right. The future of radical politics.* Cambridge: Polity Press (first print 1994).

Giddens, A. (1998). *The Third Way. The renewal of social democracy.* Cambridge and Oxford: Polity Press.

Giddens, A. (Ed.). (2001). *The global Third Way.* Cambridge: Polity Press.

Gigerenzer, G. (2002). *Reckoning with risk: learning to live with uncertainty.* London: Penguin Books.

Haak, C., &. Schmid, G. (2001). Arbeitsmärkte für Künstler und Publizisten: Modelle der künftigen Arbeitswelt? *Leviathan, 29 (2),* 157-178.

Hauser, R., & Becker, I. (2001). Lohnsubventionen und verbesserter Familienlastenausgleich als Instrumente zur Verringerung von Sozialhilfeabhängigkeit. In H.C. Mager, H. Schäfer, K. Schrüfer (Eds.), *Private Versicherung und Soziale Sicherung. Festschrift zum 60. Geburtstag von Roland Eisen* (pp. 293-312). Marburg: Metropolis.

Houseman, S. & Osawa, M. (Eds.). (2003). *Nonstandard work in developed economies. Causes and consequences.* Kalamazoo, Mich.: W.E. Upjohn Institute for Employment Research.

Koning, J. de, & Mosley, H. (Eds.). (2001). *Labour market policy and unemployment. Impact and process evaluations in selected European countries.* Cheltenham: Edward Elgar.

Marsden, D. (1999). *A theory of employment systems: Micro-foundations of societal diversity.* Oxford: Oxford University Press.

O'Reilly, J., Cebrián, I., & Lallement, M. (Eds.). (2000). *Working-time changes. Social integration through transitional labour markets,* Cheltenham, UK and Northampton, MA, USA: Edward Elgar.

Rawls, J. (1990). *A theory of justice, Oxford.* Oxford University Press [Tenth impression, first published 1972].

Rawls, J. (2001). *Justice as fairness – A restatement* (edited by Erin Kelly), Cambridge, Mass., and London: The Belknap Press of Harvard University Press.

Rodrigues, M. J. (Ed.) (2002). *The new knowledge economy in Europe. A strategy for international competitiveness and social cohesion*. Cheltenham, UK and Northampton, MA, USA: Edward Elgar.

Sarfati, H. (2002). Labour market and social protection policies: linkages and interactions. In H. Sarfati & G. Bonoli (Eds.), *Labour market and social protection reforms in international perspective. Parallel or converging tracks?* (pp. 11-57). Aldershot, England and Burlington, USA: Ashgate.

Scharpf, F. W. (2002). The European social model: coping with the challenges of diversity. In *Journal of Common Market Studies, 40*, (pp. 645-670).

Scharpf, F. W. & Schmidt, Vivien A. (Eds.). (2000). *Welfare and work in the open economy. Volume I: From vulnerability to competitiveness; Volume II: Diverse responses to common challenges*. Oxford: Oxford University Press.

Schmid, G. (2002a). Towards a theory of transitional labour markets. In G. Schmid & B. Gazier (Eds.). *The dynamics of full employment. Social integration through transitional labour markets* (pp. 151-196). Cheltenham, UK and Northampton, MA, USA: Edward Elgar.

Schmid, G. (2002b). Transitional labour markets and the European social model: towards a new employment compact. In G. Schmid & B. Gazier (Eds.). *The dynamics of full employment. Social integration through transitional labour markets* (pp. 393-435). Cheltenham, UK and Northampton, MA, USA: Edward Elgar.

Schmid, G. (2002c). *Wege in eine neue Vollbeschäftigung. Übergangsarbeitsmärkte und aktivierende Arbeitsmarktpolitik*. Frankfurt a. M. and New York: Campus.

Schmid, G. & Gazier, B. (Eds.) (2002). *The dynamics of full employment. Social integration through transitional labour markets*. Cheltenham, UK and Northampton, MA, USA: Edward Elgar.

Schömann, K. & O'Connell, P.J. (Eds.). (2002). *Education, training and employment dynamics. Transitional labour markets in the European Union*. Cheltenham, UK and Northampton, MA, USA: Edward Elgar.

Sen, A. (2001). Development as freedom, New York: Alfred A. Knopf.

Shiller, R. (2003). *The new financial order: risk in the 21st century*. Princeton: Princeton University Press.

Smith, R., McHugh, R. & Stettner, A. (2003). Unemployment insurance and voluntary quits. *Challenge 46 (3)*, 89-107.

Standing, G. (1999). *Global labour flexibility. Seeking distributive justice*. London and New York: Macmillan/St. Martin's Press.

Stiglitz, J. E. (1983). Risk, incentives and insurance. The pure theory of moral hazard. *The Geneva Papers on Risk and Insurance, 8 (26), January*, 4-33.

Supiot, A. (2001). *Beyond employment. Changes in work and the future of labour law in Europe*. Oxford: Oxford University Press.

Vandenbroucke, F. (2001). *Social justice and individual ethics in an open Society. Equality, responsibility, and incentives*. Berlin and New York: Springer.

Vandenbroucke, F. (2002). Foreword. Sustainable social justice and 'open co-ordination' in Europe. In G. Esping-Andersen with D. Gallie, A.M. Hemerijck & J. Myles, *Why we need a new welfare state* (pp. VIII-XXIV). Oxford: Oxford University Press.

Wilthagen, T. (2002). Managing social risks with transitional labour markets. In H. Mosley, J. O'Reilly, K. Schömann (Eds.), *Labour markets, gender and institutional change. Essays in honour of Günther Schmid* (pp. 264-289). Cheltenham, UK and Northampton, MA, USA: Edward Elgar.

J. PLANTENGA

DUTCH DEBATES: MODERNISING SOCIAL SECURITY BY INTRODUCING THE LIFE COURSE AS A FRAME OF REFERENCE[1]

1. INTRODUCTION

The aim of the existing social system has always been to offer citizens the security of an income in those circumstances in which it is not possible or not considered possible to perform salaried work. If we are no longer able to work due to long-term illness or a handicap, if we lose our job, and when we turn 65, we can apply for a benefit.

This seems a rather straightforward observation, yet at the beginning of the 21st century there is little consensus about the actual interpretation of this basic principle. The current system is under attack as being too expensive, too complex, too generous, too passive. Stricter screening and lower benefits for a shorter time are supposed to turn the tide and to give the impressions that the claims are – in principle – under control. The debate does not only refer to the costs, however, it also refers to the basic principles of the current social system. Critics claim that the current design offers an insufficient answer to new circumstances and trends. Changing patterns of family formation and labour market behaviour, for example, raise questions about the risks that should be covered. At this moment, the system only guarantees income security in case of traditional 'external' risks; risks that befall us like sickness and unemployment. Manufactured, self-chosen risks are not insured: loss of income as a result of caring for children is considered the result of a personal choice and is therefore not covered. The current design of the system of social security also lacks a proper answer to the increasing variation in personal circumstances and life courses. There is little scope for personal responsibility and the collective solutions no longer accommodate the dynamics and differentiation of individual choices. At the most fundamental level these questions refer to the most adequate division of responsibility between the public and the private; a new system should stimulate proactive behaviour of citizens and increase personal responsibility. A new system should also facilitate a more varied life course and cover social beneficial matters such as caring time.

1 Acknowledgements. The author wishes to thank Ivy Koopmans (USE), Loek Groot (SISWO) and Paul de Beer (AIAS) for their stimulating conversations on life course policy when writing this article.

P. de Gijsel and H. Schenk (eds.), Multidisciplinary Economics, 53–64.

Against this background, the life course has become a important frame of reference in the Dutch debate about modernising social security. Introducing a life course conscious perspective would benefit young families who suffer from the combination pressure, would increase personal responsibility, would facilitate the maintenance of human capital and, in the end, result in a more sustainable participation rate (Commissie Sociaal-Economische Deskundigen, 2001; Schippers, 2001). Despite the optimism of the proponents, there have also been a few dissident voices, stating that the expectations projected in the life course scheme are simply not realistic and that the proposition of 'all benefits, no costs' seemed simply too good to be true.

In this contribution I will start by providing arguments used in favour of life course policy, while the next section describes life course policy as the joint responsibility of the employee, the employer and the government. I will then discuss the actual government proposal and the ensuing debate. In the final section I will sketch the contours of a life course conscious modernisation of social security.

2. INTRODUCING THE LIFE COURSE; NEW PERSPECTIVES ON SECURITY

The basic principles of a new system of social security are relatively clear. A modern and activating social system should make it more convenient for citizens to bear responsibility for the content of their life. Men and women are increasingly interested in deciding for themselves how to allocate their time to working, learning, caring and other activities during various stages of life. The social security system should facilitate individual decisions whether or not to work less during the family stage and to continue working for longer once the children have left home. Obstacles to this sort of modern life course should be removed, while investments should be encouraged. The point of departure is a society in which men and women enjoy sufficient economic security to be able to address their own social and financial responsibilities, now and in the future. This calls for a different division of personal and collective responsibilities.

In this process of recalibration, a life course perspective seems essential. Life course schemes are designed to help people combine various activities (work, education, care) more effectively in different phases of their lives, allowing them to make their own individual choices. Through this emphasis on flexibility, freedom of choice and personal responsibility, life course schemes aim to address a large amount of societal trends and needs, such as (the effort towards) personal responsibility, diversity, more effective use of human capital, de-stressing, simplification, etc. The following partly overlapping issues are mentioned most often in the relevant literature and policy considerations (Ministerie van Sociale Zaken en Werkgelegenheid, 2000; Goudswaard & Riemens, 2004) .

Facilitating time to care

During the past few decades a lot has changed in the way households organise work and care duties. The strict organisation principles of the past no longer hold. Today's parents tend to negotiate the most favourable regime, choosing from a wide range of possible options with different intensities of work and care. The result has been labelled the rise of the dual earner family or, more adequate in the Dutch context, the rise of the one-and-a-half-earner family. In most modern households, both partners tend to work, though with varying intensity in terms of the number of working hours.

The search for new work and care patterns necessitates changes in government policy. In the area of paid labour, the targets are relatively clear. Paid labour plays an important part in the modern ideal of citizenship and makes up a vital element of any viable welfare state. It follows that Dutch government policy is aimed explicitly at stimulating both men and women to participate in the labour market. The targets in terms of care are more diffuse. Although recent investments in day-care would suggest a departure from the traditional breadwinner model, the government has clearly opted away from the outsourcing of (all) care. On the contrary; the policy documents place great emphasis on the importance of freedom of choice for parents and the significance of self-care. Despite the efforts towards broader labour market participation, the government aims to offer households more freedom to step back from the labour market temporarily, especially when children are still young. A life course-conscious policy should aim to provide a fitting response to this issue by facilitating the spread of work and care over the entire life course, whilst keeping the disposable income at a reasonable level. The income loss as a result of child care costs should therefore be less severe, the peak time family should be afforded a bit more breathing space and the generation living on independent means will have to do with a bit less, both in terms of time and money. The desired end-result would then be an increase in sustainable labour market participation (Plantenga, 2004).

Life long learning and participation

A second element in the debate has been an emphasis on the importance of life long learning and of reducing non-participation at the later stages of life. The achievement of a successful transition to a knowledge-based society, at the heart of the EU Lisbon strategy, is critically dependent upon the mobilisation of all skills and talents. Continuous upgrading of labour force skills and life long learning are important strategies in this respect. Moreover, up to date knowledge is an important precondition for extending the working life and combating the under-utilisation of human capital in the older age categories. Extending the working life is all the more pressing in view of the demographic changes and the ageing of the labour force. Yet, although society's interest in knowledge is steadily increasing, existing institutions do not sufficiently promote permanent investment in knowledge and skills throughout one's entire working career. (Pre-)pension schemes, especially, have led to an incentive system that does not promote sufficient investment in human capital either on the part of employers or on the part of employees (Bovenberg, 2001, 2003).

Policy goals are rather straightforward in this respect. The participation of working age population in education and training should increase in order to avoid skill gaps in the labour market. In addition, workforce participation among the elderly should increase. Employees should be able to remain productive for a longer period thus ultimately increasing workforce participation. Life course policy could provide an important instrument in this respect by generating time to maintain and accumulate human capital over the life course. A life course-conscious policy should also create an incentive structure in which people are urged to keep their employability up to scratch, by encouraging and appreciating investments in human capital.

Diversity

A third important issue refers to the growing diversity in life courses. In former days, the situation was rather clear-cut. Rites of passage, such as leaving home, getting married and having children, occurred in a strict sequence. After finishing school, men generated the income and women looked after the home and children. Standardisation was underpinned by a fairly rigid working-time regime; if people worked, they worked full-time and continuously. Much has changed, however. The straightforward division of labour is a thing of the past and there is a greater diversity in life courses. Some authors even talk of a de-standardisation of the life course, with the growth of transitions and combinations as the most characteristic element (Liefbroer & Dijkstra, 2000). The destandardisation process means that life courses bear increasingly less resemblance to each other. The cycle in which life events occur is less rigid and there is more variation in timing. In addition, the system of fixed working hours has been overtaken by more variation and differentiation in working-time patterns. The fixed-time regime is breaking down. Fixed working rhythms, such as nine to five, Monday to Friday, no longer dominate. The emphasis has shifted increasingly to more flexible working hours and 'customisation'.

This growing diversity and de-standardisation is not yet matched by accompanying changes in the system of social security which is still based on uniformity and standardisation. A life course scheme in the form of an integrated saving facility could offer citizens more say in the allocation of the premiums they have accumulated, so that they also become better acquainted with the consequences of certain choices. By introducing capital funding elements for certain social risks, a mix of generic and individual rights could be created that addresses more optimally the mixed nature of these risks as partly external and partly self chosen. Social security could therefore be applied more flexibly and would provide more custom-made solutions for the needs ensuing from diverse labour patterns and life courses. As a result, life course schemes could improve the opportunities for citizens to become the directors of their own lives.

Modernising the concept of risks

Finally, the life course perspective plays a role in the redefinition of the concept of risks. Traditionally, the social security system mainly compensated loss of income as a result of involuntary external risks, such as unemployment, illness, disability and old age. Care activities, through their element of voluntary choice, were not traditionally included here. However, organising a system on the basis of the distinction between 'external' and 'manufactured' risks is becoming increasingly difficult. The claim that only external risk should be covered seems to overlook the fact that most citizens do have some influence on the extent to which they have to rely on an unemployment or disability benefit; sometimes due to the activities that they perform while they are unemployed or incapacitated for work, and sometimes due to the way they organise their life course. 'External' risks therefore, also entail a certain amount of personal responsibility. On the other hand, the limited scope for insuring manufactured risks like the care for children and other relatives seems to overlook the fact that society as a whole benefits from citizens consciously opting for these risks; they qualify as investments in the future. The 'external effects' of citizens' decisions are therefore not taken into account, as a result of which an under-participation in care responsibilities might occur (Wilthagen, 2003).

Given the emphasis of choice and responsibility, a life course perspective offers opportunities to go beyond the rigid distinction between self-chosen and external risks. With regard to traditional, external risks, individual responsibility could take shape by introducing individual savings within the context of social security. If citizens have more say in the allocation of the premiums they have accumulated, proactive behaviour might be encouraged, aimed at investing in human capital and reducing risks. On the other hand, social benefits of manufactured risks should be taken into account by introducing collective risk coverage, for example by introducing a paid parental leave scheme. In general, insurances seem more adequate in the case of unavoidable risks or in the case of extensive social benefits. Savings are more adequate when citizens have some influence on the risks they run and when the social benefits are limited. The result would be a different definition of, and approach to, external and manufactured risks, leading to new combinations of savings and insurances (Leijnse et al, 2002).

Summarising the issues so far, it seems fair to state that the innovative aspect of the life course perspective is that it increases the coherence between the issues and choices that arise during the various states of life, thereby introducing a new perspective on individual and collective responsibilities. Life course policies increase the opportunities of citizens to become the director of their own life course, by offering greater freedom of choice in organising their working life. Life course policies imply a change in the incentive structure so that people are encouraged to invest more in socially beneficial matters like education and care. In the end, employees will then be able to remain productive for longer, thus increasing workforce participation.

3. LIFE COURSE POLICY AND THE OPTIMAL DIVISION OF RESPONSIBILITY

Given the presumed individual and collective advantages, a life course scheme has been analysed as the joint responsibility of the employee, the employer and the central government. The emphasis on diversity, for example, and on increasing individual choice, seems to be in line with a larger role for private responsibility. Employees are granted more opportunities to achieve their preferences, as a result of which they have to bear a certain degree of responsibility. Employers may benefit from the availability of qualified and motivated employees, while life course schemes may also be linked to the extension of the standard working week and the reduction of pre-pension schemes. In this case, the trade-off would therefore be fewer collective rights, but more tailor-made agreements. The government bears the responsibility of creating the conditions that enable personal choices that are in the interest of all. In the present circumstances women interrupt their career because of caring duties and may find it difficult to re-enter the labour market. Elderly workers may find it difficult to remain in the labour market because their knowledge is no longer up to date or because their job is too demanding. In both cases, life course schemes make it possible to bridge temporary periods of nonactivity. This might lead to a reduction on both the claims on social provisions due to early withdrawal from the labour market and the under-utilisation of human capital. A temporary reduction of working hours within the context of a life course programme, may therefore prove a socially and economically attractive investment in the life course, or a personal choice that also serves the common interest.

Externalities do not only apply to a more available and productive labour force. They can also be presumed to be applicable to care involvement. This refers both to the number of children that are born as to the extent of unpaid voluntary care. At the moment approximately 25% of higher educated women remain childless. In addition, the number of people currently providing informal care is estimated at 1.4 million. This is significantly more than the number of professional carers (Nimwegen, 2004). It is likely that the need for care will grow, given the ageing of the population, putting an even greater strain on, mostly female, carers. A life course scheme granting the possibility of caring at times when it is most needed might then be viewed as cost efficient and beneficial to society as a whole.

At the same time the actual extent of the externalities is difficult to estimate, generating room for debate about the most optimal division of responsibilities. It is not certain, for example, whether people will in fact be able to plan and plot their lives and will indeed take more free time now in exchange for less free time later. The life course scheme has in this respect been typified as an unrealistic 'saving for earlier' scheme which seems to contain a sequential error. It may be laudable to try to keep older employees working longer, but a life course scheme is just an ineffective gift-wrapping for abolishing social security (Jansweijer, 2004). A life course scheme may even be a waste of money because it implies a subsidy on free time while the socioeconomic state of affairs in fact demands the reverse. Indeed, available studies on the expansion of paid leave schemes indicate that this will have uncertain and possibly negative effects on the participation rate. The effect on the redistribution of formal and informal care duties does not seem to be positive either, raising doubts about the effectiveness of the life course scheme. Debates have also arisen about the actual design of the life course scheme, in particular as regards notions of solidarity and the optimal division between the private and collective responsibilities. The strong point of the life course scheme, as presenting an answer to different societal trends and challenges, also implies that the actual proposal is confronted with varying expectations and criticism.

Before turning to the actual debate, it is important to present the government proposal in more detail. After all: the expectation projected and the criticism raised can only be valued if the actual design of the life course scheme is clear.

4. THE DUTCH LIFE COURSE SCHEME

In the autumn of 2003 the cabinet submitted a proposal for a life course scheme to the lower house. The scheme is relatively straightforward. By the envisaged life course arrangement, employees are granted a statutory right to participate in a life course arrangement; participation in the life course arrangement is therefore not dependent on the employer offering such an arrangement. A maximum of twelve percent of the annual wage can be saved, for a maximum of 1.5 years of leave, which amount to 2.1 years of leave at 70% of last earned income. The deferred tax principle is applicable, implying that no taxes are paid on the saving accounts, but solely on withdrawals. In the short run, the costs are estimated at 300 million Euro – basically because of delayed tax payments. On the long run the costs are more limited and consist of the difference between the deductible tax rate on the savings and the taxation rate on the withdrawals. To prevent people using the life course savings account for prepension, the savings can only be used to finance part-time leave (up to fifty percent of the usual working hours) during the two year period prior to retirement. In the margins of the proposed life course scheme, a plan is put forward for paid parental leave. The payment consists of a tax credit of fifty percent of the gross minimum wage for the duration of the parental leave (six months on a part-time basis – or three months full time). The proposed compensation is a temporary measure, effective until December 31st, 2007. As the explanatory memorandum states: 'after this period employees are expected to have had ample opportunities to make financial provisions for a reasonable amount of leave time'.

During the autumn wage negotiations, the cabinet reached an agreement with the social partners that the life course scheme would be linked to the proposed abolition of the tax facility for early retirement and pre-pension. However, in the spring of 2004, the negotiations failed and at the time of writing the contours of the system are still uncertain. The debates (in newspapers, at conferences, and during the tripartite negotiations) can be boiled down to two issues: the effectiveness and actual design of the life course scheme.

4.1 The effectiveness: life course schemes as a sequential error

The ultimate goal of a life course scheme is to bring the distribution of working time, caring time and income in line with the preferences and needs of individuals. A life course scheme therefore allows a more balanced distribution of time and money over the life course. As a result, the linkage between work time and income become less strict. Yet, at the same time, the income paid over the life course, has to be earned somehow during that same life course. Anyone who wants more time to look after children during the peak time of life will have to work longer or save at a younger age. What is involved here is an intertemporal substitution. Less work at point A is compensated by working more at point B, or more work at point A is compensated by less work at point B. The relevant question therefore is: will this exchange in fact take place and if so are the results in line with the expectations?

Several authors are rather sceptical in this respect (see Theeuwes, 2004; Jansweijer 2004). Critics point to the fact that striving to curb early retirement and stimulate the labour participation of older employees is like ‘swimming against the tide’. Over the past century, there has been a structural trend towards earlier retirement in a period when life expectancy is increasing. The reversal of that trend implies a heroic struggle between people’s desire to retire early and the need to increase the labour force participation of the older employees. More specifically, there are severe doubts about the effectiveness or in fact the desirability of the proposed substitution. The exchange between more free time in the peak period in exchange for working longer at the end of the day introduces a break in the accumulation of human capital and does not correspond with the preferences of the population at large. The break in the accumulation of human capital is demonstrated by many empirical studies of age and income profiles of women who withdraw from the working process when they have children and return a few years later once the children are at school. The preferences are measured by inter-temporal substitution elasticity. The available studies indicate that the elasticity is small and generally insignificant, indicating that the proposed incentives for exchange in the life course policy do not work and that people do not respond in the expected manner. People simply do not exchange more free time now for less free time later (Theeuwes, 2004).

The presumed difficulties with regard to the proposed inter-temporal substitution also pose severe doubts about the effectiveness of life course policy when it comes to the reconciliation of work and care. Maybe the most obvious comment with regard to the proposed individual saving device lies in the fact that care responsibilities sometimes come unexpectedly and often exceed personal responsibility. Furthermore care responsibilities for children are mainly significant at the start of one’s working career, when the amount of accumulated credit is still relatively low. This problem is further aggravated by the fact that most households tend to opt for more than one child. A rough calculation shows that a contribution of twelve percent will allow the average employee to save up half a year’s worth of leave within a period of approximately four years. Obviously, employees can also opt to make do with a smaller salary and spread the amount out over a longer period. A twelve percent contribution may be feasible in the period before the first child is born, although this will probably prove unrealistic for those entering the labour market for the first time. Once the first child has been born, however, it will probably be entirely impossible, because the reduced number of working hours will generally have caused a drop in income. This means there will only be funds for a second period of leave in the event of a surplus in the savings account, which seems unlikely, or a long gap between the first and second child, which seems undesirable. This problem can only be addressed by means of an easily accessible collective provision, in which the duration and amount of the benefit payments are independent of the individual employment record (Plantenga, 2004).

A further objection lies in the risk that an individual saving device will intensify the differences between men and women. After all, it seems likely that women will use their savings to pay for care leave, while men tend to use their savings for educational purposes or to go into semiretirement. At present, 42 percent of all women entitled to parental leave actually make use of the scheme, as opposed to twelve percent of men (Portegijs et al, 2002: p. 112). The proposed life course scheme seems likely to further consolidate this discrepancy rather than break the trend. This observation is all the more worrying in view of the fact that the claims are inextricably linked: savings used for care leave cannot be used for educational purposes.

The conclusion must be that life course schemes in the form of savings schemes will only provide a weak incentive to reduce the workload and stress in the middle stages of the life course. In addition, it will only partially address the difficult position of care responsibilities in today's life course. The system's strong point, the facilitation of diversity and the shaping of personal responsibility, can only be put to optimal use if life course schemes are offered *in combination with and supplementary to* easily accessible collective provisions. The collective arrangement, in the form of a leave scheme, addresses the need for time and the interests of care, while the life course arrangement helps define personal responsibility and freedom of choice within a specific spectrum.

4.2 The design: life course schemes and the boundaries of solidarity

The second issue which raised considerable debate concerns the actual design; the level of organisation and the financial arrangements.

When designing a life course scheme, the actual bargaining can take place at several levels. Decentralised, bilateral negotiations between employees and employers can be taken as a starting point. From the point of view of the employee, the life course scheme becomes a savings device, with the employee deciding on how much to save and for which purpose. This may be full-time leave, but could also be taking part in a retraining program. Given that this is a bilateral agreement between the employer and the employee, there is no legal right to take periods of leave. Yet it is conceivable that within the context of a collective labour agreement some basic rules can be established, for example a parental leave facility. It is also conceivable that for some purposes – say training – the employee receives an extra bonus from the employer. The basic benefit is that a more varied life course is facilitated through the accumulation of individual rights; the actual use of the life course scheme, however, largely depends on the consent of the employer.

The impact of a life course scheme may increase if the life course scheme is developed within a statutory framework of tax possibilities, rights, and regulations, that is: if the government enters the negotiations and three parties become involved. A life course scheme that is part of a policy to reconcile work and family especially needs the introduction of rights, for example in the case of care responsibilities. Regulations about life course schemes might also be useful in order to prevent the use of the savings account as a pre-pension scheme. The public goals of life course schemes – to facilitate the combination of work and care and to prolong the working life – might be more difficult to reach in a decentralised setting, which legitimises a steering and supporting role on the part of the government.

In addition to the organisational level, life course schemes might differ in their financial arrangements and whether or not they are organised on an individual or on a collective basis. An individual arrangement means that there is room for opting in or out. The scheme is therefore not obligatory. A collective arrangement on the other hand indicates that everybody is involved and that there is no exit option.

There are several good reasons for organising a life course scheme on a individual basis. Arguments in favour – most often phrased by employers and the central government – are that uniformity and solidarity no longer apply when it comes to working, caring, learning and living. An individual arrangement takes the individual freedom of choice as a starting point and presumes that the individual can make an informed choice. Individual life course schemes allow for the maximum of flexibility inside and outside the scheme and provide tailor made solutions. Another argument is that individual arrangements may be more efficient because there are no free riders. More collective arrangements might influence the decisions of the individual about the proper working, caring and leisure patterns and lead to a sub-optimal outcome. In more economic terms: an individual arrangement minimises the efficiency losses. In addition, an individual savings account might be most easily transferable to other employers. It is therefore in line with the modern emphasis on the importance of labour market mobility.

There are also good reasons for introducing a collective arrangement as especially the trade unions have emphasised. A collective arrangement seems more adequate given the actual purposes of a life course scheme. Care responsibilities, for example, may be quite significant at the start of one working career, when the amount of accumulated credit is still relatively low. This might hinder the use of leave. In a collective scheme the connection between the deposit and the withdrawal is less strict, making it possible to grant certain rights although the individual account is not yet sufficient. A second argument is that the actual benefits from the individual saving scheme are insecure. Employees may have saved for a prepension scheme all their lives, but the actual amount saved depends on the profits of the investments. A collective scheme may provide a more stable investment, because the savings of numerous people are pooled and risks are shared. A third argument refers to the risk of adverse selection. A collective arrangement ensures that everybody is involved. This guarantees a broad support and an acceptable premium level. The final argument is paternalistic: people are short sighted and may underestimate the need to save for care or educational purposes. A strictly individual arrangement might result in a less than optimal use of a life course scheme. A collective arrangement leads to obligatory saving which might be useful later on.

It is difficult to estimate the actual weight of the arguments beforehand. Among other things, it depends on the place of the life course scheme in the whole system of social security. If, for example, there is a proper collective parental leave facility, and the life course scheme is introduced in addition to facilitate individual differences, the importance of the argument that care responsibilities are significant at the start of the life course is less serious than if the life course scheme is supposed to compensate the lack of any paid parental leave facility. Also the differences might to some extent be bridged. A collective scheme could for example, be combined with individual claims, comparable to the second pillar in the pension schemes. In fact, proponents claim that the essential innovation of the life course approach is exactly this transition from a public right financed by a pay-as-you-go-system, to individual claims, financed by a capital funded system. Leijnse (2004: D35): 'It is time to build in individual responsibility and a flexible allocation of the accumulated premiums in the old social security system. The pension scheme has shown that this is quite possible by completing the public first pillar (solidarity by pay-as-you-go) with a second pillar (solidarity by capital funded, but individual claims)'.

5. RISKS, LIFE COURSES AND SOCIAL SECURITY

Summarising the debate so far, it seems most accurate to incorporate a life course scheme in the system of social security, taking the three-pillar pension scheme as a point of reference (Leijnse et al, 2002). The first pillar would consist of generic, mandatory schemes for all citizens, providing (basic) coverage in the event of a specific situation or risk. This basic coverage can be both a provision at minimum income level as well as a (temporary) income-related benefit. The second pillar consists of (mandatory) schemes for all employees in a given sector, collective labour agreement or organisation. These schemes should increasingly take the form of mixed savings and insurance schemes that allow citizens to build up individual rights, comparable to the current pension funds system. The third pillar consists of individual savings deposits and insurance policies for citizens seeking to take out additional insurance.

For the traditional risks of unemployment, sickness and disability, this implies that the basic public provision in the first pillar will be supplemented with sectoral agreements and/or personal savings for example in a collective life course scheme. Just like the current early retirement schemes, social partners may stimulate deposits or withdrawal for specific purposes in order to encourage certain choices like education. The government can facilitate participation in the savings scheme by applying the deferred tax principle: deposits (and capital build-up) are tax-free, withdrawals from the surplus are taxed. There are no separate schemes for all sorts of new social risks, but one surplus that can be applied to different choices at the individual's discretion. The second pillar therefore is not the sum of individual saving schemes for different purposes (such as care, training, illness etc.) but an integrated device, generating individual rights within a collective framework.

New risks like care responsibilities are partly covered by second and third pillar arrangements, but also incorporated in the first pillar as activities that deserve public support, in money as well as time. The duration of the benefit, the amount and the conditions that have to be met to become eligible, still have to be established. As a first impression and in order to stimulate the discussion, the Leijnse commission suggested covering twenty percent for a period of four years, the age at which a child – in the Netherlands – enters primary school. A twenty percent coverage would then allow the employee to reduce his or her working week by a day with no loss of income, or facilitate full-time care leave during the child's first year, at a payout ratio of eighty percent. Those seeking to take more leave or higher payouts in this period can use their second-pillar savings. In this system, 'saving for care' is less problematic than in the proposed life course scheme, as savings are a supplement to the collective scheme. The first pillar scheme firmly anchors care and the responsibility for care in the social security system. New work and care patterns are supported, while care is recognised as a valuable activity within society. Supplementing this collective basis with second or third-pillar life course schemes, allows space for freedom of choice and personal responsibility. This offers employees opportunities for individual choice within their life course.

REFERENCES

Bovenberg, A.L. (2001). Een belaste levensloop. *Economisch Statistische Berichten, 23 februari,* 171.

Bovenberg, A.L. (2003). De levensloopbenadering. In J.B. Kuné (Ed.). *Leven in een ouder wordende samenleving* (pp. 151-177). Den Haag: SDU-uitgevers.

Commissie Sociaal-Economische Deskundigen (2001). Levensloopbanen: gevolgen van veranderende arbeidspatronen. *Rapport van de Commissie Sociaal-Economische Deskundigen.* Den Haag: SER.

Goudswaard, K.P. & Riemens, T.D. (2004). Levensloopbeleid: hype of noodzaak. *Economisch Statistische Berichten, Dossier levensloop*, D3-D6.

Janswijer, R. (2004). Te mooi om waar te zijn. *Economisch Statistische Berichten, Dossier levensloop*, D25.

Koopmans, I., Jaspers, A. P. C. M., Knijn, T. & Plantenga, J. (2003). *Zorg in het huidige stelsel van sociale zekerheid en pensioen: een vergelijking tussen zes landen*. Utrecht: De Graaff.

Leijnse, F., Goudswaard, K., Plantenga, J. & Toren, J.P. van den (2002). *Anders denken over zekerheid: levenslopen, risico en verantwoordelijkheid.* Den Haag: Ministerie van Sociale Zaken en Werkgelegenheid, Directie Coördinatie Emancipatiebeleid.

Liefbroer A.C. & Dijkstra, P.A. (2000). Levenslopen in verandering. Een studie naar ontwikkelingen in de levenlopen van Nederlanders geboren tussen 1900 en 1970. *Voorstudies en achtergrond V 107.* Den Haag: Wetenschappelijke Raad voor het Regeringsbeleid.

Ministerie van Sociale Zaken en Werkgelegenheid (2000), *Verkenning levensloop. Beleidsopties voor leren, werken zorgen en wonen*. Den Haag: SZW.

Nimwegen, N. van (2004). Van spitsuur naar sandwich. *Economisch Statistische Berichten, Dossier levensloop*, D19-D21.

Plantenga, J. (2004). Zorgen in en om de levensloop, *Economisch Statistische Berichten, Dossier levensloop,* D14-D17.

Portegijs, W., Boelens, A. & Keuzenkamp, S. (2002). *Emancipatiemonitor 2002*. Den Haag: Sociaal en Cultureel Planbureau / Centraal Bureau voor de Statistiek.

Schippers, J. (2001). *De vraag naar diversiteit*. Inaugural address, Utrecht University: Utrecht, Economisch Instituut.

Teeuwes, T (2004). Tegen de storm in. *Economisch Statistische Berichten, Dossier levensloop,* D22-D24.

Wilthagen, T.C.J.M. (2003). *De onvergankelijke arbeidsmarkt en het (on)vergankelijke sociale recht.* Retrieved from: http://www.tilburguniversity.nl/flexicurity

B. NOOTEBOOM

LEARNING TO TRUST[1]

INTRODUCTION

Georg Simmel proposed that trust is a mixture of rationality and feeling: it is based on certain amount of rational assessment, but also entails a leap of faith beyond that. This seems related to the 'paradox of information' associated with trust (Pagden 1988). On the one hand trust requires lack of information: if one were certain about future behaviour, we would no longer speak of trust. On the other hand, trust is based on information, in the attribution of motives and competencies to people, based on observed or reported behaviour.

This paper aims to contribute to our understanding of how this mixture of rationality and feeling, assessment and faith, and information and uncertainty may 'work' in the process of the making and breaking of trust. It examines trust from the perspective of 'embedded cognition' (Merleau-Ponty, 1942, 1964), which is supported by recent neuroscience insights (Edelman, 1987, 1992, Damasio, 1995, 2003; Lakoff and Johnson, 1999). According to this perspective, cognition is rooted in brain and body, which are in turn embedded in their external environment. Here, cognition denotes a broad range of mental activity, including proprioception, perception, sense making, categorisation, inference, value judgments, emotions, and feelings.

One core assumption is that people perceive, interpret and evaluate the world according to mental categories that they have developed in interaction with their social and physical environments. This is consistent with the view of 'symbolic interactionism' from sociology (G.H. Mead). It is particularly relevant to trust, which builds up or breaks down in processes of interaction between people. A second assumption is that rationality and emotions, and mind and body, are intertwined (see also Simon, 1983, Nussbaum 2001). This goes against the body-mind dualism of Descartes, and is more in sympathy with the thought of Descartes' contemporary Spinoza (Damasio, 2003). Events call forth emotions, rooted in the body, which give rise to feelings, which may lead to reflective thought, which may modify emotions and may yield a critical analysis of events. This is also of particular relevance to trust, where emotions play an important

1 Revised version. An earlier version of the paper was presented at the symposium 'La structure cognitive de la confiance', EHESS, Paris, September 2003 and is forthcoming in French in the book *La structure cognitive de la confiance* (edited by Albert Ogien and Louis Quéré).

P. de Gijsel and H. Schenk (eds.), Multidisciplinary Economics, 65–81.

role in the way that trust builds up or breaks down in an emotion-laden perception and assessment of threats and risks. For a further understanding of how this works, we will employ insights from social psychology.

In this paper, trust is defined as perceived vulnerability to the actions of others, with the possibility of 'things going wrong', combined with the belief that they will not go (seriously) wrong.

The paper proceeds as follows. First, it gives a summary of the basic notions of trust on which it builds, adopted from the literature (Nooteboom, 2002). Second, it gives a further discussion of the notions of knowledge and learning used, from the perspective of embodied cognition. Third, it analyses the process of trust building as a process of learning. For a closer analysis of how this works, it next employs insights derived from the theory of framing (Lindenberg 1998, 2003) and decision heuristics from social psychology (Bazerman, 1998; Tversky and Kahneman, 1983).

BASIC FEATURES OF TRUST

In line with Nooteboom (2002), trust is taken here as a four-place predicate: the trustor (1) trusts a trustee (2) in one or more aspects of behaviour (3), under certain circumstances (4). Trustees can be individual people, but also collectives, such as organisations and institutions. The relation between trust in people and trust in organisations depends on the position and roles that people have in an organisation (Ring and van de Ven, 1992, 1994) and on the organisation's mode of co-ordinating behaviour. Concerning aspects of behaviour that one may trust, it is customary to distinguish trust in competence (ability to conform to expectations) and trust in intentions (to perform in good faith according to the best of competence). Competence includes technical and cognitive competence. Trust in intentions requires commitment, i.e. attention to possible mishaps, and absence of opportunism. In the literature, absence of opportunism has been called 'benevolence', 'goodwill' and 'solidarity'. The dependence of trust on circumstances entails that trust is limited: one may trust someone (in competence or intentions) under some conditions but not in others that go beyond competence or resistance to temptations of opportunism.

Concerning the sources of trust, there are psychological causes and rational reasons. Psychological causes include emotions and may entail reflexes or automatic response. Rational reasons entail inference, on the basis of perceived behaviour, of someone's trustworthiness. An important question is how those two sources of trust are related. Can we separate rationality from emotions and feelings? As indicated above, in this article the view is that they cannot be, and that emotions, rationality and feelings are intertwined. According to Damasio (2003), perceptions may trigger emotions, which in turn yield feelings, which may yield thoughts that lead to some constraint on emotions. The question is how this works, in more detail. Assessment of someone's trustworthiness, on the basis of observed or reported behaviour, is limited by uncertainty and bounded rationality, and is mediated by mental heuristics, in the perception and attribution of motives and competences of people. Action is based on behavioural routines and their selection, according to decision heuristics. Such heuristics of inference and decision are known from social psychology (Tversky and Kahneman, 1983; Bazerman, 1998; Smith and Mackie, 2000), and will be used in this paper. Nevertheless, judgements of trustworthiness can be more or less rational, in efforts to avoid 'jumping to conclusions', to be reasonable, and to extend the benefit of the doubt to people when trouble occurs. How the psychology of trust may work will be discussed in more detail later in this paper.

The next question is why people might be trustworthy. Here, we focus on intentional trustworthiness, in particular why people might not act opportunistically. A distinction is made between 'micro' foundations that are specific to a relationship, and 'macro', institution-based foundations that lie in the social environment of a relationship. The distinction between macro and micro sources is also known as the distinction between 'universalistic' or 'generalised' sources versus 'particularistic' sources, made by Deutsch (1973: p. 55), and between impersonal and personalised sources made by Shapiro (1987) and goes back to the work of Parsons. A distinction is also made between self-interested bases and bases that go beyond calculative self-interest. In self-interested foundations, trustworthiness may be based on control or deterrence. The trustor may control opportunities for opportunism ('opportunity control'), or material incentives ('incentive control').

Opportunity control may be based on legal coercion ('macro') or on hierarchical 'fiat', within a relationship ('micro'). Beyond self-interest, and beyond control by the trustor, trustworthiness may be based on socially inculcated values, norms and habits ('macro'), or on personal feelings of empathy or identification, or routinisation of conduct in a relationship ('micro'). Empathy entails the ability to understand another's 'way of thinking' without sharing it (having mental models of other people's mental models), and identification entails that one 'thinks the same way' (having similar mental models). For trust, one needs empathy, but not necessarily identification. One needs to understand 'what makes others tick', without necessarily 'ticking in the same way'. Empathy is needed to have a sense of the limits of trustworthiness, depending on circumstances. An overview of the bases of trustworthiness is given in Table 1.

Note that in Table 1 reputation is included in the self-interested foundations of trustworthiness. Here, one behaves well because bad behaviour would become known in relevant communities, whereby one would forego possibly profitable options for future relationships.

Concerning routinisation (see Table 1), Herbert Simon a long time ago showed that routines have survival value due to bounded rationality, in the sense of bounded capacity for reflective thought. Routines allow us to keep our scarce capacity of 'focal awareness' in reserve (Polanyi, 1962), in rational, calculative thought, for conditions that are new and demand priority. When things go well for a while in a relationship, one tends to take at least some of it for granted. One may no longer think of opportunities for opportunism open to a partner, or to oneself. On the basis of experience in relations, trustworthiness is assumed until evidence to the contrary emerges. In other words, trust is a 'default'. The possibility of opportunism is relegated to 'subsidiary awareness' (Polanyi, 1962). Generally, when something out of the ordinary occurs, our awareness shifts from subsidiary to 'focal' and we look critically at what is going on. As Simon (1983) pointed out, we need emotions of danger and excitement to catapult danger or opportunity into focal awareness. Next, in the case of trouble we must control our emotions in order to give our partner the benefit of the doubt, allowing for mishaps, rather than immediately assume the worst (opportunism). In this way, routine behaviour is not necessarily blind, or more accurately: it is not unconditional.

Table 1. Sources of (intentional) reliability

	macro; universalistic	**micro**; particularistic, relation-specific
self-interest	opportunity control contracts, legal enforcement, incentive control, reputation	hierachy, managerial 'fiat', dependence: unique partner value, switching costs, hostages
altruism	values, social norms of proper conduct, moral obligation, benevolence, sense of duty, bonds of kinship	empathy, routinisation, identification, affection, friendship

Source: adapted from Nooteboom (2002).

According to the analysis so far, trust may be based on control (coercion, incentives). However, several authors have recognised that trust goes beyond control, in the direction of 'goodwill' or 'benevolence' (see e.g. the special issue of *Organization Studies* 'Trust and control in organisational relations', 22/2, 2001). As noted by Maguire et al (2001: p. 286), if we do not include the latter, we conflate trust and power. Control or deterrence is part of calculative self-interest, but benevolence is not. Many authors feel that control is foreign to the notion of trust, and that 'genuine' trust is based on other, more social and personal foundations of trustworthiness. Therefore, trust has been defined as the expectation that a partner will not engage in opportunistic behaviour, even in the face of short-term opportunities and incentives (Bradach and Eccles, 1984; Chiles and McMackin, 1996). To avoid confusion, here the term 'reliance' is used to cover all bases of trustworthiness, and 'trust' is used for motives that go beyond self-interest.

While trust can go beyond calculative self-interest, in benevolence, it does, and generally should, have its limits. Blind, unconditional trust is generally unwise. Even benevolent people need to guard their self-interest, and it is not excessively cynical to assume that resistance to temptations such as opportunism or betrayal is limited. Managers may be expected to cheat if their firm is under pressure to survive in competition. An illustration is the ENRON affair. When the overriding survival criterion of a firm is short-term (quarterly) profit, and an economic slump erodes it, the firm may feel irresistible pressure to cheat on the figures. Thus, one should maintain awareness of conditions where trustworthiness may be put under too great a strain.

Yet, as noted before, within limits trust can become routinised and be taken for granted. One does not continually scrutinise behaviour and conditions for opportunities for opportunism, for oneself or one's partner, until they are felt to be excessive. As noted before, in view of uncertainties concerning motives and conditions, trust can only operate as a default: one assumes trustworthiness, within limits, until evidence of its failure becomes manifest, and then one adjusts the limits of trust. In other words, one must trust in order to learn about trustworthiness. If one only trusted under certainty one would never trust, thereby robbing oneself of the opportunity to learn about trustworthiness and its limits.

One must learn to trust, in finding out how far trustworthiness goes, in different aspects of behaviour. How far does someone's (or a firm's) competence go? Where are the weak spots? How robust is competence under adverse conditions? How strong are the pressures of competition, and what resources does a firm under adversity have in reserve before it succumbs?

After this summary of the 'basics' of trust, this paper focuses on the 'trust process'. The question is on what heuristics of attribution and decision trust and trustworthiness are based, and how this works out in the build up and break down of trust.

KNOWLEDGE AND LEARNING

As indicated in the introduction, this paper builds on the assumption that knowledge is physically embodied and socially embedded. People perceive, interpret and evaluate the world according to mental categories (or frames or mental models) that they have developed in interaction with their social and physical environment, in 'embodied realism' (Lakoff & Johnson, 1999), with the adaptive, selectionist construction of neural nets (Edelman, 1987, 1992). The term 'knowledge' here is a broad one, and denotes any mental activity, including perception and value judgements. In other words, we see cognition and emotion (such as fear, suspicion) and body and mind as closely linked (Merleau-Ponty, 1964; Simon, 1983; Damasio, 1995; Nussbaum, 2001). The notion that cognition is embedded, arising from interaction with the environment, goes back to Vygotsky (1962) and Piaget (1970, 1974), with their idea that 'intelligence is internalised action'. In sociology, the idea that cognition arises from interaction of people with their (especially social) environment arises, in particular, in the 'symbolic interactionism' proposed by G.H. Mead (1934, 1984).

As a result of differences in physical and cultural environments and individual paths of life that are embodied in cognition, perception, interpretation and evaluation are path-dependent and idiosyncratic to a greater or lesser extent. Different people see and experience the world differently to the extent that they have developed in different physical, social and personal surroundings and have not interacted with each other. In other words, past experience determines absorptive capacity, and there is greater or lesser 'cognitive distance' between people (Nooteboom, 1999).

This yields both an opportunity and a problem. Because one cannot 'climb down from one's mind' to assess whether one's knowledge is properly 'hooked on to the world', the variety of perception and understanding offered by other people, on the basis of a variety of experience, is the only source one has for correcting one's errors. Greater distance yields greater novelty value. However, greater distance also makes it more difficult to understand each other and to agree on aims and procedures. If effectiveness of learning by interaction depends on the mathematical product of increasing novelty and decreasing understandability, it has an inverted U-shaped relationship with cognitive distance. This entails a difference between crossing cognitive distance (in understanding people who think differently) and reducing it (thinking more alike). This is the same as the difference between empathy and identification, as discussed before. As relationships last longer, cognitive distance is reduced, and identification takes place, especially if the relationship is exclusive, i.e. there are no outside relationships. That is good for trust building but bad for learning. As a result, there is also an inverted U-shaped relation between learning and the duration of a relationship. First, learning increases due to increased understanding, but then learning declines for lack of cognitive distance, in identification. For empirical tests of the hypothesis of optimal cognitive distance, see Wuyts et al (2003).

According to Damasio (2003), events, appraised in perception and interpretation, trigger emotions, seen as bodily responses, which may yield automatic response, but also yield feelings that may lead to critical reflection on the perceived event, its interpretation, consequences, and possible response.

HOW TO BEGIN, TO ADAPT AND TO END A RELATIONSHIP?

Let us turn to a more detailed analysis of the process of trust development. First, I turn to rational analysis, and psychological processes will be elaborated on later. As a transaction relation unfolds in time, one can accumulate more or less reliable information about trustworthiness. And such experience can be communicated in reputation mechanisms. The sociological literature gives extensive instructions on how to infer intentional trustworthiness from observed behaviour (Deutsch 1973). Did the partner act not only according to the letter but also to the spirit of the agreement? Did he give timely warnings about unforeseen changes or problems? Was he open about relevant contingencies, and truthful about his dealings with others who might constitute a threat? Did he defect to more attractive alternatives at the earliest opportunity? Or to use Hirschman's (1970) notions of 'voice' and 'exit': how much voice rather than exit did he exhibit?

In interaction, partners may get to understand each other better, which enables a better judgement of trustworthiness, in 'knowledge based trust'. In ongoing interaction they may first develop insight into each other's cognitive frames, or empathy. This does not entail that they always agree. There may be sharp disagreements, but these are combined with a willingness to express and discuss them more or less openly, in 'voice', extending mutual benefit of the doubt. As a result, conflicts may deepen the relationship rather than breaking it. Next, partners may develop shared cognitive frames, by which they may identify with each other's goals, in 'identification based trust', with understanding or even sympathy for weaknesses and mistakes (McAllister, 1995; Lewicki and Bunker, 1996).

How, then, does trust develop if there was none before, when there is no basis for ex ante trust based on earlier experience? The assumption here is that vulnerability cannot be avoided: to achieve its purpose the relationship entails risks of dependence. As indicated earlier (in Table 1), one solution might be to rely on reputation mechanisms. Zucker (1986) suggested that one may infer trustworthiness on the basis of social characteristics, such as upbringing and membership of social groups (such as families, clubs, associations of trade or profession, see also Putnam 2000). Let us suppose, then, that neither reputation nor reliable characteristics are available.

One view is that under those conditions one can only start with control (Lewicki and Bunker, 1996), on the basis of contracts, for example, and then shift to trust as knowledge and empathy grow. One problem with this is that in learning and innovation there is likely to be too much uncertainty to specify the conditions of an extended contract, and limited opportunities for monitoring contract execution. Another possibility is develop the relation in a careful balance of mutual dependence, so that there is a threat of retaliation when the temptation of opportunism arises. Another possibility would be to start with small steps, with limited risk, and expand vulnerability as trust grows. One problem with that is that this approach may take too long. Under present market conditions there is often a need for speed. To reduce risk and to speed up relationship development, one may also profit from the service of specialised intermediaries.

There are a host of different types of intermediaries or go-betweens whose task it is to help judge performance and to provide intermediation or arbitration in conflicts. Shapiro (1987) called these intermediaries 'guardians of trust', Zucker (1986) saw them as part of 'institutions based trust', and Fukuyama (1995) used the term 'intermediate communities'. Many of these serve to develop and police technical or professional standards with certification systems. There are also roles for go-betweens as consultants in the management of inter-organisational relationships (Nooteboom, 2002), in offering arbitration or mediation in conflict, assessing the value of information before it is traded, creating mutual understanding (helping to cross cognitive distance), monitoring information flow as a guard against the spill over of sensitive information, guarding hostages, supporting a reputation system. A further, and perhaps most crucial, role is to act as an intermediary in the building of trust. Trust relationships are often entered into with partners who are trusted partners of someone you trust. If X trusts Y and Y trusts Z, then X may rationally give trust in Z a chance. X needs to feel that Y is able to judge well and has no intention to lie about his judgment. This can speed up the building of trust between strangers, which might otherwise take too long. Intermediation in the first small and ginger steps of co-operation, to ensure that they are successful, can be very important in the building of a trust relationship. The intermediary can perform valuable services in protecting trust when it is still fragile: to eliminate misunderstanding and allay suspicions when errors or mishaps are mistaken as signals of opportunism. He may also help in the timely and least destructive disentanglement of relationships. To eliminate misunderstanding, to prevent acrimonious and mutually damaging battles of divorce, a go-between can offer valuable services, and help in 'a voice type of exit'.

FRAMING

For a deeper analysis, we need to know more about how, in the building and breaking-down of trust, people make inferences from observed behaviour, and how they act on them. In particular, we want to know how rationality and emotions are combined, and how people go beyond calculative self-interest and yet refrain from blind, unconditional trust. Here, we employ insights from the theory of framing and from social psychology.

The basic assumptions of framing are the following. People act on the basis of cognitive frames with different motives or goals. At any moment one frame tends to be salient or 'in focus' (Polanyi) while others are in 'subsidiary' awareness. Mental frames are connected with repertoires of action such as threat, attack, retaliation, defence, surrender, withdrawal, avoidance, approach, offer, receipt, negotiation, etc. In human relations, two basic repertoires of action may be those of 'voice' or 'exit', proposed by Hirschman (1970). Frames, together with situational conditions, trigger behavioural routines that enact the frame. Selection and switches of frames are typically based on emotions, triggered by events in specific contexts of action. Emotions may yield automated, reflexive behaviour, or may lead to feelings that give rise to rational considerations by which emotions may to some degree be held in check or modified. The importance of emotions here is that they trigger the frame switching.

Lindenberg (2003) proposed the following frames:

- 'Guarding one's resources', i.e. focusing on survival or self-preservation.
- 'Acting appropriately' (Lindenberg, 2003), i.e. according to norms of behaviour (in a community) or shared values (in a specific relationship), gaining social legitimation.
- 'Acting as a friend'.
- 'Hedonics', i.e. giving in to urges of gratification.

In social psychology, Smith and Mackie (2003) recognised three basic motives of human behaviour: striving for mastery, seeking connections with others, valuing yourself and other people connected with you. Damasio (2003) refers to Spinoza's thought in terms of two basic human drives: towards self perpetuation, which seems similar to Lindenberg's 'guarding one's resources', and towards perfection, which seems similar to what Smith and Mackie recognised as 'striving for mastery'. Damasio proposed a hierarchy of bodily and mental regulation, as illustrated in Table 2. Here, the 'drives', which Spinoza called 'appetites', of hunger, thirst, sex, etc., seem similar to Lindenberg's 'hedonics'.

Here, for maximum simplicity, but in broad agreement with the typologies indicated above, I assume two basic sets or families of frames: self-directed (including concern for survival, resources, gratification) and other-directed (acting appropriately, as a friend, connections with others, social legitimation). Note that this brings us close to the classification of sources of (intentional) reliability in Table 1.

Stability of relations depends on frame stability, which depends on how salient a frame is, which depends on how strongly it is held, on what frames are subsidiary and on the extent to which they are complements or substitutes to the salient frame (Lindenberg, 2003). If, for example, the salient frame is to act with regard for others, and the frame of self-interest is subsidiary, they complement each other when self-interest is served by collaboration with others. When self-interest is threatened, beyond some tolerance level, the stability of an other-directed frame is precarious. This is how I reconstruct the limits of trust in psychological terms.

Table 2. Hierarchy of bodily and mental regulation

Feelings	
Emotions:	social emotions: sympathy, embarrassment, shame, guilt, pride, jealousy, envy, gratitude, admiration, indignation, contempt, ... primary emotions: fear, anger, disgust, surprise, sadness, happiness, ... background emotions (state of being): enthusiasm, edginess, excitement, tranquillity, ...
Drives (appetites):	hunger, thirst, curiosity and exploration, play, sex, ...
Pain and pleasure:	yielding reflexes of withdrawal, attraction, protection, expression of alarm
Immune response:	basic reflexes: startle reflex, ... metabolic regulation: endocrine or hormonal secretions, muscular contraction (heart digestion, ...), heart rate, breathing, blood pressure, storage and deployment of proteins and carbohydrates, ...

Adopted from Damasio (2003).

DECISION HEURISTICS

The question now is what heuristics are used in these processes of the formation, selection and enactment of frames. Here, I turn to decision heuristics proposed in social psychology by Bazerman (1998):

- Representativeness heuristic: the likelihood of an event is assessed by its similarity to stereotypes of similar occurrences.
- Availability heuristic: people assess the probability and likely causes of an event by the degree to which instances of it are 'readily available' in memory, i.e. are vivid, laden with emotion, familiar, recent and recognisable. Less available events and causes are neglected.
- Anchoring and adjustment heuristic: Judgement is based on some initial or basic value ('anchor') from previous experience or social comparison, plus incremental adjustment of that value. People have been shown to stay close even to random

anchors that bear no systematic relation to the issue at hand. First impressions can influence the development of a relationship for a long time.

These heuristics serve to give more substance to the notion of absorptive capacity, i.e. the ability to perceive and interpret phenomena, and to the claim, made in embodied cognition, that rationality and emotions are intertwined. The heuristics are not rational in a calculative sense (*calculative rationality*). Indeed, they serve to show how bounded rationality works. However, they are 'adaptively rational' in the sense of contributing to survival under uncertainty and bounded rationality, and the need, in many situations, to decide and act quickly (*adaptive rationality*). Nevertheless, they can lead to error, as will be discussed. In the elaboration of these heuristics I present what I make of them, from the perspective of embodied cognition and framing theory, and this may deviate from established practice in social psychology.

Prospect theory (Tversky and Kahneman, 1983) has demonstrated that people are not risk-neutral, and tend to be risk-taking when a decision is framed in terms of loss, and risk-averse when it is framed in terms of gain. This entails that people will accept a greater risk of conflict when they stand to incur a loss than when they stand to gain. As a result, the frame of guarding resources, or going for material self-interest, splits up into a frame of loss and a frame of gain. Related to this effect is the *endowment effect*: people often demand more money to sell what they have than they would be prepared to pay to get it. In the first case one wants to cover for loss.

Yet another psychological mechanism is that in violation of rational behaviour sunk costs, such as sacrifices made in a relationship, are not seen as bygones that should be ignored in an assessment of future costs and benefits. They are seen as sacrifices that would be seen as having been made in vain if one pulls out after having incurred them. This yields what is known as the *non-rational escalation of commitment*. It is associated with *cognitive dissonance*: cutting one's losses and pulling out would entail an admission of failure, of having made a bad decision in the past. Deutsch (1973) gave the example of the US finding it increasingly difficult to pull out of Vietnam as the number of killed soldiers accumulated. The phenomenon is confirmed in empirical research, which shows that when the decision is to be made by someone not involved in the initial commitment, or when the threat of an admission of failure is removed, the rational decision to pull out is made. Again, one cannot say that this mechanism is always bad, because it also demonstrates perseverance in the face of setbacks, which can be a good thing, and is in fact a trait of many a successful innovating entrepreneur. This phenomenon can be connected with the effect of a loss frame versus a gain frame. The person, or group, that made the initial decision experiences a loss frame, with the inclination to accept further risk in order to prevent acceptance of the loss. The decision maker who comes onto the scene later with a fresh look at the situation experiences a gain frame, and is able to make a decision that will offer profit or prevent further loss in the future, regardless of past sunk costs.

Evolutionary psychologists claim that certain psychological features or mechanisms are 'in our genes' as a result of evolution (Barkow et al, 1992). They emerged as features that gave selective or reproductive advantage, over the millions of years that the human species evolved in hunter-gatherer societies. For example, survival required the basic ability to identify objects and movement, to categorise natural kinds (plants, animals), to distinguish the animate from the inanimate, and natural kinds from artefacts (Tooby and Cosmides, 1992: p. 71). On top of that, it required the ability to recognise objects, judge speed and distance, to avoid predators and to catch prey (Tooby and Cosmides, 1992: p. 110). Survival also required mother-infant emotion communication signals (Tooby and Cosmides, 1992: p. 39). Such instincts contribute to the heuristics of availability and representatives in our framing of the world.

These heuristics and principles from social and evolutionary psychology are consistent with the perspective of embodied cognition, and indeed serve to elucidate and extend it, in their integration with emotions, their pragmatic role in survival under conditions of radical uncertainty, and their embedding in processes of practical action.

APPLICATION TO TRUST

In my interpretation, the *representativeness heuristic* constitutes our repertoire for categorisation, i.e. what we *can* attend to, in our absorptive capacity. There is a connection with the role of 'prototypes' or 'exemplars' in language and categorisation (Rosch, 1978; Nooteboom, 2000). Since definitions can seldom offer necessary and sufficient conditions for categorisation, and meaning is context-dependent and open-ended, allowing for variation and change, we need prototypes. Prototypes are salient exemplars of a class that guides categorisation by assessing similarity to the prototype. We try to fit or assimilate observed behaviour into prototypes in our cognitive repertoire, and when we recognise some features as fitting, we tend to attribute remaining, unobserved attributes that belong to the prototype. The mechanism of attributing unobserved characteristics directly after the recognition of observed ones enables fast pattern recognition, which is conducive to survival. The downside of the representativeness heuristic is that it also yields prejudice, in the premature, erroneous application of stereotypes, in mistaken attributions. In the present framework, the representativeness heuristic regulates the *cognitive content* of frames, in terms of the categories that they employ. In the context of trust, I see the representativeness heuristic as providing benchmarks, in the form of prototypes, for efficient, fast identification of trustworthy and untrustworthy behaviour, and guidelines or exemplars for trustworthy behaviour. In organisations, such prototypes for trust are often part of organisational culture. An example is the following. In her analysis of 'trust and trouble' in organisations, Six (2004) found the precept, in one organisation, that in case of trouble, 'people should not complain *about* people but *to* them'. Here, the organisational ethic is one of voice: when trouble arises, be open about it and try to work it out together.

The *availability heuristic*, in my interpretation, regulates what we *actually* attend to, by filtering impressions, in emotions that contribute to the selection of frames. If we did not apply such filters, our consciousness would likely be overloaded. We cannot afford to pay attention to everything that is presented to our senses, and we need to select what appears to be salient and requiring attention. Much of our conduct is based on routines that are relegated to subsidiary awareness. Then, as discussed earlier, we need emotions to catapult attention back into focal awareness when a threat or new opportunity emerges. Emotions tend to be stronger when personal desires or interests are at stake than in situations where motives are more abstract and impersonal. Thus, frames of hedonism and 'guarding resources' tend to acquire salience more easily than a normative frame (Lindenberg, 2003). However, when the desire to 'act appropriately' is based on emotions of friendship or kinship, it will have greater 'availability'.

As noted before, trust may become routinised when a relationship has been going well for a while. Trustworthiness is taken for granted until something exceptional arises in observed behaviour or conditions that might yield a temptation or pressure that a partner may not be able to resist. This evokes feelings of fear, suspicion or indignation that break routinised trust open to critical scrutiny. Earlier, we noted the role of identification in trust, on the basis of shared categories concerning motives and conditions of behaviour. Here, availability is based on familiarity. It affects both one's own trustworthiness, in the willingness to make sacrifices for others, and one's trust, in the tolerance of behaviour that deviates from expectations. One will more easily help someone when one can identify with his need. One can more easily forgive someone's breach of trust or reliance when one can identify with the lack of competence or the motive that caused it. One can more easily take the blame oneself. Since one can identify with him, one may sympathise with his action, seeing, perhaps, that his action was in fact a just response to one's own previous actions. One might have reacted in the same fashion as he did.

While it is adaptively rational, the availability heuristic yields several problems. One is that anger may overshoot its function of calling attention, and prompt impulsive defensive or retaliatory conduct. Another problem is that attention is called only by extreme, emotional appeals, so that more subdued, nuanced appeals and weak signals tend to be ignored. The availability heuristic yields useful emotional triggers to create focal awareness of possible risk in relations, but after that one should be careful not to jump to conclusions, and to exercise benefit of the doubt wherever possible. This is the case, in particular, because when 'things go wrong' in a relationship, there may be a multitude of possible causes: an accident, lack of resources, lack of competence and opportunism. One may jump to assuming the worst, opportunism, while that conclusion is not justified.

The *Anchoring and adjustment* heuristic indicates that once we select a frame, with corresponding behavioural routines, we do not easily drop it. Deutsch (1973) also argued that beginnings are important and may be difficult to turn in another direction. He suggested that there is circular causation between the characteristics of participants and the results of interaction, in his 'crude law of social relations': 'The characteristic processes and effects elicited by a given type of social relationship (co-operative or competitive) tend also to elicit that type of social relationship'. Under uncertainty cognition does need such an anchor. Studies of learning and adjustment have shown that hasty and large departures from existing practices can yield chaotic behaviour (March, 1991; Lounamaa and March, 1987). It is adaptively rational to experiment with small, proximate change, to accumulate motivation for more radical change, as well as insights into directions and elements of change that are likely to be viable and worth the upheaval (Nooteboom, 2000). However, this heuristic also entails the risk of inertia: the inability to make needed drastic change in the face of a crisis.

This heuristic is related to the notions of trust as a default, and routinised trust. The notions of default and routine entail that one sticks to an established form of behaviour until new evidence compels its change.

As already noted, the heuristic of anchoring and adjustment entails that beginnings are often difficult to turn in another direction. This brings me back to the discussion of how to start a relationship when at the beginning there is no basis for trust. If one takes the advice of Lewicki and Bunker to start on the basis of control, this may be seen as a sign of distrust, which is not only likely to evoke a similar response, with the risk of a vicious circle of control upon control that constrains the scope for flexibility, improvisation and innovation in the relationship, but may also be difficult to turn into trust as the relationship develops.

These heuristics appear to complement each other. Representativeness determines how one can interpret behaviour, availability determines which interpretation is triggered, and anchoring stabilises chosen behavioural routines. Of the three, availability is the most laden with emotion, and representativeness is the most concerned with learning. Availability causes frame switches, and anchoring and adjustment serve to constrain such switches. The first is needed for survival, the latter is needed to make framing less unstable and precarious.

The notion of a *loss versus a gain frame*, from prospect theory, has important implications for the stability of relationships (Nooteboom, 2004). It was noted earlier that one way to start a relationship without prior trust is to develop it in a careful balance of mutual dependence. Then, however, the problem often is that the balance is broken by a change of circumstances, such as a change of technology or market whereby existing competences lose relevance, in different degrees for different partners, or the emergence in the arena of a new player who turns out to be a more attractive alternative for one of the partners. This partner may then want to exit while the other partner wants to hold on to him. Then, the first partner is in a gain frame (getting more out of an alternative relationship), while the other is in a loss frame (losing a valuable partner). According to the theory, the latter would go to greater extremes, in emotional and even self-destructive actions (slander, hopeless litigation), to retain the partner, than the other partner would engage in to realise his exit.

The phenomenon of *escalation of commitment* also contributes to the stability of a relationship. After a relationship has cost one partner an accumulation of sacrifice, it may become increasingly difficult for him to exit from it, since that would suggest that his past sacrifices were wasted. Such a partnership may quickly unravel under new management that is not compromised by past sacrifices.

In sum, there appear to be three mechanisms for the stabilisation of relationships: anchoring, loss versus gain, and escalation of commitment.

Evolutionary psychology claims that in the hunter-gatherer societies in which man evolved, the variance of yields, in gathering edible plants, roots, nuts, etc., and even more in hunting, when it was impossible to consume large game immediately, together with the problems of durable storage, resulted in the development of *reciprocity:* the willingness to surrender part of one's yield to others in need, in the expectation of receiving from them when they were successful (Cosmides and Tooby, 1992: p. 212).[2] This is enhanced by the supposed ability to assess such willingness among others, in a 'cheater detection mechanism', and to signal a credible, often emotion-laden threat to sanction lack of reciprocity (Frank, 1988). This purported natural inclination towards reciprocity would contribute to a solution of the problem, discussed before, of how to start a relationship without trust based on prior experience, while allowing trust to develop. Presumably, the principle works only in communities existing under stable conditions, where recipients of goodwill will 'stay around' to engage in reciprocity. A similar condition was discussed for a reputation mechanism. Reciprocity and reputation are mutually reinforcing.

The heuristics have implications not only for starting and adapting a relationship, but also for ending one. The ending of relationships is at least as important as the issue of starting one, in view of the fact that relationships may last too long, yielding too much identification, resulting in lack of cognitive variety for further innovation. Nooteboom (1999, 2004) proposed that there is a hostile and a collaborative mode of exit from a relationship. In the hostile mode, one tries to prepare one's exit, no longer engaging in relation-specific investments, retrieving hostages, and building up investments in a new relationship, as surreptitiously as one can, and then springs a surprise exit on the partner, who is left with the unforeseen damage of worthless specific investments and discontinued production. In the collaborative mode, in a 'voice mode of exit', one would announce one's intentions towards exit ahead of time, help the partner to disentangle the relationship with minimum damage, and help to find a replacement. The advantage of the latter mode would be that the partner is less in a loss frame, and hence less likely to take radical actions of binding and retaliation. A risk, however, is that the partner would have more time and opportunity to take such actions. Here, the anchoring and adjustment heuristic also kicks in. If the relationship had been collaborative, based on benevolence, that would set the norm, and a hostile mode of exit would constitute a greater shock than in a more calculative relationship, with greater risks of extreme retaliatory behaviour.

In sum, the decision heuristics and other phenomena from social and evolutionary psychology are highly relevant to the development of trust, because they affect the attribution of characteristics, expectations of trustworthiness, and choice of action.

CONCLUSIONS

A central claim of this paper is that for an understanding of how trust is built up and broken down, and how trust can go beyond calculative self-interest without becoming blind or unconditional, we may profit from the application of framing theory and decision heuristics derived from social psychology. They are consistent with the

2 The argument requires that group selection is viable. In spite of earlier arguments that group selection is dominated by individual selection, according to later arguments it can be viable. That is the case if opportunistic intruders into a reciprocity-based society are pre-empted before they get a chance to develop reproductive advantage (Ridley, 1997).

perspective of embodied cognition, and yield an elaboration of it. In particular, they elaborate the idea that rationality and emotions are intertwined, and that psychological mechanisms arise from conduct that is selected for survival. In this article, an attempt was made to combine framing theory and decision heuristics. A frame is an intentional stance, guiding perception and action, which focuses on a limited number of a range of possible other-directed or self-interested goals or motives. At any moment one frame tends to be salient while others are subsidiary, and perceptions of events may cause switches.

This helps to understand the limits of trust. Decision heuristics help to explain how this happens. The following heuristics are discussed:

- The representativeness heuristic.
- The availability heuristic.
- The anchoring and adjustment heuristic.
- The phenomenon of escalation of commitment.
- The phenomenon of cognitive dissonance.
- The notion of a loss frame versus a gain frame.
- The notion of an instinct for reciprocity, combined with a cheater detection mechanism.

The representativeness heuristic was interpreted as yielding a repertoire of possible frames and behavioural routines, constituting a cognitive repertoire, in the form of prototypes, in terms of which judgements of (un)trustworthiness are made and translated into action. The availability heuristic was interpreted as determining which frames are salient and which are subsidiary, and how switching between them occurs. This is governed by emotions and by familiarity. Emotions serve to break behavioural routines open for scrutiny. On the other hand, the heuristic of anchoring and adjustment, escalation of commitment, and the notion of a loss versus a gain frame serve to stabilise behaviour. Anchoring and adjustment clarify why it may be difficult to turn suspicion into trust and why it is difficult to take a hostile, abrupt approach to exit if the relationship was based on benevolence and voice. Instinctive reciprocity helps to start a relationship in which there is no prior trust based on experience.

Here also we find paradoxes. These heuristics and phenomena are adaptively rational, given bounded rationality and the pressure to survive under conditions of radical uncertainty and the need for speedy response. However, they can yield irrational actions, such as prejudice, blindness, injustice, inertia, lack of adaptiveness under crises, and impulsive behaviour. They help to enable and support the building of trust, but may also prevent it, and may cause unjustified breakdowns of trust.

A recurrent theme in the process of trust is openness, in a voice based approach. The importance of that was argued earlier by Zand (1972). Since there may be many causes of disappointed expectations, it is important to be open to a partner about problems that one may cause. Silence until the problem becomes manifest is likely to be interpreted as a sign of the worst possibility i.e. opportunistic behaviour. An imposition of control and requisite monitoring has adverse effects, indicated before, of a vicious circle of control that blocks scope for learning and innovation, and starts a relation on a footing of mistrust that may be difficult to turn around. If, on the other hand, one voluntarily accepts or even invites some control by the partner, and opens up to monitoring, this greatly facilitates trust building. This indicates the importance of voluntary transparency for trust relationships. A timely announcement of intentions to exit may greatly help to disentangle relationships without too much damage. If one shies away from exhibiting one's fears of relational risk, one thereby robs the partner of the opportunity to reduce that risk.

While some progress may have been made in this article, in the attempt at a coherent account of the trust process, in a combination of framing theory and decision heuristics, there is need for further research, analysing in more detail how the different psychological mechanisms mesh and compensate or conflict, and how this depends on the interaction between them and on their social contexts, such as organisational culture and institutional environments. There is much scope and need for further empirical research, to test and revise the many conjectures developed in this article. In cognitive science, research in embodied cognition may investigate the neural correlates or underpinnings of the psychological mechanisms discussed in this article.

REFERENCES

Barkow, J., Cosmides, L. & Tooby, J. (1992). *The adapted mind: Evolutionary psychology and the generation of culture.* Oxford: Oxford University Press.

Bazerman, M. (1998). *Judgment in managerial decision making.* New York: Wiley.

Bradach, J.L. & Eccles, R.G. (1984). Markets versus hierarchies: From ideal types to plural forms. In W.R. Scott (Ed.), *Annual Review of Sociology, 15*: (pp. 97-118).

Chiles, T.H. & McMackin, J.F. (1996). Integrating variable risk preferences, trust and transaction cost economics. *Academy of Management Review, 21/7*, 73-99.

Cosmides, L. & Tooby, J. (1992). Cognitive adaptations for social exchange. In H. Barkow, L. Cosmides & J. Tooby (Eds.) *The adapted mind.* (pp. 163-228). Oxford: Oxford University Press.

Damasio, A. R. (1995). *Descartes' error: Emotion, reason and the human brain.* London: Picador.

Damasio, A. R. (2003). *Looking for Spinoza.* Orlando, Florida: Harcourt.

Deutsch, M. (1973). *The resolution of conflict: constructive and destructive processes.* New Haven: Yale University Press.

Edelman, G. M. (1987). *Neural Darwinism; the theory of neuronal group selection.* New York: Basic Books.

Edelman, G. M. (1992). *Bright air, brilliant fire; On the matter of mind.* London: Penguin.

Frank, R.H. (1988). *Emotions within reason, the strategic role of the emotions.* New York: W.W. Norton.

Fukuyama, F. (1995). *Trust, the social virtues and the creation of prosperity.* New York: Free Press.

Hirschman, A.O. (1970). *Exit, voice and loyalty: Responses to decline in firms, organisations and states.* Cambridge MA: Harvard University Press.

Lakoff, G. & Johnson, M. (1980). *Metaphors we live by.* Chicago: University of Chicago Press.

Lakoff, G. & Johnson, M. (1999). *Philosophy in the flesh.* New York: Basic Books.

Lewicki, R.J. & Bunker, B.B. (1996). Developing and maintaining trust in work relationships. In R.M. Kramer & T.R. Tyler (Eds.), *Trust in organizations: Frontiers of theory research* (pp. 114-139).Thousand Oaks: Sage Publications.

Lindenberg, S. (1998). Solidarity: its micro foundations and macro-dependence: A framing approach. In P. Doreian & T.J. Farro (Eds.), *The problem of Solidarity: Theories and models* (pp. 61-112). Amsterdam: Gordon and Breach.

Lindenberg, S. (2003). Governance from a framing point of view: The employment relationship and relational signalling. In B. Nooteboom & F. Six (Eds), *The trust process in organizations* (pp. 37-57) Cheltenham (UK): Edward Elgar.

Lounamaa, P. H. & March, J.G. (1987). Adaptive coordination of a learning team. *Management Science, 33*: 107-123.

Maguire, S., N. Philips, N. & Hardy, C. (2001). When "silence=death", keep talking: Trust, control and the discursive construction of identity in the Canadian HIV/AIDS treatment domain. *Organization Studies, 22/2:* 285-310.

March, J. (1991). Exploration and exploitation in organizational learning. *Organization Science, 2/1*, 101-123.

McAllister, D.J. (1995). Affect- and cognition based trust as foundations for interpersonal cooperation in organizations. *Academy of Management Journal, 38/1*: 24-59.

Mead, G. H. (1934). *Mind, self and society; from the standpoint of a social behaviorist*. Chicago: University of Chicago Press.

Mead, G. H. (1982). *The individual and the social self, unpublished work of G.H. Mead*. D.L. Miller (Ed.). Chicago: University of Chicago Press.

Merleau-Ponty, M. (1942). *La structure du comportement*. Paris: Presses Universitaires de France.

Merleau-Ponty, M. (1964). *Le visible et l'invisible*. Paris: Gallimard.

Nooteboom, B. (1999). *Inter-firm alliances: Analysis and design*. London: Routledge.

Nooteboom, B. (2000). *Learning and innovation in organizations and economies*. Oxford: Oxford University Press.

Nooteboom, B. (2002). *Trust: Forms, foundations, functions, failures and figures*. Cheltenham (UK): Edward Elgar.

Nooteboom, B. (2004). *Inter-firm collaboration, learning and networks: An integrated approach*. London: Routledge.

Nussbaum, M.C. (2001). *Upheavals of thought, The intelligence of emotions*. Cambridge UK: Cambridge University Press.

Pagden, A. (1988). The destruction of trust and its economic consequences in the case of eighteenth-century Naples. In D. Gambetta (Ed.), *Trust, the making and breaking of cooperative relations* (pp. 127-141). Oxford: Blackwell.

Piaget, J. (1970). *Psychologie et epistémologie*. Paris: Denoël.

Piaget, J. (1974). *Introduction a l'épistémologie génétique, I and II*. Paris: Presses Universitaires de France.

Polanyi, M. (1962). *Personal knowledge*. London: Routledge.

Putnam, R.D. (2000). *Bowling alone; the collapse and revival of American community*. New York: Simon and Schuster.

Ridley, M. (1997). *The origins of virtue*. Viking Press.

Ring, P. Smith & van de Ven, A. (1992). Structuring cooperative relationships between organizations. *Strategic Management Journal, 13*: 483-498.

Ring, P. Smith & van de Ven, A. (1994). Developmental processes of cooperative interorganizational relationships. *Academy of Management Review, 19/1*: 90-118.

Rosch, E. (1978). Principles of categorization. In E. Rosch & B. B. Lloyd (Eds.), *Cognition and categorization* (pp. 27-48). Hillsdale, NJ: Erlbaum.

Shapiro, S.P. (1987). The social control of impersonal trust. *American Journal of Sociology, 93*. 623-658.

Simon, H. A. (1983). *Reason in human affairs*. Oxford: Basil Blackwell.

Six, F. (2004). *Trust and trouble in organizations*. PhD thesis, Rotterdam School of Management, Erasmus University Rotterdam, forthcoming.

Smith, E.R. & Mackie, D.M. (2000). *Social psychology*. Philadelphia: Taylor and Francis.

Tooby, J. and Cosmides, L. (1992). The psychological foundations of culture. In J.H. Barkow, L. Cosmides & J. Tooby (Eds.), *The adapted mind* (pp. 19-136). Oxford: Oxford University Press.

Tversky, A. & Kahneman, D. (1983). Probability, representativeness, and the conjunction fallacy. *Psychological Review, 90/4:* 293-315.

Vygotsky (1962). *Thought and language*. Edited and translated by E. Hanfmann & G. Varkar. Cambridge MA: MIT Press.

Wuyts, S., Colombo, M.G., Dutta, S. & Nooteboom, B. (2003). *Empirical tests of optimal cognitive distance*. Research Report, Erasmus Institute for Research in Management, Erasmus University Rotterdam.

Zand, D.E. (1972). Trust and managerial problem solving. *Administrative Science Quarterly, 17/2*: 229-239.

Zucker, L.G. (1986). Production of trust: Institutional sources of economic structure. In B. Staw & L. Cummings (Eds.), *Research in organizational behaviour, vol. 8* (pp. 53-111). Greenwich, CT: JAI Press.

INDUSTRIAL DYNAMICS AND INNOVATION ECONOMICS

H. SCHENK

INTRODUCTION

One of Europe's major, long-lasting economic questions concerns the state of innovation. In 2000, the members of the EU agreed on making their economies the most innovative of the world – overtaking or at least catching up with the US. This goal met with lots of scepticism, if not merriment. Indeed, by now, it has become clear that it will be extremely unlikely that the EU will be able to reach it.

Luc Soete's contribution to this section has been drawn against the background of such scepticism. Apparently it is not so easy to force economies to innovate more. He argues that this essentially has to do with the fact that innovation policies tend to focus on economic incentives whereas the right kind of institutional arrangements and policies matter more. Thus, he points out that concepts such as Abramovitz's technological congruence and social capability should be regarded as important policy notions. In this respect, Soete proposes that the dynamics of innovation and entrepreneurship would really thrive better if higher rewards for creativity and curiosity were to replace the high premiums on security and protection of employment. However, as Soete stresses, this issue cannot be decided on separately from discussing the desirability of giving up Europe's welfare standards in favour of those of America.

In fact, however, European politicians appear to have made up their minds already. Under the banner of freeing locked-up market systems, they have pushed through dramatic reforms in European social welfare arrangements – reforms that try to americanise the European economy more and more. But John Kay, in the opening contribution to this section, demonstrates that the politicians' idea of markets and the way they work could be a serious misunderstanding, brought about by very elegant academic ideas that, however, do notcorrespond with the real world. He reminds us also of the fact that the EU started emulating what he calls the ABM, the American Business Model, precisely at the moment when it collapsed. In the ABM, the principal determinant of economic behaviour is self-regarding materialism; financial markets are the main regulator of economic activity and the role of government is limited to the protection of property rights and the enforcement of contracts.

Reflecting on all this, it looks like European politicians get staggered again and again by American demonstrations of one part of the business cycle, a buoyant econo-

P. de Gijsel and H. Schenk (eds.), Multidisciplinary Economics, 83–84.

my, without realising that there always will be another part: one of widespread destruction of value, of pushing millions of people into poverty, of encouraging global resentment.

In the second contribution, William Shepherd joins Kay – albeit a bit more candidly – in suggesting that academic economics must share the blame for this. Economists demonstrate too much scholasticism, and they either remain tongue-tied when significant problems have to be answered or approach them with arcane, simplified and myopic theories. Shepherd draws up a list of historical features that have determined this sad state of affairs. Among them, he points at the increasing popularity of pure theory – especially game theory. Lots of valuable empirical work done in the past has thus been pushed aside. When seriously challenged, theorists often claim that their work is just meant to give insights useful for scholarly discussion, but only a few weeks later, they can be observed loudly declaring that their theories are to be considered the non-plus-ultra of economic science.

Indeed, although pure theory could be attractive in itself, our economies need models with a much greater degree of realism than is possible as long as they are based on two-player non-co-operative, simultaneous games only, where players are assumed to be pay-off maximisers. This is one of the challenges that have been taken up by Luigi Orsenigo in the concluding contribution to this section. He gathers and assesses the fundamental principles that have guided the development of historic and evolutionary studies of particular industries and sectors à la Nelson and Winter. These so-called History-Friendly Models (HFMs) start off with formulating appreciative theories that are based on inductive analyses of empirical data, and then try to translate these into logically consistent, mostly simulation models. These models can subsequently be calibrated by replicating an industry's or firm's history, as has indeed been done successfully for industries that differ as much in character as the computer and pharmaceutical industries.

The papers in this section make clear that assessing an industry's or an economy's performance in terms of innovation, or anything else, can only be adequately done if the straightjackets of mainstream theory and methodology are widened, or in some cases discarded altogether. Either way, this implies taking stock of the possible implications of other disciplines than economics, a process that results in the multidisciplinary economics that USE wishes to encourage. Driving the Bentleys of econometric method down the cow-tracks of economic data, moreover, will not get us there, either. The challenges ahead, therefore, lie in approaches that prefer relevance to elegance, and truth to precision.

Scholars who are working in industrial organisation and innovation dynamics whilst upholding these principles have meanwhile gathered in such networks as EUNIP (European Network of Industrial Policy) and EAEPE (European Association for Evolutionary Political Economy). Both networks enjoy some popularity at USE also, and it is expected that collaboration with them will be intensified, the more so since from its beginnings EAEPE in particular has opened up to scholars who are working on modern approaches to organisation theory – which is one of the main foci for research at USE.

J. KAY

THE TRUTH ABOUT MARKETS

THE ORIGINS OF THE MARKET ECONOMY

In his widely read book The Lexus and the Olive Tree, Thomas Friedman, who chronicles globalisation for the New York Times, declares that 'the world is ten years old!'[1] By this he meant that the modern, global market economy, its rules and its governance, is a product of the brief era since the Berlin Wall fell and it became apparent that market institutions were the only known route to prosperity and stable democracy.

But the modern market economy is not ten years old. It is more appropriate to search for its origins in Britain and the Netherlands in the seventeenth and eighteenth centuries. There the key institutions which characterise successful modern economies began to evolve.

That era saw the development of businesses which were more than expressions of the will and personalities of their founders. Commodity and securities markets, which allow people to trade with those they do not directly know, grew in importance. And, perhaps for the first time since classical Greece and Rome, the conduct of government fell into the hands of disinterested people who saw the economic role of the state as that of regulating the activities of private business in the social interest, rather than attempting to appropriate its produce for the benefit of those who control the apparatus of government.

These ideas came to the United States from northwest Europe. The first colonists of North America reached Massachusetts from Britain via the Netherlands, and it was British settlers in New England and the Delaware valley, and Dutch settlers in New York and New Jersey, who planted the seeds of economic development in that initially inhospitable soil, and who extended the mercantile traditions of the British and Dutch to what would become the United States.[2] The European merchants who developed these traditions were the first globalisers.

The American Civil War represented not only a political settlement in the United States, but the victory of one European economic tradition over another in north America. In 1865 bourgeois capitalism triumphed over economic systems modelled on

1 Friedman, T. (1999).
2 Fischer, D.H. (1989).

P. de Gijsel and H. Schenk (eds.), Multidisciplinary Economics, 85–102.

more feudal traditions fostered by a landed aristocracy ruling a submissive and dependent workforce.

Of course, organisational and technological developments originating in the United States, and reimported into Europe, have been central to the development of capitalism as we recognise it today. But if any states can claim to be inventors of the global trading system and the market economy, it is your country and mine, and it is in this spirit that I am pleased to be here to celebrate the opening of a centre in memory of one of the most distinguished of modern Dutch economists, Tjalling Koopmans.

I first encountered Koopmans' work as a graduate student when James Mirrlees – himself to be a fellow winner of the Nobel Prize for economics – assigned me his Three Essays on the State of Economic Science.[3] The significance for me of the extended first essay in that volume was not just that it set out the foundations of modern general equilibrium theory, but that it did so in a manner which asked how these most abstruse and yet most fundamental elements of modern economic analysis enhanced our understanding of the society in which we lived. The mathematics is of value because, and only because, of the understanding it yields of the world we inhabit. I believe we have suffered much, particularly in the ten year period that Friedman identifies, from a belief that if the world is not as economic models describe it, then the fault lies with the world, not with the model. That is an abuse of the foundations of modern neoclassical economics, to which Koopmans made such signal contributions, and an abuse which he would not have condoned. It is an abuse which leads directly to the misunderstanding of the nature of the market economy which Friedman exemplifies.

THE RISE OF THE AMERICAN BUSINESS MODEL

Friedman's thesis is the one expressed, with greater subtlety and at considerably greater length, by Francis Fukuyama in The End of History.[4] Fukuyama, more conscious of history than Friedman, would not dispute the account of the origins of the market economy which I have given. But the phrase 'the end of history' encapsulates the notion that the collapse of communism has left only one coherent account in modern political economy: a combination of lightly regulated capitalism and liberal democracy which bears a considerable resemblance to the United States at the end of the twentieth century. If other political and economic systems differ from it, then they are either in transition towards that ideal or in inevitable decline.

The triumphalism expressed in Fukuyama's careful prose was overtaken by more assertive accounts from business people and popular commentators. Walter Wriston, former chief executive of Citicorp, wrote of The Twilight of Sovereignty.[5] Wriston claimed that markets should and would undermine the traditional role of governments.

3 Koopmans (1957).
4 Fukuyama, F. (1989).
5 Wriston (1992).

By the end of the decade, this diagnosis of the subordination of government to market was shared by those – like Naomi Klein – who deplored it as well as those – like Wriston – who applauded it.[6] Business people like Wriston provide an articulate account of one view of how market economies work. Self-regarding materialism is the principal determinant of economic behaviour, and government should not restrict it. Financial markets are the main regulator of economic activity. The economic role of the state is the protection of property rights and the enforcement of contracts. I call this position the American Business Model (ABM).

Europeans have always displayed some scepticism about the universality of the American Business Model: but its inexorable rise – matched by a similarly inexorable rise in stock prices – provoked a loss of European self-confidence. In Britain and Germany, speculation in technology stocks paralleled the bubble on Wall Street. At Lisbon in February 2000 – ironically, just as the US stock market bubble reached its peak – European leaders signed up to a 'new economy' agenda – the market liberalisation required by globalisation and new technology. These ideas were also transmitted to poor countries. The phrase 'Washington Consensus'[7] came to describe the general nostrums put forward by the US Treasury and by the principal international economic agencies – the International Monetary Fund and the World Bank – whose head offices are located beside each other in downtown Washington D.C.

But globalisation and the American Business Model provoked reaction. The World Trade Organisation met in Seattle in November 1999. Rioters filled the streets and the conference ended in disarray. Every similar subsequent meeting attracted crowds of demonstrators.

Nevertheless at the start of the twenty-first century, the American Business Model (ABM) plays the role in political economy that socialism enjoyed for so long. All political positions, even hostile ones, are defined by their relationship to it. Globalisation and privatisation have displaced capital and class as the terms of discourse. The label 'market forces' immediately evokes hostile or supportive reactions. The term 'Washington consensus' is for some a statement of inescapable realities of economic life, but is demonised in many poor states as an attack on democracy and living standards.

The philosophy of the ABM, as articulated by Milton Friedman – unrelated to Thomas – is of government as referee. 'It is important to distinguish the day-to-day activities of people from the general customary and legal framework within which these take place. The day-to-day activities are like the actions of the participants in a game when they are playing it; the framework, like the rules of the game they play.... These then are the basic roles of government in a free society: to provide a means whereby we can modify the rules, to mediate differences among us on the meaning of the rules, and to enforce compliance with the rules on the part of those few who would otherwise not play the game' (Friedman, 1962, p. 25).

6 Wriston (1992), Klein (1999).

7 The phrase was first used in 1989 by John Williamson of the (Washington based) Institute for International Economics. See Williamson (1999) http://www.worldbank.org and Naim (1999) for a history.

The claims of the American Business Model are of four kinds:

- Self interest rules – self-regarding materialism governs our economic lives;
- Market fundamentalism – markets should operate freely, and attempts to regulate them by social or political action are almost always undesirable;
- The minimal state – the economic role of government should not extend much beyond the enforcement of contracts and private property rights. government should not itself provide goods and services, or own productive assets;
- Low taxation – while taxation is necessary to finance these basic functions of the minimal state, tax rates should be as low as possible and the tax system should not seek to bring about redistribution of income and wealth.

THE CASE FOR THE ABM

The ABM case is often founded on arguments of general principle and the moral issues around freedom of contract are fundamental for many people. Some supporters of the ABM see government action in economic matters as an attack on liberty, an improper use of the coercive power of the state. Freedom of contract requires a minimal state; market fundamentalism and low taxation are immediate corollaries.

Although people who believe this mostly also believe that the ABM is economically efficient, presumably they would still favour it if it were not. If it could be shown that some regulation of markets would make everyone, or very many, people better off, they would still judge it wrong for government to implement it. From a different ethical starting point others find the premise of self-interested motivation morally repugnant. Even if it is true it ought not to be true, and social institutions should restrain greed rather than accommodate it. The accountability of democracy is preferable to the anonymity of markets. If market fundamentalism, the minimal state and low taxation are necessary for economic efficiency, material sacrifices must be made to secure a just society. But people who hold this view tend also to believe that such sacrifices would not be large. This clash of moral values cannot be resolved by economics: perhaps it cannot be resolved at all.

But wider support for the ABM derives, not from these moral arguments, but from concern for economic efficiency. Faith in the efficiency of market mechanisms has been widespread amongst economists since the foundation of the subject by Adam Smith, but the relationship between market organisation and efficient resource allocation was first formally described through the fundamental theorems of welfare economics, a key element of that general equilibrium theory described in Koopmans' first essay. Arrow and Debreu established precisely the way in which individual decision-making by households and competitive firms might produce consistent outcomes. The conjecture of the 'invisible hand' became an exact mathematical result.

Arrow and Debreu worked in the context of a specific, simplified model of the economy in which preferences and production possibilities can be represented as convex sets. All markets are perfectly competitive and the households and firms which trade in them are self-regarding maximisers. Their preferences and choices are independent of those of other households and firms. If these conditions hold, there is a set of prices such that aggregate supplies will equal aggregate demands for every commodity in the economy. There will be no surpluses, and no shortages. No co-ordinator is needed to achieve a co-ordinated outcome. The manufacture of a car requires the contributions of thousands of resources and thousands of people. But it isn't necessary for anyone to oversee the whole of that process. It is sufficient that people make decisions on the basis of the prices they see and the knowledge of their own preferences and production possibilities.

The abstract nature of the model gives pause to many. This arcane mathematics seems far removed from the basic questions that motivate the study of economics. The assumptions of the theory are obviously unrealistic. Our preferences are influenced by those of other people, different production processes interfere with each other, economies of scale are widespread. But abstraction is not, in itself, a sufficient basis for criticism. Because economic systems are complex, *any* discipline model requires extensive simplifying assumptions.

A model like that of Arrow-Debreu demonstrates the possibility of spontaneous order in economic systems. It does not necessarily follow that there will *be* spontaneous order. Nor does it follow that if there is co-ordination, or spontaneous order, the Arrow-Debreu model explains it. But some approximation to spontaneous order does seem to be a feature of real market economies, and the Arrow-Debreu model offers one coherent explanation of how such spontaneous order might come about. With the demonstration of coherence and consistency comes an assertion of efficiency.

Every competitive equilibrium constitutes a Preto efficient state – one in which no one can be made better off at the expense of someone else. Any allocation that is Preto efficient can be achieved by a competitive equilibrium. These are the fundamental theorems of welfare economics that link general equilibrium theory to modern American political philosophy and provide the intellectual underpinnings of the ABM.

John Rawls' *Theory of Justice*, published in 1972, and Robert Nozick's *Anarchy State and Utopia*, which appeared in 1974, are among the most influential works of modern political theory. Both Rawls and Nozick have been influential among economists, Rawls mostly for those whose political leanings were to the left and Nozick for those who inclined to the right. There is a natural affinity between their frame of reasoning and the fundamental theorems of welfare economics, a product of the consonance between modern American individualistic political philosophy and economic models based on the maximisation of aggregations of individual preferences.

For Nozick, it is illegitimate to use the coercive power of the state to make some better off at the expense of others. His concept of justice requires the protection of property rights legitimately acquired or legitimately transferred. Nozick's government must achieve Pareto efficiency, but may not choose between alternative allocations which are Pareto efficient. The first of the fundamental theorems of welfare economics – every competitive equilibrium is Pareto efficient – could have been written for Nozick. The economic policy suggested is the creation of a framework that will permit competitive equilibrium to be achieved. No more, no less.

Rawls invites us to stand behind a 'veil of ignorance', and order states of the world without knowing our role in them. The world economic system encompasses many different types of economic experience, but we are not aware which of these experiences we ourselves will encounter. Rawls invokes what he calls the maximin principle – since we fear our position will be unfavourable, we support policies which will make the worst off as well off as possible. The Rawlsian approach not only justifies substantial redistribution, but requires it.

If the first fundamental theorem of welfare economics was written for Nozick, the second was written for Rawls. We stand behind the veil of ignorance, in search of a just mechanism for allocating scarce resources between competing ends. We are bound to choose a Pareto efficient outcome. The choice between Pareto efficient outcomes will be determined by the maximin principle. The second fundamental theorem of welfare economics – any Pareto efficient outcome can be achieved by an appropriate allocation of resources – tells us that all we need do is get the initial distribution right. Competitive equilibrium will take care of the rest. A free market economy, with income redistribution, meets the requirements of Rawls' Theory of Justice.

Nozick and the first fundamental theorem argue for the justice and efficiency of the American Business Model. A competitive market equilibrium is just simply by virtue of being a competitive market equilibrium. And Rawls and the second fundamental theorem argue for a more moderate version of political economy – redistributive market liberalism – which, while embracing the basic tenets of the American Business Model, concedes a larger role for government in addressing the distribution and redistribution of wealth. With appropriate redistribution, a competitive market system will bring about a just and efficient outcome. Rawlsian justice need not involve a discussion of how the economy operates, as long as we are satisfied that it is perfectly competitive. If society will only wind up the mechanism the market will direct us towards the desired result.

IS GREED GOOD?

Even the most enthusiastic supporters of the ABM acknowledge that it has a public relations problem. As Daniel Yergin and Joseph Stanislaw, cheerleaders for the worldwide rise of the ABM, acknowledge regretfully, 'few people would die with the words 'free markets' on their lips' (p. 398). It is not difficult to explain why people will die with Stalin, Heil Hitler, or Jihad on their lips, but will not give the same accolade to free markets. Stalin, Hitler and Bin Laden recruited followers by demonising other people. The American Business Model demonises itself. We dislike the American Business Model most of all for its unattractive account of our behaviour and our characters.

Some practitioners revel in this unflattering self description. Al Dunlap, the author of Mean Business, and (subsequently disgraced) champion of shareholder value, wrote in the euphoric 1990s 'if you want a friend, get a dog. I'm not taking any chances, I've got two'.[8] John Gutfreund, chairman of Salomon Brothers, one of the most aggressive investment banks of the 1980s, said successful traders must wake up each morning

8 Dunlap (1996), p. xii.

'ready to bite the ass off a bear'.[9] In those extreme versions of the American Business Model, which came to the fore in the last two decades of the twentieth century, it is a mistake to deplore materialism and regard selfishness as a vice. Greed is good: nice guys finish last. The rambling but strident philosophy of Ayn Rand, Alan Greenspan's former mentor, proclaims the virtues of selfishness under the title of 'objectivism'.[10] The logical conclusion of extreme individualism is that concern for others is an emotion which can properly be called on only to the extent that we feel it spontaneously. Private charity is the only proper mechanism of redistribution, and any further claim on us by the community would infringe our autonomy.

In an alternative view, ethical issues which puzzled great thinkers from Aristotle to the present day disappear in a haze of confusion and goodwill. Modern advocates of 'corporate social responsibility' and well meaning business people claim that if only self interest is interpreted sufficiently widely, there will be no conflict between self interest and the public good.[11] As when Charles Wilson asserted that 'what was good for our country was good for General Motors, and vice versa?'[12] History interpreted his remark as malign, but it was only naïve.

A more plausible argument is that there is simply a dichotomy between economic life and public morality. The values appropriate to business are just different from those appropriate to our private lives. As Goethe observed at the beginning of the industrial revolution, 'everything which is properly business we must keep carefully separate from life'.[13] Goethe's position mirrors Milton Friedman's: 'the social responsibility of business is to maximise its profits'.[14] This position is acceptable to many business people because it puts few restrictions on their behaviour. Its corollary, or certainly its consequence, is the general contempt amongst intellectuals for business and those who engage in it. The dichotomy between economic values and ordinary values achieves sophisticated expression from philosophers like Michael Walzer, who identifies 'spheres of justice':[15] criteria for distinguishing the proper boundaries of the market. In practice, these boundaries seem to imply very few restrictions on the extension of market institutions.

But the primary objection to the description of human behaviour in the ABM is not that it is immoral, but that it is incorrect. Greed is a human characteristic, but not, for most people, a dominant one. The minority for whom it is an overriding motive are not people we admire. Nor do we think of them as successful. When we read that Hetty Green, possibly the richest woman in history, dressed in second-hand clothes to secure

---

9 Cited in Lewis (1989) *Liar's Poker*, p. 54.

10 Rand (1990a 1990b).

11 See, for example OECD (2001) and, for a critique Henderson (2001).

12 Wilson's observation was made in testimony to the Senate Armed Services Committee on his nomination as Secretary for Defense in the Eisenhower administration (quoted in *New York Times*, February 24, 1953). It is often reproduced as 'what's good for General Motors is good for America', a significantly different statement.

13 Goethe (1971) p. 45.

14 *New York Times,* 13 September 1970: see also Friedman (1962) chapter VIII.

15 Walzer (1981).

admission to a charity hospital for her injured son,[16] we feel sadness and even sympathy that she made such a mess of things. At least in Europe, our sense of what constitutes a good life is based, not on an addition of material possessions, but on an account of the virtues very similar to that which Aristotle described two millennia ago.

Politics is attractive to people obsessed by financial reward. Joseph Mobutu, who looted the wealth of the Congo as its president for thirty years, was probably the greatest thief of modern times but even he was more interested in money as a means to power rather than an end in itself.[17] Productive economies have adopted systematic, and usually successful, policies to exclude such people from public life. Those who enter politics in Europe or the United States today may have other personality disorders, but not that one.

Nor is modern business truly appealing to the truly greedy. Building great businesses requires considerable abilities and hard work. Successful business people – from Andrew Carnegie, in the nineteenth century, the ruthless steel tycoon who wrote that 'a man who dies rich dies disgraced', to Bill Gates in the twentieth century – have pursued a business as a primary, not an intermediate, goal. That is what they tell us and we should not disbelieve them.[18] When Carnegie or Gates declared their intention to crush competitors, they were not trying to persuade us to like or admire them.

Even in the financial services industry, personal greed is often moderated by commitment to the activity and concern for status. Donald Trump, master of The Apprentice, is perhaps the most aggressive and high-living American trader of the last two decades. Yet Trump's autobiography begins with 'I don't do it for the money', He goes on 'I've got enough, much more money than I'll ever need. I do it to do it. Deals are my art form'.[19] What of Warren Buffett, the legendary investor and today, after Gates, America's richest man? His motives are complex. Buffett's biographer reports: 'It's not that I want money,' Warren replied. 'It's the fun of making money and watching it grow.'[20] Which is, presumably, why Buffett still lives in the same Omaha bungalow he purchased in 1956 and enjoys nothing better than a Nebraskan steak washed down with cherry coke. The aspiration of the bond traders at Salamon Brothers described by Michael Lewis was to be regarded by their peers as a 'Big Swinging Dick'. Lewis reports that 'what really stung the traders .... was not their absolute level of pay but their pay in relation to the other bond traders.'[21]

This is not to deny that self-interested materialism is an important feature of economic life. Economic systems based on appeals to work for the common good will fail. But self interest is necessarily hedged by the complex institutions of modern economic, social and political life – formal regulation and implicit rules, mechanisms of reputation and co-ordination, instincts and structures of co-operation, feelings of

16 Crossen (2001) p. 213.
17 Wrong (2000), p. 20.
18 Gates (1995, 1999).
19 Trump (1987) p. 1.
20 Lowenstein (1995), p. 20
21 Lewis (1989), p. 88.

solidarity. Modern societies did not develop ethical norms which limit and deplore self-regarding materialism out of perverse desire to restrain entrepreneurial spirits.

Economic motivations are complex, multi-faceted, and not necessarily consistent. The study of human behaviour is an empirical subject. It cannot rely solely on introspection and a priori assumption. Still less should it rely on introspection and a priori assumptions that do not correspond to experience. The best starting point is to expect that behaviour will be adaptive – that people will behave in the way they are normally expected to in the circumstances in which they find themselves. This expectation will sometimes be false. Economies would not develop otherwise.

PROPERTY RIGHTS

The ABM emphasises the central importance of property as an institution: so central that its defence is the principal function of the state. The Arrow-Debreu framework generally takes a distribution of property rights as its starting point. This assumes that the nature of property rights is obvious. But property rights are socially constructed. Property rights can be defined in many ways and allocated among individuals, households and firms in many ways. Milton Friedman, unlike many of his less sophisticated followers, understands this: 'what constitutes property and what rights the ownership of property confers are complex social creations rather than self-evident propositions.' But, he goes on 'in many cases, the existence of a well specified and generally accepted definition of property is far more important than just what the definition is.'[22]

But Friedman produces no evidence for this conjecture, and experience of economic history and geography demonstrates the opposite. The development of agriculture, of employment, and of limited liability companies is an evolution from one group of definitions of property rights to another, and without such evolution economic progress would be much less rapid than it has been. The legitimacy of property rights determined the different economic experiences of Argentina and Australia. In one country, a 'top down' assignment of property among rich individuals close to political power produced poor landlords and a political system polarised around attack and defence of illegitimate privilege: in the other, a 'bottom up' allocation created a stable and productive democracy.

Property rights are debated in many other contexts. We continue to argue over the scope of intellectual property and the nature of media regulation in a pluralist society. It is not easy to see how the current co-evolution of technology and institutions in the internet and genome will play itself out. No one could think that the outcome of these debates doesn't matter.

The leader of Russia's economic reforms in the 1990s, Anatoly Chubais, mirrored Friedman's claim that the definition of property rights is more important than their distribution when he said of the oligarchs who grasped control of many of the former state assets. 'They are stealing absolutely everything and it is impossible to stop them.

22 Friedman (1962), pp. 26-27.

But let them steal and take their property. They will then become owners and decent administrators of the property'.[23] This did not happen. Russia's economic failure in the post-communist era, which reproduces the errors of Argentina, is an enduring reproach to those who claim that the only requirement of a market economy is a system of private property rights. The quality of economic institutions – which it is too simple to characterise as property rights – is the most important difference between rich and poor states. The quality of these institutions is the product of extensive historic evolution. That is why a proper understanding of economic history is essential, and why simple attempts at the transplantation of institutions, as in Russia, inevitably fail.

The possibility of many different property rights regimes, with differing effects on economic efficiency, is a fundamental challenge to the efficiency claims of the Arrow-Debreu model. The fundamental theorems of welfare economies can be true only with respect to a particular structure of property rights. It is then no longer possible to claim that any particular competitive equilibrium is Pareto efficient. A different property rights regime could – and very probably would – make everyone better off.

THE TRUTH ABOUT MARKETS

Misunderstandings about motivation and simplifications of property rights are not the only problems. Markets function effectively only if they are embedded in social institutions which are poorly – if at all – accounted for within the ABM.

(i) Information in complex modern economies is necessarily incomplete and imperfect. Competitive markets fail when there are major differences of information between buyers and sellers. Transactions usually take place within a social context. We prefer to deal with people we know. Or we rely on trusted suppliers, or trusted brands. This social context develops, and is necessary, to deal with these asymmetries of information.

(ii) Markets for risk are not, as they are represented in the Arrow-Debreu framework, essentially similar to those for other commodities. In the face of uncertainty, asymmetries of information are not just prevalent, but the principal impetus to trade. That is why securities markets are generally not efficient, either in the standard technical sense of market efficiency nor by wider standards of social and economic efficiency. Most of the important risks of everyday life – the breakdown of marriage and relationships, redundancy, unemployment and business failure, and acute or chronic illness – are not handled through the market, but in households, among communities, and by government. Securities markets are better described as arenas for sophisticated professional gambling than as institutions which minimise the costs of risk bearing and allocate capital among different lines of business.

(iii) Most economic activity cannot be organised by negotiations between large numbers of potential buyers and potential sellers in impersonal markets. We

23 Freeland (2000), pp. 67-68.

need to work in organisations and in teams, and to co-operate in small groups. Self-interested individuals will often fail to co-operate with each other, even when it is in their mutual best interests to do so. Corporate cultures, ethical values, and the blending of working and social lives are all necessary for effective co-operation.

(iv) It is often true that co-ordination is more effectively achieved through mechanisms of spontaneous order than central direction. But spontaneous order does not emerge immediately and infallibly. Many co-ordination mechanisms are the product of government interventions, social institutions, and agreements between firms.

(v) Knowledge and information are key products in complex modern economies. They cannot be produced in competitive markets in which there are many buyers and sellers of each commodity. Non-materialist motivations – the thrill of discovery and the satisfactions of philanthropy – have generally been more important stimuli to innovation than profit seeking. Very few major twentieth-century innovations were generated by commercial companies.

The ABM is deficient for its naïve approach to issues of human motivation, its simplistic analysis of structures of property rights, its inability to maintain efficiency in the face of imperfect information, its misleading account of markets in risk, its glossing over of problems of co-operation and co-ordination, and its failure to describe the generation of the new knowledge on which its very success depends.

It encounters a further problem of practical implementation – the issue of the legitimacy of the distribution of income and wealth which results from it. The fourth premise of the ABM denies that this distribution is a proper concern of government in a market economy. If differences in income and wealth are the result of differences in productivity, and these are in turn the consequence of differences in effort, talent and skill, redistribution of income and wealth is potentially inefficient. If rewards to differences in efforts, talents and skills are suppressed then talents and skills will not be fully exploited. This is not a conclusive argument against redistribution, but it suggests that redistribution may involve a high price in economic efficiency.

Yet it is hard to believe that differences in income and wealth are completely, or even mainly, explained by differences in effort, talent and skills. Bill Gates made an important contribution to the personal computer industry, but his wealth would allow him an annuity of $5 billion per year for the rest of his life. Are his effort, talent and skills really so exceptional? Do they justify an income many thousands times greater than that of say Alan Turing, the inventor of modern computing, who never earned more than an academic salary, and ultimately committed suicide? Would Gates have put in significantly less effort if the prospective reward had been – say – only $1 billion per year?

If GDP would fall by $5 billion if Gates stayed at home, then we are all better off by paying him $5 billion to come to work. It is not very likely that this is true. We certainly don't know that it's true. And even if it were true, we might still be able to cut a deal in which he agreed to come to work for – say – only $1 billion per year. Most of Gates' reward is economic rent.

And what of the people on the trading floors of securities houses? They are valuable to their employers, which is why they receive multimillion dollar bonuses. But the profits generated from the trading activities are mainly arbitrage gains, and the value added associated with them is much smaller, if indeed it is positive at all. Corporate executives are paid a lot not because of their productivity – which is impossible to measure – but because of their bargaining power. They take a slice of the rents they control.

The complexity of the way in which market rewards are determined makes it impossible to argue that such rewards are necessarily just or efficient. Thoughtful conservatives like Friedman and Nozick do not make that claim: they assert instead that interference with the process that gives rise to them would be unjust, because it would involve illegitimate state coercion.[24]

Some people might agree with this argument. Many would not. That disagreement is itself a problem. If the distribution of income and wealth in the market economy does not meet widely shared notions of legitimacy, that distribution will be expensively disputed. The direct and indirect costs of litigation and crime may be a serious burden on the market economy. In Argentina, and modern Russia, the problems of the legitimacy of that initial distribution of property rights led to structures of politics which have blocked effective economic development for many years afterwards.

If the American Business Model is not a plausible description of how market economies function, why is the American economy so successful? The answer should by now be obvious: the ABM does not describe the American economy. We do not look to the richest countries of the world, to Norway, Switzerland or the Netherlands for societies populated by the exclusively self-interested: but nor do we look to the United States. We point instead to countries such as Nigeria or Haiti, in which there is insufficient basis of trust for market institutions to develop. Or read Colin Turnbull's description of the Ik mountain people, whose social institutions had been shattered by adversity, and among whom the resultant callous materialism had led to a spiral of economic decline.[25]

The ability to form supportive groups which enhanced the lives of individuals and households but did not involve the processes of government has always been a distinguishing feature of American society. Tocqueville identified association as a peculiarly American characteristic almost two centuries ago: 'the most democratic society on earth is found to be the one where men in our day have most perfected the art of pursuing the object of their common desires in common and have applied this new science to the most effect'.[26] The market economies of rich states depend on such institutions. The most important today is the corporation. Corporate man, the epitome of the American submergence of the individual in the company, was once the butt of jokes. Corporate

24 E.g. 'I find it difficult to justify either accepting or rejecting (the capitalist ethic) or to justify any alternative principle. I am led to the view that it cannot in and of itself be regarded as an ethical principle; that it must be regarded as instrumental or a corollary of some other principle such as freedom.' Friedman (1962) p. 165-166.

25 Turnbull (1973).

26 Tocqueville (1835).

men, and corporate women, are the social individuals who make the economic lives of Americans rich and fulfilling.

THE EUROPEAN SOCIAL MARKET IN GERMANY

There is a different European tradition, described as the social market. The phrase originates from Germany, with the ordo-liberals, or Freiburg school, led by Armand Müller-Armach.[27] A key concept of their analysis is "vollständige Konkurrenz", which seems to translate naturally into English as "perfect competition", the ideal of the Arrow-Debreu model. But German scholars[28] insist that its German meaning is wider: it implies resistance to any form of concentrated economic power, in cartels, corporations or the state, so that it embraces intellectual, political and economic pluralism, in obvious reaction to the totalitarian disasters of the Nazi era. Along with "vollständige Konkurrenz" goes an assumption that risks will be managed through public institutions as well as private businesses.[29]

In 1948 the ordo-liberal, Ludwig Erhard, was appointed director of economic affairs in the American and British occupation zones. Erhard's economic reform programme removed price controls and instituted a new currency. This provoked a Russian blockade of Berlin which was defeated by a massive allied airlift. The creation of a West German state followed in which Erhard became first Economics Minister and then Chancellor. In the two decades that followed, the rapid recovery of Germany's economy within the framework of the social market earned the label of 'economic miracle'.

Today the phrase 'social market' has two distinct meanings. This distinction is recently described by Adair Turner. He acknowledges that 'simplistic market fundamentalism can be as dangerous to sensible market liberalism as was Marxism. Capitalism can have a human face, but governments and political processes need to ensure that it does', Turner goes on to say 'two different approaches can be pursued – the classical liberal model in which wider objectives are achieved through the constraints of tax and regulation within which individuals pursue their own self-interest, or the 'communitarian' or 'stakeholder' which seeks to humanise capitalism by asking of individuals and corporations that they take upon themselves a wider set of responsibilities.'[30]

The first of these options – redistributive market liberalism – is the Rawlsian version of the American Business Model, which makes its first three premises but acknowledges a larger role for government in the distribution of income and wealth. Redistributive market liberalism (RML) makes a sharp distinction between our economic lives and our social roles as citizens and neighbours. At work, in business, through our commercial dealings, we may – even must – pursue our self-interest. We

27 Euchen (1981).
28 Watrin (1998).
29 Neaman (1990).
30 Turner (2001) p. 372.

then vote for high taxes so that the proceeds of our successful pursuit of that self-interest can be redistributed.

Few people can handle this schizophrenia. The philosophy of redistributive market liberalism is developed by individuals of high intelligence and moral calibre – like Turner – who can handle the paradoxical concept of an obligation to behave self-interestedly. It is difficult to be a beast in the boardroom and a concerned citizen at the ballot box. People who have successfully pursued commercial self-interest usually support tax and benefit policies which further advance that self-interest. Rich individuals who engage in philanthropy do so in reflection of a 'wider set of responsibilities' rather than self-interest within 'the constraints of tax and regulation'.

For capitalism with a human face to be tenable, the face must be one not two. In Brecht's parable of The Good Woman of Szechwan, the kindly prostitute Shen Te establishes a business with good intentions, but dresses as a cousin when hard-nosed decisions are required. As with Jekyll and Hyde, the inhuman face takes over.

A mild version of RML proposes that government should simply be concerned with equality of opportunity, not equality of outcome. Inequalities in access to education and other barriers to mobility are primary sources of injustice in almost any political philosophy. Could a government ever claim to have met the needs of its citizens by ensuring equality of opportunity in the market economy? Could we ever frame fair rules and institutions without knowledge or concern for their outcomes? Could we set just rules for competition policy and copyright without considering that we were giving Bill Gates $50 billion, or taking it away? Could we set policies for university admissions independent of the structure of graduate earnings? Could we determine an access regime for telecommunications by reference to general principle rather than effect on market structure, call charges, or share prices? Because markets are embedded in a social framework, the distinction between process and outcome – Friedman's distinction between the rules and the play of the game – becomes untenable.

The fundamental objections to redistributive market liberalism are the same as those used against the American Business Model. The mistaken assumptions about motivation and behaviour, the failure to acknowledge socially constructed nature of property rights, the inability of market institutions to deal with risk. The problems of securing necessary co-operation among self-interested individuals and the difficulties of handling asymmetries of information within a complex modern economy.

All these are reasons why we cannot simply wind up the mechanism of the market economy and let it run, and illustrate why market economics function only by virtue of being embedded in a social context. The real objective is not to 'humanise capitalism' by 'asking of individuals and corporations that they take upon themselves a wider set of responsibilities'. Rather it is to understand that capitalism works in practice only because it is humanised. An alternative view that more closely corresponds to that post-war German conception of the social market is the political economy of the embedded market.

THE EMBEDDED MARKET

The assumptions of the ABM are false, but that does not imply their opposites are true. There are people who think economic behaviour is mostly altruistic, political mechanisms of allocation are always preferable to the anarchy of the market, government should control and preferably own all productive assets, and highly progressive taxation should be imposed to bring about an egalitarian distribution of income and wealth.

But not many. The reality is a fuzzier, intermediate one. The economic world is complex. Self-interest is an important motivation, but not an exclusive motivation. Our other concerns influence work and business lives as well as personal lives. We need the approbation of our friends, the trust of our colleagues, the satisfaction of performing activities that are worthwhile in themselves and give others pleasure. These motives are not materialistic, but that does not mean they are not economic. They are an essential part of the mechanisms through which successful business operates. Without them business and economic systems would be impoverished – in material as well as other terms.

Markets work broadly , but not always and not perfectly. Pluralist market structures promote innovation, and competitive markets meet many consumer needs, but there is no general reason to believe that market outcomes are efficient. Social and economic institutions manage the transmission of information in market economies. These institutions depend on culture and values, laws and history. In the Arrow-Debreu framework, taken over by the simplicities of the ABM, it is obvious what the rules of a market economy should be, it is easy to enforce them, and the description of products and the definition of their properties is also obvious and easy.

Market economies have been successful relative to other societies precisely because the rules that govern them are not obvious to frame and easy to implement, and rich states have evolved complex governance structures embedded in other modern social and political institutions. That evolution allows the development of sophisticated products which consumers are confident to buy and use without needing to understand them. Market economies handle co-ordination problems associated with logistics well – co-ordination between manufacturers and component suppliers, reliable deliveries, overall balances between supply and demand. They do less well when even temporary imbalances are intolerable – as in electricity supply, when the lights go out. But markets do not necessarily succeed at all, or succeed in producing good outcomes, when other forms of co-ordination are required, as for networks and standards. Markets for risk and capital, dominated by speculative traders, are prone to bubbles and overshooting. These fluctuations in securities markets destabilise markets for goods and services, and divert resources from productive activities to the pursuit of small arbitrage gains.

The very concept of a market for labour is offensive to many people, and with cause: workers are citizens as well as suppliers of labour, and enjoy rights that are not held by apples, pears, software – or corporations. Laws that prohibit slavery, and regulate the organised sex industry are hardly controversial. They restrict freedom of contract on the grounds that even voluntary transactions may degrade society and deprive individuals of dignity. The issue is not whether the labour 'market' should be subject to social and legal regulation, but the nature and extent of such regulation. That is a matter for moral judgement, social values and empirical evidence.

Many services cannot be provided in competitive markets: public goods like lighthouses, environmental protection, police and defence, and the framework of rules within which the modern market economy operates. There are natural monopolies, in water and electricity distribution, road and rail networks, air traffic control. Other services – like education and health – could be provided by competitive markets but are not, for reasons that most people find compelling. It is desirable to find pluralist structures for these industries, but acceptable market solutions will not emerge spontaneously. The distribution of income and wealth and the process by which that distribution is established must, like the structure of market institutions itself, enjoy legitimacy if the market economy is to survive and evolve. Many failures of the market economy follow from this.

The embedded market describes the successful market systems of Western Europe – and the reality of the United States. The embedded market does not function within a minimal state. Productive economies have the largest, most powerful and most influential governments the world has ever seen. Through most of history, and in poor countries today, government rarely impinges on the everyday lives of ordinary people.

In rich states, we are always conscious of the influence of government. We pay its taxes on every transaction we make, and most of us also receive social benefits. Regulation governs everything we do, from the way we drive to the butter we spread on our bread. We look to government to provide a wide range of goods and services, from education to rubbish collection. The market economy relies on intermediate institutions greater than individuals, smaller than governments. The most important of these are corporations. But there are many others.

Because markets are embedded in social institutions, it is not only, or mainly, by voting that we influence the development of the market economy. Economic policy is not simply a list of things the government should do. We make economic policy as consumers, employers, entrepreneurs and shareholders. We influence economic policy when we conform to, or resist, the norms and values of the market economy. Economic policy is as much about social attitudes and customary behaviour as about law and regulation.

The difference between rich and poor states is the result of differences in the quality of their economic institutions. After four disappointing decades, development agencies have recognised this and used their authority to demand reforms. But the prescriptions have often been facile. What was offered to Russia was not American institutions: but the caricature of them, contained in the American Business Model. The institutions of the market – secure property rights, minimal government economic intervention, light regulation – were supposed to be simple and universal. If these prescriptions were implemented, growth would follow.

But the truth about markets is far more complex. Rich states are the product of that coevolution of civil society, politics and economic institutions which began in Britain and the Netherlands three hundred years ago. A coevolution which we only partially understand, and cannot transplant. In the only successful examples of transplantation

– the Western offshoots – entire populations, and their institutions, were settled in almost empty countries. The appeal of the American Business Model today, as of Marxism yesterday, is the suggestion that the history of economic institutions, the structure of current society, and the path of future development have a simple economic explanation and an inevitable outcome. In a curious reversal, the claims of historic inevitability and economic determinism, once made on behalf of Marxism, are today made by the political right on behalf of the American Business Model. But the failure of Marxism as economic doctrine was not that it was the wrong grand narrative, but that no grand narrative is properly descriptive of the modern market economy. The truth about markets is not revealed in one single overarching account – not the Marxist critique, not the American Business Model, nor the neoclassical model of general equilibrium – but through little stories and piecemeal observation.

BIBLIOGRAPHY

Brittan, L. (1996). *Capitalism with a Human Face.* London: Fontana Press.

Brittan, L. (1968). *Left or Right: The Bogus Dilemma.* London: Secker & Warburg.

Brittan, L. (1973). *Is there an Economic Consensus? An Attitude Survey*. London: Macmillan.

Crossen, C. (2001). *The Rich and How They Got That Way,* London: Nicholas Brealey.

Dunlap, A.J. with Andelman, B. (1996). *Mean Business: How I Save Bad Companies and Make Good Companies Great.* New York: Fireside.

Euchen, W. (1981). *The German Social Market Economies.* Oxford: Basil Blackwell.

Fischer, D.H. (1989). *Albion's Seed.* New York: Oxford University Press.

Freedland, J. (1998). *Bring Home the Revolution: How Britain can Live the American Dream.* London: Fourth Estate.

Freeland, C. (2000). *Sale of the Century: The Inside Story of the Second Russian Revolution.* New York: Times Books.

Friedman, M. (1962). *Capitalism and Freedom.* Chicago and London: University of Chicago Press.

Friedman, T. (1999). *The Lexus and the Olive Tree.* London: Harper Collins.

Fukuyama, F. (1989). The End of History. *The National Interest*, Summer.

Gates, B., with Hemingway, C. (1999). *Business @ the Speed of Thought: Using a Digital Nervous System.* Harmondsworth: Penguin Books.

Gates, B., with Myhrvold, N. & Rinearson, P. (1995). *The Road Ahead.* London: Viking.

Gilder, G.S. (1984). *The Spirit of Enterprise.* New York: Simon & Schuster.

Goethe, J.W. von, (1971). *Elective Affinities* (1809), trans. with introduction by R.J. Hollingdale. London: Penguin.

Henderson, D. (2001). Misguided Virtue: False Notions of Corporate Social Responsibility. *Hobart Paper, 142* (London, Institute of Economic Affairs).

Klein, N. (1999). '*No Logo*'. London: Flamingo.

Leadbeater, C. (2000). *Living on Thin Air: The New Economy.* London: Viking.

Lewis, M. (1989). *Liar's Poker.* London.

Lowenstein, R. (2000). *When Genius Failed: The Rise and Fall of Long-term Capital Management.* London: Fourth Estate.

Meade, J. (1964). *Efficiency, Equality and the Ownership of Property.* London: Allen & Unwin.

Naim, M. (1999). Fads and Fashion in Economic Reforms: Washington Consensus or Washington Confusion. *Third World Quarterly, 21 (3),* 505-528.

Neaman, E.A. (1990). German Collectivism and the Welfare State. *Critical Review, 4 (4),* 608.

OECD,(2001). *Corporate Social Responsibility: Partners for Progress.* Paris, Organisation for Economic Cooperation and Development.

Rand, A. (1990a). *Introduction to Objectivist Epistemology.* New York: Meridian Books.

Rand, A. (1990b). *The Voice of Reason: Essays in Objectivist Thought.* New York: Meridian Books.

Tocqueville, A. de (2000) edn. *Democracy in America (1835)*. Ed. and trans. H.C. Mansfield & D. Winthrop. Chicago: University of Chicago Press.
Trump, D., with Schwartz, T. (1987). *Trump: The Art of the Deal*. London: Century.
Turnbull, C.D. (1973). *The Mountain People*. New introd., 1994. London: Pimlico.
Turner, J.A. (2001). *Just Capital: The Liberal Economy*. London: Macmillan Publishing.
Walzer, M. (1981). Philosophy and Democracy. *Political Theory, 9 (3)*, 379-399.
Watrin, C. (1999). The Social Market Economy: The Main Ideas and their Influence on Economic Policy. In A. Kilmarnock (Ed.), *The Social Market and the State*. London: Social Market Foundation.
Williamson, J. (1999). http://www.worldbank.org
Wriston, W.B. (1992). *The Twilight of Sovereignty*. New York: Scribner.
Wrong, M. (2000). *In the Footsteps of Mr Kurtz: Living on the Brink of Disaster in the Congo*. London: Fourth Estate.
Yergin, D.L. & Stanislaw, J. (1998). *The Commanding Heights: The Battle between Government and the Marketplace that is Remaking the Modern World*. New York: Simon & Schuster.

W.G. SHEPHERD

THE STATE OF THE INDUSTRIAL ORGANIZATION FIELD

This event is a fine housewarming for a new scholarly family. The department's academic strengths will be enhanced by the Dutch scholarly style: clear analysis, high skills, impeccable manners, and a cheerful bluntness. Hans Schenk will be a notable leader in all this.

I have been asked to discuss how the field of Industrial Organization is, and how it has been changing. The field of Industrial Organization is exciting and active, but often divisive and contentious. There is an abundant flow of mainstream research into concepts and evidence. But recent decades have seen many efforts to insert doubtful 'new' ideas and methods. Tension continues between real-world research and pure theorists. The unresolved disagreements are long-lasting and deep.

I shall first summarise what the field is really about, in Section I. Then in Sections II and III, I shall explain and describe the evolution of the modern field since it emerged in the 1880s. In Section IV, I shall give details on three of the most important issues. They are:

1. How 'perfect' are actual markets? Are nearly all markets just about 'perfect'? Or do many markets have significant imperfections, while some are deeply imperfect?
2. Actual competition versus potential competition. Which matters most: actual competition (often embodied in each firm's own share of the market) or potential competition (the possibility that new firms may enter from outside the market)?
3. Research methodologies: theory versus applied research. Should we rely mainly on pure theory (especially game theory) to create and organise the field's knowledge, or rely mainly on applied research testing concepts with real-market conditions?

I shall also use an important example to illustrate these points. It is the 'Merger Guidelines' of the US antitrust agencies, especially as they were revised in 1992 and are still used now. US officials have even urged European antitrust authorities to adopt them. I shall explain why they definitely should not do so.

Finally, I shall briefly discuss how U.S. antitrust policies have become inferior to those in Europe and the U.K.

P. de Gijsel and H. Schenk (eds.), Multidisciplinary Economics, 103–126.

I. WHAT THIS FIELD IS REALLY ABOUT

This field's core is about competition and monopoly power: how much is there of each in real markets, what causes them, and what are their effects? The field also studies the policy efforts using antitrust and regulation (and deregulation) to promote effective competition in place of weak, ineffective competition. For summaries and background on the history, see William G. Shepherd and Jeanna M. Sheperd (2004), especially chapter 1, F.M. Scherer and David Ross (1991) and Almarin Phillips and Rodney E. Stevenson, (1974). In the special cases where a market is a natural monopoly, the field studies how to apply economic regulation in place of competition.

Figure 1 presents the field's format, as it is usually summarised in the U.S. literature. Note that the policies influence markets; but also, note that powerful companies in those markets tend to influence the policies. Policies are hammered out in rough political strife, rather than coolly designed and applied with cool, clinical precision.

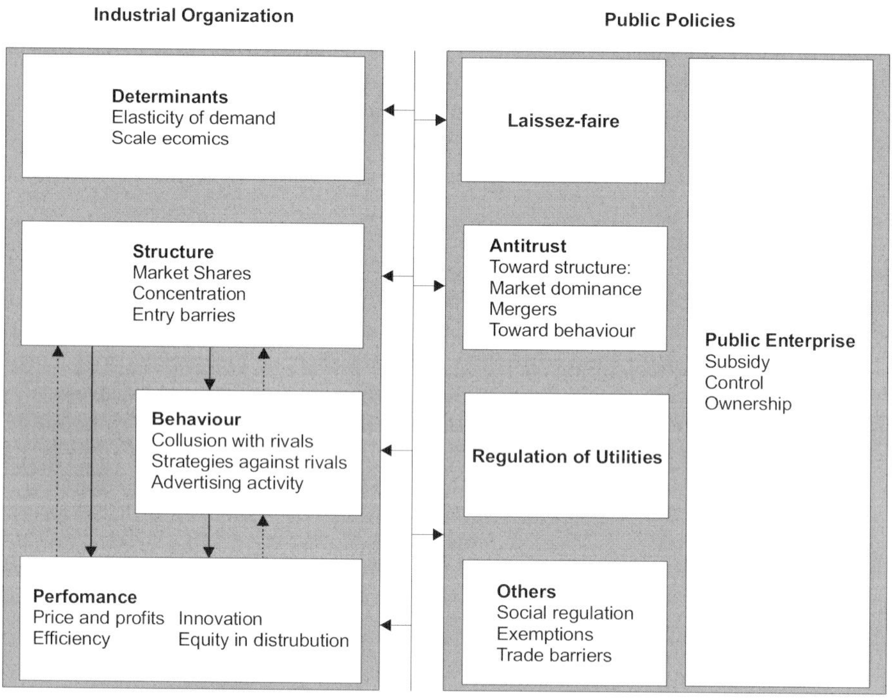

Figure 1. The Format of the Industrial Organization Field.[1]

1 Reprinted by permission of Waveland Press, Inc. from Shepherd-Shepherd, The Economics of Industrial Organization, 5/E. (Long Grove, IL: Waveland Press, Inc., 2004).

This is a big subject, reaching all corners of the economy and requiring sophisticated judgments about complex realities. Competition is crucial because it promotes innovation and protects freedom of choice and opportunity.

More than a century of research has developed four main intellectual categories of markets, differing in their degrees of competition and market power. They are summed up in Table 1, with a number of U.S. examples.

Table 1. The Main Types of Markets, from Pure Monopoly to Effective Competition[2]

Market Type	Familiar Examples
Pure Monopoly One firm has 100 per cent	Patented goods (e.g. pharmaceutical), local electric supply, water, transit
Dominant Firm One firm has over 40 per cent	Microsoft, many newspapers, Gatorade, Campbell Soup, Yellow Pages, Baby Bells, Anheuser-Busch, Boeing, De Beers, Gerber, Frito-Lay, Hallmark Greetings
Tight Oligopoly Four firms hold over 60 per cent	Nike and Adidas, cigarettes, ready-to-eat cereals, Coca-Cola and Pepsi, video games, Boeing and Airbus, jet aircraft engines, disposable diapers, FedEx and UPS, toys, garbage disposal
Effective Competition Four firms hold less than 40 per cent. Entry is free (includes loose oligopoly, monopolistic competition, and perfect competition)	Everything else; over 70 per cent of the U.S. economy

Each market has its structure, which primarily involves the market shares of the leading firms. Larger market shares almost always give more power over the market. Figure 2 illustrates the current structure of a market that has a dominant firm looming over many smaller ones. There may also be some degree of a barrier at the edge of the market, which may impede any potential new entry that might try to occur from outside the market.

2 Reprinted by permission of Waveland Press, Inc. from Shepherd-Shepherd, The Economics of Industrial Organization, 5/E. (Long Grove, IL: Waveland Press, Inc., 2004). All rights reserved.

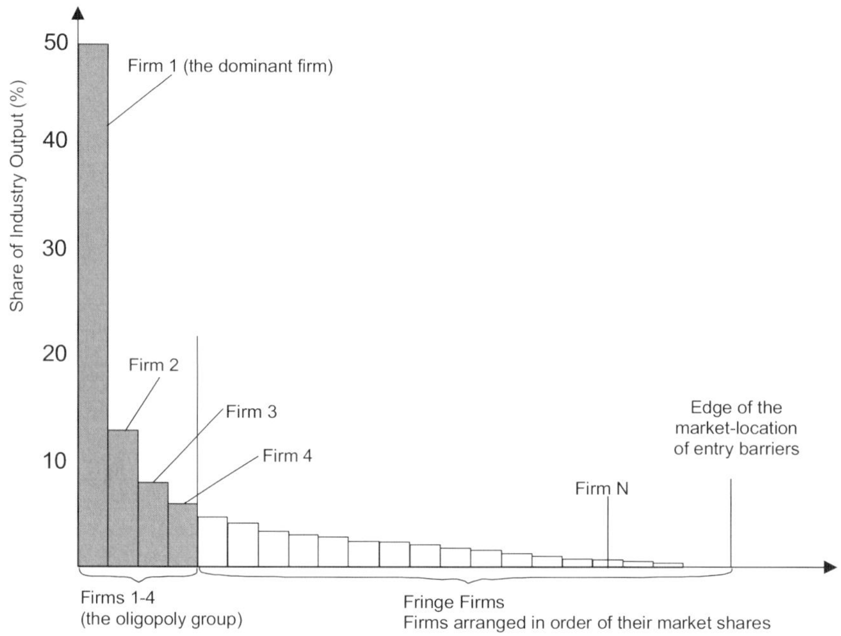

Figure 2. An illustration of Market Structure with a Dominant Firm.[3]

Each market's structure influences its performance (its innovation, efficiency, fairness, etc.). The Chicago School free-market view asserts the opposite: that each firm's performance influences its market share. The influence may range between tight or loose. If (and only if) markets are perfect, then causation might run the other way; if a firm gains a high market share because it's more efficient and innovative,and it 'deserves' the rewards.

Always, there are many goals for the economy, not just one. They include innovation, efficiency, fairness in distribution, the healthy competitive process itself, static allocational 'efficiency', freedom of choice, and others. Innovation is usually regarded as the most important goal. Table 2 sums them up.

3 Reprinted by permission of Waveland Press, Inc. from Shepherd-Shepherd, The Economics of Industrial Organization, 5/E. (Long Grove, IL: Waveland Press, Inc., 2004). All rights reserved.

Table 2. The Main Economic Goals for Markets and the Economy[4]

1. **Efficiency in Resource Allocation**
   a. Internal efficiency (also called X-efficiency or business efficiency).
   b. Allocative efficiency. Resources are allocated among markets and firms in patterns that maximise the value of total output. Prices equal long-run marginal cost and minimum average cost.
   c. Avoiding simple resource wastes.

2. **Technical Progress**
   New products and production methods are adopted rapidly.

3. **Equity in Distribution**
   There is a fair distribution (in line with the society's standards of fairness) of
   a. Wealth
   b. Income, and
   c. Opportunity.

4. **The Competitive Process**
   Competition itself provides social values of open opportunity and rewards to effort and skill.

5. **Other Dimensions**
   Including
   a. Individual freedom of choice,
   b. Security from extreme economic risks of financial and job losses,
   c. Support for healthy democratic processes, and
   d. Cultural diversity.

II. THE FIELD'S BACKGROUND

My viewpoint

I have worked throughout the field's various parts since about 1955, and I have had the remarkable good luck to know personally many of the field's most important people during this modern era.

My perspective also reflects four specific kinds of experience. First, my research has dealt with most of the field's topics, as they play out in U.S. and European markets. My textbooks have covered all parts of the field, trying to be fair and neutral.

Second, in 1967-68 I was the personal economic adviser to the mild-mannered but brilliant Donald F. Turner, then the head of the U.S. Antitrust Division in Washington DC. I gained a great deal of top-level experience and insight during that intense year of merger mania, big dominant firms, and tight oligopolies. There was much drama. We considered suing the Big 3 auto firms for their 'shared monopoly', the AT&T company

4 Reprinted by permission of Waveland Press, Inc. from Shepherd-Shepherd, The Economics of Industrial Organization, 5/E. (Long Grove, IL: Waveland Press, Inc., 2004).

for its vertical monopoly, and we did sue IBM for its near-monopoly of computers, and more. Little was actually done then, despite false claims since then that antitrust was way too active in the 1960s.

Third, for more than a decade, from 1990 to 2001, I was the General Editor of the Review of Industrial Organization. That journal encourages and publishes 'applied' research on real markets and policies, as well as on theory. The journal includes the research issues and policies of all intellectual schools and much of the world. I observed the colleagues and trends in detail, and I always dealt fairly with authors and ideas. Incidentally, because I treated all authors well, I gained only friends, not enemies.

Fourth, I'm currently preparing (with Henk de Jong) a wide-ranging book that surveys the innovative modern 'pioneers' in the Industrial Organization field, from its beginnings in the 1880s up to the mid 1980s. We've been thinking hard about past innovations, trends and controversies.

Understanding the Field's Evolution

This field is highly unusual in several ways. In fact, let me suggest 12 special features that have shaped the field's history.

1. A Pressure Cooker. The field has always been a pressure cooker of corporate power and big money. It brims with immense, megadollar cases of law and policy. The pressure rises or recedes from time to time, as big waves of government action often driven by vast waves of corporate mergers have risen and faded during the field's history. Research, debate and megacases were particularly intense during 1900-1915, the 1930s and 1940s, and in the 1960s.

   After the 1960s the pressures against antitrust and regulation intensified even more. An array of major cases arose in the U.S. and Europe, with serious effects on the field. Examples include the big U.S. v. IBM case (I formed its economic core, but then despaired as it was mishandled); the FTC In Re Xerox case of 1974-76; AT&T's astonishing break-up in 1984; two huge and increasing waves of mergers, peaking in 1986 and 2000; the British privatisation crusade after 1980, which spread to other countries; and the rapid deregulation of banking, utilities and other large industries in the U.S., Britain and Europe.

   These vast corporate pressures have made this a 'hot' field, always being pushed and often distorted by outside forces.
2. The Main Ideas Have Long Been Known. Almost all of the important ideas in this field were known and discussed as long ago as 1920. Such longstanding familiarity is true of many long-developing fields in all of the sciences, where the reality is familiar and the ideas have long been well known. Many supposedly 'new' ideas in this field haven't been new at all. Instead, ambitious authors often merely shift attention to some other well-known idea, giving it a new label or technical claims.
3. Familiar, Famous Problems. Related to this, Industrial Organization's main real subject competition, monopoly power, and various possible abuses has been widely familiar to people everywhere for many centuries. All people have had to compete and have benefited from competition to serve them. The have seen and coped with

real monopolies and market dominators since human economic life began, back beyond the mists of antiquity. We're all experts, to some degree. We know that more monopoly power comes from controlling more of the market, and that it raises prices to enrich its owners.

4. No Big Discoveries. Partly because its subject is so familiar, this field has had no seismic 'Eureka!' events or Big Discoveries during its history since the 1880s. The gains have mostly been marginal, not fundamental. In fact, many of the 'innovations' (including some of the most highly-publicised ones) have been dubious and of questionable value. Some have probably been harmful to knowledge, by displacing solid concepts and measures.
5. Innovations Have Finite Often Brief Lives. Even the innovations that are valuable have a finite period of influence. They add some value for awhile, are debated and whittled down, and are absorbed as modest additions. Soon enough (a few years, a decade or two?) they are often displaced entirely by new innovations. Damage to knowledge can occur when a modest innovation comes from ambitious authors who claim that instead it is really supreme, with huge permanent importance. Such distortions push aside other valuable ideas and methods.
6. Each Young Generation Must Come Up With 'New' Ideas Even If There Aren't Any. Yet there is a relentless pressure that generates and inflates the supposedly 'new' ideas. Here, as in every field of knowledge, the rise of young scholars requires them to replace the old, by force if necessary. The rising generation casts about for ideas and techniques to use as weapons in order to displace their seniors. The young researchers have to publish something in order to gain professional stature. The literature is often just the record of push by the young to displace the old.

   The 'new' weapons in this field's ongoing debates and strife have included the following:

1. the use of mathematics,
2. the pure theory of games and other deductive relationships in place of induction,
3. the great attention to entry barriers,
4. 'contestable markets' and 'sustainable markets' theory,
5. the 'efficient structure hypothesis', and
6. such specific items as the Hirschman-Herfindahl Index in place of concentration ratios, 'rent' instead of excess profits, Tobin's q in place of profitability, the 'SSNIP' 5 percent basis for defining markets, 'Ramsey pricing' (long known as price discrimination), 'uncommitted entrants', and other new terms.

   Each of these has some value, but each can be overblown while being employed as weapons in the battles. I'll comment on some of them below.

   The 'powerful new techniques' can be claimed to be superior to the field's established ideas and to the wisdom and judgment of the older scholars. The senior scholars have indeed learned wisdom and sophistication, after doing their own youthful exaggerations. But the young scholars commonly deride their elders' supposedly soft-minded 'judgment', belittling it as inferior to their tight (but often too simple) 'rigor'.

7. The Systematic Bias toward Theory and Against Applied Research. The process has a systematic bias toward using pure theory to displace complex real-world research. The young (and all theory using scholars, for that matter) are drawn to pure theory because it can be done so quickly and with none of that tedious effort to learn about real conditions. It takes just a few days to write up a 'theoretical insight' in 10 pages, instead of slogging for 18 months to master real markets, prepare evidence, process data, and interpret the results for an 80 page research study. Also, if the theory can be portrayed as 'new' and technically difficult and there are no reliable data at hand to test it, then the theory has a certain glamour and is immune to being tested or even disproved.

   When seriously challenged, theorists often brush off the criticism of their claims for 'powerful' and 'authoritative' theories. Oh, those are just meant as 'insights', useful for scholarly discussions, they say. Yet, weeks later the same theorists can often be observed loudly declaring that the theories sweep away all evidence and objections to the contrary.
8. High Financial Rewards for Consulting. The urge to replace established knowledge has been especially strongly intensified in this field by massive flows of money. New young experts since the 1960s could look forward to large rewards for private consulting and testimony, using their self-described 'better' ideas for clients in private consulting and at public hearings and trials. The corporate profits at stake in a single large antitrust or deregulation case often run well over $5 billion every year.

   That is enough for just one or two companies to flood the entire research field with money, buying the support or neutrality of every working expert who might otherwise oppose them.

   Thus AT&T in the 1970s retained some 30 of the field's leading scholars, some 4 to 7 of them at the highest ranked departments, just to serve as 'advisers' or actual expert witnesses. Drug firms, IBM, virtually all large merging firms, and other large corporations have also acted in this way to attract much of the field's best talent to their side. The massive payments to the scholars have been large compared to their salaries, at hundreds of dollars per hour for extended service often over many years. But to the firms the funds are mere pennies, which are extremely well spent. The process has continued as a large flow of money, going to scores of the best known scholars.

   Some colleagues have grown rich, and some list well over a hundred cases in their vitas, at the rate of 5 or 10 per year. I often marvel that the serious research in the field has been as good as it has, despite the sheer volume of these distracting temptations.
9. The Market For Ideas Sometimes Fails. The 'market for ideas' has long promoted healthy competition among concepts and beliefs in all fields, including this one. But this market is often fragile and vulnerable to distortion; its outcomes can often be seriously damaged. The market process can be biased and distorted, with a tendency toward extremism as people exaggerate or deceive in order to make a big impact. Careful, balanced thinkers can be outfoxed by aggressive claims and technical

pretences. The biases can yield ideas which actually blank out superior ideas and valid evidence. That can reduce knowledge and understanding, not enhance them.

10. Evidence in This Field Is Usually Poor and Sparse. Regrettably, the field suffers from poor information, especially about such crucial things as firms' market shares, profitability, rates of innovation, and degrees of efficiency. Firms ruthlessly hide or misrepresent this sensitive information about themselves. Moreover, any actual data that do emerge about market shares and profits are often distorted, as the accounting scandals during 2000-2003 have starkly shown. Huge dollar interests are dependent on the data, and that creates especially high pressures for secrecy and distortion.

11. A Babble of Bizarre 'Ideas' Can Flourish, With No Way to Screen Out the Genuinely Grotesque Ones. In such a vacuum of reliable data, anybody: economists, lawyers, company officials, think-tank writers or politicians can get away with propagating almost any 'new' idea, because testing those ideas is extremely difficult or impossible.

    Even more than most fields, the Industrial Organization field requires special care and great sophistication in combining pure logic with real-world amounts. Logic is important: we always need good new ideas, and *gedanken-experimenten* can often clarify the alternatives.

    Because the testing of ideas is so hard to do reliably, wild exaggerations can thrive. A tiny possibility (say, that all markets are 'perfect', or that potential entry is more important than actual competition) is first said to be 'conceivable' or 'interesting', perhaps just a 'useful insight'. Then it is restated to be 'quite possible', after all. Soon it even becomes 'often true' and also 'important'. Before long, a theorist offers the assumption that it is 'usually true'. Then we hear, 'Let's assume it is always true, but just for the sake of insight'. And then Lo! Why not say it? It's actually true! All the time. The magic of creative theory, by those with little or no practical experience or evidence!

    Such creeping exaggerations, leading to grotesque errors, have become only too frequent in the field. Their very brazenness has often misled the field into accepting pure theories that are beyond any plausibility.

12. A 'Stone Age' Before 1970? Or Even Before 1980? Meanwhile, the influx of pure theory since 1970 has reduced scholars' awareness of the field's long, rich history. 'Modern' research has often been dated back to the 1930s, when the theory of oligopoly began being analysed in detail though the important concepts were discussed long before that. Many current theorists are literally ignorant of this, and hae a tinier perspective. They say that little was done before 1970 except loose talk and fluff. Before game theory's rise in the 1970s, they think, there was a Stone Age of ignorance and incompetence. There was no theory, no rigor, no 'serious' work. Everything was defective.

    This ignorance is profound and destructive, because it wipes out many layers and eras of important understanding. Instead, significant research began in the 1880s, most of the important ideas were discussed by 1920, and a wide array of concepts and methods had advanced far by 1970.

III. THE FIELD'S HISTORY

The field's development in the U.S. is sketched in Table 3. The post-Civil War boom of 1865-1890 was followed by waves of mergers, causing rising concentration in many heavy industries. The 1880s brought the emergence of neoclassical microeconomic theory and of economics as a professional discipline. There were already hot debates about the dangers of monopoly despite the happy lessons of competition within neoclassical analysis.

Table 3. Emergence of the Field's Ideas Since the 1880s (leading issues for ongoing debate are in boldface type)

Conceptual	Devices and Lesser Concepts
1880-1910:	
Monopoly and its effects reduce efficiency and innovation	
Impediments to new entry	
Economies of scale	
Natural monopoly as a basis for regulation	
1920s:	
Multiproduct costs and price discrimination; J.M. Clark	
Regulations may harm efficiency, innovation and investment	
1930s-1940s:	
Large corporations; Berle and Means	Lerner Index of monopoly
Oligopoly theory	Concentration data
The Schumpeterian analysis, defending dominant firms; 'creative destruction'	
Pure Game Theory; von Neumann and Morgenstern	
Vertical: economies, integration and restraints that reduce competition	
Structure-Conduct-Performance causation	

Conceptual	**Devices and Lesser Concepts**
1950s:	
Monopoly causes only tiny inefficiency; Harberger, 1954	Cross-elasticity used in defining markets
Big emphasis on entry barriers; Joe S. Bain, 1956	
1960s-1970s:	
Extensive regression analysis of concentration, its causes and its monopoly effects	The Averch-Johnson effect toward excess investment
Economic analysis of regulation; the case for deregulation; A.E. Kahn's major study, 1971	X-inefficiency; Harvey Leibenstein, 1966
Market shares relate to profitability in large firms; Shepherd, 2004	Dominant-firm analysis; Darius Gaskins, 1971
Chicago 2: Perfect markets eliminate the dangers of monopoly; the 'efficient structure hypothesis'	A cost rule for judging 'predatory pricing'; Areeda and Turner, 1975
Advertising and concentration	Profits data are useless; Franklin Fisher
Game Theory revival in the 1970s; pure theory as 'New IO theory'	
1980s:	
Theory of 'contestability'; the Baumol group, 1982' sustainability and price discrimination ('Ramsey pricing')	New Merger Guidelines: Herfindahl indexes
Dominant firms; Hay and Vickers, 1987; Dennis Mueller, 1986	Tobin's q; better than profit rates?
Pure theory of IO; Jean Tirole, 1988	Market definition method; 5% rule ('SSNIP')
1990s:	
'New empirical Industrial Organization'	Scanner date; analyse to define markets and assess market power

The Great Merger Wave of 1897-1901 created near-monopolies in scores of the largest U.S. industries, ranging from twine, leather and cigarettes to metals and shipping. See John Moody (1904). Nearly all the recent justifications for rampant mergers scale economies, consolidation, market stability, international competition, etc. were claimed then, and many of them were properly deflated. See Charles J. Bullock (February 1901), among an array of articles and books.

As the fledgling U.S. Antitrust Division attacked six of the ten largest U.S. corporations during 1904-1915, there was extensive factual research into industrial monopoly power by the Bureau of Corporations. See Hans B. Thorelli (1954), and William Letwin (1965), for detailed discussion of the wide array of economic concepts that were extensively discussed. The dimensions of financial power were also studied intensively.

The field's achievements were impressive, both in ideas and policies. Early ideas and research focussed tightly on the core problems, such as dominant market shares and their solidity, monopoly profits, the damage to efficiency and innovation, the resistance to new competition, and the need for strict action. Major cases were brought and won, and the U.S. showed that firm antitrust policies could cure the worst problems. Meanwhile, progress began toward fairly effective public regulation of privately-owned utility monopolies (especially in electricity, telephones and western railroads).

Even at the field's beginnings in the 1880s, the ideas, research and policies were surprisingly extensive, focused and relevant including market definition, economies of scale, competitive processes, collusive behaviour and much else. Since then, there has been progress in some areas, especially in getting more data. However, true intellectual progress has been surprisingly fitful, and odd claims have been frequent. For reasons I noted above, some newer ideas have tended to replace or to confuse valid basic ideas and methods.

An example is oligopoly theory, starting with Chamberlin's and Robinson's contributions in the 1930s.; also William J. Fellner (1949).

Though it was interesting and significant, the excited focus on oligopoly eliminated almost all attention from the more acute problems of market dominance by single firms, such as AT&T, IBM and Xerox in the 1960s. The new vogue after 1956 for potential competition and entry barriers simply accentuated this fixation on oligopoly. It directed attention away from real competition and monopoly at the centre of the market. Instead, the market's edges became the obsession, along with supposed potential entrants who might come in from entirely outside the market.

Oligopoly theory in the 1930s and game theory after 1944 did stimulate a lot of technical activity; the sense of excitement and discovery was much like the advent of supposedly magical nuclear power at the same time. The theorizing also moved attention away from single-firm dominance and toward the secondary issue of multiple-firm co-operation. That co-operation would always be weaker than single-firm dominance. Concentration data were developed and then mined extensively on into the 1960s and 1970s. Again, the focus was away from single-firm dominance and instead toward the lesser problem of oligopoly.

Since the 1970s, some additional theories about entry conditions have diverted the field from the core issues. The clearest example is Baumol's 'contestable markets' theory of 1982 (see below). In some cases, the focus and clarity of established research have been replaced by a proliferation of vague 'new' but confusing ideas. For parallels, think of academic 'music', which exists in its own isolated world. Commonly such arcane, cerebral 'music' has no harmony, rhythm or melody. It is written only for other abstract academic specialists, in a kind of ingrown group-think. Similarly, abstract paintings with monotone canvases have been like over-abstract economic theory. Exotic economic theory can be equally extreme and empty.

As for the rise of free-market Chicago School 2 ideas in the 1960s-1970s, their proponents actually did little practical research on the basic conditions. They simply assumed that markets were perfect. Then the patterns which strongly linked market shares with profit rates were said to 'prove' their 'efficient structure hypothesis', and to disprove the presence of market power. To Chicago 2 writers, firms gained and held high market shares only because they were superior: more efficient and innovative. That claim might be logically valid, but only if the markets were quite perfect. Imperfections could instead easily let firms 'win' by using anticompetitive tactics that were deceptive or unfair. Indeed, a high market share inevitably creates or increases imperfections in the market, by tilting the competitive field against smaller firms.

Before the Chicago 2 free-market claims gained currency in the 1980s, the research field had properly given extensive study to the possibilities of market imperfections. Table 4 summarises 19 categories of market imperfections that have been covered in the literature. They are many, familiar, and important. The literature has suggested that numbers 4, 6, 8, 9, 11, 13 and 16 are particularly important. But the free-market advocates simply declared perfection, without providing reliable evidence to prove it. In the conservative Reaganesque glow of the 1980s, this optimism fitted the political trends well.

Table 4. Nineteen Categories of Market Imperfections[5]

1. ***Pecuniary Gains May Be Obtained By Some Firms.*** They occur when a firm is able to buy its inputs at cheaper prices than its competitors can. The firm can then obtain high profits based on something other than superior performance.
2. ***Consumers May Exhibit Irrational Behaviour.*** Some or many consumer preferences may be carelessly formed, unstable, or inconsistent. They may pursue goals other than maximising utility in the neoclassical manner. They may let elements other than self-interest (e.g. copying other people or complying with advertising) interfere with their decisions.
3. ***Producers May Exhibit Irrational Behaviour.*** Some or many of them may have limited or inconsistent decision making abilities. They may distort their accounts or pursue goals other than pure profit-maximising.
4. ***There May Be Large Uncertainties Which Interfere with Decisions Made By Consumers and/or Producers.*** The main criteria for decision making may be unknown, or may change unpredictably, so that consumers or producers cannot make properly informed or consistent decisions.

5 Reprinted by permission of Waveland Press, Inc. from Shepherd-Shepherd, The Economics of Industrial Organization, 5/E. (Long Grove, IL: Waveland Press, Inc., 2004). All rights reserved.

5. ***Lags May Occur In The Decisions and/or Actions of Consumers or Producers***. Actions may not be timely, permitting firms to take strategic actions that prevent competition and/or beneficial outcomes. The firms may gain advantages that don't reflect economic efficiency.
6. ***Consumer Loyalties May Be Strong***. They may be instilled or intensified by advertising and other marketing activities. The loyalties make them willing to pay higher prices, like captive customers.
7. ***Some Firm Managers Also May Hold Irrational Loyalties***. They will remain with the firm throughout their careers rather than moving freely to other employers for better pay. The loyalties may permit the firms to pay abnormally low salaries and rewards.
8. ***The Segmenting of Markets May Be Accentuated and Exploited***. If producers can segregate customers on the basis of their demand attributes, then the producers may be able to use price discrimination strategically so as to raise their monopoly power.
9. ***Differences In Access To Information, Including Secrecy***. If some firms have more information than their rivals and/or consumers, then these firms may gain excess profits without having superior efficiency. The patterns of innovation may also be distorted.
10. ***Controls Over Key Inputs and Technology***. Firms may obtain specific controls over crucial inputs, such as superior ores, specific talents of expert personnel, favourable geographic or urban locations, and patents or other access to critical technology. These controls may permit the direct exclusion of competitors and exploitation of consumers.
11. ***Barriers Against New Competition*** (see chapter 9). New entry may be blocked or hampered by a variety of conditions that raise entry barriers, Some twenty sources of barriers are known to be significant in real markets.
12. ***Risk Aversion***. Some consumers and/or producers may be strongly risk averse, which may make them unwilling to take the normal range of competitive actions.
13. ***Transaction Costs and Excess Capacity May Be Significant***. They may occur naturally or be increased by firms' deliberate actions. These costs and rigidities may cause the market to deviate from instant and complete adjustments in line with true costs.
14. ***Firms May Have Sunk Costs, Including Excess Capacity and Switching Costs That Arise From Past Commitments***. These sunk costs may prevent the firms from making free and rapid adjustments. They may also curtail or prevent new entry.
15. ***Because of 'Principal-Agent' Problems, Firms May Deviate From Profit Maximising***. Managers may seek their own personal gains, which may conflict with stakeholders' interests. The business-fraud scandals of 2000-2002 illustrate these.
16. ***Internal Distortions in Information, Decision Making, and Incentives May Cause High Costs and Distorted Decisions***. There may be misperceptions and conflicts of interest between shareowners and managers, and between upper and lower management groups. Especially in large, complex companies, there may be bureaucracy, excess layers of management, and distorted information and incentives.
17. ***Owners of a Firm's Securities May be Unable To Co-ordinate Their Interests and Actions Perfectly***. The owners may be unable to organise among themselves with perfect information and efficiency. That reduces their ability to enforce efficient behaviour by managers.
18. ***In International Markets, There May Be Artificial Exclusionary Conditions, Including Barriers at Borders***. Attempts by firms to operate freely across borders may be impeded by customs, levies, taxes, required permissions, formalities, and other artificial burdens. Also, cultural and social differences may prevent the free exchange of standardised goods among global markets.
19. ***In International Markets, Firms May Often Have Differences In Information Due To Languages and Cross-Cultural Differences***. That may give advantages to some firms and prevent the perfect-market outcomes that could occur in cross-national firms and markets. Some firms may ignore real opportunities or problems, make inefficient mergers, or incur added costs and inefficiencies.

As a result, antitrust policies and staffing in both agencies (the Antitrust Division of the Department of Justice, and the Federal Trade Commission) were cut back deeply after 1980, and some policy areas were eliminated entirely. Though theorists and free-market advocates praised this for reflecting 'superior' economics, antitrust was severely weakened. It is still fragile and passive to most developments in 2004.

Europeans have been more sceptical of the 'new IO theory' ideas, and antitrust in Europe and the United Kingdom has remained more based in reality. So Europe and the U.K. now have, on the whole, the most thorough and effective policies treating market power (see section V below). Some U.S. 'new IO' scholars claim that Europe and the U.K. are merely 'obsolete', but Europeans in particular are largely correct in keeping the focus on real markets, market shares, and the many real costs of monopoly.

IV. LEADING EXAMPLES OF ONGOING DEBATES

Among the points and debates in Table 3, several are of large long-run importance and continue to be unresolved. They define much of the current content and state of the field. I will discuss three of them, plus the current U.S. 'Merger Guidelines'.

Issue #1: Perfect Markets and 'Efficient Structure'. (This is a leading issue since the 1970s.)

The idea that most markets are essentially perfect began in the 1950s with Aaron Director, a law professor (with no economic training or research experience) at the University of Chicago. With ideological zeal, he converted his colleagues and then transformed George Stigler from scepticism to this rosy optimism, after Stigler arrived at Chicago in 1957. See also George J. Stigler (Journal of Political Economy, February 1957). Stigler created a big business funded atelier at Chicago where new young economic or legal scholars made their mark by attacking all kinds of public policies for 'distorting' markets rather than improving them. The original sceptical Chicago School became the uncritical Pangloss Chicago 2. Their claim: all high market shares are good, because they are always won in perfect markets.

'Perfect' markets actually must meet extreme requirements of perfection:

1. total information about current and future conditions, known completely by all participants, including all producers, all consumers, and all potential entrants,
2. no lags or frictions,
3. all participants are always rational, including consumers,
4. a high number of relatively equal competitors,
5. stable technology, so equilibrium can be reached.

The perfection must also hold for all capital markets, which are crucial; all firms must have equal access to ample investment funds. That requirement for perfection is particularly stringent. If capital markets have imperfections, that infects all other markets with imperfections.

Chicago 2 writers thus sought to eliminate the long, deep debates about imperfections in real markets, by simply declaring them obsolete. The writers have done very little real-world research to validate their perfect-market assumptions. It is true that some trends since the 1950s have tended to make many markets less imperfect. Better telecommunications and the rise of the Internet have recently spread information more widely. Many markets have grown more transparent and open to quick action.

There are some close limits on this. For example, the 1990s brought claims that the Internet would replace most purchasing of inputs by major industries, such as automobiles, metals and machinery. Those hopes turned out to be mostly empty, and the Internet units either folded quickly or are struggling. Markets were not drastically changed. As always, a 'radical' new idea and method turned out to have an impact ranging from zero to moderate, at best.

Chicago 2 (especially law professors like Robert Bork and Richard Posner, who are not trained in economic analysis or research) also tried to impose the restrictive claim that the only relevant goal for competitive processes is efficient static allocation. Legal analysts like Bork and Posner have commonly relied on rudimentary microeconomic theory (with its focus on allocative efficiency), wrongly thinking that it is enough. Instead, it merely encourages narrow modes of thought and argument. But static allocation is only one among many goals, and innovation is widely recognised to be more important.

Chicago 2 writers freely accepted the strong correlation of market shares with profit rates, as illustrated in Figure 3. They then flatly denied the most obvious lesson, that the correlation shows some role for monopoly power, perhaps a large role. Chicagoans asserted instead that because to them all markets seem perfect the regression line merely proves that dominant firms are more efficient. They simply deny that monopoly power exists, a rosy view that the Reagan and Bush administrations embraced during 1980-1992.

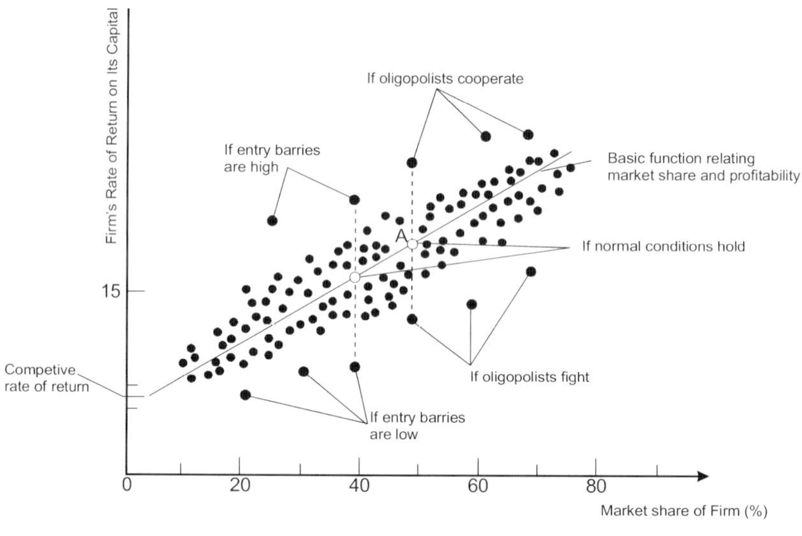

Figure 3. Illustration of the Partial Regression Relationship Between Market Shares and Profit Rates of Large Manufacturing Firms.[6]

6 Reprinted by permission of Waveland Press, Inc. from Shepherd-Shepherd, The Economics of Industrial Organization, 5/E. (Long Grove, IL: Waveland Press, Inc., 2004). All rights reserved.

This issue persists as sharp and divisive. Think for yourself how common 'perfect' markets are and whether static allocation is the only economic goal.

Issue #2: Should Research and Policy Focus On the Market's Centre (the leading firms' market shares?) or On Its Edges (its potential entry conditions)?
This has been a leading issue for half a century, and it still is. John Bates Clark had discussed new entry as long ago as 1887, and the idea has some intuitive interest, especially when there is a major specific legal barrier (a patent, ownership of key ores, the best location, etc.).

In 1956 Joe S. Bain set out to broaden the topic to several general economic sources of barriers, including large size, cost advantages, advertising intensity, and other 'capital barriers'. Bain was keen to show that barriers could increase the strength of oligopoly collusion.

Barriers are peripheral to a market, as Figure 2 illustrated, while the market shares of the leading firm or firms are central to the real competition or monopoly in the market. Smart businesspeople think that, invariably. Success means getting more of the market, and failure means losing market share.

Moreover, it quickly became clear that any efforts to define and measure entry barriers could reach only the vaguest sort of rough estimates (such as Bain's guesses of absolute, high, moderate and low). Also, the literature soon developed at least 20 significant sources of possible barriers, and virtually all of them are impossible to measure reliably; see Table 5. 'Potential competition' is even harder than that to measure. Which potential entrants might come in? How rapidly and with what new market shares? The whole exercise is sheer guesswork.

Table 5. Common Causes of Barriers Against New Entry[7]

I. **Exogenous Causes:** ***External Sources of Barriers***
   1. **Capital Requirements:** related to the MES of plants and firms, capital intensity, and capital market imperfections.
   2. **Economies of Scale:** both technical and pecuniary; require large-scale entry, with greater costs, risks and intensity of retaliation.
   3. **Absolute Cost Advantages:** many possible causes, including lower wage rates and lower-cost technology.
   4. **Product Differentiation:** may be extensive.
   5. **Sunk Costs:** any cost incurred by an entrant that cannot be recovered upon exit.
   6. **Research and Development Intensity:** requires entrants to spend heavily on new technology and products.
   7. **Equipment is Highly Durable and Highly Specialised ('Asset Specificity'):** makes entrants install costly, highly specialised equipment; entrants suffer large losses if the entry fails.
   8. **Vertical Integration:** may require an entrant to enter at two or more stages of production; raises costs and risks.
   9. **Diversification by Incumbents:** may make it possible to move resources around to defeat entrants.

7 Reprinted by permission of Waveland Press, Inc. from Shepherd-Shepherd, The Economics of Industrial Organization, 5/E. (Long Grove, IL: Waveland Press, Inc., 2004).

10. **Switching Costs:** complex systems may entail costs of commitment and training, which impede customers from switching to other systems.
11. **Special Risks and Uncertainties of Entry:** entrants' higher risks may raise their costs of capital.
12. **Gaps and Asymmetries of Information:** incumbents' superior information helps them bar entrants and may raise entrants' cost of capital.
13. **Formal, Official Barriers Set by Government Agencies or Industry wide Groups:** examples are utility franchises and foreign-trade duties and barriers.

II. **Endogenous Causes:** ***Voluntary and Strategic Sources of Barriers***

1. **Pre-emptive and Retaliatory Actions by Incumbents:** include selective price discounts targeted to deter or punish entry.
2. **Excess Capacity:** lets incumbents retaliate sharply and threaten retaliation credibly.
3. **Selling Expenses, Including Advertising:** increase the degree of product differentiation and make entry harder.
4. **Segmenting of the Market:** segregates customer groups by their demand elasticities, and makes broad entry into the whole market more difficult.
5. **Patents:** may provide exclusive control over critical or lower-cost technology and products.
6. **Exclusive Controls over Other Strategic Resources:** examples include the best ores, the best locations, and various unique talents of people.
7. **Raising Rivals' Costs:** require new entrants to incur extra costs.
8. **Packing the Product Space:** may occur in industries with high product differentiation, like cereals.
9. **Secrecy about Crucial Competitive Conditions:** specific actions may create secrecy about key conditions.

Sources: These categories are extracted from the larger literature, as discussed in the text.

Nevertheless, the excitement of 'new' barriers ideas spread in the 1960s. By the 1970s, free-market writers had reversed Bain's viewpoint. They claimed that entry was virtually free and quick in most markets, and that this nullified any efforts of oligopolists to collude or even of dominant firms to affect the market at all. In this over-optimistic view, potential competition somehow mattered more than actual competition.

Notice that a focus on entry and barriers will suit the interests of dominant firms and tight oligopolists. It diverts attention from their own powerful positions, and it creates hope that 'potential competition' will somehow nullify any market power if not immediately, then sometime in the future.

In contrast, real businesses are tightly centred on the endless struggle for market share. Almost always, high profit yields come from controlling high shares of the market. Entry barriers are an esoteric for scholarly specialists. They are rarely considered in business activity, reporting and discourse.

'Contestability'

In 1982 the fetish for entry and barriers went to the extreme. William Baumol and several colleagues (1982) announced what they said was a radically superior pure theory of entry and exit. 'Contestability' (their odd label for it) was a theoretical extreme, in which a new firm could enter instantly, and then leave instantly. That action could have a huge impact on the existing monopolist taking away all of its sales!

This carried the potential-entry focus to a pure-theory extreme; to its authors, potential entry now replaced real competition entirely! The claimed ouster was also intellectually complete: the theory of contestability even displaced the entire theory of competition itself. Because entry could take away every scrap of the monopoly firm's demand, contestability theory makes a limitless claim; it draws the demand curve to be perfectly truncated. If the monopolist raises its price even by just a penny, it will instantly lose every bit of its sales.

The Baumol group have admitted that they have no real-market examples of the theory. It's just an interesting idea, they say, that gives 'insight'. Yet they have used it frequently and emphatically in policy discussions and in sworn testimony about large corporate mergers and dominant-firm positions. The theory is powerful, they say in those settings, and it proves that there can be no monopoly effects whatever. My own main critique of the theory is in William G. Shepherd, 'Contestability versus Competition', American Economic Review, September 1984; see also my 'Contestability vs. Competition Once More', Land Economics, August 1995.

In addition, Baumol, Willig, Ordover and other colleagues have offered the idea of 'uncommitted entrants'. These are hypothetical firms in adjacent markets, whose products and costs are similar to those already in the market. These firms might shift 'easily' into the market. So the theorists treat these outside firms as so-called 'uncommitted entrants', as if they are already in the market!

Yet, despite the theoretical notion, these firms are certainly not yet in the market. The theory seeks to convert a mere possibility of entry into a definite fact that large, successful entry has already occurred.

The wider research debate continues, and you can consult your own viewpoint to see how you might decide important real cases. Has Microsoft held a virtual monopoly, extending it into other markets? Or is Microsoft a paper tiger, beset by powerful potential entry and likely to be eliminated quickly if it tries even a small exploitation of the market? The same question applies to electricity suppliers in newly deregulated power markets, to telecommunications firms that are merging to get high market shares, to Intel the dominant chip maker, to pharmaceuticals makers, and to many others.

Issue #3: Pure Theory and Game Theory versus Applied Research.

From 1932 on, Chamberlin, Fellner and Bain made oligopoly a complex topic, and they stressed that oligopoly would tend toward collusion. By 1954, Bain developed empirical tests that concentration yielded higher profits, and Weiss's major collaborative study of 1989 later affirmed it.

Neumann and Morgenstern's landmark book of 1944 immediately diverted the complex discussion into the abstract realm of game theory. Here, there are just two players: they are assumed not to collude at all, and they play only a brief two-stage game, with no thought for later stages. It's charming, and it has nothing to do with real ongoing games. During the 1950s, Shubik made extensive efforts to apply this sort of arcane, simplified and myopic theory to real markets, but he concluded in 1961 that the theory did not have practical research possibilities.

Yet surprisingly, in the 1970s, like the mythical Phoenix, game theory came back to life, especially among young pure theorists who used it as a major device to gain professional success. It also provided many with apparent credentials to qualify as expert witnesses in lucrative antitrust cases.

The new boom in game theory related also to the markets-are-perfect viewpoint; without perfection, game analyses often grow too complicated to resolve. The theorists said, as of course they still do, that game theory provided great rigor and power; it was, they said, the only logically correct basis for thinking about market power. This viewpoint became prevalent in teaching Industrial Organization on many U.S. campuses during the 1980s.

Though game theory has now passed its crest of influence, it is firmly installed in the field and in the personnel rosters of departments all over the country. How much research value it may have is a major ongoing debate. Though the theory has certain strengths and values, they are finite and limited. The field is still searching for the proper balance and focus in using game theory.

A Major Example: The U.S. Merger Guidelines

The U.S. Merger Guidelines are a special example, which links all three of these issues. The current Guidelines beautifully illustrate many of the current problems in research and policies.

I helped to write the first such Merger Guidelines while I was near the top of the Antitrust Division during 1967-1968; Donald Turner originated the idea, and he finally finished and issued them in June 1968. They focussed on the merging firms' market shares and any underlying trends toward concentration. They were compact, clear and effective. They reported policies, rather than making policies; they merely summarised what the latest Supreme Court precedents were, in economic terms.

But they were displaced in 1982, by Reagan-era antitrust officials who held strict Chicago 2 views. The new Guidelines set out to make new policy; they indicated where the merger limits should be, telling the Supreme Court about the economic 'factors' and levels to which its merger decisions should conform. Many 'factors' were stated as the bases for the criteria, making these Guidelines scarcely practical.

Moreover, the new Guidelines discussed only oligopoly price collusion as a danger from mergers. With that fixation, the Guidelines bizarrely omitted any mention of single-firm dominance entirely. Also, the long-familiar, clear concentration ratios were replaced by 'Herfindahl Indexes'. Such H indexes are entirely abstract, a pure ratio of ratios (the sum of the squares of all market shares in the market). The H index's theoretical rationale is supposedly derived 'rigorously' from game theory, as a technical matter. But H indexes have no real-world meaning or familiarity, nor any clear normative standards based on facts. Concrete information about market shares is replaced by abstractions.

Oddly, H index advocates offered an implausible refusal when other scholars applied the H index to dominant firms. For example, a market share of 60 percent gives an index value of at least 3,600. That is far above the market-power benchmark of about 2,000. It makes a strong case that dominance imposes intense monopoly power, with its well-known harms for innovation, low prices, efficiency and fairness. Yet the H index's advocates and officials brushed this off by merely declaring with no economic basis that H Indexes apply only to mergers, not to dominant firms. That was simply wrong.

The Guidelines' problems worsened in 1992, as I and others have noted; see the Special Issue on Mergers of the Review of Industrial Organization, March 1993. See also the detailed discussion in George B. Shepherd, Helen S. Shepherd, and William G. Shepherd, 'Sharper Focus: Market Shares in the Merger Guidelines', Antitrust Bulletin, Winter 2000. The Baumol Group's 'contestability' ideas were inserted into the Guidelines by Robert D. Willig, who then held the position of chief Antitrust Division economist. Even more vague 'factors' were now listed as the supposed basis for judging mergers, even though scarcely any of the factors could be defined or measured in any practical way.

Two examples are:

1. There were four listed categories of evidence for defining markets. The second category was:

> 'Evidence that sellers base business decisions on the prospect of buyer substitution between products in response to relative changes in price or other competitive variables.'

This seems to be merely a notion about the cross-elasticity of demand. It requires impossibly obscure knowledge of the inner psychology of business thinking. Such an actual measurement of the 'evidence' would scarcely be possible.

2. A discussion of 'the means of entry' was aimed to clarify if potential entry might reduce the existing firms' market power. But the Guidelines' 'evidence' would be:

> 'All phases of the entry effort will be considered, including, where relevant, planning, design, and management; permitting, licensing, and other approvals; construction, debugging, and operation of production facilities; and promotion (including necessary introductory discounts), marketing, distribution, and satisfaction of customer testing and qualification requirements. Recent examples of entry, whether successful or unsuccessful, may provide a useful starting point for identifying the necessary actions, time requirements, and characteristics of possible entry alternatives.'

This is a startling stew of vague notions, with no apparent relation to things that can be defined and measured. The rigor of theory was replaced by various immeasurable and barely intelligible 'factors'.

Here is one more example, in the discussion of the 'Likelihood of Entry'. The Guidelines say that this 'evidence' will guide its decision:

> 'Sources of sale opportunities available to entrants include: (a) the output reduction associated with the competitive effect of concern, (b) entrants' ability to capture a share of reasonably expected growth in market demand, (c) entrants' ability securely to divert sales from incumbents, for example, through vertical integration or through forward contracting, and (d) any additional anticipated contraction in incumbents' output in response to entry'. (Items a, b and d also have footnotes with fairly lengthy and complicated discussions of additional aspects).'

Faced with well over 50 such 'factors' and 'conditions' in the Guidelines that need to be defined and measured, any staff economist couldn't really do any practical research, nor reach coherent conclusions. Rather, there would be a void, to be filled only with impressions, guesses and hunches. The staff member could reach almost any judgment about a merger: for, against, ambivalent, etc. Then any official could agree or reverse the decision, and judges at an actual trial could decide just about anything they want. Therefore, merging companies actually have almost no guidance about what the agencies and the judges might do. These Guidelines don't guide, even though they claim to represent rigorous modern research.

V. COMPARING EUROPEAN AND U.S. ANTITRUST POLICIES

The U.S. has a much longer antitrust history than Europe. The U.S. began in 1890 with the Sherman Act, and the first wave of serious enforcement peaked in 1911-1913. That wave was followed by lesser waves during 1937-1952 and 1961-1968. But U.S. antitrust before the 1980s always had a minimum level of activity and degree of strictness.

Then the 1980s brought the Chicago 2 triumph of free-market doctrines in the Reagan administration. Antitrust restraints on dominance and mergers were sharply reduced, well below historical standards, and since 1992 they have recovered only mildly. In response to wide-open, indefinite merger policies, large merger waves occurred in the 1980s and 1990s. Microsoft's dominant position was scarcely touched by an antitrust settlement in 2002, in what is widely viewed as a sell-out by antitrust officials. No important new dominant-firm cases have been started.

Modern European policies began in the 1950s, with a focus against price-fixing. Since the 1970s, the policies have grown stricter against horizontal mergers and abusive actions by dominant firms. Since 1990 the European Union competition policies have ventured strict actions against a variety of dominant positions, price fixing, and mergers. They reflect a firm grasp of the mainstream applied research about monopoly power and its impacts.

There have been a number of recent judicial setbacks in Europe. Some say that this shows that European antitrust has reached too far and incorrectly, deviating from American standards of rigor. Instead, I think that the European court not the competition authority needs to improve its grasp of economic standards and research. In April 2004, the competition authority announced new economic standards, which focussed on innovation and on conditions that could be reasonably estimated. European antitrust continues to set standards of strictness and consistency that make U.S. policies look weak, whatever their self-announced 'rigor' and modernity may be.

VI. TO SUM UP

Much of the research in recent decades has enhanced the understanding of market power, at least for awhile. The mainstream of applied research continues to progress on many topics, while pure theory may have passed its main period of contribution. I've noted here some of the more debatable points. These ongoing research debates are exciting, and they have important lessons for U.S. and European policies.

This field continues to require great care in using imperfect evidence to judge imperfect markets and to frame policies that also have to be less than perfect. Perhaps Utrecht's scholars can help to cure some of the imperfections in markets and policies and in research. They'll be busy!

REFERENCES

Areeda, P.E. & D.F. Turner (1975) Predatory Pricing and Related Practices Under Section 2 of the Sherman Act. *Harvard Law Review* 88, 697-733.

Averch, H. & Johnson, L. (1962). The Behaviour of the Firm under Regulatory Constraint, *American Economic Review, December*.

Bain, Joe S. (1956). *Barriers to New Competition*. Cambridge: Harvard University Press.

Baumol, William J., Panzar, John C. , & Willig, Robert D. (1982). *Contestable Markets and the Theory of Industry Structure*. Harcourt Brace Jovanovich.

Berle, A.A., and G.C. Means (1932), *The Modern Corporation and Private Property*, rev. ed. 1968, New York: Harcourt, Brace, Jovanovich.

Bork, Robert H. (1978). *The Antitrust Dilemma: a Policy at War with Itself.* New York: Basic Books.

Bullock, Charles J. (February 1901). Trust Literature: A Survey and Criticism. *Quarterly Journal of Economics*, pp. 167-217.

Chamberlin, Edward H. (1932). *The Theory of Monopolistic Competition*. Harvard University Press 1932,

Clark, John Bates (1887). The Limits of Competition. *Political Science Quarterly 2*, 45-61.

Clark, J. M. (1923). *Studies in the Economics of Overhead Costs*. Chicago, University of Chicago Press

Fellner, William J. (1949). *Competition Among the Few*. Knopf.

Fisher, Franklin M. & McGowan, John J. (1983) On the Misuse of Accounting Rates of Return to Infer Monopoly Profits. *The American Economic Review*, Vol. 73, No. 1. (Mar., 1983), pp. 82-97.

Gaskins, Darius W., Jr. (1971). Dynamic Limit Pricing: Optimal Pricing Under Threat of Entry. *Journal of Economic Theory* 3:306-322.

Harberger, A.C. (1954). Monopoly and Resource Allocation, *American Economics Review, May, 45, 2.*

Hay, D.A. & Vickers, J. (1987). *The Economics of Market Dominance*. New York: Blackwell.

Kahn, A.E. (1988). *The Economics of Regulation: Principles and Institutions*. Cambridge, MA: MIT Press (reprint of 1970 and 1971 volumes).

Leibenstein, Harvey (1966). Allocative efficiency vs. X-efficiency, *American Economics Review, 56*, 392-415.

Lerner, A.P. (1934). The Concept of Monopoly and the Measurement of Monopoly Power, *Review of Economic Studies, June*, 157-175.

Letwin, William (1965). *Law and Economic Policy in America*. Random House.

Moody, John (1904). *The Trust About the Trusts*. Moody Publishing.

Mueller, Dennis C. (1986), United States' Antitrust: At the Crossroads, in: De Jong and Shepherd, eds. (1986), 215-241.

Mueller, D. (1985). Mergers and Market Share, *Review of Economics & Statistics 57 (2)*, 259-67.

Neumann, John von & Morgenstern, Oskar, (1944). *Theory of Games and Economic Behavior*. Princeton NJ: Princeton University Press.

Ordover, Janusz A., & Willig, Robert D. (1993). Economics and the 1992 Merger Guidelines: A Brief Survey. *Review of Industrial Organization 8 (April 1993)*.

Phillips, Almarin, & Stevenson, Rodney E. (Fall 1974). The Historical Development of Industrial Organization. *History of Political Economy 6*, 324-342.

Posner, Richard A. (1976). *Antitrust Law*. Chicago: University of Chicago Press.

Robinson, Joan, (1933). *Economics of Imperfect Competition*. Macmillan.

Scherer, F.M., & Ross, David (1991). *Industrial Market Structure and Economic Performance,* 3d ed. Houghton Mifflin.
Shepherd, W.G. & Shepherd, J.M. (2004). *The Economics of Industrial Organization*, 5th ed. Long Grove: Waveland Press Inc.
Shepherd, William G. (1984). Contestability versus Competition. *American Economic Review,* pp. 572-87.
Shepherd, William G. (1995). Contestability vs. Competition Once More. *Land Economics*, pp. 299-309.
Shepherd, George B., Shepherd, Helen S., & Shepherd, William G. (2000). Sharper Focus: Market Shares in the Merger Guidelines. *Antitrust Bulletin,* Winter *2000.*
Shubik, Martin, (1959). *Strategy and Market Structure*. New York: Wiley.
Special Issue on Mergers, *Review of Industrial Organization*, March 1993.
Stigler, George J. (1957). Perfect Competition, Historically Contemplated. *Journal of Political Economy*, p. 117.
Thorelli, Hans B. (1954). *The Federal Antitrust Policy*. University of Chicago Press.
Tirole, J. (1988), *The Theory of Industrial Organization*, Cambridge, MA: MIT Press.
Weiss, Leonard W. (Ed.) (1989). *Concentration and Price*. Cambridge: MIT Press.

L. SOETE[1]

ON THE DYNAMICS OF INNOVATION POLICY: A DUTCH PERSPECTIVE

INTRODUCTION

There is by now a substantial literature on the *raison d'être* of science and technology policy, and in particular innovation policy.[2] In recent years this literature has been strongly influenced by the perception, particularly in Europe, of a growing knowledge gap emerging between Europe and the United States. Due to this rapidly growing knowledge gap, so it has been claimed, Europe's long-term competitiveness is increasingly being eroded, questioning the long-term sustainability of Europe's social welfare model. It was the awareness of Europe's falling behind in knowledge creation, in innovation and knowledge diffusion, which induced the European heads of state to set the bold objective at the Lisbon summit in March 2000 of becoming the world's most competitive and dynamic knowledge economy by 2010. This objective was reconfirmed once more in Barcelona in the spring of 2002. The European countries were to aim to spend approximately 3% of their Gross Domestic Product on investments in research, development and innovation by 2010, a figure roughly comparable to the investment percentages in the United States and Japan today. A new voluntary, modern version of Harold Wilson's celebrated 'White Heat' science and technology policy had emerged: innovation policy as the new medicine for Europe's poor economic growth performance.

The setting of a common target figure is like a 'focusing device', sharpening existing policy priorities. It should be noted, however, that in contrast with more common economic objectives, such as public deficit, inflation or other monetary targets, the setting of objectives in the science and technology or innovation policy area raises many questions.

First and foremost they raise factual questions. How real is the so-called knowledge gap? What are its underlying causes? And to what extent has the strategy of companies and national governments played a role in the emergence of this gap?

---

1 I'm grateful to Abraham Garcia for statistical support, to Wil Foppen, Paul de Graaf and Bart Verspagen for critical comments and participants at the USE colloquium in October 2003 for helpful suggestions.

2 See e.g. the relevant Chapters in our own textbook with Chris Freeman: Freeman, C. and L. Soete, (1997).

P. de Gijsel and H. Schenk (eds.), Multidisciplinary Economics, 127–149.

Second, there are of course the more fundamental policy questions. Does it really matter? And what can be done about it?

The Barcelona objective of 3% is, above all, an investment objective; equally important, if not more so, is the question what the results – in terms of efficiency and effectiveness – of these investments will be. Incidentally, in so far as it is business enterprise investment in research, development and innovation which is lagging behind in Europe relative to the US, the question can also be raised to what extent European governments can actually do something about it and change or influence such private investment trends.

Before addressing this issue in greater detail, we first provide in this chapter a short, analytical introduction to the modern, systemic version of science, technology and innovation policies. The notion of regional or national *systems* of innovation is central here. We provide some illustrations of the relative strengths and weaknesses of the national innovation systems of various European countries. In a second section we then turn to the broader challenges which the EU, and the Netherlands in particular, are facing in the area of innovation and more generally knowledge investments. The Netherlands appears to be, so to speak, a European 'model country' both with regard to possible explanatory factors in the emergence of a knowledge gap with the US, and with regard to the identification of the most important policy challenges presenting themselves. We describe this in terms of a new version of an old, well known phenomenon: the Dutch 'knowledge' disease.

1. SCIENCE, TECHNOLOGY AND INNOVATION POLICIES

1.1 On the shift towards more systemic policy views

Over the past ten to fifteen years, there has been a major shift in one's understanding of the relationships between research, innovation and socioeconomic development. Single-factor explanations either of the technology push or demand pull kind, have by and large disappeared. Instead, it is now widely recognised that economic growth and well-being is founded on a well-functioning 'knowledge and innovation system', in which all actors perform well. The concept of a national (or regional) innovation system emerged in the 80's. It incorporated all actors and activities in the economy involved in knowledge production. It put the emphasis, as illustrated in *Box 1*, on the national institutional framework within which firms and other organisations operated and which appeared of crucial importance to the speed, extent and success by which innovations got introduced and diffused in the economy.

Box 1. Alternative definitions of national systems of innovations.

'The network of institutions in the public and private sectors whose activities and interactions initiate, import, modify and diffuse new technologies' (Freeman, 1987; p. 1).

'The elements and relationships which interact in the production, diffusion and use of new, and economically useful, knowledge… and are either located within or rooted inside the borders of a nation state' (Lundvall, 1992; p. 12).

'A set of institutions whose interactions determine the innovative performance of national firms' (Nelson, 1993; p. 5).

'The national institutions, their incentive structures and their competencies, that determine the rate and direction of technological learning (or the volume and composition of change-generating activities) in a country' (Patel and Pavitt, 1994; p. 12).

'That set of distinct institutions which jointly and individually contribute to the development and diffusion of new technologies and which provides the framework within which governments form and implement policies to influence the innovation process. As such it is a system of interconnected institutions to create, store and transfer the knowledge, skills and artefacts which define new technologies' (Metcalfe, 1995; p. 462-463).

'…. the notion of national system of innovation may be viewed as a way of encompassing these numerous facets (of the relationship between technology, trade and growth) so as to suggest that the performance of national economies depend on the manner in which organizational and institutional arrangements and linkages conducive to innovation and growth have been permitted to thrive in different countries' (Chesnais, 1992; p. 23).

'A national system of innovation is the system of interacting private and public firms (either large or small), universities and government agencies, aiming at the production of science and technology within national borders. Interaction among those units may be technical, commercial, legal, social and financial, inasmuch as the goal of the interaction is the development, protection, financing or regulation of new science and technology.' (Niosi and Bellon, 1994; p. 139).

Source: Montobbio (1999)

A common feature of all such systems – regional, national and transnational – is of course the fact that firms rarely if ever innovate alone. There is a need for a constant interaction and co-operation between the innovating firm and its external environment, which in the optimal case leads to a virtuous learning circle of better exploitation of available knowledge. As Richard Nelson (1993) e.g. noted: 'to orient R&D fruitfully, one needs detailed knowledge of its strengths and weaknesses and areas where improvements would yield big payoffs and this type of knowledge tends to reside with those who use the technology, generally firms and their customers and suppliers. In addition, over time firms in an industry tend to develop capabilities . . . largely based on practice.'

The fact that the knowledge and innovation systems of countries show marked differences associated with their individual paths of specialisation in production, has obvious policy implications. External intervention may be desirable or even necessary but must be informed by local conditions and based on the study of innovation processes, organisations and institutions and their interactions over relatively extended periods. It is crucial to identify which elements of the system are subject to inertia so that particular deficiencies can be addressed. Hence, many authors on the national systems of innovations literature, such as Freeman, Lundvall, Nelson and Edquist speak of the 'dynamic coevolution of knowledge, innovations, organisations and institutions'. From a systemic perspective, it is often the weakest chain which is the most critical one for economic growth and development, and hence also for policy intervention.

The idea that there is something to learn from institutional arrangements and policies in other, more 'advanced' environments, as exemplified today in the European obsession with the knowledge gap with the US, and that systematic comparative studies are a useful tool in this respect, is of course not a new one. Alexander Gerschenkron (1962) pioneered this kind of comparative country study. As he pointed out, some countries are at the technological frontier, while others lag far behind. Although the technological gap between the frontier country and the laggard would represent 'a great promise' for the latter (a potential for higher growth through imitating frontier technologies), there were also various problems that would prevent backward countries from reaping the potential benefits to the full. Gerschenkron actually argued that if one country succeeded in embarking on an innovation-driven growth path, others might find it increasingly difficult to catch up. His favourite example was Germany's attempt to catch up with Britain a century ago. When Britain industrialised, technology was relatively labour intensive and small scale. But in the course of time technology became more capital and scale intensive, so when Germany entered the scene, the conditions for entry had changed considerably. Because of this, Gerschenkron argued, Germany had to develop new institutional instruments for overcoming these obstacles, above all in the financial sector, 'instruments for which there was little or no counterpart in an established industrial country'.[3] He held these experiences to be valid also for other technologically lagging countries.[4]

3 In doing so Gerschenkron put the emphasis on the importance of the creation of institutions in backward countries, see also Gerschenkron, A. (1968).

4 For a more in depth analysis on the contributions of these historical contributions to modern catching up growth theory see Fagerberg, J. (2002).

In this context, Moses Abramovitz (1986), introduced the notions of *technological congruence* and *social capability* to discuss what he called the 'absorptive capacity' of latecomers. The concept of *technological congruence* referred to the degree to which leader and follower country characteristics were *congruent* in areas such as market size, factor supply, etc. The concept of *social capability* pointed to the various efforts and capabilities that backward countries possessed in order to catch up, such as improving education, infrastructure and technological capabilities (R&D facilities, etc.). He explained the successful catching up of Western Europe vis-à-vis the USA in the post-war period as the result of both increasing technological congruence and improved social capabilities. As an example of the former he mentioned explicitly how European economic integration led to the creation of larger and more homogenous markets in Europe, facilitating the transfer of scale-intensive technologies initially developed for US conditions. Improved social capabilities on the other hand were reflected in such other factors as the general increase in educational levels, the rise in the share of resources devoted to public and private sector R&D and the success of the financial system in mobilising resources for change. In a similar vein the failure of many so-called developing countries to exploit the same opportunities is commonly accounted for by their lack of technological congruence and missing social capabilities (e.g. education, financial system).

The point here is that concepts such as 'technological congruence' and 'social capability' appear to be important policy notions which might be helpful in addressing the systemic 'success' or 'failure' of science, technology and innovation policies.

1.2 Measuring national systems of innovation

But the notions and concepts developed originally by Gerschenkron and Abramovitz provide an even stronger policy handle than originally thought by national systems of innovation theorists. Reporting on some work carried out for the European Commission,[5] a short elaboration is presented here of one of the few empirical attempts at identifying European member countries' national innovation system and their respective weaknesses. The core of this analysis hinges on the notions developed by Abramovitz and subsequently many growth and development economists. While the analysis is presented here at the national level, it can easily be repeated at the regional level.

Four factors appear at the outset essential for the functioning of a national system of innovation.

First there is the investment of the country in *social and human capital*: the cement, one may argue, that holds the knowledge and innovation systems together. It is incorporated in a number of knowledge generating institutions in the public as well as the private sector such as universities, polytechnics and other skill training schools. Social and human capital is of course also likely to be involved in the creation of new innovations and the diffusion of those innovations throughout the economic system. With the

5 See Soete, L. *et al.* (2002).

development of 'new growth' models in the economics literature, the role of education and learning in continuously generating, replacing and feeding new technology and innovation has received more emphasis[6] over the last decade. An initial stock of human capital in a previous period is likely to generate innovation growth and productivity effects, downstream as well as upstream with lots of 'spillovers' and positive 'externalities', affecting other firms, regions and countries.

Higher education is itself crucial for the continuous feeding of fundamental and applied research. Many new growth models have tried to build in a more complex fashion such impacts, giving prime importance not just to education itself, but also to its by-products such as research and innovation. The second central node of any system of innovation is hence not surprisingly the *research capacity* of a country or region and the way it is closely intertwined with the country's higher education system. From a typical 'national' innovation system perspective, such close interaction appears important; from an international perspective the links might be much looser, with universities and research institutions being capable of attracting talent world wide.

In most technology growth models, these two nodes form the essential 'dynamo effects' (Dosi, 1988) or 'yeast' and 'mushroom' effects (Harberger, 1998) implicit in the notion of technological change. Knowledge and human capital act like yeast to increase productivity relatively evenly across the economy, while other factors such as a technological breakthrough or discovery suddenly mushroom to increase productivity more dramatically in some sectors than others.

The third 'node' holding knowledge together within the framework of a national system of innovation is, maybe surprisingly, geographical proximity. The regional clustering of industrial activities based on the close interactions between suppliers and users, involving learning networks of various sorts between firms and between public and private players, represents a more flexible and dynamic organisational set-up than the organisation of such learning activities confined within the contours of individual firms. Regional or local learning networks can allow for much more intensive information flows, mutual learning and economies of scale amongst firms, private and public knowledge institutions, education establishments, etc. Some innovation management authors (Chesbrough, 2003) and firms (Philips) like to refer here to the notion of 'open innovation'. The *technological and innovative performance* of firms is what can be most directly measured to approximate the degree of success of such clustering.

In a well-known study Saxenian compares e.g. the impact of Silicon Valley and Route 128 in the US. She cites Silicon Valley in California where a group of entrepreneurs, helped by research effort in the local universities, contributed to the development of a world centre of advanced technology. According to her, the success of the latter cluster is due largely to horizontal networks of both informal and formal co-operation among companies in the region. By contrast, in the Route 128 corridor outside Boston, it is the lack of Putnam's (1993) so-called 'social capital' between firms which led to

6 For a recent analysis of the growth impact of higher education see Bassanini, A. and S. Scarpetta, (2001), and a more recent exploration by Vandenbussche, J., Aghion, P., and C. Meghir, (2004).

a more traditional form of corporate hierarchy, secrecy and territoriality. The comparison shows that the innovativeness and technological performance of firms strongly depends on close interaction between them.

In addition to human capital, research and the related phenomenon of local networks, and particularly interfirm networking, the fourth and last notion essential to any innovation system approach is the '*absorptive capacity*' of firms, clients and consumers in a particular region or country. The ability of companies to learn will of course in the first instance depend on their internal capabilities, represented by the number and level of scientifically and technologically qualified staff. Firms must do enough R&D to be economically dynamic and to have the 'absorptive capacity' to conduct a professional dialogue with the public research sector and other external sources of knowledge. At the same time, consumers, clients, and citizens might be very open to new designs, products, even ideas, enabling rapid diffusion of such new products created by R&D in knowledge-intensive sectors, or very conservative, resistant to change and suspicious of novelty. The absorptive capacity amongst countries, regions, even suburbs, varies dramatically.

Schematically Figure 1 illustrates, the growth dynamics associated with such an ideal, virtuous national innovation system. The four key nodes suggested here can be represented in a simple taxonomic way, opposing the relative importance given in science, technology and innovation policy to supply versus demand on the one hand and users versus creators factors on the other. Supply will generally be dominated by public resources, demand by private resources. The focus on users will be generally characterised by broad, economy wide features, reflecting the impact of the diffusion of technologies; the focus on creators will be generally more specific. The four key elements suggested above can be represented as elements of a 'virtuous' circle mutually reinforcing each other with in the end a positive overall impact on competitiveness and sustainable growth. From this perspective, it is in the interactions between these four constituents that the most interesting and efficient set of science, technology and innovation policy initiatives can be found.

Using a combination of a variety of indicators for each of the four concepts discussed above, an attempt was made to provide some empirical evidence for the various EU countries as to the workings of their respective national systems of innovation. In doing so, one hopes to provide some first quantitative evidence on some of the direct ways in which the key concepts described above interact and provide new insights into a country's competitiveness and long term growth path.[7] We first briefly describe the way in which the concepts discussed above have been empirically approximated. The approximation is far from perfect and dominated by the availability of comparable data for each of the 15 EU member countries.

7 See the High Level Expert report of Soete et al, 2002. This is part of an ongoing research project initiated within the framework of the ETAN Benchmarking exercise of DG Research at the European Commission.

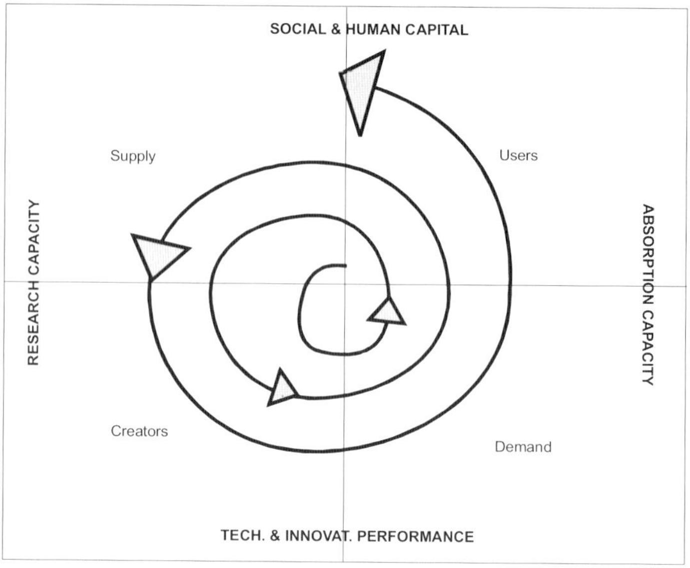

Figure 1. A National System of Innovation taxonomy.

– Social and human capital

The concept of social and human capital as discussed above is most closely related to measures of levels of education in a country and their maintenance. The human capital proxy used below will be based on an average of three indicators: a human capital investment indicator based on the educational expenditures in a country (percentage of GDP spent on education); an output-based education performance indicator (percentage of working population with third-level degrees) and an informal training indicator (participation in lifelong learning).

– Research capacity

The long term strength of a country's research system is approximated here by its capacity to deliver highly qualified researchers (scientists and engineering graduates as a percentage of working population); the amount of public resources a country is prepared to invest in R&D (GOVERD and HERD as a percentage of GDP) and the performance of its national research system (number of publications per million population).

– Technological and innovativeness performance

Technological performance is reflected in the more traditional RTD indicators such as business performed R&D (BERD as a percentage of GDP) and the number of patents obtained (triad patents per capita). In addition an innovation indicator (innovation expenditures as a percentage of total sales) has been added which provides additional information on firms' innovation efforts generally not captured in formal R&D investments or numbers of patents.

– Absorptive capacity

The concept of absorptive capacity is reflected here in the successful diffusion of new technologies throughout the economy. The measures used are: an indicator measuring a firm's capacity to renew its product range and adjust to technological change, based on the weighted average of sales of new-to-market products; a more process oriented measure of technological improvements, namely labour productivity; and a competitiveness indicator: relative trade performance in high-tech goods.

These four combined measures provide a relatively close approximation to the four concepts discussed above and identified with e.g. Abramovitz.

The proposed indicators will be presented as *relative* indices, whereby the EU average is equalized to 100. In the following figures the various indicators are compared in their various combinations for each of the EU-15 old member countries.

Figure 2 consists of a simple graphical illustration of an interlinked systemic vision of the various EU member countries' national system of innovation. The *best* performance is always indicated by points positioned towards the outside of each of the four quadrants of the graph and poor performance is reflected by the position of points near the centre. What emerges from Figure 2 is that EU countries do seem to have the supply side of their national systems of innovation well under control with, not surprisingly, substantial performance gaps between Europe's Northern and Southern member countries in human and social capital, public research efforts and private technological and innovative performance. However, quite strikingly, it is member countries' absorptive capacity which seems not to 'fit the bill' with little relationship with either technological and innovative performance, or social and human capital. Hence, Abramowitz's observation of nearly half a century ago appears as valid as ever.

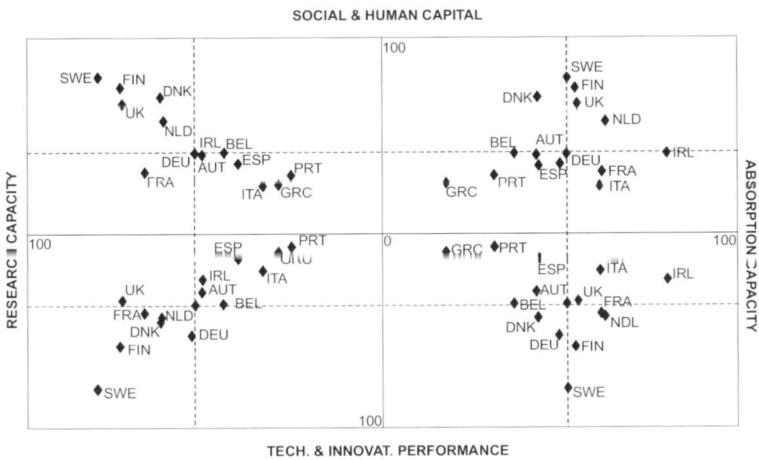

Figure 2. European N.S.I. Performance: A 'Bird's Eye' View.

In Figure 3, the analysis is pushed a step further. By simply looking at each country's position in each of the quadrants of Figure 2 relative to its position in the other quadrant, one can calculate the relative 'bias' in each country's national innovation system.

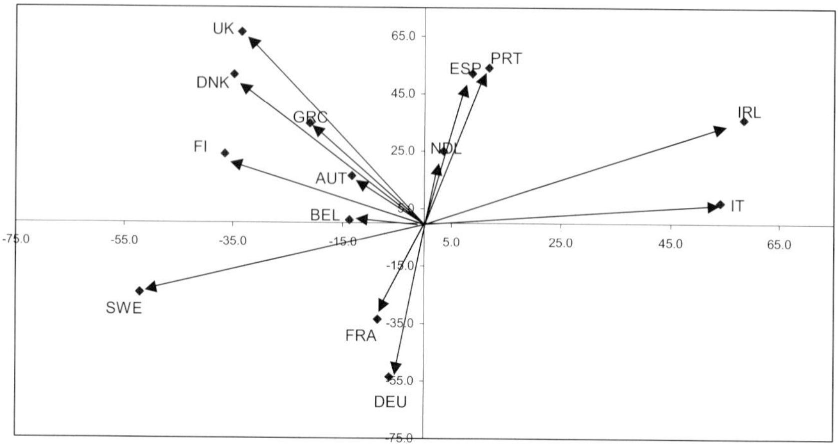

Figure 3. Biases in National Systems of Innovation.

Results are presented in Figure 3. The figure provides some interesting insights into the underlying implicit biases in individual member country's national systems of innovation. Looking at some of the most extreme positions in each of the quadrants, four features are worth noting:

- First, the UK in particular, but also Denmark appear to be characterised by a national system of innovation heavily biased towards the higher education-basic research interrelationship. The intrinsic weakness of these countries' national innovation system resides in the technological innovation-absorptive capacity linkages, which appear insufficiently strong to compensate for the heavy focus on higher education-basic research.
- Second, Sweden's NSI appears characterised by a strong bias in the research-technological performance relationship. In a much less extreme fashion Germany appears also characterised by such a bias nearer, though, to the technological performance end of the quadrant.
- Third, Ireland and Italy have a NSI strongly biased towards absorptive capacity and weak on the research side; Portugal and Spain have their NSI also biased in the same quadrant but much more towards the social and human capital end; the higher education system. These countries are weak where Sweden, in the case of Italy and Ireland, and Germany, in the case of Portugal and Spain, are strong.
- Finally, and most noticeable of all, no EU countries are located in the technological and innovative performance quadrant, pointing to a general European weakness in this area. When the data of Japan are added to the figure, Japan appears in this quadrant: a national system of innovation heavily biased towards the diffusion of technological and innovative performance.

Ideally one would like to expand the analysis in Figure 3 in a more dynamic fashion, rather than just comparing countries in a purely static way. Unfortunately the available data did not allow us to do this here: in subsequent research we hope to elaborate further on a more dynamic approach. The analysis presented here is only aimed at illustrating the importance of systemic interactions when looking at various relatively stylised aspects of a country's national system of innovation.

We turn now to the broader European debate and the particular role given to innovation policy in the so-called Lisbon strategy.

2. ON THE EMERGING KNOWLEDGE GAP BETWEEN EUROPE AND THE UNITED STATES

2.1 A knowledge and efficiency gap

The discussion about the knowledge gap between Europe and the United States is not new. In the 1960s, Jean-Jacques Servan-Schreiber, former French ambassador to the US, gained much publicity with his book *Le défi Américain,* in which he addressed the technological disadvantage of Europe relative to the US. Incidentally, a great many articles had previously been published in the international trade literature, which tried to provide an explanation for this technological gap. Characteristic of this gap was, however, the presupposition that the gap was actually the cause of the higher productivity growth rates in Europe compared to the United States. Due to imitation, international diffusion of knowledge and consumption patterns, European countries (just like Japan) were able to benefit from American innovations and effectively enter into a historically unprecedented phase of catching up growth. A large number of empirical studies confirmed this pattern, referred to by the French historian Jean Fourastier as 'les trentes glorieuses': the thirty years of rapid, 'worry-free' catching up growth following the Second World War. US growth was characterised over that same period by relatively high unemployment. In the mid-1960s, a debate took place within the US about the extent to which the high US unemployment rate was 'technological', i.e., the result of automation.

From this perspective, the technological disadvantage of Europe at that time, and particularly the lagging behind in investments in R&D, was very much considered as merely a temporary phenomenon that would disappear of its own accord thanks to technological catching up.

It is interesting to note that the Netherlands did actually not quite fit into this picture. As Figure 4a shows, in the late 1960s and early 1970s, the relative efforts of Dutch firms in the area of R&D exceeded not only the European average and Japan, but also the United States. However, in contrast to countries such as Japan, Germany (the former Federal Republic), Sweden, and to a lesser extent, France and Belgium, whose business efforts in R&D almost doubled throughout the 1970s and 1980s, the Dutch efforts over the same period hardly increased, so that Dutch business financed R&D intensity is now well below that of the US, Japan and even the EU average.

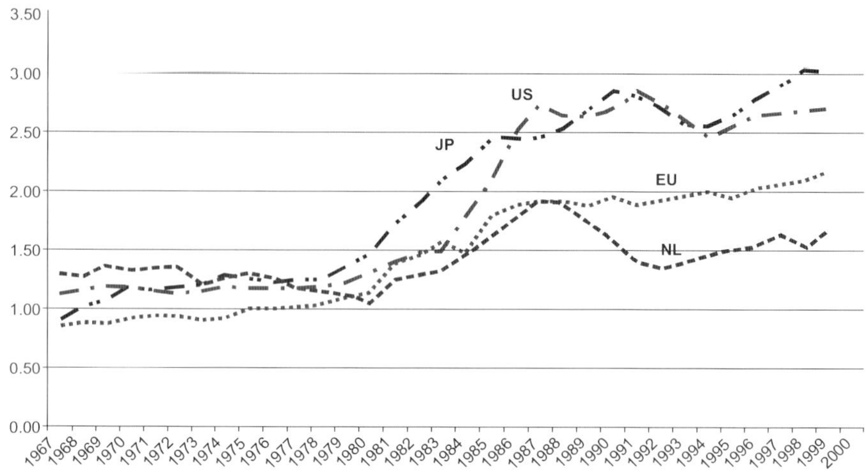

Figure 4a. Business-financed R&D efforts as a percentage of industrial added value (VS, EU, J, NL 1967-2000).

Figure 4a illustrates this long-term historical trend in business-financed R&D efforts as a percentage of the industrial added value over the period 1967-2000 for the US, Japan, the EU and the Netherlands.[8]

Apart from such business-financed R&D investments, research funded by public authorities is also conducted in the business sector – the greater part of these R&D expenditures goes to defence and aerospace research. Figure 4b, presenting the trend over the same period in the *total* business-oriented research activities but now as a percentage of GDP, shows that the United States in particular invested heavily in publicly funded business R&D expenditure in the 60s. For Europe, and the smaller member states in particular, foreign countries constitute today an increasing source of funding for national business-oriented research activities. Currently, for the Netherlands, foreign funding accounts for more than 25% of the total of business-oriented R&D activities. Nevertheless, in terms of the total business-oriented R&D intensity too, the Netherlands now lags behind Japan, the US and the European average, as Figure 4b indicates.

8 A lot of questions can be raised with respect to the reliability of international data on R&D expenditures and long-term trend comparisons of such data. Thus, in a large number of countries, the United States in particular, fiscally friendly schemes for R&D expenditures were introduced in the 1980s with respect to business-financed R&D; also, the internationally accepted definition of R&D in the Frascati Manual only became gradually accepted in the 70's. There is, hence, a strong suspicion that there exists a certain overestimation of the growth of officially reported R&D business activities in a number of countries in the 1970s and 1980s. Finally, R&D activities have a strong industrial connotation and seem to be a less appropriate indicator for services in particular.

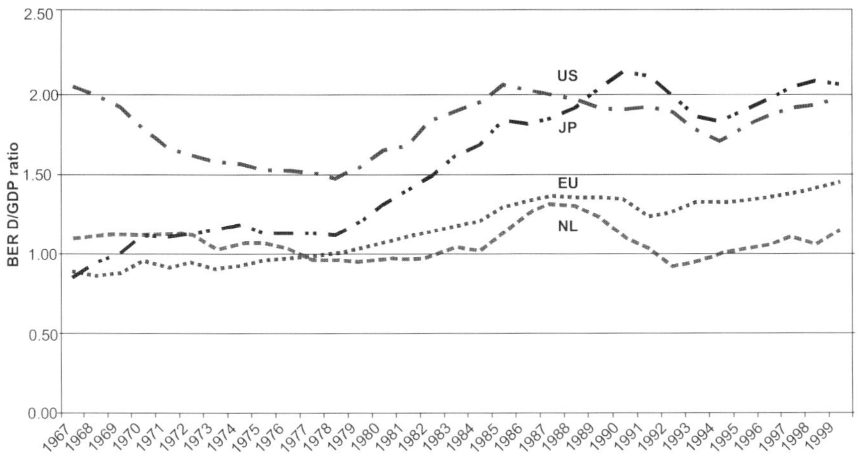

Figure 4b. Total business-oriented R&D activities as a percentage of the Gross Domestic Product (US, EU, J, NL 1967-2000).

The relation between the total of business-oriented research activities (measured here, as in Figure 4b, as the percentage of Gross Domestic Product in year 1) and the resulting domestic productivity growth (measured as the annual growth in the GDP per man-hour in the subsequent period of years 1-5) is represented in Figure 5 for two different periods: the early 'catching-up' period of 1967-72 in Figure 5a and the more recent period of 1995-2000 in Figure 5b. Both of these are periods of relatively high growth. Figure 5 shows how different the relationship was between research intensity and productivity growth in both periods. In the first period, strongly dominated by the 'catching-up' phenomenon, there appears to be no positive relationship between R&D business intensity and the resulting productivity growth, on the contrary the relationship appears rather negative (Figure 5a). By contrast, the positive relationship does seem to hold for the most recent period (Figure 5b). From this perspective, the most recent period seems to be more similar to earlier periods of 'innovation-induced' growth,[9] for example the period 1890-1913.

9 See, among others, Pavitt, K. and L. Soete, (1982), analysed and described the 1890-1977 period from the perspective of the 'entrepreneur-driven' growth hypothesis.

Figure 5. Business-oriented R&D intensity and productivity growth.

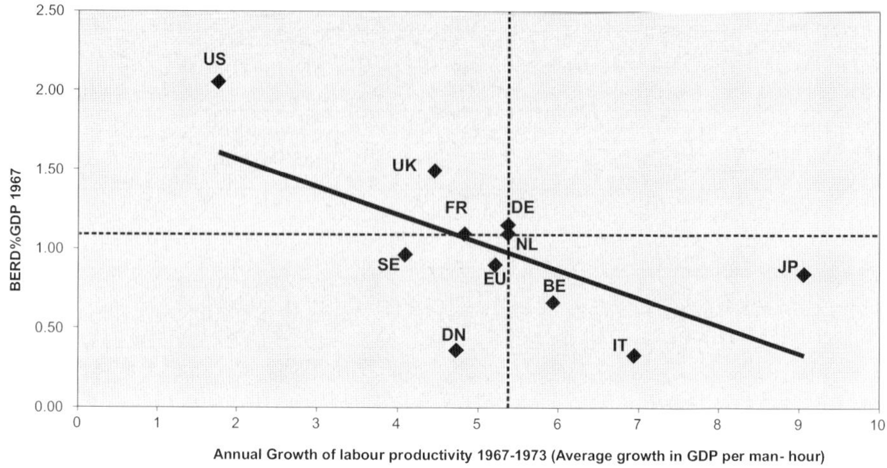

5a. 1967-1967/1972.

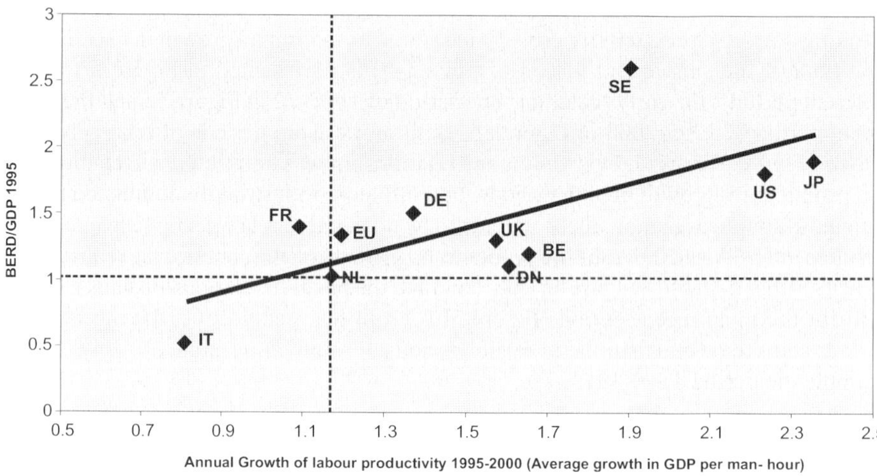

5b. 1995-1995/2000.

The Netherlands seems, in other words, to have evolved throughout the last 30 years from a technologically leading into a technologically following country in the area of private knowledge investments, at the very moment that these business-oriented investments efforts started to make an essential difference in the prosperity of a country and its international competitiveness.

From this last perspective, a focus on the Dutch trend of lagging behind in business-oriented R&D efforts in the 1970s and 1980s appears useful in that it might provide some interesting insights into the current knowledge gap of the EU relative to the US. As the Lisbon declaration recognises, Europe's technological development over the 1990s can best be described as one of 'falling behind' in the area of knowledge investments of Europe relative to the US.

Two underlying phenomena seem to be characteristic of the 'falling behind trend' in the Netherlands over the last 30 years.

1. First and foremost, the strong internationalisation of the Dutch business community and especially of the large R&D-intensive multinational companies that used to be, and still are, heavily present in the Dutch economy. Until the 1980s, the five largest Dutch industrial companies represented more than two-thirds of all Dutch business-funded R&D investments. These firms actually showed an 'over-concentration' on research and development investments in the Netherlands, certainly when compared to their international production activities. Along with the further internationalisation (and 'Europeanisation' in preparation for the European single market) of production, R&D investments also became, logically, subject to internationalisation. Initially, this was limited to R&D activities strongly linked to the maintenance and adjustment of production processes and product technology to the foreign market conditions. This was, however, further reinforced by the shift that took place in most large firms in the 1980s in the organisation of R&D activities, from autonomous laboratories directly under the responsibility of the Board of Directors to more decentralised R&D activities integrated into and part of business units. In a second phase, firms started to make more effective use of the presence abroad of possibly relevant knowledge centres. Highly qualified electronic engineers are not only available in Eindhoven. A similar development took place somewhat later in Japan. This process of internationalisation in R&D is still going on (also in the Netherlands). Not only production is being internationalised, firms will increasingly 'shop' on the world market for knowledge and choose the best locations to perform their R&D activities. In doing so they not only hope to make their own, in-house R&D more efficient, but also look to the efficiency, quality, and dynamics of the external, local knowledge institutions, such as public R&D institutions and universities. Recent survey studies on the R&D location intentions of R&D managers show that this internationalisation trend is likely to continue in the future. As such, it appears nearly a natural trend: knowledge becomes part of the globalising economy.

Without any doubt, a similar tendency to 'Europeanise' R&D activities has taken place within Europe in many of the large R&D-intensive, European and foreign firms located in Europe. From this perspective, the creation of the larger European single market in 1992 led to economies of scale not only in production and distribution, but also in the field of business R&D activities. Hence, one of the reasons for business-oriented R&D activities to lag behind in Europe relative to the US in the 1990s might well be the natural trend in Europe to rationalise existing, overlapping R&D activities in various European countries as a result of a conscious striving for efficiency on the part of the large multinational R&D-intensive companies in the new, 'integrated' European Union.

2. A second factor is related to the strongly increased international specialisation of a small open economy like the Dutch one. Over the last twenty years, firms with sometimes technologically heavy investments, such as in the aircraft construction or automobile industry, disappeared as a result of fierce, international competition or were taken over by foreign firms. The Dutch economy has been characterised more than other countries in continental Europe, by an unremitting process of de-industrialisation. This went together with the development and strong international growth of service sectors, for example the financial and insurance, logistic, and media sectors, where (industrial) R&D efforts are, by definition, limited. Interestingly, the Dutch 'falling behind' trend in business-oriented R&D investments shows many similarities to that in the United Kingdom, the other European country characterised most by de-industrialisation in the 1970s and 1980s.

In the Netherlands this led to a debate about the structural and industrial composition of R&D efforts.[10] Authors like Hendrik Snijders (1998) considered the national trend of aggregated Dutch R&D figures irrelevant: rather than 'falling behind', Dutch companies found themselves in a process of ongoing internationalisation and sectoral specialisation. On the other hand, authors like Verspagen and Hollanders[11] calculated that after checking for sectoral shifts in the Dutch R&D composition, there was, still, an important 'falling behind' trend in R&D performance. The relatively low Dutch productivity growth rates over the last decade (Figure 5b) support this latter interpretation.

A similar process of specialisation has taken place in Europe. European firms in high-tech sectors like the electronics, computer and software industries lost a large part of their European and world market share, causing the industrial structure of the European economy to become less specialised in different high-tech segments of the manufacturing industry, and in particular the IT sector. Despite the development of a European research support policy in the 1980s and 1990s, for such 'sunrise' sectors, the European technological disadvantage in these sectors further increased. In view of the size of the European market, comparable in terms of population with the American one, the structural adjustment towards fewer high-tech sectors might well have gone hand in hand with the emergence of a technological and efficiency gap, as seen in Figure 5b.

2.2 The public-private knowledge gap: an increasing mismatch?

Intensification of investments in knowledge and innovation is at the heart of Europe's Lisbon ambition. As indicated above, attention has focused mainly on business-oriented R&D investments. Although the investments in public research institutions, particularly the publicly funded higher education and research institutions, represent an easier policy domain for additional investment efforts, a comparison between the US, Japan, and

10 For a more dynamic analysis based on R&D *and* innovation indicators which also takes into more explicit consideration so-called sectoral innovation 'regimes', see the recent analysis of Marsili, O. and B. Verspagen, (2002).

11 See the discussion in *Economisch Statistische Berichten* (ESB) between Snijders, H. (1998) and Verspagen, B. & H. Hollanders, (1998).

the European Union shows that Europe does not actually fall behind in terms of R&D expenditure in the public sector. This applies both to publicly financed R&D activities, as indicated in Figure 6a, and to R&D activities performed by public institutions, as illustrated in Figure 6b. Both figures show that this also holds for the Netherlands. The Netherlands is not falling behind Europe and the United States in terms either of publicly funded R&D (Figure 6a) or R&D performed by public institutions (Figure 6b).

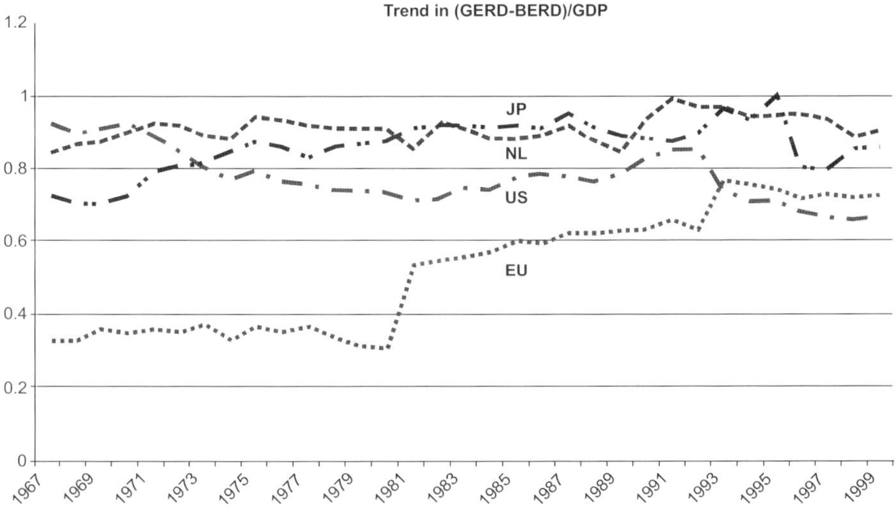

Figure 6a. Publicly financed R&D as a percentage of GDP (US, EU, J, NL 1967-2000).

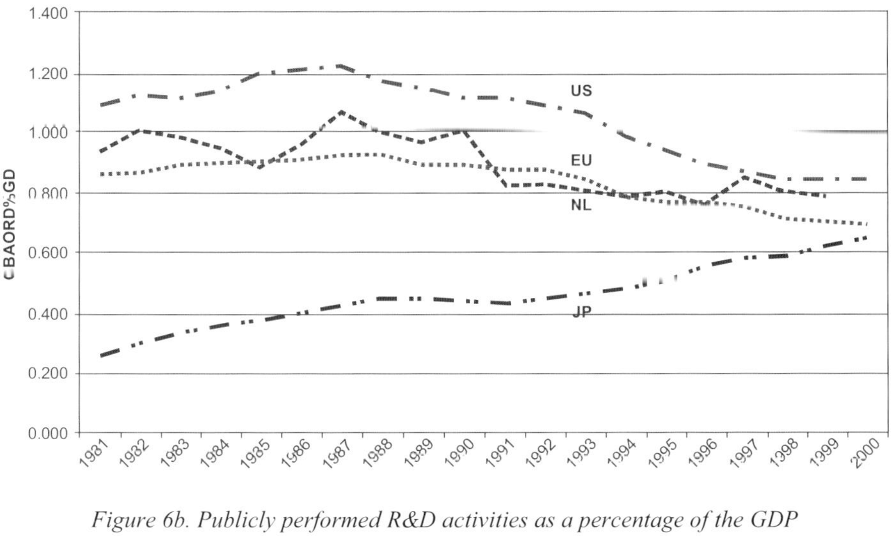

Figure 6b. Publicly performed R&D activities as a percentage of the GDP (US, EU, J, NL 1967-2000).

Comparison of Figures 4 and 6 raises the question to what extent European public research is adequately geared to private research. What does the fact that the gap in R&D expenditure between the US and the EU mainly focuses on the private sector tell us about the nature and structure of the public R&D sector in Europe? Is public research in Europe of insufficient quality? Does it have insufficient appeal for private firms to perform their research in Europe? Is it too fragmented over various European member states? These questions are essential to make a well-founded assessment of the nature of the knowledge gap between Europe and the United States.

Once again, it seems useful to look at these questions in a somewhat broader historical context. As early as the 1960s, the so-called British research paradox received a great deal of attention in response to the 'science and technology push' policy of the then British labour government (Harold Wilson's 'white heat of technology'): Britain appeared good in terms of scientific performance and technological inventions, but poor in terms of innovative, market-oriented applications. This paradox, which has been the subject of uncountable analyses throughout the 1980s, was elevated to a European paradox in the 1990s fairly quickly. To a large extent, the paradox also seems applicable to the Netherlands.

Thus, the national performance of scientific research, measured, for example, in terms of the number of publications per researcher, or per million of Euros spent on public R&D is not inferior in the case of the United Kingdom or the Netherlands (even Europe) to that of the United States. Throughout the years, with the increasing dominance of English as the language of scientific communication, the growth in the total 'production' of internationally read and reviewed, scientific articles in Europe has, incidentally, been higher than in the United States. The Netherlands, too, scores remarkably high both in terms of scientific publications and number of citations. Linked to Figure 6 this would imply that when looking at both scientific research efforts and scientific output, Europe, and the Netherlands in particular, have not been lagging behind in terms of such 'public' knowledge vis-à-vis the US. More detailed analyses of the number of references to scientific papers in patents confirm this picture and indicate that Europe has not been lagging behind in the awareness and diffusion of scientific knowledge.

However, and in line with the sets of arguments put forward above (under section 2.1), it might be argued that precisely at a time when Dutch business research was increasingly becoming internationalised and specialised worldwide, a reverse '*nationalising*' trend with respect to public research took place. Characteristic of public research is to some extent, its national embeddedness.[12] From this perspective, Dutch policy aiming at increasing 'competition' between Dutch universities and public research centres, as was the case with the formation of so-called research schools, undoubtedly produced an important quality impulse to Dutch public research, but did *not* lead to

12 See our discussion in section 1 on the concept of '*national* systems of innovation' as developed by innovation literature authors like Freeman, Lundvall or Nelson: differences between countries in the set-up and nature of *national* institutions, in particular university education and the public research infrastructure, seem to be able to explain to a large extent differences between countries in innovation strength.

specialisation of research, rather to further research duplication. Practically every university jumped on the same, new, promising research areas (life sciences, nanotechnology, information technology, new materials, etc.), competing nationally and world wide to recruit Dutch and foreign leading researchers. This resulted in a multitude of different, relatively small research groups, each of them seeking additional funding and networks through e.g. European funding programmes.

Thus, reinforcement of the link between the more business focused, specialised research knowledge and public, fundamental research hardly materialised. Awareness of this problem led to the initiative of the so-called 'Technological Top Institutes' (TTIs), aimed at steering research in the public research field on the basis of financial matching from the private and public resources, towards the long-term research needs of firms located in the Netherlands.[13] In other words, policymakers too, especially those at the Ministry of Economic Affairs, became aware over the last decade of the increasing duality between publicly oriented and privately driven research.

A similar trend has also taken place in other European member states.[14] It might be said that the European research programmes contributed insufficiently from this perspective to closing this gap. The European support for networking, the mobility of European researchers and regional cohesion are likely to have even led to increased European duplication of research in the 'new' research areas outlined in the framework programmes. This phenomenon of a growing mismatch between national public and internal private research specialisation amounts to what I have described elsewhere as the *Dutch knowledge disease*.[15] Effectively it consisted of a double 'crowding out' effect: the crowding out of applied, privately oriented research from public research institutions, in particular universities, and the crowding out of basic, fundamental research from private research establishments.

In this view, the concept of a European Research Area (ERA) clearly meets an absolute public need within Europe to make public research across European borders more specialised and more internationally competitive. As Paul David put it: 'One might do well to consider whether the present "noncompeting" style of national public agencies engaged in funding R&D is not part of the problem of the "European paradox".'[16] In this sense there is, particularly on the public supply side of the system of innovation taxonomy presented in Figure 1, no evidence of a European *system* of innovation, but rather of 15, today 25, national systems of innovation each with noncompeting national funding institutions.[17]

13 Interesting in this context was the initial negative attitude of the Dutch public research council NWO towards the initiative, and the positive attitude of the Dutch Academy of Sciences KNAW, which as a result became much more actively involved in the selection of these TTIs.

14 It should be noted here that British and French policymakers focused most on the need for this link and the risk of duality.

15 See Soete, L., (2003).

16 David, P., (2002).

17 See Caracostas, P. and L. Soete (1997) for a more in depth analysis of the nonemergence of a European innovation system.

However, the ERA need is not just limited to the domain of public research. After all, the European Research Area also comprises private research performed in Europe, and it is precisely this research that is expected to give the impulse to the future development of the EU towards a knowledge economy. Actually, an emphasis on the public research part without paying sufficient attention to the link between public and private research across European borders is likely to lead to an even larger European research paradox. It is crucially important, therefore, that when shaping and elaborating the ERA, the commission adequately considers the needs of the private sector. In this sense the first experiences with the next round of the so-called framework programmes (the current 6th one and the forthcoming 7th) do not stem hopeful. Here too, the policy initiatives taken in the Netherlands to address some of the emerging mismatches might well provide interesting examples to be readily copied, such as the foundation of European Technological Top Institutes. After all, it is this type of pan-European institute that, apart from the few areas endowed with large, expensive infrastructures (particle accelerators, cyclotrons, astronomy, JET, etc.), is currently lacking in the European public and private research area, and distinguishes the EU research landscape most from that of the US.

A different, but equally important question relates to how a 'European' research *area* is to be physically delineated. Knowledge is undergoing internationalisation, and publicly oriented knowledge in particular is likely to become much more open and developed in interaction with other countries, in *and* outside Europe. In other words, for the majority of scientists the relevant public research area is the international research area, not necessarily the European one. The *cocooning* of knowledge inside a country's physical borders, national or European, might even lead to undesirable 'diversion' effects of knowledge: researchers will prefer to network with European colleagues for the sake of European financial support. While this might have a positive impact on the reinforcement of the European research potential, it may have long-term, negative effects for the maintenance within national borders of top research. In spite of the high scientific quality of European research, it is striking that in terms of top research (Nobel prizes, Field medals in mathematics, other scientific prizes), the US have gained a significant advantage in many, if not most scientific areas. This holds all the more true for many applied areas in which American universities are leading, often with the financial support of the business community.

CONCLUSIONS

The analysis presented in section 2 focused mainly on the technological aspects of knowledge development, specifically the link between private and public research expenditure. Outside this sphere, however, as highlighted in section 1, other factors play an essential role in the innovation process: the introduction of new products into the market, the implementation of new production techniques, the setting up of new, innovative companies, the local innovative and entrepreneurial culture, the regional clustering and absorptive capacity, etc.

Certainly within Europe there are still many institutional, social and cultural barriers that may have a negative impact on knowledge development and innovation. In many reports, also those issued from within the European Commission itself, attention is focused on a number of obstacles related to the lack of harmonisation within Europe in a number of areas of particular relevance to innovation. Thus, important 'costs' of 'non-Europe'[18] still exist: costs related to inadequate harmonisation within the EU and specifically the *non*realisation of European economies of scale due to differences in national regulations.

The current patenting costs in Europe are e.g. much higher in Europe than in both the US and Japan. Patents are crucially important in the innovation process, insofar as they, if successfully obtained, ensure some degree of legal security concerning future potential flows of income with which a firm may recuperate its R&D expenses. At the same time, publication of the technical details of the invention in the patent document contributes significantly to the further diffusion of knowledge. Thus, the high European patenting costs act as a brake on Europe's innovative capacity and on the diffusion of knowledge. Similarly the availability in Europe of venture capital, which is often a crucial bottleneck for innovation and small high-tech firms, is much more limited than in the US, even though European countries vary considerably in the availability of venture capital. Here, too, the lack of European harmonisation represents an important obstacle to innovation.

However, besides these institutional barriers to the innovation process in Europe, another more fundamental question which can be raised is to what extent certain aspects of the European social welfare model might contain intrinsic obstacles to 'entrepreneurship and innovation culture', especially in light of Europe's increasing structural disadvantages in the areas of innovation and high-tech entrepreneurship. The Lisbon declaration was not only an expression of the political desire to strive for a Europe that by 2010 would belong to the world's most knowledge-intensive regions, but also of the desire for this to happen within the context of a strengthened, 'activated' social Europe that would have an eye for past social achievements. The question that was in fact *not* addressed in Lisbon is whether both objectives are always compatible and might not involve an economic trade-off in a number of specific areas.

In a recent contribution, Saint-Paul[19] analyses the relationship between labour market institutions and the development of innovations from a theoretical perspective. In doing so, he emphasises in particular the costs of dismissing employees. These costs which are much higher in Europe, particularly continental Europe, than in the US, are in many ways the most explicit manifestation of Europe's social welfare state. They have led to stability in labour relations and represent an important incentive for employers and employees alike to invest in human capital. They are central to Europe's social model.

18 Analogous to the analysis in the 1988 Cecchini report, prepared in preparation of the 'Single Market', and mapping the cost of 'non-Europe'.

19 Saint-Paul, G., (2002).

However, in terms of innovation, and in particular the Schumpeterian process of creative destruction, the cost of developing new activities crucially depends on the ease with which 'destruction' can be realised. Thus, as shown in Saint-Paul's model, the US, with much lower firing costs, will eventually gain a competitive advantage in the introduction of new, innovative products and process developments onto the market, while Europe will become specialised in technology-following activities, based on secondary, less radical improvement innovations.

In other words, the dynamics of innovation, of entrepreneurship, of creative destruction thrives better, practically by definition, in an environment providing higher rewards for creativity and curiosity than in an environment putting a higher premium on the security and protection of employment. Viewed from this perspective, the gap between Europe and the United States in terms of innovative capacity, efficiency, and wealth creation may also be the price Europe has to pay for not wanting to give up its social model and in particular its achievements in the field of social 'security'. In this respect, the Lisbon declaration was not really clearly formulated. A better way would have been: how much of the social achievements of the European model is Europe prepared to give up in order to keep up with the United States, let alone develop Europe into one of the most prosperous and dynamic regions in the world? A question which, four years after Lisbon, has not lost any of its relevance and one which will continue to challenge European policy makers in the area of innovation policy in the years to come.

REFERENCES

Abramovitz, M. (1986). Catching Up, Forging Ahead and Falling Behind. *Journal of Economic History, 46:2*, 385-406.

Bassanini, A. & Scarpetta, S. (2001). Does Human Capital Matter for Growth in OECD Countries? *OECD Economics Department Working Paper no. 2001-8.*

Caracostas, P. & Soete, L. (1997). The building of cross-border institutions in Europe: towards a European system of innovation? In C. Edquist (Ed.), *Systems of Innovation. Technologies, Institutions and Organizations.* London: Pinter.

Chesbrough, H. (2003). *Open Innovation: The New Imperative for Creating and Profiting from Technology.* Harvard Business School Press.

Chesnais, F. (1992). National systems of innovation, foreign direct investment and the operation of multinational enterprises. In B-Å. Lundvall, (Ed.), *National Systems of Innovation: Towards a Theory of Innovation and Interactive Learning.* London: Pinter.

David, P. (2002). ERA visions and Economic realities: A cautionary approach to the restructuring of Europe's research system, *EC STRATA Workshop 'New challenges and new responses for S&T policies in Europe', Brussels, 22-23 April 2002*, mimeo.

Dosi, G. (1988). Sources, Procedures, and Microeconomic Effects of Innovation. *Journal of Economic Literature, Vol. 26(3), September*, pp. 1120-1171.

Fagerberg, J. (2002). *Technology, Growth and Competitiveness: Selected Essays.* Cheltenham: Edward Elgar.

Freeman, C. (1987). *Technology Policy and Economic Performance: lessons from Japan.* London: Pinter.

Freeman, C. & Soete, L. (1997). *The Economics of Industrial Innovation, third edition.* London: Cassell.

Gerschenkron, A. (1962). *Economic Backwardness in Historical Perspective*, Cambridge, Belknap Press of Harvard University Press.

Gerschenkron, A. (1968). The typology of industrial development as a tool of analysis. In: A. Gerschenkron, *Continuity in history and other essays*, (pp. 77-97). Cambridge, Harvard University Press.

Harberger, A. (1998). A vision of the growth process. *American Economic Review, March 1998*, 1-32.

Lundvall, B-Å. (1992). *National Systems of Innovation: Towards a Theory of Innovation and Interactive Learning.* London: Pinter.

Marsili, O. & Verspagen, B. (2002). Technology and the dynamics of industrial structures: An empirical mapping of Dutch manufacturing. *Industrial and Corporate Change,. 11 (4)*, 791-815.

Metcalfe, J.S. (1995). The economic foundations of technology policy, equilibrium and evolutionary perspectives. In P. Stoneman (Ed.), *Handbook of the Economics of Innovation and Technological Change.* Oxford: Blackwell.

Montobbio, F. (1999). National Innovation Systems. A Critical Survey, paper per la ricerca CESPRI: *Sectoral Systems in Europe – Innovation, Competitiveness and Growth (ESSY), Targeted Socio-Economic Research, TSER.*

Nelson, R.R. (1993). *National Systems of Innovation: A Comparative Study.* Oxford: Oxford University Press.

Niosi, J. & Bellon, B. (1994). The Global Interdependence of National Innovation Systems. Evidence, Limits and Implications. *Technology in Society, 16 (2) 1994*, 173-197.

Patel, P. & Pavitt, K. (1994). The continuing, widespread (and neglected) importance of improvements in mechanical technologies. *Research Policy, 23 (5),* 533-545.

Pavitt, K. & Soete, L. (1982). International differences in economic growth and the international location of innovation. In H. Giersch, *Emerging Technologies. Consequences for Economic Growth, Structural Change and Employment.* Tübingen: J.C.B. Mohr.

Putnam, R. (1993). *Making Democracy Work: Civic Traditions in Modern Italy.* Princeton: Princeton University Press.

Saint-Paul, G. (2002). Employment protection, international specialisation and innovation. *European Economic Review, vol. 46*, 375-395.

Saxenian, A. (1994). *Regional Advantage: Culture and Competition in Silicon Valley and Route 128.* Cambridge: Harvard University Press.

Snijders, H. (1998). Nederlandse R&D: het valt best mee. *ESB, 6-2-1998,* 112-113.

Soete, L. et al. (2002). Benchmarking National R&D Policies: The Impact of RTD on Competitiveness and Employment. *Strata-ETAN Expert Working Group, Final Report, Brussels, June.*

Soete, L. (2002). A Dutch 'Knowledge' disease, Innovation Lecture 2002, *Closing the Gap, December 9, 2002.* The Hague: Ministry of Economic Affairs.

Soete, L. (2003). De Nederlandse Kennisziekte. *ESB, 7-2-2003, 88e jaargang, nr. 4394*, 51.

Vandenbussche, J., Aghion, P., & Meghir, C. (2004). Distance of Technological Frontier and Composition of Human Capital, January 2004. *AEA meetings in San Diego*, mimeo.

Verspagen, B. & Hollanders, H. (1998). De Nederlandse Innovatie-achterstand. *ESB, 10-4-1998,* 290-291.

L. ORSENIGO

'HISTORY FRIENDLY' MODELS OF INDUSTRIAL EVOLUTION: AN OVERVIEW

1. INTRODUCTION

'History-friendly' models (HFM) are a new style of formal evolutionary economic models. They aim to capture – in stylised form – qualitative theories, suggested by empirical research, about the mechanisms and factors affecting the evolution of various industries, technological and institutional change.

HFM have been inspired by a few fundamental methodological principles that have guided the development of the evolutionary approach:

i) realism should be considered as a merit of theoretical models and the design of formal economic models ought to proceed well informed by the empirical literature on the subject matter they purport to address;
ii) formal evolutionary theory can be a major help to empirical research in economics;
iii) formal models play a crucial role for the development of more general theories that are capable of subsuming diverse specific instances into a compact, broad and simple conceptual framework.

This paper will first discuss the basic methodological inspiration of HFM. Second, the basic structure and some applications of a model of the evolution of the computer industry will be dealt with. In the third section, a brief illustration of a model of the pharmaceutical industry will be used to suggest how one can use HFM – in an inductive way – to progress towards broader generalisations and theories. The concluding section indicates some lines for future research.

2. METHODOLOGICAL INSPIRATION

HFM are inspired by the recognition that there is a tension between richly detailed, empirical and historical accounts of specific phenomena and 'general theories', almost always formalised in mathematical models. In particular, HFM try to bring about a dialogue between different phases of the process of economic analysis, i.e. between empirical analysis, appreciative theorising, formal modelling and the attempt to construct general theories.

This is particularly the case where the study of the evolution of industries is concerned. For example, at one end a huge literature is now available that investigates the

P. de Gijsel and H. Schenk (eds.), Multidisciplinary Economics, 151–163.

history of different economic sectors, in different countries, for different spans of time. It presents empirical evidence and suggests powerful explanations, often – but not always – with a distinct evolutionary flavour. Usually these 'histories' are very rich and detailed. Actors and variables like the educational system, policies, institutions, the internal organisational structure of firms and the structure of demand play a fundamental role in these accounts. Moreover, such explanations often (although not always) imply some form of dynamic increasing returns, path-dependency and more generally nonlinear dynamics.

This literature is based on what Nelson and Winter defined in their 1982 book as 'appreciative theorising' (Nelson and Winter, 1982), i.e. nonformal explanations of observed phenomena based on specific causal links proposed by the researcher. Nelson and Winter argued that not only appreciative theorising is a true causal theory, but also a fundamental and unavoidable step in any process of 'theory-making'. However, it is sometimes hard to check the logical consistency of appreciative models, whether they are sufficient to provide an explanation, or whether they need to be augmented in certain ways.

This is particularly the case if these appreciative models embody nonlinear path-dependent processes and a variety of agents and institutions. Moreover, it is usually hard to generalise about these accounts. Each history is often treated as unique, because the details and the specific observed sequence of events make it difficult or controversial to claim that the particular case can be considered as an instance of a more general process applicable to a wider range of cases.

At the other end, one finds (with some luck) simple, general models that have precisely the ambition of identifying the basic principles explaining the facts under investigation. These models are almost always expressed in mathematical form and their virtue lies in the parsimony of their basic assumptions as well as in their elegance. However, precisely because of their generality, empirically oriented analysts often feel that these models fail to adequately consider some crucial aspect of the empirical story and / or that some assumptions are too stark and extreme, with very little connection with reality.

To a large extent, this tension is unavoidable and it is a legitimate and indeed fruitful source of progress in understanding. However, in many cases, this tension signals that the divorce between the empirical analysis of specific cases and the construction of general theories has indeed gone too far.

This is arguably the case in evolutionary economics, too. Most of the 'first generation' evolutionary models aimed primarily at broadly exploring the logic of evolutionary economic processes and at demonstrating the feasibility of the theoretical and methodological approach. Often – but not always – those models tried to explain empirical phenomena such as economic growth, the relationship between industrial structure and innovation, the diffusion processes, and other stylised facts about issues of industrial dynamics. Even if the linkage to empirical evidence was considered an essential and characterising element of the evolutionary approach, most of these 'first-generation' models were rather simple and abstract. Sometimes they had a very complex formal structure, but both the description of the phenomena under observation and the internal structure of these models were highly simplified. Thus, especially as these models progressed in mathematical sophistication, it was sometimes felt that their linkage with specific economic facts was becoming worryingly tenuous.

In this context, HFM try precisely to bridge this gap. In this vein, formal models should be considered to begin with as attempts at checking the consistency and the robustness of the verbal arguments that constitute the appreciative theory. They aim to capture the essence of the appreciative theory developed by analysts of the history of an industry or a technology, and thus to enable its logical exploration. The term 'formal' means that all of the logic that underlies model outcomes is explicit. Often, in these cases, only a simulation model can capture (at least in part) the substance of the appreciative model. But it is worth observing that a 'history-friendly' model doesn't necessarily need to be based upon simulation, nor on an evolutionary approach.[1]

On the other hand, HFM might contribute to the construction of more general theories in at least two ways. First, the construction of formal models of specific industries might be useful in forcing the theorist trying to apply a general model to a specific case to recognise that often the 'devil is in the details' and to focus attention on the specificities that characterise the evolution of such industry, calling both for more realism than is usually the case, and for stronger awareness of the distance that might exist between any 'general' theory and the case under investigation.[2]

Second, in a more inductive attitude, building different HFM for different industries may help the development of 'general theories' by prompting the analyst to clearly recognise what is similar and what is different between two or more sectors. As an example, at the very beginning of the development of a model, one must obviously identify the distinctive features of the industries under investigation. Thus, a model of the computer industry will probably have to be different from a model of the pharmaceutical industry. But what has to be different and what can remain similar in the two models is an inductive exercise, which paves the way for subsequent generalisations. In this sense, HFM try to impose a 'double' methodological discipline on evolutionary industrial organisation theory: imposing formal discipline on appreciative theorising and empirical discipline on more abstract, general theories.

3. THE MODEL OF THE COMPUTER INDUSTRY

The first attempt at building a HFM concerned the computer industry (Malerba *et al.*, 1999). The model clearly shares the distinctive characteristics of the evolutionary

1 For example, the model presented by Jovanovic and MacDonald (1993) could be considered a neoclassical antecedent of 'history-friendly' models.

2 This is particularly the case when the empirical phenomena that the theorist tries to explain are extremely generic and not sufficiently specified or conditioned to restrictions. Thus, they can result from very different dynamic processes. Phenomena like S-shaped curves in diffusion theory or skewed firm's size distributions are typical examples of this kind of 'unconditional objects' (Brock, 1999). In these instances, it might be useful to both enrich the internal structure of the model and above all to increase the number and the kind of facts that one tries to explain at the same time. The imposition of a tighter 'empirical discipline' is necessarily a more demanding test for the model.

approach. Agents are characterised by 'bounded rationality', i.e. they don't completely understand the causal structure of the environment in which they act and they are unable to elaborate exceedingly complex expectations about the future. Rather, firms' and consumers' actions are assumed to be driven by routines and rules that introduce inertia in their behaviour. Agents, however, can learn and are able to improve their performance along some relevant dimensions, in particular technology.

Given earlier period's conditions, firms act and modify their performance. Specifically, profitable firms expand, and unprofitable ones shrink. Thus, the model is mainly driven by processes of learning and selection. Jointly, the actions of all the agents determine the aggregate industry conditions, which then define the state for the next iteration of the model.

Strong nonlinearities are present in this structure. They generate complex dynamics and prevent an analytical solution of the system. Moreover, the model does not impose equilibrium conditions: on the contrary, 'ordered' dynamics emerge as result of interactions far from equilibrium.

3.1 The basic structure of the model

At the beginning of the history analysed in the model, a number of firms engage in efforts to design a computer, using funds provided by 'venture capitalists' to finance their R&D expenditures. Computers are designed on the basis of transistor technology and they are defined by two characteristics, 'cheapness' (defined as the inverse of the price of a given computer) and 'performance', which improves over time as a consequence of firms' R&D spending. Some firms exhaust their capital endowment without achieving a product and fail. Other firms succeed and begin to sell computers in the marketplace, thus opening the mainframe market.

The value that customers place on a computer design is an increasing function of its performance and its cheapness,[3] which, jointly, define the 'merit' of a particular computer in the eye of the customers.

When consumers buy computers, they value its 'merit', as compared to other products. In addition, however, markets are characterised by brand-loyalty (or lock in) effects and respond to firms' marketing policies. Moreover, there is a stochastic element in consumers' choices between different computers. Without lock-in effects or marketing, demand would be similar to a standard demand curve. It would tend to converge towards the higher quality product, even if a positive probability of survival for computers with lower quality design always remained. The inclusion of brand-loyalty and bandwagon effects *introduces inertia and forms of increasing returns in market dynamics work.*

Firms with positive sales use their profits to pay back their initial debt, to invest in R&D and in marketing. Firms are represented by sets of technological and marketing competencies that are accumulated over time, and by rules of action, trying to capture

3 Markets for mainframes and for PCs consist of a large number (a parameter in the model) of independent sub markets. They are sub-groups of purchasers with identical preferences.

elements of the theory of the firm based on 'dynamic competencies' (Winter 1987, Dosi e Marengo 1993, Teece *et al.*, 1996). Through their R&D expenditures, firms accumulate technical capabilities and design new, better computers. Outcomes of R&D activities depend on the research direction each firm decides to follow (which is assumed to be firm-specific and time-invariant) and on latent technological opportunities (i.e. the maximum levels of the two characteristics that can be achieved by a computer design), as well as on a probabilistic effect. The price that firms charge for their products is obtained by adding a constant mark-up to production costs, which in turn are determined by the technical progress function. R&D and advertising expenditures are simply determined as constant fractions of profits (after the repayment of their debt). As time goes by, successful firms grow and gain market shares, but technical advance becomes slower as they gradually approach the technological limits defined by transistor technology.

After some time, microprocessors become exogenously available, so that it is possible to achieve better computer designs, in particular as regards cheapness. Now, a new type of computer design, personal computers (PC), becomes technically achievable. A new group of firms tries to design new computers exploiting the new technology, in the same way as happened for transistors. Some of these firms fail. Some enter the mainframe market and compete with the incumbents. Others open up the PC market. PC users attribute relatively more value to cheapness than to performance, as compared to mainframe customers. Incumbents may choose to adopt the new technology to achieve more powerful mainframe computers. The adoption of new technology by old firms is however costly and time-consuming, because firms' competencies are cumulative and – as a consequence – they can face great difficulties when trying to do something radically different from their past experience. Competence traps and lock-in phenomena are distinctive features of this approach. Yet, after adoption, firms have access to the new technological frontier: they can innovate faster and may decide to diversify into the PC market.

The procedures governing diversification in the model mimic the actual strategy used by IBM, i.e. firms enter the PC market founding a completely new division, which inherits part of the competencies and budget of the mother company but then behaves exactly as a new entrant, with independent products, profits and research strategies.

3.2 The simulation runs

The model is able to replicate the industry history. A dominant transistor-based firm (IBM) emerges relatively quickly in the mainframe market and keeps its large market share even after the entry of new microprocessor firms. IBM then diversifies into the PC market, and gains a significant, but not a dominant, share.

These results are obtained with a parameter setting that reflects the basic key assumptions that economists who have studied the computer industry suggested were behind the pattern of what happened. Specifically, the dominant position of IBM in the mainframe market was due to significant effects of brand loyalty and consumer lock-in. This raised substantial entry barriers for new entrants. Second, by the time microprocessors became available, computer design under the old technology was reasonably advanced, and the leader, IBM, responded to the availability of the new technology pretty rapidly. Third, IBM's massive resources enabled it to initiate an R&D and advertising effort quickly enough to allow them to catch up with the earlier entrants into the PC market. However, in the PC market lock-in and brand-loyalty processes were less important.

The logic of the model might then be tested conducting counterfactual simulation runs. Thus, a reduction of the parameter capturing brand-loyalty effects in the demand function of mainframe market significantly lowers the market's concentration. Similarly, if the time of the introduction of microprocessor technology is anticipated, new firms break into the market before a dominant firm can emerge. Hence, the process of microprocessor adoption is slower and more costly. Facing this environment, IBM is not able to achieve a significant market share in the PC market because it must compete with firms who already have a dominant position in the new segment. Conversely, IBM is also able to dominate the PC market, if the parameters measuring the economies of scale in R&D and brand-loyalty in the PC market are increased and when the adoption and diversification processes are eased.

3.3 Further exercises: experimental users, diversification and industrial policies

After checking that the model is able to reproduce the stylised history and that it reacts appropriately to changes in the key parameters (as suggested by the theory), it becomes possible to explore new issues and questions. Here, only two of such exercises will be briefly mentioned.[4]

Experimental users

A first issue concerns the role of experimental users and/or diverse preferences among potential users in forcing the successful introduction of radically new technology in an industry (Malerba *et al.*, 2003). Typically, a new technology is inferior to the old one in its early stages and it progresses only through the R&D efforts of new entrants. But, in the absence of customers who buy (for different possible reasons) these initially inferior products, the new firms will not gain market shares and profits. Despite the

4 A further exercise concerns the question diversification strategies. For example, under what conditions would a different diversification strategy by IBM have performed better? To explore this issue, a new diversification behaviour, labelled 'competence-driven' (Malerba *et al.*, 2001) was modelled. Here, instead of starting a totally new division, diversifying firms try to apply their specific 'mainframe' competencies to the PC and set up a new internal division which develops PCs following the old trajectory of technological progress and begins its activities starting from the position reached by the parent company in the space of technological characteristics. This strategy may have the disadvantage that the new division's trajectory of advance might fare relatively badly in a market that values cheapness rather than performance. Conversely, the strategy based on the acquisition of new knowledge from external sources can be much more expensive and, in general, the new technological strategy of the parent company might well turn out to be a very bad one. Simulation results show that 'competence-driven' strategy performs relatively better if the PC design does not require a drastic re-orientation in the competencies mix (i.e. in the trajectory of technological advance) and if the PC market is not too distant from the mainframe market.

opportunities afforded by a potentially powerful new technology, the industry will stay stuck with the old one.

To explore this hypothesis, various demand contexts are analysed. In a first set of runs, the bandwagon effects in the demand equation are modified in such a way that new firms trying to introduce microprocessors are unable to get any significant market share in the mainframe market. As a consequence, established leaders in the market do not have the incentive to adopt the new technology. The same result occurs, though, even when the bandwagon effect is eliminated but customers are sophisticated and their preferences are homogeneous, in the sense that users always buy the 'best' computer currently offered in the market. Since the new technology is initially inferior to the old one, sophisticated customers continue to buy the old – currently better – designs, preventing new entrants from finding a profitable market and to develop the new technology.[5]

The situation changes if a group of customers is introduced who will buy some of the products based on the new technology, simply because they are new or if there is a group of customers with very different tastes than the customers who had been buying the old products. In both cases, the new firms, and the new technology, are able to get a foothold in the industry and to grow. Established firms now are challenged by these new ones, and they change their own practices. The result is that, as time goes by, products using the new technology come to dominate the market and in the long run even the old consumers may be significantly better off.

Antitrust policies

According to the model, the emergence of a monopolist in the mainframe market was nearly inevitable, given the presence of two interacting sources of increasing returns that tended to reinforce each other: cumulativeness in firms' efforts to advance product and process technologies and brand-loyalty and lock-in effects on the demand side. Against this background, an interesting policy question concerns the effectiveness of public policies under conditions of dynamic increasing returns.

A set of exercises focuses on antitrust policies (Malerba *et al.*, 2001a). In the model, the antitrust authority (AA) intervenes when the monopolist reaches a share equal to 75% of the market and it breaks the monopolist up into two smaller companies. The two new firms originating from the old monopolist have half of the size and resources of the mother company. AA may intervene at different periods: 1 year after the first firm has reached a share equal to 75% of the market, or after 5, 10 and 20 years.

Results show the relevance of the timing of the intervention in dynamic markets. When AA intervenes very early, the market becomes concentrated again very soon, because one company will quickly gain an advantage and grow exploiting increasing returns. In the case of later intervention the emergence of a new monopolist takes more time. Finally, if the intervention occurs after 20 years, the market will be divided into two oligopolists, which won't be able to profit any longer from the possibility of

5 This result shows that, quite paradoxically, a more 'competitive' market – with little inertia in consumers' behaviour – can generate more concentration than a market where inertia is greater.

gaining market leadership, because dynamic increasing returns are limited (technological opportunities are almost exhausted). Another interesting result is that even if the intervention has limited effects on the mainframe market, it produces noticeable consequences on a proximate market, i.e. the PC segment, where concentration is lower than in the standard case.

The reasons of this result are the following: when AA intervenes early (after 1 or 5 years), both new 'IBM children' are able to diversify into the PC market, thereby reducing concentration there. If AA intervenes 'late' (after 10 or 20 years), only one firm will be able to diversify, but it will be smaller and the overall concentration in the PC market will decrease.

This exercise suggests some considerations. First, in markets where substantial dynamic increasing returns are present there is a strong tendency towards concentration and it is extremely difficult to contrast this tendency. Small initial advantages tend to grow bigger over time and it is almost impossible to catch up. Leaders do not only have a 'static' advantage: they also run faster than laggards (assuming no imitation). Thus, antitrust intervention might be effective in modifying the degree of concentration only in the short run or in making the monopoly contestable. Policies of the kind are somehow designed to 'levelling the playing field'. But this does not seem to be enough. In order to get effective and long-lasting results, some form of 'positive discrimination' might be necessary. That is to say, in the presence of strong dynamic increasing returns, policies should make competitors able to run (much) faster than the monopolist, and not just remove static disadvantages.[6]

4. THE MODEL OF THE PHARMACEUTICAL INDUSTRY

A further attempt at building a HFM concerns the pharmaceutical industry and biotechnology (Malerba and Orsenigo, 2002). Work on the model is still in progress and therefore only some brief comments will be given here. This case differs drastically from computers in a number of respects. Thus, beyond its intrinsic interest, the pharmaceuticals model might illustrate how HFM can be used in an inductive and 'comparative' perspective to generate and test hypotheses about the determinants of market structure and its evolution.

Pharmaceuticals are traditionally a highly R&D intensive sector where, despite a series of radical technological and institutional 'shocks', the core of leading innovative firms and countries has remained quite small and stable for a very long period of time. However, differently from computers, the degree of concentration has been consistently low, whatever level of aggregation is considered.

These patterns of industrial dynamics are intimately linked to two main factors. First, the nature of the processes of drug discovery, i.e. to the properties of the space of technological opportunities and of the search procedures through which firms

6 Similar results were obtained in the analysis of policies supporting the entry of new firms.

explore it. Second, the fragmented nature of the relevant markets. Specifically, innovation processes have been characterised for a very long time by a low degree of cumulativeness and by 'quasi-random' procedures of search (random screening). Thus, innovation in one market (a therapeutic category) does not entail higher probabilities of success in another one.

The gist of the story is as follows. A number of firms competes in discovering, developing and marketing new drugs for a large variety of diseases. At the start, they face a large number of unexplored opportunities. However, the search for new promising compounds is essentially random, because the knowledge of why a certain molecule can 'cure' a particular disease and of where that particular molecule can be found is limited. Thus, firms explore the 'space of molecules' randomly until they find one which might become a useful drug and patent it. The patent provides protection from imitation for a certain amount of time and over a given range of 'similar' molecules. After discovery, firms engage in the development of the drug, without knowing how difficult, time consuming and costly the process will be and what the quality of the new drug will be. Then, the drug is sold on the market, whose notional size is defined by the number of potential patients. Marketing expenditures allow firms to increase the number of patients they can access. At the beginning, the new drug is the only product available in that particular therapeutic class. But other firms can discover competing drugs or imitate the original one. The innovator will therefore experience a burst of growth following the introduction of the new drug, but later on its revenues and market shares will be eroded away by competitors and imitators.

The discovery of a drug in a particular therapeutic class does not entail any advantage in the discovery of another drug in a different class (market) – except for the volume of profits that can be reinvested in research and development. Moreover, the various submarkets (therapeutic categories) that define the overall pharmaceutical industry are independent from one another also on the demand side: an antiulcer drug is useless for a patient suffering from Alzheimer's. As a consequence, diversification into different therapeutic categories is also purely random. Hence, firms will start searching randomly again for a new product everywhere in the space of molecules. Firms' growth will then depend on the number of drugs they have discovered (i.e. in diversification into different therapeutic categories), on the size of the markets they are present in, on the number of competitors, on the relative quality and price of their drug vis-à-vis competitors. Occasionally, a firm can discover a blockbuster. But, given the large number of therapeutic categories and the absence of any form of cumulativeness in the search and development process, no firm can hope to be able to win a large market share in the overall market, but – if anything – only in specific therapeutic categories for a limited period of time. As a result, the degree of concentration in the whole market for pharmaceuticals and in any individual therapeutic category will be low. However, a few firms will grow and become large, thanks essentially to the discovery of a 'blockbuster' and to diversification.

The advent of biotechnology starts to change this picture. In the model, a first, very rough, reduced form is introduced of the cognitive processes underlying drug discovery after the molecular biology revolution.[7]

In the model, scientific knowledge sheds some light upon the mechanism of the action of some drugs and the biochemical and molecular roots of some diseases. This improved understanding allows firms to try to 'design' compounds that might have particular therapeutic effects and to focus search in particular directions. Moreover, science makes new products potentially available.

On these bases, new science-based firms enter the market, trying to discover new drugs. Yet, science does not simply provide (imperfect) information on the properties of the search space. There might be multiple competing trajectories for eventually discovering a new drug and many of them will prove to be dead-ends. The new firms are specialised in specific techniques and applications and cannot change their trajectories and easily apply their specific competencies to different areas. Moreover, they have very little funding and – even when they succeed in discovering a new drug – they don't control the resources to developing and marketing it.

Thus, only few of the new biotechnology firms (NBFs) will succeed in discovering, developing and selling a new drug. Conversely, incumbent big pharmaceutical companies do not react immediately to the new opportunities and when they eventually adopt the new technologies they have to gradually 'learn' the new knowledge base. However, they have plenty of financial and marketing resources. Moreover, they are able – in principle – to 'screen' wider subsets of the search space: they are 'generalists' rather than 'specialists'. Against this background, big pharmaceutical companies and NBFs may find it profitable to strike collaborative agreements, whereby NBFs complete some specific project with additional funding provided by their large partners. The drug is then developed and (if successful) marketed by the big pharma corporation, paying a royalty to the NBF. As a consequence, a network of alliances begins to emerge.

As in the model of the computer industry, firms act according to very simple rules as far as investment in R&D and marketing is concerned. Also the basic structure of demand is quite similar to the previous model, except – of course – that there is now a large number of independent markets. The main difference concerns, then, the representation of the search space in which firms conduct their innovative and imitative activities: here, the discovery of a new promising drug is totally random and there is no cumulativeness in technological advances.

The results are also encouraging. The model is actually able to replicate some of the key features of the pharmaceutical industry in these periods, especially as regards the low level of concentration both in the overall market and also, to a lesser extent, in each therapeutic category. Similarly, the biotechnology revolution does not change market structure substantially, despite the significant entry of new firms. A dense network of

7 This attempt is inspired by the so-called Arrow-Nelson model about the effects of scientific research on the productivity of industrial research, but some modifications to this approach are considered, aimed at capturing the simple idea that science does not simply simplify the search space, but it deforms it and generates an explosion of alternative hypotheses to be tested (Orsenigo, Pammolli and Riccaboni, 2001).

agreements between incumbents and NBFs starts to develop, though. Collaborative relations allow for the survival of many NBFs and for the further growth of some incumbents, that benefit from collaboration for discovering better drugs.

Various counterfactual exercises show indeed that it is quite difficult to substantially increase concentration in this model unless the costs of R&D are drastically increased and technological change and marketing are made much more cumulative. Similarly, it is almost impossible, within the current structure of the model, for new biotechnology firms to displace incumbents.

Within this context, it becomes possible to start running exercises concerning e.g. the effects of alternative forms of patent protection and market regulation.

One specific investigation focuses on the factors that influence entry and survival in the age of random screening (Garavaglia, Malerba and Orsenigo, 2004). Indeed, a major puzzle in the interpretation of the history of pharmaceuticals is the question why entry was not a relevant feature of this industry – especially as regards the innovative core – until the advent of the biotechnology revolution, despite low cumulativeness in the process of drug discovery and low levels of concentration.

In these runs, the entry process is not modelled as an endogenous process. Rather, the implications of market structure and innovation of alternative patterns of entry are explored, in terms of number of entrants and timing of entry.[8] First, simulations are performed for different numbers of entrants, everything else remaining equal. Second, given an initial budget equal for all entrants and fixing the total number of entrants (50), the model explores the effects of different patterns of the timing of entry. Thus, 5 generations of equal size (i.e. 10 firms in each generation) of potential entrants try to enter the market at a pre-set timing: t_1, t_2, t_3, t_4, t_5.[9]

The main results can be summarised as follows:

a) Concentration, not surprisingly, decreases monotonically with the number of entrants.
b) Market fragmentation *per se* does not significantly matter for market concentration and entry, in the absence of strong cumulativeness in the process of discovery; however, the higher the degree of market fragmentation (in terms of the number of

8 This is clearly a major limitation. However, as a partial justification, it might be noted that most models of entry basically assume an infinite queue of would-be entrants that might decide to actually enter the industry when expected profits are positive. Yet, the assumption that the pool of potential entrants is infinite is quite strong and nothing is usually said about the determinants of the size of such a pool. In some cases, it might well be that low rates of entry are observed not (only) because of insufficient incentives (profits below the norm), but because the pool of potential entrants is too small. For example, basic scientific and technological capabilities in a given country may be too low to generate a sufficiently large number of potential entrants, for lack of adequate capabilities. Thus, the following exercise could be interpreted as a preliminary analysis of (simplified) contexts whereby the pool of potential entrants is determined exogenously by a different set of variables having to do with e.g. technological competencies, rather than with direct economic incentives.

9 More precisely, four cases are explored: – case a) timing: 0, 5, 10, 15, 20
– case b) timing: 0, 10, 20, 30, 40
– case c) timing: 0, 20, 40, 60, 80
– case d) timing: 0, 30, 60, 90, 120

therapeutic categories, given the total value of the market for drugs as a whole), the higher are the chances for late potential entrants to enter and survive.

c) The timing of entry is crucial. First entrants face an unexplored scenario, characterised by unexplored opportunities and high possibilities of profits. This leads to an increasing gap over time between the first generation of entrants and the subsequent ones. The gap becomes more significant the later the subsequent potential entrants try to enter the industry.
d) Two main factors influence the fate of entrants. First, high discovery opportunities make it easier for later potential entrants to prosper. Second, increasing search costs over time significantly obstruct survival, especially for later generations of entrants.
e) The size of the market has an important effect on survival. But, in a dynamic setting, larger market size might imply first–mover–advantages linked to 'success-breeds-success' processes which make life harder for later entrants.

5. CONCLUSIONS

The models briefly discussed here – even if very simple – appear to be flexible and 'powerful' enough to perform the tasks for which they were created. They capture in a stylised and simplified way the focal points of an appreciative theory about the determinants of the evolution of the two industries. They are able to replicate the main events of the industry histories with a parameter setting that is coherent with basic theoretical assumptions. Changes in the standard set of parameters actually lead to different results, 'alternative histories' that are consistent with the fundamental causal factors of the observed stylised facts. Furthermore, on these bases, it becomes possible to explore the effects of different hypotheses about agents' behaviour, the conditions which determine the profitability of different strategies or the impact of alternative designs for industrial policies and forms of market regulation. Finally, – in a more 'theoretical' attitude – HFM can be used to develop and analyse more general assumptions about the determinants of the evolution of market structures, like, e.g. the structure of demand and of the relevant technological regimes. The models reviewed here, thus, provide some original insights and suggestions for the study of the evolution of industrial structures,[10] particularly by examining the dynamic properties of structures characterised at the same time by several sources of increasing returns.[11]

10 For example, they support some conclusions recently proposed by John Sutton (Sutton, 1999) about the relation between innovation and market structure or by Steven Klepper about the determinants of industries life cycles (Klepper, 1996). Yet, these results are grounded on different insights and also suggest different assumptions and conclusions.

11 Until now, typically, economic literature focussed on cases where only one source of increasing returns is present. For example, some models have investigated the consequences of the cumulativeness of technical advance. Others have analysed the importance of network externalities on the demand side (Arthur 1985, David 1985, etc.). We think that the joint consideration of these aspects can be a promising trajectory of analysis, showing the possible differences in these processes and, above all, illustrating the consequences – which are not always intuitive – of their interaction.

These models are only preliminary attempts and there are many opportunities for further research along these lines. A first direction of analysis – already in progress – concerns the processes of vertical integration and specialisation and the co-evolution of an upstream and a downstream industry. More generally, there is obviously ample scope for the construction of models of different industries, which can explore different histories and investigate new theoretical questions. HFM might therefore prove to be valid tools for economists to progress at the same time towards a more general and a more empirically and historically founded theory of industrial evolution and economic change.

REFERENCES

Arthur, W.B. (1985). Competing Technologies and Lock-in by Historical Small Events: The Dynamics of Allocation Under Increasing Returns. *Technological Innovation Project Working Paper No. 4,* Centre for Economic Policy Research, Stanford University.

Brock, W.A. (1999). Scaling in Economics: A Reader's Guide. *Industrial and Corporate Change, 8,3,* 409-446.

David, P.A. (1985). Clio and the Economics of QWERTY. *American Economic Review, 75*, 332-337.

Dosi G., & Marengo, L. (1993). Some Elements of an Evolutionary Theory of Organizational Competence. In R.W. England (Ed.), *Evolutionary Concepts on Contemporary Economics*, Ann Arbor: University of Michigan Press.

Garavaglia, C. , Malerba, F. & Orsenigo, L. (2004). Entry, market structure and innovation in a history friendly model of the evolution of the pharmaceutical industry. In G. Dosi & M. Mazzucato (Eds.), *The Dynamics of the Pharmaceutical Industry*', Oxford: Oxford University Press, forthcoming 2004.

Jovanovic, B. & Macdonald, G.M. (1993). The Life Cycle of a Competitive Industry. *Working paper No. 4441,* Cambridge (MA): National Bureau of Economic Research.

Klepper, S. (1996). Entry, Exit and Innovation over the Product Life Cycle. *American Economic Review, 86(3)*, 562-582.

Malerba, F. & Orsenigo, L. (2002). Innovation and Market Structure in the Dynamics of the Pharmaceutical Industry and Biotechnology: Towards a History-Friendly Model. *Industrial and Corporate Change, 11(4)*, 667-704.

Malerba F., Nelson R., Orsenigo L. & Winter, S. (1999). History friendly models of industry evolution: the computer industry. *Industrial and Corporate Change, 1*, 3-41.

Malerba, F., Nelson, R., Orsenigo, L. & Winter S. (2001). Product Diversification in a 'History-Friendly' Model of the Evolution of the Computer Industry. In A. Lomi & E. Larsen (Eds.) *Dynamics of Organizations. Computational Modelling and Organization Theories* (pp. 349-376). Cambridge (MA): MIT Press.

Malerba, F., Nelson, R., Orsenigo, L. & Winter, S. (2001a). Competition and Industrial Policies in a 'History-Friendly' Model of the Evolution of the Computer Industry. *International Journal of Industrial Organization, 19*, 613-634.

Malerba, F., Nelson, R., Orsenigo, L. & Winter, S. (2003). Demand, Innovation and the Dynamics of Market Structure: The Role of Experimental Users and Diverse Preferences. *CESPRI Working Paper no.135.*

Nelson, R. & Winter, S.(1982). *An Evolutionary Theory of Economic Change.* Harvard University Press.

Orsenigo, L., Pammolli F. & Riccaboni, M. (2001). Technological Change and the Dynamics of Networks of Collaborative Relations. The Case of the Bio-pharmaceutical Industry. *Research Policy.*

Sutton, J. (1999). *Technology and Market Structure.* Cambridge (MA.), MIT Press.

Teece, D. & Pisano, G. (1994). The Dynamic Capabilities of Firms: An Introduction. *Industrial and Corporate Change, 3*, 537-555.

Winter, S. (1987). Knowledge and Competence as Strategic Assets. In D.J. Teece (Ed.), *The Competitive Challenge* (pp. 159-184). Cambridge (Mass): Ballinger.

FINANCING PROBLEMS OF THE WELFARE STATE

B. UNGER

INTRODUCTION

Public sector economics in a broad sense includes taxation, public debt and deficit issues, welfare economics and public choice. Nowadays, the public sector faces problems in all of these subfields. Tax compliance declines, public debt increases, demands that we should move from welfare to workfare get louder and criticism of the behaviour and choices of politicians have become newspaper evergreens. The debate on the welfare state is a good example to use in order to demonstrate the importance of public sector economics. It allows scholars to analyse problems from the point of view of different (sub)disciplines and to integrate them.

The welfare state has come under pressure. Exploding expenditures for pensions and public health, lower state income because of tax evasion and avoidance, increasing debt and deficits have led to increased scepticism about public governance. The welfare state, it is argued, cannot be financed anymore. The state has to withdraw or at least reduce its role in the economy substantially.

When seen from a multidisciplinary – political, institutional and historical – perspective, today's perception of the inefficient public sector seems pretty old. The political acceptance of the public sector has seen its ups and downs throughout history. The political goals of a leaner or a fatter state have been mirrored in economic reasoning. Most likely, today's predominant view of 'bad government' will again turn into one of 'good government' in some years time, the pendulum will swing up again. The borderlines between the public and the private sector shift over time, and so do economic ideas.

Some 30 years ago Bruno Frey brought public choice from the US to Europe. In his keynote lecture on 'Public Governance and Private Governance: Exchanging Ideas', Frey emphasises the interaction between the public and the private sector. Using a public choice approach, he turns the current negatively biased debate on the public sector upside down and shows what corporate governance can learn from public governance by creating the right incentives for people. The Frey group in Zurich deals with topics such as tax avoidance and tax resistance.

P. de Gijsel and H. Schenk (eds.), Multidisciplinary Economics, 165–166.

Rick van der Ploeg approaches the topic of public debt and deficits from a macroeconomic perspective. What can and should the public sector do? Or in modern words: to smooth or not to smooth taxes and expenditures over time, that is the question here. Van der Ploeg concludes that it is desirable that governments impose a financial tight-jacket. But unfortunately, most budget rules, including the Maastricht norms, are pro-cyclical and see only a small role for debt in smoothing intertemporal tax distortions and financing temporary increases in public spending. As former state secretary of culture, heritage and media and professor of economics at the European University Institute in Florence, Van der Ploeg links economic ideas with his political experience.

Willem H. Buiter, Chief Economist and Special Counsellor to the President of the European Bank for Reconstruction and Development, stresses the 'Joys and Pains of Public Debt' and its consequences for developing countries. He introduces a 'permanent balanced budget rule', but also stresses that first the political and institutional side of the state must be strong enough to permit the sovereign to enter into credible debt commitments.

Members of the USE's chair of Public Economics have worked in different international and interdisciplinary projects regarding the welfare state, such as the group around Fritz Scharpf and Vivienne Schmidt at the Max Planck Institute in Cologne on the development of welfare state regimes in different countries over the last 30 years. With the group around Maurizio Ferrera and Martin Rhodes at the European University Institute, the chair of Public Economics investigates labour market reforms that aim at reducing welfare and increasing workfare in different European countries. In addition, the chair members collaborate with Regnet, a research institute and network on regulation and tax systems integrity at the Australian National University. As at USE, scholars at Stanford, Berkeley, Venice and Vienna collaborate in integrating different fields of public sector economics and enriching them with an institutional perspective. Furthermore, interdisciplinary work is enhanced by networks such as the Society for the Advancement of Socio-economics (SASE), of which Professor Unger was one of the founders. Its goal is not to limit itself to pure economic reasoning but enrich it with an institutional, historical and political perspective.

B.S. FREY*

PUBLIC GOVERNANCE AND PRIVATE GOVERNANCE: EXCHANGING IDEAS

I. A RIDICULOUS IDEA?

To many economists it may appear a strange, if not queer idea, to even consider what can be learned from the public sector. Have we not, after all, a lot of negative experience with the public sector? It is often considered synonymous with large-scale inefficiency, waste, scandals and corruption. As a result, have there not been many efforts to overcome these shortcomings of the public sector by moving towards more market-oriented institutions and policies? For this reason, the 'New Public Management' was introduced in many countries. Its main message was that the public sector should imitate the market as fully as possible. In particular, the dependence of individuals on governmental services, characterised by long waiting queues and bad quality[1] was to be replaced by a service corresponding to consumer needs. Public sector wages should not be determined by seniority, but by performance. A similar movement in the United States referred to 'Reinventing Government', in the sense of introducing market mechanisms (see, for instance, Stiglitz 2002: 351).

The serious shortcomings of the public sector were also the subject of a great deal of academic writing. My own field, Public Choice or Modern Political Economy[2] can, in many ways, be characterised as the study of 'government failures' (see, for instance, Tullock et al., 2002). From the very start,[3] it concentrated on the irrationalities, inconsistencies and inefficiencies of the public sector. The 'Comparative Institutional Analysis' (see, for instance, Eggertson 1990) concluded quite generally that government failures were far more important than market failures. As a consequence, aca-

* I benefited greatly from extensive discussions on Corporate Governance issues with Margit Osterloh and Reiner Eichenberger. I am also grateful for helpful comments from Matthias Benz, Christoph Engel, René L. Frey, Bernd Helmig, Dennis Mueller and Alois Stutzer.

1 Even in a country with a relatively small public sector, like Switzerland, it is only a few years back that one had to wait for weeks to get a telephone installation and the only choice was an unattractive phone in one color only, black.

2 E.g. Frey (1978), Persson and Tabellini (2002), Mueller (1997, 2003). The shortcomings of public bureaucracy are discussed in e.g. Wintrobe (1996), and rent seeking in Tollison (1982), Tullock et al. (1988) and Tollison and Congleton (1995).

3 Arrow (1951), Black (1958), Buchanan and Tullock (1962), Sen (1970), Niskanen (1971).

P. de Gijsel and H. Schenk (eds.), Multidisciplinary Economics, 167–186.

demic literature has been keen on transferring ideas from the market (normally understood to be perfectly competitive) to the public sector. Most importantly, introducing competition and the market via privatisation and deregulation has been the major advice offered by economists to improve the working of society in general, and the public sector in particular. An example is competitive federalism, where various jurisdictions undertaking the same activity is not seen as a waste but, given the right conditions, as an incentive to raise efficiency (see, for instance, Frey and Eichenberger 1999). On a more microeconomic level, the introduction of market elements into the public sector was hailed as one of the great achievements in economics in the last century (Faulhaber and Baumol, 1988). According to Stern (2002: 337), this approach can be fairly summarised in the following manner: 'Privatise, get the government out of the economy, and let markets determine allocation and make decisions wherever possible'. Auctioning systems for allocating scarce resources, road pricing and tradable permits for pollution control are well-known examples.

There is no doubt, in my opinion, that transferring ideas and mechanisms from the private into the public sector provided fresh and valuable insights, and in many cases strongly increased the efficiency of the public sector. But in this paper I wish to do exactly the reverse: *I argue that the private sector can learn from the public sector.* I claim that, throughout its long existence, the public sector, and in particular democracy, has generated worthwhile institutions, some of which may be of great use to private governance. In order to substantiate this claim, I want to be concrete. I direct my attention to the core of the private sector, namely the management of firms. I thus wish to defend the proposition: '*Corporate Governance should learn from Public Governance*'. It will be argued that the recent large-scale scandals, fraud, inefficiencies and corruption among firms (see Osterloh and Frey, 2003) could have been reduced, and perhaps avoided, if rules and institutions existing in the public sector had been in place in private corporations. But I have to warn the reader that, in order to appreciate this approach, a change in outlook is required, i.e. it is necessary to go beyond conventional economic reasoning. Most importantly, one must depart from the view that there is one, and only one, motivation – namely extrinsic incentives – guiding human behaviour. Rather, it has to be acknowledged that intrinsic motivation also matters.

The approach followed here is mainly based on Constitutional Political Economy[4] and is also greatly influenced by Psychological Economics or Behavioural Economics.[5] The results of our alternative approach[6] suggest a very different organisation of the capitalist firm from that which traditional agency theory argues. More generally, it argues for a broader understanding of human behaviour and motivation in organisa-

4 See Buchanan and Tullock (1962), Frey (1983), Mueller (1995), Cooter (2000), Frey and Kirchgässner (2002).

5 See e.g. Kahneman, Slovic and Tversky (1982), Simon (1982), Dawes (1988), Lane (1991), Thaler (1992), Rabin (1998), Fehr and Schmidt (1999), Mullainathan and Thaler (2000), Fehr and List (2002), Frey and Stutzer (2001/2, 2002).

6 I thus seek to follow Gibbons' (1998: 130) evaluation: '...I think that the best economics on this subject (incentives in organisations, BSF) ... will exhibit stronger connections both to the broader literature on organizational economics and to other disciplines that study organizations'.

tions. The approach does not contradict classical agency theory, but rather introduces new, forgotten or neglected aspects. As a consequence, however, the ideas on organisational design differ substantially from much of what is suggested by conventional economic theory.

Corporate governance is discussed from the point of view of agency theory in section II. The following section analyses the multiple ways in which the power of actors in the public sector is restricted. Section IV argues that extrinsic incentives can be created by outside recognition and not only by monetary rewards. Section V shows how goal-oriented motivation is supported in the public sector. The last section offers conclusions. The paper, of course, does *not* argue that public governance produces ideal results – far from it. It has already been stressed that *democratic politics* and *public administration* are subject to many inefficiencies and scandals, and that distortions due to rent seeking activities are prevalent. But this does not exclude that *some* institutions of public governance may be useful for corporate governance.

II. CORPORATE GOVERNANCE AS AGENCY THEORY

Modern scholars think of corporate governance in terms of agency theory. This approach takes the firm to be a web of voluntary contracts. The major task is to find the most efficient way to align the interests of the managers as the agents to the interests of the stockholders as the principals (Jensen and Meckling, 1976). The market for corporate control is taken to work well, so that this system is self-regulating. There is no reason to assume 'contractual failure'; the collective action problems faced by (dispersed) shareholders are overcome by various processes, the most important being unfriendly stock-market takeovers.

Agency theory has sparked a huge literature, which has very ably and extensively been surveyed by e.g. Becht et al. (2002), Prendergast (1999) and Gibbons (1998). While agency theory is not a unified whole, and different opinions do exist, as in any other vigorous discipline, I take these surveys to adequately represent the state of research.

The general adoption of agency theory as the essence of corporate governance is in line with the development of the American economy which, since 1995, has grown significantly more quickly than the European and the Japanese economies. It may also be seen to correspond to the stock market boom of the 1990s and, more generally, to the adoption of the American way of life.

Agency theory has not only dominated the academic discipline, but has been accompanied by applications of its major message in business practice. Agency theory's emphasis that managers' interests must be aligned with those of stockholders has arguably been responsible for the effort to introduce performance incentive plans, in particular pay-for-performance. The idea has even spread to areas outside the market: society should be run as if it were a firm. 'New Public Management' urges nonprofit organisations and public administrations and, of course, profit-oriented firms, to adopt pay-for-performance programmes.

But there has recently been a sudden *sobering up*. The stock market has crashed, the greatest losses being experienced by the new market stocks (NASDAQ and the New Market Index). More importantly for agency theory, the corporate sector has been plagued by huge scandals relating to excessive manager compensation and fraudulent bookkeeping.[7] Performance pay, linking salaries to stock options, has led to an explosion of compensation due to the stock market boom. This trend has, in many cases, simply continued, even under changed economic conditions. Management compensation has often increased even further, though share prices have plummeted. This suggests that, in actual fact, the compensation of managers has little to do with performance. Rather, the reason for the steady increase in compensation is due to the fact that managers are able to exert considerable control over the money they get. Most importantly, they can do so by producing short-term increases in share prices, or by re-pricing their stock options. Some managers even resorted to unlawfully misrepresenting their firms' accounts in order to increase their private incomes.[8] After the event, it is possible to state that agency theory has obviously neglected the possibility of managers distorting their own standards of performance: '... much of agency theory ... unrealistically assumes that earnings and stock prices cannot be manipulated. That is a major weakness of the theory ...' (Becht et al., 2002: 47).[9]

These weaknesses and failures of both agency theory and actual practice suggest that it might be useful to approach the issue from a *new perspective*, namely the way democratic government and public administration are organised.

III. RESTRICTIONS ON POWER[10]

'Disciplining agents' is a central task of democratic government. The same goal is shared by corporate governance with respect to 'disciplining management' (Becht et al., 2002: 21-22). In the case of public governance, not only the government politicians, but also the members of parliament and administration, must be constrained from misusing their power. The major reason for the accumulation of uncontrolled discretion in both areas of governance is the strongly asymmetric state of information of the persons occupying leading positions. This accumulation of power threatens the interests of citizens, as well as of shareholders, and leads to authoritarian, or even dictatorial, forms of governance.

---

7 Corporate Scandals were e.g. discussed at an Academy of Management special presidential panel entitled 'The Crisis in Corporate Confidence', see Bartunek (2002), Kochan (2002), Gioia (2002), Child (2002), Adler (2002).

8 See e.g. Benz and Stutzer (2003), Müller (2003) and, more generally, Lutter (2001).

9 Other authors, not surprisingly among them major contributors to agency theory, tend to defend the existing corporate governance system. But most of them admit major weaknesses in the approach. An example is Holmstrom and Kaplan (2003: 2) stating that: '... while parts of the U.S. corporate governance system failed under the exceptional strain of the 1990's, the overall system, which includes oversight by the public and the government, reacted quickly to address the problems'. It should, in particular, be noted that the idea of a self-regulating corporate system, based on competitive markets, is not seen to suffice.

10 This section is based on joint work with Reiner Eichenberger.

For centuries, democracies have developed various efficient institutions to restrict the accumulation of power. Three are most important:

1. Division of Power

Democratic states distribute the right to act among the three classical decision-making bodies: the executive, legislative and jurisdictive branches. The constitutions actively promote the principle of checks and balances. It does not prevent one branch from dominating for some time, but it ensures that the other branches can reassert themselves in due time. This principle is clearly visible in the American constitution.

A close analogy has often been seen between private corporations and the public sector: the CEO corresponds to the head of government; the shareholder meeting to parliament.[11] A more appropriate analogy would be to look at the shareholder meeting as a town council meeting, in which the citizens themselves convene and no representatives are needed. The company board may be seen to correspond to the members of the cabinet. In corporate governance, the division of power between the top agents (CEOs) and the principles (shareholders) is much less strict than in democratic public governance. It is often the case that, in many countries (for instance in the USA, France and Switzerland), the CEO of the firm is at the same time the president of the board and therewith of the shareholder meeting. This has arguably often led to catastrophic consequences. There are many cases of CEOs, either with particularly strong personalities, or who have been in office a long time, who then started to dominate their firms in an almost dictatorial way. Absolute power also corrupts in the corporate sector.

There is another important division of power in public governance. There is an independent institution controlling the executives: the court of accounts, Rechnungshof or Rechnungsführungskommissionen. Unfortunately, in many countries, their competencies are quite restricted. In Germany, for instance, the Rechnungshöfe may only inform the parliament and the public about the way the executive performs his or her task, but may not interfere. The courts of accounts derive their independence from being part of the jurisdictive branch, while the Rechnungsprüfungskommissionen in Switzerland derive their independence from being directly elected by the citizens.[12] The corporate sector often does not clearly separate the executive and external auditing functions. In most cases, the CEO determines the auditing firm, which is supposed to control him or her. At the same time, the auditing firms are paid for advising jobs for the CEO and general management. As a result of the huge scandals produced by this system, there are now government-imposed rules in many countries, more clearly separating the executive from the auditing branch. This is an area where corporate governance learned directly from public governance – but only after having incurred huge costs.

11 This analogy stood indeed at the beginning of the Corporate Governance literature (see Mead 1922, for a survey Becht et al., 2002: 6-10), but has largely been forgotten.

12 See more fully Schelker and Eichenberger (2003), who empirically show that directly elected Rechnungsprüfungskommissionen induce governments to misuse their power less, and to act more strongly in the citizens' interests.

2. *Rules*

Democratic constitutions constrain their agents by extensive rules of law. Suffice it to mention three:

a) *Restricted terms of office*
   The members of parliament and directly elected presidents are (normally) elected for four years. At the end of this period, their term in office ends *automatically*; no further decision is needed.
b) *Re-election restrictions*
   Many constitutions know the provision that a president may only be re-elected for one additional term. This is a very strong constraint; it can safely be assumed that many, if not most, presidents would have been re-elected for more terms.
c) *Rotation of positions*
   Some parties (again the German Green party is an example) instituted an automatic change in positions between those inside and those outside parliament and government. The Japanese MITI, a regulatory authority, automatically rotates its leading members in order to make corruption more difficult.

These rules are not only able to effectively restrict the power of public agents. They also open positions to newcomers, and therefore to fresh ideas.

Corporate governance also knows either self-imposed or government-imposed rules, but they are much less far reaching than those used in public governance, mainly because the market is supposed to control firms. These rules may, to some extent, be used by 'shareholder suits' (see Becht et al., 2002: 92-93). The term of office of all agents in private corporations is limited. But this is very often just a formal provision, of no real consequence. Automatic reelection is the rule, as long as the agents work well and, if they don't, dismissal within terms is undertaken.[13] Indeed, today, CEOs are in office less than four years on average. An effective term limit of four years, with the possibility of one re-election, would therefore not constrain corporate life[14] much.

3. *Institutionalised Competition*

Democratic governance can be understood to be the competition by parties for votes (Schumpeter, 1942; Downs, 1957). This competition is closely regulated. There are three main features:

a) *Voting rights.*
   Only citizens may participate, and each citizen has one vote.[15] Elections are individually oriented, as the voters can determine which persons will sit in parliament. In some cases (especially at the local and provincial level), the voters are also able

13 For a discussion of CEO succession, see Hambrick and Fukutomi (1991), Ocasio (1999), Westphal and Zajac 1995).

14 They are indeed enforced in some well-known firms, such as McKinsey. Mandatory rotation of external auditors is discussed in Arrunada and Paz-Ares (1997) and Summer (1998).

15 But the concept may be generalised, see Frey (2003).

to choose the persons in the executive branch. In contrast, pay-for-performance is more collectively oriented, because the performance measures (company profits, share prices) are not the product of a particular individual.

b) *Competitive process.*
It must be open and the citizens must have a choice between several different options, i.e. parties and persons.

c) *Voting rules.*
Various mechanisms for aggregating votes are used, the best known being 'first past the post', leading to strong majorities, but tending to exclude minorities (the UK system) and the proportional system (used in most European countries). The latter sometimes guarantees seats for minorities, or excludes parties with less than a certain percentage of votes (e.g. 5% in Germany).

There are similar vote and representation processes in stock companies. There is also a collective action problem with dispersed share ownership (see Becht et al., 2002: 6-7, 20-21). The board is elected by the shareholder meeting, and the top management and the external auditing firm are elected by the board. But there is a very big difference to the election process, as we know it, in democratic countries: in most corporations, the voting processes are opaque (to say the least) and there is generally *no choice between various alternatives*. As a matter of course, the shareholders are offered *one* person to be elected for one position on the board, and only *one* external auditing firm can be chosen.

Corporate governance could learn from public governance with respect to the following aspects:

a) Voting rights

In principle, each share has one vote. However, this principle is often violated by privileged shares or by nonvoting shares. Such devices are often used to prevent unfriendly takeovers. Recently, much emphasis was placed on *'independent' directors* (members of the board), who are supposed to protect the interests of minority shareholders from actions by both the CEO and blockholders. Empirical research has, however, found that independent directors have little influence on firm performance (Becht et al., 2002: 42-3). An important reason may be that they have less information at their disposal than 'inside' directors.

Voting rights may also be given to *nonshareholder groups*, giving rise to a considerable theoretical literature on multiconstituency boards (Becht et al., 2002: 48-57). One group which may be represented are the *employees*. This could be seen as a formal recognition of 'corporate citizenship' or, more broadly, of 'organisational citizenship'. Agency theory (e.g. Roberts and Van den Stehen, 2000) has recognised that such employee participation may be efficient in firms with much job specific human capital. It has also recognised (e.g. Holmström, 1999) that such codetermination may be an effective way of reducing costly strikes. As seems to be the rule, the many contributions to the topic stemming from German-speaking countries are totally neglected in surveys on agency theory.[16]

Another group, which may be given a formal voting right for corporate decisions, are the creditors and customers. Even more broadly, environmentalists and other action groups may be accorded participation rights in firms, thus formally integrating 'stakeholders'.

So far, corporate governance theory has not provided any systematic analysis of these issues. 'What is worse, this literature mostly considers highly stylised models of multiple constituencies' and there is, at best, sketchy empirical evidence on the role of boards (Becht et al., 2002: 48, 97). This is no doubt an area where closer collaboration between agency theorists and political economists would be fruitful. The various interests have some analogy to political parties and distinguish themselves, for instance, with respect to the time frame or the role attributed to profits.

b) Competitive process

Democracy is not well developed within corporations. The essential element of competition, namely that the voters can *choose between relevant alternatives,* hardly exists. For instance, for a truly democratic process, the persons with voting rights in the firm must have the option of choosing between several competing firms offering external auditing. Similarly, they must be able to choose between various persons willing to serve as directors. In both cases, the competitors must be willing to clearly state their interests and programme, and must be able to convince the corporate voters that they are capable of fulfilling the required tasks. It is difficult to see why such a competitive process exists in the political sphere, but is often taken to be impossible within corporations.

A further step can be imagined. Instead of the board members being faced with a choice of managers chosen by the CEO, and possibly a small group of directors aided by head hunters, the selection could be made in an open competition. Anybody who is reasonably competent as a manager should be able to participate. Even more extreme, the whole management group may be opened to competition by individuals or firms prepared to fill certain positions (for instance the CEO). Already now, there are firms competing to manage a particular corporation for a fixed number of years and for a specific price. In Germany, for instance, firms are hired from outside to manage hospitals and other organisations in the health sector. The electoral competition then serves to select the most efficient group (it may be the former managers), i.e. the group the corporate voters believe to be the most capable relative to the compensation demanded. In difficult situations, the price asked may be high but, unlike today, such compensation truly reflects expected performance rather than rent sharing.

---

16 At least in Becht et al. 2002, Prendergast 1999, Gibbons 1998. It should be noted that formal codetermination is not only a German phenomenon, but is also important in Austria, the Netherlands, Denmark, Sweden and Finland. A recent empirical analysis of codetermination in German firms is, for example, Schank et al. (2002).

c) New Voting rules

Public governance tends to be rather conservative. It is difficult to extend the area of democratic participation[17] or to introduce new voting rules. The major reason is that the established politicians, parties and interest groups fear to lose from such changes. The corporate sector is proud of being more dynamic. It should therefore be willing to consider new voting mechanisms. Examples are voting by veto (Mueller, 1978) or storable votes (Casella, 2002), but there are many others. Firms can choose the respective innovative voting rules where they are most appropriate, while sticking to simple majority, qualified majority or unanimity elsewhere.

Evaluation

The many different institutional devices developed in democratic public governance to restrict the power of managers can serve as a pool of ideas to improve corporate governance. The latter has relied too much on the notion that competitive market forces are quite capable of effectively restricting executives. This belief is difficult to maintain in the face of the huge management scandals recently observed. Many corporate actors, and certainly public decision-makers, have grasped the lesson to be learned. They have indeed already co-opted some of the mechanisms of public governance, including the division of power between management and external auditing firms, and also between the CEO and the president of the board.

IV. EXTRINSIC INCENTIVES BY OUTSIDE RECOGNITION

Public governance also relies on externally mediated incentives to align agents' behaviour with the goals of the organisation. Unlike traditional agency theory, it is not committed to only one motivational force. While agency theory favours monetary incentives, because they are the most fungible, and therefore seem to be the most efficient, public governance uses *various different kinds* of extrinsic motivations.

Three types of institutions are used in public governance as extrinsic motivators:

1. Titles

People like titles to clearly indicate their place in the hierarchy.[18] They have much added value when they are transferable to life outside of the organisation they work in, especially in their social life with family and friends, as well as with strangers. In former times, this condition was perfectly met by conferring such titles as 'Geheimrat'

17 See, for instance, the great difficulties of introducing elements of direct voter participation via initiatives and referenda. Compare Kirchgässner et al. (1999).

18 The importance of positional competition for individuals has been empirically shown by many scholars, e.g. Frank (1985).

in Germany and Austria, or 'Sir' or 'Lord' in Britain.[19] Titles are transferable if persons outside the organisation have a sense of the distinction conferred. They do not necessarily have to know exactly what they mean, but they have to be impressed.[20] Therefore they must be conferred in a restricted way.[21]

In recent years, most leading private corporations have given up conferring transferable titles. Instead, they use 'functional' titles of little or no use outside of the organisation. It is difficult to brag in social circles about the title 'group leader' when nobody has a clue whether this means that one is in charge of ten people, or ten thousand people, as both can be, and are, called 'groups'.

2. *Orders*

Public governance confers 'orders' on people extensively as an incentive device. They are often given at the end of bureaucratic careers as a tribute to the life-long devotion to one's tasks, and not for specific performance.[22] Orders are not contractible when one enters a public career, but they are given on the basis of clear rules. They are transferable to social life, as they are virtually worn outside, on the dinner jacket and even on normal suits (e.g. the French Legion d'Honneur).

Corporations know a similar institution when they choose 'The manager of the year', 'The employee of the month' or 'The dishwasher of the day'. But these 'orders' are designed to relate directly to specific performance. They are therefore understood to be solely instrumental. Moreover, they are difficult to transfer outside of the organisations (and often are considered to be rather ridiculous). Finally, they tend to be handed out in such an inflationary way that those not receiving them are demotivated.

3. *Ceremonies*

Titles and orders are almost invariably handed out in a ceremony. Public governance knows of many other occasions when agents in the public sector participate in publicly visible ceremonies. Examples are the reception of foreign dignitaries, parading the troops or coronations. They provide the agents working in the public administration, or politicians, with prestige and visibility in the public sector, which is an important extrinsic reward.

Such ceremonies are much more rare in the private sector.[23] They tend to be considered a waste of time for all the people concerned. They do not correspond to the

19 Note that banks in German speaking countries until recently used the title 'Bankdirektor' or even 'Bankbeamter', therewith adopting a title belonging to the public administration.

20 Thus, it is not important for outsiders to know whether a 'Ministerialdirektor' is more or less than a 'Ministerialdirigent', or a 'Major General' more or less than a 'Lieutenant General'.

21 Corporations do not seem to be good at that. When a considerable percentage of managers are 'vice-presidents', the title is no longer worth as much (it must be amended by adding 'senior', 'executive' etc.). A similar inflation can be observed even with the title 'Chief Executive Officer'. Today, many firms have several CEOs, for instance one for each division.

22 Exceptions are the few orders conferred on the battlefield, but they are small in number.

23 For a discussion of ceremonies in organisations, see Dandridge et al. (1980).

image of an 'efficient' manager. It therefore can happen that a new CEO takes over a firm without the employees ever having seen him or her. To some extent, corporations seek to imitate public ceremonies, but they tend to be instrumental and nontransferable outside of the firm. As a consequence, they are of limited use in bolstering motivation.

Evaluation

The extrinsic incentives[24] provided by public governance are directed to lifelong devotion to one's tasks and achievements. They represent an overall evaluation, and are of an ex post noncontractual nature. They do not relate to any specific performance, and are therefore designed not to be (directly) instrumental. The incentive structure applied by public governance skilfully combines the production of outside recognition and status with crowding-in goal oriented intrinsic motivation. It might be argued that titles and orders have lost importance. This is certainly true, but may be attributed to the fact that they have partly been abolished. It is interesting to note how many leading economic economists were, and still are, obviously delighted to have titles bestowed on them, Lord Keynes and Sir Tony (Atkinson) being just two such examples.

There are major differences between conferring titles and orders and giving money as compensation for performance:

- Conferring titles and orders are intended to honour long-term, even lifelong performance, while almost all of necessity performance pay relates to short-term achievements. As employees have to earn their living by getting paid, if this money is given in relation to performance, it must be adjusted according to short-term considerations.
- Titles and orders are mainly given in a process-oriented way, serving as a reliable feedback for performance. This feedback tends to raise intrinsic motivation (see Deci and Ryan 1985, Frey 1997). Performance pay is outcome-oriented. But outcomes are subject to many other systematic and random effects beyond the influence of the recipient. The feedback is therefore less reliable, and does not contribute to crowding-in intrinsic motivation.
- Titles and orders tend to be more absolute than monetary income which is easy and straightforward to compare. When monetary pay is explicitly given to reward performance, employees are inclined to compare the amount they get with the total profits of the firm. They easily see that their share is normally only a tiny fraction of the total profits, a comparison which decreases their dedication to their firm.

This discussion suggests that conferring titles and orders, as well as honouring employees by holding specific ceremonies, has quite different motivational implications from monetary compensation, in particular to pay-for-performance. In many cases, the incentives produced by conferring titles and orders, especially the increase in intrinsic

24 For the terms intrinsic and extrinsic, see Frey and Osterloh (2001), Osterloh et al. (2002). An application of an extrinsically oriented 'public choice' theory to bureaucratic organisations has been undertaken in business economics e.g. by Spicer (1985). However, intrinsic motivation of managers and employees is traditionally emphasised by such approaches as 'stewardship theory' (Davis et al., 1997).

motivation induced, is most valuable for an organisation and should therefore be part of management.

V. SUPPORTING GOAL-ORIENTED INTRINSIC MOTIVATION

Traditional agency theory builds primarily, or exclusively,[25] on extrinsic motivation. In contrast, *intrinsic motivation* is attributed a substantial role in *public governance*. A substantial number of institutions have been designed in the public sector, serving to shape agents' intrinsic motivation so as to produce the desired outcomes. The fact that such institutions exist is an important, but often neglected, aspect of politics and public administration.

Four institutions serve this purpose, the first one relating to politicians, the second one relating to both politicians and public officials, and the two remaining ones relating to public administrators.

1. Popular Participation Rights

Democracies are defined by giving citizens clearly determined participation rights. In representative democracies, the citizens can determine the parties, and often the persons, represented in parliament. In direct democracies, citizens can also determine substantive issues via initiatives and referenda. The citizens' participation rights have important consequences for the behaviour of the politicians:

a) Identification

The more extensive the right to participate politically is, the stronger the extent of interaction between the citizens and the (professional) politicians. The constant tendency for the leaders to establish a 'classe politique' is reduced.[26] Codetermination in firms also raises identification, not least because the managers are induced to interact more intensively with their employees than they otherwise would.

25 Becht et al.'s survey (2002) and Gibbons (1998) virtually disregard intrinsic motivation, not to mention the interaction between extrinsic and intrinsic motivation. Prendergast (1999) devotes half a page (on p.18) of his 56 page survey to intrinsic motivation, but dismisses it with the remark: '... there is little empirical evidence'. He seems to overlook the fact that the situation is not better for agency theory, according to his own evaluation: 'All in all, the available empirical evidence on contracts does not yet provide a ringing endorsement of the theory' (p. 56). Moreover, today there is substantial empirical evidence on the relationship between intrinsic and extrinsic motivation, see the survey by Frey and Jegen (2001).

26 See e.g. Frey (1997), Bohnet and Frey (1999), Eichenberger and Oberholzer (1998).

b) Feedback

The reaction of the voters to the actions of the politicians constitutes an essential part of the democratic political process. In referendum democracies, the politicians get a direct feedback on how the voters evaluate specific policies. This feedback is of an informative, rather than a controlling nature, and therefore[27] tends to raise the intrinsic motivation of politicians to pursue policies in the interests of the citizens.

2. Fixed Position and Income

The career path and the income corresponding to the various positions are governed by formal rules. Advancement is regular and mostly by seniority. Promotion does not depend on any *specific* output performance. The job is guaranteed for life; the members of the public administration cannot be dismissed by their superiors. Public employees are therefore able to make suggestions for improvement, and to criticise the course of events, even if their superiors do not necessarily agree.[28]

Tournament theory has identified such bureaucratic rules as an optimal response to the dysfunctional behaviour, due to evaluation procedures occurring in multitasking situations (Holmström and Milgrom 1991, 1994). Agency theory responds by suggesting 'subjective performance evaluation' (see Prendergast 1999: 29-33, Gibbons 1998: 120-123). But such subjective evaluation in firms shifts the discretion over employees' pay to the superior. This dependence of employees on the goodwill of their superior weakens or even totally suppresses their incentives to monitor and criticise the behaviour of their superiors. Indeed, whistle-blowing has proved to be rarely used under a regime in which the superiors are able to determine the wages of the persons working for them. But such monitoring of the superiors by their inferiors plays an important function, because the inferiors are normally well informed about the tricks played and wrongdoings committed by the management. This problem is mitigated in public administration. While there is a well-defined bureaucratic hierarchy, the superiors have to follow well-defined rules and have, in principle, no discretion concerning the pay of their inferiors. This advantage is indeed seen by Prendergast (1999: 37), when he states with respect to bureaucracy: '... rules are used to allocate resources rather than allowing individuals discretion over resource allocation'.

An administrative career according to seniority and with fixed compensation allows its members to concentrate on *work content.* Fixed incomes serve as 'redistribution constraints' (Hansmann 1996, Osterloh and Rota 2003). They free employees from fighting over earnings and so contribute to the organisations' common good. In contrast, the system characterised by pay-for-performance strongly induces employees to devote time and effort to influencing their variable income. The employees rationally engage

27 Deci and Ryan 1985, Thomas and Velthouse 1990.

28 This is, of course, the reason for life tenure of professors, who are given a position independent of government.

in rent seeking activities in order to manipulate the performance standards and therewith their income. While they *can* seek higher income by increased effort, it is often easier and less demanding to influence the measuring rod, even by distorting and falsifying the figures. Agency theory has, to a large extent, failed to see this rational reaction by employees subjected to pay-for-performance (Becht et al., 2002: 47). Corporate governance also seems to have neglected a more aggregate response to performance wages, again diverting the efforts of employees in unproductive directions. Pay-for-performance systems concentrate the attention, especially of managers, on compensation rather than on effort. It aligns the interests of all employees to one specific goal, namely to jack up profits, or share prices, as much as possible. No manager or other employee has any incentive to inform the shareholders or the public whether these goals are reached by illegitimate, or even illegal means, because they all benefit from the system. The result of this arrangement is an explosion of managers' compensation, which is consistent with what we have observed ever since pay-for-performance was widely introduced.

The administrative approach to the allocation of career and pay avoids the fundamental problems connected with pay-for-performance. It suffices to list them (see also Osterloh and Frey 2000): (1) Performance is rarely easily defined, but is subject to interpretation and influence;[29] (2) In many cases, only some aspects of performance are measurable, leading to the multitasking problem; (3) The employees must constantly be monitored in order to be able to pay them, leading to a perception of being controlled. This tends to crowd out any existing intrinsic motivation; and (4) The work content as such is no longer of interest to employees, but is regarded as instrumental to pay. This induces distributional fights and negative sum games.

3. *Extensive Selection Process of Agents*

To become a member of the classical public bureaucracy is a *formalised and arduous process*. It takes many years. Before a person can become a full member (ein Beamter), he or she has to pass through many, clearly regulated stages, similar to being accepted into a religious order. The prospective members must have passed exams specifically

29 The few existing empirical studies analysing the effect of pay on performance, Lazear (1999, 2000) and Paarsch and Shearer (1999), relate to very simple jobs, like windshield fitting and tree planting. The same holds for the recent study by Fehr and Goette (2002), relating to bicycle couriers. But Prendergast (1999: 57) rightly criticises '... the excessive focus on the contracts of workers for whose output measures are easily available ... to put it simply, most people don't work in jobs like these'. An exception is Lavy (2002), in his analysis of performance wages for schoolteachers.
Obviously, because it is generally taken to be impossible to measure the performance of political executives in a reasonable way, the proponents of pay-for-performance do not advocate that the president of the United States is paid according to the increase in real GNP, or the rise in the Dow Jones Share Index produced during his administration, but it has recently been proposed by a proponent of the Deutsche Gewerkschaftsbund in Saxony, see Leipziger Volkszeitung (2003). But why is it taken to make sense for CEOs, who often command larger 'realms' than nations? This is only possible if the share value is taken to be the only criterion. But such a measure is hotly debated by all persons taking a broader view of the role of corporations in society.

designed as initiations into this select profession. In many cases, these exams have little or nothing to do with the task to be later performed as a member of public administration. The famous Chinese bureaucracy required people to be able to prepare poems (see Tullock, 1964); in Germany a public official had to have, and still to some extent has to have, an education in law, while France puts more emphasis on formal (mathematical) education in the *Grandes Ecoles*.

The long and arduous process promotes a specific *self-selection* for anyone wanting to become a member of public bureaucracy. Because of the 'deferred compensation', persons with very highly developed intrinsic motivation to work in the public sector are attracted, while short-term materialists have no incentive to engage themselves.[30] The difficult and long-drawn out process strongly *socialises* the persons to the specific culture of the public sector. The goals of the organisation are at least partly internalised. The members develop a distinct and often marked sense of loyalty.[31] The process thus tends to *crowd in* intrinsic motivation.

The long formal selection process, moreover, provides the successful applicants with self-confidence in their own abilities.[32] This sense of competence is not so much based on outcome related performance (it already exists before the applicants take up their position), but on having got through the process. This feeling sometimes results in arrogance, a trait often attributed, for instance, to top-level French public officials coming from ENA (*Ecole Nacionale d'Administration)*, or *Enarques*.

The democratic process also leads to a particular selection of traits in politicians. Voters have a strong tendency to evaluate contenders for political office in terms of their presumed characters (see Brennan and Hamlin 2000, Cooter 2003). Decentralised democracies allow voters to better select the characters of politicians they want, because there are a large number of elections in which the contenders have to present themselves to the citizens. The same holds for elections of specific persons, rather than closed lists prepared by the parties. Firms should pay more attention to selecting the appropriate characters for the tasks at hand, rather than to mainly or exclusively relying on external incentive systems (Cooter and Eisenberg, 2000-2001).

4. *Autonomy Within Rules*

Bureaucratic rules provide directions, but *within* them public employees enjoy a clearly defined measure of autonomy. They have room to evaluate and to make decisions based on what they see to be correct and appropriate for the long-term goals of the organisation. As long as public employees adhere to the rules, they ideally are protected from

30 Agency theory has noted the important function of deferred compensation for the selection of desired workers (already Salop and Salop 1976). But, in the empirical study by Lazear (1999, 2000), the opposite effect is studied: the offer of introducing incentive wages to workers induces persons with above-average productivity in fitting windshields to join the firm, i.e. the more extrinsically oriented materialists tend to newly enter the firm.

31 The third part of Hirschman's *Exit, Voice and Loyalty* (1970) reappears.

32 Social psychology emphasises competence as an important innate need. See Deci and Ryan's (1985) self-determination theory.

intervention by their superiors, as illustrated by the story of Frederick the Great, who was unable to make one of his low-level bureaucrats obey an order which he judged to violate the law. Such autonomy contributes to intrinsic motivation as a deep innate need in individuals (see Deci and Ryan, 1985, 1987).

Employees in capitalist firms do not have such autonomy, as there are no such well-defined rules. As long as the superiors do not violate the law, they can to a large extent order an employee to do anything they like. The only option open to a dissenting employee is to leave the firm, an action which often involves substantial costs. The bookkeeping scandals have made clear that, in practice, CEOs are even able to order their employees to commit illegal actions (such as fiddling the accounts). The few dissenting employees who took the decision not to obey the orders, preferring to leave the firm, had very high costs to pay.

Evaluation

Public governance uses a completely different system to align agents' behaviour to principals' goals. It relies on self-selection and socialisation to bring about an *internalised intrinsic behaviour* of agents consistent with the *goals of the public organisation.* Traditional agency theory seeks to produce this alignment exclusively by setting the right extrinsic (most importantly monetary) incentives.[33] Bureaucratic rules may appear inefficient ex post but are not necessarily *ex ante.* This point has been noted in accepted agency theory, but is only related to an effort to avoid inefficient rent seeking activities.[34] The approach on which public governance is based places more emphasis on guiding agents' behaviour by intrinsic motivation, which has the considerable advantage that the problems arising by having to appropriately and fully measure performance standards (among which multitasking has received most attention in agency theory) are avoided.

VI. CONCLUSIONS

Counterarguments against the very idea of transferring elements from public governance to private governance, and even more against specific institutions, are quite possible. It should also have become clear that the public institutions already discussed have been presented in a favourable light. This has been done on purpose, because only then is it possible to see the *potential* of the mechanisms for firms.

33 A notable exception is the paper by Holmström and Milgrom (1994: 989): 'The use of low-powered incentives within the firm, although sometimes lamented as one of the major disadvantages of internal organization, is also an important vehicle for inspiring cooperation and coordination'. But the two authors do not take the next step of fully considering the alternative 'power' of intrinsic motivation and crowding-in.

34 '... while rules harm ex post efficient allocations, they improve the incentives for agents to allocate their activities correctly, by avoiding influence activities' (Prendergast 1999: 38; more extensively Milgrom and Roberts, 1988; Tirole, 1992).

The objective of this paper has *not* been to discuss in any depth the problems existing when institutions of public sector are introduced into the private sector. Rather, the goal has been to introduce some unconventional ideas. Nor does this paper suggest that the ideas derived from public sector *should* be applied in the private sector. There are situations in which they are unnecessary. This is, for instance, the case in a perfectly competitive market in which managers have no discretionary room whatsoever; the goods, managers and financial markets align their incentives perfectly with those of the shareholders. But such ideally competitive markets are certainly the exception rather than the rule. Practically all markets allow for substantial discretionary behaviour of the executives, sometimes going as far as illegal actions. It should not be forgotten that a large number of organisations acting on markets are not-for-profit, but take an intermediate position between shareholder wealth maximisation and pure public ownership. It is argued here that in this broad area, insights and institutional ideas derived from public governance are of substantial interest.

This paper has proposed the basic idea that *the private sector can learn from the public sector. In particular, corporate governance can learn from public governance.* Three main ideas derived from public governance and potentially useful for orporate governance are discussed:

1) *Division of power, rules* and *institutionalised competition* effectively constrain managerial power. These features have been either treated too lightly, or have been altogether neglected, by corporate governance.
2) *Extrinsic motivation* can be induced by institutions conferring titles and orders on people and holding ceremonies. Corporate governance focuses too exclusively on monetary incentives.
3) Many institutions produce *goal-oriented intrinsic motivation.* Most important are an extensive and formalised selection process, fixed position and income, and autonomy within rules. These institutions have the added advantage of producing *loyalty* to the firm. The private sector relies excessively on extrinsic incentives to align the interests of principals and agents.

REFERENCES

Adler, Paul S. (2002). Corporate Scandals: It's Time for Reflection in Business Schools. *Academy of Management Executive 16(3),* 148-149.

Arrow, Kenneth J. (1951). *Social Choice and Individual Values.* New York: Wiley.

Arrunada, B. & Paz-Ares, C. (1997). Mandatory rotation of company auditors: A critical examination. *International Review of Law and Economics 17,* 31-61.

Bartunek, Jean M. (2002). Corporate Scandals: How Should Academy of Management Members Respond? *Academy of Management Executive 16(3),* 138.

Becht, Marco, Bolton, Patrick, & Röell, Ailsa. (2002). Corporate Governance and Corporate Control. *ECGI Working Paper Series in Finance 02/2002, 30 September 2002.* Also in: George Constantinides, Milton Harris & René Stulz (Eds), Handbook of Finance, North Holland.

Benz, Matthias & Stutzer, Alois. (2003). Was erklärt die gestiegenen Managerlöhne? *Die Unternehmung 57,* 5-19.

Black, Duncan. (1958). *The Theory of Committees and Elections.* Cambridge: Cambridge University Press.

Bohnet, Iris & Frey, Bruno S. (1999). The sound of silence in prisoner's dilemma and dictator games. *Journal of Economic Behavior and Organization 38*, 42-58.

Brennan, Geoffrey & Hamlin, Alan. (2000). *Democratic Devices and Desires.* Cambridge: Cambridge University Press.

Buchanan, James M. & Tullock, Gordon. (1962). *The Calculus of Consent. Logical Foundations of Constitutional Democracy.* Ann Arbor: University of Michigan Press.

Casella, Alessandra (2002). Storable Votes. *NBER Working Paper No. 9189.*

Child, John. (2002). The International Crisis of Confidence in Corporations. *Academy of Management Executive 16(3),* 145-147.

Cooter, Robert D. (2000). *The Strategic Constitution.* Princeton: Princeton University Press.

Cooter, Robert D. (2003). Who Gets on Top in Democracy? Elections as Filters. Mimeo, School of Law, University of California at Berkeley.

Cooter, Robert D. & Eisenberg, Melvin A. (2000-2001). Fairness, Character, and Efficiency in Firms. *University of Pennsylvania Law Review 149*, 1717-1733.

Dandridge, Thomas C., Mitroff, Ian, & Joyce, William F. (1980). Organizational Symbolism: A Topic to Expand Organizational Analysis. *Academy of Management Review 5(1),* 77-82.

Davis, James H., Schoorman, F. David, & Donaldson, Lex. (1997). Toward a Stewardship Theory of Management. *Academy of Management Review 22 (1),* 20-48.

Dawes, Robyn M. (1988). *Rational Choice in an Uncertain World.* San Diego and New York: Harcourt, Brace, Yovanovich.

Deci, Edward L., & Ryan, Richard M. (1985). *Intrinsic Motivation and Self-Determination in Human Behavior.* New York: Plenum Press.

Deci, Edward L. & Ryan, Richard M. (1987). The Empirical Exploration of Intrinsic Motivational Processes. *Advances in Experimental Social Psychology 10,* 39-80.

Downs, Anthony. (1957). *An Economic Theory of Democracy.* New York: Harper and Row.

Eichenberger, Reiner & Oberholzer, Felix. (1998). The Role of Fairness in Democratic Economic Politics. *Public Choice* 94 *(1-2),* 191-210.

Eggertson, Thrainn. (1990). *Economic Behavior and Institutions: Principles of Neoinstitutional Economics.* Cambridge: Cambridge University Press.

Faulhaber, Gerald F. & Baumol, William J. (1988). Economists as Innovators: Practical Products of Theoretical Research. *Journal of Economic Literature 26,* 577-600.

Fehr, Ernst & Goette, Lorenz. (2002). Do Workers Work More if Wages Are High? Evidence from a Randomized Field Experiment. *Working Paper No. 125, Institute for Empirical Research in Economics,* University of Zurich.

Fehr, Ernst & List, John A. (2002). The Hidden Costs and Returns of Incentives – Trust and Trustworthiness among CEOs. *Working Paper No. 134, Institute for Empirical Research in Economics*, University of Zurich.

Fehr, Ernst & Schmidt, Klaus. (1999). A Theory of Fairness, Competition and Cooperation. *Quarterly Journal of Economics 114*, 817-868.

Frank, R.H. (1985). *Choosing the Right Pond.* Oxford University Press.

Frey, Bruno S. (1978). *Modern Political Economy.* Oxford: Blackwell.

Frey, Bruno S. (1983). *Democratic Economic Policy.* Oxford: Blackwell.

Frey, Bruno S. (1997). *Not Just for The Money. An Economic Theory of Personal Motivation.* Cheltenham, UK and Brookfield, USA: Edward Elgar.

Frey, Bruno S. (2003). Flexible Citizenship for a Global Society. *Politics, Philosophy & Economics* 2, *1,* 93-114.

Frey, Bruno S. & Eichenberger, Reiner. (1999). *The New Democratic Federalism for Europe. Functional, Overlapping, Competing Jurisdictions.* Cheltenham UK and Northampton, MA, USA: Elgar.

Frey, Bruno S. & Jegen, Reto. (2001). Motivation Crowding Theory: A Survey of Empirical Evidence. *Journal of Economic Surveys* 5, *15*, 589-611.

Frey, Bruno S. & Kirchgässner, Gebhard. (2002). *Theorie demokratischer Wirtschaftspolitik.* Munich: Vahlen.

Frey, Bruno S. & Osterloh, Margit. (Eds.). (2001). *Successful Management by Motivation. Balancing Intrinsic and Extrinsic Incentives*. Berlin, Heidelberg: Springer-Verlag.

Frey, Bruno S. & Stutzer, Alois. (2001/2). Economics and Psychology: from Imperialistic to Inspired Economics. *Philosophie économique, No. 4.*

Frey, Bruno S. & Stutzer, Alois. (2002). *Happiness and Economics*. Princeton: Princeton University Press.

Gibbons, Robert. (1998). Incentives in Organizations. *Journal of Economic Perspectives 12, 4 (Fall)*, 115-132.

Gioia, Dennis A. (2002). Business Education's Role in the Crisis of Corporate Confidence. *Academy of Management Executive 16(3)*, 142-144.

Hambrick, Donald C. & Fukutomi, Gregory D.S. (1991). The Seasons of a CEO's Tenure. *Academy of Management Review 16(4)*, 719-743.

Hansmann, Henry. (1996). *The ownership of enterprise*. Cambridge: Belknap Press of Harvard University Press.

Hirschman, Albert O. (1970). *Exit, Voice and Loyalty*. Cambridge: Harvard University Press.

Holmström, Bengt. (1999). Managerial Incentive Problems – A Dynamic Perspective. *Review of Economic Studies 66, 1*, 169-182.

Holmström, Bengt & Kaplan, Steven N. (2003). The State of U.S. Corporate Governance: What's Right and What's Wrong? *NBER Working Paper Series 9613*.

Holmström, Bengt & Milgrom, Paul. (1991). Multitask Principal Agent Analyses: Incentive Contracts, Asset Ownership and Job Design. *Journal of Law and Economic Organization 7*, 24-52.

Holmström, Bengt & Milgrom, Paul. (1994). The Firm as an Incentive System. *American Economic Review* 84, 972-91.

Jensen, Michael C. & Meckling, William H. (1976). Theory of the Firm: Managerial Behavior, Agency Costs and Ownership Structure. *Journal of Financial Economics 3*, 305-60.

Kahneman, Daniel, Slovic, Paul, & Tversky, Amos (Eds). (1982). *Judgement under Uncertainty: Heuristics and Biases*. Cambridge: Cambridge University Press.

Kirchgässner, Gebhard, Feld, Lars & Savioz, Marcel R. (1999). *Die direkte Demokratie: Modern, erfolgreich, entwicklungs- und exportfähig*. Basel et al.: Helbing and Lichtenhahn/ Vahlen/ Beck.

Kochan, Thomas A. (2002). Addressing the Crisis in Confidence in Corporations: Root Causes, Victims, and Strategies for Reform. *Academy of Management Executive 16(3)*, 139-141.

Lane, Robert E. (1991). *The Market Experience*. Cambridge: Cambridge University Press.

Lavy, Victor. (2002). Paying for Performance: The Effect of Teachers 'Financial Incentives on Students' Scholastic Outcomes. Mimeo, Hebrew University Jerusalem.

Lazear, Edward. (1999). Personnel Economics: Past Lessons and Future Directions. *Journal of Labor Economics 17*, 199-236.

Lazear, Edward. (2000). Performance Pay and Productivity. *American Economic Review 90(5)*, 1346-61.

Leipziger Volkszeitung. (2003). DGB will Leistungsprämien für Politiker. 18. März 2003.

Lutter, Marcus (Ed.). (2001). *Der Wirtschaftsprüfer als Element des Corporate Finance*. Düsseldorf: Idw-Verlag.

Mead, E. S. (1922). *Corporation Finance*. New York and London: Appleton.

Milgrom, Paul & Roberts, John (1988). An Economic Approach to Influence in Organizations. *American Journal of Sociology 94*, 154-79.

Mueller, Dennis C. (1978). Voting by Veto. *Journal of Public Economics 10*, 57-75.

Mueller, Dennis C. (1995). *Constitutional Economics*. Cambridge: Cambridge University Press.

Mueller, Dennis C. (Ed.) (1997). *Perspectives on Public Choice*. Cambridge: Cambridge University Press.

Mueller, Dennis (2003). *Public Choice III*. Cambridge: Cambridge University Press.

Müller, Christian. (2003). Bilanzskandale. Eine institutionenökonomische Analyse. *Perspektiven der Wirtschaftspolitik* 4, forthcoming.

Mullainathan, S., & Thaler, R. (2000). Behavioral Economics. Mimeo No. 00-27, MIT, Cambridge.

Niskanen, William A. (1971). *Bureaucracy and Representative Government*. Chicago and New York: Aldine Atherton.

Ocasio, William. (1999). Institutionalized Action and Corporate Governance: The Reliance on Rules of CEO Succession. *Administrative Science Quarterly 44(2)*, 384-417.

Osterloh, Margit & Frey, Bruno S. (2000). Motivation, Knowledge Transfer, and Organizational Form. *Organization Science 11*, 538-50.

Osterloh, Margit & Frey, Bruno S. (2003). Corporate Governance for Crooks? The Case for Corporate Virtue. In: Anna Grandori (Ed). *Corporate Governance and Firm Organization*. Oxford: Oxford University Press (forthcoming).

Osterloh, Margit, Frost, Jetta, & Frey, Bruno S. (2002). The Dynamics of Motivation in New Organizational Forms. *International Journal of the Economics of Business 9*, 61-77.

Osterloh, Margit & Rota, Sandra. (2003). Open Source Software: New Rules for the Market Economy? *Working Paper, Institute for Empirical Economic Research*, University of Zurich.
Paarsch, Harry & Shearer, Bruce (1999). The Response of Worker Effort to Piece Rates: Evidence from the British Columbia Tree-Planting Industry. *Journal of Human Resources* 34 (4), 643-667.
Persson, Torsten & Tabellini, Guido. (2002). *Political Economy: Explaining Economic Policy* Cambridge: MIT Press.
Prendergast, Canice. (1999). The Provision of Incentives in Firms. *Journal of Economic Literature 37 (March)*, 7-63.
Rabin, M. (1998). Psychology and Economics. *Journal of Economic Literature 36 (1),* 11-46.
Roberts, John & Stehen, Eric Van den. (2000). Shareholder Interests, Human Capital Investments and Corporate Governance. Mimeo, Stanford University Graduate School of Business.
Salop, Steven & Salop, Joanne. (1976). Self-Selection and Turnover in the Labor Market. *Quarterly Journal of Economics 90, 4*, 619-27.
Schank, Thorsten, Schnabel, Claus, & Wagner, Joachim. (2002). Works Councils – Sand or Grease in the Operation of German Firms? *IZA Discussion Paper No. 648.*
Schelker, Mark & Eichenberger, Reiner. (2003). Starke Rechnungsprüfungskommissionen: Wichtiger als direkte Demokratie und Föderalismus? Ein erster Blick auf die Daten. Mimeo, University of Fribourg.
Schumpeter, Joseph A. (1942). *Capitalism, Socialism and Democracy*. 1st edn., New York: Harper.
Sen, Amartya K. (1970). *Collective Choice and Social Welfare*. San Francisco: Holden-Day.
Simon, Herbert A. (1982). *Models of Bounded Rationality*. Cambridge: MIT Press.
Spicer, Michael W. (1985). A Public Choice Approach to Motivating People in Bureaucratic Organizations. *Academy of Management Review 10 (3),* 518-527.
Stern, Nicholas. (2002). Towards a dynamic public economics. *Journal of Public Economics 86,* 335-339.
Stiglitz, Joseph E. (2002). New perspectives on public finance: recent achievements and future challenges. *Journal of Public Economics 86,* 341-360.
Summer, M. (1998). Does mandatory rotation enhance auditor independence? *Zeitschrift für Wirtschafts- und Sozialwissenschaften 118,* 327-359.
Thaler, Richard H. (1992). *The Winner's Curse. Paradoxes and Anomalies of Economic Life*. New York: Free Press.
Thomas, Kenneth W. & Velthouse, Betty A. (1990). Cognitive Elements of Empowerment: An 'Interpretive' Model of Intrinsic Task Motivation. *Academy of Management Review 15(4),* 666-681.
Tirole, Jean (1992). Collusion and the Theory of Organizations. In: Jean-Jacques Laffont (Ed.). *Advances in Economic Theory: Sixth World Congress.* Cambridge: Cambridge University Press.
Tollison, Robert D. (1982). Rent Seeking: A Survey. *Kyklos* 35 *(4),* 575-602.
Tollison, Robert D. & Congleton, Roger. (Eds). (1995). *The Economic Analysis of Rent Seeking.* Aldershot: Edward Elgar.
Tullock, Gordon.(1964). *Politics of Bureaucracy.* Washington D.C.: Public Affairs Press.
Tullock, Gordon, Seldon, Arthur, & Brady, Gordon. (2002). *Government Failure: A Primer in Public Choice.* Washington D.C.: Cato Institute.
Tullock, Gordon, Tollison, Robert D., Rowley, Charles K. (Eds). (1988). *The Political Economy of Rent Seeking.* Boston: Kluwer.
Westphal, James D. & Zajac, Edward J. (1995). Who Shall Govern? CEO/Board Power, Demographic Similarity, and New Director Selection. *Administrative Science Quarterly 40(1),* 60-84.
Wintrobe, Ronald. (1996). Modern Bureaucratic Theory. In: Dennis Mueller (Ed.), *Perspectives in Public Choice: A Handbook* (pp. 429-454). Cambridge: Cambridge University Press.

F. VAN DER PLOEG

MACROECONOMICS OF FISCAL POLICY AND GOVERNMENT DEBT*

1 INTRODUCTION

Why do fiscal policy and government debt matter? Macroeconomists of various breeds debate whether a fiscal expansion leads to boom or recession and whether government debt matters for real macroeconomic outcomes or not. Politicians switched from using fairly Keynesian practices in policy making during the sixties and seventies to a classical doctrine of trimming government during the eighties and early nineties. In addition, a variety of OECD countries attempt to make their public finances healthier by not only cutting taxes and the size of the public sector but also by reducing the ratio of government debt to national income. Here we explain the arguments of the various strands of macroeconomists and try to understand why politicians often ignore advice offered to them.

Under the classical view labour markets clear instantaneously. Fiscal expansions in the form of a rise in public spending harm the economy if they are financed by taxes on labour. The larger wedge between the producer wage and the consumer wage causes a drop in economic activity. The erosion of the tax base threatens survival of the generous welfare state of many OECD countries. The classical view focuses on structural labour market policies – cutting labour taxes, cutting benefits, abolishing minimum wages, training, R&D, removing barriers to labour market participation and bashing union power. The rise in public spending is more than fully crowded out by falls in other components of aggregate demand. The rise in the interest rate and appreciation of the real value of the currency dampens private investment and net exports. Monetary policy is, according to classical economists and their New Classical successors, neutral. Most of these insights carry over to a framework of monopolistic competition as well (Layard, Nickell and Jackman, 1991; OECD, 1993; Nickell, 2004). Keynesians stress that market failures and nominal rigidities may cause idle capacity and unemployment in the long run. Governments should act countercyclically; spend or cut taxes in a recession but cut public spending or raise taxes in a heated economy.

* Based on a review of the macroeconomic effects of fiscal policy and government debt, written for the Public Economics Division of the Economics and Statistics Department of the OECD in 1994. The author thanks members of the Public Economics Division of the Economics and Statistics Department, OECD, Ben Heijdra, Janet Sartorius and Brigitte Unger for helpful comments. All errors and omissions are mine.

P. de Gijsel and H. Schenk (eds.), Multidisciplinary Economics, 187–208.

Countercyclical policy works better if leakages arising from saving, paying taxes and buying imports as well as financial crowding out are small. There are many automatic stabilisers which act in a countercyclical fashion, albeit less at the community level in Europe than in the US. Supply-friendly fiscal expansions raise aggregate demand and output, which is good from Keynesian and classical points of view. For example, tax cuts and public infrastructural projects fight cyclical downturns and improve the structure of the economy.

Section 2 focuses on the adverse effects of looser budgetary policies on economic growth if all markets clear. Four ingredients are necessary: (i) overlapping generations without intergenerational bequest motive, so government debt matters for real economic outcomes; (ii) constant returns to scale with respect to all reproducible factors of production at the aggregate level, so that there is endogenous growth; (iii) adjustment costs for investment to ensure a finite investment rate and nontrivial explanation of the stock market; and (iv) a risk premium on foreign debt which drives a wedge between the domestic and the world interest rate. A higher national income share of public consumption or ratio of government debt to national income then pushes up the interest rate, runs up foreign debt, and depresses the stock market and economic growth. Traditional macroeconomic arguments say that financial crowding out of investment and net exports eventually leads to lower growth and higher interest rates. Section 3, in contrast, discusses Ricardian debt equivalence. If they are right, government debt does not matter for real economic outcomes and thus the adverse effects arising from financial crowding out do not occur. The empirical evidence is mixed. Some conclude that debt equivalence is a good first-order approximation; others conclude that it is an oddity. Many critiques can be levelled at debt equivalence, hence traditional policy analysis deserves the benefit of the doubt. As a benchmark, it is helpful to examine the role of public debt in a world where debt equivalence holds approximately.

Section 4 considers the sustainability of the public sector's finances. Government debt matters. If it is too high, the government may not honour its obligations to redeem its debt. To avoid default or debt repudiation, there is an upper limit on the budget deficits that a government can run. We discuss a number of targets that can be used to ensure sustainability and critically discuss the norms agreed upon in Maastricht. Section 4 also discusses the role government debt plays in smoothing tax distortions over time. This leads to the prescription that taxes should finance permanent rises in public consumption and losses on public sector capital and foreign exchange reserves, while the government must borrow for temporary rises in public consumption and public investment with a market rate of return. This neoclassical public finance policy prescription and Keynesian countercyclical policies argue that governments run unbalanced budget deficits and assign a crucial role to government debt.

Government debt matters if there is a danger that it gets monetised and causes higher inflation. This may cause unpleasant monetarist arithmetic; tight money now may yield high inflation now. Section 5 discusses these issues and focuses on the credibility of central banks and reneging on public debt. One can ensure credibility by appointing a conservative central banker, tying the currency to a strong currency, indexing government debt, or selling government debt in hard foreign currency. These arguments may justify an independent central bank, which is less inclined to use unanticipated inflation to wipe out the real market value of public debt. It may also help to have fines and penalties like the ones of the Stability and Growth Pact. Section 5 argues that government debt matters if it is used strategically by the incumbent political party to tie the hands of a potential future government. This is why conservative governments run larger deficits if they fear being booted out of office by a left wing party. There is also evidence that, in democracies with a large amount of inequity, left wing governments come to power who implement a variety of Robin Hood policies. Inequity may be responsible for lower economic growth and higher inflation. Section 6 concludes with a brief summary.

2. GOVERNMENT DEBT, GROWTH AND THE EFFECTIVENESS OF FISCAL POLICY

Here we consider the longrun macroeconomic effects of fiscal policy taking account of the government budget constraint. We assume that all markets clear and focus at the processes of economic growth and accumulation of debt and wealth. To generate real effects of government debt, we assume overlapping generations of households (Blanchard and Fischer, 1989, Chapter 3; Weil, 1989). Combined with the traditional view of economic growth with diminishing returns to capital at the macro level, one finds that expansionary budgetary policy crowds out private investment and induces less capital-intensive production. If extended with the new theories of endogenous growth (Romer, 1989; Grossman and Helpman, 1991; van der Ploeg and Tang, 1992), one can demonstrate that a higher national income share of public consumption or a higher ratio of government debt to national income depresses economic growth (Saint-Paul, 1992) and increases the ratio of foreign debt to national income (Alogoskoufis and van der Ploeg, 1991; Buiter and Kletzer, 1991; van der Ploeg, 1996). A higher national income share of productive government spending may boost the rate of economic growth despite some crowding out (Barro, 1990).

2.1 Bond finance versus money finance

The size of the Keynesian multiplier depends on how public spending is financed. A tax-financed rise in public spending depresses disposable income and private consumption, so leads to a smaller expansion of employment and national income than a bond-financed increase in public spending. Money finance is on impact more expansionary than bond finance; there is not only an expansion of aggregate demand for goods but also a boost to money supply. With money finance the LM curve shifts out; with bond finance the LM curve shifts inwards. Money finance thus dampens the rise in the interest rate and induces less financial crowding out than bond finance. Once we take into account the government budget constraint, bond finance in a Keynesian world with rigid wages and prices is more expansionary than money finance (Blinder and Solow, 1973). In the long run the government books must be balanced. National income and the tax base rise to generate just enough tax revenues to finance the rise in public spending. The money-financed multiplier is thus one over the income tax rate. After the impact effects of the rise in public spending, the government must print money to finance the initial deficit. Households thus become wealthier which boosts goods and money demand. Since the elasticity of money demand with respect to wealth is less than unity, the LM curve shifts out. Combined with the outward shift of the IS curve, the second-period effect is a further rise in employment and economic activity. The rise in national income continues until just enough tax revenues are generated to finance the deficit. Money finance is clearly a stable mode of finance.

With bond finance tax revenues, the tax base and thus national income must rise sufficiently to cover not only the rise in public spending but also the interest on government debt accumulated in the interim period. The long-run bond-financed multiplier is thus greater than the inverse of the income tax rate, and exceeds the long-run money-financed multiplier. Bond finance is thus less expansionary in the short run but more expansionary in the long run than money finance. However, bond finance is likely to lead to unstable escalation of government debt. After the impact effects of the rise in public spending, the deficit must be financed by selling debt to the public. This makes households wealthier and raises private consumption and the demand for goods, but also raises money demand. The second-period effect is thus a higher interest rate. Only if the wealth effect in money demand is minor relative to the wealth effect in private consumption will national income and thus the tax base rise in the second period. Stability of bond finance is only guaranteed if wealth effects in money demand are small and in goods demand are large. If the process is unstable, the government eventually has to raise taxes or print money to prevent government debt exploding. Both policy changes dampen the long-run multiplier.

The above analysis can be extended to allow for capital formation, expectations and flexible prices (Buiter, 1990, Chapter 10 with J. Tobin; Marini and van der Ploeg, 1988). The above discussion about the effectiveness of fiscal and monetary policy applied only to the Keynesian short run. A money-financed rise in public spending gives a bigger long-run rise in prices than a bond-financed expansion due to the associated rise in the money supply and the smaller expansion of real output. Money finance is thus inadvisable as it leads to a smaller employment benefit and a bigger long-run inflation cost.

2.2 Overlapping generations and debt policy

Since government debt is part of private wealth, a tax cut and the accompanying rise in government debt leads to higher private consumption. Private agents do not fully discount the higher taxes the government must levy in the future to finance interest and principal on accumulated government debt. Otherwise, they realise that the increase in financial wealth is exactly offset by the fall in human wealth, leaving private consumption unaffected. To avoid debt irrelevance, macroeconomists employ the Diamond-Samuelson or Yaari-Blanchard-Weil overlapping generations framework (Blanchard and Fischer, 1989, Chapter 3; Weil, 1989). If there is a positive birth rate (β=n+p>0 where n stands for population growth and p is the probability of death) and no intergenerational bequest motive, current generations can pass some of the burden of future taxes on to future, yet unborn generations. Finite lifetimes are not essential, since debt neutrality prevails if population growth equals the death probability. A temporary bond-financed tax cut thus boosts private consumption, since part of the future tax hike is paid for by future generations.

With a unit elasticity of intertemporal substitution and a constant subjective rate of time preference ($\theta>0$), the marginal propensity to consume out of human wealth (H) plus financial wealth (A) is the rate of time preference plus the death rate ($C=(\theta+p)(H+A)$). Impatient and short-lived households consume a greater proportion of their total wealth. The growth in aggregate private consumption is boosted if there is a large incentive to save, i.e., if the market interest rate (r) rises relative to the rate of time preference (θ), population growth (n) is high, and relative to private consumption there is little financial wealth, that is $\Delta C/C \equiv \gamma = r - \theta + n - \beta\,(p+\theta)\,(A/C)$ where γ is the growth rate. This specification assumes life-cycle maximising households and a competitive insurance industry. If households own few financial assets, households rebuild assets by saving and postponing consumption. However, if government debt does not matter, i.e., if the birth rate is zero ($\beta=0$), financial wealth and thus government debt do not affect growth of aggregate private consumption.

2.3 Debt, deficits and growth

We focus on the new theories of endogenous growth with overlapping generations. New growth theories assume constant returns to scale with respect to all reproducible factors of production. At firm level companies face diminishing returns to capital and constant returns to all adjustable production factors. At the macro level, however, production is proportional to a very broad measure of the capital stock (say, K). This broad measure includes physical and knowledge capital, public and private infrastructure, and land reclaimed from the sea. Production is proportional to this very broad capital measure. Long-run growth is not exogenous, but depends on national income shares of investment, education and R&D. Knowledge and infrastructure capital generate positive externalities, since they benefit productivity of rival firms. New growth theories stress knowledge spillovers and market failures arising from difficulties in patenting discoveries. Such market failures provide a rationale for education and R&D subsidies and public investment in the material and immaterial infrastructure. Here we focus on the adverse effects of demand-side policies on economic growth.

New theories of economic growth suggest that the equilibrium capital-output ratio is constant. Financial wealth consists of equity (qK where K denotes physical capital and q is the value of the stock market), government debt (D) minus net foreign liabilities (F). Using lower-case letters to denote fractions of national income, we obtain: $\gamma = r - \theta + n - \beta\,(p+\theta)\,(qk+d-f)/c$. If the birth rate is zero ($\beta=0$), this gives the Keynes-Ramsey rule of economic growth (Blanchard and Fischer, 1989, Chapter 2). This famous rule says that per capita growth (γ-n) amounts to the market interest rate minus the rate of time preference ($r-\theta$). If there is a positive birth rate, there is a positive relationship between economic growth (γ) and the national income share of private consumption (c) – the SG locus in Figure 1. Intuitively, a low value of financial assets relative to consumption induces households to save and postpone consumption. Given

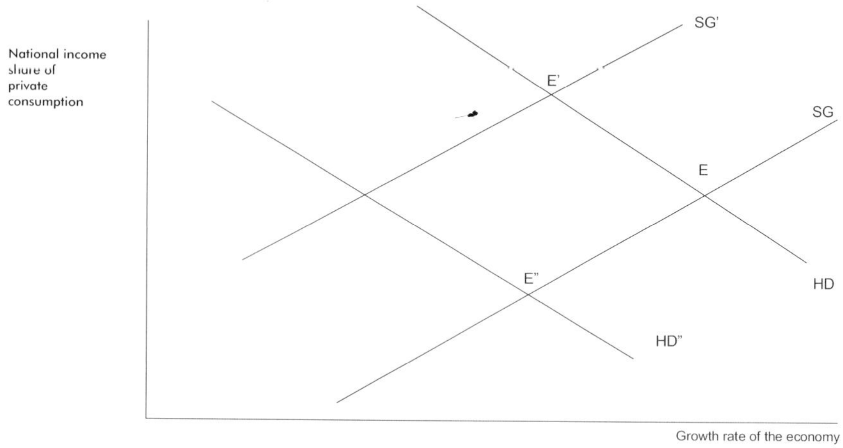

Figure 1. Debt, deficits and growth.

Key: A higher ratio of government debt to national income (or a lower ratio of foreign debt to national income) shifts E to E′ , raising the national income share of private consumption and depressing economic growth. A higher national income share of public consumption shifts E to E″, with less than 100 per cent crowding out of private consumption and lower growth.

that government debt matters if the birth rate is positive, a rise in ratio of public debt to national income stimulates the national income share of private consumption and thus shifts up the SG locus. Similarly, a fall in foreign indebtedness pushes up the SG locus.

The other condition for determining macroeconomic outcomes is the accounting identity that national income, domestic income from production minus interest payments on foreign debt (rF), minus domestic absorption (private and public consumption and investment plus internal adjustment costs for investment) equals the current account deficit (ΔF). This identity generalises the Harrod-Domar condition, namely that economic growth (suitably modified to allow for internal costs of adjusting investment) equals the average propensity to save divided by the capital-output ratio (k). The average propensity to save equals one minus the sum of the national income shares of private consumption and public consumption minus interest payments on foreign debt (1-c-g-(r-n)f). Since a higher share of private consumption leaves fewer resources for investment, there is a negative relationship between the share of private consumption and the rate of economic growth. This is captured by the downward-sloping HD locus in Figure 1. The HD locus shifts inwards if the national income share of public consumption or the degree of foreign indebtedness rises. A tax-financed rise in the national income share of public consumption crowds out resources for private investment and shifts down the HD locus in Figure 1. The result is lower growth and a lower national income share of private consumption. Public spending, unless it boosts productivity of private capital, depresses economic growth. A temporary tax cut leads to a rise in government debt. This raises private financial wealth and boosts private consumption, thereby shifting upwards the SG locus. Consequently, a rise in public debt boosts private consumption, crowds out private investment and depresses economic growth – see Figure 1.

2.4 Sovereign debt, the stock market and growth

Higher foreign debt has two effects. First, it cuts private financial wealth and reduces private consumption, shifting down the SG locus. This leaves more resources for saving and investment, and thus boosts economic growth. Second, it burdens the economy with higher interest payments to foreign holders of debt. Clearly, this leaves fewer resources for investment and lowers economic growth, witness the downward shift in the HD locus. If the country is not stifled by having to service a huge foreign debt, the first effect dominates the second effect. Hence, foreign indebtedness bolsters the growth rate so we plot in Figure 2 an upward-sloping SF locus. Section 2.3 tells us that the SF locus shifts down if the national income share of public consumption or the ratio of government debt to national income rises. To understand the relationship between investment and foreign indebtedness, we need to explain the domestic interest rate. A country burdened by a large foreign debt faces a higher interest rate, so that the domestic interest rate (r) equals the foreign interest rate (r^*) plus a country risk premium that rises with foreign indebtedness ($r=r^*+\Omega(f)$, $\Omega'>0$). High levels of foreign debt imply a danger of default. The investment rate rises with Tobin's q, the discounted value of the stream of present and future (constant) marginal products of capital. The stock market (q) falls if the interest rate rises, since this depresses present and future marginal products of capital. A higher degree of foreign indebtedness pushes up the domestic interest rate, which causes a fall in the stock market and thus a decline in the investment rate and the growth rate – see the downward-sloping IF locus of Figure 2.

A bigger national income share of the public sector shifts the SF locus in Figure 2 downwards. This leads to a fall in the national income share of private consumption, the investment rate and the growth rate, a larger foreign debt, a higher domestic interest rate and a fall in the stock market. The greater interest payments on foreign debt contribute to the fall in private consumption. Hence, a bigger public sector goes at the expense of economic growth and crowds out activities in the private sector. A temporary tax cut, accompanied by a higher ratio of government debt to national income, also shifts down the SF locus. Hence, bigger public debt pushes up the interest rate and depresses the stock market. This reduces the rate of investment and economic growth. The higher ratio of foreign debt to national income raises the risk premium on sovereign debt and thus the interest rate. The temporary tax cut benefits the old at the expense of the young and constitutes a transfer from future to current generations. This reduces the national saving rate, which implies a lower domestic investment rate, temporary current account deficits and a higher interest rate. In summary, looser budgetary policies push up interest rates, raise the foreign debt, and depress the stock market and the growth rate.

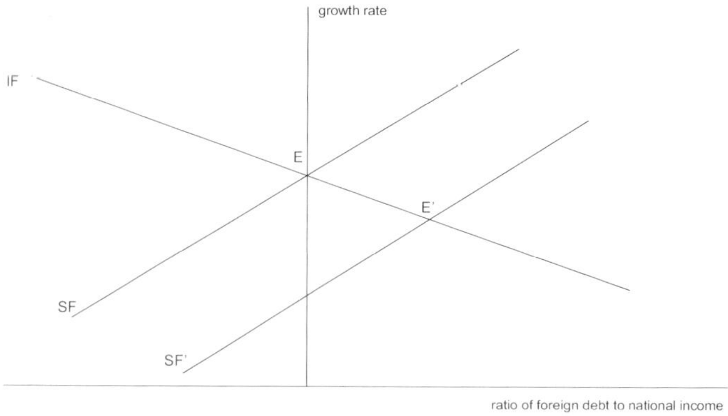

Figure 2. Foreign indebtedness, the stock market and growth.

Key: A higher ratio of government debt to national income or higher national income share of public consumption shifts E to E′, thereby depressing economic growth and the stock market while pushing up the domestic interest rate and boosting foreign indebtedness.

3. DOES GOVERNMENT DEBT MATTER?

Government bonds may not be part of private wealth (Barro, 1974). It may matter whether a given stream of present and future levels of primary public spending is financed by taxes today or taxes tomorrow. Finance by future taxes amounts to debt finance, so there is no difference between tax finance and debt finance as far as real outcomes are concerned. Why then care about public debt?

3.1 Critique of Ricardian debt equivalence

1) Politicians argue that government debt unfairly burdens future generations and is immoral. Such rhetoric highlights only one side of the cion. It ignores the fact that our grandchildren not only inherit the burden of higher future taxes but also government debt. With one hand the government levies taxes on our grandchildren and with the other hand the government hands out interest and principal to our grandchildren. There is thus no problem of intergenerational inequity, but one of intragenerational inequity. Rich kids inherit government debt, but poor kids do not. Higher government debt thus benefits offspring of rich parents at the expense of offspring of poor parents. One may argue that intermarriage among families makes all households one happy altruistic dynasty, thereby negating such distributional effects. This defence seems rather far-fetched.
2) Households are short-lived while government is infinitely-lived. Households may not live to shoulder the future burden of higher taxes (cf. Blanchard and Fischer, 1989, Chapter 3). If there is population growth, new generations help to carry the burden of the future tax rise (Weil, 1989) – see section 3. Barro (1974) showed that

this critique requires absence of intergenerational bequest motives. Debt equivalence breaks down if children threaten to behave badly unless parents are generous. The dynasty defence of Ricardian debt equivalence also breaks down due to the growth of childless families.

3) Households are liquidity constrained and cannot borrow against future income, so a temporary tax cut may boost private consumption. The present value of the future tax increase (the future receipt of interest and principal by households) is less than the value of the current tax cut. On balance there is an increase in wealth and a boost to private consumption. The boost to aggregate demand pushes up interest rates and causes capital losses on assets of the good-risk households as well as substitution away from current towards future consumption. The net effect on aggregate consumption is thus attenuated.
4) A popular argument is that government debt matters if it has been sold to foreigners. In the future our children face a burden, because they have to pay higher taxes in order for the government to pay interest on and redemption of government debt to the children of foreigners. A rise in government debt is thus thought to constitute a transfer of wealth abroad. However, the original sale of government debt to foreigners leads to an inflow of foreign assets whose value equals the present value of the future amount of taxes levied on home households which is then paid as interest and principal to foreigners. Hence, this critique of Ricardian debt equivalence is a red herring.
5) If the long-run interest rate falls short of the growth rate, the government has a 'free lunch'. It can forever roll on debt to cover principal and interest as this would be less than the expansion of the tax base. This situation is unlikely to prevail in the long run, so this critique does not carry much force.
6) A temporary tax cut, accompanied by a rise in government debt, acts as an insurance policy and leads to less precautionary saving and a rise in private consumption (Barsky, Mankiw and Zeldes, 1986). The future rise in the tax rate reduces the variance of future after-tax income, so that risk-averse households engage in less precautionary saving. A temporary tax cut thus has real effects, because it is better to have one bird in the hand than two in the bush. This critique of Ricardian debt equivalence relies on absence of complete private insurance markets. A related reason for failure of debt equivalence is that people are uncertain of what their future income and their future bequests will be (Feldstein, 1988); people thus value differently spending a sum of money now and saving and bequeathing it.
7) A temporary bond-financed cut in distortionary taxes, followed by a future rise in distortionary taxes, causes Ricardian debt equivalence to fail except if the tax base is totally insensitive to intertemporal changes in the tax rate. This non-neutrality is due to intertemporal substitution effects induced by changes in marginal tax rates over time.
8) Households may have bounded rationality or find it too costly to do the calculations required to offset the tax implications of government debt policy.

Most of the critics argue that government debt matters, because it redistributes between heterogeneous private agents who differ in expected lifetimes, access to capital markets, propensities to consume out of current disposable income and financial wealth.

Despite the theoretical doubts about Ricardian debt equivalence, it is tough to empirically find substantial departures from it (Seater and Mariano, 1985; Kormendi, 1983, 1985). Government debt has no discernible effects on private consumption or investment and, if anything, has a negative effect on the interest rate (Evans, 1988). However, there are severe data problems and the empirical results so far are not strong enough to decide against or in favour of debt equivalence (e.g., Poterba and Summers, 1987; Heijdra, 1993). Hence, we must be careful in making statements about adverse effects of government debt on the interest rate, investment and economic growth, because they rely largely on prejudice. Even though Seater (1993) concludes that debt equivalence is a good approximation, Bernheim (1987) in his survey comes to the conclusion that debt equivalence is at variance with the facts. Even though debt equivalence may be theoretically invalid and empirically invalid as well, supporters of debt equivalence must, for the time being, be given the benefit of the doubt. Hence, in the following sections we see what role there is for government debt if government debt has no real effects in the long run.

3.2 Playing with definitions

Some argue that the discussion on budget deficits and government debt is artificial and conceptually flawed. It is difficult to distinguish between debt finance and other schemes for implementing intergenerational transfers (Auerbach and Kotlikoff, 1987; Kotlikoff, 2002). Running a deficit by issuing government bonds financed by taxes on young citizens redistributes resources from the young to the old. However, redistributing resources from working young to pensioners can also be achieved by running a balanced budget and operating an unfunded (PAYG) social security system. Government debt is thus like an unfunded old-age pension scheme as it also represents a claim to future transfers from the government. Concepts such as the budget deficit thus lose their meaning. All that matters is the present value generational accounts. Although there is considerable appeal in the logic of these arguments, it is easy to think of economies with liquidity constraints, distortionary taxes and uncertainty in which these various claims to future payments are not equivalent (Buiter, 1993).

4. TO SMOOTH OR NOT TO SMOOTH?

Even if public debt barely affects real economic outcomes, there is a role for government debt in smoothing tax and inflation rates and smoothing private consumption over time. Such neoclassical views give prescriptions for government budget deficits and debt that superficially are observationally equivalent to Keynesian countercyclical demand management. In the light of our discussion of tax smoothing we comment on golden rules of public finance and critically discuss the norms agreed upon in the Treaty of Maastricht. We also discuss how foreign debt and the current account are used to smooth temporary shocks in national income and public spending and to finance investment projects with a market rate of return. The Feldstein-Horioka puzzle says that empirically there is little support for the proposition that the current account of a nation is used in this way.

4.1 Intertemporal public sector accounts

To analyse sustainability of government debt, one must examine intertemporal aspects of the public sector budget constraint (Buiter, 1990, Chapters 3-5, 1993; Blanchard, 1993). We consider the consolidated budget constraints of the general government and central bank. The government budget deficit (B_D) is financed by issuing interest-bearing government debt (ΔD), selling public assets to the private sector ($p_G \Omega$ where p_G is the real sale price of privatised capital in terms of the national income deflator – assuming no adjustment costs for public investment – and Ω stands for revenues from sales of public sector capital), printing money (μM where μ is the nominal rate of growth in money supply and M is nominal money supply), or sales of foreign exchange reserves ($-E\Delta F^*$ where E is the spot exchange rate and F^* the stock of official foreign exchange reserves). The government budget deficit equals total outgoings minus incomings. Total outgoings are public consumption (G_C), gross public investment (G_I) plus debt service of outstanding government debt (iD where i is the nominal interest rate). Total incomings are tax revenues (T) plus return on public sector capital (ρK_G where ρ is the cash rate of return on public sector capital K_G) and the return on foreign exchange reserves ($i^* EF^*$ where i^* is the rate of return on foreign exchange reserves). Using lower-case letters to express fractions of nominal national income in local currency, we have:

$$\Delta d + (\pi+\gamma)\, d + p_G\, \omega + \mu\, m - \Delta f^* - [\pi+\gamma-(\Delta E/E)]\, f^* =$$

$$b_D \equiv g_C + g_I + id - t - \rho k_G - i^* f^* = id - i^* f^* - b_{PS}$$

where π is the inflation rate, γ the real growth rate, and $b_{PS} \equiv t+\rho k_G-g_C-g_I$ the primary budget surplus. The terms $(\pi+\gamma)d$ and μm are the inflation-cum-growth tax on government debt and seigniorage revenues, respectively. Since sales of public assets are $\omega=g_I-(\gamma+\delta_G)k_G-\Delta k_G$ with δ_G the depreciation rate of public sector capital and Δk_G net investment in public sector capital, we can rewrite the public sector budget constraint in terms of the public sector's net liabilities ($n \cong d-k_G-f^*$):

$$\Delta n = (r-\gamma)n - (t-g_C) + (r+\delta_G-\rho)k_G + (1-p_G)\omega + [i-i^*-(\Delta E/E)]f^* - \mu m$$

where $r \equiv i-\pi$ is the real interest rate. If the primary current surplus ($b_{PC} \cong t-g_C$) plus seigniorage revenues (μm) exceed growth-corrected interest on the government's outstanding net liabilities ($(r-\gamma)n$) plus losses due to public sector capital being privatised too cheaply ($(1-p_K)\omega$) and losses due to the user cost being less than the cash return on public sector capital ($(r+\delta_G-\rho)k_G$) and losses due to foreign exchange reserves not earning a market return, then net liabilities as a fraction of national income fall over time.

If there are no losses on privatisation and a market return is charged for use of public sector capital ($\rho = r + \delta_G$), public sector investment and public sector capital can be netted out of the government budget constraint. This justifies the Golden Rule of public finance: the government should borrow for public investment projects *with a market rate of return*. In general, there is no reason to privatise public sector capital unless it is better run in the private sector. Conversely, if competition or effective regulation can be ensured, there is no reason to keep such activities in the public sector unless they are clearly better run there. Revenues from privatisation lessen the need for debt finance but they do not make public sector finances healthier as future dividends no longer come in. Since foreign exchange reserves earn close to a market rate of return, i.e., the return on foreign exchange reserves roughly matches the opportunity cost of borrowing plus the expected rate of appreciation of the exchange rate ($\widetilde{i^*}$ i-(ΔE/E)), we can net them out of the consolidated budget constraint of the government and the central bank. We assume that losses on foreign exchange reserves are small. We also assume that the consolidated public sector is solvent and does not engage in Ponzi games. This requires no explicit default on the government debt that is inherited from past government and that the growth rate of government debt and net government liabilities is less than the interest rate. A country with a positive stock of government debt and a positive real interest rate must run primary public sector surpluses. If the public sector is solvent, we write its present value budget constraint as follows:

$$d \leq PV_{r-\gamma}[b_{PS} + p_G\omega + \mu m] \quad \text{or } n \leq PV_{r-\gamma}[b_{PCS} - (r+\delta_G-\rho)k_G - (1-p_G)\omega + \mu m]$$

where $PV_{r-\gamma}[x]$ denotes the present value of the stream of present and current values of x using the discount rate r-γ. Hence, outstanding government debt must not exceed the present value of the stream of present and future primary surpluses, receipts from the sale of public sector capital and seigniorage revenues. Alternatively, outstanding net government liabilities cannot exceed the discounted value of present and future primary current surpluses plus seigniorage revenues minus the losses arising from privatising and operating public sector capital too cheaply.

4.2 Sustainability of the government finances

Sustainability of government finances can be viewed in different ways. The simplest one is to fix a value at which the ratio of government debt to national income should be stabilised (d*) and to agree on a target for the ratio of the government budget deficit to the national income (b_D*) consistent with no explosion of public debt.

This target for the public sector deficit equals the growth-cum-inflation tax on outstanding government debt plus privatisation revenues plus seigniorage revenues, that is $b_D^* = (\pi+\gamma)d^* + p_G\omega + \mu m$. Something like this underlies the norms for the budget deficit and government debt agreed upon in the Treaty of Maastricht. For example, if the growth rate in nominal national income is 5 percent ($\pi+\gamma=0.05$) while seigniorage and revenues from privatisation are insignificant, the budget deficit should be 3 percent of the national income for government debt to be stabilised at 60 per cent of national income. It is difficult to find an economic theory to back up such norms.

Indeed, some argue that the Maastricht norms amount to 'voodoo' economics (Buiter, Corsetti and Roubini, 1993). A disadvantage of this way of stabilising government debt is that public investment projects suffer. A less short-sighted strategy is to stabilise the ratio of public sector net liabilities as a fraction of the national income (n^*), so that running up public debt does not matter if it is used to build up public sector capital or foreign exchange reserves.

Stabilisation of the ratio of public sector net liabilities to national income then implies the following target for the budget deficit $b_D^{**} = b_D^* + \Delta k_G - [\pi + (\Delta E/E) + \gamma] f^*$. The target for the budget deficit is loosened if there is more net investment in public sector capital or if the growth-cum-inflation subsidy on holdings of foreign exchange reserves falls. In addition, the government may borrow to finance public investment projects that provide a stream of services (rather than income) and are worth doing. In that case, expenditures on these projects add to future social welfare so that a bigger target for the budget deficit can be tolerated.

Blanchard (1993) and Buiter (1993) suggest the *permanent primary gap* as a measure of the permanent fiscal correction that is required to avoid debt repudiation or default. It is defined as:

$$GAP \equiv (r-\gamma)_L \, [d - PV_{r-\gamma}(b_{PS} + p_G\omega + \mu m)]$$

where the long-run growth-corrected rate of interest equals $(r-\gamma)_L \equiv 1/PV_{r-\gamma}(1)$. The adjusted primary surplus includes privatisation and seigniorage revenues. The *planned* permanent adjusted primary surplus corresponds to that constant value of the adjusted primary surplus whose present discounted value is the same as the present discounted value of the stream of adjusted primary surpluses that are expected to prevail in the future. The *required* permanent adjusted primary surplus is what is necessary to cover servicing (using the long-run growth-corrected real interest rate) of outstanding government debt. The permanent primary gap then amounts to the excess of the *required* permanent adjusted primary surplus over the *planned* permanent adjusted primary surplus.

4.3 The Feldstein-Horioka puzzle

The current account of the balance of payments or saving surplus of the nation may be used to smooth private consumption (Sachs, 1981). If the country is in temporary recession or public spending is temporarily high, a country should borrow from abroad to smooth the stream of consumption. This is different from Keynesian predictions that in recession expenditures and thus imports are cut back, driving the current account into surplus. The life-cycle view of the current account predicts, in contrast, that in a temporary boom the current account shows a surplus, i.e., the country saves by buying foreign assets. Another strong prediction of the life-cycle view is that, if private and public investment projects have a market return, they should be financed by borrowing from abroad. The current account should go into deficit to finance private or public investment projects with a market return. Sensible use of the current account thus implies that domestic investment is unconstrained by domestic saving. However,

Feldstein and Horioka (1980), using cross-country OECD data, cannot reject the hypothesis of a zero coefficient in regressions of the saving rate on the investment rate. Indeed, a quick glance at the data suggests that there is a high correlation between saving and investment rates and later empirical studies confirm this observation (e.g., Tesar, 1991). Roubini (1988) shows that the optimal current account amounts to the temporary component in national income minus the temporary component in public spending minus investment projects with a market rate of return. This helps to explain part of the Feldstein-Horioka puzzle, but not all of it.

Given that onshore and offshore interest rates move close together for countries with liberalised capital movements, it is hard to argue that the Feldstein-Horioka puzzle implies imperfect capital mobility across international borders. Why does in a global economy with integrated capital markets capital not flow from countries with a high propensity to save to countries with attractive investment opportunities? One explanation is that saving and investment rates are highly correlated, because shocks in, say, population or productivity affect saving and investment rates similarly. This explanation is implausible, since Bayouomi and Rose (1993) find no correlation between regional saving and regional investment rates on data for the UK. Given that governments do not target *regional* current accounts but seem interested in *national* current accounts, a more reasonable explanation of the Feldstein-Horioka puzzle is that government policy is aimed at a particular outcome for the current account and thus at a high correlation between domestic saving and domestic investment rates. The targeting may occur via changes in budgetary policy, but also through restrictions on private saving. Often pension funds face upper limits on the amount of foreign assets they may have in their portfolio. If this is correct, transition towards EMU in Europe implies that individual governments stop targeting their current accounts which yields a more efficient allocation of saving to investment projects.

4.4 Stabilisation policy and solvency of the public sector

Both the Keynesian view on countercyclical demand management and the public finance approach make a case for unbalanced government budget deficits. Keynesians fight temporary recession with a tax cut or a boost to public spending while tax smoothers allow temporary budget deficits to cover the fall in tax revenues and rise in unemployment benefits. If the recession is structural (think of hysteresis in labour markets), Keynesian demand management is ineffective. Hence, tax rates must rise to ensure a balanced public sector budget and stop escalation of public debt. In practice, situations occur where the recession is structural from the outset but not recognised as such by politicians and others. For example, there is a danger that stagflation caused by supply shocks is wrongly combatted with Keynesian demand management.

The literature offers almost no integration of Keynesian demand management and the neoclassical public finance prescription of smoothing intertemporal tax distortions. Indeed, Keynesian policies have largely been discredited because of their neglect of public sector solvency and also their assumption that workers can be fooled all the time. Politicians have been keen to cut taxes and increase spending to combat Keynesian unemployment, but seem unwilling to raise taxes or cut spending if the economy is in a boom. This is related to the 'culture of contentment' (Galbraith, 1992) and has given rise to large levels of public debt. It is therefore crucial to supplement any countercyclical policy rule with an autonomous solvability component. In temporary recession the solvability component of the tax rule rises to meet the annuity value of the foregone tax revenues on account of the lower tax base and the higher level of benefits. The countercyclical component of the tax rate falls during a recession and outweighs the rise in the solvability component of the tax rate. Any *temporary* cut in the tax rate in order to fight a temporary recession mast be followed by a modest *permanent* rise in the tax rate to ensure solvability of the public sector's finances – see van der Ploeg (1995b).

4.5 Critique of the norms of Maastricht

It is hard to justify the 3% and 60% Maastricht norms for the public sector deficit and gross government debt (van der Ploeg, 1991; Buiter, Corsetti and Roubini, 1993). In light of our discussion of tax smoothing, these norms are odd. Why not correct definitions for the budget deficit for growth-cum-inflation taxes? Poor countries with higher growth rates (e.g., Portugal) may sustain a higher ratio of the budget deficit to national income. Why not attempt to use a norm for net liabilities rather than for gross debt? Some countries (the Netherlands) have funded pensions for civil servants, but other countries (Germany, France) do not. If corrected for public pensions, the ratio of government debt to GDP drops by about 50 percentage points in the Netherlands (Bovenberg, Kremers and Masson, 1991). With unfunded pension systems net debt is underreported in the official debt statistics. Neither official gross debt nor net debt statistics tell the whole story about the debt burden, but the Treaty of Maastricht only considers gross debt. Why agree on a procyclical straitjacket? Why not allow for countercyclical elements in demand management? Why impose a norm for government debt at all? Why not let the market discipline countries with unsound government finances? Where do the numbers 3 and 60 come from? Why create intertemporal tax distortions by forcing countries to use temporary tax hikes or cuts in public spending to force down the ratio of government debt to national income? Why, just when European economies are suffering a cyclical downturn, impose a severe contraction in demand and cause even more Keynesian unemployment? Why not have *lower* bounds as well as *upper* bounds on public sector deficits and debt? Why is convergence of budget deficits and government debt desirable? International co-ordination of policies is not the same as convergence and conditions differ among the countries of Europe. Convergence may thus be harmful.

Although the Treaty of Maastricht contains a golden rule of finance to allow governments to borrow for investment projects with a market return, most countries do not apply it and the subsequent Stability and Growth Pact does not provide for it. The Maastricht norms are meant to avoid bail out of insolvent members of the EU (Bovenberg, Kremers and Masson, 1991). Indeed, the Treaty specifies there will be no bail out if one of its members cannot service its debt. This argument relies on markets not demanding a sovereign risk premium from countries with unhealthy government finances (also section 3.4). A related rationale for the Maastricht norms is that they avoid the ECB having to monetise budget deficits and push up inflation. The danger of monetisation is further reduced by the explicit *independence* of the ECB. A danger of monetisation remains with an independent ECB, since central bankers need to go back to their capitals after their term of office.

5. CREDIBILITY, INFLATION AND THE POLITICAL ECONOMY OF PUBLIC FINANCE

Here we focus on three other aspects of government debt. First, if government debt is unsustainable, the government is tempted to monetise the deficit (Buiter, 1993). Subsequently, monetary growth and inflation are substantially higher as seigniorage must cover the initial budget deficit *and* the interest on accumulated government debt. People anticipate that tight money now results in higher inflation in the long run. Expected inflation thus rises and real money demand falls. The resulting fall in the base of the inflation tax and loss in revenues demands higher inflation. This unpleasant monetarist arithmetic suggests that with unsustainable deficits, an upper bound on public debt and forward-looking agents, tight money today may result in high inflation today (Sargent and Wallace, 1981).

Second, a large nominal government debt invites wiping it out with unanticipated inflation (Barro, 1983; Obstfeld, 1991; van der Ploeg, 1991). In the absence of commitment inflation will be higher. This argues for a conservative central banker (Rogoff, 1985b; van der Ploeg 1995a), tying the currency of a country with a weak monetary authority to a strong currency (Giavazzi and Pagano, 1988), indexing government debt, and issuing some government debt in hard foreign currency (Bohn, 1990, 1991; Watanabe, 1992). This is particularly the case if: (i) there is a large stock of nominal public debt; (ii) the base of seigniorage revenues is small as then the loss in revenues resulting from lower (foreign) inflation is small; (iii) aversion to inflation is large; and (iv) the black economy is small (cf., Canzoneri and Rogers, 1991), so it is efficient to extract (nonmonetary) tax revenues. If there are other nominal contracts, e.g., nominal wage contracts, the incentive to have an independent central bank is even bigger. Delegating monetary policy to a central banker who is less inclined to renege allows one to tie the hands of a government wishing to please the electorate. The majority does not appoint a central banker with the *sole* task of price stability. Similarly, the minister of finance should have greater say in cabinet decisions than his spending colleagues. Another way of avoiding repudiation of government debt through unanticipated inflation is to index public debt (and wages) to prices. Since private agents are likely to be more risk averse than the government, indexing debt has the added advantage of a lower risk premium as the risk of a change in inflation is shifted to the government. Indexed debt thus lowers the burden of debt service. Yet another alternative to overcoming untrustworthy monetary policy is to issue government debt in hard foreign currency. If authorities renege through unanticipated inflation, they hurt themselves as the interest on the public debt has to be paid in hard currency while the own currency has depreciated. Issuing foreign-currency denominated government debt ensures monetary discipline. Domestic-currency bonds give incentives for surprise inflation while foreign-currency bonds provide incentives for surprise deflation. The optimal mix of domestic-currency and foreign-currency bonds balances these two incentives. More price rigidity and a longer maturity of public debt strengthen the inflationary but weaken the deflationary incentive. The share of foreign-currency bonds increases with more price rigidity and a longer maturity of public debt. Watanabe (1992) suggests that for the US economic welfare rises if one continues to issue almost 100 per cent of T-bills in US dollars and at the same time cuts the share of US dollars in long-term bonds.

Third, the incumbent political party can use government debt strategically to tie the hands of a potential successor. Politicians are neither benevolent dictators nor only look after the interests of the median voter. They are self-interested and strategic animals concerned with survival. This explains why conservative governments have looser budgetary policies than they would normally have (Persson and Svensson, 1989; Alesina and Tabellini, 1990; Persson and Tabellini, 1990; Tabellini and Alesina, 1990).[1] These models rely on a *partisan* view of the political process, i.e., there are poor favouring left-wing policies and politicians and rich who favour right-wing politicians. Left-wing parties try to shift from policies protecting property in the broadest sense to Robin Hood policies. A large degree of political polarisation leads to big budget deficits. Government debt also matters, because in democracies the majority votes for a conservative central banker (e.g., van der Ploeg, 1995a). In addition, countries with unequal distribution of private wealth and government debt, typically, vote for populist governments which yield lower economic growth (Alesina and Rodrick, 1994; Persson and Tabellini, 1992a; Perotti, 1992) and higher inflation (Beetsma and van der Ploeg, 1996). Alesina and Tabellini (1992) compare political economy and public finance approaches to government debt. Partisan explanations of the political business cycle stress that left-wing governments run larger deficits than right-wing governments. Also, democracies with coalition governments end up with bigger budget deficits and higher government debt (Borooah and van der Ploeg, 1983; Alesina, 1989; Roubini and Sachs, 1989; Alesina and Roubini, 1992). Finally, asymmetric information may yield political business cycles (Rogoff and Sibert, 1988; Rogoff, 1990). Democracies with many political parties and proportional voting often have coalition governments. Political decision making is then a lengthy process, because consensus is hard to arrive at. It is then hard to resolve budgetary problems, especially as coalition governments tend to fall apart, leading to high budget deficits and high public debt (Roubini and Sachs, 1989). Politicians of different colours may play a war of attrition ('game of chicken'), which may explain why stabilisation programmes are often delayed (Alesina and Drazen, 1991).

1 Forward-looking financial markets anticipate higher budget deficits and higher short rates of interest under a future left-wing government. Already during the conservative rule, the exchange rate appreciates and the long rate of interest rises, throwing the economy in recession. The conservative incumbent fights the recession with a looser budgetary policy than without a left-wing takeover (van der Ploeg, 1987).

6. CONCLUDING REMARKS

Fiscal policy and government debt matter. First, looser budgetary policies crowd out private investment and lead to more foreign debt, a higher domestic interest rate and lower economic growth. Also, taxes on economic activity have adverse supply-side effects. Second, even if debt equivalence holds, higher public debt due to an intertemporal shift in taxation causes intragenerational inequity. In practice, heterogeneity among households (due to differences in age or number of children), liquidity constraints, uncertainty, precautionary saving, and distortionary taxes ensure that government debt affects real macroeconomic outcomes. Third, even if government debt and public consumption do not affect employment, output and growth, government debt smoothes intertemporal tax distortions and finances temporary rises in public spending or public investment projects with a market return (section 5). Fourth, unsustainable budget deficits matter because they may necessitate a switch from bond to money finance, leading to unpleasant monetarist and fiscal arithmetic. Alternatively, unsustainable budget deficits may cause explicit default. Fifth, without reputation or explicit binding contracts for the monetary authorities, the presence of long nominal government debt induces a higher equilibrium rate of inflation due to the danger of repudiation through unanticipated inflation. These time inconsistency problems can be partially overcome by appointing a conservative central banker, indexing public debt or issuing long debt in foreign currency.

It is desirable that governments impose a financial straitjacket. Most cabinets have many spending ministers and only one finance minister. To give more power to the minister of finance, norms are imposed on budgetary policies. Unfortunately most, including the Maastricht norms, are procyclical and give debt little role in smoothing intertemporal tax distortions and financing temporary increases in public spending. Furthermore, most norms apply to government debt rather than to net government liabilities. Governments should borrow for temporary increases in government spending and for *net* investment in projects with a market return, but the government should levy taxes for permanent increases in government spending and for losses on public investment projects, privatisation issues and operating foreign exchange reserves. In addition, governments may borrow for projects which yield a stream of services over a number of years. A high ratio of government debt to national income matters, since high taxation is needed to service debt. However, it is inadvisable to have a severe fiscal contraction (e.g. a temporary tax hike) to cut the ratio of government debt to national income. The government should care about net government liabilities rather than gross government debt, since deficits do not matter if they are used to build up assets (e.g., public sector capital, provisions for future pensions of civil servants, or foreign exchange reserves) with a market (or social) return. To ensure that politicians do not try to count everything as investment, a national accounting body must be installed to verify that public projects for which the government wishes to borrow indeed have a market (or social) return. Many public investment projects (e.g. missiles) may not qualify, while some forms of public consumption (e.g., student loans or primary education) do. Not much rationale for the Maastricht norms for the ratio of the public sector deficit to national income (especially if they are not corrected for growth-cum-inflation taxes) can be found. Politically, it is understandable if governments agree on a norm for the ratio of public consumption (including debt service corrected for growth and inflation but excluding investment projects with a market or social rate of return) as this determines the national income share of taxation: a 'double lock' on public sector finances.

To avoid the danger of monetising excessive budget deficits and causing inflation, monetary authorities may be given some independence from day-to-day politics and have central bankers that are more conservative than the majority of the electorate. In effect, this introduces an additional 'lock' on the monetary authorities' ability to fund deficits or to affect the aggregate demand for goods. Alternatively, it may be worthwhile to tie the currency to the currency of a country with a much tougher monetary discipline. Other ways of reducing the monetary authorities' incentive to use unanticipated inflation are to issue indexed bonds, to shorten the maturity structure of government debt, and to issue a proportion of bonds in hard currency, but these instruments are dangerous in that they give a signal that the government is less concerned about price stability. Yet another disciplining device is to impose fines and penalties if government have too high public sector deficits and debt; see Beetsma and Uhlig (1999) or Beetsma (2001) for a political economy rationale for the fines of the Stability and Growth Pact.

Keynesian demand management was largely discredited during the late seventies and eighties. Undoubtedly, this had something to do with many old-fashioned Keynesians relying on money illusion and naive expectations to justify demand management, politicians being keen to expand demand in a recession and reluctant to contract demand in a boom, and most of the shocks in this era being supply-side rather than demand-side shocks (OPEC hike in oil prices). However, currently the European economies suffer from deficient aggregate demand. It is hard to believe that the recent upsurge in European unemployment rates is a consequence of a higher level of benefits or a bigger tax wedge. In that case, Keynesian demand management may be called for. However, the underlying structural problems of European labour markets are important as well. Europe has become addicted to fairly generous welfare states that reward economic inactivity rather than stimulate people to look for work and firms to take on extra labour. This is why a two-handed approach to economic policy – supply-friendly demand expansion – is called for. For example, a cut in the income tax rate to reduce the wedge between consumer and producer wages, because this boosts disposable income, private consumption, aggregate demand and employment. Alternatively, governments could invest more in R&D, transboundary education programmes, international infrastructure projects and coordinated investment in pollution abatement. The attack on Keynesian policies has succeeded, because the point is taken that it is bad to stimulate public consumption. However, there may still be a case for a supply-friendly expansion of aggregate demand in a cyclical downturn if the underlying economy badly needs improvement. In addition, a policy of trimming public consumption, transfers and subsidies and at the same time cutting tax rates (a policy of fiscal consolidation) is an effective policy for improving labour market participation from a classical point of view and not too bad from a Keynesian point of view.

REFERENCES

Alesina, A. (1989). Politics and business cycles in industrial economies, *Economic Policy*, *8*, 55-98.

Alesina, A. & Drazen, A. (1991). Why are stabilizations delayed?, *American Economic Review*, *81, 5,* 1170-1188.

Alesina, A. & Rodrik, D. (1994). Distributive politics and economic growth, *Quarterly Journal of Economics*, *109*, 465-490.

Alesina, A. & Roubini, N. (1992). Political cycles in OECD economies, *Review of Economic Studies*, *59*, 663-688.

Alesina, A. & Tabellini, G. (1990). A positive theory of fiscal deficits and government debt, *Review of Economic Studies*, *57*, 403-414.

Alesina, A. & Tabellini, G. (1992). Positive and normative theories of public debt and inflation in historical perspective, *European Economic Review*, *36,* 337-344.

Auerbach, A.J. & Kotlikoff, L.J. (1987). *Dynamic Fiscal Policy*, Cambridge: Cambridge University Press.

Alogoskoufis, G. & Ploeg, F. van der. (1991). On budgetary policies, growth and external deficits in an interdependent world, *Journal of the Japanese and International Economies*, *5, 4,* 305-324.

Barro, R.J. (1974). Are government bonds net wealth?, *Journal of Political Economy*, *82*, 1095-1117.

Barro, R.J. (1983). Inflationary finance under discretion and rules, *Canadian Journal of Economics*, *41,* 1-16.

Barro, R.J. (1990). Government spending in a simple model of endogenous growth, *Journal of Political Economy*, *98*, S103-S125.

Barsky, R.B., Mankiw, N.G., & Zeldes, S.P. (1986). Ricardian consumers with Keynesian propensities, *American Economic Review*, *76, 4*, 676-691.

Bayoumi, T.A. & Rose, A.K. (1993). Domestic savings and intra-national capital flows, *European Economic Review*, *37, 6,* 1197-1202.

Beetsma, R.M.W.J & Ploeg, F. van der. (1993). Does inequality cause inflation? The political economy of inflation, taxation and government debt, *Public Choice*, *87, 1-2,* 143-162.

Beetsma, R.M.W.J. & Uhlig, H. (1999). An analysis of the Stability and Growth Pact, *Economic Journal*, *109, 458*, 546-571.

Bernheim, B.D. (1987). Ricardian equivalence: An evaluation of theory and evidence, in S. Fischer (Ed.), *NBER Macroeconomics Annual*, Cambridge: MIT Press.

Blanchard, O. & Fischer, S. (1989). *Lectures on Macroeconomics*, Cambridge: MIT Press.

Blanchard, O. (1993). Suggestions for a new set of fiscal indicators. In H.H.A. Verbon & F.A.A.M. van Winden (Eds.), *The Political Economy of Government Debt*, Amsterdam: North-Holland

Blinder, A.S. & Solow, R.M. (1973). Does fiscal policy matter?, *Journal of Public Economics*, *2*, 319-338.

Bohn, H. (1990). A positive theory of foreign currency debt, *Journal of International Economics, 29*, 273-292.

Bohn, H. (1991). Time consistency of monetary policy in the open economy, *Journal of International Economics*, *30,* 249-266.

Borooah, V.K. & Ploeg, F. van der. (1983). *Political Aspects of the Economy*, Cambridge: Cambridge University Press.

Bovenberg, A.L., Kremers, J., & Masson, P. (1991). Economic and Monetary Union in Europe and constraints for national budgetary policies, *IMF Staff Papers*, *38*, 374-398.

Buiter, W.H. (1990). *Principles of Budgetary and Financial Policy*, Cambridge: MIT Press.

Buiter, W.H. (1993). Public debt in the USA: How much, how bad and who pays?, *discussion paper no. 791, CEPR,* London.

Buiter, W.H., Corsetti, G., & Roubini, N. (1993). Excessive deficits; sense and nonsense in the Treaty of Maastricht, *Economic Policy, 16*, 57-100.

Buiter, W.H. & Kletzer, K. (1991). Persistent differences in national productivity growth rates with a common technology and free capital mobility, *Journal of the Japanese and International Economies*, *5, 4,* 325-353.

Canzoneri. M.B. & Rogers, C.A. (1990). Is the European Community an optimal currency area? Tax smoothing versus the costs of multiple currencies, *American Economic Review*, *80, 3*, 419-433.

Evans, P. (1988). Are consumers Ricardian? Evidence for the United States, *Journal of Political Economy*, *96, 5*, 983-1004.

Feldstein, M.S. (1988). The effects of fiscal policies when incomes are uncertain: A contradiction to Ricardian equivalence, *American Economic Review, 78, 1*, 14-23.
Feldstein, M. & Horioka, C. (1980). Domestic saving and international capital flows, *Economic Journal, 90*, 314-327.
Galbraith, J.K. (1992). *The Culture of Contentment*, Penguin, Hammondsworth, Middlesex.
Giavazzi, F. & Giovannini, A. (1989). *Limiting Exchange Rate Flexibility*, Cambridge: MIT Press.
Giavazzi, F. & Pagano, M. (1988). The advantage of tying one's hands: EMS discipline and central bank credibility, *European Economic Review, 32, 5*, 1055-1082.
Grossman, G.M. & Helpman, E. (1991). *Innovation and Growth in the Global Economy*, Cambridge: MIT Press.
Heijdra, B.J. (1993). Ricardian equivalence in the Dutch economy?, *discussion paper no. 93-152*, Tinbergen Institute.
Kormendi, R.C. (1983). Government debt, government spending, and private sector behavior, *American Economic Review, 73, 5*, 994-1010.
Kormendi, R.C. (1985). Does deficit-financing affect ecoomic growth? Cross-country evidence, *Journal of Banking and Finance (Supplement), 2*, 243-255.
Kotlikoff, L.J. (2002). Generational policy, Chapter 27. In A.J. Auerbach and M. Feldstein (Eds.), *Handbook of Public Economics, Volume 4*, Amsterdam.: North-Holland
Layard, R., Nickell, S., & Jackman, R. (1991). *Unemployment*, Oxford: Oxford University Press
Marini, G. & Ploeg, F. van der. (1988). Monetary and fiscal policy in an optimizing model with finite lives and capital accumulation, *Economic Journal, 98*, 772-786.
Nickell, S. (2004). Taxes and employment, in J. Agell and P.B. Sørensen (eds.), *Tax Policy and Labor Market Performance*, Cambridge: CESifo and MIT Press.
Obstfeld, M. (1991). Dynamic seigniorage theory: An exploration, *discussion paper no. 519, CEPR,* London.
OECD (1993). *Taxation and unemployment*, Working Party No. 2 on Tax Analysis and Tax Statistics of the Committee of Fiscal Affairs, Paris.
Peltzman, S. (1992). Voters as fiscal conservatives, *Quarterly Journal of Economics, 107*, 327-361.
Perotti, R. (1992). Income distribution, politics, and growth, *American Economic Review, 82,* 311-316.
Persson, T. & Svensson, L. (1989). Whu a stubborn conservative government would run a deficit: policy with time-inconsistent preferences, *Quarterly Journal of Economics, 104*, 325-345.
Persson, T. & Tabellini, G. (1990). *Macroeconomic Policy, Credibility and Politics*, Harwood Academic Publishers, Chur.
Persson, T. & Tabellini, G. (1992a). Growth, distribution and politics. In A. Cukierman, Z. Hercowitz & L. Leiderman (Eds.), *The Political Economy of Business Cycles and Growth*, Cambridge: MIT Press.
Persson, T. & Tabellini, G. (1992b). The politics of 1992: Fiscal policy and European integration, *Review of Economic Studies, 59*, 689-701.
Ploeg, F. van der (1987). Optimal government policy in a small open economy with rational expectations and uncertain election outcomes, *International Economic Review, 28, 2*, 469-491
Ploeg, F. van der (1988). International policy coordination in interdependent monetary economies, *Journal of International Economics, 25*, 1-23.
Ploeg, F. van der (1991). Macroeconomic policy coordination during the various phases of economic and monetary integration in Europe, chapter 7, 136-164. In M. Emerson (Ed.), *The Economics of EMU, Volume II, European Economy, 44, special edition no. 1*, Commission of the European Communities, Brussels.
Ploeg, F. van der (1995a). Political economy of monetary and budgetary policy, *International Economic Review, 36, 2*, 427-439.
Ploeg, F. van der (1995b). Solvency of counter-cyclical policy rules, *Journal of Public Economics, 47,* 45-65.
Ploeg, F. van der (1996). Budgetary policies, foreign indebtedness, the stock market and economic growth, *Oxford Economic Papers, 48,* 382-396.
Ploeg, F. van der & Tang, P. (1992). The macroeconomics of growth: An international perspective, *Oxford Review of Economic Policy, 8, 4*, 15-28.
Poterba, J.M. & Summers, L.H. (1987). Finite lifetimes and the effects of budget deficits on national saving, *Journal of Monetary Economics, 20, 2,* 369-391.
Rogoff, K. (1985a). Can international monetary policy cooperation be counterproductive?, *Journal of International Economics, 18,* 199-217.

Rogoff, K. (1985b). The optimal degree of commitment to an intermediate monetary target, *Quarterly Journal of Economics*, 1169-1189.

Rogoff, K. (1990). Equilibrium political budget cycles, *American Economic Review*, *80*, 21-36.

Rogoff, K. & Sibert, A. (1988). Elections and macroeconomic policy cycles, *Review of Economic Studies*, *55*, 1-16.

Romer, P. (1989). Capital accumulation in the theory of long-run growth. In R.J. Barro (Ed.), *Modern Business Cycle Theory*, Cambridge: Harvard University Press.

Roubini, N. (1988). Current account and budget deficits in an intertemporal model of consumption and taxation smoothing. A solution to the Feldstein-Horioka puzzle?, *working paper no. 2773, NBER*, Cambridge.

Roubini, N. & Sachs, J. (1989). Fiscal policy, *Economic Policy*, *8*, 99-132.

Sachs, J.D. (1981). The current account and macroeconomic adjustment in the 1970s, *Brookings Papers on Economic Activity*, *12*, 201-268.

Saint-Paul, G. (1992). Fiscal policy in an endogenous growth model, *Quarterly Journal of Economics*, *107*, 1243-1259.

Sargent, T.J. & Wallace, N. (1981). Some unpleasant monetarist arithmetic, *Federal Reserve Bank of Minnaepolis Quarterly Review*, 1-17.

Seater, J.J. (1993). Ricardian equivalence, *Journal of Economic Literature*, *XXXI*, 142-190.

Seater, J.J. & Mariano, R.S. (1985). New tests of the life cycle and tax discounting hypotheses, *Journal of Monetary Economics*, 195-215.

Tabellini, G. & Alesian, A. (1990). Voting on the budget deficit, *American Economic Review*, *80*, 37-49.

Tesar, L. (1991). Savings, investment and international capital flows, *Journal of International Economics*, *31*, 55-78.

Watanabe, T. (1992). The optimal currency composition of government debt, *Bank of Japan, Monetary and Economic Studies*, *10*, *2*, 31-62.

Weil, P. (1989). Overlapping generations of infinitely lived agents, *Journal of Public Economics*, *28*, 183-198.

W.H. BUITER

JOYS AND PAINS OF PUBLIC DEBT [1]

1. INTRODUCTION

If public debt did not exist, it would most certainly be invented soon. Whether it ought to be invented depends on one's view on the objectives pursued by those who determine the path of public debt issuance, their competence, their capacity for making binding credible commitments (or its counterpart – their proclivity for indulging in opportunistic behaviour) and the institutional (including cultural), political and economic constraints they face.

The Ultimate Welfare Rationale for Public Debt and Deficits

The normative case for government borrowing and lending, as for all borrowing and lending, ultimately rests on consumption smoothing in a market economy. Often, income and/or nonconsumption expenditures (investment, military expenditure)[2] vary significantly over time. People prefer a more even pattern of consumption over time. They can achieve this by building up financial assets or paying down debt during periods of exceptionally high current income or exceptionally low nonconsumption expenditure. This can also be done by running down financial assets or increasing their debt during periods of exeptionally low current income and/or exceptionally high nonconsumption expenditure.

Ultimately and fundamentally, all loans are consumption loans. Loans can be direct private consumption loans among heterogeneous private consumers, generally intermediated through specialised financial institutions. The Allais-Samuelson's pure consumption loans model (Allais (1947), Samuelson (1958)) is an elegant early demonstration of both the benefits and limitations of intertemporal trade between households. Loans can also be indirect private consumption loans, when enterprises borrow to fund capital formation in excess or enterprise saving and households benefit as owners of these

1 The view and opinions expressed are those of the author. They do not represent the views and opinions of the European Bank for Reconstruction and Development.

2 In the national accounts, military expenditure and expenditure on public administration (law and order, the civil service etc.) are classified as consumption. From an economic point of view these are expenditures on intermediate public goods and services, not spending on final goods and services. However valuable or essential they may be, they should not be counted as part of value added or GDP. Their contribution to GDP is already counted in the true consumption and investment totals.

P. de Gijsel and H. Schenk (eds.), Multidisciplinary Economics, 209–224.

enterprises. Or they can be public consumption loans. The public authorities can borrow to smooth public consumption directly, or to smooth public consumption indirectly by financing public sector capital formation.[3] If some (but not all) private agents face binding liquidity constraints at some point in their life cycle, the public authorities can also can borrow to smooth private consumption indirectly by using public debt issuance and retirement together with taxation and transfer payments, to smooth private consumption across the lifetime of one or more generations or to redistribute resources (and thus consumption) across generations. Public sector deficits and surpluses can be used to smooth the excess burden of distortionary taxes over time, thus minimising the aggregate social welfare loss inevitably associated with the need to use distortionary taxes: few governments attempt to finance wars with a balanced budget.

The issuance of financial claims permits both consumption smoothing over time and across states of nature. I will focus on trading over time, although risk trading is often inextricably tied to intertemporal trade.

2. SUSTAINABILITY: THE FEASIBILITY OF THE FISCAL-FINANCIAL-MONETARY PROGRAMME OF THE STATE

It will come as no surprise that I will not attempt to develop here a general framework for optimal dynamic fiscal policy – spending, taxation, borrowing and monetary issuance over time. Optimality is beyond me. The subject matter I will address is feasibility – a logical prerequisite for optimality. I will, from time to time, make reference to properties or attributes of the fiscal-financial-monetary-programme of the state that I consider to be sensible or desirable, but that is as close to optimality as I shall get in this lecture.

Consider first, consumption smoothing over time. Government borrowing permits government saving to be uncoupled from government investment. Of course, government borrowing, that is, a government's ability to run a financial deficit, requires the existence of other economic agents – the domestic private sector, the foreign private sector, foreign governments or international financial institutions – willing and able to lend, that is, to run a matching financial surplus. A basic premise of finance theory is that there is no Santa Claus. Lenders lend because they expect to be compensated for giving up, for a while, the command over the resources they part with.

The fiscal-financial-monetary programme of the state is sustainable if the implementation of the programme does not threaten the solvency of the state, now or in the future.[4] The definition of (in)solvency of the state is, in principle, no different from that of the (in)solvency of any other economic agent. It is true that, if we restrict ourselves

3 I have often wondered how the construction of the pyramids was financed. There must be a Ph D topic there somewhere.

4 In an uncertain world, nothing can be taken for granted, and there can be no absolute certainty that the state will not become insolvent. A strict but rather pedantic restatement of the sustainability criterion is therefore that an FFMP is sustainable if the implementation of the programme does not result in an unacceptable risk of insolvency for the state.

to natural persons, the state is longer-lived than most private agents, but private institutions with legal personality like firms or charities can have a lifespan exceeding that of natural persons. It is also true that the state has revenue raising instruments that are (or ought to be) unique within a given national jurisdiction. The state can raise taxes and it can declare some of its liabilities to be legal tender. Both these powers are a reflection of the state's unique position as the repository of the legitimate use of coercive power in a society. If one private person tried to tax another one, that is, if he tried to extract a *quid* from the other party without offering in exchange a *pro quo* deemed to be of at least equal value by the other party, it would be considered theft or extortion. If legal tender – generally a monopoly of the state, often issued by its agent the central bank – has been accepted in settlement of a financial obligation, there is a strong presumption that this is the end of the matter – the seller or creditor retains no further claim on the buyer or debtor. The capacity to tax and to issue legal tender makes the state an unusual borrower, but below the surface, it is subject to the same pains and joys of borrowing experienced by private sector borrowers.

2a. What are the right boundaries of the public sector for analysing fiscal sustainability?

In principle, the answer to this question should be clear. We are interested in the solvency of the state, that is, the sovereign – the agent with the power to tax and to declare one or more of its financial liabilities to be legal tender. At the very least, this includes the consolidated general government sector and central bank. It is important that the central bank be included. The central bank may be operationally independent, that is, it may not be an agent of the government of the day in the setting of the short nominal interest rate, it is always an agent of the state. General government includes the central or federal government, state or provincial government and local or municipal government. The question of the inclusion of an economic agent, organisation or entity in a fiscal sustainability analysis arises if the answer to at least one of the two following questions is 'yes': (a) is the state ultimately responsible for its debt? and (b) does the state appropriate the profits of the entity and make up its losses? If the answer to at least one of these two questions is affirmative, the income-expenditure and profit and loss accounts and balance sheet of the entity in question must be consolidated with that of the state for the purpose of sustainability analysis. If only one of the boxes is ticked, or if there is uncertainty attached to the answers, judgement enters. The central bank qualifies on both criteria. So do the social security and state pension, health and disability funds.

A further advantage of considering the consolidated general government and central bank is that this ensures that the quasi fiscal deficit of the central bank is fully included in the fiscal sustainability analysis. The central bank has many instruments at its disposal, including multiple exchange rates, reserve requirements, subsidised borrowing rates; de facto grants to state enterprises or private enterprises that, for a while, masquerade *de jure* as loans. If a 'loan' is economically equivalent to a grant or a subsidy, the formal, legal niceties are irrelevant.

It is key that the fiscal sustainability auditor see through off balance sheet items and special purpose vehicles. The public sector has had, and continues to have, too many Enrons of its own. The auditor must see through legal and accounting veils to get to the economic substance underneath. Everything goes in the pot.

2b. Which financial instruments should be included in the fiscal sustainability assessment?

The simple answer is: all of them, that is, all contractual liabilities and assets of the state must be included. This includes, on the liability side, such familiar instruments as Treasury Bills or Bonds and other foreign currency-denominated, domestic currency-denominated or index-linked instruments. These liabilities should be valued at their 'default-risk-free values'. For variable rate government bonds (with a fixed notional value), that would simply be the face value of the bond. For fixed-interest longer maturity bonds whose default risk-free value can vary as the level of current and anticipated future risk-free interest rates varies, an estimate must be made if either there is no readily available, deep and liquid secondary market on which the bond is traded, or if the price in such a market reflects the presence of default risk. For concessional debt, the present discounted value of all future debt service (interest and repayment of principal) should be included. This can be significantly lower than the notional or face value of the debt.

The net debt figure also includes a fair valuation of any exchange-traded, OTC or nontraded contingent contractual liabilities the government may have. The words 'off balance sheet' (or 'off budget') are irrelevant. For fiscal sustainability, everything is 'on balance sheet' and 'on budget'. Of course, the valuation of non-market-traded contingent claims is often not straightforward. How does one value such commitments as the government's support for a deposit insurance scheme, government guarantees and other types of government support, or different types of 'comfort' offered to domestic or foreign investors?

On the asset side, a comprehensive fiscal sustainability analysis includes the valuation of state owned assets such as natural resources, infrastructure and other state property. These assets should be 'marked to market', and where no market exists, they should be valued by the estimated present discounted value of the future net cash flows they will generate for the government. The historical cost of these assets is irrelevant in this valuation, as is the valuation of the noncash social benefits these state assets may produce. It follows that, from the point of view of fiscal sustainability, some state 'assets' must be assigned a negative value. A public road or railway system that does not cover even its running cost (let alone its total cost) would be an example. They may be useful and their social benefits may well far exceed their costs, but for sustainability only pecuniary returns and outlays matter.

In a study of fiscal sustainability in 10 transition economies (Buiter, 1998), I adopted the convention to treat all loans from the central bank to the state enterprise and private sector as grants. The stock of such loans was therefore valued at zero: there would be no collection of interest due nor any recovery of principal. I believe this was a wise valuation, and the subsequent (non)performance of these loans bore this out.

Current and future income and expenditure streams that are noncontractual will be considered in Section 2c.

2c. What is the meaning of solvency and sustainability when the state and its financial assets and liabilities live on, even though governments may come and go?

If the world were known to come to an end at some fixed future date, solvency for the state would be easy to define. When the last trumpet sounds, the state cannot leave any net debt. It is less straightforward to define solvency when there is no obvious terminal date. Things are further complicated by the fact that solvency assessments require one to reduce current and future expenditures and revenues to a common denominator. When markets are incomplete, as they are, pricing uncertain future payments and receipts requires a lot of hand waving. When there is no finite terminal date, solvency is conventionally defined by the requirement that the state cannot engage in Ponzi finance. Ponzi finance means always borrowing at least as much as is required to service the debt (interest plus repayment of principal). The growth rate of the debt will be at least as high as the (average effective) interest rate on the debt. The commonly accepted concept of solvency rules out such everlasting pyramid schemes. The finite-horizon solvency criterion requires the terminal debt to be nonpositive. The infinite-horizon concept of solvency requires that the present discounted value of the terminal debt be nonpositive in the limit as the terminal date retreats infinitely far into the future.[5]

Let us begin with a little bit of accounting arithmetic. We distinguish between the contractual obligations and claims of the state and its noncontractual or discretionary expenditures and revenues. Contractual obligations include the net domestic currency-denominated nonmonetary debt of the consolidated general government and central bank, B, its net foreign currency-denominated debt, B^* (which is net of the official foreign exchange reserves held by the central bank) and the monetary liabilities of the central bank, the stock of base money, M. Let the nominal exchange rate (the spot price of foreign currency in terms of domestic currency) be S. Domestic currency debt has a nominal interest rate i and foreign currency a nominal interest rate i^*. Base money has a zero nominal interest rate. Noncontractual or discretionary expenditures as a share of GDP are denoted g and ρ denotes noncontractual revenues as a share of GDP. Real GDP is Y and P is the GPD deflator – the general price level. The difference operator Δ is defined by $\Delta x \equiv x - x(-1)$. The budget deficit of the consolidated general government and central bank, as a fraction of GDP, is given by:

$$\frac{\Delta M + \Delta B + E\Delta B^*}{PY} \equiv g - \rho + i\frac{B}{PY} + i^*\frac{EB^*}{PY} \tag{1}$$

5 This definition of solvency is not as self-evident as it may seem. Buiter and Kletzer (1998) show the kind of limitations that must be imposed on the government's ability to tax for the conventional solvency constraint in an infinite-horizon economy to be rationalisable from acceptable primitive assumptions.

The primary surplus of the state, as a fraction of GDP, denoted σ, is the excess of noninterest revenues over noninterest expenditures (as a fraction of GPD), that is, $\sigma \equiv \rho - g$. Let r be the domestic real interest rate, π the domestic rate of inflation, n the growth rate of real GDP, ε the proportional rate of depreciation of the nominal exchange rate. Total (domestic and foreign currency-denominated) debt as a share of GDP is b, base money issuance as a share of GDP is μ and the share of foreign-currency nonmonetary public debt in total nonmonetary public debt is denoted α.[6]

It follows that

$$\Delta b \equiv -\left(\sigma + \mu + [i - (i^* + \varepsilon)]\alpha b\right) + (r - n)b \tag{2}$$

I will define the augmented primary surplus, $\hat{\sigma}$ as the conventional primary surplus, σ, plus monetary base issuance as a fraction of GPD, $\mu \equiv \dfrac{\Delta M}{PY}$ (which I will refer to as seigniorage) plus the stock of net foreign currency-denominated debt (as a share of GDP), αb, times the deviation of the domestic interest rate from the level it would be at if uncovered interest parity (UIP) applied, $i - (i^* + \varepsilon)$, that is,

$$\hat{\sigma} = \sigma + \mu + [i - (i^* + \varepsilon)]\alpha b \tag{3}$$

The change in the public debt to GDP ratio can therefore be written as

$$\Delta b \equiv -\hat{\sigma} + (r - n)b \tag{4}$$

Note again the net public debt is the net nonmonetary public debt of the consolidated general government and central bank. Government debt held by the central bank is netted out: it is irrelevant from the point of view of fiscal sustainability analysis, as it is a claim of one agency of the state on another agency of the state. Likewise, state revenues do not include any payments made by the central bank to the government or any payments or capital transfers going the other way when, say, the government recapitalises the central bank.

Consider (3) and (4). From the point of view of the state, seigniorage is like other current revenue, like taxes. Base money is viewed as a financial asset by the private sector, but since base money is irredeemable, it is not, in any meaningful sense a liability of the state: it creates no future debt servicing obligations: it bears a zero nominal interest rate and the principal never has to be repaid.

In equation (4) the domestic real interest rate, r, is imputed to the entire public debt, regardless of whether that debt is denominated in hard currency or in local currency. The term ® – $n)b$ will therefore overstate (understate) the true real interest burden on

6 $\pi = \dfrac{\Delta P}{P}; n = \dfrac{\Delta Y}{Y}; \varepsilon = \dfrac{\Delta E}{E}; b = \dfrac{B + EB^*}{PY}; \mu = \dfrac{\Delta M}{PY}; \alpha = \dfrac{EB^*}{PYb}$. The formulae are exact only in continuous time. The correct discrete time analogues are slightly messier. The proper discrete time analogues should be used, however, whenever π, ε, n, i or i^* are large, as the continuous time approximation becomes very bad.

the state if the domestic nominal interest rate exceeds its UIP level, given by the foreign interest rate plus the expected proportional rate of depreciation of the domestic currency. The term $[i-(i^*+\varepsilon)]\alpha b$ corrects for this. It is often the case in developing countries and emerging markets, that the domestic interest rate is much higher than its UIP level. In that case, switching from domestic currency denominated debt to hard currency debt would be attractive to the state as a borrower. However, for many developing countries and emerging markets, the interest rate on its outstanding stock of foreign currency debt will often be a highly concessional one. The government will be rationed at that rate, that is, it will not be able to borrow more at anything like that rate, which therefore does not represent (and understates) the true opportunity cost of foreign borrowing.

It follows from (4) that the public debt–GDP ratio will be constant when

$$\hat{\sigma}=(r-n)b \tag{5}$$

If the real interest rate is, say, 8 percent, the real growth rate 5 percent and the debt to GDP ratio 50 percent, then an augmented primary surplus of 2.5 percent of GDP will stabilise the debt GDP ratio.

The solvency constraint that the present discounted value of the terminal government debt goes to zero as the terminal date recedes into the future implies that the present discounted value of current and future augmented primary surpluses be at least as large as the (default-free or notional) value of the state's outstanding debt. This intertemporal budget constraint of the state can be rewritten in a form that is very similar to the condition for a constant public debt to GDP ratio, given in (5). It is

$$\hat{\sigma}^p \geq (r^p-n^p)b \tag{6}$$

Here $\hat{\sigma}^p$ is the permanent (augmented) primary surplus as a fraction of GDP, r^p the permanent or long-run domestic real interest rate and n^p is the permanent or long-run growth rate of real GDP. 'Permanent' is used in the sense of 'permanent income', that is, it means, roughly, 'average (long-run) expected'.[7]

Equation (6) tells us that any given debt to GDP ratio can be sustained with a lower permanent surplus to GDP ratio, the lower the long-run real interest rate and the higher the long-run real growth rate. Conversely, for any given permanent surplus to GDP ratio, a higher debt to GDP ratio can be sustained the lower the long-run real interest rate and the higher the long-run real growth rate.

Note once more that these accounts must be comprehensive and transparent.

---

7 Strictly speaking $\hat{s}^p(t)\equiv\left(\int_t^\infty e^{-\int_t^v[r(u)-n(u)]du}dv\right)^{-1}\int_t^\infty e^{-\int_t^v[r(u)-n(u)]du}\hat{s}(v)dv$ and

$$r^p-n^p\equiv\left(\int_t^\infty e^{-\int_t^v[r(u)-n(u)]du}dv\right)^{-1}.$$

2d. What is a safe level of the debt to GDP ratio?

While something less than rocket science must be used to try to answer this question, the key point for a developing nation or early emerging market economy is that the maximum public debt burden that can be carried safely is likely to be a much lower figure than one might think by contemplating the debt burdens carried by developed nations. Italy, Belgium and Greece had (gross) public debt-to-annual GDP ratios near and often above 100 percent for the past 10 years.[8] The EU has a ceiling (more often violated than not) of 60 percent for the general government gross debt to GDP ratio, for countries wishing to join the EMU. The only known rationalisation for this 60 percent number is the fact that this was the historical average figure for the EU at the time the debt ceiling was promulgated in the Maastricht Treaty (in 1992). Why the criterion involves gross rather than net debt remains a mystery.

In a recent paper, Reinhart, Rogoff and Savastano (2003) argue that developing countries and emerging markets with a poor track record as borrowers, that is, with a history of default, have but a very limited capacity for carrying public debt, internal or external. For external debt, they calculate that the 'safe' threshold for highly debt intolerant emerging markets may be as low as 15 to 20 percent of GDP. While such countries may be able to borrow more (even significantly more) at times, when the markets suffer one of their episodes of collective euphoria and selective amnesia, the risk of a loss of confidence, a sudden sharp reversal in capital inflows, a debt rollover crisis and a rollover, standstill, moratorium or default by any other name, is uncomfortably high. Fear of default will raise sovereign risk premiums and with it the risk of actual default.

A government's capacity to carry debt is determined by the assessment of existing and potential lenders of that government's capacity and willingness to generate future primary budget surpluses, $\hat{\sigma}^{p}$, and by the prevailing views about future real growth potential, n^{p}, and the path of future real interest rates summarised in r^{p}. Generating primary surpluses is painful and politically challenging because it involves some combination of public spending cuts, tax increases and increased monetary financing.

Lest anyone believe that increased recourse to the printing presses is the obvious way out of what would be a painful dilemma, let me point out that the extraction of additional real resources through increased growth in the nominal money stock will be subject to rapidly diminishing real revenue returns and rapidly increasing inflationary costs. Unanticipated increases in inflation can be used in the short term to make large real resource transfers to the state, especially if there is domestic currency denominated fixed rate debt outstanding, but once the surprise element is gone, the monetary authorities are fighting against the seigniorage Laffer curve: higher monetary growth leads to higher expected inflation, which leads to currency substitution out of domestic money into domestic inflation-proof assets or foreign currency-denominated assets.

8 These figures refer to gross general government debt, not to the net debt of the consolidated general government and central bank, but the difference is not very large for the countries in question.

This undermines and ultimately destroys the inflation tax base (see Buiter (1983, 1985, 1990, 1998) and Buiter and Patel (1992)). It is a fight the authorities cannot win.

For the state to be able to borrow a significant amount, at home or abroad, it must be capable of credible commitment vis-à-vis its current and potential future creditors. A government that borrows must not only be able to commit itself to service the debt; it has to be able to commit its successors also. Unless the obligation to service the debt is assumed ('inherited') automatically by the successor government (regardless of whether this government is politically friendly or hostile towards its predecessor, and regardless of the modalities of the succession), there will be few willing lenders forthcoming. In many developing countries and emerging markets, such credible commitments cannot yet be made, because the institutions of the state are too weak. Indeed, as Reinhart, Rogoff and Savastano (2003) speculate, a government's default may further weaken domestic institutions, making subsequent defaults more likely, and so on, in a vicious cycle of serial default. The likelihood of such a vicious cycle developing is enhanced by a factor not under the control of the borrowing government: the notable cycles in the cost and availability of foreign capital to emerging markets and developing countries, amplified by bouts of alternating euphoria and depression among the lenders.

For many developing countries and emerging markets without a long track record of successful debt servicing and fiscal and monetary restraint, borrowing is risky, even dangerous. There is no doubt in my view that time and again, and right into this new century, sovereign governments have been persuaded, seduced and sometimes almost cajoled to borrow too much. The persuaders are to be found in the private sector but also among the international financial institutions, including the multilateral development banks.

In the private financial markets, the half-life of the collective memory of a major sovereign debt default appears to be no more than three years. Five years after a major default on its GKO debt, the Russian sovereign obtains an investment grade rating! I would not be hugely surprised (although still somewhat surprised) if, despite finding itself, in 2002, at the debtor end of the largest ever sovereign default (and despite a long history of prior sovereign defaults), the Argentine sovereign were to regain an investment grade rating before the end of the decade. It is true that, from the point of view of the ability to pay, the best credit risk is a borrower who has just defaulted on all his debt. Of course, the default may convey information about unobservable characteristics of the borrower that determine his willingness to pay. One inference from the study of Reinhart, Rogoff and Savastano (2003) and from the more extensive IMF (2003) study that covers similar ground, is that past default is a very useful predictor of future default. This is consistent with the hypothesis that markets don't learn – ever.

As regards official lending to developing countries and emerging markets, the bureaucratic imperative – the organisational instinct for self-preservation and, where possible, self-aggrandisement – can drive private and national or international public bureaucracies to pursue size as a primary objective. When the institutionally relevant measure of size is the volume of new lending or the size of the loan portfolio, strong incentives are created for excessive lending, with the ordinary citizens of the borrowing countries and the shareholders of the lending institutions (that is, in the case of public lending institutions, the tax payers of the countries that provided their capital) footing the bill when things go pear-shaped.

The vast majority of the twenty-seven heavily indebted poor countries (HIPCs) that have reached the decision point of the Initiative (out of 38 countries that potentially qualify for assistance under the HIPC) owe most of their external debt to bilateral and multilateral official creditors. None of the EBRD's countries of operation are among these HIPC Initiative eligible countries. However, each of the five EBRD countries of operation for whom poverty and high external debt pose especially acute problems and policy dilemmas, (the CIS countries Armenia, Georgia, Kyrgyz Republic, Moldova and Tajikistan) owes more than half its external debt to official bilateral and multilateral creditors (see Buiter and Lago (2001)).

When debt burdens become unsustainable, or sustainable only at an intolerable human cost, and when there have been no major adverse exogenous shocks that unexpectedly impaired the borrowers' ability to service the debt, it is clear that either both the borrower and the lenders have made mistakes, or that at least one side of the debt bargain has acted dishonestly. A resolution that is fair and provides the right incentives to prevent a recurrence of these debt sustainability problems should impose a cost on both the borrower and the lenders. Regrettably, the borrowing governments and the ruling elites that support them, are often able to pass their share of the cost on to the disenfranchised and often poor and defenceless citizens of their countries. Those that were on the lending side of the bad loans have often moved on to pastures new and greener by the time the chickens come home to roost.

2e. What happens when fiscal sustainability is not achieved? Why do sovereign borrowers ever service their debt?

When *ex-ante* the government cannot satisfy its solvency constraint and intertemporal budget constraint one or more of the following will happen. (1) Realised public spending will be lower than planned public spending; (2) realised tax revenues will be higher than originally planned; (3) inflation will turn out to be higher than expected because the government tries to appropriate more resources through the anticipated and unanticipated inflation taxes; or (4) the public debt (domestic and/or external) will be defaulted on, in part or comprehensively.

The first three options are clearly painful and politically unpopular for the borrowing government. What is the cost of sovereign default to the borrower?

One reason why a borrower, private or sovereign, might service his debt on the originally agreed contractual terms, is that he believes it is the right thing to do. Paying your debts, like telling the truth, can be viewed not instrumentally as something that may or may not be individually rational, but as something intrinsically valuable – not a tactical or even a strategic option, but something worth doing for its own sake. I believe that societies and cultures where such norms predominate and prevail are likely to be both more pleasant and more prosperous that those where the citizens and the state take a purely instrumental view of honesty and commitment.

Back in the economic textbook world of a-moral, selfish economic man and woman, borrowers honour their debt obligations because, if and when it pays to do so. In countries with a well-functioning judiciary and efficient law enforcement, private parties often choose to fulfil their debt obligations because of credible 'third party' enforcement of debt contracts. The situation is less clear for sovereign borrowers. While governments explicitly forego key sovereign immunities when they enter into external debt contracts, taking a government to court is a costly and lengthy process. The kind of gunboat diplomacy that used to be a popular mechanism for sovereign debt collection by imperial powers on behalf of their creditor citizens, is no longer fashionable. Other sanctions against a defaulting government include the risk of attachment of the government's assets located in foreign jurisdictions, and the need to engage in costly cash-in-advance international trading relationships because all trade financing dries up.

One reason a government may opt for servicing and paying down a debt today is the expectation that it may have to borrow again in the future, because desired public spending and domestic revenue bases are not well-aligned over time. Default means at least temporary loss of access to new external financial resources. Governments of export-dependent countries facing highly variable terms of trade will therefore be able to borrow more and on better terms than governments for whom future access to external finance is less valuable. Such self-enforcing, time-consistent or sub game-perfect debt contracts are undoubtedly part of the explanation of why sovereign debt gets serviced at all.

One cost of sovereign default, especially default which is viewed as 'discretionary' and 'voluntary' rather than an unfortunate but unavoidable consequence of bad luck, is the damage it does to respect for the law, to the 'sanctity' of contracts, and to trust among private agents and between private agents and the state. If the state, the ultimate arbiter and enforcer of contracts, can choose to play fast and loose with its own contractual obligations, why should ordinary citizens not try the same? Of course, such considerations are unlikely to weigh heavily with a government that chooses to default when alternative options remain available, but it can inform our understanding of the wider economic and political pathologies that are often encountered in countries that have a history of public debt default.

2f. When should a borrower run the required primary surpluses?

The solvency criterion requires that the outstanding debt be no larger than the present discounted value of current and future primary (augmented) surpluses. It is silent about when in the future any future primary surpluses are to be run. When there is no terminal date (or even if there is one but it is far in the future), there is an obvious temptation for a debtor to put off the day of reckoning as long as possible. Even after 200 years of deficits, our debtor can always argue that he has all of the rest of eternity to run the necessary primary surpluses. Such a debt service strategy would lack credibility. Both creditors and debtors know that talk is cheap, that actions speak louder than words and that seeing is believing. Governments with either a very limited or a poor track record of debt servicing will be required to demonstrate early on the capability and willingness to service their debt by running primary surpluses.

The more recent the arrival of the government in the global capital markets or the more recent its latest encounter with problems servicing its debt, the earlier evidence of debt servicing ability and willingness will have to be provided to the markets, through the early generation of significant primary surpluses. Many developing countries and emerging market economies are in such a position. It inevitably reduces the value to the country of access to the capital markets.

2g. Domestic debt and external debt.

There is, in principle, a wide range of alternative public debt instruments available to governments. Debt can be denominated in domestic currency or in foreign currency, or it can be index-linked to some domestic price index. It can be fixed rate or variable rate. It can come in different maturities. It includes bank loans and OTC or exchange-traded securities. Bonds may have collective action clauses attached to them. Any of these instruments can be held by domestic residents or by foreign residents or offshore creditors.

Very few developing countries and emerging markets can borrow abroad using financial instruments denominated in their own domestic currency. The situation is different for the governments of many of the industrial countries. The world's largest international debtor government, the USA, borrows almost exclusively in US dollars. The world's creditors clearly trust Alan Greenspan and his eventual successors not to engage in any high-inflation experiments. The 'original sin' that prevents emerging market and developing countries from selling domestic currency debt to foreign creditors is a long history of unanticipated (hyper) inflation and its devastating effect on the real returns earned by the holders of such debt. Many of today's advanced industrial countries were a part of this history during past centuries. As regards today's emerging market economies, the markets' collective memory is often not discriminating enough to distinguish between countries with a penchant for inflationary financing and bastions of monetary rectitude; 'original sin' taints them all. This situation will change only if and when sustained low and stable inflation rates have become a familiar and natural part of the economic landscape also in the developing world and in emerging market economies.

When domestic and international financial markets are segmented, through capital controls and other man-made obstacles to cross-border capital flows, there are frequent and often quite sustained spells during which domestic real interest rates (real interest rates on domestic currency-denominated public debt held by residents) are significantly higher than on foreign currency-denominated external debt. This is especially likely to be the case if the domestic economy is booming, say because of a natural resource boom in a natural-resource-rich country or because of the introduction and implementation a set of business-friendly reforms. If the government is not rationed in the external capital market, this creates strong incentives for borrowing abroad rather than at home, and even for retiring outstanding domestic debt and refinancing with a Eurobond issue.

Such a decision can turn out to be an expensive mistake. Servicing domestic public debt involves only an internal transfer, that is, a transfer of resources from the domestic private sector to the government, through higher taxes (including higher seigniorage) or lower public spending. Servicing external public debt involves a dual or double transfer: an internal resource transfer from the domestic private sector to the government (through the augmented primary surplus of the government) and an external resource transfer from the domestic economy to the rest of the world (through the nation's external primary surplus (the current account surplus exclusive of interest payments). The external transfer often requires a worsening of the external terms of trade and a depreciation of the real exchange rate. For long periods, the external transfer may take place smoothly and in orderly fashion. If, however, there is a sudden loss of confidence in the domestic currency or in the fiscal probity of the government, there can be a run on the currency, a run on the public debt (that is, a refusal to roll over maturing debt and to provide additional external funds) and, often, a run on the domestic banking system. Real interest rates on both foreign currency- and domestic currency-denominated debt issued by domestic residents shoot up, and even at these much higher rates, very little refinancing or new lending takes place. Credit is rationed. A sharp depreciation of the nominal and real exchange rate is the result and the real burden of the external debt can more than double in a matter of days as ex-post real interest rates on foreign currency debt explode when the exchange rate collapses. Central banks can act as lender of last resort for domestic currency debt but not for foreign currency debt. This is the story of Argentina in 2002/2003, and the story of countless emerging markets before it.

Vulnerability to a sudden loss of confidence and reversal of capital inflows is greater when the maturity of the debt is short and when there is a bunching of debt repayments in a short period of time. This can become a natural focal point for a speculative attack. Crises and default can, however, occur even when the debt is optimally structured along all relevant dimensions.

2h. Asset sales, including privatisations

Asset sales (including *de facto* partial privatisations such as PSAs (Production Sharing Agreements) only improve the financial sustainability of the government if the proceeds from the sale exceed the present discounted value of the future cash income these assets would have produced for the government under continued public ownership (the assets' continuation value in the public sector). If the sale price equals the continuation value, asset sales are equivalent to borrowing; they neither add to nor subtract from the government's fiscal sustainability. Of course, if the government encounters temporarily unfavourable borrowing conditions in the markets, such short-term liquidity or debt roll-over constraints can be relaxed through asset sales.

As a rule, privatisation should be done for efficiency reasons rather than for deficit financing reasons. The fact that the sales price exceeds the continuation value in the public sector of a public sector asset may, but need not, reflect greater efficiency in the management of the asset in the private sector. It could also, wholly or in part, reflect a more intensive exploitation of monopoly or monopsony power by the new owners of the privatised assets.

3. WHAT WOULD A SENSIBLE STATE DEFICIT RULE LOOK LIKE?

As an example of an intuitive fiscal-financial rule that (a) guarantees fiscal sustainability and (b) makes sense under a number of practically relevant contingencies, I will, immodestly, offer the Permanent Balance rule proposed by Clemens Grafe and myself (Buiter and Grafe (2003) and Buiter (2003)).

Total current revenues as a share of GDP, ρ, are the sum of taxes τ and other revenues, κ, which includes any capital income the state may receive, seigniorage revenue, μ, and the 'deviations from UIP correction term' $[i-(i^*+\varepsilon)]\alpha b$, all as shares of GDP. Government spending g is the sum of consumption spending g^c, gross capital formation, g^I, and transfers and subsidies, g^T, all as shares of GDP.

The permanent balance rule is a 'tax-smoothing rule' in the spirit of Barro (1979): tax revenues are planned to be a constant share of GDP, the permanent tax rate or share. This share is the lowest constant share of tax revenues in GDP that would, in the absence of news and surprises, ensure the long-run solvency of the government. It is given by sum of (1) the permanent share of noninterest public spending in GDP (roughly the long-run average share of noninterest public spending in GDP, looking forward) and (2) the permanent government interest bill, as a share of GDP, calculated as the product of the debt-to-GDP ratio and the excess of the long-run real interest rate over the long-run growth rate of real GDP. It is given in (7)

$$\tau \geq \tau^P \equiv g^P - \kappa^P + (r^P - n^P)b \tag{7}$$

Under the permanent balance rule, the public sector deficit, as a share of GDP, d, behaves as follows:

$$d \leq (n+\pi)b + g - g^P + \kappa^P - \kappa + \left[\left(r - r^P\right) - \left(n - n^P\right)\right]b \tag{8}$$

The permanent balance rule therefore implies that the permissible general government budget deficit as a fraction of GDP is the sum of four components. The first is the reduction in the debt-to-GDP ratio due to nominal GDP growth (inflation and real GDP growth), $(n + \pi)b$. For example, if annual real GDP growth and annual inflation are both 2.5 percent and the debt-to-annual GDP ratio is 40 percent, this component would permit a deficit of no more than 2 percent of GDP. The second component is the excess of the actual share of government spending in GDP over its permanent share, $g - g^P$. The third is the excess of permanent non-tax revenue over current non-tax revenue (both as shares of GDP), $\kappa^P - \kappa$. The fourth is the excess of the actual (inflation-and-growth-corrected) interest bill over the permanent interest bill (which is itself (long-run) inflation- and – (long-run) growth-corrected).

The permanent balance rule has some key attractive properties. It ensures the solvency of the state and the sustainability of its fiscal-financial-monetary programme. It is 'inflation and real growth corrected', that is, the permissible deficit allows for the effect of inflation and real growth on the capacity of the economy to carry debt; it does not confuse issues having to do with deficit financing (intertemporal priorities) with issues having to do with the size of the public sector; it avoids procyclical behaviour of the fiscal policy instruments; it allows for important differences in economic structure and initial conditions; it does not incorporate the 'golden rule' fallacy that borrowing for public sector capital formation is inherently more financially sound and safe than borrowing to finance public sector consumption or transfer payments. Borrowing to finance public sector investment is permitted, by the rule, if and to the extent that current public sector investment exceeds permanent (long-run average) public sector investment (as shares of GDP). But the same holds for public consumption and transfer payments. Any excess of current public spending over permanent public spending (all as shares of GDP) can be financed by borrowing, regardless of whether it is public consumption spending, public sector transfer payments or public sector investment. Any shortfall of current spending relative to permanent spending should be reflected in repayment of debt.

4. CONCLUSION

Without fiscal sustainability, no economic development strategy can succeed. Unfortunately, in many emerging markets and developing countries, weak political institutions and incompetent and corrupt public administrations impose very strict limits on the amount of public debt, internal and external, that can be carried. In principle, tight constraints on a government's borrowing and debt capacity need not prevent it from reaping the benefits of consumption smoothing. A government could manage an on-average positive net financial asset position instead of an on-average positive net financial liability position. A government can smooth consumption over time by managing the liability side of its financial balance sheet: incurring debt when spending is unusually and temporarily high or when the tax base is unusually and temporarily depressed, and servicing and paying down the debt when spending is unusually low and the revenue base unusually strong. Or it can smooth consumption over time by managing the asset side of its financial balance sheet: by building up its stock of financial assets during unusually good times and running it down during unusually lean times. It is easier to be a credible manager of your own assets than of your own liabilities. Some of the natural resource rich nations faced with both sharp high frequency fluctuations in their external terms of trade and the long-term problem of managing an exhaustible resource, have created national oil funds other stabilisation funds to smooth public and private consumption over commodity price cycles and across generations.

For the poorest countries, the challenge of first building up a sufficiently large stock of public sector assets is likely to prove too much. Countries that could, in principle, smooth consumption through the asset side of the public sector balance sheet rather than through the liability side, may find that having a sizeable stock of financial assets under public control may create irresistible pressures for wasteful expenditure, graft and corruption; an oil fund or gas fund may present a prime target for rent seekers and other predators. With weak domestic political and judiciary institutions and a lack of effective accountability of the leadership to its citizens, a country's access to the global capital markets will remain highly restricted, and domestic markets for public debt will remain underdeveloped.

Once the body politic and the institutions of the state have become strong enough to permit the sovereign to enter into credible commitments over time, a nation, through its government, can experience the true joys and pains of public debt within a set of rules that ensures sustainability. The kind of 'Permanent Balance' rule I have sketched in Section 3 provides a useful benchmark.

Unless a government can stick to the rules of sustainable budget finance when it involves paying down debt and running (primary) surpluses, it should not venture anywhere near the internal or external debt markets. Many developing countries and even some highly touted emerging market economies have economic institutions that are so weak and political institutions and regimes that are so corrupt and oppressive, that sovereign borrowing is unlikely to increase and may well diminish the well-being of the vast majority of the citizens. This has not stopped their sovereigns from borrowing when they could; nor has it stopped the private and public lending community from extending the hand of finance. This combination of market failure and political failure should give us all pause for thought.

REFERENCES

Allais, Maurice. (1947). *Economie et Intérêt*. Paris: Imprimerie Nationale.

Barro, Robert J. (1979). On the Determination of the Public Debt, *Journal of Political Economy, October*.

Buiter, Willem H. (1983). Measurement of the Public Sector Deficit and its Implications for Policy Evaluation and Design. *International Monetary Fund Staff Papers, 30, June 1983,* pp. 306-49.

Buiter, Willem H. (1985). A Guide to Public Debt and Deficits. *Economic Policy, 1, November,* 13-79.

Buiter, Willem H. (1990). Some Thoughts on the Role of Fiscal Policy in Stabilization and Structural Adjustment in Developing Countries.In W.H. Buiter, *Principles of Budgetary and Financial Policy* (pp. 407-448). MIT Press.

Buiter, Willem H. (1998). Aspects of Fiscal Performance in Some Transition Economies under Fund-Supported Programs. In Gary Saxonhouse, & T.N. Srinivasan (Eds.), *Development, Duality, and the International Economic Regime: Essays in Honor of Gustav Ranis* (Chapter 15 pp. 398-451). Ann Arbor, MI: University of Michigan Press.

Buiter, Willem H. (2003). Ten Commandments for a Fiscal Rule in the E(M)U. *Oxford Review of Economic Policy, Vol. 19, No. 1, Spring 2003,* 84-99.

Buiter, Willem H. & Grafe, Clemens. (2003). Reforming EMU's fiscal policy rules; some suggestions for enhancing fiscal sustainability and macroeconomic stability in an enlarged European Union. Forthcoming in Marco Buti (Ed.), *Monetary and Fiscal Policies in EMU: Interactions and Coordination.* Cambridge University Press.

Buiter, Willem H. & Lago, Ricardo. (2001). Debt in Transition Economies: Where is it Heading, What can be Done About it? *Revue D'Économie Financière, Special Issue, Ten Years of Transition in Eastern European Countries, Achievements and Challenges, 2001*, 191-213.

Buiter, Willem H. & Patel, Urjit. (1992). Debt, deficits and inflation: an application to the public finances of India. *Journal of Public Economics, 47, 1992*, 171-205; also in Amaresh Bagchi & Nicholas Stern (Eds.). (1994). *Tax Policy and Planning in Developing Countries* (pp. 94-131). Oxford University Press.

IMF (2003), Public Debt In Emerging Markets: Is it Too High? *World Economic Outlook 2003,* Chapter III (pp. 49-88).

Reinhart, Carmen M., Rogoff, Kenneth S., & Savastano, Miguel A. (2003). Debt Intolerance. *Working Paper No. 9908, August*. NBER.

Samuelson, Paul A. (1958). An Exact Consumption-Loan Model of Interest with or without the Social Contrivance of Money. *Journal of Political Economy, 66*, 467-482.

EU INTEGRATION AND THE NEW ECONOMIC GEOGRAPHY

J.H. GARRETSEN

INTRODUCTION

In recent years academic research in mainstream economics has showed a (renewed) interest in geography. Thanks to the so called New Economic Geography (NEG) or Geographical Economics literature, spatial distribution and the growth of economic activity figure prominently on the research agenda within economics. So far, the emphasis in NEG has been on theory. It is only fairly recently that progress is being made as to its empirical relevance. In a nutshell, NEG is the attempt to endogenise the location decisions of mobile factors of production using the tools of general equilibrium theory where optimising individual behaviour and the analysis of equilibria are key ingredients. This attempt has met with some serious criticism both from within and from outside economics (as to the latter, economic geographers are rather critical of the NEG enterprise). Harry Garretsen (2005) explains the background of the NEG in more detail. One line of criticism has been the lack of empirical research. At the same time it is clear that many important (policy) issues in economics could benefit from NEG-inspired research. In particular, issues dealing with the effects of economic integration on the spatial allocation of economic activity spring to mind. The impact of, for instance, EU enlargement, the EMU or globalisation on the economic geography of Europe is a major concern for policymakers. Without empirical research to back up the theoretical insights from NEG about the relationship between spatial allocation and economic integration, the NEG will be of limited use.

For the research into the empirical relevance of NEG (at least) the following three issues stand out:

- The measurement of the spatial or geographic concentration of economic activity.
- The tension between the simplicity of the formal NEG models and the complexity of the forces that shape 'real world' economic geography.
- The search for testable hypotheses that really discriminate between NEG and alternative theories of location.

These 3 issues are at the heart of the research carried out at the Utrecht School of Economics (USE) as to the role of geography within economics. The research is firmly rooted within the NEG approach and hence within mainstream (international) economics but it also explicitly tries to take on board insights from economic geography at

P. de Gijsel and H. Schenk (eds.), Multidisciplinary Economics, 225–226.

large. The longstanding collaboration of economics in Utrecht with the economic geographers at Utrecht University is definitely a bonus in this respect. The NEG-inspired research at the Utrecht School of Economics will also benefit from the research contacts with other scholars from national as well as international research institutions. The idea is that USE is well-placed to become part of the internationally recognised 'agglomeration' of research at the crossroads between economics and geography. The co-operation and contacts with fellow economists and geographers from the University of Cambridge, LSE, Brown, Munich, Hamburg, Erasmus University and Groningen University, to name a few, are an essential part of this effort.

The papers in the present volume are good examples of the present and future research that will be carried out at USE. All contributions mentioned below were part of the seminar that took place on October 23rd 2003. The seminar preceded the inaugural lecture of Garretsen (2005). The introduction to the paper by Marius Brülhart and Rolf Traeger (2005) that is included here deals with the measurement issue, whereas the contribution by Ron Martin (2005) uses the example of European integration to inter alia assess the relevance of NEG and to argue that economic geography at large offers a better alternative to deal with European integration and the prospects for regional convergence. The 3rd issue mentioned above was also part of the seminar: the inaugural lecture by Garretsen (2005) gives an introduction to the search for testable hypotheses and the study by Steven Brakman, Harry Garretsen, Joeri Gorter, Albert van der Horst and Marc Schramm (2005), not included here, is the full-blown final-product that stemmed from the initial results presented at the seminar.

REFERENCES

Brakman, S., Garretsen, H., Gorter, J., van der Horst, A. & Schramm, M. (2005). *New Economic Geography, Empirics, and Regional Policy*. The Hague: Netherlands' Bureau for Economic Policy Analysis (CPB)/ Sdu publishers, forthcoming.

Brülhart, M. & Traeger, R. (2005). An Account of Geographic Concentration Patterns of Europe: Introduction and Summary, this volume.

Garretsen, H. (2005). From Koopmans to Krugman: International Economics and Geography, inaugural lecture, Utrecht University, this volume.

Martin, R. (2005). European Integration and Economic Geography: Theory and Empirics in the Regional Convergence Debate, this volume.

R. MARTIN

EUROPEAN INTEGRATION AND ECONOMIC GEOGRAPHY: THEORY AND EMPIRICS IN THE REGIONAL CONVERGENCE DEBATE*

1. INTRODUCTION

Over the past decade or so, there has been a veritable explosion of academic and policy interest in regional economic growth: why regional growth rates differ, what makes some regions more competitive than others, whether regional economic inequalities narrow or persist over time, and what sort of policies are most likely to raise the economic prosperity of lagging regions. These issues have attracted the attention of both economic geographers and the new breed of 'geographical economists'. To be sure, the approach adopted to advance our understanding of these questions differs markedly between the two groups.[1] Nevertheless, notwithstanding sharp differences in methodology and epistemology, both camps agree on one central tenet: geography matters for economic performance.

This recognition has acquired a particular relevance in the context of the European Union. Interest in the economic geography of the European Union has expanded apace in recent years. There are several reasons for this. Since the beginning of the 1980s, the European Union has made major strides towards its goal of economic integration: in particular, abolishing the remaining obstacles and barriers to a single market for goods and services, establishing a single currency (the Euro), and creating a unified monetary space (Euro zone).[2] The recent enlargement of the EU from 15 to 25 members repre-

---

* Based on an invited paper presented at the Inauguration of the New School of Economics, University of Utrecht, 23 October 2003

1 Compare, for example, M. Storper (1997) *The Regional World*, and A.J. Scott (1998) *Regions and the World Economy*, both economic geographers, on the one hand, with M. Fujita, P. Krugman and A. Venables (1999) *The Spatial Economy*, M. Fujita and J-F. Thisse (2002) *Economics of Agglomeration*, and R. Baldwin et al (2003) *Economic Geography and Public Policy*, all 'new economic geographers' on the other.

2 The twelve members of the single currency area are: Austria, Belgium, Finland, France, Germany, Greece, Ireland, Italy, Luxembourg, the Netherlands, Portugal, and Spain. Britain, Denmark and Sweden – together with all of the new enlargement states (see next footnote) – remain, for the moment, outside the formal Eurozone.

P. de Gijsel and H. Schenk (eds.), Multidisciplinary Economics, 227–257.

sents the latest stage in this process of deepening and widening integration.[3] These developments – together with the challenges posed by accelerating globalisation and technological change – have profound implications for the structure and evolution of the economic landscape of the EU. For such 'shocks' are by no means necessarily neutral in their geographical effects, but rather are more likely to impact differently on different EU regions. At the same time, the European Commission puts great emphasis on the pursuit of regional 'cohesion' or convergence, that is the reduction of regional disparities in economic performance and welfare. Indeed, regional cohesion is itself an important element of integration; after all, the existence and persistence of wide regional disparities is hardly consistent with 'harmonious and balance regional development'.[4]

Yet further, the regional dimension has assumed heightened salience in relation to the concern over the growth performance of the EU. According to the Commission, and other observers, EU economic growth – particularly productivity growth – has been disappointingly slow in recent years, especially in comparison to the USA.[5] As set out in the Lisbon and Nice summits of 2000, a primary objective of the Commission is to close this gap with the United States, and make the European Union the 'most competitive knowledge-based economy in the world' by 2010. Whether this highly ambitious aim is feasible is debatable. What is important about it, however, is that the Commission puts great emphasis on the need for all regions to contribute to this imperative:

> If the EU is to realise its economic potential, then all regions wherever they are located, whether in existing Member States or in the new countries about to join, need to be involved in the growth effort... The cost of not pursuing a vigorous cohesion policy to tackle disparities is, therefore, measured not only in terms of a loss of personal and social well-being but also in economic terms, in a loss of the potential real income and higher living standards. Given the interdependencies inherent in an integrated economy, these losses are not confined to the less competitive regions... but affect everyone in the Union. Strengthening regional competitiveness throughout the Union and helping people fulfil their capabilities will boost the growth potential of the EU economy as a whole to the common benefit of all. And by securing a more balanced spread of economic activity across the Union, it will reduce the risk of bottlenecks as growth occurs and lessen the likelihood of inflationary pressures bringing growth to a premature end.[6]

3 The ten accession states that joined the EU in May 2004 are the eight Central and East European countries (CEECs), – the Czech Republic, Estonia, Hungary, Latvia, Lithuania, Poland, Slovakia, and Slovenia – together with Cyprus and Malta. Bulgaria and Romania are anticipated to join in 2007. Negotiations have yet to get underway with Turkey, as a possible thirteenth applicant.

4 European Commission (2000) *Unity, Solidarity, and Diversity for Europe, its People and its Territory: Second Report on Economic and Social Cohesion,* p. 13.

5 For example: European Commission (2004) *A New Partnership for Cohesion: Convergence, Competitiveness, Cooperation, Third Report on Economic and Social Cohesion*; A. Sapir et al. (2003) *An Agenda for a Growing Europe: Making the EU Economic System Deliver*, Report to the President of the European Commission.

6 European Commission (2004) *A New Partnership for Cohesion: Convergence, Competitiveness, Cooperation, Third Report on Economic and Social Cohesion*, pp. vii-viii.

Given these various shocks and challenges to the European regions, it is not surprising that there has been heated discussion about the role, scale, impact and future allocation of the structural, cohesion and other policies that are intended to assist the process of regional cohesion and convergence.

For all these reasons, the competitive performance of EU regions has attracted considerable academic attention and debate. Indeed, the implications of progressive economic integration for the regions of the EU has itself been one of the factors behind the 'geographical turn' within economics. As Fujita, Krugman and Venables, some of the prime movers of this development, have put it:

> The field has been given an enormous boost in particular by plans to unify the European market and the attempt to understand how this deeper integration will work by comparing international economics within Europe with interregional economics in the United States.[7]

However, this is not to say that there is general consensus amongst either economists or geographers about what has been happening to regional disparities in the EU, nor about what the impact of economic and monetary integration on the regions has been thus far, and is likely to be in the future. My argument in this paper is that this lack of agreement derives from two main sources. One problem is that there is no one single, generally accepted, theory that best predicts the evolution of the economic landscape under increasing EU integration. Different theories predict quite different outcomes and impacts. Another problem is that the interpretation of empirical trends in regional economic performance across the EU is equally diverse and debatable, and attributing these trends explicitly to the integration process itself is in any case problematic. These issues are clearly of some importance since they have implications for attempts to assess the likely impact of integration on the regions of the new enlargement states.

2. THEORETICAL PERSPECTIVES ON THE REGIONAL IMPLICATIONS OF ECONOMIC AND MONETARY INTEGRATION

As noted above, in the quote from Fujita, Krugman and Venables, the EMU experiment has played a significant role in stimulating new theoretical developments within economics that assign central importance to the location of economic activity and the evolution of regional economies. Three main streams of recent work can be distinguished: the application of standard Neoclassical growth theory and its new endogenous growth variants to regional convergence; the 'new economic geography' models of spatial agglomeration; and the so-called 'new intranational or regional macroeconomics' (Table 1).

7 M. Fujita, P. Krugman and A. Venables (1999) *The Spatial Economy: Cities, Regions and International Trade*, p. 2.

Table 1. Three Theoretical Perspectives on the Regional Implications of EMU

Theoretical Framework	Predicted Implications for EU Regions
New Growth Theory	According to standard growth model, removing barriers to trade and factor mobility, harmonising regulatory environments, and creating monetary union, should all promote regional convergence in per capita GDP and productivity. In endogenous growth variants, existence of marked regional disparities in innovation and technological change, and evidence of spatially limited knowledge spillovers suggest that regional convergence will at best be conditional, slow and possibly non-existent, with differences in per capita GDP and productivity persisting over time.
New Economic Geography	EMU will boost trade and lower transactions costs, hence stimulate spatial concentration and regional specialisation. Core-periphery pattern likely. Increased regional specialisation will accentuate region-specific shocks, which given increased factor mobility could amplify regional disparities in growth and employment so that regional divergence a possibility.
New Intranational Macroeconomics	EMU will increase trade between and specialisation of regions and expose them to more intense shocks. Lack of labour mobility in EU, compared to USA, will mean that regions in EU not as fully integrated as regions in USA, and will not adjust as easily to demand, technological and policy shocks. No necessary reason for regions to converge, and are likely to depend much more on interregional and other fiscal transfers payments to overcome adverse shocks.

Given its assumptions of constant returns to scale, diminishing returns to factors of production, and exogenous technological change, standard neoclassical (Solow-Swan) growth theory predicts that countries or regions that initially have low per capita incomes and low productivity will experience faster rates of growth than countries and regions that initially have higher per capita incomes and productivity, so convergence takes place. Economic integration is assumed to promote such convergence by increasing the flows of labour, capital and technology from high productivity regions to low productivity regions. These flows speed up the process of factor price equalisation across regions and nations. Thus, it is argued that EMU should accelerate national and regional convergence.

However, this model takes little account of significant and persistent differences in economic structure, technology, tastes and so on between nations, and in the presence of such differences convergence to a common long-run level of productivity or per capita income need not occur. Barro and Sala-i-Martin argue that such 'absolute' convergence is most likely to occur across regions within a single nation rather than between nations, because regions within a country will tend to be more similar than nations in terms of institutional, technological and other characteristics:

> Although differences in technology, preferences and institutions do exist across regions, these differences are likely to be smaller than those across countries. Firms and households of different regions within a single country tend to have access to similar technologies and have roughly similar tastes and cultures. Furthermore, regions share a common central government and therefore have similar institutional set-ups and legal systems. This relative homogeneity is more likely to apply across regions within countries than across countries.[8]

This could be interpreted as an argument that the more regions have similar structural, institutional and cultural characteristics (i.e. are 'homogeneous'), the more likely absolute regional convergence is to occur, so that the regions could be said to constitute an optimum currency area (OCA).[9] Geographers would argue, however, that regional differences in institutional, social and technological characteristics can be substantial and may persist for long periods, so that regional convergence may not in fact be of the absolute type. Such regional differences in economic, social and institutional structures will be even more pronounced between the regions of different members states across the EU. Indeed, there is agreement that economically, socially, culturally and politically, the EU will never be as integrated as the USA, and that regional differences – especially as between different member states – will continue to exert an influence on growth and prosperity. For one thing, the linguistic and cultural diversity of the EU is marked compared to that found in the USA. Second, there are political limits to the regulatory, fiscal and monetary harmonisation for which EU member states will be willing to cede their autonomy and sovereignty. For example, there is no centralised EU-wide fiscal stabilisation system of the sort that operates across US regions, and tax harmonisation seems a long way off indeed. Third, and crucially, there is copious evidence that rates of interregional labour mobility are much lower within EU countries than in the USA (see Table 2) and they are even lower between EU member states – in part because of the linguistic and cultural differences referred to above. Thus there are grounds for believing that EU countries are unlikely to become as integrated as regions within those countries are already. EU wide regional convergence could therefore be very slow and limited.

Since the mid-1980s, however, the assumption of exogenous technical change in the Solow-Swan model has been replaced by so-called endogenous growth wherein technical change is the result of purposive R&D activity and learning by firms and workers, and where spillovers of knowledge occur between producers.[10] This prevents

8 R. Barro and X. Sala-i-Martin (1995) *Economic Growth*, p. 382.

9 See, for example, R.A. Mundell (1961) A Theory of Optimum Currency Areas, *American Economic Review, 51*, pp. 657-665.

10 The incorporation of R&D theories and imperfect competition into the growth theory framework began with Romer. See P.M. Romer (1986) Increasing Returns and Long-Run Growth, *Journal of Political Economy, 94*, pp. 1002-1037; P.M. Romer (1987) Growth Based on Increasing Returns due to Specialisation, *American Economic Review, 77, 2*, pp. 56-62; P.M. Romer (1990) Endogenous Technological Change, *Journal of Political Economy, 98, 5*, Part II, pp. S71-S102.

diminishing returns to capital accumulation, and permits regional growth rates to differ, so that per capita GDP and incomes need not converge. In this theory the relative immobility – the slow or limited spillover – of technological innovation between regions, is a major source of increasing returns and of resultant persistent differences in the innovativeness of regions. Technological innovation is assumed to depend, at least in part, on relatively immobile tacit knowledge and localised collective learning, and locally-specific institutional structures (for example, university research expertise and university–business linkages). Regions that initially have advantages on these fronts will tend to attract mobile educated labour and research-orientated capital, thereby increasing their comparative advantages as areas of technological and innovative leadership yet further. Regional inequalities in the innovative-based economic development tend to become self-reinforcing. High rates of innovation and technology spending per capita tend to be significantly positively correlated with high per capita incomes, and in such models, regional divergence or persistence of regional inequalities are more likely outcomes of economic integration than is regional convergence. While this endogenous growth variant can be linked to the conditional convergence of standard Neoclassical theory, the recognition that innovation and technological change are often very localised, giving rise to equally localised increasing returns, and that the diffusion of knowledge and technology is slow and spatially restricted, implies that regional growth may actually diverge.[11]

Table 2. Average Net Interregional Migration in three EU countries versus and the USA (per cent of Regional Population)

Period	US	Germany	Italy	UK
1970-79	1.20	0.27	0.37	0.47
1980-89	0.84	0.34	0.33	0.26
1990-95	0.87	0.31	0.40	0.20

Note: Figures are population-weighted averages over regions. For the period concerned, each regional figure is calculated as the average absolute value of the change in regional working age population (measured net of national working-age population growth).
German figures are for western Länder only, excluding Berlin.
Source: Obstfeld and Peri (2000)[12]

Indeed, in endogenous variants of the Neoclassical growth model, EMU of itself need not produce regional convergence at all, but might even accentuate preexisting regional

11 For a survey of the application of different forms of endogenous growth models to regional development, see. Martin and P. Sunley (1998) Slow Convergence? The New Endogenous Growth Theory and Regional Development, *Economic Geography*, 74, 201-227.

12 M. Obstfeld and G. Peri (2000) Regional nonadjustment and fiscal policy, in G.D. Hess and E. van Wincoop (*op cit*), pp. 221-271.

economic disparities.[13] There are no obvious or compelling reasons to suppose that economic integration across the EU will stimulate the diffusion or dispersal of innovative technological advance any more quickly or widely than occurs across the integrated economies of individual member states. As the European Commission itself has documented, R&D activity is highly localised within the EU: some 50 per cent of R&D expenditure is accounted for by just 28 of the 211 NUTS2 regions, and 50 per cent of patent activity by just 13 regions. These 'islands of innovation' appear to have established 'first mover' advantages that will prove difficult for other regions to emulate. These same islands of innovation also rank amongst the EU's most prosperous regions in terms of levels and growth rates of per capita GDP.

The operation of increasing rather than constant returns to scale is also a key assumption underpinning much of the 'new economic geography'.[14] Thus, as Paul Krugman and others have argued, economic integration allows regions to specialise, increasing returns to be realised and geographical concentration to occur. The process of EMU reduces the transaction costs between regions, and will make it more likely that any given degree of external economies will be sufficient to lead to increased spatial concentration of an industry. Regional economies are predicted to become more dependent on export clusters held together by Marshallian economies of localisation. Increased regional specialisation in turn means that, being less diversified, regions will be more subject to idiosyncratic technology and demand shocks. This leads to a greater risk of severe region-specific recessions. It also leads, in the presence of high factor mobility, to regional divergence over the longer term.

In support of these predictions, Krugman suggests that US states and cities are more economically specialised than member countries and regions of the EU. Further, not only are US regions more specialised than those in the EU, but the high mobility of capital in the former magnifies regional economic fluctuations, and combined with the high mobility of labour, tends to produce spatial agglomeration and divergent regional economic growth over time.[15] The existence of the heavily federalised US fiscal system

---

13 G. Bertola (1993) Models of economic integration and localised growth, in F. Torres and F. Giavazzi (Eds) *Adjustment and Growth in the European Monetary Union*, pp. 159-179.

14 See, in particular: P. Krugman (1991a) *Geography and Trade*; P. Krugman (1991b) Increasing returns and economic geography, *Journal of Political Economy, 99*, pp. 483-499; P. Krugman (1995) *Development, Geography and Economic Theory*; P. Krugman (2001) Where in the world is the 'New Economic Geography'? In G.L. Clark, M. Feldman and M. Gertler (Eds) *Handbook of Economic Geography*, pp. 49-60; and M. Fujita, P. Krugman and A. Venables (1999) *The Spatial Economy: Cities, Regions and International Trade*; Other work in this vein includes S. Braman, H. Garretsen, and C. van Marrewijk (2001) *Geographical Economics* (an attempt to make Krugman type models more relevant to real-world data); and M. Fujita and J-F. Thisse (2002) *Economics of Agglomeration: Cities, Industrial Location and Regional Growth,* and R. Baldwin et al. (2003) *Economic Geography and Public Policy* (both highly mathematical treatments).

15 This argument is best illustrated in P. Krugman (1993) The Lessons of Massachusetts for EMU, in F. Torres and F. Giavazzi (Eds) *op cit,* pp. 241-269. In fact the evidence that the US states are more economically specialised than EU regions is far from convincing.

offers a partial solution to this problem.[16] According to Krugman, then, both theory and available evidence from the US suggest that with the Single Market (1992) and EMU, European regions will become more economically specialised, and hence more vulnerable to regional specific shocks. Since regions are unable to respond with countercyclical monetary or exchange rate policies, they will be faced with new stabilisation problems.

Whether such shocks will produce long-run regional divergence as Krugman-style new economic geography models would predict, will depend on what happens to factor mobility. Although increases in labour mobility across the regions of the EU may be limited by enduring linguistic and cultural barriers, capital mobility will almost certainly increase substantially under EMU. And, as mentioned earlier, the EU has no centralised fiscal system, so unless there is some massive change in EU institutions, this automatic cushion will be absent. In contrast to the neoclassical growth models, therefore, the new economic geography is far less optimistic about the prospects for regional convergence under EMU. As Sapir et al. argue:

> In reality... economic activity does not diffuse uniformly across integrated territories within each Member State, and within each region, production agglomerates in cities and industrial districts. Agglomeration tendencies reflect locally increasing returns to scale... In the EU economic integration context, such phenomena can endanger cohesion objectives. If relatively advanced regions attract an even larger share of the overall economic activity, an increase in the scale and intensity of continent-wide interaction could well cause relatively backward regions to lag further behind rather than catch up within the more advanced portions of the integrated economic area.[17]

In fact, under new economic geography models, EU integration could well intensify the spatial concentration or agglomeration of economic activity at a variety of spatial levels: from local industrial districts and clusters, to cities, to the EU's large-scale core-periphery structure.

Furthermore, regional economic development is known to be strongly path dependent, that is long-run regional outcomes are dependent on the historical adjustment paths taken to them. Prosperous regions tend to remain prosperous for long periods of time, and likewise for less successful regions. The pervasive nature of path dependence in the economic landscape is recognised in much of Krugman's work (his argument that 'history matters'), and in the related location models developed by Brian Arthur.[18] Similarly, it is a key feature of Kaldorian cumulative causation models of selfreinfor-

16 It has been estimated for example, that in the USA as much as one third of a negative demand shock in a state is cushioned by interstate transfers operating through the Federal tax and transfer system: see X. Sala-i-Martin and J. Sachs (1991) Fiscal Federalism and Optimum Currency Areas: evidence for Europe from the United States, *NBER Working Paper 3855*.

17 A. Sapir et al. (2003) *Agenda for a Growing Europe: Making the EU Economic System Deliver*, Report of a High Level Study Group to the President of the European Commission, p. 56.

18 See P. Krugman (1991) History and industrial location: The case of the Manufacturing Belt, *American Economic Review (Paper and Proceedings), 81*, pp. 80-83; B. Arthur (1994) *Increasing Returns and Path Dependence in the Economy*.

cing regional development.[19] Here, the key driver of increasing returns is demand, especially for a region's exports. Increased demand for a region's exports raises total regional output (through export multiplier effects), and this increase in output in turn raises productivity though economies of scale induced technological improvements and so on (the Verdoorn effect). Provided this productivity boost is not eroded by excessive wage increases, the region's efficiency wage falls and this raises the competitiveness of the region's exports and the cumulative, self-reinforcing process is repeated. Under this model, therefore, regions that already have a significant competitive advantage will benefit most from the expanded market and trade opportunities created by EMU and regional divergence is likely.

However, we know from empirical evidence that while self-reinforcing cumulative path-dependent regional development is a common feature, it does not continue indefinitely: we do not observe unlimited regional divergence over the long run. Rather, historical evidence indicates that while some regions do indeed manage to remain high income leaders over very extensive periods of time, in general different regions tend to rise and fall in relative growth terms. Increasing returns models of regional development and the spatial agglomeration of economic activity – whether of the Krugman or Kaldorian type – may predict hysteretic or path dependent regional trajectories, but they are not necessarily evolutionary. The possibility of varying regional evolutions over time requires that we allow for processes of technological and institutional innovation, and lock-in. A number of evolutionary and institutional models attempt to do this.[20] The central messages of these perspectives are, first, that that there is no single long-run steady state equilibrium of regional inequalities; second, issues of regional convergence and divergence can only be explained with reference to a specific historical institutional and technological 'regime'; and that the impact of major technological and institutional shocks (such as EMU, and EU enlargement) on the pattern of regional development depends on whether such shocks set off endogenous processes of change. Such models are thus ambivalent about whether EMU will promote regional convergence or divergence.

The third form of geographical economics that has been stimulated, in part at least, by the process of EMU, and which like the new economic geography, has tended to take the USA as the model type of continental-sized integrated economy of the sort the EU aspires to, is what has recently been labelled the 'new intranational macroeconomics'.[21] The rationale for this subfield is that the relevant geographical borders for understanding how the international economy works are no longer necessarily national but increasingly regional:

---

19 M. Setterfield (1997) *Rapid Growth and Relative Decline*.

20 See for example: J. Cornwall and W. Cornwall (2001) *Capitalist Development in the Twentieth Century: An Evolutionary Keynesian Perspective*

21 This can be traced to two seminal papers: O. Blanchard and L. Katz (1992) Regional Evolutions, *Brookings Papers in Economic Activity, 1*, pp. 1-75 and T. Bayoumi and B. Eichengreen (1993) Shocking Aspects of European Monetary Integration, in F. Torres and F. Giavazzi (Eds) *Adjustment and Growth in the European Monetary Union*, pp. 193-229. More recent developments can be found in G. Hess and E. van Wincoop (Eds.) (2000) *Intra-national Macro-economics*.

> An approach that has recently been adopted by researchers to better understand how economic interactions *between* countries will evolve as national borders decline in importance is to analyse economic interactions across regions *within* a country, whose economies are already highly integrated... a new field which we refer to as intranational macroeconomics... Regions within a country share a common currency, tax system legal foundation, accounting system and language. They provide, therefore, a proper benchmark for understanding macroeconomic relationships within an economically integrated geographic area.[22]

Much of the work on this theme has been concerned with the implications of economic and monetary integration for how regions adjust to key macroeconomic shocks – such as business cycles, demand and technology shifts, and changes in monetary and fiscal policy. There are many reasons to expect both business cycles and long-run growth patterns to depend on the extent of integration among regions. A higher degree of factor market and goods market integration implies that business cycles should have a larger common component across regions. A higher degree of monetary and fiscal policy co-ordination, particularly in the form of a single currency and fiscal regime, could also lead to a larger common component to regional business cycle volatility. On the other hand, if, by extending the size of the market and stimulating trade, economic integration increases regional specialisation, regional shocks are likely to become more idiosyncratic and asymmetric, which could lead to greater regional variation in the timing and severity of business cycles.

Again, of key importance to these questions of regional economic fluctuation and adjustment are the issues of labour mobility and relative price (wage) responses.[23] The low rate of labour mobility in the EU, as compared to the USA, suggests that Euroland may not be an optimal currency area (OCA) in this sense. Magnifico made this point over thirty years ago, in a curiously neglected but highly prescient study of the regional dimensions and implications of European monetary union. He argued that to the extent that European regions differ in productivity and interregional wage flexibility is limited, regions will not only react differently to economic shocks but also differ in their 'inflation propensity'. The process of EMU could as a consequence not only open up major regional disparities in unemployment, but also frustrate EU monetary stability and policy. Recall that this is precisely one of the reasons why the European Commission has recently stressed the importance of regional cohesion (convergence) for succeeding in its goal of closing the producivity gap between the EU and the USA.

Low levels of labour mobility and relative price inflexibility in turn imply a greater reliance on interregional fiscal transfers ('intranational risk sharing') in alleviating the regional impacts of shocks. The need for fiscal risk sharing in the EU was emphasised by Delors in his report on EMU:

> In all federations the different combinations of federal budgetary mechanisms have powerful 'shock absorber' effects dampening the amplitude either of economic difficulties

22 G. Hess and E. van Wincoop (*op cit*), p. 2.

23 See A. Fatas (2000) Intranational labour migration, business cycles and growth, in G. Hess and E. van Wincoop (*op cit*) pp. 156-188; M. Obstfeld and G. Peri (2000) Regional nonadjustment and fiscal policy: lessons for EMU, in G. Hess and E. van Wincoop (*op cit*) pp. 221-271.

> or of surges in prosperity of individual states. This is both the product of, and the source of the sense of national solidarity which all relevant economic and monetary unions share.[24]

Channelling income from prosperous regions to depressed regions can help to attenuate asymmetries in the cyclical fluctuations of different regions belonging to a integrated economic space, and produce a more even economic development across all regions. Starting with the McDougall Report, many economists have argued that a successful EMU must be vested with instruments for regional redistribution comparable to those existing in the USA. The basic argument, that the loss of an exchange rate channel for adjustment to asymmetric shocks must be compensated by an appropriate fiscal policy tool in order to avoid large and protracted regional swings in economic growth and unemployment.

The main conclusion of this discussion is that there is no one single or superior theoretical perspective for predicting the impact of EMU on regional inequalities across the EU. The impacts are likely to be complex, and to differ for different groups of regions. Whilst EMU might well stimulate convergence amongst certain types of region, it could just as well lead to increased inequalities amongst and between others. But what does the empirical evidence suggest on this issue? Here too there is debate.

3. THE CONTESTED EMPIRICS OF REGIONAL CONVERGENCE IN THE EU

This question of regional convergence is hardly a new one. It can be traced back at least to the early work of Borts and Stein (1964) on regional growth paths in the US.[25] Similarly, Williamson's (1965) study of regional income inequalities for a number of advanced countries was concerned with this topic.[26] In his paper, Williamson explored the evolution of the dispersion of regional per capita incomes (using the coefficient of variation) as economic development proceeds, using cross-section data for several countries and time series information for others. His results suggested that regional per capita income inequalities change over time as the level of economic development increases (stylised in Figure 1). In the earlier stages of economic development, regional inequalities widen (diverge), then reach a peak and thereafter narrow (converge) at higher levels of economic development. His explanation for this pattern was mainly drawn from the work of Myrdal and Hirschman, namely that in the early stages of development there is geographical polarisation of incomes as regions that had initial competitive advantages benefit most from the expansion of the market and trade and from increasing integration of the economy more generally. After a certain point, however, when factor markets are fully integrated, the advantages of the leading areas

24 J. Delors (Ed.) (1989) Regional Implications of Economic and Monetary Union, *Report on Economic and Monetary Union in the European Community*.

25 G.H. Borts and J.L. Stein (1964) *Economic Growth in a Free Market*.

26 J.G. Williamson (1965) Regional Inequalities and the Process of National Development, *Economic Development and Cultural Change, 13*, pp. 1-84.

wane, and growth becomes more geographically diffused across the economy, so that other regions catch up and regional inequalities decline.

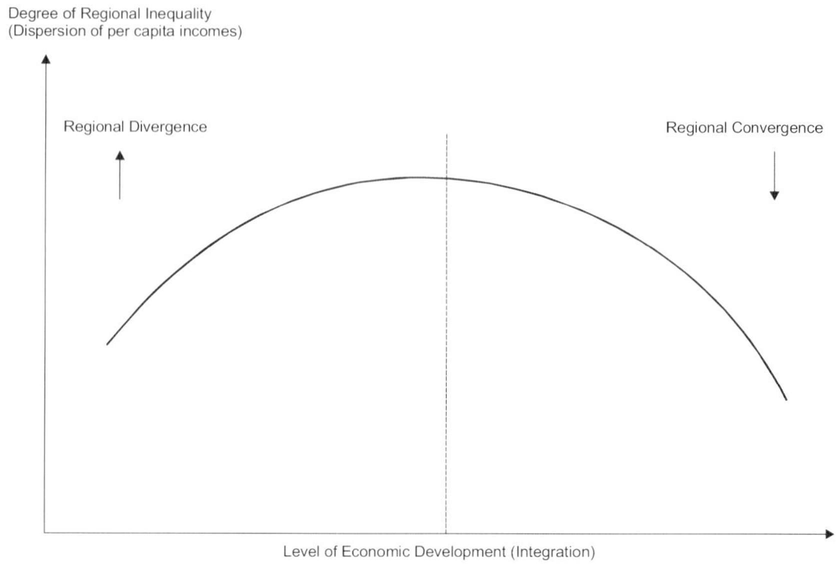

Figure 1. Williamson's Model of the Rise and Fall of Regional Inequality.

Interestingly, Williamson's early paper is not referred to by the authors of any of the three variants of the 'new geographical economics' summarised above. But the problem they seek to answer, namely what will happen to regional disparities in the EU as it becomes increasingly integrated economically and monetarily, is obviously not dissimilar. In terms of Williamson's curve, three pertinent questions arise. First, where on the curve was the EU before the introduction of the single currency: were regional inequalities already narrowing? Second, what effect will EMU have on regional inequalities: will it induce convergence or divergence? And third, what effect will the additional of the new, lower income enlargement states have on regional inequalities? How far will enlargement widen disparities across the enlarged EU, and how long will such a widening last?

What in fact has been happening to regional economic disparities across the EU over the past two decades of increasing integration? Looking at relatively simple indices of regional socioeconomic welfare, the European Commission has tended to the view that regional disparities in the EU have been narrowing over the past quarter-century, in other words that there has been regional convergence and thus increasing regional cohesion.[27] However, the situation is far from clear-cut. In fact, numerous studies have examined the regional convergence issue in the EU, and the findings admit of various interpretations: much depends on the index of regional economic performance that is examined, the statistical technique employed to measure convergence, and the time period over which the analysis is conducted. While many studies find some evidence for convergence, some commentators argue that no significant convergence has occurred at all, and some that perhaps there has even been some divergence.[28]

Essentially, two main methods have been used to test for regional convergence: the so-called growth regression (or β-convergence) approach and variance analysis (σ-convergence). The former, popularised by Barro and Sala-i-Martin, and since widely used by various authors, including the European Commission itself.[29] takes the form of the regression

$$G(y_r) = \alpha - \beta y_{r0} + \lambda' x_r + \varepsilon_r$$

where $G(y_r)$ is the average growth rate, defined as $(1/T)\log(y_{rt} / y_{r0})$, of per capita output in region r over the period t=0 to t=T, y_{r0} is the logarithm of regional per capita output in the initial year t=0, x_r is a vector of region-specific structural factors and conditions, α and β are parameters, λ a vector of parameters, and ε_r an error term. A significantly negative estimate of β, the convergence parameter, is interpreted to imply that a high (low) initial level of regional per capita output if followed by a (low) high growth in regional output per capita, and hence that per capita output across regions converges to a common trend. By contrast, an estimate of β insignificantly different from zero is interpreted to imply that regions do not converge towards a common trend, and indeed have different trend growth rates if λ is estimated to be significantly different from the zero vector. If the model does not include any conditioning variables, then a significant negative value of β is said to denote the presence of 'absolute' convergence, as predicted by standard growth theory; a significant negative value of β in the presence of significant x-variables is said to denote 'conditional' convergence (to different region-specific per capita GDP trends), and can be given an endogenous growth interpretation.

Different studies report differing rates of absolute β-convergence for the EU regions, but most are very slow, ranging from 0% to about 2% per annum. A rate of 1%

27 Commission of the European Communities (1999), *Sixth Periodic Report on the Social and Economic Situation and Development of the Regions of the European Union*; Commission of the European Communities (2001), *Unity, Solidarity, Diversity for Europe, its People and its Territory: Second Report on Economic and Social Cohesion.*

28 For surveys of these studies, see, for example, H. Armstrong and R. Vickerman (Eds.), *Convergence and Divergence among European Regions* (1995); R. Martin and P. Sunley, 'Slow Convergence? New Endogenous Growth Theory and Regional Development', *Economic Geography, 74*, (1998) 201-227; K. Button and E. Pentecost, *Regional Economic Performance within the European Union* (1999); R. Martin, 'EMU versus the Regions? Regional Convergence and Divergence in Euroland', *Journal of Economic Geography, 1*, (2001) 51-80.

29 R. Barro and X. Sala-i-Martin (1995) *op cit*. See also R. Barro (1997) *Determinants of Economic Growth.*

per annum implies a convergence half-life (the average time taken to halve an initial regional disparity) of around 70 years; a 2% rate around 35 years. Estimates of conditional convergence do not fare much better. Such slow rates hardly provide overwhelming support for the standard growth model of regional economic evolution under progressive integration.

There are in fact several potential problems with this growth regression approach. In the first place, it estimates an average rate of convergence across all of the regions – in effect it assumes a common rate of convergence. The enormous heterogeneity of regions across the EU – in terms of economic, social, cultural and institutional characteristics – makes this assumption difficult to accept. Thus growth regressions tell us nothing about geographical variations in the rate of regional convergence. The incorporation of so-called 'conditioning' x-variables is meant to respond to this problem, by recognising that different regions might be converging not to a common per capita GDP trend but to different region specific trends that reflect geographical variations in the conditions that influence regional economic performance. However, the inclusion of such factors in the model potentially introduces problems of simultaneity, in that such factors may themselves be influenced by and dependent on regional per capita incomes (output). Indeed, it is difficult to think of conditioning factors that are not influenced by regional growth in some way. For example, regional leadership in technological change – arguably a key determinant of regional growth in per capita GDP – is well known to be itself a positive function of regional prosperity, similar to expenditure on higher education. These feedback effects are after all precisely what endogenous growth theory emphasises. Resorting to the use of instrumental variables or lagged versions of the x-variables to estimate the regression does not necessarily solve the problem.[30]

A further issue relates to the frequent presence of spatially auto-correlated error terms in growth regressions. Spatial autocorrelation in the error terms may arise simply because of the effects of common omitted x-variables, such as similar reactions by neighbouring or nearby regions to common exogenous demand, technology or policy shocks. But they may also reflect genuine spatial 'contiguity' or spillover effects in the regional growth process. Indeed, the growth regression approach to testing for regional convergence actually allows very little role for geography, for space, other than assuming geographical mobility of factors and technology as drivers of the convergence process. In contrast both endogenous growth models of regional development, and the new economic geography models of spatial agglomeration, explicitly emphasise localisation effects, that is spatial contiguity effects arising from geographical clustering of linked, similar and networked firms, from local labour commuting flows, from spillovers of knowledge through local competition, trade, technology transfer and local institutions, and the like. As Davis and Weinstein argue in their study of regional productivity convergence in Japan, the role of location, relative distance and market

30 See P. Evans (2000) Income dynamics in regions and countries, in G. Hess and E. van Wincoop, *op cit*, pp. 131-155.

accessibility needs to be explicitly analysed.[31] In the EU context, for example, one of the recurring themes in discussions of regional development has been the idea of a core from South East England through the Benelux countries and southern Germany into northern Italy, versus a southern and northern periphery. Maps of accessibility confirm the comparative – if not absolute – advantage of the core countries and regions in the EU.[32]

Such are the potential problems and limitations of convergence regressions that a few authors have urged that we should focus instead on the cross-region variance, or σ-convergence. More than a decade ago Milton Friedman argued that inferences drawn from growth regression are invalid.[33] At more or less the same time, Quah also criticised growth regressions and argued that the temporal dynamics of the cross country and cross region distribution of per capita output over time afford better insight into the convergence issue. More recently Evans has demonstrated that the cross-country and cross-region variance of GDP per capita can be used to distinguish between endogenous and exogenous models of growth and convergence.[34] In the EU context, the cross-region variance is defined as

$$V_t = 1/N\Sigma_r (y_{rt} - y_{EU,t})^2$$

where the summation is across all N regions, and y_{EU} is the EU mean per capita GDP. Regional convergence requires that regional disparities, $(y_{rt} - y_{EU,t})$, decline over time, so that V_t will drift downwards; and vice versa for regional divergence. If regional disparities are untrended (stationary) over time then the variance will itself be stationary and fluctuate around a constant value. One of the advantages of the cross-region variance is that it is easily decomposed into different regional groupings, and unlike the growth regression can reveal the extent of regional differences at each point in time. The obvious disadvantage is that this approach, being basically descriptive rather than explanatory, is unable to test for the relative role of different factors in accounting for the temporal movements in the cross regional dispersion of per capita GDP.

Most studies of regional convergence have focussed on the growth regression approach, using per capita GDP as the indicator of economic performance. Rather than repeat these studies, it may be more instructive to look at regional productivity, especially since this is a critical factor behind regional variations in competitiveness across the EU.[35] To this end, convergence regressions were estimated for regional labour productivity for NUTS2 level regions in the EU-15 states over the period 1980-

31 D.R. Davis and D.E. Weinstein (2001) Market size, linkages and productivity: a study of Japanese regions, National Bureau of Economic Research *Working Paper 8518*.

32 European Commission (2004).

33 M. Friedman (1992) Do old fallacies ever die? *Journal of Economic Literature, 30*, pp. 2029-2032.

34 P. Evans (1996) Using cross-country variances to evaluate growth theories, *Journal of Economic Dynamics and Control, 20*, pp. 1027-1049. Other studies that have used cross-country variances in this way include: W.J. Baumol, S.A.B. Blackman and E.N. Wolff (1989) *Productivity and American Leadership: the Long View*; S.L. Parente and E.C. Prescott (1993) Changes in the wealth of nations, *Federal Reserve bank of Minneapolis Quarterly Review, 17*, pp. 3-16.

35 European Commission (2004) *op cit.*

2001, where labour productivity was computed as GDP per hour worked rather than per employee.[36] The plot of productivity growth against initial productivity levels is shown in Figure 2. The estimate of the regional convergence parameter, β, in Table 2 is negative as required, and statistically significant, but it is small, suggesting an average annual convergence rate of less than 1 per cent.

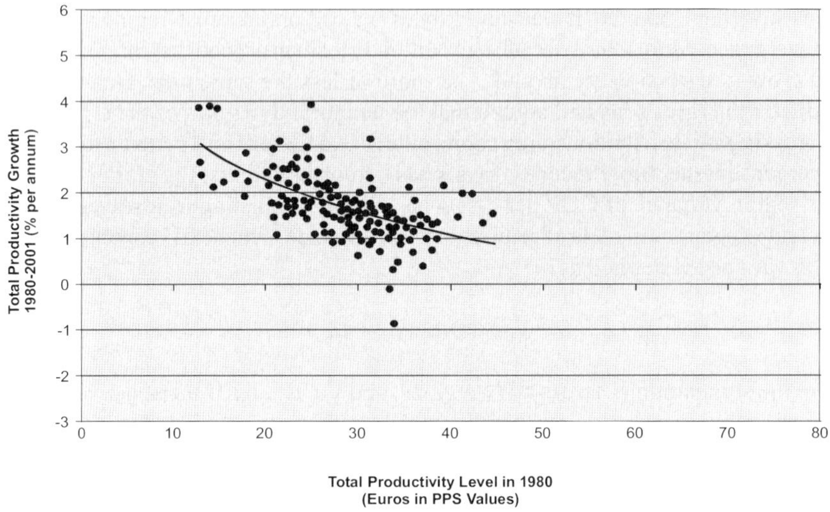

Figure 2. Regional Productivity across the EU-15, 1980-2001.

A recurring theme in the various theories of regional growth under progressive integration is that the latter increases trade which in turn promotes regional convergence in productivity. The supposition is that openness should expose the sectors in question to pressures that make for constant improvements in technology, efficiency, investment, product design and so on if a region's exporting firms are to remain competitive. Regional nontraded activities, that serve local markets, are not exposed to such external competitive pressure. Thus the expectation is that regional convergence in productivity should be faster in traded sectors than in nontraded ones.

Sectoral data limitations at the regional level prevent a detailed evaluation of this issue, but a preliminary analysis is possible in the case of the EU-15 states by recalculating regional productivity separately for two aggregate sectors that correspond in broad terms to 'traded' and 'nontraded' activities. The former was defined to include manufacturing, energy, business services, and intermediate services; and the latter to

36 For the construction of these data, which use Labour Force Survey estimates of hours worked, including part time workers, see B. Gardiner, R. Martin and P. Tyler (2004) Competitiveness, Productivity and Economic Growth across the European Regions, *Regional Studies, 38* (forthcoming).

include construction, household services and public sector services.[37] This is obviously only an approximate decomposition, since not all local manufacturing industries need export, while some local construction activities and household services are exported out of regions. Nevertheless, these broad divisions should be sufficient to reveal any significant differences in regional convergence between the traded and nontraded sectors of the economy.

Table 2. Absolute (Unconditional) Convergence Parameters for Regional Productivity across the EU-15, 1980-2001

Model (Estimated on 197 NUTS2 regions)	Convergence parameter (β estimate)	R^2	Standardised Moran statistic
Total productivity	-0.0095* (0.0011)	0.282	0.673
Traded sector productivity	-0.0089* (0.0013)	0.275	0.710
Nontraded sector productivity	-0.0104* (0.0009)	0.324	1.023

Notes: Standard errors in parentheses
* statistically significant at 95 per cent level
Expected value of Moran's statistic is –0.005 in all cases

The results are quite instructive. First, as perhaps expected, initial regional productivity levels were noticeably higher in traded activities than in nontraded (Figures 3 and 4). Second, the evidence suggests that regional productivity convergence in traded activities has been no faster, in fact slightly slower, than that in the nontraded sector (Table 2). This is, perhaps, surprising, given that traded activities are likely to be much more exposed to external competition and influences. On the other hand, since the composition of household and public services tends to be similar across regions, we might expect productivity differences to be small and to diminish over time. Interestingly, productivity levels in nontraded activities were noticeably less variable across regions to begin with. In both cases, however, rates of convergence over the 1980-2001 period remain very slow.

In Table 2, the Moran statistics indicate the presence of positive spatial autocorrelation in the errors terms in all three regressions. As discussed above, this may reflect important omitted variables, common influences or genuine spatial contiguity/agglomeration effects.

37 The analysis excludes agriculture.

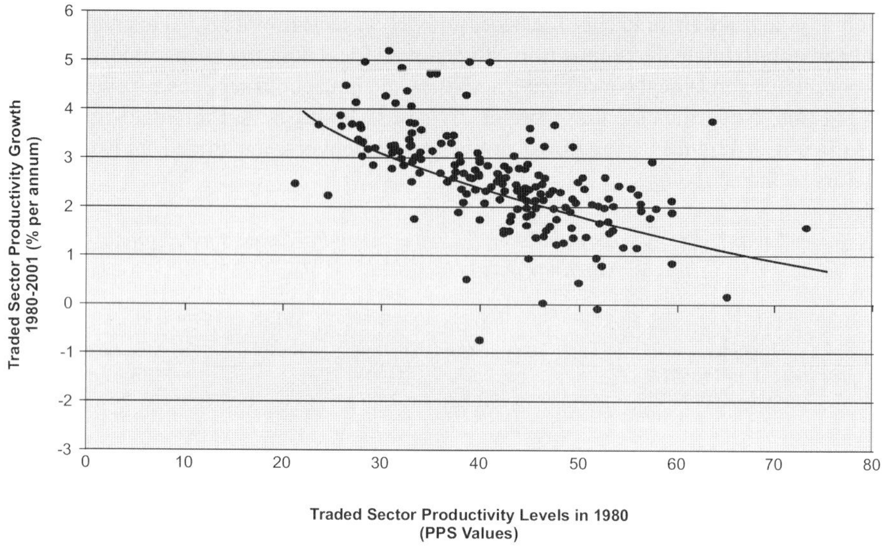

Figure 3. Regional Productivity in Traded Sectors, EU-15, 1980-2001.

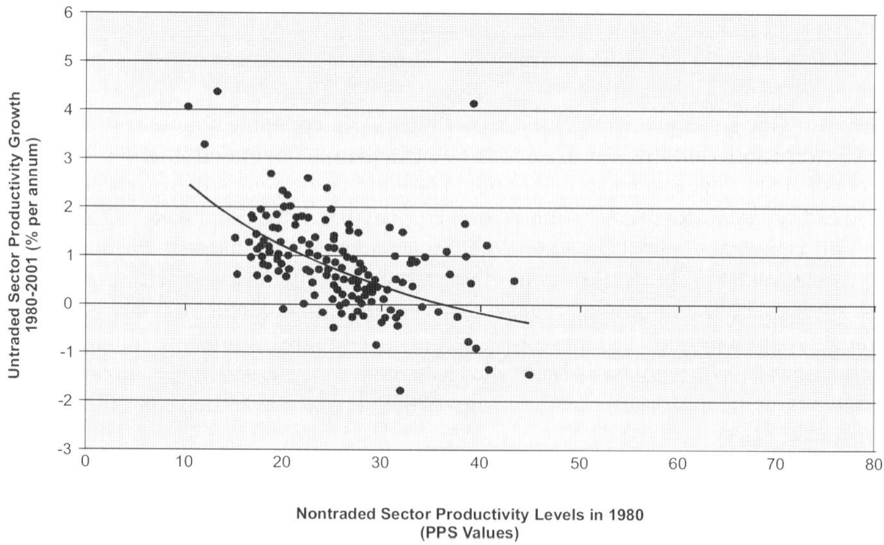

Figure 4. Regional Productivity in Nontraded Sectors, EU-15, 1980-2001.

Table 3. Conditional Convergence Regression for Regional Productivity

Model (Estimated on 197 NUTS2 regions)	Coefficient	Standard error	t-ratio
Initial productivity level (1980) (β)	-0.0013*	0.0018	-7.28
Proportion of tertiary educated students 1985)	0.0002	0.0006	0.33
Share of high-tech employment (1990)	-0.0003	0.0005	0.60
R&D spending as proportion of GDP (1990)	0.0014*	0.0003	4.66
Market potential (1990)	0.0082*	0.0022	3.72
R^2	0.396		
Standardised Moran statistic	0.350		

Notes: * statistically significant at 95 per cent level
Expected value of Moran's statistic is –0.005

Table 3 illustrates the effect of expanding the basic absolute convergence model to include a range of variables suggested by the endogenous growth and new economic geography models discussed in the previous section: namely, human capital factors (proportion of tertiary educated students in the local population and the proportion of workers in high-tech jobs), R&D intensity (spending as a proportion of GDP), and a market potential/accessibility variable, defined as[38]

$$MP_r = k\Sigma_s(GDP_s / D_{rs})$$

where

$$k = [\Sigma_{r,s}(GDP_s / D_{rs})]^{-1}$$

For simplicity we assume that the influence of other regions on a given region declines with the inverse of the distance, D, between their centroids.

Both R&D intensity and market potential emerge in this model as significant 'conditioning variables', but the human capital variables appear to be irrelevant. The convergence parameter is increased slightly, as is R^2, and the degree of spatial autocorrelation in the residuals is reduced. But the overall fit of the model is hardly high, and the estimated rate of regional convergence remains very slow.

Thus these results for regional productivity mirror many of those found for regional per capita GDP. They provide little overwhelming support for theories that predict increasing regional convergence as a result of progressive economic and monetary integration in the EU. Of course, it might be argued that other shocks to the European regions over the past two decades arising from rapid technological change and accelerating globalisation have complicated and hindered the process of regional convergence.

38 Here we follow the definition used by Davis and Weinstein (*op cit*).

The fact that regional convergence in the USA ceased in the 1980s and early 1990s may possibly support this argument.[39] Added to this, given the potential problems that surround the use of the growth regression approach, referred to above, the question arises as to how much confidence can be placed in estimates of β-convergence in any case. Thus it is useful to compare these results with the cross-regional variance of productivity over the same period.

The very slow β-convergence in regional productivity is also borne out by trends in the cross-regional variance.[40] The coefficient of variation declined only marginally between 1980 and 2001, from 0.39 to 0.38. The regional dispersion in productivity actually widened slightly in the first half of the1980s, then narrowed during the second half of that decade. Since then it has remained more or less untrended. Equally interesting, decomposing the total variation in regional productivity across the EU-15 into between country and within-country parts reveals that whilst the between-member state inequality has declined since 1990, regional inequalities within member states have actually widened slightly (Figure 5). This implies that caution is needed in interpreting the overall cross–region variance, and that different trends may at work in different member states.

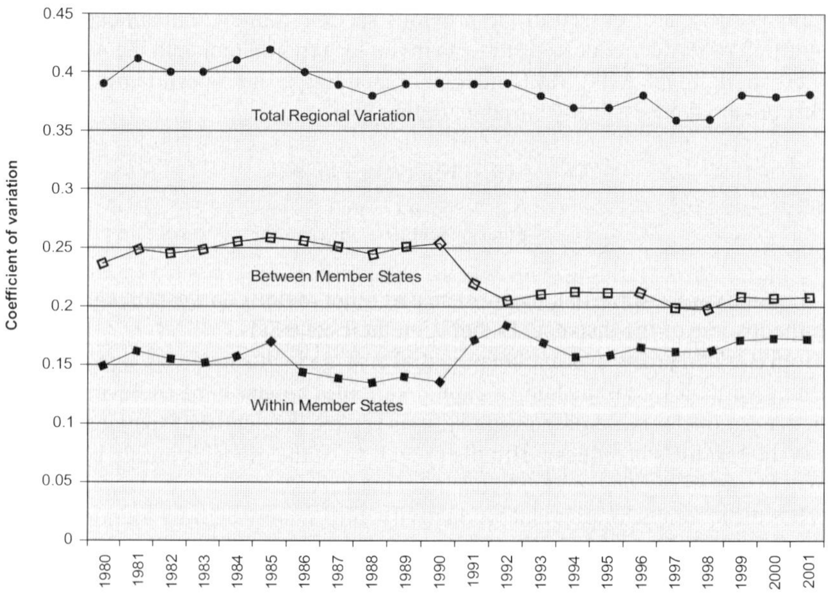

Figure 5. Cross-region variance of productivity, EU-15, 1980-2001.

39 See Barro and Salai-i-Martin, *op cit.*

40 The coefficient of variation is used instead of the variance as a measure of σ-convergence in order to remove the effects of rises in the EU-wide productivity level over time.

In fact, as Figure 6 shows, regional inequalities in productivity have behaved differently in different countries. In some member states, such as Austria and Greece, the cross-region variance has declined over time, indicating regional convergence on this measure of economic performance. In others, however, inequalities have been widening, resulting in regional divergence: Ireland and Sweden for example illustrate this pattern. In still others, like Belgium, Italy and the UK, regional inequalities have remained more or less stable. These different national trends in regional convergence considerably weaken the value of a growth regression estimate of a single EU-wide rate of regional convergence, and point to a complex picture in which it is far from straightforward to generalise about the regional responses to economic integration or to favour one theoretical model over another.

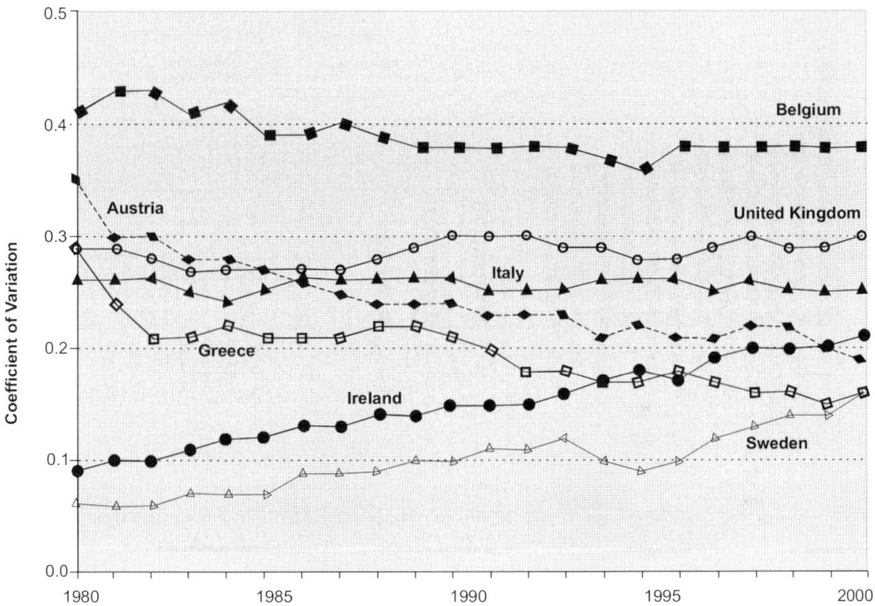

Figure 6. Cross-region variance of productivity in selected EU-15 member states, 1980-2001 (NUTS2 regions).

4. THE CHALLENGE OF ENLARGEMENT TO REGIONAL CONVERGENCE IN THE EU

The eastwards enlargement of the EU represents no less a shock to the regional system of the Union than the formation of the Eurozone. At a stroke, enlargement has doubled the per capita income gaps between countries and regions. The average GDP per head of the new accession states is less than 50 per cent of that in the former EU-15 (see Figure 7). Thus enlargement has lowered the average per capita income across the EU considerably. On current data, none of the new member states has average per capita incomes that exceed the new (lower) EU-26 mean.[41] In fact, at this national level, enlargement has produced a three-tiered EU. The most prosperous group of member states consists of a 'core' of 12 leading countries (the former EU-15 minus Spain, Portugal and Greece), all with average per capita incomes around 20 per above the new EU-26 average. This is followed by a middle group of 7 states (Spain, Portugal, Greece, together with Cyprus, Malta, Slovenia and the Czech Republic), with average per capita incomes around 80 per cent (actually between 68 per cent and 95 per cent) of the EU-26 figure. The real change, however, is a third group of member states, comprising the 8 remaining enlargement countries, where average income per head is only around 40 per cent of the EU-26 mean.

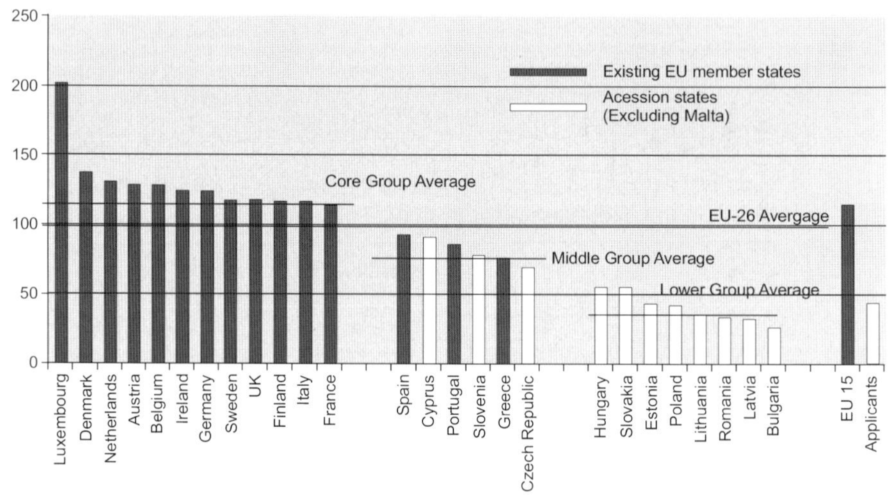

Figure 7. Relative GDP per capita across EU-15 Member States and new Enlargement Countries, 2001 (EU26 = 100, Excludes Malta).

At the regional scale, enlargement has not increased the overall degree of disparity (between regional extremes) that significantly (see Figure 8), but it has increased the number of regions with low per capita incomes dramatically.[42] This threatens regional convergence (cohesion) in three ways. First, the number of regions with average incomes below 75 per cent of the EU average – the threshold at which regions become eligible for Objective 1 Structural Fund assistance – has risen. If the former EU-15 average per capita GDP is used as the base, the number of such regions jumps from 46

41 We include the candidate countries, Bulgaria and Romania, here, but exclude Malta for which data are unobtainable.

42 Dunford, M. and Smith, A. (2001) Catching Up or Falling Behind? Economic Performance and the Trajectories of Economic Development in an Enlarged Europe, *Economic Geography*.

to 97 (Table 4). Even if the new lower EU-26 average per capita GDP figure is used, the number still rises markedly from 46 to 70. Put another way, with enlargement, the population living in low-income regions has risen from 71 million to 174 million.

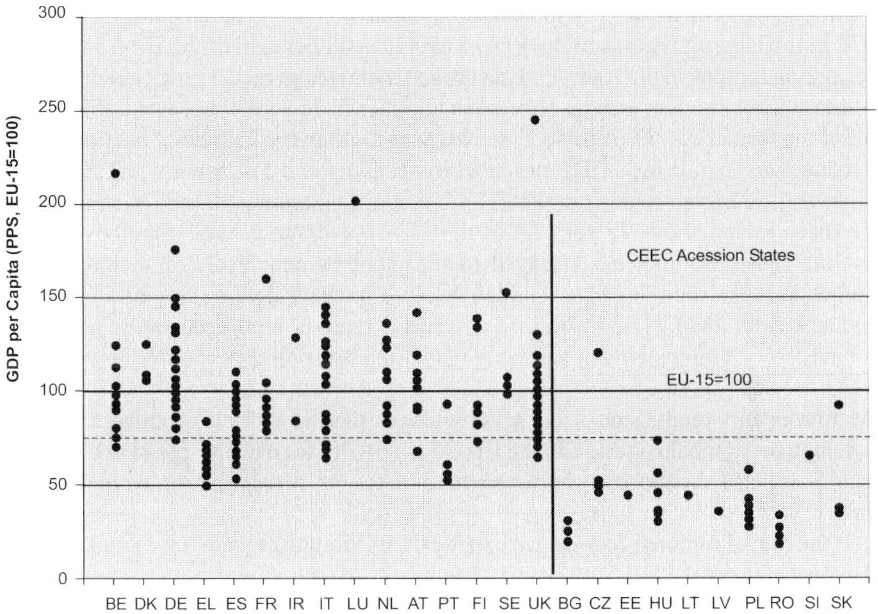

Figure 8. Regional GDP per capita, by EU Member State including the Central and Eastern Europe Enlargement Countries, 2001.

Table 4. The Implications of Enlargement for Low Income EU Regions

Index Used	EU-15	EU-26	
	EU-15 as index base	EU-15 as index base	EU-26 as index base
Number of Regions falling below 75% of average	46	97	70
Population in those Regions (Millions)	71	174	125
Population as proportion of EU total	19%	36%	26%
Average GDP per head (PPS) of regions falling below 75%	66	48	46

Source: Eurostat (DG Regio). EU-26 is used instead of EU-27 because of lack of data on Malta.

This represents an increase from 19 per cent of the population in the former EU-15 to 36 per cent of that in the EU-26 if the EU-15 average GDP per capita index is used as the base, or to 26 per cent if the new, lower EU-27 average income is used. Thus, either way, the *extent* of regional inequality in the EU has increased substantially. Second, in addition, enlargement has also increased the *intensity* of regional disparity. Per capita GDP in the lagging regions of the EU-15 averages 68 per cent of the EU-15 mean. In the lagging regions in the enlargement states, it averages around 37 per cent of the EU-15 mean. Thus the two groups of regions together have a GDP per head of less than half of the former EU-15 average.[43] But because the statistical effect of enlargement is to reduce the EU average GDP per head by an estimated 18-20 per cent, on current values some 27 or so regions in the EU-15, containing around 50 million inhabitants, have been raised above 75 per cent of the EU-26 average income. Obviously, in an absolute sense, nothing has changed to the incomes and levels of socioeconomic welfare in these regions. Their sudden relative improvement is simply a statistical product of the addition to the union of several regions with even lower per capita incomes: poor regions are not suddenly made rich by adding yet poorer regions.

The European Commission itself acknowledges that as a result of enlargement the challenge to regional cohesion in the EU-25 is now 'twice as widespread and twice as large'.[44] It is, furthermore, a challenge that is likely to persist for some considerable time.

If the rate of regional convergence in the CEEC countries were to be similar to that estimated across the EU-15 over the past decade or so (see above), it would take at least two generations for the increased regional income gap created by enlargement to be halved. Even if GDP per capita growth rates in the CEEC states well above the average in the EU-15 can be sustained in the long term, for most of these countries and many of their regions, catching up to the EU average GDP per capita is likely to be a drawn out process. For example, the European Commission estimates that if growth is maintained in these countries at 1.5 per cent a year above the EU average, which is the differential achieved between 1995-2002, it would still take until almost 2040 for average GDP per head in the CCECs to exceed 75 per cent of the predicted EU-27 average. At this rate of growth, Bulgaria and Romania would still have a level of GDP per capita below 75 per cent of the EU average in 2050.

Of equal concern, there are already clear signs that the rapid growth recorded in the CEECs in recent years has been not been widely spread geographically, but spatially focused in particular (usually the more urbanised) regions. In fact, what limited evidence is available on regional GDP per capita for these states suggests that they are likely to experience growing regional inequality as they experience increasing economic integration within the EU and the restructuring this is bound to promote: thus Hungary and the Czech Republic – arguably more advanced down the path of eco-

43 These calculations are those made by the European Commission.

44 Commission of the European Communities, *Unity, Solidarity, Diversity for Europe, its People and its Territory: Second Report on Economic and Social Cohesion, Vol 1* (2001) p. 9.

nomic and structural conversion than other Central and East European accession states – have seen regional divergence over the past decade (Figure 9). It may be they have begun to follow the regional divergence limb of the Williamson curve discussed earlier (Figure 1).

Some – inclining to the predictions of neoclassical growth theory – have argued that the applicant countries have considerable growth potential precisely because their low cost and unproductive industries offer considerable opportunities for new investment, and incomes could indeed grow much faster than has been typical across the EU-15 in recent years.

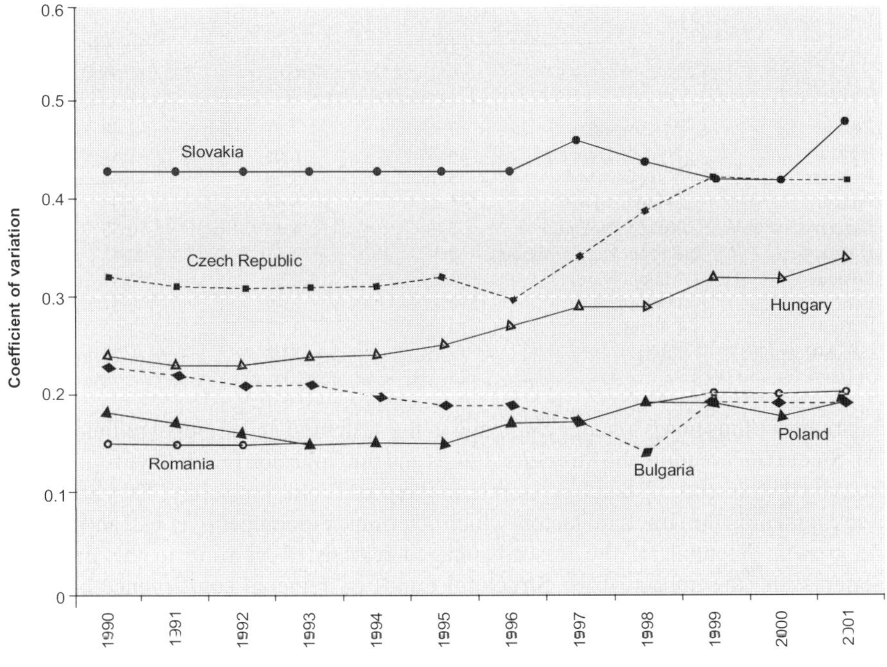

Figure 9. Cross-region variance of per capita GDP in the Central and East European Enlargement States, 1990-2001.

The success of Ireland might be taken as an exemplar in this respect, though as Figure 6 shows, rapid growth there has also been accompanied by regional divergence. Against this view, however, one can point to the run-down industries, poor infrastructures, backward agriculture, lack of skilled labour and outmoded institutions in the CEECs as major obstacles to their rapid development. It seems likely that, because of their preexisting endogenous advantages, economic activity and wealth creation will continue to agglomerate in the 'core' regions of the EU-15, and that economic catch up in the poor regions throughout most of the enlargement countries will be slow and limited.

Convergence towards the EU level of GDP in these regions will require nothing short of a dramatic change in their underlying structural conditions (in terms of capital of all kinds and different labour force skills). The inevitable industrial rationalisation and restructuring that will take place is bound to have highly disruptive effects on the labour markets in many of the regions of the enlargement states. Thus in all of the fastest growing regions in the Central and East European enlargement states, rapid productivity advance has so far been at the expense of employment (Table 5).

Table 5. Productivity Growth and Employment Rate Decline in Top Ten Growth Regions in the CCE enlargement states, 1993-2001 (Annual percentage rates)

Country	Region	GDP/hd Growth	Productivity Growth	Emp Rate Growth
Poland	Mazowieckie	7.93	7.81	-2.48
Hungary	Nyugat-Dunántúl	5.78	6.05	-1.84
Bulgaria	Yugoiztochen	5.45	5.78	-1.96
Poland	Wielkopolskie	5.44	5.63	-2.05
Hungary	Közép-Dunántúl	5.04	4.43	-0.55
Hungary	Kozép-Magyarország	4.57	4.53	-0.41
Poland	Malopolskie	4.23	4.50	-2.37
Poland	Pomorskie	4.22	3.99	-0.51
Poland	Lódzkie	4.10	3.77	-3.12
Czech Republic	Praha	4.10	3.93	-1.26

Enlargement thus poses a major challenge to the structural and regional policies of the EU. Since their creation, the Structural Funds and the Cohesion Funds have represented the main instruments of social, economic and regional cohesion policy. They are aimed at strengthening the structural factors which determine the competitiveness, and thereby the growth potential, of the less advantaged regions. According to the European Commission, the impact of the Structural Funds on regional convergence has been positive, contributing to an improvement in the relative per capita incomes of the poorest and lagging regions. The slow rates of regional convergence discussed above casts some doubt on this conclusion. In fact, a growing number of commentators have been much less positive in their assessment of the impact of the Structural Fund, and are sceptical that they are adequate to prevent geographical polarisation of growth and prosperity given the twin shocks of monetary union and enlargement. There is criticism that the Structural and Cohesion Funds have not been that successful and radical suggestions that they should be refocused and allocated to low income countries rather than low income regions.[45]

45 See for example, T. Dignan (1995) Regional Disparities and Regional Policy in the European Union, *Oxford Review of Economic Policy, 11*, pp. 64-95; P. Braunerhjelm, R. Faini, V. Norman, F. Rauner and P. Seabright, (2000) Integration and the Regions of Europe: How the Right Policies can Prevent Polarisation, *Monitoring European Integration 10*; M. Boldrin and F. Canova (2001) Inequality and Convergence: Reconsidering European Regional Policies, *Economic Policy, 16*, pp. 207-253; D. Puga (2002) European regional policies in the light of recent location theories, *Journal of Economic Geogra-*

This debate over the efficacy of the Structural Funds has arisen at the very time that political disagreement has broken out amongst the member states over the scale of those Funds and their allocation between the 'old' EU-15 and the new enlargement countries. Given that the resources dedicated to the Structural Funds are likely to remain pegged or even reduced beyond 2006, there will almost certainly be several unhappy assisted regions within the old EU-15. The need for development support in these regions will not suddenly have disappeared, but they will cease to figure within the regional cohesion policies of the EU: there will be fewer 'old' EU regions supported, even though they will remain economically depressed. At the same time, there is some doubt over whether the funds to be allocated to the CEECs will be sufficient to promote a faster rather than slower rate of catch up there.

What is clear is that a major rethink of structural policy will be called for beyond 2006, not just to accommodate enlargement itself but also to respond to the new types of cohesion problems presented in the CEECs, and the impact of withdrawal of aid from many existing cohesion regions. The fundamental question is what the role of cohesion policy should be in an enlarged Union of nearly 30 member states, containing within itself an 'inner' monetary union, in a context of rapid economic, technological and social change.

5. A CONCLUDING COMMENT ON THE ECONOMIC GEOGRAPHY OF EUROPEAN INTEGRATION

In one sense, the process of EMU provides a unique opportunity for observing the impacts of progressive economic integration on regional growth and development. As we have noted, this fact has played a significant role in stimulating a 'geographical turn' within economics in recent years: in effect, the EU has become a sort of laboratory for elaborating and evaluating alternative theories of the economic landscape. In practice, however, this focus on the regional dimensions and implications of EMU has generated as much debate as insight. At the heart of the debate is the question of whether EMU will lead to regional convergence or to increased regional agglomeration and concentration of economic activity, growth and prosperity. This question is of more than just academic interest since it relates directly to the European Commission's concern over, and desire to secure, regional cohesion. One problem is that several alternative 'geographical' economic models of regional development under progressive European integration have been proposed, and these yield rather different predictions and views of what the regional implications of EMU are likely to be. A second problem is that the empirical evidence is itself open to debate and disagreement, not only on the question of regional convergence, but also on related issues of whether – as some models predict – regions are becoming more economically specialised across the EU, and thus more prone to region-specific shocks. A further issue is that not enough is

phy, 2, 4, pp. 373-406. A. Sapir et al., (2003) *op cit*; Between Development and Social Policies; The Impact of the European Structural Funds in Objective 1 Regions, *Regional Studies, 38* (Forthcoming).

known about just how long it takes for regions to adjust to major integrative shocks such as a single market, monetary union and enlargement, especially when these follow quickly on the heels of one another. In this context, it is also difficult to construct meaningful counterfactuals against which to try to assess what the regional impact of EMU (or the Structural Funds, come to that) has thus far been.

Perhaps for these reasons, comparison is often made between the EU experiment and the historical experience of the USA, on the grounds that the latter has long been a continental-sized integrated space economy of the sort that the EU is moving towards. But, as has been noted, real reservations must be expressed against using the USA as a comparator in this way, not just because the EU is never likely to be as socioeconomically or institutionally integrated as the USA, but also because economic integration in the USA has been spread over a much longer historical time span than is the case in the EU. In any case, not only has regional divergence actually stopped in the SA over the past two decades, claims that its regions and cities are more specialised than those in the EU remain unconvincing.[46] In short, it is tempting but also misleading to use the US as a predictor of what to expect in the EU as the latter becomes increasingly integrated.

To compound these criticisms, the formal models used by growth theorists and the 'new economic geographers' within economics to theorise about the possible regional implications of EMU have their own limitations.[47] Despite their mathematical sophistication, these models are unable to capture the immense complexity of actual regional growth and development of the sort found across the EU. Indeed, to be mathematically solvable, these models are forced to make highly simplifying and heroic assumptions, not least regarding the spatial structure of the economic landscape itself. To a large extent their predictions about the geographical outcome of economic integration are preconditioned by the highly stylised geographies they employ to begin with. The more complex the spatial structure of the economic landscape is made in these models the less tractable they become. But the economic geography of the EU *is* highly complex. General models can provide some useful insights, but this is done at the cost of neglecting and excluding regional specificities, the scale-dependent nature of economic and political processes, and a range of social, institutional and cultural factors that are difficult to express in formal mathematical terms or to capture in aggregate statistical modelling, but which shape local economic activity and performance in crucial, locally dependent ways. Understanding the different regional responses and growth trajectories under EMU ultimately requires a detailed appreciation of this diversity of local conditions and reactions. Thus different regions can exhibit convergence of their per capita

46 For example, Krugman himself has acknowledged that regional specialisation may have declined in recent decades: see P. Krugman (1991) *Geography and Trade*.

47 See R.L. Martin and P. Sunley (1996) Paul Krugman's 'Geographical Economics' and its Implications for Regional Development Theory: A Critical Assessment, *Economic Geography, 72*, pp. 259-292; R. Martin and P. Sunley (1998) Slow Convergence? The New Endogenous Growth Theory and Regional Development, Economic Geography, 74, pp. 201-227. G.A. Dymski (1999) On Krugman's Model of Economic Geography, *Geoforum*, 27, pp. 439-452; R.L. Martin (1999) The New 'Geographical Turn' in Economics: Some Critical Reflections, *Cambridge Journal of Economics, 23*, pp. 65-91.

incomes to the EU average for quite different reasons, and as a result of quite different processes. Similarly, different regions are linked differently to the global economy, and are subject to different shocks, while the same shock or process can impact on different regions in markedly divergent ways. Likewise, the intriguing question of spatial spillovers of growth and technology requires far more research. The issue of regional convergence across the EU has certainly helped to stimulate a much greater awareness of economic geography amongst economists, but in so doing it has also exposed the limitations of formal models based on endogenous growth theory or the 'new economic geography' in helping to understand the complexity of regional growth patterns and processes in the European Union. The next phase of research must focus on those regional complexities and specificities, and to a reconsideration of our theories accordingly.[48]

REFERENCES

Armstrong, H. & Vickerman, R. (1995) (Eds). *Convergence and Divergence among European Regions*, London: Pion.

Arthur, B. (1994). *Increasing Returns and Path Dependence in the Economy*. Ann Arbor: University of Michigan Press.

Baldwin, R. et al. (2003). *Economic Geography and Public Policy*. Princeton University Press.

Barro, R. & Sala-i-Martin, X. (1995). *Economic Growth*, New York: McGraw-Hill. p. 382.

Barro, R. (1997). *Determinants of Economic Growth*, Cambridge, MA: MIT Press.

Baumol, W.J., Blackman, S.A.B. & Wolff, E.N. (1989). *Productivity and American Leadership: the Long View*, Cambridge, MA: MIT Press.

Bayoumi, T. & Eichengreen, B. (1993). Shocking Aspects of European Monetary Integration. In F. Torres & F. Giavazzi (Eds), *Adjustment and Growth in the European Monetary Union*, (pp. 193-229) Cambridge: Cambridge University Press.

Bertola, G. (1993). Models of economic integration and localised growth. In F. Torres & F. Giavazzi (Eds), *Adjustment and Growth in the European Monetary Union*, Cambridge: Cambridge University Press (pp. 159-179).

Blanchard, O. & Katz, L. (1992). Regional Evolutions, *Brookings Papers in Economic Activity, 1*, 1-75.

Boldrin, M. & Canova, F. (2001). Inequality and Convergence: Reconsidering European Regional Policies, *Economic Policy, 16*, pp. 207-253;

Borts, G.H. & Stein, J.L (1964). *Economic Growth in a Free Market*, New York: Columbia University Press.

Brakman, S., Garretsen, H. & Marrewijk, C. van (2001). *An Introduction to Geographical Economics*. Cambridge University Press.

Braunerhjelm, P., Faini, R., Norman, V., Rauner, F. & Seabright, P. (2000). Integration and the Regions of Europe: How the Right Policies can Prevent Polarisation, *Monitoring European Integration, CEPR Annual Report 10*, London: CEPR.

Button, K. & Pentecost, E. (1999). *Regional Economic Performance within the European Union*, Cheltenham: Edward Elgar.

Commission of the European Communities (1999). *Sixth Periodic Report on the Social and Economic Situation and Development of the Regions of the European Union.*

Commission of the European Communities (2001). *Unity, Solidarity, Diversity for Europe, its People and its Territory: Second Report on Economic and Social Cohesion, Vol 1*, p. 9.

48 For a suggestion of the direction this might take, see M. Dunford (2003) Theorising regional economic performance and the changing territorial division of labour, *Regional Studies, 37*, pp. 839-854.

Cornwall, J. & Cornwall, W. (2001). *Capitalist Development in the Twentieth Century: An Evolutionary Keynesian Perspective,* Cambridge University Press.

Davis, D.R. & Weinstein, D.E. (2001). Market size, linkages and productivity: a study of Japanese regions, *National Bureau of Economic Research Working Paper 8518,* Cambridge, MA: NBER.

Delors, J. (Ed.) (1989). Regional Implications of Economic and Monetary Union, *Report on Economic and Monetary Union in the European Community*, Luxembourg: Office for Official Publications of the EC.

Dignan, T. (1995). Regional Disparities and Regional Policy in the European Union, *Oxford Review of Economic Policy, 11*, pp. 64-95.

Dunford, M. & Smith, A. (2000). Catching Up or Falling Behind? Economic Performance and the Trajectories of Economic Development in an Enlarged Europe, *Economic Geography, Vol 76, no. 2,* 169-195.

Dunford, M. (2003). Theorising regional economic performance and the changing territorial division of labour, *Regional Studies, 37*, pp. 839-854.

Dymski, G.A. (1999). On Krugman's Model of Economic Geography, *Geoforum, 27*, pp. 439-452.

European Commission (2000). *Unity, Solidarity, and Diversity for Europe, its People and its Territory: Second Report on Economic and Social Cohesion.*

European Commission (2004). *A New Partnership for Cohesion: Convergence, Competitiveness, Cooperation: Third Report on Economic and Social Cohesion,* pp. vii-viii.

Evans, P. (1996). Using cross-country variances to evaluate growth theories, *Journal of Economic Dynamics and Control, 20*, pp. 1027-1049.

Evans, P. (2000). Income dynamics in regions and countries. In G. Hess & E. van Wincoop, (Eds.), (2000). *Intra-national Macro-economics,* Cambridge University Press. (pp. 131-155).

Fatas, A. (2000). Intranational labour migration, business cycles and growth. In G. Hess & E. van Wincoop (Eds.), *Intra-national Macro-economics,* Cambridge University Press. (pp. 156-188).

Friedman, M. (1992). Do old fallacies ever die? *Journal of Economic Literature, 30*, 2029-2032.

Fujita, M., Krugman, P. & Venables, A. (1999). *The Spatial Economy: Cities, Regions and International Trade.* Cambridge: MIT Press.

Fujita, M. & Thisse, J-F. (2002). *Economics of Agglomeration: Cities, Industrial Location and Regional Growth.* Cambridge University Press.

Gardiner, B., Martin, R. & Tyler, P. (2004). Competitiveness, Productivity and Economic Growth across the European Regions, *Regional Studies, 38*, (forthcoming).

Krugman, P. (1991a). *Geography and Trade.* Cambridge, MA: MIT Press.

Krugman, P. (1991b). Increasing returns and economic geography, *Journal of Political Economy, 99*, 483-499.

Krugman, P. (1995). *Development, Geography and Economic Theory*; The Ohlin Lectures, Cambridge, MA: MIT Press.

Krugman, P. (2001). Where in the world is the 'New Economic Geography'? In G. L. Clark, M. Feldman & M. Gertler (Eds.), *Handbook of Economic Geography*, Amsterdam: North Holland (pp. 49-60).

Krugman, P. (1991). History and industrial location: The case of the Manufacturing Belt, *American Economic Review (Paper and Proceedings), 81*, 80-83.

Krugman, P. (1993). The Lessons of Massachusetts for EMU. In F. Torres & F. Giavazzi (Eds.), *Adjustment and Growth in the European Monetary Union,* Cambridge University Press (pp. 241-269).

Martin, R.L. & Sunley, P. (1996). Paul Krugman's 'Geographical Economics' and its Implications for Regional Development Theory: A Critical Assessment, *Economic Geography, 72*, pp. 259-292.

Martin, R.L. & Sunley, P. (1998). Slow Convergence? New Endogenous Growth Theory and Regional Development, *Economic Geography, 74*, 201-227.

Martin, R.L. (1999). The New 'Geographical Turn' in Economics: Some Critical Reflections, *Cambridge Journal of Economics, 23*, pp. 65-91.

Martin, R. (2001). EMU versus the Regions? Regional Convergence and Divergence in Euroland, *Journal of Economic Geography, 1*, 51-80.

Mundell, R.A. (1961). A Theory of Optimum Currency Areas, *American Economic Review, 51*, 657-665.

Obstfeld, M. & Peri, G. (2000). Regional non adjustment and fiscal policy: lessons for EMU. In G. Hess & E. van Wincoop (Eds.), *Intra-national Macro-economics,* Cambridge university Press. (pp. 221-271).

Parente, S.L. & Prescott, E.C. (1993). Changes in the wealth of nations, *Federal Reserve bank of Minneapolis Quarterly Review, 17*, 3-16.

Puga, D. (2002). European regional policies in the light of recent location theories, *Journal of Economic Geography, 2, 4*, 373-406.

Romer, P.M. (1986). Increasing Returns and Long-Run Growth, *Journal of Political Economy, 94*, 1002-1037.
Romer, P.M. (1987). Growth Based on Increasing Returns due to Specialisation, *American Economic Review, 77, 2*, 56-62.
Romer, P.M. (1990). Endogenous Technological Change, *Journal of Political Economy, 98, 5, Part II*, S71-S102.
Sala-i-Martin, X. & Sachs, J. (1991). Fiscal Federalism and Optimum Currency Areas: evidence for Europe from the United States, *NBER Working Paper 3855,* Cambridge, MA: NBER.
Sapir, A. et al. (2003). *An Agenda for a Growing Europe: Making the EU Economic System Deliver*, Report to the President of the European Commission.
Sapir, A. et al. (2004). Between Development and Social Policies; The Impact of the European Structural Funds in Objective 1 Regions, *Regional Studies, 38* (forthcoming).
Scott, A.J. (1998). *Regions and the World Economy, the coming shape of global production competition and political order.* Oxford University Press.
Setterfield, M. (1997). *Rapid Growth and Relative Decline: modelling macroeconomic dynamics with hysteresis.* Basingstoke: MacMillan.
Storper, M. (1997). *The Regional World: Territorial Development in a Global Economy.* New York: Guilford Press.
Williamson, J.G. (1965). Regional Inequalities and the Process of National Development, *Economic Development and Cultural Change, 13*, 1-84.

M. BRÜLHART AND R. TRAEGER[1]

AN ACCOUNT OF GEOGRAPHIC CONCENTRATION PATTERNS IN EUROPE

INTRODUCTION AND SUMMARY[2]

Empirical research in spatial economics is flourishing. The recent theoretical advances of the new economic geography and the empirical reality of eroding distance- and border-related transaction costs give rise to a demand for both stylised facts and rigorous hypothesis tests on the location of economic activity. This demand is particularly strong in Western Europe, where the spatial concentration forces that characterise the recent location models are perceived by some as a looming threat. Numerous researchers have therefore examined the data in a quest for robust evidence on geographic concentration patterns in Europe.[3]

It has proven difficult to distil strong stylised facts from this research. Sectoral relocation in Europe is a slow and multifaceted process that does not leap out from the data. Overman, Redding and Venables (2003) summarise the available evidence as follows: 'In contrast to the US, EU countries are becoming increasingly specialised (...), although the changes are not particularly large'. This diagnosis of a slowly more concentrated European industrial geography is supported by the majority of analyses, but there are numerous exceptions.[4] Furthermore, most of the available evidence relates to the distribution across *countries* of *manufacturing* sectors. Yet, rather little is still known

1 Any opinions expressed in this paper are those of the authors and do not necessarily reflect those of UNECE or its member countries.

2 Printed with permission from Elsevier. The complete version of this paper is published in *Regional Science and Urban Economics*. For more information on the paper see Brülhart's homepage at http://www.hec.unil.ch/mbrulhar. An earlier version of the paper is available as HWWA discussion paper, see www.hwwa.de.

3 For studies of geographic concentration patterns in Europe using sectoral output or employment data, see Aiginger and Davies (2001), Aiginger and Leitner (2002), Aiginger and Pfaffermayr (2004), Amiti (1999); Barrios and Strobl (2004); Brülhart (2001a, 2001b); Clark and van Wincoop (2001); Haaland, Kind, Midelfart Knarvik and Torstensson (1999); Hallet (2000); Helg, Manasse, Monacelli and Rovelli (1995); Imbs and Wacziarg (2003); Kalemli-Ozcan, Sorensen and Yosha (2003); Krugman (1991); Midelfart Knarvik, Overman, Redding and Venables (2002); Paci and Usai (2000); Peri (1998); and Storper, Chen and De Paolis (2002). Combes and Overman (2004) provide a comprehensive survey.

4 Decreasing trends in sectoral specialisation of countries and/or geographic concentration of sectors have also been found by Aiginger and Davies (2001), Aiginger and Leitner (2002), Aiginger and Pfaffermayr (2004), Hallet (2000), Midelfart-Knarvik et al. (2002), Paci and Usai (2000), and Peri (1998).

P. de Gijsel and H. Schenk (eds.), Multidisciplinary Economics, 259–263.

about geographic concentration of sectors at subnational level and across the full range of economic activities. In addition, existing studies use a number of different concentration measures that are chosen largely for their intuitive simplicity; they are based on data with varying coverage and disaggregation; and they do not attempt to gauge the statistical significance of observed patterns.

The aim of this paper is therefore to provide a comprehensive and methodologically rigorous account of sectoral concentration patterns across Western European regions, in a quest for empirically well-founded stylised facts. Our study distinguishes itself from the existing literature in four principal respects.

First, we apply entropy indices to measure geographic concentration. These indices have distinct advantages over the conventional measures in this literature. One advantage lies in their suitability to inequality decomposition analysis. This allows us to compare within-country concentration to between-country concentration in conceptually rigorous fashion. In addition, we can quantify how much each sector contributes to the geographic concentration of aggregate activity, by decomposing aggregate concentration into the 'factor contributions' of individual sectors.

Second, we employ bootstrap inference to test the statistical significance of changes in observed concentration measures. These tests have been shown to be particularly accurate when used in conjunction with entropy measures.

Third, we address aggregation biases that arise in regional data and are often overlooked. Consideration of this issue leads us to compute separate indices for 'relative' concentration, where we measure the degree to which sectors are concentrated relative to the geographic distribution of aggregate activity, and for 'topographic' concentration, where we measure the degree to which sectors are concentrated relative to physical space. Our results show that this conceptual distinction has substantial empirical relevance.

Fourth, our study is based on comprehensive regionally and sectorally disaggregated data. Our main data set provides us with a balanced panel of employment in eight economic sectors in 236 NUTS-2 and NUTS-3 regions belonging to 17 Western European countries over the 1975-2000 period.[5] The eight sectors of this dataset cover the full range of economic activities, including agriculture and services. Through the use of employment as the size measure we can avoid problems of currency conversion inherent in value data. As a complement to the main data set, we use a second data set that disaggregates manufacturing value added into nine industries for 116 EU-15 NUTS-1 and NUTS-2 regions over the 1980-1995 period.

Some existing studies use similar methodologies to ours, but none covers all four elements. Indeed, while entropy indices are common in the income distribution literature (see e.g. Cowell, 2000), their use in spatial contexts has remained relatively rare.

5 NUTS (Nomenclature of territorial units for statistics) is Eurostat's classification of subnational spatial units, where NUTS-0 corresponds to the country level and increasing numbers indicate increasing levels of subnational disaggregation.

A number of researchers have used entropy measures and their decompositions to describe the spatial inequality of *aggregate income* in Europe (e.g. de la Fuente and Vives, 1995; Duro and Esteban, 1998; Duro, 2001; and Combes and Overman, 2004). The application of entropy measures to *sectoral* data for Europe has been pioneered by Aiginger and Davies (2000) and Aiginger and Pfaffermayr (2004). These studies are based on *country*-level data, they do not exploit the indices' decomposability, and they perform no statistical inference. Finally, the paper by Mori, Nishikimi and Smith (2004) resembles ours in some key respects: topographic concentration patterns are described using an entropy index and exploiting its decomposability. Mori *et al.* (2004) do not, however, explicitly address regional aggregation biases, and they use a method for statistical inference that requires strong assumptions.[6]

Our main results are as follows.

We find that the topographic concentration of *aggregate* employment has not changed significantly over our sample period. The concentration of European *manufacturing*, however, has indeed changed statistically significantly: manufacturing has become more geographically concentrated relative to the spatial spread of total employment (increased relative concentration, see Figure 1), but it has become less geographically concentrated relative to physical space (decreased topographic concentration). This likely explains the differences in diagnoses of European concentration trends cited above. The implied story is that manufacturing employment is relocating towards economically peripheral locations. Furthermore, the observed topographic spread of manufacturing in part explains our observation that the contribution of this sector to the topographic concentration of aggregate employment has fallen from 26% to 13% over our sample period.

As to *services*, we detect a statistically significant decrease in concentration, both in relative and topographic terms, for the transport and telecommunications sector. The geographic concentration of the remaining market service sectors (financial services, distribution, and other services), however, has not changed significantly over our sample period (see Figure 1 for relative concentration patterns).

The main aims of this paper are to propose versatile measures for the description of geographic concentration patterns, and to provide a characterisation of locational trends in Western Europe. We believe that a rigorous and detailed description of changing concentration patterns is of interest in itself. Yet, conjectures of relevance to related studies are possible. For example, Ciccone (2002) has estimated the extent to which the topographic concentration of total employment increases regional labour productivity, which he called 'agglomeration effects'. Using regional cross-section data sets for the five largest West European countries, he found that productivity significantly rises in topographic concentration, with a remarkably robust elasticity of around 4.5 percent. Our analysis shows no significant change in the topographic concentration of total

6 Furthermore, Mori et al. (2004) base their study on data for *Japanese* regions.

employment over time, but statistically significant changes in the topographic concentration of individual sectors. Hence, it might be revealing to extend Ciccone's study to changes agglomeration effects over time, based on sectorally disaggregated data. Additional extensions to our work are not difficult to conceive. For example, it would be interesting to describe evolutions of the full distribution of sectoral location patterns including transitions over time of region-sector observations inside those distributions, and to compute measures of spatial separation so as to assess the contiguity of sectoral clusters. The biggest constraint on the quality of research on location patterns in Europe, however, is the quality of available subnational data. Our analysis cannot entirely escape the spatial and sectoral aggregation biases inherent in conventional regional statistics, even though we do our best to minimise their distorting impact. If it were possible to merge plant-level micro geographic data sets that have been collected in several European countries, ideally encompassing services as well as manufacturing establishments, the description of the European economic geography could take a quantum leap in terms of accuracy, comparability and potential for theory-based inference.

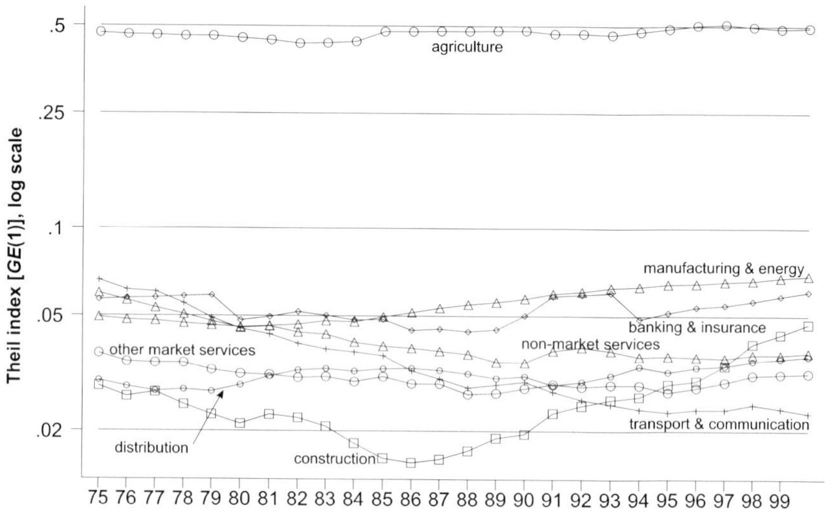

Figure 1. Relative Concentration of Sectors across Western European Regions, 1975-2000.

REFERENCES

Aiginger, Karl & Davies, Steve W. (2001). Industrial specialisation and geographic concentration: Two sides of the same coin? *Working Paper #23*. University of Linz.

Aiginger, Karl & Leitner, Wolfgang. (2002). Regional concentration in the United States and Europe: who follows whom? *Review of World Economics (Weltwirtschaftliches Archiv), 138(4)*, 652-679.

Aiginger, Karl & Pfaffermayr, Michael. (2004). The Single Market and geographic concentration in Europe. *Review of International Economics, 12(1)*, 1-11.

Amiti, Mary. (1999). Specialisation patterns in Europe. *Review of World Economics (Weltwirtschaftliches Archiv), 135(4)*, 573-593.

Barrios, Salvador & Strobl, Eric. (2004). Industry mobility and geographic concentration in the European Union. *Economics Letters, 82(1)*, 71-75.

Brülhart, Marius. (2001a). Evolving geographic concentration of European manufacturing industries. *Review of World Economics (Weltwirtschaftliches Archiv), 137(2)*, 215-243.

Brülhart, Marius. (2001b). Growing alike or growing apart? Industrial specialisation of EU countries. In: C. Wyplosz. (Ed.) *The impact of EMU on Europe and the developing countries*, Oxford University Press.

Ciccone, Antonio. (2002). Agglomeration effects in Europe. *European Economic Review, 46(2)*, 213-227.

Clark, Todd & & Wincoop, Eric. (2001). Borders and business cycles. *Journal of International Economics, 55(1)*, 59-85.

Combes, Pierre-Philippe & Overman, Henry G. (2004). The spatial distribution of economic activities in the European Union. In V. Henderson & J.F. Thisse (Eds.), *Handbook of Regional and Urban Economics, vol. 4*. North Holland: Elsevier.

Cowell, Frank A. (2000). Measurement of inequality. In: A.B. Atkinson & F. Bourguignon (Eds.) *Handbook of Income Distribution, vol. 1*. North Holland: Elsevier.

De la Fuente, Angel & Vives, Xavier. (1995). Infrastructure and education as instruments of regional policy: evidence from Spain. *Economic Policy, 20*, 11-40.

Duro, Juan A. (2001). *Regional income inequalities in Europe: an updated measurement and some decomposition results*. Mimeo, Institute for Economic Analysis, Universitat Autònoma de Barcelona.

Duro, Juan A. & Esteban, Joan. (1998). Factor decomposition of cross-country income inequality, 1960-1990. *Economics Letters, 60(3)*, 269-275.

Haaland, Jan I., Kind, Hans J., Midelfart Knarvik, Karen H., & Torstensson, Johan. (1999). What determines the economic geography of Europe? *Discussion Paper #2072*. CEPR

Hallet, Martin. (2000). Regional specialisation and concentration in the EU. *European Commission Economic Papers, No. 141*.

Helg, Rodolfo, Manasse, Paolo, Monocelli, Tommaso, & Rovelli, Ricardo. (1995). How much (a)symmetry in Europe? Evidence from industrial sectors. *European Economic Review, 39(5)*, 1017-1041.

Imbs, Jean & Wacziarg, Romain. (2003). Stages of diversification. *American Economic Review, 93(1)*, 63-86.

Kalemli-Ozcan, Sebnem; Sorensen, Bent E. & Yosha, Oved. (2003) Risk sharing and industrial specialization: regional and international evidence. *American Economic Review, 93(3)*, 903-918.

Krugman, Paul. (1991). *Geography and Trade*. MIT Press.

Midelfart Knarvik, Karen H., Overman, Henry G., Redding, Stephen J., & Venables, Anthony J. (2002). The location of European industry. European Economy, *Special Report 2/2002*, European Commission, Brussels.

Mori, Tomoya, Nishikimi, Koji, & Smith, Tony E. (2004). *Relative entropy index of industrial localization: a statistic for large sample analysis*. Mimeo, Institute of Economic Research, Kyoto University.

Overman, Henry G., Redding, Stephen & Venables, Anthony J. (2003). The economic geography of trade, production and income: a survey of empirics. In: Choi E. Kwan, & J. Harrigan (Eds.) *Handbook of International Trade*. Blackwell.

Paci, Raffaele and Usai, Stefano. (2000). Technological enclaves and industrial districts: an analysis of the regional distribution of innovative activity in Europe. *Regional Studies, 34(2)*, 97-114.

Peri, Giovanni. (1998). Technological growth and economic geography. *Working Paper #139*, IGIER, Bocconi University.

Storper, Michael, Chen, Yun-chung, & De Paolis, Fernando. (2002). Trade and the location of industries in the OECD and European Union. *Journal of Economic Geography, 2(1)*, 73-107.

PAST AND FUTURE OF THE GLOBAL FINANCIAL ARCHITECTURE

C.J.M. KOOL

INTRODUCTION

Over the past two decades, the industrialised world has become more financially developed and integrated than it has ever been. Moreover, less developed countries – in particular the group of emerging economies – are urgently trying to catch up with the global capital market. Overall, the growth of the financial services industry, the development of new financial instruments and the emergence of new – international – financial markets will all contribute to a more efficient operation of the global financial system. In turn, this should lead to better resource allocation and higher economic growth and welfare. Nevertheless, many unsolved issues remain.

In this volume, Kool (2005) provides an overview of the costs and benefits of fast economic development and of interesting topics for further research. Kool demonstrates that fast financial development is typically accompanied by increased financial instability. Moreover, countries at a lower stage of economic development are more likely to be hit by a financial crisis – be it an exchange rate or banking crisis or a combination of the two – and, when hit, to experience more severe costs. On the other hand, the more developed countries appear to reap most of the benefits of increased global financial integration. In general, Kool argues that a deeper analysis of the link between financial development and economic growth in an international context is required. In particular, the historical and institutional characteristics of both national and global financial systems appear crucial in the analysis. The different players and the constraints under which each of the players operates deserve separate attention. To be more precise, financial instability often appears to be caused by some combination of an unwise choice of exchange rate regime, inappropriate macroeconomic demand policies, incorrect sequencing of internal and external financial liberalisation, insufficient regulatory and supervisory institutional frameworks, and inappropriate incentives for national and multinational banks, and national and supranational supervisors and policy makers.

Goodhart (2005), Hovanov et al (2005) and Fratianni & Pattison (2005) all complement the analysis made by Kool. Goodhart elaborates on the question of what role central banks should play in the conduct of financial regulation both nationally and internationally. With respect to the international dimension, Goodhart also discusses

P. de Gijsel and H. Schenk (eds.), Multidisciplinary Economics, 265–266.

the desired balance of power and responsibilities between national central banks – like the ECB – and supranational formal (IMF) and informal (BIS) financial supervisors. He pays ample attention to both the historical and institutional context of financial supervision in an attempt to shed more light on problems and solutions. Fratianni (2005) focuses on the role of the IMF from a corporate governance perspective. He qualitatively investigates the extent to which the IMF's major shareholders, the large industrialised countries, or the IMF's staff determine the IMF's mission and policy. Kolari (2005) analyzes the institutions of money. More specifically, he investigates the potential role of a synthetic 'world currency'. The idea of a world currency has been around since Keynes. Problems associated with the concept of a global currency have to do with the lack of a unified political entity backing such currency and lender of last resort issues. The SDR, which was not truly successful, is the closest we ever got. Kolari argues that a 'synthetic' global currency can do better than the SDR. In his view, synthetic money can be of relevance in financial markets for reasons of political economy.

Overall, the articles in this chapter share a focus on the historical, legal and institutional aspects of the operation and development of financial instruments, markets and systems and on strategies and policies of private and public financial institutions. As such, they are good examples of the present and future research performed by USE's finance and financial markets group. Financial researchers at USE, moreover, are part of important national and international networks which will help promote this type of research. Existing contacts and co-operation with other institutions include the Universities of Maastricht, Nijenrode and Rotterdam (the Netherlands), Antwerp (Belgium), Tuebingen (Germany), and Texas A&M and Indiana (USA), as well as De Nederlandsche Bank, the Bundesbank and the Federal Reserve Bank of St. Louis.

REFERENCES

Fratianni, M. & Pattison, J. (2005). Who is runnning the IMF, this volume.

Goodhart, C.A.E. (2005). Regulation and the Role of Central Banks, this volume.

Hovanov, N.V., Kolari, J. & Sokolov, M.V. (2005). Synthetic Money, this volume.

Kool, C.J.M. (2005). The Global Market for Capital: Friend or Foe, inaugural lecture, Utrecht University, this volume.

C.A.E. GOODHART

REGULATION AND THE ROLE OF CENTRAL BANKS IN AN INCREASINGLY INTEGRATED FINANCIAL WORLD

1. INTRODUCTION

My focus in this paper will be primarily on the constitutional and institutional issues of what should be the role for central banks in the conduct of financial regulation, both nationally and internationally. This focus, of course, abstracts from many other important and fascinating questions about the substance, and justification, for such regulations. But space and time constraints prevent such a wider canvass.

Regulation is about rule (i.e. law) making; supervision is about the monitoring of such rules, and, potentially, the imposition of sanctions for their infringement.

Let me raise a few questions ata the outset:
The central bank can advise on regulation, but should it be given delegated powers, by the government, to go further and be enabled to issue 'secondary regulatory requirements' at the national level? Moreover, what might be the locus for a central bank in the process of supervision, should it be carrying that out, to impose penalties – e.g. closure, fines, naming and shaming – on the supervised, its charges, at the national level? Note, in particular, that the central bank is usually unelected, and often operationally independent of the government. Is there a 'democratic deficit'?

If we turn next to issues of *international* regulation and supervision, there is no equivalent corpus of law available. There is, instead, 'soft law', now largely imposed on the rest of the world by a self-appointed group of central bankers, meeting in the Basel Committee of Banking Supervision. Such 'soft law' is, however, backed up by the sanction of exclusion from major world financial centres for the banks of any countries refusing to abide by such regulations. Moreover, international regulations, and supervision, are increasingly undertaken by the International Monetary Fund (IMF), with its Financial Stability Assessment Program (FSAP), and also by the Financial Stability Forum (FSF) at the Bank for International Settlements (BIS) at Basel.

P. de Gijsel and H. Schenk (eds.), Multidisciplinary Economics, 267–278 .

2. AN EVOLUTIONARY HISTORY OF REGULATION

Central banks were initially founded by governments, largely to support government financing, (to finance war, manage public sector debt, maintain the gold, or silver, standard, to process public sector expenditures/receipts), in return for certain monopoly advantages, such as the privilege of being the only joint-stock bank either in the country, or in the capital.

The central bank was otherwise perceived, in the early 19th century, as an ordinary private bank. But naturally it became the biggest and most powerful of such private sector banks. Hence, the small country banks came to bank with the central bank, and it became the bankers' bank. The central bank would lend to banks who were its customers, just as they, the smaller commercial banks, lent in turn to their own customers. Because of its size, and central role, the central bank became the lender of last resort. Now what do banks need as a basis for making loans? What they need is information on the prospects of the borrower, and the protection of collateral against their loans. Throughout the centuries, central banks have always been concerned with the quality of collateral for such loans, of last resort, and also with the status and solvency of those banks to whom they might lend.

But central banks have inevitably other, macro and systemic, responsibilities as well. These include:

1) to prevent domestic liquidity crises;
2) to maintain the gold (or silver) standard.

An early problem was that the achievement of these two responsibilities appeared to clash. In order to prevent domestic liquidity crises, the need was for the injection of additional liquidity into the system, i.e. large loans or expansionary open market operations, and low interest rates. In order to maintain convertibility against an external drain, a speculative attack on the currency, the opposite need was to have tight money, and high interest rates.

The way to combine these two, apparently conflicting, objectives was taught in the early half of the 19th century by two great British economists. The first and greatest of these was Henry Thornton, who in 1802 wrote perhaps the greatest book on monetary economics ever published, *The Paper Credit of Great Britain*. The second, of course, was Walter Bagehot, with his book *Lombard Street* (1873). What both of these advocated was that the onset of a dual crisis, i.e. both an internal and an external simultaneous drain, should be met by a combination of credit expansion, but at a high rate of interest. During these same decades, the Bank of England also developed certain rules of thumb, somewhat like the Taylor rule currently for the adjustment of interest rates, for determining its own monetary operations; these were known as the Palmer rules. Under the Palmer rules, the Bank of England would tighten, or ease, credit restrictions by its market operations depending on the level of its gold reserves, notably the ratio of gold to other paper assets.

One particular problem was making its own interest rate the effective level for all short-term money market rates. During periods of tight money, especially in crises, the bank had no such problem in making its own bank rate effective, because other banks would want to borrow from it. On the other hand, in the first half of the 19th century, the bank found it difficult to make its rate effective in circumstances when there was considerable liquidity, and easy money in the markets. It was not until the latter part of the 19th century that the bank discovered how to use open market operations (OMO), to withdraw excess monetary base, and squeeze liquidity, so as always to be able to force the commercial banking system into the bank, to borrow from the bank at the bank's desired rate.

The bank still faced, however, a number of additional problems in operating increasingly in the role of a central bank to maintain internal and external convertibility of the currency, and macro economic stability.

There were three such main problems. The first was that the central bank at that time remained essentially a private sector bank, and was therefore concerned about profitability. The difficulty was that the objectives for maintaining convertibility and financial stability required it to withdraw credit during good periods, when every other bank was lending, and to make loans during domestic financial crises, when every other bank was trying to withdraw, or limit, such credit extension. Clearly, this was not consistent with a single-minded focus on maximising profitability. Eventually what occurred was that it became realised that a central bank should *not* seek to maximise profits. In the UK, for example, dividends from the bank ceased to vary with profits, but instead became fixed at a given nominal level. This, in effect, meant that the shareholders found the nature of their asset shifting from an equity asset to a debenture/bond-type holding. Certainly, by the beginning of the 20th century, it had become generally recognised that central banks could and should not, be profit-maximisers, irrespective of the formal nature of their ownership structure.

The second problem was that, insofar as they remained a private, commercial bank in their own right, they continued to be competitors of the other commercial banks. This led to an artificial situation, in which the central bank both controlled, in a sense, and also regulated, the same commercial banks with which it competed. This led to certain conflicts of interest on both sides. For example, it has been suggested that one reason that the Bank of England was relatively slow in trying to deal with the crisis caused by the collapse of Overend & Gurney in 1866 was that the latter firm represented a clear competitor to the bank, and that the bank was not displeased to see the collapse take place. Another example in the United States in 1907 was that the panic in that year was largely caused by the commercial bank which acted as the clearing bank for the Knickerbocker Trust Company refusing to clear for the Knickerbocker, in conditions where there was some possibility of one of the directors of the Knickerbocker having business connections with some firms that had failed. In fact the Knickerbocker, as became clear later on, was solvent; the suspicion was clearly there that the bank refused to clear for the Knickerbocker, and therefore brought down the system, partly because there was competition between the commercial banks in the clearing house arrangement, (which acted as a substitute for a Central Bank), and the Trust Companies which had certain legal advantages in bidding for business.

Similarly, in the UK at the end of the 19th century and beginning of the 20th century, the commercial banks and the Bank of England were very unwilling to deal directly with each other because of such competitive pressures. The rather arcane and curious arrangement of discount houses was largely initiated by the bank to provide a buffer between the commercial banks and itself, so that transfers of liquidity and open market operations could take place without the bank and the major commercial banks ever having to deal directly and face-to-face with each other. The solution that was found for this particular difficulty was for central banks to abandon commercial banking altogether. In the UK, again, there was an (unwritten) agreement that the Bank of England would freeze all its private commercial banking operations on the one hand, and that the commercial banks would accept the general market leadership of the Bank of England on the other, an agreement which came into operation in the first decade of the 20th century.

The third problem was that the central bank, although it could create base money, nevertheless had limited capital. This meant that its lender of last resort loans had to be limited, because the central bank could not afford a sizeable loss, in the event of a borrower becoming bankrupt. That meant that LOLR was somewhat limited. The solution to this problem was either to require full, and additional, collateral, or, frequently, to organise a consortium of other commercial banks, along with itself, to provide potential loans and guarantees. This, for example, was done in the case of the first Barings crisis in 1890. An alternative solution, if the commercial banks could not, or would not, club together to support the central bank, was to seek government support. Indeed there *had* to be resort to such government assistance in the case of the major potential crisis, which was in the event controlled, at the outbreak of World War I in August 1914. The British financial system had a massive short-term creditor claims on the, now hostile, central countries of Germany and Austro-Hungary. It had to be assumed that such claims were now valueless, and writing down such claims effectively meant that the British financial system became insolvent. Effectively the crisis was met by the Government promising that it would repay the lost value of those claims.

What the central bank did *not* do then was bank supervision, as it is currently known. Instead the protection of depositors, and governance arrangements for commercial banks, were a function generally of central government. There were many facets to such governance arrangements. These included:

1) Unlimited, or double, liability for shareholders, combined with measures to ensure that a shareholder selling his shares would still be liable, if the purchaser in turn defaulted, for a period of months after the sale.
2) The allowance that banks could undertake joint-stock governance arrangements.
3) Regular publication of accounts. For example, at the beginning of 1890, shortly after banks had been allowed to adopt a limited liability structure, the then Chancellor of the Exchequer, Goschen, insisted on regular call reports from commercial banks, following the practice of the Office of the Comptroller of the Currency in the United States.
4) Required backing for the note issue, (both for commercial banks, (e.g. in the US National Banking System), and of central banks in other countries).

One of the problems with the regular publication of accounts was that, unless all the accounts of all banks were related to the same single day, there was the possibility that the accounts would become heavily window-dressed. Indeed this happened. There was, for example, some convergence towards a desired level for both the cash ratio and the liquid assets ratio in the UK, which was regarded as 'best practice' for banks to publish. By about 1930, for example, the general level of cash ratio which was shown in the books was 8%, and for the liquid assets ratio about 30%. In practice, however, these numbers were heavily 'window-dressed', because the accounts of the different banks were drawn up on different days, so that effectively the cash assets, and indeed the liquid assets, just got passed through interbank markets from bank to bank, in practice allowing each bank to operate normally to much lower ratios than they publicly showed.

Unlimited liability, especially with such liability potentially continuing for some months after a sale of the shares, was, indeed, a strong incentive for shareholders to monitor the banks in which they held shares carefully, and to restrict the riskiness of such activities. Nevertheless such risk control could not be perfect, and failures did occur from time to time in the 19th century, notably the failure of the City of Glasgow Bank in the 1870s. This led to the ruin of many of its shareholders and losses to its other creditors. The effect of that was to raise the risk premium on the purchase of equity in commercial banks to such a high level that it became exceedingly difficult to fund new banks, or bank expansion. Accordingly it was decided that bank equity had to be in limited liability form. But that removed that particular incentive for prudent behaviour. So what alternative external control mechanisms could then be available to help promote good behaviour?

George Rae, the author of *The Country Banker*, wrote that book in the aftermath of that crash, and thought that such an alternative had indeed now been found, primarily in the guise of more transparency, which was introduced in the 1879 Act.

Let me provide quotes from pages 259 and 263.

> 'But the Act, whilst it thus effectually protects the depositor, still further safe-guards his interest in other ways. Every bank, as we have before stated, which registers under the Act, has to publish a balance-sheet, which shall set forth its exact financial position at least once a year.
>
> It has further to submit the whole of its books and accounts, its money and securities, to the investigation of public auditors, in order that they may certify, or decline to certify, as the case may be, to the correctness of the figures of the balance-sheet.'
>
> 'No doubt there will be banking losses in the future; but they can never attain to vast and overwhelming totals again, because hereafter they will be checked in time. There can never again be successful concealment of evil-doing stretching over periods of time. You will have to render an annual account of your stewardship, and that account must henceforth be verified by the sharpened vision of skilled accountants. The nursing of doubtful accounts by means of fraudulent book-keeping to figures more and more portentous, year after year, will no longer be possible. The enormities of our banking past, can never be re-enacted; the banking misfortunes of the future will be trifles light as air compared with the devastating experiences of the past.'

These quotes indicate, alas, that the merits of both transparency and of external audit can be much overstated.

As remarked earlier, the onset of World War I required direct government intervention in the combatant countries, in order to overcome the fragmentation of the global system that took place at the outset of the war in August 1914. Note that that war had not been anticipated, so that there was an enormous network of claims and liabilities outstanding among the hostile parties. Furthermore, the scale and duration of the war effort in the combatant countries required the authorities to direct and concentrate resources for the purpose of pursuing the continuing hostilities. This meant that finance was further controlled by the direct intervention of government authorities. In this way, the central bank became subsidiary to the Ministry of Finance in all the combatant countries (except the USA) for the duration of World War I.

After the war there was some considerable reversion to a system of central banks, which were at least nominally independent of their Ministries of Finance. The Bank of England played a major role in trying to re-establish such a system, especially in central Europe. There was also an attempt to revert to the Gold Standard. But, as is well known, there was a subsequent collapse, starting in 1929, back into depression, with disorganised floating exchange rates. Following a massive rise in unemployment, there was a turn in most countries towards a more controlled and centralised economic system. Central banks again became subsidiary to the Ministry of Finance, this time for the purpose of financing public sector deficits at the lowest feasible interest rates.

The financial systems of many countries at this time also faced collapse, with many of the major banks failing. The response in the United States, for example, was new legislation to restrict the function of commercial banks (the Glass-Steagall Law) with new government bodies, such as the Federal Deposit Insurance Company (FDIC), together with additional new organisations and supporting mechanisms. There was, however, no extra role for the central bank, except insofar as it lent its good offices towards the attempt to provide industrial consolidation, and to encourage cartels which might, in periods of weak demand, maintain stronger profits and more viable companies. Indeed in the UK there was a move back towards fixing interest rates by official fiat, as indeed there also was in the United States.

The subsequent outbreak of war in 1939, and the economic recovery that was in part associated with such wartime expenditures, led to monetary expansion. To prevent inflation, and to conduct war at the minimum possible interest rates, direct credit controls were then imposed on banks. This limited their ability to take up private sector debt, and therefore left them more room to purchase government debt. In this exercise the central bank became the (often unwilling) junior assistant to the Ministry of Finance in deciding on the amount and allocation of rationed credit that the banks could provide to the private sector.

Such limited and rationed credit was usually directed to large manufacturing industry. The result of all this was that bank assets were mainly concentrated in holdings of government debt and claims on major firms. Such assets were relatively safe. One result of this was that there was no serious bank crisis in almost any country from about 1936 until about 1966.

But, as a result, commercial banks did not monitor their borrowers, and no one, including the central bank, really monitored the commercial banks. At the Bank of England the entire staff dealing with supervision of banks, and monitoring what they were doing, was represented by the principal of the discount market, together with a small handful of other officials. They focussed on monitoring the condition of the discount market and of the accepting houses, because it was bills that were endorsed by the accepting houses and then rediscounted by the discount houses to the Bank of England, which formed the assets purchased by the Bank of England from the private sector.

Although safe, this system of rationed private sector credit, was both inefficient and conservative. Those firms which were innovative, and could make most use of credit, found it difficult to get access to such credit. There was virtually no competition, little innovation and little conscious assumption, or assessment, of risks involved in the whole exercise. The system of credit rationing eventually broke down, from competition which arose both from internal competitors, which unlike the main commercial banks were not regulated or controlled, and also increasingly from international competition. The advent of new information technologies (IT) sharpened the capacity to compete; and competition was also encouraged by an emerging rebirth of belief in the free market system.

But liberalisation, in one country after another, then led on to financial crises. Neither the banks, nor the central bank, knew exactly how to behave once they had been freed to take more risk, and then crises led to bank failures. In my own country, the UK, the advent of liberalisation was marked by the passage of the paper on *Competition and Credit Control* in 1971. There was, (a history to be followed in many other countries), then a subsequent asset price boom which reached a peak in 1973. This was followed by what became known as the Fringe Bank Crisis in 1974/75, during which a number of small and middle-sized banks failed, and concerns were even expressed over the solvency of one of the main commercial banks.

These failures, often in the course of collapses following asset price bubbles, which in turn were set off by liberalisation, resulted in added responsibilities for banking supervision being placed on central banks. Indeed, it can be argued that the requirement for an extra central bank supervisory role largely developed and occurred in the course of the last few decades, since the 1970s. Before then, measures, such as they were, to limit bank risk taking had largely been the responsibility of direct government measures. After about 1970, banking supervision became seen as one of the responsibilities of a central bank. Central banks were given this largely new role in part by default, since there was no other body capable of undertaking this particular function.

This central bank supervisory role, however, has had numerous problems:

1) The coverage and scale of responsibilities involved has increasingly gone beyond the commercial banking sector to encompass the whole financial system, because there has been an increasing blurring of dividing lines between banking, insurance and securities houses. In order to maintain a level playing field to prevent regulatory arbitrage, it is, therefore, becoming increasingly necessary to supervise the whole of the financial system; but this takes central banks beyond their particular area of expertise; it leads them into fields and sectors, such as insurance and capital markets, in which they have been relatively unwilling, and unskilled, in getting involved.

2) There are severe reputational problems. Regulation is always unpopular with the regulated, since by definition it is forcing them to take actions that they would not otherwise voluntarily do. Moreover, regulation neither should, nor can, prevent all failures. But, once an institution is regulated, then anyone who loses money from such a failure will blame the regulators for that failure. All failures will be blamed on the regulators. So, at best, the regulators will barely be noticed; at worst, the regulators will be held responsible for everything that goes wrong within the financial system. But, if the regulators who are being blamed are central bank officials, then this will be held to tarnish the reputation of the central bank itself. Indeed, in the UK, the failings of the central bank to avert the collapses of Johnson Matthey, Barings and BCCI, were used as arguments against granting operational independence to the Bank of England.
3) During these last decades, central banks have become more (operationally) independent of government. That raises the question of how far such an independent body should also be responsible for monitoring and sanctioning private sector entities. Put another way, would a central bank which had both the power to set interest rates, and the power to supervise and control the whole of the private sector financial system, become an excessively powerful independent entity? Insofar as a central bank becomes separate from government, should it have such wide-ranging powers? Indeed there have been some indications that the greater the operational independence of a central bank, the less likely it is also to have supervisory responsibilities.
4) There is also a question of possible conflicts of interest between monetary and prudential policies. Might the supervisory wing of a central bank, with combined responsibilities, seek perhaps greater financial ease, because of potential problems of financial instability, at a time when there was a need to tighten monetary policy to restrain inflation? In my own experience, such conflicts of interest are extremely rare. More often, when there are signs of serious financial fragility, as in Japan in the 1990s and the United States in the early 1930s, the problem with monetary policy has been that it was too tight, not too expansionary. Nevertheless, there is widespread concern about such possible conflicts of interests, particularly among academics.
5) With a well-functioning money market system, it is rare for a bank to face problems of illiquidity, unless there are lurking concerns about its possible insolvency. Otherwise such a bank can borrow in the money market to meet its short-term liquidity problems. So, when a bank comes to a central bank for lender of last resort assistance, it is usually because there are insolvency problems in the background. But, when there are such problems about insolvency, nowadays a central bank cannot meet these on its own, because it has limited capital. Consequently it really *has* to involve the government in all the major issues connected with the rescue of a failing bank. So a central bank has to go into partnership with the Ministry of Finance in any such rescue or bail-out event. The central bank can no longer act on its own to resolve a crisis.

There are, of course, many arguments tending in the other direction, i.e. that support the inclusion of the supervisory function within the central bank. Again, constraints of time and space prevent me from going into them in any detail. That said, I have, however, outlined the arguments both for and against, central bank operation of the supervisory function in my earlier paper, entitled 'The Organisational Structure of Banking Supervision'.

3. THE INTERNATIONAL DIMENSION

Once exchange controls were removed, an integrated, global financial system emerged. It is no longer possible within one country, in the absence of exchange controls, to introduce regulations independently. The result of that simply would be to drive the restricted financial intermediation offshore, to the benefit of banks in other countries, rather than to domestic banks, without in any way being able to limit the financial process subject solely to domestic credit controls.

One of the problems, however, with the emerging global financial system has been that supervision, monitoring and sanctions remain at the national level, although the functioning of the financial system, at least for wholesale purposes, has become international. With international competition, but national systems for regulating and supervising the financial system, there was obviously a need to try to co-ordinate the supervisory arrangements, at least in the major countries. That appreciation dawned on central banks in the early 1970s. The Basel Committee on Banking Supervision was set up in 1974, after the failures of Herstatt Bank in Germany and Franklin National Bank in America, both of which had transnational repercussions. Among the first issues that this committee considered was the need for consolidated banking supervision after the failure of Banco Ambrosiano later in the decade.

The greater competition introduced by all these developments, however, led to a decline in capital. Greater competition led to margins being pared, and greater risks being taken led to more nonperforming loans. Smaller margins and more NPLs led to a reduction in profitability; a reduction in profitability led to a steady decline in capital ratios. A decline in capital ratios was making the banking and financial systems in all countries perceptibly more fragile. There was a need to halt this trend. The Basel Committee on Banking Supervision tackled this problem in the agreement that became known as Basel I, in 1988, which established that all major countries would require certain minimum capital ratios, and would require subsidiaries of foreign banks seeking to operate in these host countries to apply equivalent ratios. There were, however, problems with Basel I. For example, there was no attempt to distinguish the relative riskiness of loans to differing kinds of private sector borrowers. All were given the same risk ratio. This meant that low-risk safe borrowers were being required to be backed by the same amount of (equity) capital as extremely risky borrowers. Consequently the cost of lending to safe borrowers was overstated, and that to very risky borrowers understated. The effect of this was to lead to lending to safe borrowers becoming transferred off banking loan books, by securitisation and credit risk transfers of various kinds to nonbank lenders; whereas risky borrowers remained on bank loan books. The effect of this, in practice, was to make banks into 'bad' banks, because their loan books were now filled with the relatively riskier loans.

So the problems of Basel I have led to Basel II; and there are many concerns about Basel II, in the guise of procyclicality, complexity, undesirably detailed intervention into banking business, and a host of other more technical concerns. All this suggests that the process of regulation and reregulation have yet much further to go.

This Basel system is, indeed, a curious one; it is 'ad hoc', but quite effective. This has worked in part because central banks are collegial and tend to work together much more easily than governments seem to do. Their agreements are no in any sense 'hard law', but they are 'soft law'. They are also based on sanctions, because bank subsidiaries or branches from countries that do not abide by these agreements will not be allowed into the major countries' markets. On the other hand, it is not really effective for the major countries themselves. For example, it is widely thought that Japan did not really apply either appropriate accounting techniques, or enforce the Capital Adequacy Ratios rigorously, during the period of banking weakness in the last decade. Similarly, the US seems to be having certain concerns about the application of Basel II in its own country; and has, more or less unilaterally, decided that it will apply a somewhat different set of rules to its own domestic banks than are being required to be adopted in Europe and the rest of the developed world.

Is this role as unofficial, and unelected, legislators of 'soft law' for the rest of the world really a proper role for central banks? Without legislative and statutory support, how do they even manage to commit the banks of their own country? In reality, there is a degree of 'capture' in that each central bank will tend to put forward a position which it thinks will be reasonably favourable to its own domestic banks. Is this necessarily a bad thing? Also, how do central banks, and the others involved in the Basel Committee, manage to commit their own governments, and indeed other relevant quasi governmental bodies, such as the Office of the Comptroller of the Currency in the United States? In the course of the Basel negotiations, it became noticeable that the representative of the US came from the Federal Reserve System, but that the main objections to the adoption of Basel II came from the OCC, (and J. Hawke), which latter were not directly represented in these discussions. Certainly the whole of the Basel II process represented a lengthy exercise in indirect politicisation and 'horse trading'. Moreover, the Basel Committee has had to be expanded, involving the co-option of specialised financial supervisors, even though these in many cases have moved outside central banks, such as the Financial Services Authority (FSA) in the United Kingdom.

So the main negotiations, discussions and subsequent agreements on financial regulation and supervision at the global level continue to be made by the representatives of the leading national supervisory bodies, both central banks and specialised FSA. What about the international institutions? The Bank for International Settlements (BIS) has an important role as secretariat to the Basel Committee, and facilitator of negotiations, discussions and meetings amongst central banks. But it is not yet really a major independent player. The IMF is, however, now becoming such an independent player in the international supervisory system, especially after the Asian crisis in 1997/98. The Asian crisis itself was largely attributed to weaknesses in the financial systems in those countries, and in particular to weak supervisory systems. Consequently, and in turn, the focus of the IMF has switched somewhat from purely macroeconomic concerns about monetary aggregates and fiscal policies, to paying increasing attention to the methods and procedures for ensuring financial stability. These include, for example, the Financial Sector Assessment Programmes (FSAPs), which all countries are now being encouraged to undergo in conjunction with the IMF and World Bank. Through such FSAPs, and by other routes, the IMF is now attaching far greater importance to external assessment of the standards of financial supervision and assessing the extent of financial strength in each economy. But should an even greater executive role in global financial regulation go to the IMF? This question will remain, even if it has been somewhat sidetracked in the last couple of years by issues connected with the resolution of sovereign debt default.

But how about the European dimension? In the past, the directives related to financial stability and banking supervision have essentially simply taken their line from the Basel Committee. But should there now be a separate role for the European Central Bank (ECB) and indeed the wider ESCB? Questions have been asked, for example by Padoa-Schioppa, on:

a) Whether it is possible to separate the domain of monetary and prudential control? The domain of monetary control now covers the whole of the Euro-zone. Is it sensible to have the domain of prudential control effectively still separated amongst the various national authorities of the Euro-zone?
b) What about crisis overlaps between countries? This will become increasingly important as the EU retail financial system becomes less nationally separate. It has been mainly nationally separate, with the retail system dominated by local banks, until quite recently. This is increasingly less so, with such overlaps becoming more common in the smaller Euro-zone countries. In particular there are significant overlapping institutions within Scandinavia, and again between Belgium, Netherlands and Luxembourg; this trend is also occurring in Austria, and it is most pronounced of all in the Accession Countries.

4. CONCLUSIONS

The structure of financial regulation and supervision has been evolving rapidly and quite dramatically, especially so in recent years. But the structure is still far from being coherent, or common amongst countries.

Starting perhaps some twenty or thirty years ago, central banks became allocated, in part by chance, in part by seizing the initiative, a larger role in this regulatory and supervisory exercise, especially grouped together collegially in Basel, than they perhaps either could or should maintain. They have a number or problems:

a) Central banks do not have enough capital resources to be able to sustain their financial system through periods of serious fragility. They will, therefore, need to rely on the Ministry of Finance.

b) There remains the question of the role of the ECB within the Euro-zone in the field of supervision. What will be the division of responsibilities and competences between them and the national central banks (NCBs)?
c) Then there is the question of the consistency between the operational independence of central banks and their continuing to maintain a major supervisory role. Where the roles of supervision and operational independence have been separated, then there is a further emerging question of the relationship between the separate central bank and its associated FSA.

On the international front, there is the question of whether a second focal centre (besides the IMF), probably at the BIS, may grow up as an alternative centre for deciding on international issues; and what should be the division of responsibilities between the IMF and the World Bank here? But the IMF has only just begun to turn its attention to such supervisory issues. So the question of where the locus of power and influence at the international level in this area will be remains uncertain. Equally uncertain, however, is the question of whether decisions on such regulatory issues will continue to be made by collegial groupings of national authorities, or might move to the international authorities.

There certainly remain a lot of questions ahead.

REFERENCES

Bagehot, Walter (1873). E. Johnstone & Hartley Withers (Eds.). *Lombard Street: A description of the Money Market*. London: Henry S. King & Co.

Goodhart, C.A.E. (2001). The Organisational Structure of Banking Supervision. In Financial Stability and Central Banking. Bank of England: Routledge.

Rae, George (1885). *The Country Banker: His Clients, Cares and Work.* Rochester, N.Y.: The L.C.P. Co.

Thornton, Henry (1802): *An Enquiry into the Nature and Effects of the Paper Credit of Great Britain.* London: J. Hatchard.

M. FRATIANNI AND J. PATTISON

WHO IS RUNNING THE IMF: CRITICAL SHAREHOLDERS OR THE STAFF?

I. INTRODUCTION

The International Monetary Fund (IMF), as one of the Bretton Woods institutions, was designed to provide the public good with an efficient international monetary system. But over the years, the IMF has transformed itself into a multiproduct institution: its output ranges from a good housekeeping seal of approval for member countries through so-called surveillance and conditionality lending, all the way to technical assistance. Presiding over this wide array of activities are member governments, the shareholders of the IMF. But, as is true of privately-owned corporations, these shareholders face a monitoring problem and may not be able to fully achieve what they wish through the IMF. The purpose of this paper is to examine who is in charge at the IMF: the principal, the agent, or both. The key questions are: who decides on the mission, who controls the agenda, who implements decisions, and how independent are management and staff from shareholders. These are core corporate governance issues bearing on the strategies and effectiveness of the IMF.

The theme is not new. Vaubel (1986), for example, is an early proponent of bureaucratic growth of international organisations (IO) due to the fact that shareholders have small incentives for monitoring. Vaubel et al. (2003) corroborate this finding by estimating a larger-than-unity elasticity of staff size with respect to member states, without however controlling for the size and complexity of the output. Along the same lines, Barnett and Finnermore (1999) posit that international organisations, once created, develop their own agenda. Staff autonomy is grounded on the ability of the staff to retain control over vital information. Frey (1997), instead, emphasises prestige and influence with reference groups as the main forces motivating the staff of IOs. Using this insight, Willett (2001, p. 323) reasons that 'the environment of the IMF is much like that of central banks and finance ministries. As such, there would seem to be relatively little incentive for key decision makers at the IMF to maximise staff size.' Nielsen and Tierney (2003) hypothesise that the IO agent (in their case the World Bank) retains some degree of autonomy so long as his actions are not greatly at odds with the principal's preferences. When significant differences emerge, the principal finds an incentive to reassert his authority and to bring about a change in the agent's behaviour. Martin's (2003) study of the IMF combines elements of informational asymmetries and preference alignment between principal and staff. The principal

P. de Gijsel and H. Schenk (eds.), Multidisciplinary Economics, 279–292.

delegates more autonomy to the staff when issues become more complex and the environment is riskier to the principal, for example during financial crises. On the other hand, if staff actions divert significantly from the principal's preferences, staff autonomy declines. If shareholders trusted the agent completely, delegation would be complete and so would agent autonomy (Majone 2001). Clearly, we have not reached this stage at the IMF. The central message of our paper is that a core of shareholders at the IMF is in full control of the institution's mission on the big issues and that staff autonomy is restricted to areas of marginal interest to the critical shareholders.

The rest of the paper is organised as follows. Section II presents general considerations on the principal-agent relationship in the public sector. The key point there is that, while agency problems tend to be more serious in the public sector than in the private sector, the nature of the production function of the international institution determines the size and incidence of agency costs and the restrictions placed on the agent by the principal. Section III discusses two sharp alternative hypotheses concerning the governance of the IMF: critical shareholders in charge versus management/staff in charge. We also explore the fact that the two hypotheses can co-exist for different states of the world. Section IV presents evidence obtained from the literature. The sum total of the evidence is more qualitative than quantitative given the nature of the topic. Conclusions are drawn in the last section.

II. AGENCY COSTS AND THE PUBLIC SECTOR

Casual observation suggests that agency problems and effective monitoring of the agent are more serious in the public sector than in the private sector. To begin with, corporations seek profit or shareholders' wealth maximisation. Government agencies, instead, have multiple objectives and have to resolve the difficult task of assigning a weight to each of those objectives. Furthermore, objectives or the weight assigned to them change because of the political process and the power of interest groups. While privately held corporations remain focused on the maximisation of profits or shareholders' wealth, the political process changes the rules of the game as political parties or groups, with different ideological agendas, alternate in power. In democracies, political control is contested at fixed dates or within fixed intervals. Elections are the equivalent of takeover bids in the private sector. Political takeovers can be interpreted in either of two ways. The first is that they give an opportunity to replace inefficient bureaucrats with more efficient ones (Breton and Wintrobe 1982, p. 97). The second is that elections serve the purpose of altering the ideological make-up of the civil service, either by replacing top management, as in the U.S. tradition, or by demanding that the civil service fully adhere to the policies of the new government, as in the U.K. tradition. According to the second interpretation, political takeovers are different from private takeovers. Private takeovers are motivated by profit, political takeovers by ideological agendas. This is the reason why government agencies suffer from time inconsistency and their commitment to a given policy is weak (Tirole 1994, p. 5; Majone 2001, pp. 106-7).

Pecuniary incentives play a smaller role in government agencies than in the private sector. The multiplicity of objectives, the fuzziness of weights associated with them, and the lack of observable output and product prices make it difficult to remunerate the civil servant according to his or her marginal value product. This, in turn, gives rise to low powered incentives and the potential for capture by interest groups (Laffont and Tirole 1993). The principal, on the other hand, is the electorate or its representatives, one best characterised as being small, relatively uninformed and consequently at a big disadvantage in monitoring the agent. To offset these tendencies, government agencies tend to leave less discretion to their management and employees than their counterparts in the private sector. The extent of these restrictions depends on the production function of the agency and on the extent of conflicts of interest. A procurement agency faces more restrictions than a central bank.

The same principle applies to IOs. The potential for capture by interest groups is stronger for the World Bank than the IMF, the reason being that the former has a more specialised production function than the latter (Willett 2001, pp. 321-2). The World Bank lends for specific infrastructure projects that affect the income and wealth of identifiable, homogeneous, and well-organised interest groups. The IMF, in contrast, deals with macroeconomic issues and lends with macroeconomic conditions that impact on broad, heterogeneous, and relatively poorly organised constituencies. In a typical IMF standby arrangement, a member government draws hard currency against its own for a period of up to five years and pays an interest rate that historically has been lower than the interest rate on Special Drawing Rights.[1] The borrowing country receives an implied subsidy from the loan but 'pays' for it by accepting a set of restrictions on its policy making.[2] While the conditions may turn out to be too harsh or too lenient relative to the implied subsidy, the central point is that IMF loans have a pecuniary and a nonpecuniary cost. Loan pushing, which is a key aspect of bureaucratic or capture theories, involves the softening of conditions below the equilibrium value of the subsidy. But who is responsible for the softening? The testable implication of bureaucratic growth theory is that the staff does the pushing against the wishes of the shareholders. The alternative is that the shareholders themselves do the pushing, in which case there is no agency problem. So, again, it is important to examine whether the actions of the bureaucracy are aligned with the shareholders' preferences.

III. ALTERNATIVE EXPLANATIONS OF IMF GOVERNANCE

In a formal sense the highest decision-making body of the IMF is the Board of Governors, consisting of one governor and one alternate governor for each of the 184 member countries. In practice, this body is too large and unwieldy and has delegated in fact much of the policy making to the Interim Committee, now called the Interna-

1 The SDR interest rate is a weighted average of money market interest rates in the US, Euroland, Japan, and the UK.

2 It is customary to argue that the IMF does not bear a credit risk because its loans enjoy senior status. Under this assumption, the subsidy is given by the difference between the SDR interest rate and the rate of charge, which is quantified by Jeanne and Zettelmeyer (2000) at less than one per cent of borrowers' GDP.

tional Monetary and Financial Committee (IMFC), consisting of 24 governors. The IMFC meets twice a year and directs the Executive Board (EB) to consider specific issues. The real power behind the IMFC and the Board of Governors is the small, powerful, and agile group of G-7 Finance Ministers who are the critical shareholders of the IMF; more on this below.[3] The EB is made up of 24 directors and the Managing Director who chairs the EB.

Voting power in the EB is asymmetric and reflects the size of the quota of each member state. At present, the United States has 17.14% of the total votes, Japan 6.15%, Germany 6.01 %, France and the United Kingdom 4.96% each, Italy 3.26%, and Canada 2.95%; the G-7 countries, as a group, hold 45.43% of the votes. Nothing of substance in the IMF can take place without the approval of the G-7 countries, or for that matter the United States. Given the distribution of votes within the G-7 group and the history of the institution, the United States is *primus inter pares* among the G-7 countries. While some decisions require a simple majority, for example the approval of a loan, the EB in practice works by consensus (Boughton 2001, p. 1032). Other decisions require a 70% majority, for which the G-7 has veto power. Still other decisions require a supermajority of 85%, for example quota increases, for which the United States has veto power.

The staff of the IMF produces a steady flow of position papers and reports, interacts with and advises officials in member countries, is involved in surveillance activities, and designs (after negotiation with national officials) the conditions attached to loans. This output, with policy recommendations, flows up first to management and then to the EB who can either approve a position, not approve it, or ask for changes. The entire process is supervised by the Managing Director who, as the Chair of EB meetings, controls the agenda. Martin (pp.13-14) takes the view that this bottom-up information flow gives management and staff considerable influence, a sort of first-mover advantage plus agenda-setting power. Rieffel (2003, ch. 11), instead, sees the process more as a top-down flow from the G-7 to the IMFC, the EB, and ultimately the management and staff; more on this below.

The governance issue at the IMF is an old one and goes back to the very roots of the institution. The United Kingdom (that is, Keynes) and the United States (that is, White), the two countries responsible for the architecture of the IMF, had sharply different views on who should be in charge of the institution. Mikesell (1994, p. 52), at the time an U.S. Treasury economist who was intimately involved with the Bretton Woods meetings, recalls that:

> 'White had wanted control of the Fund to be in the hands of a board of directors whose members represented their governments and who would be continuously involved in decisions on exchange rates, drawings and other matters'.

Keynes, on the other hand, wanted an international secretariat to manage and direct day-to-day operations. Mikesell goes on to say that:

3 The G-7 group consists of the United States, Japan, Germany, France, the United Kingdom, Canada, and Italy. The first three countries form the G-3, and the first five the G-5.

'White's position, and that of the U.S. administration generally, reflected a desire to have the Fund heavily influenced by the United States in order to promote the U.S. economic objectives of stable exchange rates, nondiscrimination in trade, and international financial equilibrium'.

It is not surprising that the Articles of Agreement of the IMF were never clear on the matter, a convenient resolution of the differences.

On the basis of both the history of the institution and the above discussion, two alternative hypotheses emerge to explain governance at the IMF. The first is that residual control rights at the IMF are vested with the critical shareholders, a small group of industrial nations, one that certainly includes the United States, Germany and Japan but can stretch to the G-7 finance ministers and possibly, but less likely, to G-10 finance ministers. This group controls vast economic and financial resources and enjoys the highest regulatory and governance standards. Furthermore, critical shareholders own significant numbers of shares, or have similar influence, in all important international financial institutions (e.g. World Bank and Bank for International Settlements) and thus can effectively co-ordinate their strategies by relying on a portfolio of international institutional and financial assets in addition to their national assets. Critical shareholders meet regularly during the year and delegate execution of policy to the national directors. Executive directors at the IMF are simply an extension or a proxy of their finance ministers. Agency costs are small and management and staff behave in accordance with the preferences of the critical shareholders.

An implication of this hypothesis is that benefits are distributed asymmetrically across shareholders. In privately owned companies, controlling shareholders may capture a disproportionate share of the profits by inducing management to deal preferentially with companies owned or controlled by the shareholder (Hart 1995, p. 683). The capture of excess profits is the return from monitoring by the controlling shareholder. Corporate and securities laws are designed in part to reduce the scope for abuse and to protect minority shareholders. At the IMF, critical shareholders may obtain a disproportionate share of the benefits by persuading directors and management to divert a disproportionate share of the institution's resources to governments that are friendly to those shareholders, or to use such resources to assist these governments to achieve their policy goals.

The sharp alternative to the critical shareholder hypothesis is that management and staff make important decisions that are at odds with the preferences of the shareholders. Costly monitoring, including specialised staff knowledge, may be the reasons for agency costs. Management and staff, under this alternative, would seek self-preservation and aggrandisement, and would cater to the interest of client governments, the borrowing countries.

It is also possible that the two hypotheses can co-exist for different states of the world. Critical shareholders may face multiple types of agency costs: low for big issues, that is issues that are important to the critical shareholders; and high for small issues, that is issues that are of marginal value to the critical shareholders and where monitoring by them is thus less effective. Since monitoring has both fixed and variable costs, the per unit cost of monitoring a few big or high-value products is smaller than for many low-value activities involving countries or circumstances of less political urgency.

In sum, decisions reached by the IMF can be interpreted as implications of three different hypotheses: either critical shareholders are the driving force behind the decisions without much dilution in representation by management and staff, or management and staff are the driving force even when they do not reflect shareholders' preferences, or a mix of the two depending on the importance of the issues to the critical shareholders. In what follows, we review the evidence on governance that already exists in the literature to arrive at a qualitative assessment of whether the IMF is run by the critical shareholders, the staff or both.

IV. EVIDENCE FROM THE LITERATURE

In this section we review the literature that bears directly on the hypotheses discussed in the previous section. We start with studies that favour an interpretation along the lines of the critical shareholders' model, then continue with those favouring staff autonomy, and finally with the evidence that indicates that the two hypotheses can co-exist depending on the states of the world.

Critical shareholders

Solomon (1977, p. 5), in his analysis of the international monetary system from 1945 to 1976, remarks that 'to call it a system is to impute more formality to it than it deserves.' Yet he identifies in the G-10 Ministers and their Deputies an important group:

> 'the IMF Executive Board was expected to do the preparatory work and to receive the views – in practice, the decisions – of the Interim Committee' (p. 303).

The Interim Committee was formed in 1974 to replace the Committee of Twenty and was renamed IMFC in 1999. As we have mentioned it in the previous section, members of the IMFC have played the role expected of corporate directors, which is advising and recommending strategies to management for them to implement.

Williamson (1977, p. 60) goes a step further on the role of the G-10:

> 'The G-10 had filled the role of discussing such issues for the previous decade and it had been active … as the natural body in which to negotiate the exchange rate realignment'.

For Plumptre (1977, p. 281):

> '[the Interim Committee] is to stand between the Board of Governors – massive and cumbersome, with more than 125 members who deliver set speeches to audiences of thousands at annual meetings – and the twenty Executive Directors…In short, the intention was to introduce a more effective political influence into the Fund's decision-making'.

Even more direct is Rieffel (2003, pp. 28-9):

> 'The other mistake is to view the IMF as an independent authority. The IMF is an instrument of the G-7 countries. There is no example that comes easily to mind of a position taken by the IMF on any systemic issue without the tacit, if not explicit, support of the United States and the other G-7 countries'.

In contrast, the EB of the IMF is described by Solomon (1977, p. 87) as 'reflecting the diverse views of 20 Executive Directors from Europe, Asia, Africa, and North and South America, [and] was inevitably bland in its recommendations, overt or implied.' The irrelevance of the EB is also emphasised by Woods (2001, p. 87):

> '... real debates over policy and issues are conducted outside of the Board. Controversial cases and stand-off debates are rare. For example, a loan that did not meet with US approval would seldom be presented to a Board for discussion.'

Boughton (2001) has an extensive discussion of the relationship between the IMF and its critical shareholders. In chapter 5, he examines the review process under Article IV of the Articles of Agreement between the IMF and each of the G-5 countries. The opening sentence of the chapter sets the tone for what follows: 'Nowhere is the difficulty of conducting surveillance more apparent than in the relationship between the IMF and the major industrial countries' (p. 135). The G-5 countries are too powerful to mind the advice of the IMF, and this is especially true of the United States. In chapter 7, Boughton tells the history of policy co-operation, starting with the creation of the G-10 and the General Arrangements to Borrow in the early 1960s, then G-5 and its enlargement to G-7 in the mid-1970s, then the Plaza Accord of 1985, and finally Louvre of 1987.[4] In retrospect, the critical shareholders were acting quite co-operatively in the 1980s, although there were signs that even the G-7 was too large a group and had its own 'super-co-operative' core of G-3 countries (the United States, Germany and Japan).[5] In all of this activity, the IMF played a subsidiary and technical role. Boughton candidly acknowledges that 'the Fund participated only at the pleasure of the countries' officials and had no real standing to guide the process' (p. 186). In sum, the G-7 countries stand out from the rest of the shareholders of the IMF, and behave as controlling shareholders.

The International Financial Institution Advisory Commission (2000, p. 48) laments the undue influence of the critical shareholders:

> '[the] IMF should not be used as a 'slush fund' to satisfy decisions of the G-7 finance ministers or other groups of powerful members'

The Commission's main recommendation of setting a rule whereby the IMF would lend only short term, at penalty rates, and conditional on ex-ante standards of financial

4 G-10 consists of G-7 plus Belgium, the Netherlands, Sweden and the affiliated Switzerland (the 11th member of the Group).

5 The core within the core comes out loud and clear in Funabashi (1988).

soundness (p. 8) may be interpreted as a mechanism to rein in the disproportionate influence exercised on the IMF by its critical shareholders (Tarullo 2001, pp. 625-6).

According to Blustein (2001), who covers the period of the currency and banking crises of the 1990s, the G-7 finance ministries, but in particular the US Treasury, control the agenda of the IMF (p. 9). With a touch of irony, Blustein calls the critical shareholders '...the guardians of global financial stability [who] were often scrambling, floundering, improvising, and striking messy compromises' (p. 14). The messy compromises are often driven by incentives to rescue the creditors of industrial countries. Like the International Financial Institution Advisory Commission, Blustein is concerned that the 'High Command' encourages moral hazard behaviour with large country bailouts.

Momani's (2002) Ph D dissertation develops an informative case study of the influence of the United States on IMF loans to Egypt. By relying on internal IMF documents covering approximately ten years of IMF staff reports on IMF-Egyptian agreements, as well as on archival material from the U. S. Department of State, the study arrives at the conclusion that the U.S. government was instrumental in pushing for lenient terms in the 1987 and 1991 agreements despite contrary opinions by IMF staff.

Further evidence on the critical shareholders' hypothesis is offered by Rieffel's (2003, chap. 11) careful review of the history of so-called private sector involvement (PSI). At the root cause of PSI is the search for a solution to moral hazard behaviour. One way to do it is to let creditors and debtors agree on debt restructurings. These can be facilitated either by changing sovereign bond covenants or through a new international agreement on restructuring established by international law and likely requiring new statutes in national financial systems. While each solution has its own advocates, both approaches aim at reducing the cost of debt restructuring; for a review see Eichengreen (1999).

Collective action clauses – the contractual solution – were first mentioned as a possible solution to facilitate debt restructuring in a report by the G-10 finance ministers following the G-7 Halifax summit meeting of 1967 (Rieffel, p. 223). A more structured approach to the problem came to light during the meeting of the G-7 finance ministers in Cologne in 1999. Their report includes a section on 'Framework for PSI', aimed at reducing the risk of moral hazard, without giving additional incentives to debtor countries to renege on their commitments (p. 239). The First Deputy Managing Director of the IMF endorsed the statutory approach in 2001 (Krueger 2001). In the following year, the Krueger proposal became the official IMF management position, recommending a Sovereign Debt Restructuring Mechanism (p. 253). But as soon as US Treasury Secretary John Snow related his opposition to the statutory approach during the April 1993 meeting of the IMFC, the initiative was quickly dropped (p. 256). In the meantime, the contractual approach gained credibility when Mexico, South Africa and Brazil issued new sovereign bonds in the United States' markets with collective action clauses. Collective action clauses have long been included in the documentation for international bonds under English law. The account of these events, to sum up, indicates unequivocally that the *primus inter pares* of the critical shareholders prevailed over senior management on an important issue.

More systematic evidence on the critical shareholders' hypothesis is provided by Barro and Lee (2002) who test econometrically whether the probability and size of an IMF loan is a positive function of the 'closeness' of the borrowing country to an important IMF member country. Using panel data encompassing 130 countries over five-year intervals from 1975 to 1999, these authors estimate Tobit and probit models to explain the size of IMF programmes, and the frequency with which a member country benefited from an IMF programme. The explanatory variables include country-specific economic factors (e.g., per capita GDP), time dummies to account for shifts in global shocks, the borrowing country's clout with the IMF, and the borrowing country's political-economic closeness to critical shareholders. The borrowing country's influence with the IMF is measured by the relative size of its quota and by the relative size of nationals among IMF professional staff; closeness to critical shareholders by fraction of votes at the U.N. General Assembly that agrees with the positions taken by critical shareholders and by the ratio of the bilateral trade between borrowing country and critical shareholder to borrowing country's GDP. There are four critical shareholders in the sample: the United States, France, Germany, and the United Kingdom. While the empirical findings differ from equation to equation, the overall pattern is that both clout and closeness to critical shareholders matter for participation in IMF programmes.

Finally, a more balanced view of the role of critical shareholders is provided by Bird (2003, ch. 3) who acknowledges that powerful members exert influence on IMF lending but cautions 'not to get overexcited about their consequences for prediction. Since IMF agreements are present in only about 20 per cent of the observations, in most large sample econometric studies a prediction of 'no agreement' would be correct about 80 per cent of the time' (p. 60). However, for the purpose of this paper the relevant issue is not whether the prediction of 'no agreement' is 0.8, but rather what effect political considerations have on the 20 per cent of the cases where agreements have been reached.

Staff autonomy and capture

Vaubel (1991) argues that the rapid expansion of the IMF's loan programmes was fuelled by bureaucratic self-preservation, power, and prestige, an outcome that is consistent with the implications of the capture hypothesis. Meltzer (1999) is even more explicit on this theme:

> 'IMF officials are judged partly on their contacts with high officials of borrowing governments. Critical reports by an IMF task force reduce the welcome the IMF team can expect on its next visit...Borrowing governments recognise this power, so they are able to restrain criticism and prevent or delay information from reaching the IMF's top management.'

Bordo and James (2000, p. 7) echo similar concerns and speak of 'clientism' among Fund staff. These authors also emphasise how the IMF branched into development work that went beyond the original function (p. 20) and for which it was not well prepared. In the private sector, moving into a new business without directors' approval, without proper controls and without adequate disclosure to shareholders generally would be considered a serious governance failure. Moreover, IMF shareholders cannot exit by selling their shares.

Mussa (2002, p.70) finds a pro-borrower bias among the staff of area departments:

> '...by the nature of their responsibilities and because of their need and desire to maintain close cooperative relations with the authorities of member countries, this bias toward the member tends to be particularly strong in the Fund's area departments.'

This bias, in turn, is neither compensated for, nor controlled by other departments that work with the area departments, nor by management that 'normally sides with the area departments in their efforts to be as co-operative with members as possible' (p. 70). The friction between area departments and the Research Department of the IMF is underscored in a report of a group of independent experts commissioned by the IMF to assess IMF surveillance (IMF 1999). For the experts, disagreements between the two departments:

> '...were at least in part responsible for the fact that that concerns about the health of Korea's financial system were not properly reflected in surveillance nor communicated to the Executive Board' (p. 32).

Coexistence of the two hypotheses

The literature reviewed seems to agree that noneconomic considerations enter into IMF loan decisions, but it is more ambiguous whether the main source of the problem lies with the critical shareholders or with the IMF management and staff. Fratianni (2003) argues that both elements are present. Consider again IMF conditional lending. The single most important goal of conditionality lending, seen from the viewpoint of the IMF, is to restore external balance while preserving long-term internal balance. Governments of borrowing countries, instead, consider external balance a constraint on their domestic economic policies, which have a plethora of political, social and economic objectives. Also, governments want to remain in power or win the next election. Thus, it may pay off politically for a government to ignore temporarily the balance-of-payments constraint and embark on fast-growth policy, which implies above-average output growth rates, balance-of-payments deficits and a rising inflation rate. An unsustainable external deficit will put an end to the expansionary policy and will start an adjustment programme financed by the Fund.[6]

The logic of conditional lending is to set restrictions that translate into costs in terms of output and employment. Costs of the programme occur typically before benefits. Most borrowing governments are aware of the intertemporal cost-benefit trade-off implied in conditionality lending. They may accept the conditions set by the IMF but find them unpalatable politically and are ill-disposed to implement them. This outcome is consistent with the view of those critics – typically from the political left – who claim

6 The policy of Peru in 1986-87 is a good example of this illustration (Boughton 2001, p. 612).

IMF conditionality lending is too costly for the borrowing countries. There is, however, a second possibility. Governments of borrowing countries are aware of the intertemporal cost-benefit trade-off but feel they can improve it by claiming extenuating circumstances. This outcome is consistent with the view of those critics – typically from the political right – who claim that IMF conditionality lending ends up encouraging repeated lending and moral hazard behaviour.

Both paradigms may co-exist because the IMF discriminates between rich and poor, large and small, geopolitically important and irrelevant members. This discrimination is to a large extent driven by the preferences of the critical shareholders who use the IMF as a multilateral agency of foreign policy and foreign aid. Critical shareholders bear heavily on IMF management when their interests are at stake; otherwise, for small and unimportant countries, their monitoring activity is low and opinions of Fund staff have a much larger influence on outcomes. An illustration of the selective activity exercised by critical shareholders at the IMF is provided by Blustein's (2001, pp. 101-102) account of the IMF's mission to Indonesia during the 1997 currency crisis:

> 'The reason for the turnaround was pressure from members of the IMF board representing Western industrial countries. Karin Lissaker, the U.S. representative, was particularly assertive. ... "The mission went out [to Jakarta] with the usual recipe -tweak a little on monetary policy here and fiscal policy there," Lissaker recalled. "We stepped up the heat, the more we found out about the issues, hearing about these massive subsidies to cronies and family members...This was clearly pushing the outside of the envelope".'

Evidence that the two hypotheses co-exist, in different states of the world, can be gleaned from Martin's (2003) review of the power swings between the EB – representing shareholders – and management and staff over decisions on conditional lending. The US government was an early advocate of conditionality in opposition to the United Kingdom and other member governments. The United States, in the end, had its way. In the early years of conditionality the EB called the shots. By the 1950s, Martin finds that the staff had gained a degree of autonomy from the EB. As new conditionality guidelines were introduced in 1969, after developing countries complained of unfair treatment compared to industrial countries,[7] power shifted back to the EB. Conditions were streamlined in 1979 with a further shift in power in favour of the EB. In sum, much of the evidence is consistent with the implications of the critical shareholders' hypothesis.[8] When shareholders feel that the staff shares their preferences, delegation is deeper without raising agency costs. But other evidence is not. For example, when shareholders are polarised, as happened in the 1960s, the evidence favours the alternative hypothesis of the staff gaining more autonomy from shareholders.

Do countries benefit from IMF loans? One of the sharpest criticisms levelled against the IMF is the high failure rate of conditional lending programmes. For Boughton (2001, p. 617), some borrowing countries do not benefit from the loans because of their unwillingness or inability to make adjustments and because the IMF staff misforecast

7 The case in point was the 1967 loan to the United Kingdom.
8 Martin does not actually distinguish critical shareholders from the EB.

the extent of the needed adjustments. Furthermore, these patterns repeat over time. For example, in 1990, the number of countries that had borrowed five or more times in the preceding 10 years and with outstanding credit of at least 100 per cent of their quota had quadrupled compared to 1980 (Boughton 2001, Figure 13.6, p. 619). The International Financial Institution Advisory Commission (2000, p. 28) reports that four countries were in debt to the IMF for 40 to 49 years, 20 countries for 30 to 39 years, 46 for 20 to 29 years , 25 for 10 to 19 years and 29 for less than ten years. Bird (2003, Table 4.2) provides further evidence of recidivism: over the 1980-96 period Argentina, Central African Republic, Democratic Republic of Congo, Costa Rica, Ivory Coast, Ecuador, El Salvador, Hungary, Jamaica, Kenya, Madagascar, Malawi, Mali, Mauritania, Morocco, Niger, Philippines, Senegal, Togo, Uganda, and Uruguay had tapped IMF resources at least seven times, an average of almost a programme every two years. The consensus is that for the bulk of the above-mentioned countries IMF programmes serve the undeclared purpose of economic aid. Clearly, shareholders are responsible for this state of affairs. Without their explicit or tacit consent, recidivism would peter out. But not all countries fall under the economic assistance category; for example, Argentina and Uruguay. What is the failure there?

Mussa (2002), an insider, gives a straightforward assessment of the IMF failure with regard to Argentina, a country that '...throughout the 1990s...operated under the auspices of a Fund-supported programme' (p. 3). The IMF made two egregious mistakes: the first was to overlook Argentina's profligate fiscal policy in the first half of the 1990s and the second was to provide the country with a huge financial package of $40 billion in 2001, despite the evidence that the crisis could not be averted (p. 4). Mussa blames both the critical shareholders and IMF staff for this state of affairs. In the eyes of the critical shareholders,

> '...Argentina was generally seen as a country deserving sympathy and support; and the Argentine authorities were certainly willing to draw on this sympathy and support' (p. 47).

This support has continued to these days. In January, 2003 the IMF approved an eight-month standby credit to Argentina for $ 2.98 billion, a decision pushed by the G-7 against strong opposition on the part of IMF's management (Financial Times, January 20, 2003). But Mussa also blames IMF management for acting 'too much as a sympathetic social worker' (p. 69) and the staff for indulging in advocacy instead of hard-nose analysis (pp. 80-81).

V. CONCLUSIONS

We have analysed the IMF from the viewpoint of the principal-agent relationship. Our point of departure is that residual control rights in this institution are vested with a small group of shareholders, the G-7 governments. This group controls vast financial resources and enjoys the highest regulatory and governance standards among IMF members. The critical shareholders face an agency cost at the IMF, stemming from costly monitoring and complex issues that give staff and management a degree of autonomy. The cost tends to be smaller at the IMF than at the World Bank because of the nature of the production function. The World Bank deals with micro issues where interest groups are homogeneous and well-organised. The IMF, in contrast, deals with macro issues where interest groups are heterogeneous and poorly organised.

We relied on two sharp alternative hypotheses to understand IMF governance. The first implies that critical shareholders are in charge and generally face small agency costs. The second is that management and staff are in charge. The two hypotheses can co-exist for different states of the world. In fact, the IMF discriminates between rich and poor, large and small, geopolitically important and irrelevant members. This discrimination is to a large extent driven by the preferences of the critical shareholders who use the IMF also as a multilateral agency of foreign policy and foreign aid. Critical shareholders bear heavily on IMF management when their interests are at stake; otherwise, for small and unimportant countries, their monitoring activity is low and opinions of Fund staff have a much larger influence on outcomes.

The evidence marshalled in the paper suggests that a core of shareholders at the IMF is in full control of the institution's mission on the big issues and that staff autonomy is restricted to areas of marginal interest to the critical shareholders. This evidence, on the whole, is qualitative and obtained from a broad cross section of the literature. There was no effort to quantify and estimate econometrically the implications of the hypotheses. It is a drawback of the study that one hopes can be remedied in future work.

REFERENCES

Barnett, Michael N. & Finnermore, Martha (1999). The Politics, Power, and Pathologies of International Organizations, *International Organizations 53, 4*, 699-732.

Barro, Robert J. & Lee, Jong-Wha (2002). IMF Programs: Who Is Chosen and What Are the Effects?, *Working Paper 8951* (May), NBER.

Bird, Graham (2003). *The IMF and the Future: Issues and Options Facing the Fund.* London: Routledge.

Bordo, Michael D. & James, Harold (2000). The International Monetary Fund: It's Present Role in Historical Perspective. In International Financial Institutions Advisory Commission, *Expert Papers*. Washington: Treasury Department.

Boughton, James M. (2001). *Silent Revolution The International Monetary Fund 1979-1989*. Washington: International Monetary Fund.

Blustein, Paul (2001). *The Chastening: Inside the Crisis that Rocked the Global Financial System and Humbled the IMF*. New York: Public Affairs.

Breton, Albert & Wintrobe, Ronald (1982). *The Logic of Bureaucratic Conduct*. Cambridge: Cambridge University Press.

De Gregorio, Jose, Eichengreen, Barry, Ito, Takatoshi & Wyplosz, Charles (1999). *An Independent and Accountable IMF*. Geneva: International Center for Monetary and Banking Studies.

Eichengreen, Barry (1999). *Towards a New International Financial Architecture: A Practical Post-Asia Agenda*. Washington, D.C.: Institute for International Economics.

Financial Times (2003). The G7 Blinks over Argentina, *Financial Times*, North American Edition, January 20, 10.

Fratianni, Michele (2003). The Fund and Its Critics. In Michele Fratianni, Paolo Savona & John Kirton (Eds.), *Sustaining Global Growth: Prosperity, Security and Development Challenges for the Kananaskis G8*. Aldershot, Hampshire: Ashgate.

Frey, Bruno S. (1997). The Public Choice of International Organizations. In Dennis C. Mueller (Ed.), *Perspectives on Public Choice: A Handbook*. Cambridge: Cambridge University Press.

Funabashi, Yoichi (1988). *Managing the Dollar: From the Plaza to the Louvre*. Washington, D.C.: Institute for International Economics.

Hart, Oliver (1995). Corporate Governance: Some Theory and Implications, *The Economic Journal 105*, 678-689.

International Monetary Fund (1999). *External Evaluation of IMF Surveillance*. Report by a Group of Independent Experts. Washington, D.C.: International Monetary Fund.

International Financial Institution Advisory Commission (2000). *Report of Commission Chaired by Allan H. Meltzer*, Washington, D.C.: U.S. Treasury Department.

Jeanne, Olivier & Zettelmeyer, Jeromin (2000). International Bailouts, Domestic Supervision and Moral Hazard, mimeo.

Laffont, J.J. & Tirole, Jean (1993). *A Theory of Incentives in Regulation and Procurement*. Cambridge: MIT Press.

Majone, Giandomenico (2001). Two Logics of Delegation, *European Union Politics, volume 2(1)*, 103-122.

Martin, Lisa (2003). *Distribution, Information, and Delegation to International Organizations: The Case of IMF Conditionality*. Department of Government, Harvard University.

Meltzer, Allan H. (1999). What's Wrong With the IMF? What Would Be Better? In William C. Hunter, George G. Kaufman, & Thomas H. Krueger (Eds.), *The Asian Financial Crisis: Origins, Implications, and Solutions*. Norwell: Kluwer Academic Publishers.

Mikesell, Raymond F. (1994). *The Bretton Woods Debates: A Memoir*, Essays in International Finance, 192, Princeton: International Finance Section.

Momani, Bessma (2002). The Role of the International Monetary Fund in American Foreign Economic Policy Towards Egypt, 1985-1998. *Ph D dissertation*. University of Western Ontario.

Mussa, Michael (2002). *Argentina and the Fund: From Triumph to Tragedy*. Washington, D.C.: Institute for International Economics.

Nielsen, Daniel L. & Tierney, Michael J. (2003). Delegation to International Organizations: Agency Theory and World Bank Environmental Reform, *International Organization 57, Spring*, 241-276.

Plumptre, A. F. W. (1977). *Three Decades of Decision*, Toronto: McClelland and Stewart.

Rieffel, Lex (2003). *Restructuring Sovereign Debt: The Case for ad-hoc Machinery*, Washington, D.C.: Brookings Institution Press.

Solomon, Robert (1977). *The International Monetary System 1945-1976*, New York: Harper and Row.

Tarullo, Daniel K. (2001). Rules, Discretion, and Authority in International Financial Reform, *Journal of International Economic Law*, 613-682.

Tirole, Jean (1994). The Internal Organization of Government, *Oxford Economic Papers 46*, 1-29.

Vaubel, Roland (1986). A Public Choice View of International Organizations, *Public Choice*, 39-57.

Vaubel, Roland (1991). The Political Economy of the IMF: A Public Choice Analysis. In Roland Vaubel & Thomas D. Willett (Eds.), *The Political Economy of International Organizations: A Public Choice Approach*, Westview Press, 1991.

Vaubel, Roland, Drexel, Axel, Müller, Stephan, & Soylu, Ugurlu (2003). *Staff Growth in International Organizations: A Principal-Agent Problem? An Empirical Analysis*, unpublished paper.

Willett, Thomas D. (2001). Upping the Ante for Political Economy Analysis of the International Financial Institutions, *The World Economy 24,3*, 317-332.

Williamson, John (1977). *The Failure of World Monetary Reform 1971-1974*, New York: New York University Press.

Woods, Ngaire (2001). Making the IMF and the World Bank More Accountable, *International Affairs 77, 1*, 83-100.

N. V. HOVANOV, J.W. KOLARI, M.V. SOKOLOV[1]

SYNTHETIC MONEY[2]

1. INTRODUCTION

The main purpose of this paper is to provide a methodology for constructing synthetic money. We define synthetic money as a currency basket whose composite value closely mimics the value of a single currency but does not contain this currency. We begin by reviewing two currency indexes proposed by Hovanov, Kolari, and Sokolov (HKS) (2004): (1) a currency invariant index (denoted *NVal*), and (2) an optimal currency basket (or stable aggregate currency denoted *SAC*) that has minimum variance for a fixed set of currencies and for a fixed period of time. These currency index concepts are used to solve the problem of finding a currency basket with maximum correlation with the U.S. dollar. We also report empirical results for a synthetic dollar composed of six currencies. Other types of synthetic money could be readily constructed using these methods. Finally, we discuss the practical significance of synthetic money in terms of a number of potential real world applications, including currency pegging, global bonds, and currency analysis.

2. CURRENCY INVARIANCE

Consider a simple exchange model wherein for any pair (g_i, g_j) of currencies g_i, g_j, taken from a fixed set $G = \{g_1, ..., g_n\}$, currency g_i may be exchanged for currency g_j *directly* (i.e. without the necessity of any medium of exchange in the form of another currency or commodity). This direct exchange of currencies g_i, g_j, is quantitatively defined by a positive *exchange coefficient* $c(i, j)$ (see Kolari *et al.* (2001)). This coef-

1 This paper was under review at the International Review of Economics and Finance at the time of going to press.

2 Acknowledgements
The authors gratefully acknowledge financial support from the Eurasia Foundation, U.S. Information Agency, Russian Foundation of Fundamental Researches, the Center for International Business Studies in the Mays Business School at Texas A&M University, and Utrecht School of Economics at Utrecht University. Helpful comments were received from Julian Gaspar, Jaap Bos, Clemens Kool, Michele Fratianni, Peter Schotman, Michael Koetter, Allard Bruinshoofd, Robert Israel and other participants at the Inaugural Conference (Nul-Lustrum), Utrecht School of Economics, Utrecht University, Netherlands (October 2003).

P. de Gijsel and H. Schenk (eds.), Multidisciplinary Economics, 293–303.

ficient gives the amount of the jth currency that can be exchanged for one unit of ith currency. In other words, a coefficient $c(i, j)$ is a *rate of exchange* of ith currency in relation to the jth currency. Thus, matrix $C = (c(i, j))$ forms a cross-currency table of exchange rates. Assuming that matrix C is transitive (i.e. the equality $c(i, j) \cdot c(j, k) = c(i, k)$ holds among every three currencies $g_i, g_j, g_k \in G$), an exchange coefficient $c(i, j)$ can be represented by the form

$$c(i, j) = \frac{Val(i)}{Val(j)}, \tag{1}$$

where magnitude $Val(i)$ is interpreted as the *value in exchange* of the ith currency, $i = 1, ..., n$ (HKS (2004)). Eq. (1) determines $Val(i)$, $i = 1, ..., n$ up to a multiplicative constant, so, without loss of generality, we can assign $Val(i) = c(i, j)$, where the jth currency becomes a *numeraire* (unit of account, standard of value, base currency, etc.). To emphasise the role of a base currency g_j, we use the notation $Val(i) = c(i, j) = Val(i / j)$.

The value in exchange dependence on the choice of a base currency introduces difficulties in examining the dynamics of values $Val(i / j)$, $i = 1, ..., n$, taken at different moments of time. Suppose that we consider three currencies: U.S. dollar (USD), European euro (EUR), and Japanese yen (YEN). The series USD over time is different using EUR versus YEN as the base currency. Thus, the value of USD is dependent on base currency choice.

To overcome this base currency problem of the function $Val(i / j)$, HKS (2004) proposed a *normalised value in exchange*:

$$NVal(i / j) = \frac{Val(i / j)}{\sqrt[n]{\prod_{r=1}^{n} Val(r / j)}} = \frac{c(i, j)}{\sqrt[n]{\prod_{r=1}^{n} c(r, j)}} = \sqrt[n]{\prod_{r=1}^{n} c(i, r)}. \tag{2}$$

The most important property of $NVal(i / j)$ is its independence from the choice of a standard currency g_j: $NVal(i / j) = NVal(i / k)$ for any $j, k \in \{1, ..., n\}$. Since the normalised value in exchange $NVal(i / j)$ is independent of a standard currency g_j, HKS use the notation $NVal(i) = NVal(i / j)$. The normalised value in exchange $NVal(i)$ can be rewritten as a *reduced* (to the moment t_0) *normalised value in exchange*:

$$RNVal(i; t / t_0) = \frac{NVal(i; t)}{NVal(i; t_0)}. \tag{3}$$

The time t_0 is the starting point chosen by the investigator (e.g., $t_0 = 1$). An important implication of currency invariance is that the same value of any particular currency is obtained no matter which base currency is chosen. This property is advantageous whenever base currency choice leads to ambiguity.

3. MINIMUM VARIANCE CURRENCY BASKETS

The derivation of an optimal (minimum variance) currency basket is problematic because different base currencies would yield different optimums. Applying HKS's currency invariance to solve the problem of constructing an optimal currency basket, a composite currency index can be defined as a weighted arithmetical mean:

$$Ind(w;t) = \sum_{i=1}^{n} w_i \; RNVal(i;t/t_0), \tag{4}$$

with reduced normalised values in exchange $RNVal(i;t/t_0)$, $i = 1,..., n$, $t = 1,..., T$, of the currencies $g_1,..., g_n$, and *weight-vector* $w = (w_1,..., w_n)$ (i.e. non-negative weight-coefficients $w_1,..., w_n$, $w_1 + ... + w_n = 1$) associated with the reduced currency invariant valuations of the n currencies.

The currency index $Ind(w;t)$ can be viewed as a measure of exchange value of a complex (composite, aggregate) currency $ACU(q) = ACU(q_1,..., q_n)$ defined by a set (basket) of simple currencies, which are taken from a fixed set $G = \{g_1,..., g_n\}$ in suitable fixed amounts $q_i > 0$, $i = 1,..., n$. There have been a number of well-known aggregate currencies in practical use in the second part of the 20th century: *EUA* (European Unit of Account), *ECU* (European Currency Unit), *Euro*, *SDR* (Special Drawing Rights), *XAM* (Asian Monetary Unit), *TR* (Transferable Ruble of Comecon), etc.

Let's suppose that a value in exchange *Val* (*ACU*(*q*)) of a bundle *ACU*(*q*) of simple currencies is determined by the weighted sum

$$Val(ACU(q)) = \sum_{i=1}^{n} q_i \, Val(i) \tag{5}$$

of values in exchange $Val(i)$, $i = 1,..., n$, of the simple currencies. For a fixed moment t and base currency j we can rewrite Eq. (5) as:

$$Val(ACU(q);t) = \sum_{i=1}^{n} q_i \; c(i,j;t). \tag{6}$$

As such, we can rewrite Eq. (4) as (see Hovanov (2000)):

$$Ind(w;t) = \frac{Val(ACU(q);t)}{Val(ACU(q);t_0)} \sqrt[n]{\prod_{r=1}^{n} \frac{c(r,j;t_0)}{c(r,j;t)}}, \tag{7}$$

where currency weights w are defined by the equalities

$$w_i = \frac{q_i \cdot c(i,j;t_0)}{\sum_{k=1}^{n} q_k \cdot c(k,j;t_0)}, \quad i = 1,\dots,n.$$

The index *Ind* (w; t) is a *reduced* (to the moment t_0) *normalised* (being divided by corresponding geometric mean) *value in exchange of the aggregated currency ACU (q) for the moment t* , or

$$Ind(w;t) = RNVal(ACU(q);t/t_0), \tag{8}$$

where currency weights w and corresponding amounts q are related by equalities

$$q_i = \mu\, w_i / c(i,j;t_0), \ i = 1,\dots,n, \tag{9}$$

for some positive factor μ (hereafter, for specificity, we will use $\mu = 1$, which provides equality $Ind(w;t_0/t_0) = RNVal(j;t_0/t_0) = 1$).

HKS proceeded to construct an aggregated currency $ACU(q^*)$ with minimal volatility of the corresponding time series $Ind(w;t) = RNVal(ACU(q);t)$ (for a fixed set of goods $G = \{g_1,\dots,g_n\}$, for given exchange rates $c(i, j; t)$, $i, j = 1,\dots, n$, $t = 1,\dots, T$ and for a fixed period of time $[1,T]$). Volatility of the time series is measured by the sample variance

$$S^2(w) = \mathrm{var}(w) = \frac{1}{T}\sum_{t=1}^{T}[Ind(w;t) - MInd(w)]^2, \tag{10}$$

where

$$MInd(w) = \frac{1}{T}\sum_{t=1}^{T} Ind(w;t) \tag{11}$$

is the sample mean.[3] The optimal weight-vector $w^* = (w_1^*,\dots, w_n^*)$ is determined by the requirement of variance $S^2(w) = \mathrm{var}(w)$ (or standard deviation $S(w)$) minimisation, $\min_w \mathrm{var}(w) = \mathrm{var}(w^*) = \mathrm{var}(w_1^*,\dots,w_n^*)$, with constraints $w_i \geq 0,\ i = 1,\dots,n,\ w_1 + \dots + w_n = 1$.

Hence, the optimisation problem is reduced to the quadratic form $S^2(w)$ minimisation under linear constraints (which is the standard task of quadratic programming). There exist many numerical methods to solve this problem. Here we use the modified Newton's method embodied in Solver.xla by MS Excel 2000.

The optimal amounts $q_1^*,\dots, q_n^*$ of the currencies, which are contained in the *optimal aggregated currency* $ACU^* = ACU(q^*)$, $q^* = (q_1^*,\dots, q_n^*)$, can be found from

3 To make our calculations statistically correct we should assume weak stationarity of multivariate time series $c(i,j;t)$, $i, j = 1,\dots,n$.

Eq. (9). So, any vector of the currencies' amounts $q = (q_1,..., q_n)$ with components proportional to the numbers $w_i */c(i, j;t_0)$, $i = 1,...,n$, determines a required optimal aggregated currency $ACU^* = ACU\ (q^*)$ that is associated to *time series* $Ind^*(t) = Ind(w^*;t) = RNVal(ACU^*;t)$, $t = 1,...,T$, *with minimal variance*. HKS dubbed this optimal basket currency *SAC* (*Stable Aggregate Currency*).

To illustrate the stability of *SAC* over time, we collected daily exchange rate data from January 1, 1999 to May 30, 2001 (after the euro's introduction) for the European euro (EURO), British pound sterling (GBP), Japanese yen (JPY), and U.S. dollar (USD) (source: Pacific Exchange Rate Service http://fx.sauder.ubc.ca/data.html). These exchange rates are normalised using Eq. (2) and reduced to begin at the value of 1.0 on January 1, 1999 using Eq. (3). Eqs. (10) and (11) are then utilised to solve minimum variance weights w^* (for the reduced normalised currency values) and q^* (for the amount of each currency in its own denomination), which are shown in Table 1.

Table 1. SAC results for four hard currencies: January 1, 1999 to May 30, 2001

Optimal weights	EURO	GBP	JPY	USD	SAC
w*(i)	26.94%	26.70%	23.23%	23.13%	
$c(i,j;t_0)$	1.1668	1.6428	0.0088	1.0000	
q*(i)	0.2694	0.2670	26.3174	0.2314	
Standard deviation (i)	0.0510	0.01980	0.0583	0.0315	0.000689

Note: European euro (EURO), British pound sterling (GBP), Japanese yen (JPY), and U.S. dollar (USD).

Table 1 also shows that, within the in-sample period, *SAC* has a standard deviation that is 28 times smaller than the pound and 73 times smaller than the Euro. Hence, *SAC* is very stable relative to individual major currencies. To further demonstrate the stability of *SAC* over time, Figure 1 plots *SAC* and the International Monetary Fund's *SDR* (i.e. the Special Drawing Right contains the same four major currencies with trade-based weights adjusted every five years) for both the in-sample period January 1, 1999 to May 30, 2001 and the out-of-sample period June 1, 2001 to October 31, 2003.

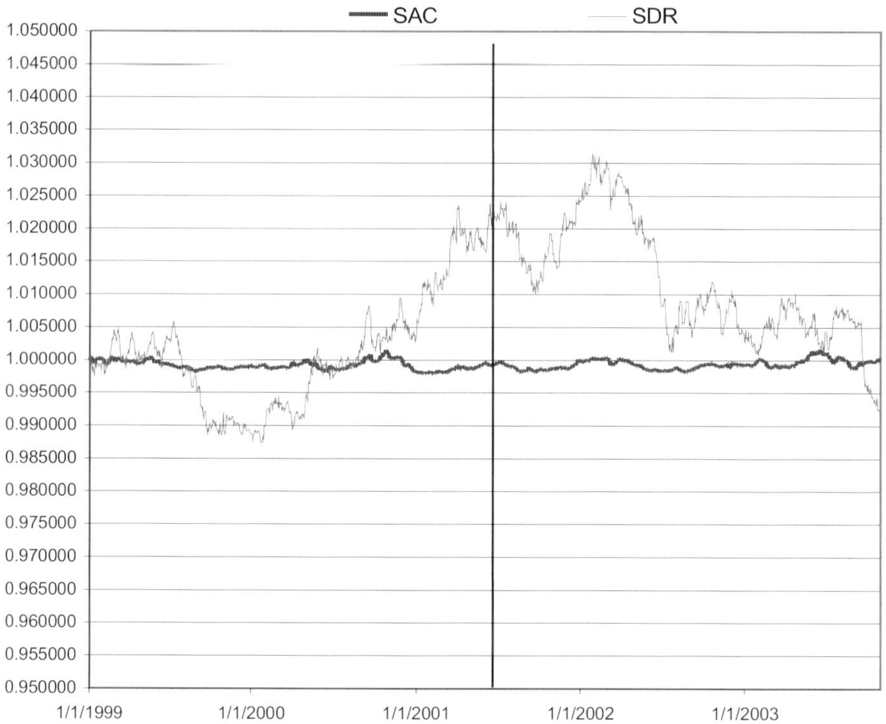

Figure 1. SAC and SDR based on four major currencies over time: In-sample period January 1, 1999 to May 30, 2001 and out-of-sample period June 1, 2001 to October 31, 2003.

The results indicate that *SAC* is more stable than the *SDR* over time (i.e. comparing the in-sample and out-of-sample periods, the standard deviation of *SDR* (SAC) is 0.0092 (0.0007) and 0.0090 (0.0007) respectively). We infer that *SAC* maintains its stability in the out-of-sample period in which the optimal weights from the in-sample period are used for its computation.

4. CONSTRUCTION OF SYNTHETIC MONEY

We next apply HKS' currency indexes *NVal* and *Ind* to the problem of constructing a *synthetic* currency, which has maximum correlation coefficient with given simple currency (e.g. the U.S. dollar). Consider the problem:

$$corr(Ind(w),USD)=\frac{\text{cov}(Ind,USD)}{S(USD)\,S(Ind)}\propto\frac{\sum_{i=1}^{n}w_i\,\text{cov}(i,USD)}{\sqrt{\sum_{i,j=1}^{n}w_iw_j\,\text{cov}(i,j)}}=\frac{a^{\text{T}}w}{\sqrt{w^{\text{T}}\Sigma w}}\xrightarrow[w]{}\max,\quad(12)$$

$$\sum_{i=1}^{n}w_i=\mathbf{1}^{\text{T}}w=1,\;w\geq 0,$$

where $a^{\text{T}}=(\text{cov}(1,USD),...,\text{cov}(n,USD))$ – n x 1 vector of value in exchange covariations of simple currencies with USD; and $\Sigma=(\text{cov}(i,j))$ – n x n value in exchange covariation matrix of currencies contained in the basket.

In the significant case in which the requirement on non-negativity of weights w is relaxed and the covariation matrix Σ is nonsingular, the solution to the optimisation problem in Eq. (12) can be found explicitly.

Indeed, since the restriction $\mathbf{1}^{\text{T}}w=1$ is not significant (as any solution of the problem can be identified up to a positive multiplier), it can be replaced simply by the requirement $w\neq 0$.

Moreover, as the maximum and minimum in optimisation problem (12) (without restriction $\mathbf{1}^{\text{T}}w=1$) is achieved at the same absolute value of the objective function, without loss of generality, one can consider the same maximisation problem but for the objective function $corr^2(Ind(w),USD)$. If the matrix Σ is nonsingular (i.e. positive definite), then from general Cauchy-Schwarz inequality one gets:

$$(a^{\text{T}}w)^2\leq\left(a^{\text{T}}\Sigma^{-1}a\right)\left(w^{\text{T}}\Sigma w\right),\quad(13)$$

where the equality holds if and only if w is proportional to vector $\Sigma^{-1}a$.

Hence, one can conclude that the solution to Eq. (11) (which admits requirement $\mathbf{1}^{\text{T}}w=1$) is:

$$w^*-\frac{\Sigma^{-1}a}{\mathbf{1}^{\text{T}}\Sigma^{-1}a},\quad(14)$$

with optimal correlation coefficient value $corr(Ind(w),USD)=\sqrt{a^{\text{T}}\Sigma^{-1}a}\Big/S(USD)$.

5. APPLICATION TO SYNTHETIC DOLLARS

Based on the solution in the previous section, we develop a synthetic dollar currency basket comprised of six major currencies: Australian dollar (AUD), Canadian dollar (CAD), Swiss franc (CHF), European euro (EUR), British pound (GBP), and Japanese yen (JPY). Daily exchange rate data are gathered for the period January 1, 2002 to December 31, 2002 (i.e. 251 data points). The optimal w^* and q^* weights are shown in Table 2. Correlation coefficients are shown in Table 3.

Table 2. Optimal structure of the synthetic U.S. dollar currency basket

	AUD	CAD	CHF	EUR	GBP	JPY
Optimal weights w*(i)	15.19%	20.64%	13.90%	14.42%	20.40%	15.45%
Optimal values q*(i)	0.2953	0.3298	0.2282	0.1596	0.1411	20.3934

Note: Australian dollar (AUD), Canadian dollar (CAD), Swiss franc (CHF), European euro (EUR), British pound (GBP), and Japanese yen (JPY).

Table 3. Correlation coefficients between RNVal's of simple and aggregated currencies

	AUD	CAD	CHF	EUR	GBP	JPY	USD	Synthetic USD
AUD	1	0.69	-0.70	-0.69	-0.62	-0.40	0.51	0.52
CAD	0.69	1	-0.98	-0.96	-0.38	-0.12	0.93	0.94
CHF	-0.70	-0.98	1	0.97	0.37	0.05	-0.92	-0.93
EUR	-0.69	-0.96	0.97	1	0.41	-0.02	-0.90	-0.91
GBP	-0.62	-0.38	0.37	0.41	1	-0.28	-0.05	-0.06
JPY	-0.40	-0.12	0.05	-0.02	-0.28	1	-0.18	-0.18
USD	0.51	0.93	-0.92	-0.90	-0.05	-0.18	1	0.99
Synthetic USD	0.52	0.94	-0.93		-0.06	-0.18	0.99	1
Std. Deviation	0.0204	0.0312	0.0213	0.0194	0.0130	0.0148	0.0372	0.0018

Note: Australian dollar (AUD), Canadian dollar (CAD), Swiss franc (CHF), European euro (EUR), British pound (GBP), and Japanese yen (JPY).

Figure 2 rescales our synthetic USD and shows that it closely mimics the USD during the in-sample period January 1, 2002 to December 31, 2002 (i.e. their correlation is 0.99). This result implies that the six different currencies contained in the synthetic USD move up and down in systematic ways, which enables us to build a currency basket that closely tracks the USD. Well-known purchasing power parity and interest rate parity conditions in international trade and finance are likely explanations for the systematic behaviour of currency values over time. Likewise, the stability of *SAC* is likely due to currencies' systematic co-movements over time.

Based on the synthetic dollar constructed from 2002 daily data, Figure 2 also shows out-of-sample results for the period January 1, 2003 to October 16, 2003. Here we see that the synthetic dollar tracks the U.S. dollar closely in the first three months of 2003. Thereafter, the synthetic dollar diverges considerably from the dollar's value over time. We infer that the optimal weights for the synthetic dollar need to be periodically revised (e.g. every few months) in order for it to closely follow dollar movements.

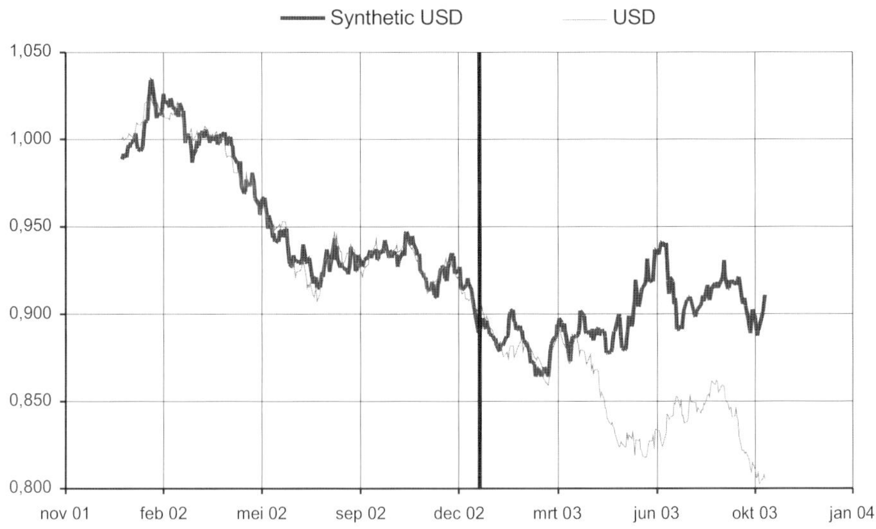

Figure 2.Dynamics of reduced normalised values for the U.S. dollar, or RNVal(USD;t), and the synthetic dollar, or linear positive transformation of RNVal(Synthetic USD;t): In-sample period January 1, 2002 to December 31, 2002 and out-of-sample period January 1, 2003 to October 16, 2003.

6. POTENTIAL USES OF SYNTHETIC MONEY

The creation of synthetic money opens up interesting possibilities for real world applications. For example, consider a country that pegs its currency to the dollar (or euro, etc.) but (for political, cultural, social, or other reasons) would prefer to peg to a basket currency that does not contain the dollar but whose value moves with the dollar over time. This synthetic dollar could be engineered to closely follow the U.S. dollar as a hard peg or some threshold correlation coefficient could be specified that is lower (e.g., 0.70) to soften the peg. The latter quasi-synthetic dollar would emulate but not mimic the dollar's movement over time.

Another potential application is the issuance of global bonds by large firms and national governments. Investors in some parts of the world may prefer to purchase bonds denominated in synthetic dollars instead of U.S. dollars. Currencies are inevitably nationalistic and investor preferences or political realities may offer the strongest case for synthetic money, albeit synthetic dollars, synthetic euros, synthetic pounds, synthetic yen, etc.

Additionally, there is also the possibility of using synthetic currencies to study currency movements. As discussed above, in the out-of-sample synthetic dollar results shown in Figure 2, we see that the dollar diverged from its synthetic currency basket after about three months in 2003. Was this divergence due to a change in foreign exchange policy by the United States at that time? The out-of-sample time series of the synthetic dollar in 2003 gives the value of the dollar assuming the relationships between the six currencies in 2002 were maintained in 2003. In this regard, notice the sharp decline in the dollar (relative to the synthetic dollar) in April 2003 and the large difference in their values over the subsequent six months. One plausible interpretation of these results is that U.S. policy shifted in spring 2003 to allow a lower value of the dollar in world currency markets. A lower dollar value would tend to reduce the large trade deficit and stimulate the slow economy. At that time the Treasury Department had been signalling that it would not be displeased if the dollar declined in value. Some experts commented on this 'benign neglect' policy as being as effective as direct intervention in foreign currency markets (e.g. currency traders sold dollars short in an attempt to profit on its expected decline in value). Thus, the synthetic dollar enables some perspective in evaluating recent dollar movements.

Our list of potential uses is not intended to be exhaustive. It is likely that there are other practical uses of synthetic money, which are left for future research.

7. CONCLUSIONS

In this paper we reviewed HKS's currency invariance and optimal currency basket concepts, illustrated their application to currency data, and extended their analyses to the construction of synthetic money. To demonstrate the notion of synthetic money, we empirically derived a synthetic dollar using six major currencies (excluding the dollar). The results showed that our synthetic dollar is highly correlated with the U.S. dollar and could be used as a substitute currency.

Synthetic money has a number of potential real world applications. For example, in currency pegging operations, a country could tie their currency to a synthetic dollar, rather than the U.S. dollar. This possibility may be relevant to China, which currently pegs the yuan to the dollar. Due to concerns among its major trading partners, the Bank of China has been considering an alternative pegging system to a basket of currencies. A synthetic dollar could be constructed with less than perfect correlation with the U.S. dollar (i.e. partially mimicking the dollar). This basket currency would be consistent with China's previous currency policy but provide some flexibility vis-à-vis the dollar/yuan exchange rate. Other implications of synthetic money to the issuance of global bonds and currency movement analyses are possible also. Future research is needed to further explore potential applications of synthetic money.

REFERENCES

Hovanov, N. (2000). Stable units of account – A base of an informational support in financial economics. *Abstracts of the 7th International Conference on Regional Informatics, St. Petersburg, Russia (December 5-8)* p. 95 (in Russian).

Hovanov, N.V., Kolari, J.W. & Sokolov, M.V. (2004). Computing currency invariant indices with an application to minimum variance currency baskets. *Journal of Economic Dynamics and Control* (forthcoming).

Kolari, J., Sokolov, M., Fedotov, Y. & Hovanov, N. (2001). A simple model of exchange: Indices of value in exchange. *Proceedings of St. Petersburg State University, No. 13,* 141-147 (in Russian).

ECONOMICS AND AGEING

R.J.M. ALESSIE

INTRODUCTION

Population ageing largely defines the economics environment in Europe in the 21st century and places a heavy financial burden on society as a result of the pay-as-you-go financed Social Security, pension, health and long-term care systems. These problems are more severe in Europe than in other developed countries because Europeans retire much earlier. In order to deal with these challenges for public policy, one should investigate how the design of pension, social insurance and health care systems affect labour market behaviour (including retirement choices), household saving and portfolio choice. Moreover, one needs to understand the complex interactions between economic, health, psychological and social factors that determine the well-being of the elderly.

This volume contains two papers, which shed some light on these research questions. The paper by Hurd and Kapteyn investigates the relationship between health and socioeconomic status (SES). This relationship has been explored earlier by, for instance, sociologists, epidemiologists and economists. The literature suggests that the positive relation between health and SES can be explained by either a causal flow from SES to health or a causal flow vice versa. Moreover, the positive correlation between health and SES can be explained by correlated unobserved heterogeneity: unmeasured factors like fitness, tastes, childhood environment etc., which might explain both good health and a high SES. In their econometric model, Hurd and Kapteyn take all three mechanisms for the positive correlation between health and SES into account. Moreover, Hurd and Kapteyn stress that the causal links between health and SES are affected by the institutional environment in which people function. Therefore they consider panel data from two countries with very different social insurance and health care systems. In the Netherlands access to health care is universal whereas in the U.S. the greater use of health care services is associated with higher income. The empirical results indeed suggest that the change in health is more strongly related to income level in the United States than in the Netherlands. On the other hand, the relationship between income change and health is stronger in the Netherlands.

The inaugural lecture by Alessie uses longitudinal survey data to address the question of how much the introduction of, and changes in, Social Security (in Dutch: AOW) have crowded out private household saving. He basically finds a limited level

P. de Gijsel and H. Schenk (eds.), Multidisciplinary Economics, 305–306.

of displacement: the estimated displacement effect (-0.10) is much smaller than the simple life cycle model predicts. Alessie provides some explanations for this phenomenon. For one of these explanations (hyperbolic discounting) he uses insights from psychology.

At USE several researchers (both macro- and microeconomists) are very interested in issues around population ageing. They are involved in several important research networks on this topic. The first one is the Network of Studies on Pensions, Aging and Retirement (Netspar). The initiative to establish Netspar was taken by Lans Bovenberg, Theo Nijman and Arie Kapteyn of Tilburg University (see the website http://www.tilburguniversity.nl/netspar/ for more information). Alessie is involved in the Survey of Health, Ageing and Retirement in Europe (SHARE) and Economics of Ageing in Europe (AGE). SHARE is an ambitious project which collects data about Europeans aged 50 and older in order to shed light on one of the most dramatic challenges in the years to come – population ageing. SHARE has assembled teams of first-rate researchers in demography, economics, epidemiology, psychology, sociology, and statistics (see website http://www.share-project.org/). The AGE network is funded by the EU (see http://www.dise.unisa.it/csef/age.htm). Finally, several USE researchers work in collaboration with the Netherlands Interdisciplinary Demographic Institute (NIDI) and the Institute for Labour Studies (OSA).

M. HURD AND A. KAPTEYN

HEALTH, WEALTH, AND THE ROLE OF INSTITUTIONS[1]

I. INTRODUCTION

A positive relationship between socioeconomic status (SES) and health has been observed over many populations and many time periods.[2] SES can be assessed in many ways including occupation, social class, education, income, and wealth. Health can be measured as a reduced level of mortality, morbidities, health-related functional limitations, mental and emotional problems as well as in other ways, and, broadly speaking, the positive relationship still obtains. The literature has identified a number of causal mechanisms, and their relative strengths vary over the life course, populations, and the level of economic development. In broad generality causality could flow from SES to health, from health to SES, or from a third latent factor to both SES and health. A major object of investigation has been to find the dominant flow of causality and to quantify the causes of the relationship between SES and health.

Until recently the main contributions to the literature have been from the disciplines of sociology, epidemiology and public health, and in this literature the dominant flow of causality has been thought to be from SES to health (Robert and House 2000). An obvious example would be access to health care services that greater economic resources would purchase, but many other mechanisms have been proposed. A prominent view in the literature is that higher SES leads to reductions in psychosocial and environmental risk factors. Examples of risk factors are unstable marriages, smoking, excessive alcohol consumption, stress, work-related pathogens, chemicals and dangers,

1 The Journal of Human Resources. Copyright 2003.38(2): 386-415. Reprinted by permission of The University of Wisconsin Press.
Support from the National Institute on Aging is gratefully acknowledged. Many thanks to Megan Beckett for helping us access the literature, and to two anonymous referees and the editor for very helpful comments.
Michael D. Hurd is Senior Economist, RAND, Santa Monica, California. His E-mail address is mhurd@rand.org.
Arie Kapteyn is Senior Economist, RAND, Santa Monica, California. His E-mail address is kapteyn@rand.org.
The data used in this article can be obtained beginning November 2003 through October 2006 from Arie Kapteyn, RAND, 1700 Main Street, PO Box 2138, Santa Monica, CA 90407-2138.

2 See Kitagawa and Hauser (1973); Berkman (1988); Marmot et al. (1991); and Feinstein (1993) and Smith (1999).

P. de Gijsel and H. Schenk (eds.), Multidisciplinary Economics, 307–332.

neighbourhood effects, and a lack of social support networks. SES acts to reduce these risks in various ways. Education could induce better health behaviours such as less smoking; better, less physically demanding occupations could lead to safer, healthier work environments; income can be used to purchase housing in clean, quiet neighbourhoods.

This theory has been used to explain the finding that the relationship between SES and health (the SES gradient) seems to reach a maximum in late middle or early old age: at least as operating through occupation the cumulative effect builds over the working life, but with retirement many SES-related psychosocial mechanisms no longer operate. Were the main causal pathway relating SES to health to operate through psychosocial and environmental risk factors, policy to increase incomes or education, or to improve the structure of occupations would also eventually lead to an improvement in health.

The sociological literature uses the terms selection, mobility selection, and reverse causality to address in a limited way the effects of health on SES (Robert and House 1994; Goldman 2001). In its simplest form it supposes that those with better underlying health will be upwardly mobile in social class. For example, someone with better health will receive better education, which will lead to a better occupation and, hence, higher income. It is unclear whether health is causal in the sense that altering health after the completion of education would change economic outcomes, or whether it is purely selection.

Selection is said to have only a minor affect on the SES gradient (Wilkinson 1999). However, it is important to distinguish the measure of SES. If it means social class as it is given at birth, health would have little effect on the gradient. If it means income, it would seem obvious that health would have an important effect particularly in economies in which most income is from earnings rather than from public transfer programs: even holding occupation and education constant more robust individuals will be able to work longer and more intensively, leading to greater incomes in the future. Furthermore, in a dynamic setting the flow of causality from health to SES is directly observed, at least in the U.S.: health events such as a heart attack lead directly to worsened health and directly to income loss because of labor market interruptions; the income loss in turn leads to reduced wealth accumulation over a lifetime (Smith 1999; McClellan 1998). In this example the health shock will increase the cross-sectional correlation between health and SES as measured by income or wealth. This mechanism can explain the increasing SES gradient with age until the age of retirement: as health shocks accumulate for some individuals, their health levels will increasingly fall below the average, and at the same time their income and wealth levels will decline relative to the average.

Despite this obvious and observable explanation for at least part of the correlation between SES and health, the sociological literature, with its focus on selection as the only way in which health can influence SES, has lacked investigation of this direct causal mechanism. A possible explanation for this focus is the poor quality of income data and the complete lack of wealth data in data sets such as the National Health Interview Survey and in the Americans' Changing Lives study, which are often used by sociologists for SES-health research. Not having good economic measures may have led to an emphasis on education where selection is a plausible and possibly important mechanism.

A third mechanism for the positive relationship between SES and health is based on a latent model of health. Individuals have unmeasured variation in fitness, tastes, attitudes, the childhood environment, and so forth. These unmeasured factors produce individuals who both have good health and the ability to succeed in life. Possibly because of the complexity of this mechanism, little attention has been paid to it in the sociological literature, even though it would seem to be a good explanation for some of the leading findings. For example, a common finding is that SES is positively related to health throughout the range of SES, not just at the lower end of the SES scale: in the Whitehall studies health increases with grade in the British civil service even at the highest grades (Marmot et al. 1991). A model based on latent fitness would explain this outcome as those with better latent fitness are more successful in their working careers and they are healthier.

A more structural model, which in principle is amenable to testing, is an economic model which emphasises the role of the subjective time rate of discount (Grossman 1972; Fuchs 1982). An individual with a low time rate of discount will invest in health and in human capital, and later in life these investments will produce better-than-average health and higher income. In addition such an individual will save more out of income leading to even higher wealth than would be produced from the income alone.

Although we may not have good measures of many of the components of latent health, an intervention could still change some components, leading to an alteration in some SES outcomes such as income and wealth and even social connections. The fact that such an intervention would lead to a change in SES, even rather late in the life cycle, distinguishes the latent health model from the model of selection.

An important complication in assessing the quantitative importance of the flow of causality is that the importance is likely to vary across populations. In less-developed populations giving people additional economic resources is likely to improve their health via improved nutrition and access to health care services, whereas such effects are likely to be much smaller in developed economies. Within a population, giving economic resources to those who are economically deprived may similarly improve their health but it would not do so for those who are better off. Yet, improvements in health could affect income over the entire range of the income distribution. Thus, there could be nonlinearities in the relationship between SES and health depending on the measures that are used and on the main direction of the causal flow. Because of the complexity of the problem it is not surprising that there are no widely agreed-upon estimates of the relative importance of the three broad explanations of the correlation between SES and health.

As for data requirements, it is not realistic to expect that these explanations can be separated in cross-sectional data. Even in panel data, it is very difficult to separate them because the data requirements are substantial. At a minimum one needs good data on a number of indicators of health status, on economic status and on other SES measures such as education, occupation, and social network.

At a conceptual level, it seems reasonable to say that SES causes health if individuals with higher SES have improvements (or slower deterioration) in health compared with individuals who have lower SES, and to say that health causes SES if individuals in better health have greater increases (or slower declines) in SES than individuals in worse health. Of course the empirical implementation of these concepts is complex, but if we have data on transitions in health status and economic status that are functions of health and economic status, it may be possible to attribute causality. An example is the work of Adams et al. (forthcoming) who test for Granger causality based on data from three waves of the AHEAD. They use 19 health conditions such as cancer, heart attack, and self-rated health to explain wealth change; and wealth, income and education to explain mortality and incidence of the 19 health conditions. They cannot reject the null hypothesis of no causal link from SES to mortality and to the onset of most acute conditions; but there is some evidence of a possible link from SES to the gradual onset of chronic conditions. They find some evidence for a causal link from health to changes in SES as measured by wealth change.

As far as we know, the work of Adams et al. is the most extensive and systematic study of causality based on a large nationally representative panel data set. Yet, the study has the limitations of any study based on nonexperimental data. In our view a natural extension is an international comparison where social programs may alter the relationship between SES and health that we observe in U.S. data. Our goal in this paper is to find whether variation in institutional structure as measured at the national level could help us understand more about the flow of causality. The Netherlands has an institutional structure that aims to shield, at least in the short run, individuals from the economic consequences of a decline in health. In the U.S., while there are programmes to reduce the severity of the consequences of a decline in heath, the consequences are certainly not eliminated. In the Netherlands access to health care is universal whereas in the U.S. the greater use of health care services is associated with higher income.

We will use data from the American Health and Retirement Study (HRS), from the Dutch Socio-Economic Panel (SEP), and from the Dutch CentER Savings Survey (CSS) to find qualitatively whether the institutional structures have the expected effect on the relationships between SES and health; and quantitatively whether the effects are important.

We will use the panel nature of these data sets in conjunction with the differences in institutional environment to shed light on the positive relationship between health and wealth that exists in both countries. The panel nature of the data sets allows us to address causality issues, whereas the differences in institutional settings make it possible to assess some common explanations for the observed relationship.

In 1992 the HRS surveyed about 12,600 persons approximately aged 51-61 and their spouses with subsequent waves in 1994, 1996, 1998, and 2000. We use data from the five waves of HRS. The SEP is a longitudinal household survey representative of the Dutch population, excluding those living in special institutions like nursing homes. We will use the years 1994-1997 of the SEP. The CSS is an annual panel of about 4000 persons. We use waves 1993 through 1998.

Our measures of SES will be both income and wealth because of the possible differing relationships between them and health as a function of age.

Institutional differences should affect some of the following explanations for the observed positive relationship between wealth and health:

- *Out-of-pocket health expenses:* In the Netherlands such expenses are on the order of 1 or 2 per cent of total expenditures, with no discernible relation with age (Alessie et al.1999b). In the age range of HRS out-of-pocket expenses are rather skewed: for example, between waves one and two about 33 per cent had no out-of-pocket expenses whereas 7 per cent had from $1,000 to $5,000 in out-of-pockets expenses and 2 per cent had more than $5,000 (Hill and Mathiowetz, 1998).
- *The role of earnings interruptions*: The U.S. and the Netherlands differ in their income maintenance provisions, and hence earnings interruptions may be expected to have different effects on wealth accumulation in the two countries. In the Netherlands generous income maintenance provisions aim to mitigate any adverse effect of health related earnings interruptions.
- *Differential access to health care*: The Netherlands has essentially a universal health care system. Thus in the Netherlands, such an explanation would be of limited importance. We investigate this issue by estimating equations that explain subsequent health on the basis of past wealth. The extent to which we find differences in this relationship between the U.S. and the Netherlands can be seen as an indication of the importance of differential access to health care. Our results indicate that conditional on baseline wealth and health, there is a significant effect of wealth and income on subsequent health status both in the U.S. and the Netherlands, but in the Netherlands the relation is weaker than in the U.S. This lends some credence to this explanation.
- *Mortality risk:* Individuals (or couples) with a higher life expectancy have more reason to save (see for example, Hurd 1987, 1989, 1998). Hence, we expect healthier individuals to save more, other things being equal. In the Netherlands, however, annuity income is the dominant source of income among the elderly, more so than in the U.S. This should lead to a weaker relationship between health and saving (and hence wealth) in the Netherlands than in the US.

The remainder of the paper is organised as follows. In Section II we present a small conceptual model that will help to organise the empirical analysis and which facilitates interpretation of empirical results. The model consists of three differential equations: one equation relating income changes to health levels, one equation relating health changes to spending on health, and one equation relating spending on health care to income. The solution of the differential equations allows us to characterise in broad terms the relation between dynamic and cross-sectional correlations between health and income and wealth. In Section III we describe the data, present several descriptive statistics, and document the strong cross-sectional relationship between health and income and wealth. Sections IV and V present the empirical counterparts of the differential equations presented in Section II. In Section IV we consider income and wealth changes as a function of health, whereas in Section V we consider health transitions as a function of income and wealth. In the concluding Section VI, we provide an interpretation of the empirical results in the light of the theoretical model and draw some general conclusions.

II. AN ILLUSTRATIVE MODEL

To motivate the empirical analysis, we analyze a three-equation model of earnings, spending on health, and health status. The model is at the individual level, which will allow us to make comparisons within a population. The model specifies that health spending depends on income but the dependence can vary across institutional settings. The dependence on income should be thought of more broadly than out-of-pocket spending, at least also incorporating work-related health care insurance and perhaps other spending with a health effect (for example buying a house in an area with good air quality). The evolution of health is assumed to depend on the amount of spending for health care. Again, spending should be thought of broadly as spending on nutrition, housing and other attributes that are thought to influence health. The model specifies that income growth depend on health status, which incorporates the idea that the healthier will be able to work harder and so have greater income growth.

Let y_t be earnings, h_t health status, and s_t spending on health, all at age t. Then consider the following simple system of differential equations:

$$\frac{dy_t}{dt} = y'_t = b + \alpha h_t \tag{1}$$

$$\frac{dh_t}{dt} = h'_t = a + \delta s_t \tag{2}$$

$$s_t = c + \tau y_t \tag{3}$$

By substituting (3) into (2) we can write the system in terms of y and h only:

$$\frac{dy_t}{dt} = y'_t = b + \alpha h_t \tag{1}$$

$$\frac{dh_t}{dt} = h'_t = d + \gamma y_t \tag{4}$$

with $d=a+\delta c$ and $\gamma=\delta\tau$.

The generic solutions to the differential equations are

$$h_t = k_h e^{\theta t} + l_h \tag{5}$$

$$y_t = k_y e^{\theta t} + l_y \tag{6}$$

By differentiating the generic solutions with respect to t and comparing parameters we obtain that the solution can be written in terms of the original parameters as follows:

$$h_t = \sqrt{\gamma}k\, e^{\theta t} - b/\alpha \tag{7}$$

$$y_t = \sqrt{\alpha}\, ke^{\theta t} - d/\gamma \tag{8}$$

with $\theta = \sqrt{(\alpha\gamma)}$ and k a scale parameter, essentially fixing the origin of the t-axis. To fully determine the solution, we have to specify initial conditions for h_t and y_t. Let the initial values for h_t and y_t at time zero be equal to h_0 and y_0. We then have five parameters in (7) and (8), α, γ, b, d, k. If we choose one initial condition, this fixes k and thereby removes any indeterminacy. The value of the other initial condition is then determined as well. Somewhat arbitrarily, we fix the initial condition for y_t at y_0. This implies:

$$k = \frac{y_0 + d/\gamma}{\sqrt{\alpha}} \tag{9}$$

(7) and (8) can then be written as:

$$y_t = (y_0 + d/\gamma)e^{\theta t} - d \tag{10}$$

$$h_t = \sqrt{\frac{\gamma}{\alpha}}(y_0 + d/\gamma)e^{\theta t} - b/\alpha \tag{11}$$

Let us now use this framework to investigate the nature of the relation between income and health in the population. To do so, we introduce individual heterogeneity. Assume that y_0 varies randomly across individuals with mean zero and variance σ^2. Furthermore, let b and d be random variables with mean zero and covariance matrix Σ, both un correlated with y_0. The parameters α and γ are assumed to be fixed, i.e. the same for all individuals. Consider the regressions of h_t on y_t, y'_t on h_t and h'_t on y_t. Write:

$$h_t = \sqrt{\frac{\gamma}{\alpha}}\, y_t + u_t,\; u_t \equiv \sqrt{\frac{\gamma}{\alpha}}d/\gamma - b/\alpha \tag{12}$$

Let observations on y_t, u_t, and h_t be stacked in n-vectors y, u, and h. Then the least squares coefficient in the regression of h_t on y_t is

$$\frac{h'y}{y'y} = \sqrt{\frac{\gamma}{\alpha}} + \frac{u'y}{y'y} \tag{13}$$

We have

$$plim\frac{1}{n}y'u = (e^{\theta t} - 1)\left[\sqrt{\frac{\gamma}{\alpha}}\frac{V(d)}{\gamma^2} - Cov(b,d)\right] \tag{14}$$

where $V(.)$ denotes variance and $Cov(.)$ denotes covariance.

$$plim\frac{1}{n}y'y = V(y_0)e^{2\theta t} + \frac{V(d)}{\gamma^2}(e^{\theta t} - 1)^2 \tag{15}$$

For positive θ and t sufficiently large, this implies that

$$\frac{h'y}{y'y} \approx \sqrt{\frac{\gamma}{\alpha}} \tag{16}$$

Similarly, for large enough t the regression of y on h will give

$$\frac{h'y}{h'h} \approx \sqrt{\frac{\alpha}{\gamma}} \tag{17}$$

A similar analysis shows that a regression of h'_t on y_t will approximately estimate γ, whereas a regression of y'_t on h_t will approximately estimate α.

We can make a number of observations on the system of differential equations and their solutions. First of all, we note that the scales of the variables 'earnings' and 'health' have not yet been defined. So for instance health can be defined in deviation of some 'average' age trajectory in a population. The exponential form of the solutions (10) and (11) therefore does not imply that health will get exponentially better or worse over the life cycle, but rather that health paths diverge with increasing age. Somewhat similarly, we can define earnings in levels, logs or some other transformation that may fit the data.

Secondly, note the tight connection between income inequality and health inequality. The regression coefficient in the regression of h_t on y_t is approximately $\sqrt{(\gamma/\alpha)}$. The parameters α and γ represent the strength of the feedback between earnings and health in the dynamic equations (cf. (1) and (4)). Thus we could have either large or small regression coefficients in the cross section, when both dynamic feedbacks are small or when both dynamic feedbacks are large. Assuming, for example, that in the Netherlands both feedbacks are small, while they are larger in the U.S. we would still see similar cross section coefficients in both countries. If the cross section regression coefficients are of similar magnitude in both countries then a larger income inequality in the U.S. will translate into a larger health inequality as well. Several papers have documented a positive relation between health inequality and income inequality across countries. See for instance, Van Doorslaer et al. (1997).

Thirdly, the model assumes that health is a continuous and observable variable, yet health is actually a latent unobservable variable. What we observe are health status indicators corresponding to the interval in which latent health falls. We shall base estimation on a logistic model of the determination of health categories and transitions between health categories. To see how this will affect the interpretation of the results, suppose that latent health is given by the following equation:

$$h_t = \beta' x_t + \lambda u_t \tag{18}$$

where u_t is a logistically distributed error term, x_t is a vector of explanatory variables and λ a scaling parameter to account for the fact that the variance in health, conditional on observables, could be different in two populations. If we have an indicator variable $I_t = 0$ when $h_t < l$, then

$$Pr(I_t = 0) \quad Pr(\beta' x_t + \lambda u_t \leq 1) \quad \frac{1}{1 \quad e^{\left(\frac{1}{\lambda} + \frac{\beta' x_t}{\lambda} \right)}} \tag{19}$$

Thus the parameter on x has the interpretation β/λ. So if for instance λ is larger in the U.S. the estimate of β is attenuated relative to the Netherlands.

Fourthly, much of the literature is concerned with the relationships between health and both income and wealth, particularly at older ages. Wealth is an accumulation of savings over a lifetime, so that variation in wealth across individuals will reflect variation in income across individuals over a lifetime. We can show how health might be related to wealth by augmenting our model with a simple model of consumption behaviour.

Suppose that consumption is proportional to income: $c_t = \eta y_t$. Over the short run there will be deviations in this relationship due to unexpected events and transitory income. But over longer periods this may be a reasonable approximation to consumption behaviour. In the context of our model we then obtain

$$w_t \approx (1 - \eta) e^{rt} y_t + v_t \tag{20}$$

where w_t is wealth and r is the constant real rate of interest; v_t depends on θ and r and on d/γ, so that it will vary across individuals. This relationship shows that variation in income will induce variation in wealth, and that the variance in wealth will grow at a faster rate than the variance in income. We would expect that populations with high variance in wealth will have high variance in health.

III. DATA DESCRIPTION

We use three data sets: HRS/AHEAD for the U.S. and CSS and SEP for the Netherlands. The Health and Retirement Study is a panel survey of individuals born from 1931 through 1941 and their spouses or partners. At baseline in 1992 the HRS had 12,652 respondents. It was nationally representative of the target cohorts, except for oversamples of blacks, Hispanics and Floridians (Juster and Suzman 1995). This paper uses data from waves one through five that were fielded in 1992, 1994, 1996, 1998, and 2000. The limitation of the birth cohorts to 1931-1941 naturally limits the age range in the sample. To have a simple cutoff rule in choosing the age range for all three samples used in the analysis, we only retain individuals in the sample who are between 51 and 65 years of age.

Household income is income of an individual and spouse or partner. Its components as measured in the HRS are earnings, asset income, pensions, Social Security, SSI, worker's compensation, unemployment, other government income (veterans' benefits, welfare, food stamps). Wealth is financial wealth, business and real estate wealth, and housing wealth.

The CentER Savings Survey (CSS) derives from annual interviews with participants in the so-called CentERpanel. The CentERpanel is run by CentERdata, a subsidiary of CentER at Tilburg University. The CentERpanel comprises some 2,000 households. These households have a computer at home, either their own or one provided by CentERdata, and the respondents in the CentERpanel answer questions that are downloaded to their computer every weekend. Typically the questions for the CSS are asked in May of each year, but in some years the timing of the CSS has deviated considerably from this. In particular in the first year (1993) technical difficulties delayed the survey to the extent that some parts of the questionnaire were administered in early 1994. As a result some parts of the 1994 questionnaire were not administered at all, including the health questions used in this paper. Initially, the CSS had two parts: a representative panel of about 2,000 households and a so-called high-income panel of about 1,000 households, but in 1997 the distinction was abandoned.

The total questionnaire of the CSS is quite long. To reduce respondent burden the questionnaire is split up in five 'modules' that are administered in five separate weekends. The modules are: demographics and work; housing and mortgages; health and income; assets and liabilities; and economic psychology. We will be using the waves 1993 and 1995-1998.

Although the technology might suggest otherwise, the CSS is *not* restricted to households with (initial) access to the Internet. Respondents are recruited by telephone using random digit dialing and if they do not have Internet access (or a computer) they are provided with Internet access (and if necessary a computer) by CentERdata. Panel members are selected on the basis of a number of demographics so as to match the distribution of these demographics in the population. The presence of the high-income panel in the earlier years, of course led to an overrepresentation of high income/ high wealth households in those years. Whenever presenting sample statistics, we will therefore employ household weights.

The Socio-Economic Panel (SEP) is conducted by Statistics Netherlands. The SEP is a longitudinal household survey representative of the Dutch population, excluding those living in special institutions like nursing homes. The first survey was conducted in April 1984. Information collected includes demographics, income, labor market participation, hours of work, and (since 1987) assets and liabilities. In some years (1994-1997) respondents were also asked to assess their own health status. We will use the years 1994-1997 of the SEP.

An evaluation of the quality of the SEP data and a comparison with macro statistics or other micro data sets is reported in Alessie, Lusardi and Aldershof (1997). We can briefly summarise their findings as follows: the data on some major components of wealth, such as housing, mortgage debt, and checking accounts are well reported in the SEP and compare reasonably well with aggregate statistics. However, some other components, in particular stocks, bonds, and savings accounts seem under-reported in the SEP, and the level of measurement error may also change over time. This problem is typical of wealth surveys and can be found in other similar data sets.[3]

We have deleted from the sample those cases with missing or incomplete responses in the assets and liabilities components and in the demographics.[4] We have also excluded the self-employed from the sample, since wealth data for the self-employed are not available after 1989. Due to these selections, we find that both low and high wealth households have a tendency to drop out of the sample. Also for the SEP we will use household sample weights when presenting sample statistics.

A. Descriptive Statistics

To facilitate comparability across the three data sets, we have restricted observations in the HRS, SEP, and CSS to individuals older than 50 and younger than 65 (for example the highest age is 64). Table 1 presents a number of descriptive statistics for the three data sets. We observe that the Dutch samples exhibit a somewhat lower average and median age than the HRS. One should note that given the way the original HRS cohort has been drawn, average age in the HRS should increase over time, as no new younger individuals are added to the sample we are using if time progresses. Household size is somewhat higher in the HRS.

3 See Davies (1979); Avery, Elliehausen, and Kennickell (1988); Avery and Kennickell (1991); and Hurst, Luoh, and Stafford (1998).

4 In some cases, missing data on assets and liabilities could be imputed. See Camphuis (1993) for more details on the data imputation and Alessie, Lusardi and Aldershof (1997) for a description of the criteria used to calculate total net worth.

Table 1. Descriptive statistics for three data sets

	HRS		CSS		SEP	
	Mean (sd)	Median (N)	Mean (sd)	Median (N)	Mean (sd)	Median (N)
Age	58.0	58	57.0	57	56.9	57
	(3.6)	(41998)	(4.1)	(6464)	(4.1)	(6175)
HH-size	2.7	2	2.2	2	2.0	2
	(1.6)	(29020)	(1.04)	(3659)	(.89)	(2884)
Assets	302.2	126.7	161.6	125.3	103.3	85.3
	(993.0)	(29020)	(206.6)	(3099)	(128.9)	(2884)
Liabilities	30.0	3.3	40.3	10.1	22.5	2.6
	(75.6)	(29020)	(68.1)	(3099)	(40.2)	(2884)
Net worth	272.2	99.5	121.3	81.0	80.7	49.9
	(991.1)	(29020)	(175.6)	(3099)	(108.4)	(2884)
HH income	56.7	38.6	25.8	22.2	24.2	21.5
	(94.7)	(29020)	(26.8)	(3753)	(13.6)	(2791)
Education l.t.	.22	0	.48	0	.47	0
High School		(41939)		(6444)		(5632)
High School	.55	1	.22	0	.37	0
		(41939)		(6444)		(5632)
More than	.23	0	.30	0	.16	
High School		(41939)		(6444)		(5632)
Employed	.62	1	.43	0	.40	0
		(41923)		(5454)		(6175)

Explanation: For each variable the first row shows sample mean and median; the second row shows standard deviation and number of observations in parentheses. Money amounts are in thousands of dollars for HRS and thousands of euros for SEP and CSS. Household incomes in CSS and SEP are after tax; for HRS incomes are before tax. Education definitions vary across the three samples, so that distributions of education level are only approximately comparable across samples. Money amounts are all reported at the household level. Fractions are reported at the respondent level. Numbers of observations vary as a result of this, but also as a result of varying numbers of missing observations. Entries for education and employment status are fractions. All sample statistics are weighted.

Income in the HRS is measured before tax, while in the Dutch data income is measured after tax, all in 1998 currencies. Although at first sight the different treatment of income in the Netherlands and in the U.S. may seem to cause problems, we believe that the way we use income in the quantitative analyses (by constructing quartiles of the distribution) is robust against the different treatment of taxes in both countries. For the use of quantiles it is only necessary that the ranking of incomes before and after tax is the same, which would appear a reasonable approximation in most cases.

Income in CSS is somewhat higher than in SEP. This is consistent with a suspicion of underestimation of income in SEP (comparison with external sources suggests an underestimation in SEP by about 10 per cent on average). More strikingly, net worth and assets are much higher in CSS than in SEP. To a fairly large extent this can be ascribed to underestimation in SEP as well, as noted above. The CSS questionnaire is much more detailed than the SEP questionnaire, which makes it likely that more components of wealth are picked up than in the SEP. Furthermore, self-employed are included in CSS, but not in the SEP. Alessie and Kapteyn (1999a) compare the SEP wealth data with external data published by Statistics Netherlands and find that average net worth in SEP may be underestimated by about 20 per cent. Comparing this to sample means and medians reported for CSS in Table 1 would then suggest some overestimation in the CSS (even taking into account the omission of the self-employed from the SEP). This may point to a less than perfect reweighting of the data by means of the sample weights used in the CSS, resulting in an over-representation of high wealth households. Altogether, one may surmise that CSS and SEP provide respectively an upper and a lower bound on the wealth holdings of Dutch households.

Finally, with respect to Table 1, we should note that the definitions of education used in the two Dutch data sets differ, so that the distributions across education levels are not comparable. In the empirical analyses using education, we will therefore always distinguish between the education definitions in CSS and SEP.

Table 2. Distribution of Self-Assessed Health

	HRS		CSS		SEP	
	Frequency	%	Frequency	%	Frequency	%
Excellent(hrs,css)/very good(sep)	7845	18.8	841	19.7	858	13.8
Very good(hrs)/good(css,sep)	12963	31.1	2389	56.2	3239	52.1
Good(hrs)/fair(css, sep)	11876	28.5	820	19.3	1814	29.2
Fair(hrs)/not so good(css)/bad(sep)	6029	14.5	180	4.2	268	4.3
Poor(hrs,css)/very bad(sep)	2926	7.0	23	0.5	38	0.6
Total	41640	100	4254	100	6218	100

Frequencies are weighted; the definitions of the health categories vary by sample and are indicated in the category names in the table.

Table 2 provides the distribution of self assessed health. The verbal labels associated with the categories are given in the table as well. Clearly, the definitions of the health categories vary by data set. The frequency distribution of health categories is more similar between the two Dutch data sets than between the HRS on the one hand and the Dutch data sets on the other hand. Taken at face value, the distribution of health levels is more dispersed in the American data. These differences may reflect true differences in health dispersion across the two countries or just be the effect of different wordings or different meanings attached to the verbal labels in different cultures (cf. for example Finch et al. 2002). These possibilities will have to be kept in mind when analyzing the different patterns across socioeconomic groups in the two countries.

The relation with education is qualitatively similar across the data sets (see Table 3) and shows the familiar pattern that the distribution of health shifts in the direction of better health if education goes up.

Table 3. Education and Self-Reported Health

	HRS			CSS			SEP		
	<HS	HS	>HS	<HS	HS	>HS	<HS	HS	>HS
Excellent(hrs,css)/ very good(sep)	8.7	18.7	28.9	16.6	21.8	22.6	11.4	13.3	21.1
Very good(hrs)/ good(css,sep)	18.7	33.0	38.4	53.8	58.9	57.5	49.6	55.6	53.2
Good(hrs)/ fair(css,sep)	30.2	29.7	24.1	23.4	15.4	16.3	33.3	26.6	22.7
Fair(hrs)/ not so good(css)/bad(sep)	25.7	13.4	6.4	5.3	3.7	3.1	4.9	4.1	2.3
Poor(hrs,css)/ very bad(sep)	16.6	5.2	2.3	0.8	0.1	0.5	0.7	0.4	0.6
Total	100	100	100	100	100	100	100	100	100

Frequencies are weighted; the definitions of the health categories vary by sample and are indicated in the category names in the table. HS means high school; the definitions of education are only weakly comparable across data sets.

Tables 4, 5, and 6 show the relation between self-reported health and BMI, smoking, and alcohol consumption. These health behaviours are not available in SEP, so comparisons only involve HRS and CSS. Table 4 suggests that the Dutch weigh less than the Americans and confirms that a high BMI is bad for health (with minor non-monotonicities in some places).

Table 4. BMI and Self-Reported Health

	HRS		CSS	
	Mean	Median	Mean	Median
Excellent(hrs,css)	25.6	25.1	24.9	24.7
Very good(hrs)/good(css)	26.7	26.2	25.2	25.0
Good(hrs)/fair(css)	27.9	27.3	26.0	25.5
Fair(hrs)/not so good(css)	28.7	27.9	24.8	24.2
Poor(hrs,css)	28.4	27.4	29.7	26.0

Means and medians are weighted.

Table 5. Distribution of Self-Reported Health by Smoking or Non-Smoking

	HRS		CSS	
	No	Yes	No	Yes
Excellent(hrs,css)	20.6	13.3	21.8	15.2
Very good(hrs)/good(css)	32.3	27.5	56.2	56.0
Good(hrs)/fair(css)	27.8	30.7	17.6	23.2
Fair(hrs)/not so good(css)	13.3	18.3	4.0	4.9
Poor(hrs,css)	6.0	10.3	0.4	0.8
Total	76.7	23.3	69.2	30.8

'Yes' means the respondent smokes now; 'No' means the respondent does not smoke now. The bottom row gives the percentages of smokers and nonsmokers in both samples. All percentages are based on weighted data.

Table 6. Distribution of Self-Reported Health by Alcohol Consumption

	HRS		CSS	
	No	Yes	No	Yes
Excellent(hrs,css)	16.8	11.2	19.5	21.7
Very good(hrs)/good(css)	32.1	24.8	56.1	56.5
Good(hrs)/fair(css)	28.9	36.0	19.5	17.6
Fair(hrs)/not so good(css)	15.2	20.4	4.3	4.0
Poor(hrs,css)	6.9	7.5	0.6	0.3
Total	97.8	2.2	89.6	10.4

'Yes' means the respondent drinks more than four glasses of alcohol per day; 'No' means the respondent drinks less or not at all. The bottom row gives the percentages of both groups in both samples. All percentages are based on weighted data.

The Dutch between fifty and sixty-five appear to smoke a bit more than the Americans (Table 5). Smoking is bad for health in both countries. According to Table 6, the Dutch drink more than the Americans. With some exaggeration, one could say that drinking more than four glasses of alcohol is bad for health in the U.S. and good for health in the Netherlands.

Table 7. Health and Wealth

	HRS		CSS		SEP	
	Mean	Median	Mean	Median	Mean	Median
Excellent(hrs,css)/ very good(sep)	477.2	233.5	160.1	121.0	96.7	82.0
Very good(hrs)/ good(css,sep)	408.5	192.2	131.4	93.2	93.7	70.2
Good(hrs)/fair(css, sep)	272.3	126.1	119.6	73.9	76.8	47.3
Fair(hrs)/not so good(css)/ bad(sep)	184.6	66.2	99.4	60.5	63.9	15.3
Poor(hrs,css)/very bad(sep)	98.8	30.0	62.8	.9	46.3	11.2

Money amounts are in thousands of dollars for HRS and thousands of Euros for SEP and CSS. Wealth is household net worth

Table 8. Health and Income

	HRS		CSS		SEP	
	Mean	Median	Mean	Median	Mean	Median
Excellent(hrs,css)/ very good(sep)	85.6	60.2	29.1	27.0	29.5	27.2
Very good(hrs)/good (css,sep)	70.1	52.3	26.8	23.8	28.1	26.2
Good(hrs)/fair(css, sep)	54.8	40.8	25.0	20.6	23.6	20.9
Fair(hrs)/ not so good(css)/bad(sep)	38.5	26.7	22.8	19.6	19.8	18.1
Poor(hrs,css)/ very bad(sep)	24.9	15.6	20.9	13.0	17.1	17.5

Money amounts are in thousands of dollars for HRS and thousands of Euros for SEP and CSS. Household incomes in CSS and SEP are after tax; for HRS incomes are before tax.

There is a monotonic relationship between health and wealth in both countries (Table 7). The same is true of the relation between health and income (Table 8), but the relation is less steep in the Netherlands than in the U.S. Partly this simply reflects the more equal income distribution in the Netherlands.

Table 9. The Cross Section Association Between Health and SES In the Two Countries

	HRS	Odds Ratios	CSS/SEP	Odds Ratios
Income low, w medium	0.797	2.22	0.098	1.10
	(14.55)**		(0.80)	
Income low, w high	1.681	5.37	0.059	1.06
	(18.55)**		(0.33)	
Income med, w low	0.971	2.64	0.277	1.32
	(18.36)**		(2.40)*	
Income med, w medium	1.389	4.01	0.603	1.83
	(28.38)**		(5.74)**	
Income med, w high	1.814	6.13	0.615	1.85
	(30.99)**		(4.96)**	
Income high, w low	1.406	4.08	0.451	1.57
	(12.71)**		(1.86)	
Income high, w medium	1.829	6.22	0.742	2.10
	(30.97)**		(6.07)**	
Income high, w high	2.153	8.61	0.902	2.46
	(36.61)**		(7.18)**	
High School	0.681	1.98		
	(17.85)**			
More than High School	1.058	2.88		
	(21.98)**			
High School (SEP)			0.051	1.05
			(0.61)	
More than High School (SEP)			0.375	1.45
			(3.06)**	
High School (CSS)			0.315	1.37
			(2.52)*	
More than High School (CSS)			0.168	1.18
			(1.42)	
Observations	42193		9423	
pseudo-R2	0.07		0.03	
chi2 Income/wealth	1520.32		84.38	
p-value	0.00		0.00	

Robust z statistics in parentheses
* - Significant at 5%
** - Significant at 1%

Explanation: The table presents ordered logits of the self-reported health categories on a number of characteristics. Controls not reported here include year dummies, a cubic in age, marital status, household size, gender. The last column presents results for pooled data of SEP and CSS, where education level is not pooled, since education definitions differ across the two data sets.

This point is even more clearly demonstrated by Table 9. Table 9 reports ordered logits of health categories on income wealth quartiles, education, and a number of other controls, which are not reported (but mentioned at the bottom of the table). To allow for nonlinearities in the relation between health and income or wealth we define nine income-wealth categories: for each of income and wealth we distinguish low, medium, and high, where low is the lowest quartile, medium is either the second or third quartile, and high is the highest quartile. The coding of income and wealth by quartiles is done separately for each year and for each data set.[5] The purpose of the tables is not to suggest any causality, but rather to characterise the strength of the relationship between health and SES in both countries. In the table we show results for the Netherlands based on pooled data of CSS and SEP. When pooling CSS and SEP we retain different education dummies for the two data sets in light of the differences in definition, as discussed earlier. A test of equality of the income/wealth dummies across the two data sets does not lead to rejection ($\chi^2(8)$ 9.37 p=0.31), which justifies the pooling. Table 9 shows a much steeper gradient of health with SES for HRS than for CSS/SEP (for instance the odds ratio of income high and wealth high is 8.61 for HRS and 2.46 for CSS/SEP), although the relation is statistically highly significant in all data sets. Education also has a highly significant relation with health, but again in the Netherlands the relation is less steep.

IV. THE IMPACT OF HEALTH ON WEALTH AND INCOME CHANGES

We have established that in both the U.S. data and the Dutch data there is a strong positive cross section association between health and indicators of socioeconomic status. In keeping with the theoretical model we now consider the effect of health status on income and wealth changes. The relation between health status and income changes would be similar to equation (4) above.

Table 10 shows a strong effect of health level on percentage wealth changes in the U.S. data. For instance, relative to people in excellent health, wealth changes of people in poor health lag by 16 per cent. The relation between wealth changes and health is much weaker in the Dutch data sets. In the pooled CSS/SEP data we find statistically significant, but small effects. For instance, relative to people in the healthiest category, the wealth change of people in the not so good/ fair category lags by 3.6 per cent. For the separate Dutch data we find some weak effects, but these are only statistically significant in the SEP. Also note that a test for equality of health effects on wealth in the two Dutch data sets leads to rejection at the 2 per cent level. Thus the pooled results are in principle based on a misspecified model. Hence we report both results based on the separate data sets and results based on the pooled data.

5 We have not combined income and wealth data of CSS and SEP in overlapping years, in view of the clear differences in measurement properties of income and wealth in the two data sets.

Table 10. Health Levels And Wealth Changes

	(1) HRS	(2) CSS	(3) SEP	(4) CSS/SEP
Health=very good(hrs)/ good(css,sep)	0.380	3.125	1.577	1.901
	(0.34)	(1.74)	(1.25)	(2.12)*
Health=good(hrs)/fair(css, sep)	-2.004	-1.058	0.905	-0.052
	(1.76)	(0.47)	(0.65)	(0.05)
Health=fair(hrs)/not so good(css)/bad(sep)	-6.747	-2.008	-3.941	-3.598
	(4.90)**	(0.52)	(1.68)	(2.02)*
Health=poor(hrs,css)/very bad(sep)	-16.029	-8.973	-0.239	-2.177
	(8.87)**	(0.85)	(0.04)	(0.47)
High School	9.924	1.483	1.823	
	(10.01)**	(0.78)	(1.91)	
More than High School	14.111	6.387	3.839	
	(11.60)**	(3.80)**	(3.18)**	
Divorced/Separated	-15.140	-9.740	-2.008	-4.062
	(11.95)**	(2.72)**	(1.10)	(2.76)**
Widowed	-12.804	0.975	-0.131	-0.504
	(8.34)**	(0.24)	(0.07)	(0.31)
Not Married	-9.500	-5.380	1.144	-0.182
	(5.37)**	-1.71	(0.95)	(0.18)
High School (SEP)				1.662
				(1.94)
More than High School (SEP)				2.916
				(2.59)**
High School (CSS)				3.404
				(2.82)**
More than High School (CSS)				7.922
				(7.83)**
Observations	30625	2509	3918	6518
F-test health	27.76	2.00	1.92	4.19
p-value	0.00	0.09	0.00	0.00
F-test education	73.90	7.72	5.34	15.85
p-value	0.00	0.00	0.10	0.00

Absolute value of t statistics in parentheses
* - significant at 5%
** - significant at 1%

Explanation: The table presents median regressions of percentage wealth changes from one period to the next. Controls not reported here include a cubic in age, gender and household size. The last column presents results for pooled data of SEP and CSS, where education level is not pooled, since education definitions differ across the two dat asets. A chi-squared test for equality of the health dummies across CSS and SEP yields a p-value of .02.

The effects of health on income are statistically marginally significant in the HRS and significant in the pooled SEP/CSS data (Table 11). A test for equality of the health effects in CSS and SEP leads to acceptance (p=.55). This outcome is somewhat surprising, in view of the relatively extensive income maintenance programs in the Netherlands. The significance of the effects in the Netherlands seems to be largely driven by the relatively large effect for poor/very bad health. For the other health categories the effects are about equal to those for the U.S. data, if not smaller.

Table 11. Health Levels And Income Changes

	(1) HRS	(2) CSS	(3) SEP	(4) CSS/SEP
Health=very good(hrs)/good(css,sep)	-0.331	-0.273	-1.221	-0.946
	(0.57)	(0.27)	(2.11)*	(2.19)*
Health=good(hrs)/fair(css, sep)	-0.151	-0.991	-0.245	-0.201
	(0.26)	(0.76)	(0.38)	(0.40)
Health=fair(hrs)/not so good(css)/bad(sep)	-1.882	4.059	-1.224	-0.503
	(2.67)**	(1.80)	(1.14)	(0.58)
Health=poor(hrs,css)/very bad(sep)	-0.303	-7.701	-2.082	-5.189
	(0.33)	(1.20)	(0.81)	(2.29)*
High School	1.319	0.026	0.002	
	(2.63)**	(0.02)	(0.00)	
More than High School	2.266	1.022	0.457	
	(3.64)**	(1.07)	(0.82)	
Divorced/Separated	-2.134	1.804	1.751	1.766
	(3.35)**	(0.89)	(2.10)*	(2.48)*
Widowed	-2.607	3.026	0.673	2.561
	(3.39)**	(1.35)	(0.73)	(3.23)**
Not Married	0.739	0.876	1.046	1.010
	(0.84)	(0.49)	(1.87)	(1.98)*
High School (SEP)				0.215
				(0.50)
More than High School (SEP)				0.827
				(1.45)
High School (CSS)				-0.717
				(1.31)
More than High School (CSS)				-0.188
				(0.40)
Observations	31226	2895	3643	6624
F-test health	2.31	1.39	1.96	2.75
p-value	0.06	0.50	0.10	0.03
F-test education	6.77	0.70	0.39	1.32
p-value	0.00	0.17	0.68	0.26

Absolute value of t statistics in parentheses
* Significant at 5%
** - Significant at 1%

V. THE IMPACT OF WEALTH AND INCOME ON HEALTH TRANSITIONS

We will quantify the effects of wealth and income on health changes via ordered logit estimation of the rate of health transition from one wave to another. We consider transitions from three initial health levels: from health being in the top-two categories, from health being in the middle category and from health being in the two bottom categories.

Table 12. Ordered Logits: Health In TheTop-Two Categories At Baseline

	(1) HRS	(2) Odds Ratios	(3) CSS/SEP	(4) Odds Ratios
Income low, w med	0.389	1.48	-0.166	0.847
	(3.65)**		(0.98)	
Income low, w high	0.911	2.49	0.088	1.09
	(7.18)**		(0.38)	
Income med, w low	0.405	1.50	-0.025	0.975
	(4.00)**		(0.16)	
Income med, w med	0.671	1.96	0.198	1.22
	(7.58)**		(1.50)	
Income med, w high	0.949	2.58	0.338	1.40
	(10.03)**		(2.27)*	
Income high, w low	0.760	2.14	0.153	1.17
	(4.36)**		(0.62)	
Income high, w med	0.935	2.55	0.236	1.27
	(9.69)**		(1.54)	
Income high, w high	1.038	2.82	0.320	1.38
	(10.99)**		(2.07)*	
High School	0.553	1.74		
	(9.85)**			
More than High School	0.770	2.16		
	(12.55)**			
Health==very good(hrs)/good(css,sep)	-1.476	0.228		
	(36.73)**			
High School(SEP)			-0.031	0.969
			(0.28)	
More than High School (SEP)			0.376	1.46
			(2.58)**	
Health=good(SEP)			-2.007	0.135
			(15.02)**	
High School (CSS)			0.015	1.02
			(0.13)	
More than High School (CSS)			-0.116	0.890
			(1.01)	
Health=good(CSS)			-2.522	0.080
			(19.50)**	
Observations	16272		4408	
pseudo-R2	0.08		0.13	
chi2 inc/wealth	205.32		16.66	
p-value	0.00		0.03	

Robust z statistics in parentheses
* - Significant at 5%
** - Significant at 1%

Explanation: The table presents ordered logits of next period's self-reported health status. Controls not reported here include a cubic in age, gender, year dummies, marital status, gender, and household size. The last column presents results for pooled data of SEP and CSS, where education level is not pooled, since education definitions differ across the two data sets. A chi-squared test for equality of the income and wealth coefficients in SEP and CSS yields a p-value of .60.

Tables 12 through 14 present the results. As in Section III, we also consider estimation results if we pool the CSS and SEP data (while keeping separate education dummies). Since in all three cases we accept the null that income and wealth effects are the same across SEP and CSS we only present the pooled results for the Dutch data.

Table 12 gives the estimated effects on the transition from excellent/very good health in HRS or from excellent or good health (CSS) or from very good or good (SEP) to each of the possible five destination or, in the event of a transition, that the transition will be to the middle category rather than to the bottom categories. We have added a dummy for health being very good (HRS) or good (CSS, SEP) to indicate where in the top categories one is at baseline.

Income and wealth have a significant influence on health transitions in both countries, but the effect appears to be considerably larger in the U.S. than in the Netherlands. This would suggest γ (cf. equation (4) to be bigger in the U.S. than in the Netherlands. In both countries it also appears that wealth is more important than income. In the Netherlands the combined effect of income and wealth is dominated by wealth. In the U.S. we observe a nonlinearity in the effect of income and wealth: an increase in wealth at all income levels increases the odds of remaining in the top health category; but an increase in income only increases the odds when wealth is low or medium, not when wealth is high.

In Table 13 the baseline category is good health for HRS and fair health for both CSS and SEP. As before, a positive coefficient increases the probability of a transition to better health or reduces the probability of a transition to worse health. The wealth income interactions are statistically significant in both countries. As before, the economic variables appear to have a stronger effect in the HRS than in the Dutch data, but the differences are fairly minor.

In Table 14, the baseline category is fair or poor for HRS, not so good or poor for CSS, and bad or very bad for SEP. The effects of income and wealth on the health transitions are now totally insignificant in the Dutch data, possibly due to the modest number of observations.

Table 13. Ordered Logits: Health In The Middle Category At Baseline

	(1) HRS	(2) Odds Ratios	(3) CSS/SEP	(4) Odds Ratios
Income low, w med	0.327	1.39	0.154	1.17
	(3.52)**		(0.79)	
Income low, w high	0.573	1.77	-0.143	0.867
	(3.44)**		(0.51)	
Income med, w low	0.407	1.50	0.181	1.20
	(4.46)**		(0.84)	
Income med, w med	0.587	1.80	0.327	1.39
	(7.20)**		(1.87)	
Income med, w high	0.785	2.19	0.179	1.20
	(7.79)**		(0.82)	
Income high, w low	0.640	1.90	-0.699	0.497
	(3.73)**		(1.28)	
Income high, w med	0.720	2.05	0.537	1.71
	(7.36)**		(2.22)*	
Income high, w high	0.769	2.16	0.818	2.27
	(7.90)**		(3.36)**	
High School	0.277	1.32		
	(5.44)**			
More than High School	0.459	1.58		
	(6.93)**			
High School (SEP)			0.021	1.20
			(0.14)	
More than High School (SEP)			0.367	1.44
			(1.70)	
High School (CSS)			0.440	1.55
			(1.50)	
More than High School (CSS)			0.406	1.50
			(1.74)	
Observations	9857		1568	
pseudo-R2	0.02		0.02	
chi2 inc/wealth	88.09		20.24	
p-value	0.00		0.01	

Robust z statistics in parentheses
* - Significant at 5%
** - Significant at 1%

Explanation: The table presents ordered logits of next period's self-reported health status. Controls not reported here include a cubic in age, gender, year dummies, marital status, gender, and household size. The last column presents results for pooled data of SEP and CSS, where education level is not pooled, since education definitions differ across the two data sets. A chi-squared test for equality of the income and wealth coefficients in SEP and CSS yields a p-value of .61.

Table 14. Ordered Logits: Health In The Bottom Two Categories At Baseline

	(1) HRS	(2) Odds Ratios	(3) CSS/SEP	(4) Odds Ratios
Income low, w med	0.214	1.24	-0.243	0.784
	(2.94)**		(0.51)	
Income low, w high	0.161	1.17	0.456	1.56
	(0.85)		(0.74)	
Income med, w low	0.332	1.39	-0.195	0.823
	(4.29)**		(0.33)	
Income med, w med	0.436	1.55	0.271	1.31
	(6.27)**		(0.57)	
Income med, w high	0.619	1.86	-0.554	0.575
	(5.98)**		(0.80)	
Income high, w low	0.520	1.68	-0.986	0.373
	(2.14)*		(1.06)	
Income high, w med	0.803	2.32	0.389	1.48
	(6.57)**		(0.59)	
Income high, w high	0.913	2.50	0.621	1.86
	(7.31)**		(0.72)	
High School	0.174	1.19		
	(3.53)**			
More than High School	0.256	1.29		
	(2.81)**			
Health==fair(hrs)/not so good(css)/bad(sep)	1.803	6.06		
	(29.78)**			
High School (SEP)			-0.230	0.795
			(0.64)	
More than High School(SEP)			-0.405	0.667
			(0.55)	
Health=bad(SEP)			1.704	5.50
			(2.20)*	
High School (CSS)			-0.442	0.642
			(0.85)	
More than High School(CSS)			0.186	1.20
			(0.31)	
Health=not so good(CSS)			3.181	24.1
			(4.35)**	
Observations	7799		296	
pseudo-R2	0.09		0.11	
chi2 inc/wealth	87.45		7.73	
p-value	0.00		0.46	

Robust z statistics in parentheses
* - Significant at 5%
** - Significant at 1%

Explanation: The table presents ordered logits of next period's self-reported health status. Controls not reported here include a cubic in age, gender, year dummies, marital status, gender, and household size. The last column presents results for pooled data of SEP and CSS, where education level is not pooled, since education definitions differ across the two data sets. A chi-squared test for equality of the income and wealth coefficients in SEP and CSS yields a p-value of .27.

VI. INTERPRETATION AND CONCLUSIONS

The conceptual model presented in Section 2 refers to the relationship between health and income. The theoretical relationship between wealth and health is considerably more complicated involving the propensity to consume out of income and the interest rate. We have not fully developed that theory beyond the observation that in populations where there is large variation in wealth there should be large variation in health. Therefore, when discussing the results in relation to the model we will concentrate on the results relating income and health. We should reiterate, however, the observation in the introduction that healthier individuals have more reasons to save for retirement, but that this reason is substantially less prominent in the Netherlands, where most retirement consumption is financed out of annuity income. We do indeed find that the effect of health on wealth is considerably smaller in the U.S. than in the Netherlands.

Based on the cross section estimations of the effects of income and wealth on health status (Table 9) we can calculate the average change in relative risk-holding constant wealth by averaging the relative risk over each wealth category. For example, in the HRS the average risk of being in a higher health category for someone in the top income quartile is computed to be 2.49 greater than the risk of someone in the lowest income quartile. In the Netherlands the relative risk is 1.90. Relating this result back to our conceptual model (cf. equations (11) and (16)), it indicates that γ/α is somewhat greater in the U.S. That is, the change in health is more strongly related to the income level in the U.S. than in the Netherlands.

Based on the three panel estimations (Tables 12, 13, and 14) we may calculate an estimate of γ in a similar way, by assuming that these equations are the empirical counterpart of (4). The estimations do not only hold wealth constant, but also baseline health constant in one of the three health status categories. In the HRS among those in the top income quartile the average relative risk of transiting to a higher health state can be calculated as 1.66 greater than the risk of someone in the lowest income quartile. In the Netherlands the risk is 1.23 greater. Thus the panel transitions indicate a higher level of γ in the U.S. than in the Netherlands.

By combining these findings we can estimate γ to be 0.27 for the U.S. and 0.34 for the Netherlands. These estimates can be compared to the estimation results presented in Table 11. According to our theoretical model, the coefficient on health for panel changes in income has the interpretation of α. Given the categorical nature of the health measure and the definitional differences between the categories in the two countries a comparison is somewhat tenuous, but qualitatively it appears that α, as derived from Table 11, is greater in the Netherlands than in the U.S., at least as measured by the largest of the coefficients (on poor health). Thus, we find broadly consistent estimates of the underlying parameters of our theoretical model. However, we clearly need better measures that can be compared with more confidence across the countries. The current data sets do not provide such comparable measures. Also we note that these calculations ignore possible differences in the variance of unobserved heterogeneity in both countries (λ in equation (19)).

We began the cross-country comparison with the observation that if national policies alter both the financing of health care services and other inputs into health production, and the relationship between health and income, we should find predictable differences in the relationship between health and income in cross section and in panel. In the Netherlands health care is universal and practically independent of income whereas that would not be the case in the U.S. In the Netherlands income redistribution programmes reduce the strength of the relationship between health and income. We found differing relationships between health and income in the two countries, and the differences are consistent with what our conceptual model would predict.

Clearly our analysis invites several improvements. On the conceptual side a more complex model relating health, wealth, and income in a three-equation system of differential equations appears to be natural extension. On the data side, one would want to consider more countries and a much wider array of health measures. Although at this moment micropanel data sets measuring health, income and wealth are only available in a very limited set of countries, the movement in various countries to emulate the U.S. Health and Retirement Study provides an exciting perspective on making progress in quantifying the relation of health and SES and the role of institutions in amending this relationship.

REFERENCES

Adams, Peter., Hurd, Michael D., McFadden, Daniel., Merrill, Angela., & Ribeiro, Tiago (2003). Healthy, Wealthy and Wise? Tests for Direct Causal Paths between Health and Socioeconomic Status. *Journal of Econometrics*, *112*: 3-56.

Alessie, Robert., Lusardi Annamaria, & Aldershof, Trea. (1997). Income and Wealth over the Life Cycle: Evidence from Panel Data. *The Review of Income and Wealth, 43*: 1-32.

Alessie, Robert., & Kapteyn, Arie. (1999a). *Savings, Pensions and Portfolio Choice in The Netherlands.* Free University Amsterdam.

Alessie, Robert., Lusardi, Annamaria, & Kapteyn, Arie. (1999b). Saving after Retirement: Evidence from Three Different Surveys. *Labour Economics 6*: 277-310.

Avery, Robert. B., Elliehausen, Gregory E., & Kennickell, Arthur B. (1988). Measuring Wealth with Survey Data: An Evaluation of the 1983 Survey of Consumer Finances. *The Review of Income and Wealth 34*: 339-369.

Avery, Robert, & Kennickell, Arthur. (1991). Household Saving in the US. *Review of Income and Wealth 37*: 409-432.

Berkman, Lisa F. (1988). The Changing and Heterogeneous Nature of Aging and Longevity: A Social and Biomedical Perspective. In George L. Maddox & M. Powell Lawton (Eds.) *Annual Review of Gerontology and Geriatrics, 8,* (pp. 37-68).

Boffetta, Paolo, & Garfinkel, Lawrence. (1990). Alcohol Drinking and Mortality among Men Enrolled in an America Cancer Society Prospective Study. *Epidemiology 1(5)*: 343-48.

Camphuis, Herman. (1993). Checking, Editing and Imputation of Wealth Data of the Netherlands Socio-Economic Panel for the period 87-89. *VSB Progress Report n. 10,* CentER, the Netherlands: Tilburg University.

Davies, James. (1979). On the Size Distribution of Wealth in Canada. *Review of Income and Wealth 25*: 237-259.

Feinstein, Jonathan. (1993). The Relationship between Socioeconomic Status and Health: A Review of the Literature. *The Milbank Quarterly 71(2)*: 279-322.

Finch, Brian K., Hummer, Robert A., Reindl, Maureen, & Vega, William A. (2002). *The Validity of Self-Rated Health among Latino(a)s*. Berkeley: School of Public Health, University of California, Mimeo.

Fuchs, Victor R.(1982). Time Preference and Health: an Exploratory Study. In *Economic Aspects of Health.* Chicago: University of Chicago Press.

Goldman, Noreen. (2001). Social Inequalities in Health: Disentangling the Underlying Mechanisms. In Maxine Weinstein, Albert I. Hermalin, & Michael A. Stoto, (Eds.), *Population Health and Aging – Strengthening the Dialogue Between Epidemiology and Demography*. Annals of the New York Academy of Sciences. 954: 118-139.

Grossman, Michael. (1972). *The Demand for Health-Atheoretical and Empirical Investigation*. New York: National Bureau of Economic Research.

Hill, Daniel H., & Mathiowetz, Nancy A. (1998). *The Empirical Validity of the HRS Medical Expenditure Data: A Model to Account for Different Reference Periods*. Ann Arbor: HRS Working Paper Series.

Hurd, Michael D. (1987). Saving of the elderly and desired bequests. *American Economic Review 77*: 289-312.

Hurd, Michael D. (1989). Mortality risks and bequests. *Econometrica 57*: 779-813.

Hurd, Michael D. (1998). *Mortality risk and consumption by couples*. Santa Monica: RAND Working Paper DRU-2061.

Hurd, Michael D., & McGarry, Kathleen. (1995). Evaluation of the Subjective Probabilities of Survival in the HRS. *Journal of Human Resources 30*: S268-S292.

Hurst, Erik., Ming Ching Luoh, & Stafford, Frank P. (1998).Wealth Dynamics of American Families: 1984-1994. *Brookings Papers on Economic Activity 1*: 267-337.

Juster, F. Thomas & Suzman, Richard M. (1995). An Overview of the Health and Retirement Study. *Journal of Human Resources 30 (supplement)*: S7-S56.

Kitagawa, Evelyn M., & Hauser, Philip M. (1973). *Differential Mortality in the United States: A Study in Socioeconomic Epidemiology*. Cambridge, Mass.: Harvard University Press.

Marmot, Michael G., Smith, George Davey., Stansfeld, Stephen., Patel, Chandra., North, Fiona., Head, J., White, Ian., Brunner, Eric & Feeny, Amanda. (1991). Health Inequalities among British Civil Servants: The Whitehall II Study. *Lancet, June 8*, 1387-93.

McClellan, Mark. (1998). Health Events, Health Insurance and Labor Supply: Evidence from the Health and Retirement Survey. In David Wise (Ed.), *Frontiers in the Economics of Aging* (pp. 301-346). Chicago: University of Chicago Press.

Robert, Stephanie & House, James. (1994). Socioeconomic Status and Health Over the Life Course. In Ronald P. Abeles, Helen C. Gift & Marcia G Ory, (Eds.), *Social Structures, Quality of Life, and Aging*, (pp. 253-274). New York: Springer Publishing Company.

Robert, Stephanie & House, James. (2000). Socioeconomic Inequalities in Health: Integrating Individual-, Community-, and Societal-Level Theory and Research. In Gary Albrecht, Ray Fitzpatrick and Susan Scrimshaw, (Eds.), *Handbook of Social Studies in Health and Medicine*, (pp. 115-135). London: Sage Publications.

Shaper, A. G. (1990). Alcohol and Mortality: A Review of Prospective Studies. *British Journal of Addiction 85*: 837-47.

Smith, James P. (1999). Healthy Bodies and Thick Wallets: The Dual Relationship between Health and Economic Status. *Journal of Economic Perspectives 13*: 145-166.

Van Doorslaer, Eddy., Wagstaff, Adam., Bleichrodt, Han., Calonge, Samuel., Gerdtham, Ulf G.G., Gerfin, Michael., Geurts, José., Gross, Lorna., Häkkinen, Unto., Leu, Robert E., O'Donnell, Owen., Propper, Carol., Puffer, Frank., Rodriguez, Marisol., Sundberg, Gun., & Winkelhake, Olaf. (1997). Income-related inequalities in health: some international comparisons. *Journal of Health Economics 16*: 93-112.

Wilkinson, Richard G. (1999). Health, Hierarchy, and Social Anxiety. In Nancy E. Adler, Michael Marmot, Bruce S. McEwen, & Judith Stewart, (Eds.) *Socioeconomic Status and Health in Industrial Nations*, Annals of the New York Academy of Sciences, 896: 48-63.

INAUGURAL ADDRESSES

H. SCHENK

ORGANISATIONAL ECONOMICS IN AN AGE OF RESTRUCTURING, OR: HOW CORPORATE STRATEGIES CAN HARM YOUR ECONOMY[1]

'If the allegation of the priority of rationality over habit
is itself simply a matter of habit then it is by that fact undermined'.
Geoff Hodgson (1998)

During the second half of the 1990s (i.e. 1995-1999), North American and West European firms expended about nine thousand billion U.S. dollars on acquisitions. At the time, by way of comparison, these acquisition expenditures in total were about seven times larger than Britain's Gross Domestic Product and more than twenty times Dutch GDP. On average, they amounted to about one-fifth of U.S. GDP during 1995-1999 (see Appendix, Table A1). Relative to the size of their home economies, this so-called fifth merger wave was dominated by firms from the U.S., the U.K. and the Netherlands.

Put differently, over the period 1995-1999 investments in acquisitions were approximately equal to sixty per cent of gross investments in machinery and equipment and they easily outpaced those in Research and Development (see tables A2 and A3 in the Appendix). Investments in acquisitions were no less than about eight times higher than business enterprise expenditures on R&D (which amounted to approx. US$ 1237 bln over the same period).

Thus, it is no surprise that mergers and acquisitions were by far the largest call on the typical CEO's time during most of the 1990s. Almost every board meeting, as casual observation confirms, was devoted to merger-related questions. Newspapers and

1 This article is the revised text of the author's Inaugural Address at Utrecht University, 21 October 2003. Many of the data used are from Schenk 2002a and 2002b; these sources provide more details in, and origins of, the data. I shall not distinguish between mergers, acquisitions and takeovers and will use these terms interchangeably.

P. de Gijsel and H. Schenk (eds.), Multidisciplinary Economics, 333–365.

business magazines followed at full tilt so that it was hard to find a single day without new announcements. Yet, government officials, when discussing the state of the economy or economic policy options, did not mention mergers at all.

In this contribution, I would wish to demonstrate that policy makers' negligence of merger issues was, and still is, unjustified, if not dangerous from a welfare point of view. Obviously, the sheer size of the merger phenomenon lifts it up to macro proportions. However, the attendant macro effects have only seldom been studied. An implication of this is, that I cannot take recourse to the literature so that my efforts will bear the characteristics of an exploration rather than an intervention in a debate, and will inevitably be a bit speculative here and there. Discussing the macro effects of a typically micro phenomenon also requires that I jump from the micro to the macro level, and back. Moreover, as will become clear, I will need to cross disciplinary boundaries. The exercise will therefore be rather risky, too, but I hope interesting nevertheless. In any case, it allows us to develop hitherto unexplored avenues for research and to chart the domain of Organisational Economics, a field of academic inquiry that focuses on the economic analysis of organisations and organisational behaviour. I will first discuss some principles of this rapidly growing subdiscipline of economics and argue that it seems most suitable for investigating the problem at issue.

THE FOCUS OF ORGANISATIONAL ECONOMICS

According to Neil Kay, the notion of Organisational Economics (OE) is an oxymoron. Say 'organisation', he writes, and it conjures up pictures of social groups and structures; say 'economics' and it triggers thoughts of impersonal (unorganised) markets and prices (Kay 2000: 684). Thus, it comes as no surprise that one of the field's most proliferate textbooks annex research monographs (Milgrom & Roberts 1992), in its own words, has 'unrelentingly' adopted 'an economic perspective in which people make self-interested choices and enter agreements only when they expect a mutual benefit' (1992: xiv). Milgrom and Roberts add, that their model of human behaviour even goes further in that it posits that people 'will be fundamentally amoral, ignoring rules, breaking agreements, and employing guile, manipulation, and deception if they see personal gain in doing so' (*ibid.*: 42).

Besides – but also in line with the previously mentioned point – OE à la Milgrom and Roberts has focused on the role of contractual relations within organisations (firms) rather than on the economics of the organisation of organisations. Thus OE has come to focus on the problems of firms as firms, and not on the problems of the structures within which firms operate and that they themselves – through sometimes quite uncoordinated collective behaviour – create.

It could be argued, though, that this is merely a matter of the division of labour among economics subdisciplines. More in particular, it would be the task of the related subdiscipline of Industrial Economics or Industrial Organisation (IO) to focus on organisational issues that are external to individual organisations. Indeed, IO has typically focused on the organisation of markets and its effects upon pricing. Then again, it has done so almost exclusively while interpreting markets as constructs that accommodate rational conduct, as structures in which individual actors can only survive by sticking to tight disciplinary rules. IO has effectively ruled out that firms might also be able to survive – at least for some time – by behaving as if they had been given a choice – e.g. to depart from constrained profit maximising behaviour, i.e. from behaviour that is the rational outcome of the wish to maximise monetary returns. According to IO, sins against the rational logic of structures are immediately punished; there is no time for corrections.

Thus, IO gives special attention to issues of industry structure and structurally defined market power while presuming economically rational behaviour among players. Evidently, this has been caused by the fact that to economists, the firm is not something to be studied for its own sake, but for its role in the price system and market exchange.[2]

For explaining what I have in mind, neither OE nor for that matter IO, as specified above, would be adequate vehicles. But these specifications are what they are merely because some academics have made them like that – they are not so by definition. Indeed, in terms of Augier *et al.* (2000), OE should be appreciated as the branch of economics that transforms theories of rational action into theories of rule-based action, emphasising not the efficiency of history but its inefficiencies. They recall that none of the powerful ideas that have grown from extensions to the theory of rational action and efficient history, like transaction cost economics, game theory, principal-agent theory and contract theory, has sacrificed those two pillars. Even the managerial theory's mainstay of bounded rationality in the end simply assumes that players are *intendedly* rational, but only limited by human and organisational properties in achieving rationality. My own perception of OE follows the one of Augier *et al.* closely in the sense that I allow an appreciation of firm behaviour as an expression of applying rules that adapt through conscious intent, learning, selection and imitation. In terms of Augier *et al.* (2000), who themselves in this respect refer to North (1990), March (1994) and Dosi & Marengo (1992), I supplement the assumption of rational action, confounded by uncertainty, human limitations and conflicts (such as those between agents and principals), with the assumption of identity-based, rule-based action. In this view, actions may be related less to their monetary consequences than to their consistency with the demands of identity and the rules of appropriate behaviour.

In this specification, OE, in actual fact, reintroduces what could be called the 'human side of organisational decision making'. The task for OE, therefore, is to study the market behaviour of firms (and – less relevant for this contribution – the formation of prices) as dependent also on the existence of social groups and structures, more particularly as determined – perhaps only in part – by the behaviour of human decision makers instead of anonymous system mechanics.

2 Only very recently, the introduction of game theory has changed this focus somewhat. It has maintained the field's strict rationality assumptions, however. See further below.

Coming back to the first sections of this contribution, it now becomes clear that an adequate study of mergers must take into account that they may have to do less with rational, profit-maximising behaviour than is usually assumed. Under the profit-maximising assumption, mergers are normally studied as static, time-invariant phenomena whereas the really interesting thing about them is that their intertemporal incidence is so erratic and that they bunch together. The organisation of our economies is not *continuously* being transformed by waves of mergers and acquisitions, but rather *periodically*, and then, as many of these mergers and acquisitions are undone, it is transformed again. Mergers and demergers occur in waves that therefore can be dubbed 'restructuring waves'. Whereas IO and EO, in the established interpretations described above, would tend to see those waves as anonymous programmes directed at efficiency improvement, this need not be the case in the real world. Rather than contributing to the welfare of nations, why would mergers not be able to block its creation?

The last century has seen five restructuring waves, three of which occurred after World War II: during the late 1960s and the late 1980s and during the second half of the 1990s, peaking in 2000.[3] In the build up, which takes on average about four to five years, hundreds of firms engage in a spending process that gains momentum quickly, as can be seen from Figure 1. In the downturn, which on average takes a year less, on average about one in three, but sometimes as many as seven out of ten, of the acquisitions made during the previous years are sold off again or dissolved in another manner.

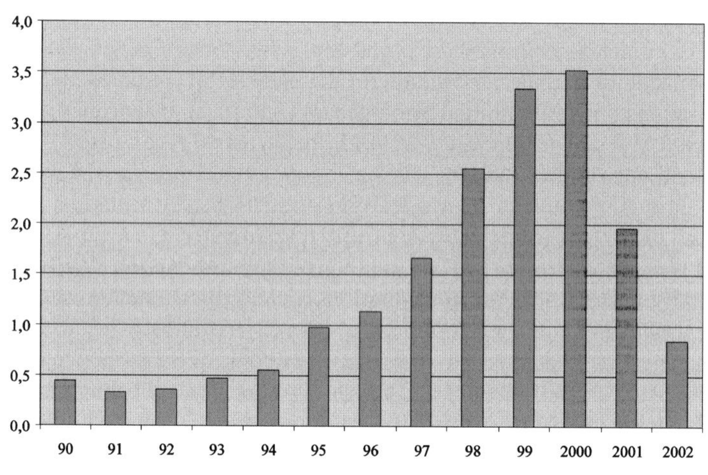

Figure 1: Value of global mergers and acquisitions, 1990-2002 ($trn)

The recurrent character of restructuring waves, of mergers and demergers, gives rise to two questions. First, why do firms acquire other firms only to sell them off a little

3 The period 1995-1999 rather than 1995-2000 (which would have covered the full upswing) has been chosen for further analysis in the article for reasons of data availability.

while later? Secondly, why do firms display this sort of behaviour in a format that has been likened to waves? Below, I will suggest that the answers to these two questions are strongly intertwined. Since a necessary part of the argument is that mergers are only rarely able to create wealth, I will discuss the evidence on merger performance first.

THE PERFORMANCE OF MERGERS

In early 2000, Numico, a top-100 Dutch food and nutrition firm with approx. 30,000 employees, acquired the American producer of vitamins Rexall Sundown for approximately € 2 bln. The deal was announced just before the fifth merger wave reached its pinnacle, and according to Numico was a once in a lifetime chance to improve both productive efficiency and its position as one of the world's leaders in the nutrition industry. Yet, only a year later, when the merger wave had receded, it announced that maybe the acquisition was not so smart after all. Rexall Sundown was sold off again for € 218 mln in 2003.

This huge loss in only a few years' time appears to be quite common, either in terms of real losses, i.e. when parts of the acquiring firm are sold off indeed, or in book losses, i.e. when acquisitions are revalued downwardly but remain part of the acquiring firm. A dramatic example of the latter case involves Britain's Vodafone. After having spent more than US$ 200 bln on various acquisitions during the second half of the 1990s, it had to write off no less than US$ 45 bln in assets in 2003 alone when it appeared that the acquisitions could not possibly generate a positive return.

To those who have studied the performance of mergers, all this should not come as a surprise. For example, Dickerson *et al.* (1997) found for a panel of almost 3000 UK-quoted firms that acquisitions have a systematic detrimental impact on company performance as measured by the rate of return on assets. Not only was the coefficient on acquisition growth much lower than that on internal growth, but there appeared to be an additional and permanent reduction in profitability following acquisition as well. More specifically, for the average company, the marginal impact of becoming an acquirer was to reduce the rate of return relative to nonacquirers by 1,38 percentage points (i.e. in the year of the first acquisition). Taking all subsequent acquisitions into account, acquiring firms experienced a relative reduction of 2,90 percentage points per annum. Since the mean return across all nonacquiring firms was 16,43 per cent, this translates into a shortfall in performance by acquiring firms of 2,9/16,43 which is around 17,7 per cent per annum.

This finding is not an exception. On the contrary, the most common result of merger performance studies is that profitability and productivity, variously measured, do not improve as a result of merger (see e.g. Ravenscraft and Scherer (1987) for the US; Bühner (1991) for Germany; Simon *et al.* (1996) for the advertising industry; and Berger and Humphrey (1992) and Rhoades (1994; 1998) for the banking industry).[4] If they do show profit improvements, these are usually due to the creation of additional market power rather than efficiency (Gugler *et al.*, 2003).

It is also likely that mergers and acquisitions have a negative effect on R&D investments, R&D investments relative to the industry average, and R&D output except for some industries, most notably the chemical industry (Scherer, 1984; Ravenscraft and Scherer, 1987; Hitt *et al.*, 1991). Market share growth seems to slow down after a merger, and acquired firms lose market share against a control group of firms that remain independent (Mueller 1986). For instance, among the world's 18 largest pharmaceutical firms, 11 out of 12 that participated in mergers lost combined market share between 1990 and 1998 whereas all six of those that had not merged gained market share (*The Economist* 22 January 2000).

Similar results are obtained when the focus is on shareholder instead of real wealth. A review of 33 earlier studies by Mueller (2003) finds that while target shareholders usually gain from acquisitions, acquirer shareholders almost always lose, especially in the long run. Generally, the longer the post-merger assessment period, the more negative shareholder returns become. Usually, positive abnormal returns are only evident for a few days around the event (and even then only when pre-event build-ups of share prices are underestimated), but taking this as evidence requires a strong belief in the Efficient Market Hypothesis. Another review of the most important studies confirmed this finding (Schenk 2002b) before testing it for a sample of 110 very large acquisitions – among them the most prolific of the century – undertaken during 1993-2001 (thus, including years that both preceded the beginning of the merger wave and followed its demise). We found that for several different models – varying only in terms of event windows – the outcomes were all negative in terms of cumulative abnormal returns (CAR) on the acquirer's side, running from minus 3,4 to minus 8,5 per cent (see Figure 2).

4 Notice that most studies have used control groups, so that it would be a bit too easy to justify ongoing mergers by arguing that firms might have performed even worse without a merger. Such a proposition would imply a generalisation that is unlikely in the face of the overall findings, though in individual cases it might, of course, apply.

Models (t in calendar days)	t = [–1, 0]	t = [–1, 5]	t = [–10, 5]	t = [–20, 5]	t = [–40, 5]
CAR acquirer	– 3,41	– 4,48	– 5,12	– 4,99	– 8,48
T-value *	– 4,691	– 4,764	– 4,422	– 3,764	– 5,174

* all T-values significant at 5%

Includes

Domestic M&As		Cross-Border M&As
AOL–Netscape	Starwood–ITT	Telefonica–Endemol
Terra Networks–Lycos	Chevron–Texaco	Mannesmann–Orange
Verizon–GTE	Exxon–Mobil	Deutsche Telekom–Voice-Stream
AT&T–McCaw Cellular	Total Fina Elf–Petrofina	Glaxo–Smithkline Beecham
QWest–US West	Weyerhouser–Willamette	Reed Elsevier–Harcourt
Compaq–Digital	Carrefour–Promodes	Daimler-Benz–Chrysler
Gener. Electric–Honneywell	E.On–Viag	Unilever–Bestfoods
Pfizer–Warner-Lambert	United Airlines–US Airways	Diageo–Grand Metropolitan
Paramount–Viacom		Vivendi–US Filter
		Suez Lyonnaise–Tractebel

Figure 2: Shareholder Value Effects of 110 Very Large Acquisitions, 1993-2001 (%)

In another study, we investigated the effects of 87 much-advertised cross-border acquisitions by Dutch multinationals. These mergers initially appeared to do better than the benchmark but as time went by turned into the red as well (see Figure 3). Notice, that mergers that were undertaken in the years immediately preceding the fifth merger wave were over-represented in the second study whereas the first focused on mergers from this fifth merger wave. The first found negative returns for short event windows while the second would have found only positive returns if the analysis had been constrained to similarly short windows as well. This suggested the possibility of intertemporal variations in merger performance. Therefore, we subdivided another sample of 100 (European) mergers into five year-cohorts (beginning with 1995 and ending with 1999) and studied their performance for 400 post-merger days each. The study revealed that 'earlier' acquisitions perform better (or less badly) than 'later' acquisitions. Figure 4 shows that the 1995 cohort reached positive results but that all others were in the negative, the 1999 cohort performing worst of all; it saddled its shareholders with an average cumulative loss of almost 25 per cent.

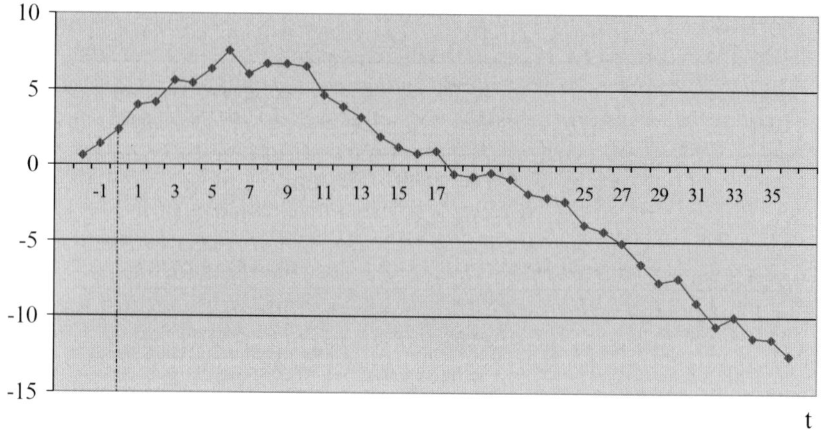

Figure 3: Shareholder Returns of Foreign Acquisitions by Dutch firms, 1990-1995 [-2, +36 m]

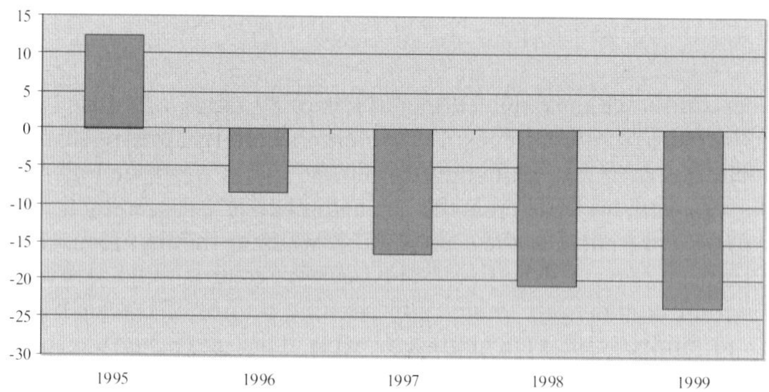

Figure 4: Shareholder Returns of European Mergers, 1995-1999 (Annual cohorts)

Similarly, in a study of about 12,000 acquisitions from 1980 to 2001, Moeller *et al.* (2003) found that while shareholders lost throughout the sample period, losses associated with acquisitions after 1997 were 'dramatic'.

These findings are consistent with newer work by Carow *et al.* (2004) who investigate stockholder returns for 520 acquisitions over 14 industry-defined merger waves during 1979-1998. They find that the combined returns for target and acquiring shareholders were higher for mergers that took place during the early stages of these waves. Well-performing acquirers all made their acquisitions during these same stages.

Summing up the evidence, we may conclude that, generally, mergers and acquisitions perform badly with respect to economically relevant real variables such as productivity, profitability, market share growth and innovation, as well as with respect to shareholder value.[5] Quoting one of the field's most reputable researchers: 'The picture that emerges is a pessimistic one: widespread failure, considerable mediocrity, and occasional successes' (Scherer with Ross 1990: 173). Scherer was referring especially to the merger wave of the late 1960s (the so-called third wave), but meanwhile it has become clear that his conclusion applies to the fourth and particularly the fifth merger wave too. Older as well as retrospective studies have also found that many mergers undertaken during the first two merger waves failed significantly, too, (see e.g. Borg *et al.,* 1969; Dewing 1921) thus illustrating that the occurrence of unsuccessful mergers is a structural event.

With respect to success and failure rates, the conclusions appear dependent on the sample taken. Most studies find failure rates of between 65 and 85 per cent. Merger success appears to correlate with method of payment (cash instead of paper payments show superior performance, but are difficult to sustain in large merger cases); size differential (the larger the size difference between acquirer and target, the more likely it is that the merger will end up in failure – obviously because small increments are less likely to create substantial market power increases); degree of diversification (horizontal mergers are less likely to become failures than conglomerate mergers – perhaps because they more easily create market power); and last but not least, with the opportunities for creating market power (see Gugler *et al.,* 2003). It would appear, however, that the most robust discriminator is intertemporality: the further down the merger wave, the more disappointing economic results become.

RESEARCH QUESTIONS

The reported findings suggest that a form of behaviour is common that contradicts the fundamental assumption of (mainstream) economic theory mentioned previously. Apparently, firms – at least periodically – engage in forms of behaviour that are known to result in profit increases in a minority of cases only. On average, profitability decreases in relative terms, i.e. in comparison to best estimates of the counterfactual. This gives rise to the following questions:

- Why do firms recurrently engage in uneconomic behaviour?
- What are the (indirect, long-run) effects of this behaviour on (a) the actors themselves; and (b) the economy as a whole?

5 For further discussion of the evidence, also see Tichy (2001).

- To minimise the occurrence of such behaviour, what can be done (a) at the level of the actors; and (b) at the level of government, including such bodies as competition commissions?

The first question is essentially a matter of theory, meant to solve the 'merger paradox', i.e. the phenomenon that most mergers have inefficient outcomes and yet are sometimes so vigorously pursued. The underlying behaviour of actors (firms) should be classified as uneconomic in the sense that it disagrees with economic theory's assumptions of maximising behaviour. The second question involves measurement and a test to which I refer as a triviality test, in order to ascertain whether intervention by firms and/or government institutions or pseudogovernment institutions is desirable at all. Finally, the third question searches for the sort of intervention that would be needed in order to prevent firms from pursuing uneconomic behaviour (if the effects of such behaviour have been found to pass the triviality test).

Clearly, answering these questions would amount to a full research programme. Therefore, I will not be able to come up with clearly cut answers straight-away. Yet, the following remarks would seem appropriate.

WHY DO FIRMS RECURRENTLY ENGAGE IN UNECONOMIC BEHAVIOUR?

Approaches that rest on economic utilitarianism and methodological individualism have great difficulties in coping with economic subjects that repeatedly engage in modes of conduct that do not maximise economic returns. This is especially the case if – for example, based on historical evidence – it is common knowledge that the chances for wealth creation are systematically small – so that one cannot speak of aberrations – and if the particular modes of conduct are widespread – as is the case with mergers. Two solutions to the merger paradox have meanwhile come to be accepted on a fairly broad scale.

Already back in the 1930s, Berle and Means (1932) observed that for joint-stock firms ownership had come to be largely separated from control. This opened the possibility of a conflict of interest between principals (owners) and their agents (managers). Whereas owners were assumed to have as their sole interest the maximisation of profits, managers might aim for the maximisation of personal utility, for example through steadily pushing for larger size (which was assumed to be positively correlated with managerial income) or for perquisites (which would add to managerial status). Faced with disappointing merger results, agency theory soon proposed that managers were undertaking mergers in order to boost their firm's size rather than profits while using up funds that should have been distributed to shareholders.

In addition, whereas principals are expected to be risk-neutral since they can diversify their shareholdings across multiple firms, agents are assumed to be risk-averse as their jobs and incomes are inextricably tied to one firm. This would imply that – apart from the size effect on income – uneconomic mergers would be undertaken in order to prevent loss of job and/or status.

To a certain extent, the empirical evidence is consistent with agency theory expectations. Managerial income and perks, as well as status, indeed, rise with the size of the firm, especially if size has been generated by acquisitions (Schmidt & Fowler 1990). But mergers may threaten agents' employment security as becomes evident from the fact that many CEOs are laid off once the merger wave is over and firms come to realise that many acquisitions have been a waste of funds or have even brought counterproductive results. Moreover, the picture that is depicted of managers is particularly negative. It is somehow hard to believe that the large number of uneconomic mergers should be explained by the fact that managers are disguising and distorting information and misleading or cheating their principals. On the contrary, managers may be just like ordinary people, i.e. they may enjoy performing responsibly because of a personal need for achievement, while interpreting responsibility as something that is defined in relation to others' perceptions. More generally, if the principal-agent relationship is conceived in terms of enlightened self-interest, it may be difficult to decouple an agent's goals from those of her principal (see Wright *et al.*, 2001). Finally, there is not much evidence that managers would only cheat their principals when they are faced (or are expecting to be faced) with rising profits that should be kept away from them. In fact, many of the most proliferate cases of cheating occurred when profits were decreasing rather than increasing (see Brenner 2002).

Others have tried to explain the apparent paradox by suggesting that hubris may lead managers to expand company size through mergers beyond that which maximises real shareholder wealth, and/or to disregard dismal experiences with earlier mergers. According to Roll, 'If there are no aggregate gains in takeover, the phenomenon depends on the overbearing presumption of bidders that their valuations are correct' (1986: 200). Such overconfidence may grow when past success (even if this was quite coincidental) leads to a certain degree of arrogance and a feeling of supremacy which in turn leads to overpayment. Indeed, the height of bidding premiums appears to depend on whether the bidders can boast a successful premerger record in terms of market-to-book and price-to-earnings ratios (Raj & Forsyth 2003). Prior success breeds overpayment, smaller bidder returns and higher target returns, thus relative failure. Not only were the premiums paid by hubris firms on average 1,5 times higher, their acquisitions were also paid with paper in 64 per cent of the cases whereas the control group managed just 23 per cent.

An earlier project by Hayward and Hambrick (1997) had used two more indicators of hubris, viz. the extent of recent media praise for the CEO and the size difference between the CEO's pay and the other executives' pay in their firms. They reached similar conclusions.[6] Malmendier and Tate (2003) classified CEOs as overconfident when they held company options until expiration. Such CEOs were found to be more likely to conduct mergers while the market reacted more negatively to their takeover bids relative to those of others.

6 Interestingly, the CEO's pay divided by the average pay for other officers was significantly greater for bankrupt firms five years before they failed than for a matched group of survivor companies (Hayward & Hambrick 1997).

In conclusion, it seems evident that both agency and hubris theory, and the latter one in particular, would play an important part in an explanation of uneconomic mergers and acquisitions. However, both are static theories. Clearly, in cross-sections empire-builders as well as hubris CEOs will be found to run the highest risk of merging their firms to the brink of failure. But this cannot account for the fact that empire building and overconfidence become manifest only under particular circumstances. Also, they take an individualistic point of view, tacitly assuming that a decision maker's actions are independent from those of others. Thus, while possibly correct in a substantial number of cases, agency and hubris theories cannot by themselves clarify why mergers should occur in waves.[7]

What is needed, therefore, is a theory that can explain why firms display uneconomic behaviour – or at least uneconomic mergers – erratically and why they do so at approximately identical intervals. The following section, which draws on Schenk (2000b), endeavours to develop such a theory of mergers. Rooted in both agency theory and game theory – but interpreted with the comments that have been made in mind – this theory suggests that many mergers are undertaken for purely strategic instead of economic motives. For reasons to be developed, these so-called 'purely strategic mergers' call for a special policy approach, provided that the problem is sufficiently serious.

A THEORY OF PURELY STRATEGIC MERGERS

According to DiMaggio and Powell (1982), uncertainty or lack of understanding with respect to goals, technologies, strategies, payoffs, et cetera – all of them typical for modern industries – are powerful forces that encourage imitation. Following Cyert and March (1963), they suggest that when firms have to cope with problems with ambiguous causes or unclear solutions they will rely on problemistic search aimed at finding a viable solution with little expense. Instead of making decisions on the basis of systematic analyses of goals and means, organisations may well find it easier to mimic other organisations. Most 'important' mergers are undertaken by large firms. These firms normally operate in concentrated industries and are usually active in several of those industries at the same time (see e.g. Karier 1993). In the typical situation of single market or multimarket oligopoly, which involves both interdependence of outcomes and strategic uncertainty, adopting mimetic routines is therefore a likely way for solving strategic decision-making problems. Moreover, organisations with ambiguous or (potentially) disputable goals will be likely to be highly dependent upon appearances for legitimacy.

7 Notice that the relationship between merger waves and stock market dynamics is ambiguous. Sometimes stock market cycles correlate with merger waves; sometimes they do not, whereas if they do it remains uncertain what causes what. Evidently, merger waves must be preceded by periods of economic prosperity. But neither historical evidence nor economic logic would lead one to qualify this as the fulfilment of a sufficient condition.

Reputation. This latter point is also implied in Scharfstein and Stein (1990). Their model assumes that there are two types of managers, 'smart' ones who receive informative signals about the value of an investment (e.g. a merger), and 'dumb' ones who receive purely noisy signals. Initially, neither these managers nor other persons (i.e. stakeholders) can identify the types, but after an investment decision has been made, stakeholders can update their beliefs on the basis of the following two pieces of evidence:

- Whether their agent has made a profitable investment; and
- Whether their agent's behaviour was similar to or different from that of other managers.

Given the quite reasonable assumption that there are systematically unpredictable components of investment value, and that whereas 'dumb' managers will simply observe uncorrelated noise, 'smart' managers tend to get correlated signals since they are all observing 'a piece of the same "truth"' (Scharfstein & Stein 1990: 466), it is likely that the second piece of evidence will get precedence over the first. Since these signals might be 'bad' just as well as 'good', 'smart' managers may, however, all have received misleading signals. Since stakeholders will not be able to assess or even perceive these signals they will refer to the second piece of evidence in assessing the ability of 'their' managers. Now, if a manager is concerned with her reputation with stakeholders, then it will be natural for her to mimic a first-mover as this suggests to stakeholders that she has observed a signal that is correlated with the signal observed by the first-mover – which will make it more likely that she is a 'smart' manager.

The more managers adopt this behaviour, the more likely it will be that 'bad' decisions will be seen as a result of a common unpredictable negative component of investment value. The ubiquitousness of the error in other words will suggest that all managers were victims of a 'bad' signal. Erring managers will subsequently be able to share the blame of stakeholders with their peers. In contrast, a manager who takes a contrary position will ex ante be perceived as 'dumb'. She will therefore be likely to pursue an investment opportunity if peers are pursuing that – even if her private information suggests that it has a negative expected value. Thus, Scharfstein and Stein's model explains why conventional wisdom teaches that 'it is better for reputation to fail conventionally than to succeed unconventionally' (Keynes 1936: 158).

Rational herding. This result, however, is not generally dependent on reputational considerations. Whereas Scharfstein and Stein's model is essentially an agency model in which agents try to fool their principals and get rewarded if they succeed, Banerjee (1992) and Bikhchandani *et al.* (1992) have addressed the imitation phenomenon as a consequence of informational externalities. In these models each decision maker looks at the decisions made by previous decision makers in taking her own decision and opts for imitating those previous decisions because the earlier decision makers may have learned some information that is important for her. The result is herd behaviour, i.e. a behavioural pattern in which everyone is doing what everyone else is doing.

These models are essentially models, which explain why some person may choose not to go by her own information, but instead will imitate the choice made by a previous decision maker. Following Banerjee (1992), suppose that – for some reason – the prior probability that an investment alternative is successful is 51 per cent (call this alternative i_1), and that the prior probability that alternative i_2 is successful is 49 per cent. These prior probabilities are common knowledge. Suppose further that of ten firms – i.e. firms A, B, ..., J – nine firms have received a signal that i_2 is better (of course, this signal may be wrong) but that the one firm which has received a signal that i_1 is better happens to choose first. The signals are of equal quality, and firms can only observe predecessors' choices but not their signals. The first firm (firm A) will clearly opt for alternative i_1. Firm B will now know that the first firm had a signal that favoured i_1 while her own signal favours i_2. If the signals are of equal quality, then these conflicting signals effectively cancel out, and the rational choice for firm B is to go by the prior probabilities, i.e. choose i_1. Her choice provides no new information to firm C, so that firm C's situation is not different from that of firm B. Firm C will then imitate firm B for the same reason that prompted firm B to imitate firm A, and so on: all nine follower firms will eventually adopt alternative i_1. Clearly, if firm B had fully relied on her own signal, then her decision would have provided information to the other eight firms. This would have encouraged these other firms to use their own information.

Thus, from a broader perspective, it is of crucial importance whether firm A's decision is the correct decision. If it is, then all firms will choose for the 'right' alternative, but if it is not, all firms will end up with a 'wrong' decision. Also, the result of this game is dependent on chance: were firm B, ..., J to have had the opportunity to choose first, things would have come out entirely different. However, when translated into our merger problem, if alternative i_2 is set equal to 'do not undertake a merger' then A's action ('merger') will always be the first to be observed as a deviation from actual practice, thus prompting firms B, ..., J to respond. The mechanism is especially clear when a first and a second firm have both chosen the same i … 0 (where the point 0 has no special meaning but is merely defined as a point that is known, i.e. observable, to the other firms). That is, the third firm (firm C) knows that firm A must have a signal since otherwise she would have chosen $i = 0$. Firm A's choice is therefore at least as good as firm C's signal. Moreover, the fact that B has followed A lends extra support to A's choice (which may be the 'wrong' choice nevertheless). It is therefore always better for C to follow A.

The main virtues of Banerjee's model are (a) that some aspects of herd behaviour can be explained without invoking network externalities, i.e. without requiring that a decision maker will actually benefit from imitating earlier decision makers (which would be the case if undertaking some action is more worthwhile when others are doing related things); and (b) that it is possible that decision makers will neglect their private information and instead will go by the information which is provided by the actions of earlier decision makers (or the prior probabilities).

Cascades. Bikhchandani *et al.* (1992) use the metaphor of a cascade to stress essentially the same point. The process is depicted as a cascade since with increasing numbers of decision makers adopting a particular action, it becomes increasingly, i.e. more than proportionally, likely that the next decision maker will follow suit. According to Bikhchandani *et al.*, a cascade will start if 'enough' predecessors have all acted in contradistinction to a subsequent decision maker's own information and if there is no a priori reason to expect that the signals received by the earlier decision makers are less valuable than the signal received by the subsequent decision maker. The first condition is dependent on the specification of the model. The latter condition is an assumption of the model (but can be adapted by introducing variations in signal strength). Ultimately, the reason that a decision maker will tend to disregard her own information is that she is sufficiently uncertain about the value of her signal to act upon it when faced by the decisions of others. Alternatively, it could be argued that she is simply economising on the costs that are involved in gathering and processing information. Observing the choices of others and imitating these may be a cheap and helpful alternative in the light of the many uncertainties that are involved with strategic decisionmaking.

Regret. The models discussed so far make clear that the intricacies of information diffusion in sequential games can cause imitation despite the fact that a follower's private information would indicate a deviation from the trajectory that seems to have been started. Notice, however, that they are couched in a positive payoff framework. Furthermore, they make use of binary action sets implying that only correct and incorrect decisions are possible and that a small mistake incurs the same loss as a large mistake. The introduction of a regret framework relaxes these conditions and increases the plausibility of models of herding behaviour. In a seminal series of experiments Kahneman and Tversky (1979) found that people systematically violate two major conditions of the expected utility model's conception of rationality when confronted with risk, viz. the requirements of consistency of and coherence among choices. They traced this to the psychological principles that govern the perception of decision problems and the evaluation of options. Apart from the fact that it appears to matter substantially in which frame a *given* decision problem is couched (or presented; formulated), even to the extent that preferences are reversed when that frame is changed, choices involving gains are often risk averse and choices involving losses risk taking. Thus, it appears that the response to losses is more extreme than the response to gains. Kahneman and Tversky's 'prospect theory', of course, is consistent with common experience that the displeasure associated with losing a sum of money is greater than the pleasure associated with gaining the same amount.

Consequently, it is likely that the contents of decision rules and standard practices will be 'biased' in such a way that they favour the prevention of losses rather than the realisation of gains. Thus, behavioural norms that carry this property are more likely to be 'chosen' as Schelling's so-called focal points (Schelling 1960). In practice, this will mean that firms are likely to adopt routines that imply a substantial degree of circumspection. A similar degree of circumspection is likely to develop if the decision maker is concerned with the regret that she may have upon discovering the difference between the actual payoff as the result of her choice and 'what might have been' the payoff were she to have opted for a different course of action. Regret in this case may be defined as the loss of pleasure due to the knowledge that a better outcome may have been attained if a different choice had been made. Under conditions of uncertainty a decision maker will modify the expected value of a particular action according to the level of this regret.

Minimax-regret. Dietrich and Schenk (1995), building on Savage (1951) and Loomes and Sugden (1982), have suggested that one way of expressing this is by adopting a minimax-regret routine. Let us assume that a decision maker knows the payoffs for each decision alternative but that she is completely ignorant as to which state of nature prevails. The minimax-regret routine then prescribes that she select that strategy which minimises the highest possible regret assuming that the level of regret is linearly related to the differences in payoff. The minimax-regret criterion thus puts a floor under how bad the decision maker would feel if things go wrong. Moreover, doing so will protect her against the highest possible reproach that can be made by those stakeholders who assess the decision's utility on the basis of the true state of nature.

When put into a framework of competitive interdependence this develops as follows. Given a particular action of firm A which is important enough to be monitored by her peers (rivals) – i.e. a merger or an acquisition – firm B will have to contemplate what the repercussions for her own position might be. Suppose that there is no way that firm B can tell whether A's move will be successful. A's move could be genuinely motivated by a realistic expectation that her cost position will improve, or by a realistic expectation that her move will increase her rating with stakeholders or even her earnings. That is, A's competitiveness position vis-à-vis her peers may be ameliorated as a result of that move, say in terms of a first mover advantage. But then again, it may not. For example, A's move might be purely motivated by the pursuit of managerial goals, or it may simply be a miscalculation caused by hubris. What is firm B to do?

Suppose that A's move will be successful, but that B has not reacted by imitating that move herself (which we will call scenario α). To what extent will B regret not having reacted? Alternatively, suppose that A's move will not be successful but that B has imitated it solely inspired by the possible prospect of A's move being a success (scenario β). To what extent will B regret this when the failure of A's move becomes apparent? Within a minimax-regret framework, it is likely that B's regret attached to scenario α will be higher than the regret attached to scenario β. For in scenario α, B will experience a loss of competitiveness, while in scenario β her competitive position vis-à-vis A will not have been harmed. Of course, B could have realised a competitive *gain* in scenario β had she refrained from imitation, but in terms of the minimax-regret model her regret of having lost this potential gain is likely to be relatively small. The implication is that under conditions of uncertainty a strategic move by firm A will elicit an imitative countermove by her rivals – even if the economic payoffs are unknown.

The models discussed assume that a decision maker's payoffs do not depend on what subsequent decision makers do, so that there is no incentive to cheat in an effort to influence a later player. Moreover, decision makers are not allowed to have heterogeneous values of adoption. Yet, these models allow us to conclude that it is likely that a decision maker who is using a minimax-regret routine will imitate actions of earlier decision makers that are regarded as significant. Thus, if – for some reason – a first decision maker within a strategic group has decided to undertake a merger, a second decision maker may follow suit even if her own information suggests otherwise. Evidently, such imitation may lead to cascades that will last very long if not forever. In a sense, mergers and acquisitions have then become 'taken-for-granted' solutions to competitive interdependence. It implies that firms may have become locked into a solution in which all players implicitly prefer a nonoptimal strategy without having ready possibilities for breaking away from it.

Even if some firms do not adopt minimax-regret behaviour, it will be sensible for them to jump on a merger bandwagon too. For, cascading numbers of mergers and acquisitions imply that the likelihood of becoming an acquisition target increases. Thus, given the finding that relative size is a more effective barrier against takeover than relative profitability (Hughes 1993; Dickerson *et al.*, 2003), firms may enter the merger and acquisition game for no other reason than to defend themselves against takeover (also see Greer 1986). Needless to say, such defensive mergers will amplify the prevailing rate of mergers and acquisitions. The cascade will inevitably stop as soon as (a) the number of potential targets diminishes, which is a function of the intensity of the cascade, and (b) the disappointing merger returns decrease the chances for obtaining the financial means that are necessary for further merger investments.

In conclusion, it would seem that the high incidence of non-wealth creating mergers is not the result of failed implementation techniques, or diverging organisational cultures, as many management scholars would like us to believe (e.g. Haspeslagh & Jemison 1991). Rather the existence of strategic interdependence under uncertainty, conditioned by the availability of funds, may compel managements to undertake mergers even if these will not increase economic performance. Inertia may prevail for long periods, but as soon as an initial, clearly observable move has been made by one of the major players, it is likely that other players will rapidly follow with similar moves. With multimarket oligopoly omnipresent, and given the increasing weight assigned to stock market performance appraisals, the ultimate result may be an economywide merger boom. Eventually, many firms will find themselves stuffed with acquisitions that were neither meant nor able to create wealth. As a consequence, after the strategic imperatives have receded, firms will start licking their wounds by undertaking corrective actions. In the short run, they are likely to look for cheap and easy alternatives, like economising on all sorts of expenses (e.g. labour; R&D). In the medium run they will likely spin off the acquisitions made during the boom – sometimes at great cost. Figure 5 depicts the different stages of the restructuring wave.

Stage 1	**Preconditional Stage** A booming economy provides the necessary means (cash; stock appreciations; borrowing facilities), but is not sufficient
Stage 2	**Event Stage** A single (random) merger ignites the game
Stage 3	**Response Stage** Minimax-regret and defensive routines lead to bursts of merger activity
Stage 4	**Depletion Stage** The merger boom levels off as a result of lacking and/or lagging productivity and profitability gains, and price rises for targets
Stage 5	**Recovery Stage** Reconstitution management sets in (selloffs, divestitures, demergers; layoffs)
Stage 6	**Normalisation Stage** The pool with targets is refilled

Figure 5: Stages of the Restructuring Wave

I propose to call such mergers 'purely strategic mergers'. These are mergers that are intended to create strategic comfort when faced with the uncertain effects of a competitor's moves, rather than economic wealth (or, for that matter, monopoly rents). It is precisely for this reason that it would be futile to wait on the so-called learning capacities of organisations to improve economic merger performance. In a system that is dominated by the few, uneconomic mergers are simply part of the game.

HOW PURELY STRATEGIC MERGERS COULD BE HARMFUL TO THE ECONOMY

Traditionally, negative welfare effects of mergers and acquisitions, if any, would be expected in the area of allocative efficiency. That is, mergers might increase market concentration to such an extent that firms could raise prices beyond the competitive level, or restrict output, so that an efficient allocation of resources would be thwarted. Inexpedient behaviour of firms in the area of mergers, however, carries important social costs even when allocative effects remain at bay. In terms of this paper, these costs would be the result of foregone improvements of, or actual decreases in, productive (or internal) and dynamic (or innovation) efficiency respectively. The finding that mergers do not lead to improvements in profitability, or merely lead to improvements that are smaller than would have been possible without merger, suggests that mergers, on average, lead to X-inefficiency (in terms of Leibenstein 1966) or relative X-inefficiency.[8]

More generally, the development of productivity and innovativeness may be harmed as merger decision making consumes an important fraction of investment funds as well as managerial time, talent, and energy, both ex ante and ex post, that cannot be spent anymore on investment projects that are more likely to create wealth in the long run, such as investment in machinery and equipment, and investment in R&D, training and schooling.

Unfortunately, it is difficult to say precisely to what extent productive and dynamic efficiency will be harmed in practice. There are, however, two reasons for expecting that the (opportunity) losses of purely strategic mergers may be significant. First, losses due to X-inefficiency extend over the entire output range rather than simply to the output contraction that would be the relevant range for determining the importance of allocative inefficiencies.

Secondly, if merger-active firms as a collectivity are sufficiently large relative to the economy as a whole and/or their merger expenditures big enough relative to total economic activity, then their inexpedient behaviour may have macroeconomic repercussions. What exactly should be understood by 'sufficient' and 'enough' is not clear, however. Merger-active firms rank among the largest (and virtually all of the largest firms are merger-active). As a group, these firms – while only being a tiny fraction of the population of firms in numbers – contribute significantly to economic development. For instance, the largest one hundred manufacturers in the EU and the U.S. – i.e. those firms that are most likely to engage in purely strategic mergers – accounted for, respectively, 28,2 and 42,3 per cent of manufacturing employment in 1990 (data upwardly biased because the numerator, in contradistinction to the denominator, includes foreign employment). When measured as sales over GDP, the figures are 19,5 and 23,8 per cent respectively (see Schenk 1997). No more recent data for Europe are known, but aggregate concentration in the U.S., after having been rather stable in the early 1990s, has increased again since then. Similarly, although the shares of the very largest firms may not have increased, the relative importance of the larger size classes has. As a result, the size distribution of firms has become more skewed toward larger firms; whereas the top 100 firms have decreased somewhat in average size between 1977 and 1992, the next 900 have increased in average size (Pryor 2001; White 2002).

Also, and as we have seen, merger investments periodically reach enormous proportions – certainly in comparison to other investments. Of course, these two factors are intertwined. Although the specific details are lacking, one can be certain that the lion's share of merger expenditures is to the account of, say the largest 2000 or 3000 firms from the U.S. and the EU. Thus, if their investments turn out well, the economy

8 Notice that X-inefficiency is normally defined as being the excess of actual cost over minimum possible cost in a given situation. Thus, in principle, it could be removed by economising on inputs (especially in the form of managerial expense) or by working harder. I use the term productive efficiency in a broader sense to include excess costs that, in a given situation, cannot be removed but are simply the result of merger-induced diseconomies of scale such as control loss.

will benefit perceptibly. But if they fail to the extent that we have discussed, the economy will suffer perceptibly.

Establishing by how much, however, is quite another matter. As far as I know, only Ravenscraft and Scherer (1987) have tried to estimate the harm done to the (U.S.) economy. Assuming that profitability movements are reflections of changes in operating efficiency relative to industry norms, they studied the efficiency effects for 634 manufacturing acquisitions done in 1968, 1971 and 1974, separating out those acquisitions that were sold off later from those that were retained. Calibrating the results for 1975-1977, they came up with total efficiency losses per annum of between 2,41 and 3,32 bln U.S. dollars, i.e. after having taken into account the gains that were generated by, especially, mergers of equals (see Table 1).

Table 1: Annual Impacts of U.S. Manufacturing Mergers, 1975-1977 (US$ bln)

	Lower bound	**Upper bound**
Loss on retained pooling mergers	-74	-133
Loss on retained purchase mergers	-42	-74
Gain on mergers of equals	+ 0,53	+ 0,53
Loss on sold off acquisitions	-178	-178
Total	-241	-332

Source: Ravenscraft & Scherer 1987

Relating these losses to expenditures on mergers in the years mentioned, amounting to about US$ 57 bln (see Schenk 2002a), gives negative returns on merger investments of between 4 and 6 per cent annually during 1975-1977. Total (cumulative) efficiency losses will have been higher, but it is not possible to say by how much.

Speculating a bit further on this, one can also take the failure estimates as an opening wedge. Recall that studies have found that between 65 and 85 per cent of mergers fail. As the lower estimate has also been frequently found in various management surveys, it is hardly questioned anymore. For the years 1995-1999, this would imply that out of total merger investments of about US$ 9000 bln, between roughly US$ 5500 and 7500 bln would have been invested with either zero or negative returns, or positive returns that were judged to be too small to be called a success (by the respondents in survey research). The last year of the rising part of the wave (i.e. 2000) adds merger expenditures of more than US$ 2000 bln. In turn, this leads to failure estimates of between 7000 and 9250 bln U.S. dollars. Part of this is a real (efficiency) loss; another part is mainly opportunity cost. Unfortunately, the distribution is unknown so that it is near to impossible to estimate which gains might have been generated by alternative deployments of investment funds.

However, applying the same proportions as used above (after having eliminated the gains from mergers of equals as we are now exclusively dealing with failure, leading to 5,2 and 6,8 per cent, respectively), we would get estimates of annual efficiency losses of somewhere between US$ 350 and 600 bln. The fifth merger wave (again including the year 2000) might therefore have implied efficiency losses to the amount of US$ 2100-3600 bln, with the lion's share falling towards the end of this five-year period. Since these losses would be real efficiency losses rather than figures that are based upon perceptions of failure, they would seem quite impressive. For example, they amount to between 2,1 and 3,6 per cent of collective and cumulative GDP of those countries that have acquiring firms present in the merger data base (Appendix, Table A1 plus a totalised GDP for 2000 of US$ 17709 bln).

Losses of this size might be large enough to have recessionary impact, certainly for the leading countries, the United States, Great Britain, and the Netherlands. Obviously, applying proportions that were valid in the 1970s to the 1990s requires some quite heroic assumptions. Especially in view of the inflated stock prices during the latter part of the fifth merger wave, returns on merger investments are likely to have been even worse.

The estimations thus far have referred to real (and opportunity) effects. Can we also infer the macroeconomic impact from the effects that mergers had on stock prices? Moeller *et al.* (2003a) have calculated the shareholder value losses for a sample of 12023 domestic acquisitions within the U.S., spanning 1980-2001, at about US$ 219 bln. There were about 44250 mergers in the U.S. during the fifth merger wave (1995-2000), so that by extrapolation we would find a total loss in shareholder value of approximately US$ 800 bln due to mergers. The effects were calculated, however, using a short event window (three days) so that the true loss of wealth is underestimated significantly. Again, quite heroic assumptions are necessary. We have found in our studies that three-year losses are typically seven times larger than 2-day losses. If it were justified to use this ratio here, the estimate of true wealth losses would amount to roughly US$ 5500. In terms of U.S. GDP, this would be approximately ten per cent.

In a more recent paper Moeller *et al.* (2003b) demonstrate that almost all of these losses appear during 1998-2001, that is, when the fifth merger wave was peaking. From data supplied to me by the authors, it can readily be seen that 3772 mergers lost US$ 240 bln for the acquiring shareholders, with an average loss of US$ 64 mln per merger. When the gains to target shareholders are subtracted, the net effect appears to be a loss of US$ 134 bln. Again by extrapolation, I find that for the approx. 36350 mergers that took place in the U.S. during 1998-2001, US$ 1290 bln was lost. Evidently, when multiplied by seven, the wealth losses when based on the most recent fifth wave mergers appear dramatic, at about 16 per cent of GDP.

It is uncertain, however, what a wealth loss implies in terms of real effects. It is likely, that investors, be they firms, institutional investors, or private investors, will react in some way to such a dramatic change in wealth but whether such reactions are significant enough to encourage a recession, for example, is an open question. However, if reactions to these losses were as severe as they were to the wealth gains that were realised when the stock market was booming, then the answer would be affirmative. Bulmash (2002), for example, estimated that the effect of the wealth gain of US$ 6000 bln over the period 1997-1999 on consumption spending in the U.S. was more than US$ 120 bln in 1998 and 1999. Over 40 per cent of the growth in consumer spending in 1999 was attributable to gains in the stock market in 1997 and 1998. The wealth losses reported above may have had similar real effects. Assuming gain and loss symmetry, the real effect of wealth losses due to mergers on American consumer spending would have been between US$ 110 and 180 bln annually. Generally, however, the regret attached to losses is much higher than the joy attached to gains (Kahneman & Tversky, 1979) so that it is likely that the effect on consumption spending has been much higher. Notice, that in order to reach correct conclusions these losses must be added to the efficiency losses estimated above, to opportunity costs and to retardations in investment spending.

In this respect it should perhaps be recalled that opportunity costs are, in contradistinction to what one might think, important. If funds do not generate wealth, this implies that they do not create economic growth. It could be argued that the billions expended on mergers do not vanish from the economic process. Indeed, it may be so that shareholders at the receiving end instead of creating a consumption bubble, or overindulging themselves in Veblen-type conspicuous consumption (Veblen 1899), will reinvest their newly acquired pecuniary wealth in investment projects that do create economic wealth. If so, then we would merely have to worry about a retardation effect. Still, such an effect may be significant, since a accumulation of retardation effects – and this is exactly what is likely to happen during a merger wave – is what economists call a recession. [9]

In conclusion, it appears that the high incidence of non-wealth creating and wealth-destroying mergers can easily have macroeconomic repercussions of a size that may contribute, or even cause, recessions. According to Mueller (1999), the vigorous pursuit of what he calls 'unprofitable' mergers may be one of the factors that contribute to the decline of nations. When professional managers as well as a whole industry of investment bankers, stock analysts, lawyers 'and even economists' are occupied with transferring assets instead of creating them, when cash flows get used to buy existing plants rather than build new ones, then decline is almost inevitable.

Although Mueller may be stretching it a bit too far, it is evident that his propositions find at least some support in the calculations that we have made, no matter how preliminary and speculative they may be. Noticing that, indeed, all merger waves were followed by years of economic distress and restructuring, it would therefore seem unjustifiable at the least to neglect the importance of the productive and/or dynamic

9 I will not elaborate on another potentially important welfare loss as a result of mergers. This may result from the fact that a significant number of SMEs appear to languish after having become part of a large acquirer (see Chakrabarti *et al.*, 1994). As small and medium sized firms in general are relatively innovative and/or efficient with respect to innovation (see e.g. Acs 1996; Nooteboom & Vossen 1995), one implication may be that some of society's most innovative institutions are simply eliminated from the competitive system as a result of takeover. By having stayed 'alive', these firms might have been able to challenge those firms that are too occupied with merger, but in the event they were not allowed to play this role. For example, in the U.S., SMEs as a group have been found to be slightly less than 2,4 times more innovative than large firms when innovativeness is measured as the number of innovations per employee (Acs & Audretsch 1990). Also, it appears that SMEs are able to more effectively utilise the knowledge spillovers from universities (Acs *et al.,* 1994). In general, there does not appear to be any evidence that increasing returns to R&D expenditures exist in producing innovative output. In fact, with only a few exceptions, diminishing returns are the rule.

losses that result from mergers. Uneconomic mergers pass the triviality test with flying colours.

POLICY IMPLICATIONS

Clearly, in a perfectly competitive economy, firms would not be able to undertake purely strategic mergers. That is, in the product market, firms that invested in higher-return projects would presumably be able to outcompete rivals that merely invested in lower-return projects. In the capital market, investors would presumably prefer firms that realise higher returns over those that do not. And in the market for corporate control, managements of higher-return firms would presumably take over those firms whose managements are apparently not able to realise the full potentials of their firms. The fact that non-wealth creating mergers keep occurring on a large scale is therefore in itself sufficient evidence of the poor operation of these mechanisms. While the takeover threat in particular is frequently regarded as a pre-eminent mechanism to keep firms alert and/or as a mechanism that takes care of replacing inefficient managements by more efficient ones (see e.g. Jensen 1988), it would rather appear that firms' acquisition behaviour implies a perversion of this mechanism.

Policy actions should therefore focus on making these market mechanisms work more effectively and eliminating those forces that could be considered responsible for their defective operation. This would seem to extend to three domains: corporate governance policy, competition policy, and industrial policy.

Corporate governance. Owners of acquiring firms would presumably be less willing to accept the managerial rationales that create merger waves if they only were better informed about what happens after a particular merger or acquisition has been realised. For, a particular firm's record in mergers and acquisitions often remains obscure, as all information on acquisitions normally vanishes into consolidated reports and forms. Thus, Ravenscraft and Scherer (1987: 227) have recommended that acquiring companies should file with the Securities and Exchange Commission (SEC) a report 'detailing all acquisitions made during the prior year, the consideration paid, the book value of the assets acquired, the method of accounting used, a description of each unit sold off during the year, and the loss or gain recorded in connection with each such divestiture'. They also recommend that certain acquisitions should be designated as distinct industry segments for which disaggregated sales, assets and operating income information would have to be disclosed in annual reports. These recommendations can only be supported. Yet, shareholders might easily get caught up in the same minimax-regret games as their agents, especially when they represent large institutional holdings. Therefore, one should not expect quick results from these recommendations. Still, and assuming that monitoring the success of mergers and acquisitions is a necessary element of good business practice and that the gathering of pertinent information should therefore simply be seen as part of normal business practice, requiring that such information be shared with the general public would be a welcome governance innovation.

Competition policy. In a market economy there is a presumption that private agents should be free to pursue their own interests as they see fit up till the point at which this pursuit has (significantly) adverse consequences for economic welfare. It is the purpose of current competition (or antitrust) policies in both the U.S. and the EU to prevent mergers that have, or are likely to have, such consequences. Under certain conditions (mostly relating to market share, as in the U.S., or size of the merger, as in the EU), mergers must at present be reported to competition authorities in order to be investigated and, possibly, challenged. These investigations, however, do not examine whether a particular merger is likely to have adverse welfare consequences as a result of productive and/or dynamic inefficiencies. Rather, the investigations are meant to establish whether a particular merger is likely substantially to lessen competition. It is correct that in the EU several more factors are taken into account, but as in the U.S. the pertinent procedures eventually end up in testing whether a merger will substantially increase market concentration (measured by means of either a concentration ratio or the Herfindahl-Hirschman Index) beyond a certain competitive level and, if so, in estimating whether that can be sustained.[10] The underlying assumption is that growing beyond a certain threshold may deliver market power, or market dominance, which is consistently defined as the ability to maintain prices above competitive levels profitably, or above long-run average costs, for a significant period of time (see, for example, FTC 1997). Such market power is expected to result in a transfer of wealth from buyers to sellers or a misallocation of resources. Therefore, what is being ultimately tested is whether a merger is likely to harm allocative efficiency.

Apart from the fact that this is not an easy task (some would say: an impossible task; see for example, Dewey, 1996) as a result of both conceptual and measurement problems – related to delineating the relevant product and geographic market as well as to estimating demand substitutability, the likelihood of new entry, and the power of potential competition – these procedures overlook the possibility that mergers may be motivated neither by the prospect of monopoly profits nor by the prospect of productive or dynamic efficiency gains. The underlying presumption is that mergers that are not motivated by the prospect of financial gains will not occur or, if they do, will only be short-lived. As we have seen, this presumption cannot be sustained.

As current merger control policies are focused on only part, and probably the minor part, of the potential problems that mergers may create for economic welfare, they should be qualified as half-hearted. It therefore follows that an adequate form of merger control should include what I call a 'Full Efficiency Test' (FET), i.e. a procedure in which a proposed merger is not just tested for allocative effects but for productive and dynamic effects as well.

Merger candidates could be required to join an efficiency protocol or prospectus with their request for allowance, i.e. a memorandum that demonstrates whether and

10 The HHI is calculated by adding up the squares of the individual market shares of all participants in a particular market thus reflecting the distribution of market shares whereas the concentration ratio only reflects the shares of the top-*n* (usually four) firms. Since the HHI gives proportionately greater weight to the largest firms, it is not necessary to know the market shares of all participants.

how productive and dynamic efficiencies will be realised. As it is in the merger candidates' interest to come up with a plausible efficiency protocol, it will be evident that the burden of proof in productive and dynamic efficiency cases will rest on them. Small mergers, i.e. mergers in which both (or all) parties are small or medium-sized, should be excluded from assessment for two reasons. First, mergers among SMEs are less likely to originate from the non-wealth creating strategies that are played in small number games. Secondly, SMEs are more likely to operate below Minimal Optimal Scale so that there is at least some likelihood of realising economies of scale. Notice that focusing on all mergers in which a large firm is implicated would also allow an assessment of piecemeal creations of market dominance, or as it is formulated in the U.S., the creation of market dominance in its incipiency.

Thus, mergers that are unlikely to create productive and/or dynamic efficiency would be blocked while mergers that are likely to have positive efficiency effects would be allowed if no negative allocative efficiency effects are to be expected. Two practical points deserve special attention, however. First, at least during the initial years of an FET regime, the numbers of mergers that would have to be investigated may be large, especially since takeovers of SMEs would need assessment, too. A pragmatic solution, to be adapted as the FET regime becomes more established, would be to limit screening to only those mergers that are proposed by the very largest firms from the U.S. and the EU respectively. For example, Dewey (1996), who has made similar suggestions, proposes to limit control to those mergers that are proposed by the 500 largest U.S. industrial firms or so. These firms should not be allowed to grow by merger 'unless it can be shown that the merger is likely to confer some non-negligible consumer benefit through cost reduction, product improvement, increased research outlays or more rapid innovation' (Dewey 1996: 397).[11] Mueller (1997), while keeping up a market share criterion, has proposed to disallow mergers that lead to a combined market share of more than 25 per cent in any one market, or to total sales in excess of US$ 600 mln, *unless* it can be demonstrated that a particular merger is likely to yield substantial efficiency gains in excess of its anticompetitive effects. Dewey's proposals imply the more radical departure from established practice but a substantial simplification of it as well, as there is no need whatsoever to assess any longer a merger's impact on competition. An added advantage would be that there is no need either to establish whether a merger is horizontal, vertical or conglomerate. While Mueller's proposals still require estimating the allocative efficiency effects of a merger, though apparently only in cases where firms can come up with a plausible efficiency prospectus, Dewey's proposals would perhaps fit in best with the present article's gist. The present EU thresholds may be adequate as far as large mergers are concerned, while the acquisitions of SMEs by large firms could be investigated at the level of individual member states.[12] Besides, and given the empirical evidence on mergers, it may be expected that

11 In this respect, also see Brenner (1990) who stresses the importance of a test for the effects of a merger on innovation performance.

12 At present, the EU Merger Control Regulation applies to mergers in which the parties when taken together have worldwide sales in excess of 5 bln euro while at least two of them have Community-sales in excess of 250 mln euro, unless all parties have more than two-thirds of their EU-sales within one and

the number of mergers that will have to be vetted will eventually be reduced dramatically once firms are to come up with a plausible efficiency protocol.

Secondly, one may rightfully ask whether the present investigating skills of the merger authorities would allow conducting a sufficiently sophisticated FET. As Scherer (1997) has noted, the detailed analysis of plant-specific and product-specific scale economies, and the technological and organisational determinants of productivity, does not belong to the regular bag of tools of an antitrust economist. Applying an FET would, indeed, require staff with solid management consultancy experience or training. Such skills, according to Scherer, would be expensive to obtain. While Scherer's doubts may be justified, applying an FET would be less demanding if the burden of proof is, as has been suggested here, on the shoulders of those firms that wish to undertake a merger or acquisition.

Also notice that the transparency of merger controls would be increased substantially by using an FET, which should be welcomed both by the firms involved and by those wishing to investigate the decisions taken by the authorities. The chances for opportunistic settlements and regulatory capture would be reduced significantly. Finally, a rather important advantage of the type of merger control proposed here would be that it reduces the complexities of gearing international merger policies to each other. Apart from the jurisdictional questions involved, there is presently much confusion over the interpretations of different merger control procedures and institutional arrangements (see e.g. Waverman *et al.*, 1997). The steadily increasing number of international mergers and acquisitions implies that firms will increasingly have to report their mergers to different national authorities. Moreover, given the internationalisation of the world economy, it becomes increasingly possible that domestic mergers will have foreign repercussions. Indeed, the recent takeover of McDonnell Douglas by Boeing became the subject of cross-Atlantic confusion as the European Commission decided, for good reasons, to leave its mark on the finalisation of the deal. The transparency of the pertinent discussions would have benefited substantially from an assessment that included an FET.

Industrial policy. More would be needed, though, to address the problem in full. Governments have historically displayed a persistent love affair with mergers and corporate bigness so that the introduction of an FET in merger control may well meet up with unjustified but vested instincts and may eventually be confronted with lax enforcement. As is evidenced by consolidation programmes in the car industry, the

---

the same member state. In the latter case, the merger would be subject to national merger control. In the course of 1998, a revised scheme became effective which adds to the previous conditions that mergers should be reported to the Commission if parties have combined worldwide sales in excess of 2,5 bln euro, as well as sales in excess of 100 mln euro in each of at least three member states, while at least two of them have aggregate sales within the EU of at least 100 mln euro each, provided that at least two of the parties have sales of at least 25 mln euro in the three member states that were meant above. The new scheme has become this cumbersome as a result of negotiations between those member states (and the Commission) that preferred lowering the thresholds while others appeared quite satisfied with the 1989-regulation.

steel industry, the aircraft industry, the transport industry (railways; airlines), electricity generation and distribution, and the telecommunications industry, merger predilections on the side of government have survived the ages, too.

For example, the Dutch government was instrumental in the takeover of DAF Trucks by America's Paccar in late 1996, and attempted – though in vain – to consolidate all four electricity generators into one big firm in 1998. In 1996, it tried rather desperately to sell Fokker Aircraft to Korea's Samsung, even after it had become expressly clear that the earlier strategy of consolidating Fokker into Daimler-Benz had failed dramatically and the German conglomerate wanted to get rid of Fokker again. All these mergers had at best dubious effects on productive and dynamic efficiency.

Consequently, rather than inducing and supporting mergers and acquisitions, industrial policies, if anything, should advocate demergers and management buy-outs as socially beneficial corporate strategies (Thompson *et al.,* 1993; Schenk *et al.,* 1997).

Secondly, governments should support the independent survival of those firms that are potentially capable of challenging the apparent *modus vivendi* of corporate capitalism, viz. small and medium sized enterprises. Such support should contribute to strengthening these firms' negotiating position vis-à-vis large acquirers. Many SMEs now succumb to acquisition proposals because these seem to offer better facilities for growth, capital in particular, than elsewhere obtainable. It is well known that SMEs still face great difficulties in finding sufficient amounts of growth capital, especially equity, even with western economies running at full speed (Hughes & Storey 1995). Increasing concentration in the financial services industry, especially acute during the 1980s and 1990s, has reinforced the orientation of banks toward the wholesale market to the detriment of the retail market (Schenk 2000a). SMEs are likely to be presented with the bill of obviously merger-related diseconomies in the banking industry. Moreover, banks appear to be quite reluctant to provide funds for innovative but risky firms if these firms cannot provide hard collateral.

CONCLUSIONS

According to Lazear (2000: 99), maximisation, equilibrium, and efficiency lift economics to the status of a 'premier social science'. Perhaps it is for fear of losing this status that for decades the profession has fought vehemently against alternative interpretations. Yet, there is no getting away from the fact that Lazear-type economics is not capable of explaining one of the most captivating and quantitatively important phenomena of our modern economy: waves of uneconomic mergers. In this contribution I have tried to find a solution to the merger paradox by adopting the tradition that the Utrecht School of Economics and its Tjalling C. Koopmans Research Institute wish to further: applying methodologies and findings from a whole array of scientific endeavours, among them game theory, organisation theory, and decision theory, while continually invoking the traditions of institutional economics (à la Hodgson 1998) and evolutionary economics (à la Nelson & Winter 2002).

I have concluded, that uneconomic mergers, thus waves of restructuring, are rooted in a kind of behaviour that I have called minimax-regret behaviour. When firms, i.e.

their decision makers, attach more regret to having overlooked a successful action of one of their competitors – either in the product market or in the capital market – than to having made a mistake when this mistake has also been made by these competitors, then they will most likely imitate a first mover when this first mover, for whatever reason, undertakes a major, i.e. immediately observable, merger. The more imitative actions are taken, the more remaining firms will feel compelled to imitate as well, if only because of defensive reasons. I refer to such non-economically motivated mergers as 'purely strategic mergers'. These mergers do not only create the typical wave pattern, but have meanwhile become so voluminous that their effects on the economy are likely to be hazardous.

Since the mechanics of the merger game do not allow single firms to withdraw, a solution to the problem may lie in restructuring current merger control procedures. In this respect, I have concluded that the commonly shared principles of competition policy suggest the adoption of a Full Efficiency Test.

Almost fifty years ago, Tjalling Koopmans asked why one would prefer a theory that conflicts with the 'apparent immediate determinant(s) of business behavior' if in fact it is possible to build a theory directly upon what appear to be the actual determinants of business behaviour (1957: 140). In this contribution, I hope to have shown that it is high time we followed our patron's recommendation in an area that is of utmost importance for the welfare of modern economies.

REFERENCES

Acs, Zoltan J. (1996). Small Firms and Economic Growth. In Admiraal (Ed.), pp. 1-62.

Acs, Zoltan J. & Audretsch, David B. (1990) *Innovation and Small Firms*. Cambridge: MIT Press.

Acs, Zoltan J., Audretsch, David B. & Feldman M.P. (1994). R&D Spillovers and Recipient Firm Size, *Review of Economics and Statistics* 76 (2): 336-340.

Admiraal, Piet Hein (Ed.) (1996). *Small Business in the Modern Economy*. Oxford: Blackwell.

Augier M., Kreiner K. & March J.G. (2000). Introduction: Some Roots and Branches of Organizational Economics, *Industrial and Corporate Change* 9 (4): 555-565.

Banerjee A.V. (1992). A Simple Model of Herd Behavior, *Quarterly Journal of Economics* CVII (3): 797-817.

Bartel, Jan-Cees, Frederikslust, Ruud van & Schenk, Hans (Eds.) (2002). *Mergers and Acquisitions: Fundamental Aspects* (in Dutch). Amsterdam: Elsevier

Berger A.N. & Humphrey D.B. (1992). Megamergers in banking and the use of cost efficiency as an antitrust defence, *Antitrust Bulletin* 37 (Fall): 541-600.

Berle A.A. & Means G.C. (1932). *The Modern Corporation and Private Property*, rev. ed. 1968. New York: Harcourt, Brace, Jovanovich.

Bikhchandani S., Hirshleifer D. & Welch I. (1992). A Theory of Fads, Fashions, Custom, and Cultural Change as Informational Cascades, *Journal of Political Economy* 100 (5): 992-1026.

Bishop, Matthew & Kay, John (Eds.) (1993). *European Mergers and Merger Policy*. Oxford: Oxford University Press.

Borg J.R., Borg M.O. & Leeth J.D. (1989). The Success of Mergers in the 1920s. A Stock Market Appraisal of the Second Merger Wave, *International Journal of Industrial Organization* 7 (1): 117-131.

Brenner, Reuven (1990). Innovations and Anti-trust. In: Dankbaar, Groenewegen & Schenk (Eds.), 235-257.

Brenner R. (2002). *The Boom and the Bubble. The US and the World Economy*. London/New York: Verso

Bühner R. (1991). The success of mergers in Germany, *International Journal of Industrial Organization* 9 (4): 513-453.

Bulmash S.B. (2002). A new paradigm: the wealth effect of the stock market on consumption, in a context of interacting bio-systems, *Journal of Socio-Economics* 31: 75-100.

Carow K., Heron R. & Saxton T. (2004). Do Early Birds Get The Returns? An Empirical Investigation Of Early-mover Advantages In Acquisitions, *Strategic Management Journal* 25: 563-585.

Chakrabarti A., Hauschildt J. & Süverkrüp C. (1994). Does it pay to acquire technological firms?, *R&D Management* 24 (1): 47-56.

Cyert R.M. & March J.G. (1963). *A Behavioral Theory of the Firm*, 2nd ed. 1992. Cambridge, MA: Blackwell.

Dankbaar, Ben, Groenewegen, John & Schenk, Hans (Eds.) (1990). *Perspectives in Industrial Organization*, Studies in Industrial Organization, vol. 13. Dordrecht/Boston/London: Kluwer Academic Publishers.

Dewey D. (1996). Merger Policy Greatly Simplified: Building on Keyes, *Review of Industrial Organization* 11: 395-400.

Dewing A.S. (1921). A Statistical Test of the Success of Consolidations, *Quarterly Journal of Economics* 36: 84-101.

Dickerson A.P., Gibson H.D. & Tsakalotos E. (1997). The Impact of Acquisitions on Company Performance: Evidence From a Large Panel of UK Firms, *Oxford Economic Papers* 49: 344-361.

Dickerson A.P., Gibson H.D. & Tsakalotos E. (2003). Is attack the best form of defence? A competing risk analysis of acquisition activity in the UK, *Cambridge Journal of Economics* 27: 337-357

Dietrich, Michael & Schenk, Hans (1995). Co-Ordination Benefits, Lock-In, and Strategy Bias, *Management Report* 220, Rotterdam: Rotterdam School of Management, Erasmus University Rotterdam.

DiMaggio P.J. & Powell W.W. (1983). The Iron Cage Revisited: Institutional Isomorphism and Collective Rationality in Organizational Fields, *American Sociological Review* 48: 147-160.

Dosi, Giovanni & Marengo L. (1992). Towards a Theory of Organizational Competence, *Unpublished Paper*.

Elsner, Wolfram & Groenewegen, John (Eds.) (2000). *Industrial Policies After 2000*, Recent Economic Thought Series. Boston/Dordrecht/London: Kluwer Academic.

FTC, Federal Trade Commission (1997). *1992 Horizontal Merger Guidelines [With April 8, 1997, Revisions to Section 4 on Efficiencies]*, Washington: Federal Trade Commission (ftc.gov/bc/docs/horizmer.htm).

Greer D.F. (1986). Acquiring in order to avoid acquisition, *Antitrust Bulletin* Spring: 155-186.

Gugler K., Mueller, Dennis C., Yurtoglu B.B. & Zulehner C. (2003). The effects of mergers: an international comparison, *International Journal of Industrial Organization* 21: 625-653.

Haspeslagh, Philippe C. & Jemison D.B. (1991). *Managing Acquisitions. Creating Value Through Corporate Renewal*. New York: Free Press.

Hayward M.L.A. & Hambrick D.C. (1997). Explaining the Premiums Paid for Large Acquisitions: Evidence of CEO Hubris, *Administrative Science Quarterly* 42: 103-127Hitt M.A., Hoskisson R.E., Ireland R.D. & Harrison J.S. (1991). Effects of Acquisitions on R&D Inputs and Outputs, *Academy of Management Journal* 34 (3): 693-706.

Hodgson, Geoffrey M. (1998). The Approach of Institutional Economics, *Journal of Economic Literature* XXXVI: 166-192

Hughes, Alan (1993). Mergers and Economic Performance in the UK: A Survey of the Empirical Evidence 1950-1990. In Bishop & Kay (Eds.), 9-95.

Hughes, Alan & Storey D.J. (Eds.) (1995). *Finance and the Small Firm*, London: Routledge.

Jensen M.C. (1988). Takeovers: Their Causes and Consequences, *Journal of Economic Perspectives* 2 (1): 21-48.

Kahneman D. & Tversky A. (1979). Prospect Theory: An Analysis of Decision Making Under Risk, *Econometrica* 47 (2): 263-291.

Karier T. (1993). *Beyond Competition. The Economics of Mergers and Monopoly Power*. Armonk: M.E. Sharpe.

Kay N. (2000). Searching for the Firm: The Role of Decision in the Economics of Organizations, *Industrial and Corporate Change* 9 (4): 683-707.

Keynes J.M. (1936). *The General Theory of Employment, Interest, and Money*. London: Macmillan.

Koopmans, Tjalling C. (1957). *Three Essays On The State Of Economic Science*. New York: McGraw-Hill.

Lazear E.P. (2000). Economic Imperialism, *Quarterly Journal of Economics* 115: 99-146.

Leibenstein H. (1966). Allocative Efficiency versus X-Efficiency, *American Economic Review* 56: 392-415.

Loomes G. & Sugden R. (1982). Regret Theory: An Alternative Theory of Rational Choice Under Uncertainty, *Economic Journal* 92: 805-24.

Malmendier U. & Tate G. (2003). Who Makes Acquisitions? CEO Overconfidence and the Market?s Reaction. *Mimeo* Stanford University, Graduate School of Business (Draft).

March J.G. (1994). *A Primer on Decision Making: How Decisions Happen*. New York: Free Press.

Milgrom P & Roberts J. (1992). *Economics, Organization and Management*. Englewood Cliffs, NJ: Prentice-Hall.

Moeller S.B., Schlingemann F.P. & Stulz R.M. (2003a). Do Shareholders of Acquiring Firms Gain From Acquisitions?, *Working Paper* 9523, NBER

Moeller S.B., Schlingemann F.P. & Stulz R.M. (2003b). Wealth Destruction on a Massive Scale? A Study of Acquiring-Firm Returns in the Recent Merger Wave, *Working Paper* 10200, NBER

Mueller, Dennis C. (1986). *Profits in the Long Run*. Cambridge/New York: Cambridge University Press.

Mueller, Dennis C. (1997). Merger Policy in the United States: A Reconsideration, *Review of Industrial Organization* 12: 655-685

Mueller, Dennis C. (1999). On the Economic Decline of Nations. In Mueller, Haid & Weigand (Eds.) (pp. 351-381).

Mueller, Dennis C. (2003). The finance literature on mergers: a critical survey. In Waterson (Ed.) (pp. 161-205).

Mueller, Dennis C., Haid A. & Weigand J. (Eds.) (1999). *Competition, Efficiency and Welfare. Essays in Honor of Manfred Neumann*. Boston etc.: Kluwer Academic.

Nelson R.R. & Winter S.G. (2002). Evolutionary Theorizing in Economics, *Journal of Economic Perspectives* 16 (2): 23-46.

Nooteboom, Bart & Vossen R.W. (1995). Firm Size and Efficiency in R&D Spending. In Van Witteloostuijn, (Ed.) (pp.69-86).

North D.C. (1990). *Institutions, Institutional Change and Economic Performance*. Cambridge MA: Harvard University Press.

Pryor F.L. (2001). Dimensions of the Worldwide Merger Boom, *Journal of Economic Issues* XXXV (4): 825-840.

Raj M. & Forsyth M. (2003). Hubris Amongst U.K. Bidders and Losses to Shareholders, *International Journal of Business* 8: 1-16.

Ravenscraft D.J. & Scherer, F. Michael (1987). *Mergers, Sell-offs, and Economic Efficiency*. Washington, D.C.: Brookings Institution.

Rhoades S.A. (1994). A Summary of Merger Performance Studies in Banking, 1980-1993, and an Assessment of the 'Operating Performance' and 'Event Study' Methodologies, *Staff Study* 167. Washington, DC: Board of Governors of the Federal Reserve System.

Rhoades S.A. (1998). The efficiency effects of bank mergers: An overview of case studies of nine mergers, *Journal of Banking and Finance* 22: 273-291.

Roll R. (1986). The Hubris Hypothesis of Corporate Takeovers, *Journal of Business* 59 (2): 197-216.

Rothschild K.W. (2002). The absence of power in contemporary economic theory, *Journal of Socio-Economics* 31: 433-442.

Savage L.J. (1951). The Theory of Statistical Decision, *Journal of the American Statistical Association* 46: 55-67.

Scharfstein D.S. & Stein, J.C. (1990). Herd Behavior and Investment, *American Economic Review* 80 (3): 465-479.

Schelling T. (1960). *The Strategy of Conflict*. Cambridge Mass: Harvard University Press.

Schenk, Hans (1997). Mergers, Efficient Choice, and International Competitiveness, *Mimeo* GRASP/Erasmus University Rotterdam.

Schenk, Hans (2000a). The performance of banking mergers: Propositions and policy implications, *Background Report, The impact of mergers and acquisitions in Finance* (pp. 24-43). Geneva: UNI-Europa.

Schenk, Hans (2000b). Policy Implications of Purely Strategic Mergers. In Elsner & Groenewegen (Eds.) (pp. 199-234).

Schenk, Hans (2001). The Repositioning of Firms (in Dutch). In Hans Schenk (Ed.). *The Repositioning of Firms. Pre-Advises to the Royal Dutch Economics Society 2001* (in Dutch) (pp. I-XVII). Utrecht: Lemma.

Schenk, Hans (2002a). Mergers: incidence and trends – an international overview (in Dutch). In Bartel, Van Frederikslust & Schenk (Eds.) (pp. 37-61).

Schenk, Hans (2002b). Economics and strategy of the merger paradox (in Dutch). In Bartel, Van Frederikslust & Schenk (Eds.) (pp. 62-133).

Schenk, Hans, with Warmenhoven, Jean-Paul, Van Velzen, Marco & Van Riel, Cees (1997). The Demise of the Conglomerate Firm (in Dutch), *Economisch Statistische Berichten* 82 (4122): 736-740.

Scherer, F. Michael (1984). *Innovation and Growth: Schumpeterian Perspectives*. Cambridge, Mass.: MIT Press.

Scherer, F. Michael (1997). Comment on 'Merger Policy in the United States', *Review of Industrial Organization* 12: 687-691.

Scherer, F. Michael & Ross D. (1990). *Industrial Market Structure and Economic Performance*. Boston: Houghton Mifflin.

Schmidt D.R. & Fowler K.L. (1990). Post-Acquisition Financial Performance and Executive Compensation, *Strategic Management Journal* 11 (7): 559-569.

Simon J.L., Mokhtari M. & Simon D.H. (1996). Are Mergers Beneficial or Detrimental? Evidence from Advertising Agencies, *International Journal of the Economics of Business* 3 (1): 69-82.

Thompson S., Wright, Mike & Robbie K. (1993). Buy-Outs, Divestment, and Leverage: Restructuring Transactions and Corporate Governance, *Oxford Review of Economic Policy* 8 (3): 58-69.

Tichy, Günther (2001). What Do We Know about Success and Failure of Mergers?, *Journal of Industry, Competition and Trade* 1: 347-394

Van Witteloostuijn, Arjen (Ed.) (1995). *Market Evolution. Competition and Cooperation*, Studies in Industrial Organization 20, Dordrecht/Boston/London: Kluwer Academic Publishers.

Veblen T.B. (1899). *The Theory of the Leisure Class: An Economic Study of Institutions*. New York: Macmillan.

Waterson, Michael (Ed.) (2003). *Competition, Monopoly and Corporate Governance. Essays in Honour of Keith Cowling*. Cheltenham: Edward Elgar.

Waverman, Leonard, Comanor, William S. & Goto A. (Eds.) (1997). *Competition Policy in the Global Economy. Modalities for cooperation*, London/New York: Routledge.

White L.J. (2002). Trends in Aggregate Concentration in the United States, *Journal of Economic Perspectives* 16 (4): 137-160.

Wright P., Mukherji A. & Kroll M.J. (2001). A re-examination of agency theory assumptions: extensions and extrapolations, *Journal of Socio-Economics* 30: 413-429.

APPENDIX

Table A1: Gross Domestic Product (bln US$, current exchange rates)

Country acronym	1995	1996	1997	1998	1999	Totaal
B	226	229	237	243	249	1184
CAN	555	563	588	607	635	2948
CH	245	245	249	255	259	1253
D	1992	2008	2036	2079	2112	10227
DK	159	163	168	172	175	837
F	1310	1325	1350	1392	1432	6809
GB	1296	1330	1376	1412	1443	6857
I	1106	1118	1138	1155	1171	5688
LUX	15	16	17	18	19	85
N	135	142	149	152	153	731
NL	343	353	367	380	394	1837
S	217	219	224	232	241	1133
SU	106	111	118	124	129	588
USA	7889	8173	8540	8916	9237	42755
Total	15594	15995	16557	17137	17649	82932

Source: 1995-1998 calculated, and 1999 compiled from OECD (2001) *Historical Statistics 1970-1999*, Paris

Table A2: Gross Fixed Capital Formation (bln US$, current exchange rates)

Country acronym	1995	1996	1997	1998	1999	Total
B	45	45	48	51	53	242
CAN	91	96	111	114	126	538
CH	49	48	49	51	52	249
D	403	400	424	437	451	2115
DK	28	29	32	34	34	157
F	239	239	239	254	272	1243
GB	194	204	219	241	256	1114
I	195	202	204	213	222	1036
LUX	3	3	3	3	4	16
N	27	30	34	36	34	161
NL	70	75	79	83	88	395
S	34	35	35	38	41	183
SU	18	19	21	23	24	105
USA	1289	1397	1520	1683	1836	7725
Total	2685	2822	3018	3261	3493	15279

Source: 1995-1998 calculated, and 1999 compiled from OECD (2001) *Historical Statistics 1970-1999*, Paris

Table A3: Business Expenditure on Research and Development (Bln US$ current PPP)

Country acronym	1995	1996	1997	1998	1999	Total
B	27	29	31	33	36	156
CAN	68	68	74	83	84	377
CH	Na	3,4	Na	Na	Na	Na
D	26,2	26,4	26,2	29,5	33,2	141,5
DK	1,3	1,4	1,6	1,8	1,9	8
F	16,9	17,1	16,9	17,3	18,5	86,7
GB	14,2	14,6	14,9	15,8	17,3	76,8
I	6,2	6,5	6,3	6,6	7,3	32,9
N	1	Na	1,1	Na	1,2	Na
NL	3,4	3,6	4	4,1	4,7	19,8
S	4,5	Na	5,1	Na	5,8	Na
SU	14	17	19	22	26	98
USA	1321	1447	1575	1692	1828	7863
Total	**2167**	**2291**	**246**	**2581**	**2873**	**1237,2***

* row total only

Source: compiled from OECD (2001) *Main Science and Technology Indicators 2001/2*, Paris

R.J.M. ALESSIE

DOES SOCIAL SECURITY CROWD OUT PRIVATE SAVINGS?

1. INTRODUCTION

The Netherlands' population is rapidly ageing. Between 2000 and 2050 the old-age dependency ratio – i.e. the number of persons aged 65 or over relative to the working population – will increase from 20 per cent to 40 per cent. It is often claimed that due to population ageing the current Dutch pension and health care systems will be unsustainable in the near future. In order to understand this claim, one should know something more about the Dutch pension system. The pension system consists of three tiers. The first tier is Social Security (SS): everyone in the Netherlands is covered by a flat rate general old age pension (SS) starting at the age of 65.[1] The second tier of the pension system consists of funded occupational pension plans. Finally, some retired people (e.g. the ex-self-employed) have privately bought pension insurance in the past (this is the third tier of the pension system). As a result, they receive an annuity income from this insurance policy. The SS benefits are financed on the basis of pay-as-you-go and only those under 65 years of age pay SS taxes. Due to the ageing of the population, the SS tax will increase considerably if the government does not take any measures.

The Netherlands is better placed than most other OECD countries to meet these pressures as it has a large, mandatory, occupational pension system (the second tier).

Nonetheless, the ageing of the population still poses serious problems. Therefore, the government has made the following proposals to restructure the pension system: firstly, the tax preferred nature of occupational early retirement schemes is to be abolished. Secondly, the government is considering increasing the statutory retirement age from 65 to 67. People have advised the government to announce such a policy measure at an early stage so that current workers can prepare for this by investing more in either human or financial capital (see e.g., Don ,1996; and Bovenberg and Meijdam, 1999). Finally another policy measure could be a decrease in the SS benefit e.g. by changing the indexation rules.

1 The level of the SS benefits is independent of other income but does depend on household composition. In principle, every individual older than 65 receives a SS benefit equal to 50% of the minimum wage. This rule implies that a couple of which both head and spouse are older than 65, receives a SS benefit equal to the minimum wage.

P. de Gijsel and H. Schenk (eds.), Multidisciplinary Economics, 367–380.

In my inaugural speech I will address the following questions: as a reaction to the policy measures described above, will consumers change their economic behaviour? Will they save more and, if so, how much more? In order to answer these questions, I will first present a simple economic model. This model can be used to predict the effects of changes in SS rules on household wealth. Subsequently, I will present the results of an empirical analysis in which I measure the level of displacement between Social Security and household wealth. I am able to measure this displacement effect by using a panel data set covering the period 1987-2001 and by considering the effect of the introduction of the SS law and the changes therein over the years.

2. THE LIFE CYCLE HYPOTHESIS

I use the Life Cycle Hypothesis[2] developed by Franco Modigliani, who died recently, as the theoretical framework of my empirical analysis. In this framework it is assumed that the consumer is rational and forward looking. To be more precise, the LCH says that the individual arranges current and future consumption in such a way that he/she maximises an expected intertemporally additive lifetime utility function subject to a lifetime budget constraint using the information available to him as efficiently as possible. Like in most other studies, I assume that the individual does not have perfect foresight, but lives in a risky environment. We need to make some further assumptions about how consumers deal with this uncertainty in order to arrive at a testable model. These extra assumptions concern the preference structure and the formation of expectations. I make the standard assumptions that the expected lifetime utility function is quadratic and that the agents hold rational expectations. Finally, I assume that the retirement date is a parameter, which cannot be manipulated by the household. Obviously, this last assumption is not realistic and I will discuss the relaxation of this assumption later on.

Figures 1a and 1b summarise the prediction of the simple version of the life cycle model.[3] On the horizontal axis, the variable 'age' is displayed.[4] In figure 1a, I assume that the individual starts working at the age of 22 and dies at the age of 80. Income is an increasing function of age until the statutory retirement age (65). In figure 1a, I assume that the consumer does not receive any income like SS after the age of 65. The model predicts that consumption is constant over the life cycle and equal to 'permanent income'; see the flat line in figure 1a. In other words, agents accumulate wealth to smooth consumption over the life cycle. Permanent income is a function of lifetime income, this is the discounted sum of current and future income which the agent expects to receive. The model also implies a relationship between wealth and age: during the pre-retirement phase agents accumulate wealth in order to smooth consumption over the life cycle, see figure 1b.

2 For a thorough description of the LCH, see Browning & Lusardi (1996).
3 Browning & Lusardi (1996) call the model illustrated above, the certainty equivalent model.
4 In these figures, I assume (without loss of generality) that the consumers live in an environment of complete certainty and that the rate of time preference is equal to the real interest rate.

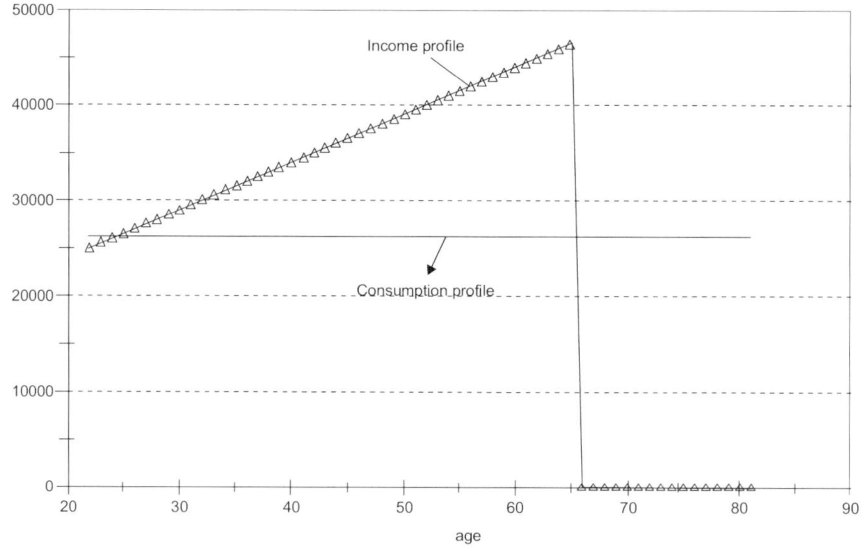

Figure 1a. The Life cycle Hypothesis (LCH).

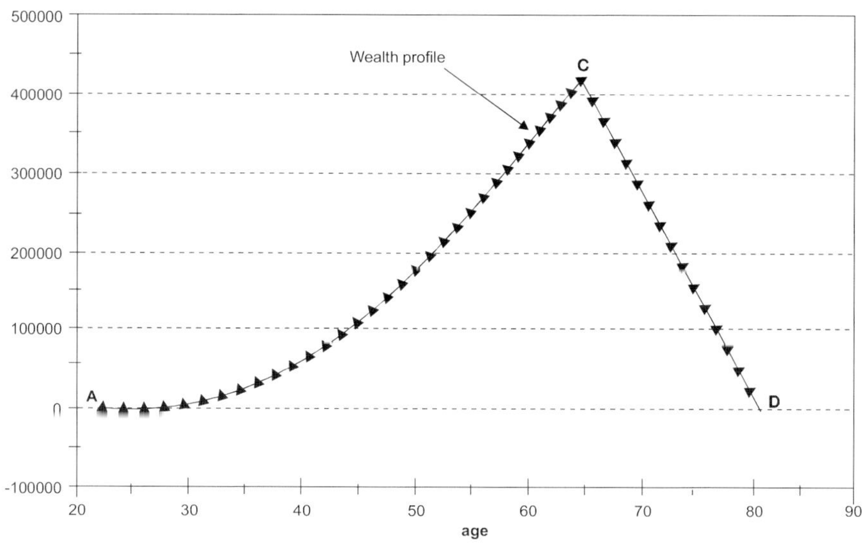

Figure 1b. The life cycle model: the age wealth profile.

In a paper with Arie Kapteyn and Annamaria Lusardi I have investigated in detail the effect of the introduction and changes in SS on consumption and wealth accumulation in the framework of the LCH (see Kapteyn et al. (2004)). In the Netherlands, the SS benefit system was instituted in 1957 and our data set includes households who were in the labour market well before the introduction of the system.[5] In figure 2a, I only sketch the main argument. I consider the effect of the introduction of SS only and ignore the changes in SS benefits, which have been effected after 1957. Obviously, in the empirical application I take the changes in SS into account (see Kapteyn et al. for more details concerning the empirical implementation). The key assumption is that the introduction of SS leads to a permanent and unanticipated increase in income at retirement. We consider two cases; in the first one, pre-retirement income is unchanged and in the second, pre-retirement income falls because a payroll tax is levied to finance SS. We start by considering the case where pre-retirement income is unchanged. In figure 2a I consider 3 different individuals. The first individual, who represents the so-called old generation, lived in a time without SS. In figure 2b the flat line displays the consumption profile of this person. The second individual was born in 1907 and was 50 years old when the SS law was introduced. The third person was 35 years old. I assume that these persons have the same pre-retirement income and their other characteristics (education etc.) also do not differ. By keeping these other characteristics constant, I am able to identify the pure effect of the introduction of SS on saving behaviour.

The individuals born in 1907 and 1922 heard in 1957 that after the age of 65 they would receive extra income, namely a flat rate SS benefit, see figure 2a. Due to the introduction of SS, lifetime income has increased for these generations. This, in turn, implies that consumption of the person born in 1907 increased from the age of 50 onwards. Consumption of the person born in 1922 also increased from the age of 35 onwards but not by as much as for the middle aged individual, since the increase in lifetime resources had to be spread out over a longer remaining lifetime.

Obviously, these shifts in consumption affect saving behaviour. Since pre-retirement non-capital income is not affected by the introduction of SS, pre-retirement saving goes down by the same amount consumption goes up. Thus, pre-retirement wealth decreases by an amount, which is equal to the compounded sum of past and current changes in permanent income (or consumption). The implied wealth profiles are given in Figure 2b. In comparison with the old cohort, the effect of SS on wealth for the middle-aged cohort at different ages is given by the vertical difference between the curve ACD and the curve AFGD. This effect can be summarised in a substitution variable DSS_t, see figure 3. Similarly, in figure 2b the vertical difference between ACD and ABED represents the effect of the introduction of SS on the wealth accumulation of the youngest cohort. In Kapteyn et al. (2004), we show that the substitution variable can be written as a function of the SS benefit levels, the interest rate, the retirement age, and the age of death.

5 The General Old Pension Act (AOW) of 1957 introduced Social Security to the entire Dutch population. Some pension provisions were present from 1947 onwards, but they were restricted to some small groups of the population, mainly the very poor and civil servants. See, also, van Ark, de Haan & de Jong (1996).

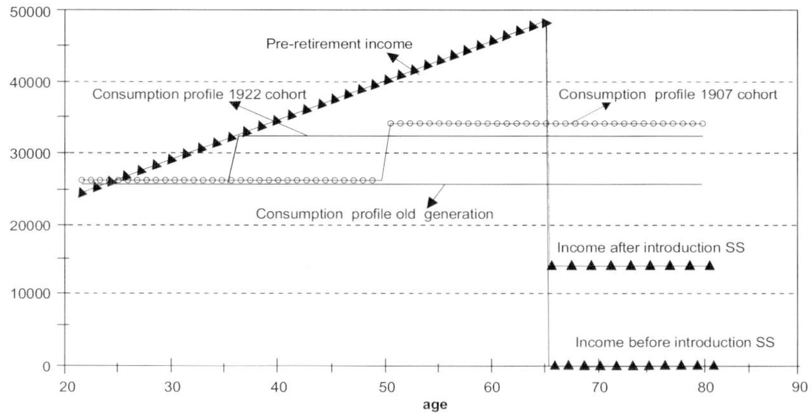

Figure 2a. The effect of the introduction of SS introduction on consumption.

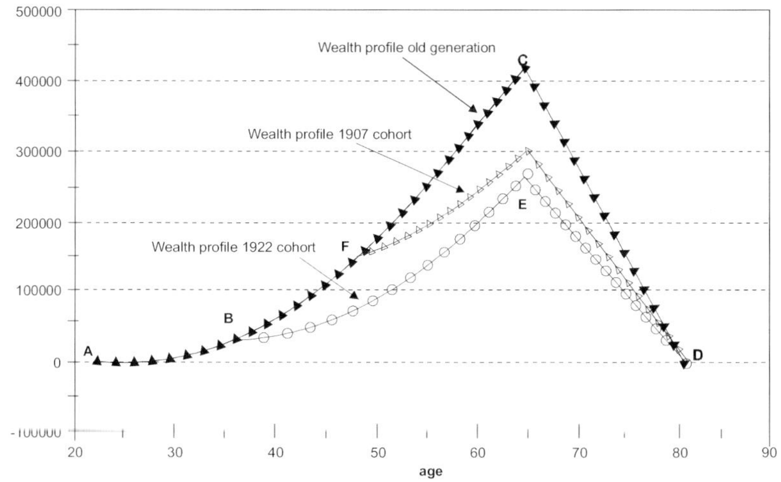

Figure 2b. The effect of the introduction of SS on wealth.

We next consider the case where pre retirement income falls because SS is financed through a payroll tax. The effects on wealth accumulation are qualitatively the same. This follows directly from the certainty equivalent setup. Given the age of retirement, savings during the working life are simply a function of the difference in income between retirement and the working life. An increase in income during retirement therefore has the same effect as a reduction in income during the working life. Consequently, the age wealth profiles of the 1907 and 1922 generations are somewhat flatter than the ones presented in figure 2b. This, in turn implies that the displacement effect, i.e. the value of the substitution variable, is somewhat bigger than indicated in figure 3 (again, see Kapteyn et al., 2004 for more details).

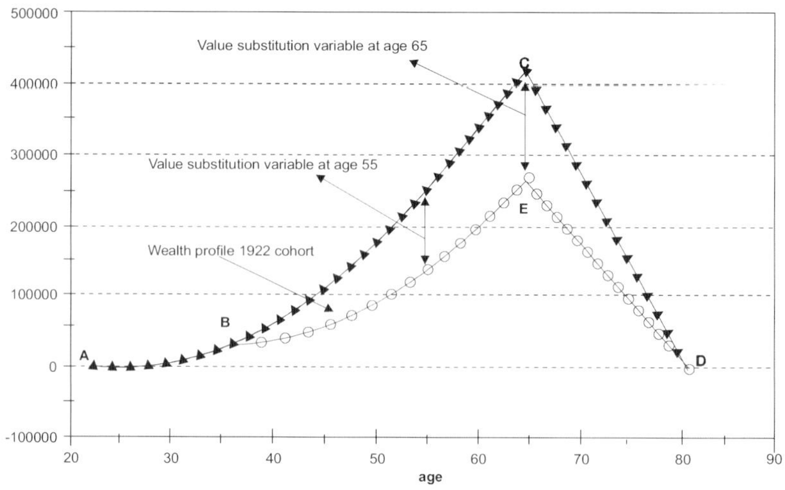

Figure 3. The substitution variable.

As in other studies on the subject (see e.g. Feldstein, 1974; and Attanasio and Rohwedder, 2001) our empirical analysis is based on the life cycle model, which I just presented. We have carried out a regression analysis in which we explain wealth holdings by a number of regressors. The most important one is the substitution variable whose construction I have described in figure 3. Under the assumptions that the life cycle model effectively describes household saving behaviour and that net income is not affected by the introduction of SS, we would expect that the parameter corresponding to the substitution variable would take a value of minus one. In the construction of the substitution variable, we did not take into account the possibility that pre-retirement income falls due to a payroll tax. Given some plausible assumptions, one can show that the displacement coefficient would take a value of around −1.2 (see Kapteyn, Alessie and Lusardi, 2004).

3. EMPIRICAL ANALYSIS

Before I present the results of our empirical analysis, I would like to comment on empirical work done by other economists. Almost all studies use the life cycle model as theoretical framework of analysis. However, as Gale (1998) effectively points out, not all implications of the theoretical are translated in a correct way in the empirical model. Given time constraints, I will not discuss this issue. I will pay attention, however, to another issue associated with these studies: they often use data which are not suited to investigating the displacement effect of SS. Martin Feldstein (1974) was one of the first economists who investigated the relationship between social security and saving behaviour. Like many other studies, his empirical analysis was based on aggregate time series. As Feldstein later admits in a survey paper with Liebman, because of aggregation problems one cannot estimate the displacement effect by using time series data.[6] By means of an example I will show the correctness of this claim. Consider a stationary economy without population growth. Moreover, assume that the wage rate remains constant over time. The simple life cycle model then predicts that in absence of a PAYG SS scheme, saving of the young part of the population is completely compensated by dissaving by the old part. Total household saving is equal to zero in such a stationary economy. However, households would also be equal to zero in such an economy even if an SS law had existed. In other words, although the life cycle model predicts substitution effects between SS and saving, in aggregate time series we cannot observe the level of substitution. Obviously, the assumption of a stationary economy is not realistic. Nonetheless the example above clearly illustrates the problems associated with the use of time series data. By the way, Feldstein (1974) finds that the level of displacement is 50 per cent smaller than the life cycle model predicts.

Next to the time series studies, many papers have used cross section data to investigate the level of displacement between SS and household saving (see e.g. Munnell (1976) and Feldstein and Pellochio (1979)). Cross section data are typically based on household surveys done in one specific year, e.g. 1990. Contrary to time series data, one does not face aggregation problems if one uses cross section data. The problem, however, with cross section data is, that one cannot disentangle generation effects from age effects. The graphical analysis (cf. Figure 3) highlights another important aspect of the introduction of SS. The displacement effect created by SS depends not only on the year when SS was introduced but also on the age of the individual at the time. In other words, there is an interaction between age and cohort effects.

The question now is: what type of data should we use to investigate the relationship between SS and savings? The first possibility is: use a time series of cross sections. Preferably the time series of cross sections should contain years in which Social Security is changed considerably. Ideally, these reforms should affect different groups of individuals differently in order to assess in a precise way the impact of changes in SS on household saving rates. Such data are seldom available: as far as I know, only two studies have used such data.[7] Attanasio and Rohwedder (2001) use the British Family Expenditure Survey to estimate the displacement effect between two types of Social Security pension – the Base State Pension (BSP) and the State-Earnings Related Pension Scheme (SERPS) – and the saving rate. For reasons, which I will explain below, Attanasio and Rohwedder (2001) allow the substitution effect to be age-specific. They find considerable displacement effects between SERPS and the saving rate, especially for elderly employees (in the age range 54-64) and no evidence for displacement between BSP and saving.

The second possibility is to use household panel survey data. In case of household panel data, the same households are interviewed yearly. The use of panel data has an important advantage: one can take into account the phenomenon of 'nonobserved

6 See Feldstein & Liebman (2001) for a review of the relevant literature.
7 See Attanasio & Rohwedder (2001) and Attanasio & Brugiavini (2003).

heterogeneity'. Apart from Social Security, saving depends on many factors. Some explanatory factors are typically observed such as income, family size and composition. But some variables are difficult to measure like time preference and risk aversion. The nonobserved factors represent the 'non-observed heterogeneity'. The problem with these nonobserved factors is that they are possibly correlated with the observed explanatory variables such as income and dummy variables indicating the employment status (self-employed, employee etc.): for instance people who are risk averse, are less likely to be self-employed. If one ignores these correlations, one estimates the displacement effect, for example, inconsistently. Only in the case of panel data do regression techniques exist, which take these correlations into account.

In my paper with Arie Kapteyn en Annamaria Lusardi, use is made of the 1987 until the 1998 wave of the Dutch Socio Economic Panel (SEP). In our regression analysis wealth holdings are explained by, among other things, age, family size and composition, education level, income and, obviously, the displacement variable. Without explicitly modelling them, we allow for macro shocks such as the developments on the housing and stock markets. We also allow for productivity growth (young generations have a higher lifetime income than old ones) and for an unobserved household effect, which is possibly correlated with the time varying right-hand-side variables. Recently, more waves of the SEP have become available. I have therefore re-estimated the models of Kapteyn et al., by using the SEP, covering the period 1987-2001. In general, the estimation results do not change dramatically by the extension of the sample period.

During the sample period, the SS (AOW) law changed a bit but not dramatically. One might wonder whether it is possible to identify the displacement effect. However, one should realise that our sample contains households whose members were born at the beginning of the twentieth century. The oldest generation in our sample was born in 1911. When the members of these generations were young, the SS law either did not exist or SS benefits were rather low (during the 1960's). Therefore, the members of these generations had a strong incentive to save for retirement. These saving decisions in the past are translated in wealth holdings as observed between 1987 and 1998 because wealth holdings are equal to accumulated saving in past and present. The SEP also contains households whose members were born after, say, 1950. These generations started working when the SS law was fully in place. As I explained before, the age wealth profiles of these young generations should differ considerably from that of the old generations. This difference is summarised in the substitution variable. Therefore we can identify the displacement effect although our sample does not cover a period with dramatic changes in the SS law.

And now the most important result of our empirical analysis: based on the extended SEP data covering the period 1987-2001, I find an estimate of the coefficient corresponding to the displacement variable which is equal to –0.10.[8] This estimate differs significantly from 0. In other words, we find some evidence of displacement between

8 Kapteyn et al. (2004) report a displacement effect of -0.115. As I said before, the analysis of Kapteyn et al. (2004) is based on the SEP covering the period 1987-1998.

Social Security and private wealth holdings: due to the introduction of SS in 1957 and of more generous SS-benefits after that date, people have saved more. However, the estimated displacement effect (-0.10) is much smaller than the simple life cycle model predicts. As I said earlier, one would expect a coefficient of around –1 if the simple version of the LCH predicts household saving behaviour correctly.

We have checked the validity of these predictions. As I explained before, the LCH predicts that due to the introduction of SS the relationship between private wealth and age is generation-specific (see figure 2b). In other words the introduction of SS has induced an interaction between age and cohort effects. By means of a statistical test, we have checked whether, apart from SS, there are other cohort effects. We do not find evidence for remaining cohort effects.

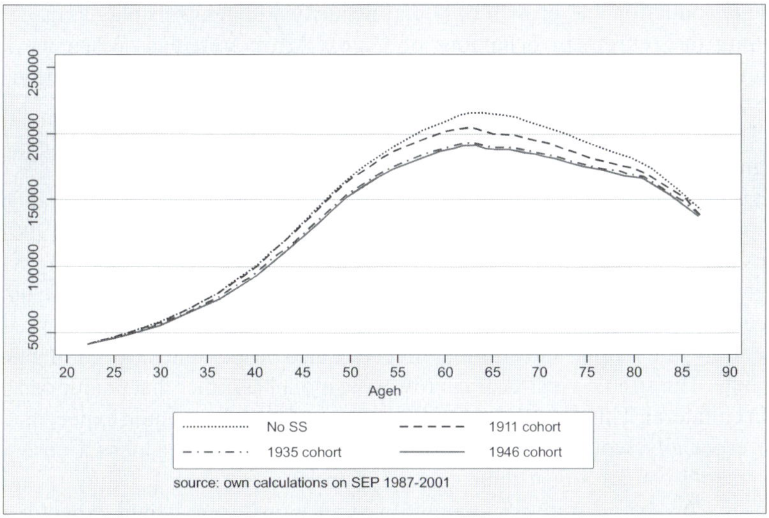

Figure 4. Age net worth profiles for different cohorts.

By modelling the generation effect explicitly, we are able to disentangle age-, time and cohort effects. Without such modelling, this is not possible because someone's age is equal to the difference between the present year and the year of his birth. In figure 4, I show the age wealth profiles of 4 different generations. Our results confirm some predictions of the life cycle model: firstly, the age wealth profiles are somewhat flatter for the younger generations. Secondly, according to our model estimates, people dissave after the age of 63.

To summarise, we find a small displacement effect of Social Security on saving behaviour. One may argue that this is not a surprising result. However, for instance Attanasio and Rohwedder (2001) find that displacement effect of SERPS on saving behaviour is considerable for some demographic groups, especially the middle aged.

4. WHY DO WE FIND A SMALL SUBSTITUTION-EFFECT?

One may wonder why we find such a small displacement effect. This can be explained in many ways. Below, I will provide three possible explanations. Firstly, in our model we do not take into account labour supply responses, as utility is assumed to depend on consumption only. In a model with both consumption and leisure in the utility function in a nonseparable way, one expects the introduction of SS to have an effect on the retirement age since the introduction of SS increases lifetime resources for the older cohorts (the expected present discounted value of their SS benefits is greater than the value of the extra payroll tax). This increase in lifetime resources may conceivably be consumed in the form of more leisure, e.g., through early retirement. This in itself increases the need to save for retirement and hence may offset the depressing effect of SS on savings. For example, Costa (1995) looks at pension data for the US and finds that the introduction and growth of Social Security and pensions play a major role in explaining the retirement behaviour of Union Army Veterans. When we look at historical data for the Netherlands, we find that the labour force participation rate of people aged 65 and older dropped from 20% in 1947 to 11% in 1960 and to 4% in 1975. The decline is quite strong for men. Male labour force participation after the age of 65 goes from 36% in 1947 to 11% in 1971.

It has been proposed to stimulate labour participation of the elderly by increasing the mandatory retirement age from 65 to 67. Some people (see e.g. Don, 1996) argue that this policy measure might not be effective because people will start to save more after the announcement of this policy measure. My estimation results suggest, however, that people adjust their saving behaviour rather marginally.

Secondly, the limited substitution effect can also be explained by binding liquidity constraints. The simple version of the life cycle model assumes that people can borrow without collateral. This assumption might not be realistic. One would expect that young people, especially, would have trouble in obtaining uncollaterised loans. Consequently, young people cannot adjust their consumption profile upward if they receive new information on extra future SS income. In other words, one would expect a smaller displacement effect of SS for young people. I have checked this prediction by estimating a model in which the displacement coefficient depends on age. I indeed find that the level of displacement is especially small for the young (see Attanasio and Rohwedder, 2001 for a similar result).

The third possible explanation of the small displacement effect, is that the LCH does not explain consumer behaviour in an adequate way. Psychologists like Ainslie (1992), and economists like Laibson (1997) argue that people procrastinate. They argue that people do not like to think about financial matters like pensions and that they therefore postpone such activities. For example, a person who procrastinates, might reason in the following way: 'Of course it is important to save for my pension, but at the moment I do not want to put money aside for this purpose. From next year onwards, I will start saving for my pension.' But the year after, this person might procrastinate again. Obviously, this leads to dynamic inconsistent behaviour. Laibson argues that this type of behaviour can be described effectively by means of the hyperbolic discounting model of Strotz (1956).[9] This model differs in one important respect from the standard life cycle model. People discount the near future with a high discount rate whereas in the longer run they use a low discount rate. This leads to an inconsistency in how events at two consecutive time periods are evaluated. If the periods t and $t+1$ are far-off, they are weighed according to the low long-term discount rate, but once one arrives in period t they are weighed according to the high short-term discount rate. In the life cycle model it is assumed that that people use one discount factor (exponential discounting). Obviously, the hyperbolic discounting model predicts a smaller displacement effect of SS than the standard life cycle model.

Due to the work of Laibson (1997) the hyperbolic discounting model has become more popular among economists. Inspired by work of O'Donoghue and Rabin (1999), Lusardi (2000) has extended Laibson' model by allowing for an extra decision variable: 'effort of planning'. This effort of planning causes disutility in the present, but may yield a better return on assets in the future. In this setup, individuals choose the optimal amount of effort by equating the marginal costs of planning to the marginal benefits of planning. Agents that face relatively low costs will exert high effort and obtain high returns. For some preference specifications, these high returns lead households to save more (i.e. the substitution effect is greater than the income effect). In other words, individuals with low planning costs end up accumulating higher amounts of wealth than other individuals.

Due to the availability of subjective data in her sample (the 1992 wave of the Health and Retirement Survey), Lusardi (2000) has been able to investigate the importance of procrastination. She reports the following evidence: approximately one third of the respondents have 'hardly thought' about retirement. This fraction is large especially if one realises that the HRS sample consists of U.S. households whose head is only a few years away from retirement (i.e. born between 1931 and 1941). She also presents evidence for the fact that education is more conducive to planning (search costs are lower). Consistent with this fact and with the model sketched above, respondents who do not think about retirement are more likely to have a low education. Her most important result is that households, who have hardly thought about retirement, have less wealth than the other households. They also hold different wealth portfolios and, most specifically, they are less likely to hold stocks. These results hold good even if she accounts for many other background characteristics and for the fact that lack of planning may be endogenous. Finally she gives some prima facie evidence for the fact that those who do not plan are also more likely to face difficulties in retirement. However, one can explain Lusardi's results by using a conventional life cycle model. One may argue that people, who have never thought about retirement, have a high rate of time preference.

9 Thaler & Shefrin (1981) have proposed an alternative model to explain procrastination behaviour, the so-called behavioural life cycle model.

Akerlof (1991) argues that the small displacement effect of Social Security on saving provides evidence in favour of the hyperbolic discounting model. But I have just argued that the limited displacement effect can also be explained by the existence of binding liquidity constraints and interactions between labour supply and saving behaviour. In order to investigate somewhat further, I have extended my econometric model by allowing the displacement coefficient to dependent on education level. Given the results of Lusardi (2000), one would expect that, ceteris paribus, on average the highly educated are better planners and consequently should react stronger to changes in SS (higher displacement coefficient in absolute value). However, a formal statistical test suggests that the displacement coefficient does not differ significantly across education levels. This finding suggests at least that apart from procrastination other explanations for the limited substitution effect should be taken seriously.

5. WHAT TO DO?

To summarise the empirical evidence, one could state that it is not clear yet which of the two models – the life cycle model or the hyperbolic discounting model – describes saving behaviour better.

Further research on this topic is important because the two models imply different policy recommendations for pension reform. An adherent of the life cycle model (e.g. Feldstein) may argue for restructuring the Dutch pension system by allowing for more freedom of choice, especially on the amount of pension saving. It is interesting to know that in the US mandatory defined benefit pension schemes have often been replaced by voluntary 401k plans.

Supporters of the hyperbolic discounting model may argue that mandatory pension schemes counteract the perverse effects of procrastination and lead to higher welfare of the consumers.

In order to discriminate between the two models we need better data on time preference. Time preference, however, is hard to measure. People have tried to come up with survey questions on time preference but the answers on these questions can be interpreted in different ways. However, some progress has been made on this point recently.[10]

Next to this, we need more information on how people form expectations about future retirement income. Like many other authors, we have assumed static expectations. That is, they plan their consumption as if the level of SS remains constant at its current level during the course of their lifetime. In other words, consumers do not anticipate changes in SS benefit levels. If such changes occur, we assume that consumers perceive these income shocks as permanent. These assumptions might be incorrect. We need subjective data on income expectations to test our assumptions. Dominitz, Manski and Heinz (2003) have formulated survey questions, which measure the subjective probability distribution of future pension income. Apart from checking

10 See Loewenstein & Prelec (1993), Barsky, Kimball & Shapiro (1997) and Kapteyn & Teppa (2003).

our assumption on expectation formation, such information can be used to assess the importance of the precautionary saving motive, which arises from uncertainty about future SS benefits. Given the ageing of the population, the level of uncertainty about future pension income might be substantial in some households.

REFERENCES

Ainslie, G. (1992). *Picoeconomics*, New York: Cambridge University Press.

Akerlof, G. (1991). Procrastination and Obedience, *American Economic Review Papers and Proceedings, 81,* 1-19.

Alessie, R, Kapteyn, A., & Klijn, F. (1997). Mandatory pensions and personal savings in the Netherlands, *de Economist, 145, no. 3,* 291-324.

Attanasio, O.P., & Brugiavini, A. (2003). Social security and household saving, *The Quarterly Journal of Economics, vol. 118,* 1075-1119.

Attanasio, O.P. & Rohwedder, S. (2001). Pension wealth and household saving: evidence from pension reforms in the UK, Institute for Fiscal Studies, *IFS working paper WP01/21*, to appear in *the American Economic Review.*

Barsky, R.B., Juster, F.T., Kimball, M.S., & Shapiro, M.D. (1997). Preference Parameters and Behavioral Heterogeneity: an Experimental Approach in the Health and Retirement Study, *The Quarterly Journal of Economics, 112,* 729-758.

Bovenberg, A.L. & Meijdam, L. (1999). The Dutch Pension System, Tilburg University, mimeo.

Browning, A., & Lusardi, A. (1996). Household saving: micro theories and micro facts, *Journal of Economic Literature, 34,* 1797-1855.

Carey, D. (2002). Coping with population ageing in the Netherlands, *OECD economics department working paper, ECO/WKP(2002)11*, OECD, Paris.

Dominitz, J.F, Manski, C.F., & Heinz, J. (2003). Will Social Security be there for you? How Americans perceive their benefits, *NBER working paper w9798*, National Bureau of Economics Research, Cambridge.

Don, H. (1996). Pensioen, overheid and markt, *Economische Statistische Berichten, no. 4065*, 585-608.

Euwals, R. (2000). Do mandatory pensions decrease household savings? evidence for the Netherlands', *de Economist, 148, no. 5,* 643-670.

Feldstein, M. (1974). Social Security, induced retirement, and aggregate capital accumulation, *Journal of Political Economy, 82,* 905-925.

Feldstein, M. & Pellechio, A. (1979). Social Security and Household Wealth Accumulation: New Microeconometric Evidence, *Review of Economics and Statistics, 61*, 361–368.

Feldstein, M. & Liebman, J.B. (2001). Social Security, *NBER working paper no. w8451*, National Bureau of Economics Research, Cambridge.

Gale, W.G. (1998). The effects of pensions on household wealth: a reevaluation of theory and evidence, *Journal of Political Economy, vol. 106, no. 4,* 706-724.

Heckman, J. & Robb, R. (1985). Using longitudinal data to estimate age, period and cohort effects in earnings equations. In: W. Mason & S. Fienberg, (Eds.), *Cohort analysis in social research beyond the identification problem*, New York: Springer-Verlag.

Hurd, M. (1990). Research on the elderly: Economic status, retirement, and consumption and saving, *Journal of Economic Literature, 28*, 565-637.

Imrohoroglu, A., Imrohoroglu, S., & Joines, D.H. (2003). Time-inconsistent preferences and social security, *The Quarterly Journal of Economics, vol 118*, 745-783.

Kapteyn, A., Alessie, R., & Lusardi, A. (2004). Explaining the wealth holdings of different cohorts: productivity growth and social security, *the European Economic Review* (forthcoming).

Kapteyn, A., & Teppa, F. (2000). Hypothetical Intertemporal Consumption Choices, *CentER Discussion Paper*, CentER, Tilburg University.

Laibson, D.I. (1997). Golden Eggs and Hyperbolic Discounting, *Quarterly Journal of Economics, 112*, 443-478.

Laibson, D.I., Repetto, A., & Tobacman, J. (1998). Self-control and saving for retirement, Brookings Pappers on Economic Activity, vol. 1998(1), 91-172.

Lindeboom, M.(1999). Het arbeidsmarktgedrag van oudere werknemers, *inaugural lecture*, Vrije Universiteit Amsterdam.

Loewenstein, G., & Prelec, D. (1993), Preferences for Sequences of Outcomes, *Psychological Review, 100*, 91-108.

Lusardi, A. (2000). Explaining why so many households do not save, University of Chicago, mimeo.

Munnell, A.H. (1976). Private Pensions and Saving: New Evidence, *Journal of Political Economy*, *84*, 1013–1032.

Thaler, R. & Shefrin, H. (1981). An Economic Theory of Self-Control, *Journal of Political Economy*, *89,* 392-406.

Woltjer, J.J. (1992). *Recent verleden: Nederland in de twintigste eeuw*, Amsterdam: Rainbow.

B. UNGER

WILL THE DUTCH LEVEL OUT THEIR ONE AND ONLY MOUNTAIN?[1]

The Pietersberg Paradox and Mountains of Debt

'Ons bin zuunig' – 'We are thrifty'
TV ad for 'Zeeuws Meisje' margarine

INTRODUCTION. THE PIETERSBERG AND MOUNTAINS OF DEBT

The Dutch seem to like levelling mountains. Believe it or not, they are quarrying away one of the few 'mountains' they have: the Sint Pietersberg – the 109m high 'Saint Peter mountain' – located to the south of Maastricht. The Dutch insist in hollowing out this hill, which they proudly call mountain, to use it for cement production. Eventually it will become the lowest point of the country, to be filled with water.[2] The Dutch made water into land, now they make land into water.

The Dutch also want to level that other little mountain that they have: their 'mountain' of public debt. The Dutch worry about debts, though they have one of the lowest public debts in the EU. Can it be that they dislike mountains of debts, because they are not used to mountains at all?

The metaphor of the Sint Pietersberg will guide us in asking questions and looking for answers to this strange 'levelling' behaviour:

1 This article is a shortened and revised version of my inaugural lecture 'Graaft Nederland zijn bergje af'. The longer version has been published under ISBN 90-9017545-8 and can be found on my homepage. For helpful comments I thank Frans van Waarden, Bruno Frey, Rick van der Ploeg, Willem Buiter, Antoon Spithoven, Bas van Groezen and Joras Ferwerda.

2 'The Pietersberg is falling apart, is being sold and disappearing. Things are going badly with the Pietersberg. Because of chalk quarrying, the Limburg hill area threatens to become the lowest point in the Netherlands. Ridiculous that nature has to be sacrificed for some years of concrete production' (NRC Handelsblad, Monday, 4th February 2002, translation BU).

P. de Gijsel and H. Schenk (eds.), Multidisciplinary Economics, 381–403.

1. IS THE DUTCH EAGERNESS TO LEVEL THEIR DEBT MOUNTAIN, IN LINE WITH THE INTERNATIONALLY PREDOMINANT PERCEPTION OF PUBLIC DEBT?

In order to outline the predominant view on public debt, I will search for answers in the economic literature on public debt of both the distant and more recent past. Some answers given in the past are still quite relevant in this day and age, but they seem to have been forgotten in the current public debate.

1.1 The historic ups and downs of public debt and of views on public debt

Throughout history, the pendulum of opinions seems to reflect the cycles and sizes of the public debt. Not only the US, but also the Netherlands has known periods of high and increasing debts and periods of lower debt. 230% of GDP in 1944, around 52% now (see chart 1). The historic development shows that there is room to manoeuvre for making debts, for as diverse purposes as war and oil or for social security and people. There seem to be degrees of freedom, possibilities of political choice by governments.

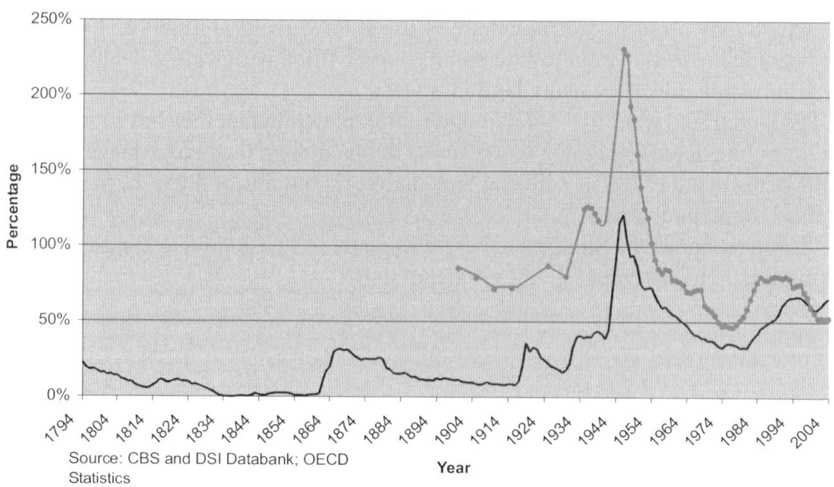

Chart 1. Government Debt of the Netherlands and USA as % of GDP.

In the development of public debt, ups and downs are mirrored in the economic debate on the virtues or vices of public debt. At times, public debt was seen as an important investment in the future, at other times it was considered the result – and indicator – of wasteful and useless government spending.

1.1.1 Enthusiasm about public debts in the 18th and 19th century

Debts were seen as assets, as a means of creating wealth, and not as something that would weaken the economy, in the mercantilist doctrine of the 18th century. *'Public debts augment the riches of a country'*, the Dutch-Portuguese writer Pinto wrote enthusiastically. '*Public debts are a mine of gold*', according to Berkeley (see Paul-Leroy Beaulieu (1906, p. 223) quoted in Buchanan (1958, paragraph 2.2.27)). *'The debts of a state are debts which the right hand owes to the left hand, and, which therefore, do not weaken the body at all'*, the French economist Melon (1734, p. 479) wrote in his political essays.

In the 19th century the public debt euphoria continued, among others by the German writers Gustav Cohn (1889, pp. 740-743), Knut Wicksell (1896, p. 131) and Adolf Wagner (1877, p. 122). Wagner's Law stated that state expenditure in percent of GDP would have to increase as the economy develops. And Lorenz von Stein (1842) considered a government without public debt as careless: '*A state without public debt either does not care enough about the future or it demands too much from the present generation*'.

His idea was that a state without public debt either does not invest in infrastructure for the future – then it does not care about the next generation – or lets the present generation pay for it, in which case this generation has to pay too much, also for the benefit of the next generation.

1.1.2 The classical hostility towards public debt

The three major classics, Adam Smith (1776), David Ricardo (1817), and John Stuart Mill (1848) all stress the evil of public debt. Jean Baptiste Say put it in a nutshell when he said: *'The very best of all plans of finance is to spend little and the best of all taxes is that which is least in amount'* (quoted in Ricardo 1817, p. 159). The best budget deficit is for him no budget deficit.

The classics were hostile to the mercantilist doctrine and they opposed the idea of a large public sector or of large public debts. All government expenditure was considered to be wasteful and unproductive. The real evil of public debt was that government used up capital, not the debt itself.

The classics assumed full employment. Hence intervention of the state for business cycle purposes was considered unnecessary or even disturbing. A government which borrows money crowds out private sector initiatives (for a survey of the crowding out debate see e.g. Buiter 1977 and 1985). Crowding out means that the positive effect of public expenditure on national income is counteracted by negative effects on the private sector. If the state invests more it uses up resources from the private sector which has less to invest.

Adam Smith (1776) devoted quite some attention to the tasks of the government and to public debt. He was far more revolutionary than many of his followers who cited only his 'invisible hand' argument. For him the state is important for law and order, for supporting business and trade, and for the provision of education (Adam Smith 1776, Vol II, p. 249).

David Ricardo, 1772-1823, wrote in 1817 in 'The Principles of Political Economy and Taxation' that it is the current generation and not the future, which bears the debt burden. He claims that it is the *taxpayer* and not the public bond purchaser who bears the primary burden of the debt. This burden is placed on the taxpayer, because he writes down the value of his capital assets in anticipation of his obligation to pay future taxes to service the debt.

'The third major figure among the English classical economists was hopelessly confused. J.S. Mill. tried to combine elements of contrasting views. This led him to claim that the public debt has a double burden, one which is borne by the current generation of labourers because resources which would otherwise be used to support labour are withdrawn from private employments, and one which is shifted forward to future generations because of the taxes required for the interest payments.' (Buchanan 1958, 1999, Chap. 8, paragraph 2.8.7).

1.1.3 The Keynesian view in favour of public debt 1936-1955

With Keynes public debt euphoria had a revival. He reserved an active role for the state. Spending was considered a virtue not a vice. Digging holes in the ground, building two pyramids rather than one, was still better than if the state did nothing! (Keynes 1936, p. 131). Keynes praises spending, wastefulness, and shows the dangers of thrift for the aggregate economy. If everybody saves more, his Savings Paradox states, then people will not consume enough. With lower demand, business will not sell enough products, will have to dismiss people, the unemployed have less income, can consume even less goods and services, so that finally the national income will decline and so do aggregate savings. The original plans of high savings cannot be realised by the individuals due to the recession that their joint decision produces at the aggregate level. The state must intervene and guarantee that there is enough demand in the economy to buy up all the products and keep people employed.

Keynes does not distinguish between investment and consumption expenditures of the public sector, he calls both 'loan expenditures' (Keynes 1936, p. 128f, Footnote), a distinction that gets far more attention in today's debate, since it is important to consider what the government spends its money on.

From the appearance of Keynes' seminal book 'The General Theory of Employment, Interest and Money' in 1936 until 1955, economists were strongly in favour of public debt. The prevalent view was that: A. public debt does not burden future generations at all; B. individual borrowing is not the same as public borrowing, because the state cannot go bankrupt, and in the aggregate each generation owes the public debt to itself as long as, C. there is no borrowing from abroad. There was agreement and enthusiasm about the virtues of public debt as long as it was domestically financed. Authors such as Lerner (1948), Hansen (1941), Harris (1947), Pigou (1949), and Meade (1945) were convinced that public debt would not create any problem.

What were the arguments of the Keynesians in favour of public debt? In the next sections I will go over them.

A. The creation of public debt does not burden future generations

In order to run a debt, the government has to use resources from the private sector of *this* generation. The private sector can spend less and must save more in order to lend money to the government. Not the future generation. There is not much difference between public expenditures financed by debt or by taxation. In either case the 'real' burden has to be borne by the current generation.[3]

Neither do interest rates on public debt burden future generations, because debt issues leave 'future' generations with a heritage of both claims and obligations. Some citizens hold bonds and earn interest rate income from it, others, maybe even the same ones, have to pay taxes in order to pay these interest rate expenditures on public debts.

B. Public debt differs from private debt

Private debt differs from national debt in being external. It is owed by one person to others. That is what makes it burdensome. But this does not hold for national debt, which is owed by the nation to citizens of the same nation. There is no external creditor. '*We owe it to ourselves*' Lerner, Abba P. (1948, p. 256).

For Keynesians public debt is eternal. It does not have to be repaid. The state either issues government bonds with eternal duration as Keynes assumes in his General Theory (1936), or the state repays old debts by issuing new bonds and making new debts in order to pay the old ones off. The mountain of debt can, according to this view, always be passed on into eternity as long as individuals trust the government and are willing to buy and hold government bonds. The limits of debt are reached when the government loses its reputation and no one wants to hold government bonds anymore. In this case, the citizens holding old government bonds will go bankrupt.

C. Domestic public debt differs from foreign public debt

The payment of interest does represent a real burden in the case of foreign debt, because interest rate payments will have to be paid abroad and future generations will find their incomes reduced by such transfers.

If one compares the share of foreign and domestic debts, the Netherlands follows the advice of the Keynesians perfectly. It has not issued government bonds in foreign currencies since the 1970s. Of course the problem in an international world is that foreigners can buy Dutch bonds. There is no statistic of who holds which kind of bonds. Dutch government bonds are traded in Amsterdam and London.

3 In today's debate one would add that this holds only for a closed, not for an open, economy. In neoclassical economics problems of tax distortions, dead weight losses from taxation because of the change of relative costs, disincentive effects for the private sector would be stressed. Furthermore, distribution problems may occur when taxpayers and bondholders are not identical.

1.1.4 The Ricardian equivalence theorem

The Ricardian train of thought that taxes and loans can exert identical effects on the economy has become the central element of the current debate.[4]

The public sector hostility of the classics was back, but at its perfection. According to Ricardo-Barro, debts are neutral, they have no effect on aggregate consumption or saving.

Economic agents with rational expectations believe that government deficits imply no real change in wealth in the long run. Government assets do not make them feel richer, because each dollar of debt means an additional dollar of future taxes to them. Furthermore, consumption will also remain unchanged, because individuals will increase savings to be able to pay the higher taxes they expect in the future. Theories must come at the right time to be diffused. Barro's ideas got popular in the 1980s, when, for the first time since the war, public debt problems occurred in the US and Europe.

A question raised by Barro's theory is, why does the government issue bonds at all? If there is no difference between levying taxes and issuing bonds, and if expenditure has no effect, why should a government bother to make debts? Neither its form nor its level affects the economy. Barro (1979) answered that taxation has transaction costs, that the higher the tax rate, the higher the transaction costs of tax collection. Furthermore, higher marginal tax rates produce greater distortions of the private sector and greater dead weight losses due to these distortions.

Blinder and Stiglitz (1983) criticised Barro's equivalence theorem and the conclusion that the public sector's activities are irrelevant because they are foreseen by ultra-rational individuals who consider them as being too far-fetched and therefore do exactly the opposite:

1. the repayment of the public debt can take place very late in the future. Thus intergenerative neutrality is not necessary there. We do not care for the children of the children of the children of the children of our children 200 years ahead.
2. the assumption of perfect capital markets is questionable. 'But people cannot borrow freely at the government's interest rate, and for a very good reason: they might default.' (Blinder/Stiglitz 1983, p. 299)
3. the taxes people assume they will have to repay in the future, must be perfectly distributionally neutral. (Maybe somebody else, hopefully somebody richer than I, will have to repay the government debt arising from the education of my child).

4 Ricardo himself did not believe in this equivalence theorem, as Musgrave (1985, p. 50) put it aptly. He rejected this proposition as unrealistic, because loan financing tends to make us less thrifty, blinds us to our real situation, whereas taxes have to be paid all at once (Ricardo 1817, p. 247). In 1974 Barro reintroduced Ricardo's concept of equivalence into mainstream economics. It was Buchanan (1976) who pointed out the similarity between Barro's and Ricardo's work and gave it the name Ricardian equivalence.

1.1.5 Public choice

Public choice theory introduced methodological individualism into the public debt debate. One cannot talk about public debt in general, its proponents, most prominently 1986 Nobel prize winner James Buchanan, claimed. Instead, one has to focus on the individual and his or her opportunity costs when lending to the government, or paying taxes. The same holds for the government, which makes choices between the tax financing and debt financing of public expenditures as well as choices regarding the amount of public expenditure. And in these choices it must be guided by the sum of individuals in a community, who can best decide themselves what they want and whether they want public or private goods and express these desires. Buchanan (1958, reprint 1999) reintroduced the classical theory, but this time built on the premises of rational individual choice.

Buchanan (1958, 1999) claims the validity of three basic propositions which are diametrically opposed to those accepted in his time but which are very common today:

1. There is no essential difference between the debt and tax financing of public expenditure. Both mean a reduction of resources available for the private sector.
2. There is no essential difference between private and public debt. To what Lerner had described as '*We owe it to ourselves*' (Lerner, 1948 p. 256), Buchanan's reacts with: '*What's that WE business'?* Buchanan 1958, paragraph 2.13.4). According to his view the future generation consists of individuals who either receive interest payments or have to pay taxes. The former could make a deliberate choice of how to postpone consumption, the latter have no free choice.
3. There is no important conceptual difference between internal and external debt. (Buchanan 1958, Chapter 12, paragraph 2.12.3). Since it is the taxpayer and not the interest payment receiver who has no choice, it does not make much difference whether the debt is domestic or foreign.

1.1.6 The international trend and the Dutch view on public debt

Where is the international debate heading for today, and where are Dutch economists located on the map of views on public debt?

What do the Dutch think of public debt? In the Netherlands, this country of compromise, we are lucky. The experts do not seem to disagree fundamentally. There is broad consensus among Dutch economists that public debt has to be reduced (an exception is Thio 2002). However, they differ in degree. The controversial issues are: when should it be reduced: now or later; how much should it be reduced: whether completely or only down to 25% of GDP or more (see table 1 on the views of Dutch economists). Most of them did not agree with Prime Minister Balkenende's plan to reduce debt down to 25% now. But there seems to be hardly any disagreement on the issues of whether the public debt has to be reduced at all or why budget consolidation and debt repudiation have become goals in themselves and have replaced topics such as reaching full employment, improving education, health care, WAO (Wet op de Arbeidsongeschiktheidsverzekering i.e. Disablement Insurance Act), or public pensions. The major concern of Dutch economists is that the public debt has to be reduced in order to create more room to manoeuvre for future pension payments.

Table 1 gives an overview of the views of leading Dutch economists on public debt repayment. For this, we took the Polderparade 2002. The Polderparade ranks Dutch economists according to their importance in Dutch publications and is published annually by the journal ESB, Economisch-Statistische Berichten (see ESB January 2003 for the Polderparade 2002). The first column lists the rank number in the parade (the same number with a and b means that two candidates share one rank), the name of the authors, the institution where they work and, as far as mentioned in the newspapers, the political party to which they belong. The second and third columns refer to an e-mail survey in which we asked the 25 economists to answer the questions: 1. Do you think that the Public Debt ever has to be paid back, may be in a very far away future? 2. Do you think that public debt should develop in such a way that each generation will be equally burdened with tax payments for this debt (tax smoothing)? The fourth to sixth columns refer to a literature survey done in a selection of Dutch newspapers and on the internet over the last three years. Column four lists the source(s) where the statement about debt was found. The fifth column lists whether they agree with Prime Minister Balkenende about starting to pay back the public debt now. The sixth column lists an important argument of the author with regard to public debt found in the newspapers. Few Dutch economists are of the opinion that the public debt should not be reduced. But only 3 explicitly said that they think public debt does have to be paid entirely back in some future. One of them even thinks that this is out of question (Fase). Most outspoken against public debt repayment is Wijnbergen who finds it a macho-idea. Some find debt repudiation harmful for growth (Theeuwes). De Beer is of the opinion that taxes should be raised instead of expenditures cut.

Though the majority of authors do not support the government proposal of debt repudiation, few of them support the Keynesian view that the debt should be high. Some give a margin (30% of GDP, Boot), some think that the public debt has to be paid back entirely (Haan, Fase). Most Dutch economists argue that we have to save in good times for bad times. There seems, however, to be disagreement about whether the present is 'good times' (Bovenberg) or 'bad times' (Keuzenkamp). The debate is future oriented. Public debt has to be brought down, because in the future: 1. room to manoeuvre is needed (Bovenberg, Scholtens), 2. an explosion of uncontrolled expenditures might occur (Teulings), 3. ageing will increase future deficits (Cnossen), 4. high interest payments will burden future generations (de Kam). Many economists find other problems, such as a lack of investment in education or research and development more important than worrying about debts (Kleinknecht, Boot, Eijffinger, Damme, Hartog, Buiter).

The majority of e-mail answers said that public debt did not have to be paid back entirely at some date, may be in the very far future. But half of the people interviewed answered, that they believed in tax smoothing. If we look at Barro's definition of tax smoothing that there must be a finite day t where the debt has to be paid back in order to calculate tax smoothing, Dutch economists seem to have a different view on tax smoothing or on the conditions for it. Some are for welfare smoothing between generations instead of tax smoothing (Theeuwes, van der Ploeg).

Are Dutch economists in line with the international trend? The majority thinks that some debt can persist. This is in line with the EU. Only, the Dutch seem to like to overdo it. 60% of GDP are the limits set by the Maastricht criteria but the Dutch want to go below this level. As Hofstede's answer expresses it aptly, this is the Dutch thriftiness over which the Belgians mock us ('de Nederlandse zuinigheid waarover de Belgen moppen maken'). But, somehow the EU and the Dutch have maintained a little hidden secret touch of Keynesianism, within all their neoclassical sophisticated models and thinking: they do not believe that the public debt has to be paid back entirely. The mountain of debt, whether a little bit higher or lower, can persist in the landscape of flatness around them.

Table 1. Views on public debt of the leading 25 Dutch economists (according to the 'Polderparade' 2002)

Name, Institution(s), and (Political Allegiance)	**Does public debt ever have to be paid back?**	**Should public debt develop so that each generation will be equally burdened with tax payments? (tax smoothing)**	**Source(s) in press**	**For or against debt repayment now?**	**Argumentation**
1. A.L. Bovenberg UvT FEW/ CentER, EUR-Ocfeb (CDA)	No, this depends on the result of tax smoothing (see next answer).	Yes, external shocks taken in account.	NRC, Intermediair, www.groenlinks.nl, Friesch Dagblad, Carrière Contact	For	Public debt has to be reduced in good economic times for bad economic times to come.
2. M.M.G. Fase emeritus	Yes, of course, this is out of question.	In the case of tax smoothing economic circumstances must be taken in account.			
3. C.N. Teulings Tinbergen Instituut, EUR-Ocfeb (PvdA)			NRC	For	Without control over public debt, the spending of politicians can get out of control.
4. C.A. de Kam RUG (PvdA)	Yes		De Telegraaf, NRC	For	Lower public debt means lower interest costs and we have to look at future generations.

5. A.H. Klein-knecht TU Delft (Groen Links)	No, the absolute public debt is not that important, it's the relative public debt that counts.	No, the future generation gets possessions and infrastructure along with public debt.	www.ocnv.nl	Against	Public debt is not the most important issue. Investment in education is much more urgent.
6. A.W.A. Boot UvA (No political party)	A public debt of 30% is never a problem. The repayment or not is just a way of accounting.	Yes, but this is not realistic in a mobile world.	NRC	Against	Public debt is not the most important issue. Investment in education is much more urgent.
7. P.T. de Beer WRR (PvdA)	No	Yes (comment; public debt is not a conflict of generations).	Het Financiële Dagblad	Against	Since the rise of taxes is inevitable, cuts in public spending is not a good decision.
8. J. de Haan RUG	Yes, this is a good way to finance the ageing problem.	Yes, I am against active business cycle policy.	www.rug.nl	Against	As long as the interest over the public debt can be paid, it is no problem to borrow more money.
9a S. Cnossen UM, Ocfeb			De Volkskrant	For	A smaller public debt is important, because in the future there will be high costs because of the large group of old people.
9b S.J.G. van Wijnbergen UvA (PvdA)	No, there is no economic reason for repaying public debt. Especially not within a generation.	Tax smoothing has efficiency advantages, but this depends on the expected income distribution between generations.	De Volkskrant, www.leidenuniv.nl, NRC, www.dotcom-business.nl	Against	A fast decrease of public debt is only possible through huge payments.
11. G. Hofstede emeritus	No. This is Dutch thriftiness over which the Belgians mock us.	No.			

12. J. Hartog UvA	No, there is no need to repay it all back.	No, this depends on the spending of income.	Noordhollands Dagblad	Against	It is more urgent that government invests in education rather than cutting back financial subsidies.
13. E.C. van Damme UvA	If public investments are efficient, they should continue.		Http://center.uvt.nl	Against	If public investments are efficient, they should continue.
14. J.J.M. Theeuwes UvA, WRR	No, as long as the investments have more return than the interest costs.	No, I prefer welfare smoothing.	NRC	Against	Reduction of public debt does not stimulate economic growth.
15. H.W. de Jong emeritus	–				
16. J.J. Graafland UvT	–				
17.S.C.W. Eijffinger UvT FEW/CentER (CDA)	No, public debt must be controllable, not necessarily zero.	Perfect tax smoothing is impossible, but tax smoothing must prevent big tax differences between generations.	NRC	Against	Now is not the time to work on public debt. Stimulation of education is much more important.
18. J. Swank DNB/EUR (OCFEB)	–				
19. W.C. Boeschoten TPG KPN Pensioen/ RUG	–				
20a W.H. Buiter EBRD/UvA	No, like Andy Williams told the bear: not now; now ever; never.	No, I would prefer welfare smoothing. Why should I care about future generations? What have future generations ever done for me?	Not found in the sources, but in div. articles	Against	Public debt is sustainable, Maastricht criteria are odd.

20b F. van der Ploeg EUI (Florence)/UvA PvdA	No, but higher expenditures in the future (like ageing) have to be taken in account.	I would prefer welfare smoothing above tax smoothing.	Financieel Dagblad, NRC	Against	Reduction of public debt in a fixed number of years is not based on anything and can be harmful.
22a Nooteboom EUR	No	Yes			
22b. L.J. Scholtens RUG	No	No, tax smoothing is not possible in real life.	www.groen links.nl	For	An increase of public debt will create financial problems in the future
24. H.A. Keuzenkamp UvA	No	Yes	De Volkskrant, NRC	Against	No financial cuts in bad times, the Zalm norm which linked expenditures to growth, worked well.
25. H. Huizinga UvT FEW/centER	Yes, private capital has low return, so repaying the public debt is better.	Yes, but impossible in real life, because of too large transfers between generations.			

Source: Bram van Helvoirt, 'Visions of Dutch economists on public debt', seminar paper, course 'economie van de publieke sector' supervised by Brigitte Unger, October 2003 and the author's own additions. The e-mail survey was done with the help of my student assistant Joras Ferwerda.

2. IS IT NECESSARY AND/OR SENSIBLE TO LEVEL THE DEBT MOUNTAIN AT ALL?

As individuals we may worry about being able to pay our debts off. Therefore we should be careful with taking up loans, with spending, don't waste resources, and make sure we earn enough to pay back any loans. Hard work and thriftiness are values with which we have been raised. The Dutch in particular have a reputation in Europe and in the world of being thrifty. Typical English expressions involving the Dutch: 'to go Dutch', 'Dutch treat', 'Dutch comfort', Dutch bargain', 'Dutch bookie', testify to this.

When political leaders, such as prime minister Balkenende, say that the public debt is too high, all these moral sentiments and existential fears are raised. If we overspend, we may not be solvent in the future, not be able to pay for our children, or even more dreadful, they may have to pay for us, or we might not have enough money when wc are old . Debt may also be seen as *a symbol of failure*, of not having made it in life; as individuals as well as the collective. The public household has to be kept as clean as our own at home. But this involves a major mistake in reasoning.

For one, the state cannot go bankrupt, only citizens can. The state is the only one who, in principle, can always, at any moment, pay back the whole mountain of debt, if it wants to. History testifies to that. It can do so thanks to its state power, its monopoly over taxation and over the legitimate exercise of force. With these, it can take it from others.

The most drastic way is to annul the debt outright, as occurred in the monetary reforms in Germany in 1948 (Roeper, H. and W. Weimer 1996). Another way is through inflation (Calvo 1988). This happened very often after wars, for example after World War One in Germany and Austria.

Of course state power has its limits. Tax increases have confronted states in the past with tax resistance and even outright revolution. The revolutions that created the Dutch and the American states started as tax revolts. The Dutch revolted against the Spanish Habsburgs, the Americans revolted against the British.

But in principle the state can repay old debt with new debt. A private person cannot do this. He has to pay back old debts first before the bank will give him a new loan. The state, with its power to enforce taxes, is more creditworthy than individuals are, because it cannot fail.

States also differ from individuals in that they are 'large' players in the economy. Therefore, their actions have macroeconomic effects. State action affects our income, our savings, our consumption, our well-being, and the well-being of our children. And, therefore, we must first analyse what macroeconomic effects a reduction of public debt has.

Can we leave the mountains standing? Keynesians always claimed that government debts can be eternal debts, that never have to be paid back. Old debts can be paid back by issuing new bonds and the mountain of debt can be passed on to the next generation and so forth and so forth in eternity.

According to these economists a mountain of debt should persist except if there are unwanted macroeconomic side effects such as higher inflation, higher interest rates, exchange rate dangers, etc. But such problems would not have to be a concern for the Dutch. Their public debt is low by international standards. Such problems might occur in Brazil or Argentina. Even Italy, with a mountain twice as high as the Dutch mountain, does not have these unwanted side effects of public debt.

By contrast, Ricardian equivalence (RE) defenders claim that every public debt has to be paid back at some finite date even if it is in the very very far future, when the state stops to exist, when the 'last judgement' has come, or whenever. The then-generation will have to pay back the interest rates on debts, which earlier generations spent, and they will also have to pay the debt back. Debts are future taxes, is today's mainstream opinion.

And they assume that rational people know this. This assumption is combined with the assumption that our generation cares for what happens to all future generations. If we care today for the very very far future, for the fact that the children of the children of the children of the children of the children of the children of our children will have to pay higher taxes in order to pay back our public debt of today, than, this theory argues, we want to save today, to bequeath them enough money to pay back our public debt at the 'last judgement'. Furthermore, the theory assumes that the then-living generation will really get our money. We must be able to shift consumption from today to the far future, to save today in order to repay public debt and higher taxes some time ahead. For this, capital markets must function perfectly and not break down between now and 'then'.

Otherwise our calculated expected future values are wrong, we make false decisions today, and end up with more or less consumption in the future. If capital markets fail, such as with bank and stock market crashes, we end up with nothing in the period when we had planned to pay the debt back.

The Ricardian equivalence theorem assumes a no Ponzi game. Charles Ponzi (1877-1949) was a Boston swindler, who borrowed considerable amounts of money by promising a high rate of interest. 50% for 45 days, 100% for 90 days. With the money of a new lender B he paid back the old debt to lender A, with even more money from C he paid back B etc. In eight months he ended up with 10 million dollars of certificates and 14 million dollars of debt (see Ricciuti 2003). The Ricardian equivalence theorem assumes that the government cannot play a Ponzi game.

But some of the assumptions of the Ricardian Equivalence Theorem seem unrealistic. The assumption of ultra rational individuals is nothing but a replacement of the assumption of perfect foresight by the assumption of perfect expected foresight, of perfect foresight on average. Individuals do not make persistent mistakes. But in a long-term setting over so many years, several hundred perhaps, there is uncertainty. Uncertainty about future incomes (Feldstein 1988), precautionary savings for unexpected circumstances, and bounded rationality are the reality.

We do not overlook almost infinite time horizons. In Barro's model consumers must be able to make rational forecasts on their future income, they must distinguish between permanent and temporary changes in taxes and deficits, and they must rapidly adjust to changes in nominal and real variables. Consumers must be experts on public debt. Some people might not have children and, therefore, care less about the income of future generations (Buiter 1988). Some consumers might be liquidity constrained. For them it might make a big difference whether they have to pay 1 dollar tax now or whether the government runs a 1 dollar deficit.

Allers, De Haan and De Kam (1998) did a survey in the Netherlands on people's knowledge about government indebtedness. They questioned respondents about the size of government debt and deficits. Only 30% gave a fairly correct answer. Only 12% answered that they did save more to be able to pay back higher taxes in the future when debt increases. Among first year and second year students of public sector economics at Utrecht School of Economics in 2003, only about 20% gave a correct estimate of the Maastricht criterion of public debt. Most of them thought that the limit was much lower than 60%, around 15% or 20%. And they thought that the Dutch figures exceeded the Maastricht debt criterion, whereas the true value for 2002 was 52% of GDP.

Another criticism on the Ricardian equivalence theorem regards imperfect capital markets. If there are inefficiencies in the capital market, some consumers can borrow only at a higher rate than the government. A tax cut makes them better off than a tax now plus a higher interest rate for borrowing.

An interesting application of experimental games to Ricardian equivalence testing has been done by Di Laurea and Ricciuti (2002). They tested how agents react when they are liquidity constrained and uncertain about their future income. For this they used an overlapping generations (OLG) experiment. Students in first and second year economics with no prior knowledge about optimal intertemporal consumption and Ricardian equivalence, were selected at random and played games in which they were either the older or the younger generation. The game lasted three periods: in period 1 only one young generation lived. Descendants and elderly people played together in period 2, and in period three only descendants played. They got a certain disposable income and an extra income which represented the tax cut in the Ricardian story, and a period later they again got their disposable income and a transfer from the government. Descendants in the third period started with a bequest inherited from the elderly who had died in the second period, their own disposable income and had to repay the debt of their parents. Everybody in the game had to decide on how much to consume, how much to save and how much to bequeath.

The game was repeated with changing settings of rich or poor parents, rich or poor descendants, and high or low debt. When uncertainty about future incomes and liquidity constraints were introduced in the game, the Ricardian equivalence theory failed. Agents fail to make precautionary savings with an uncertain income profile, and they spend the government transfer instead of saving it, when they are liquidity constrained.

The argument that agents change their behaviour today because they anticipate that the debt will have to be repaid one day in a very far future, seems to be based on weak grounds.

Most Dutch economists do not believe that the mountain of debt has to be levelled completely. They are not Barro-Ricardian.

More concern is given to the old fear that *debts might explode*. Domar addressed this question during World War II, in 1944. One of the five Maastricht criteria, which a EU country has to meet in order to join the European Monetary Union, specifies that the gross public debt in % of GDP shall not exceed 60%. Buiter (1993) showed the nonsense of these criteria. The Maastricht formula followed a very simple Domar (1944) model for the limits of debt. Domar did not claim to establish a theory of debt. He just wanted to find figures that would guarantee that if nothing else happened, the public debt would not explode. The Domar formula states that the debt-output ratio stays constant, if the deficits in % of GDP do not grow faster than nominal GDP. The average debt-output ratio of the EU countries in 1991, when the members of the committee fixed the criteria, happened to be 60%, the forecast for the long-term nominal growth rate (real growth plus inflation rate) was then 5%, and all the Maastricht committee members had to do was to calculate the net deficit in % of GDP:

Debt/GDP = (deficit/GDP)/ nominal growth rate of GDP
60% = 3% / 5%

Today there is an intense discussion about whether the budget criteria are reasonable or necessary. The debt-output ratio in itself is already a very doubtful measure. It is a stock (the mountain of debt) divided by a flow (the yearly GDP) which does not tell us much. But they have had an enormous political effect: Public Debt is considered as something bad, dangerous and punishable. And the Maastricht criteria make it legitimate for politicians to cut expenditures, for which they, otherwise, would not get domestic support.

Domar's idea of limits for public debt was followed by the concept of sustainability. Blanchard (1984) defined sustainability by the *maximum level of debt* which the government can sell without having to repudiate (part of the) debt. As Mongelli (1996, p. 4) pointed out, this definition ignores the fact that acceptable debt and deficits may change in the public opinion due to institutional arrangements such as joining the EU. Radaelli (2003) e.g. pointed out that the open method of co-ordination, such as bench marking, which the EU has adopted, has led to more shared norms vis à vis taxation and deficits. As a result, now EU member states find deficits less acceptable now than 10 years ago. But this might change again in the future when social expenditure needs make debts more acceptable than pension cuts.

3. IF THE MOUNTAIN OF DEBT HAS TO BE LEVELLED, SHOULD THIS GENERATION DO IT?

Even if we are of the opinion that the public debt has to be paid back at some finite date t, it still does not follow that it has to be paid back or reduced today. As we have seen from Table 1, most Dutch economists think that this generation should bring the debt down in order not to burden future generations, or in order to maintain room to manoeuvre for worse times.

3.1 Equity

But why should we pay for the benefit of the future generations? And carry the burden of the past generations too? The debt that we would have to pay back is the total debt that has accumulated since the founding of the Dutch kingdom in 1815. Public Choice theory argues that the current generation did not have the choice of determining the level of debt, which has piled up in the past and, therefore, it would not be fair to make them pay it back.

Furthermore, our past and present debts have been used to co-finance the society that we have created over the course of time: our physical, societal, legal, and political infrastructure, the built-up environment, the transport- and communication infrastructure, the knowledge that we have accumulated, our education and training systems, our educated population, our health care system, our pension schemes, our cultural heritage, etc. These will all be of benefit to the future generations, just as we benefit from the work of earlier generations. We and they also benefit from the high debt that was incurred to finance the victory over the Germans during the Second World War, as Buchanan (1958, Chapter 13) points out. War debts should be made permanent, because all future generations profit from this historic event. (What Buchanan does not tell us is what should happen to the losers. If we apply this same reasoning for the debt of the war losing countries, then also all future generations should be punished for the bad deeds of their ancestors).

If we paid off the public debt now, we would pay off the burden of both former, present, and future generations. Why should we do that? If the future generations have some of the benefits of today's public expenditures, why should they also not contribute in the costs, i.e. inherit some debt? Is that so unfair? Lorenz von Stein, who wrote a treatise on intergenerational fairness in 1842, argued that a state without public debt either does not invest enough in future generations, or it charges too much from the present generation. We do not have only to be fair to the future generations, but also to ourselves.

3.2 Diminishing marginal utility of income

Another reason for not paying off all public debt now is seen in the diminishing utility of income and money. The richer people are and the richer generations become, the less use they derive from additional income. Public debt can then be paid back slowly via a progressive income taxation from the rich. They suffer least from it. Future generations will be richer and can hence be more easily deprived of income to pay back the debt. And generations even further in the future will be even richer. That is, it is most economic if the last generation of mankind pays off all the debt. But for whom on earth?

3.3 Should this generation pay off the debt so that future pensions and health care are still payable?

Those who argue that this generation should pay back the public debt, or at least bring it substantially down, claim that room for manoeuvre should be maintained for the future instead of using up all the freedom and capacity to manoeuvre in the budget today.

The Dutch debt repayment debate is strongly rooted in the fear of the greying of the population. Coming from Austria, who together with Italy is called 'the old sick man of Europe', the ageing problem in the Netherlands sounds modest. But the Dutch expect the ageing problem to come later and wisely want to solve the problem some 40 years ahead.

But the pension problem cannot be solved through lower public debt. The pension problem occurs because an increasing share of the population gets older and its pensions have to be financed by a smaller and smaller number of younger workers and not because the public debt is high or because of public pensions.

The pension problem occurs both in a public and in a privately financed pension system. It does not solve the problem to switch from a public pay-as-you-go system, where the young generation pays the pensions of the old generation, in the form of the AOW (de Algemene Ouderdomswet, i.e. the public flat rate basic pension in the Netherlands), to a privately financed system, where each individual saves for his or her own pension. This is because in both cases the young working generation has to produce the goods and services for both the young and the old generation. The young generation will have to produce the food, the clothing, the transportation and health services for the old. A savings book is only a frozen claim on interest rate income, the income has to be produced in the future, in each period. If the young generation did not work, the older could not eat or dress or travel or have medical treatment, but could only eat up their then worthless savings books.[5]

Pension problems should not be mixed up with public debt problems. If the pensions cannot be financed because of an increase in old age population, neither public nor private pensions, funded or nonfunded, will solve the problem. Other policies, such as immigration policies, population steering policies or longer working years have then to be considered (see van Groezen, 2003).

One way to help to solve the pension problem (for the public and the private pension system) is to transfer real resources, that the public sector invests today in infrastructure in a broad sense. Infrastructure investments make it possible to really save for the future: the public sector invests today and the goods will be used in the future. The depreciation of infrastructure investments is the only real transfer possible, because they can be produced today and consumed in the future. Typical infrastructure investments in a broad sense are housing, good education, knowledge, transport and communication, a stable legal system, low corruption, and trust in political and economic institutions.

If we look at international comparisons, regarding pensions problems, the Dutch have a higher increase in future expenditures due to a greying population to expect, than most other European countries. But this is accompanied by a higher expected increase in revenues from old age contributions as well, leaving the Dutch with less pension problems than most other countries in forty or fifty years ahead.

The OECD (1998) has tried to estimate the impact of the increased greying of the population on government spending, taking into account the pension reforms already enacted.

The Dutch spend relatively little on public pensions, 5.2% (as compared to 8.9% EU average), but will experience a doubling of their pension expenditures by 2040. With expected revenue increases of 3.2% of GDP – which are much higher than in all other countries of comparison – this leaves the same gap as in the US, a widening of the budget deficit by 2.1% of GDP. With this gap the Netherlands stays below the expected EU average of -3.5% widening of deficits. Furthermore, it is doubtful whether the OECD assumptions that early pensions (VUT-regeling, vervroegde uittreding) will lead to such high expenditures will still hold, since the participation rate of the elderly is increasing, due to more flexible pension arrangements (Huygevoort, 2003, p. 7).

A second problem that the Netherlands shares with the US is the public health care financing problem. Both countries find themselves confronted with steeply rising health care costs. The Dutch have tried to combat this by price and capacity control. The government has limited the number of treatments that hospitals and doctors can carry out every year. Thus, an artificial shortage of capacity has been created, which manifests itself in the 'waiting list' problem. In the US such a check on costs is not

5 If the savings of the elderly are invested in real assets and increase the stock of physical capital, then productivity can increase and the elderly can actively contribute to the production of goods. I owe this point to Bas van Groezen. But in the extreme case that the young generation does not work at all, the elderly would end up with no interest payment income on their savings.

possible, with the result that costs of medical treatment are at least twice as high. Liability law, liability lawyers, liability insurance, and preventive medicine also contribute to these rising costs.

Health care is a sector characterised by many market failures. There are severe asymmetric information problems and principal/agent problems. The principal, the patient, has an information disadvantage relative to the agent, the doctor. Is the operation really necessary? Are the expensive pills really good for this treatment, or could a sea salt bath and other grandma's recipes also get rid of the complaint? Furthermore, there are spill over effects. If parts of the population suffer from a disease they might affect other parts of the population. Healthy workers also represent human capital, important for productivity and growth. Sick workers and their families have to be cared for. Finally there is the equity issue: all citizens should have equal access to something as fundamental for their existence as health care.

For all these reasons sooner or later the government gets involved in regulating, organising, financing, or even providing health care. Bismarck wanted healthy workers, and laid the basis for the Bismarckian, continental welfare state. Health can partly be privatised, as private doctors and private health insurance demonstrate. But it is a sector which can not and has not been left entirely to the private economy.

State involvement will probably even increase, as health care will still increase in importance in the future. We get older and older. At the moment the average life expectancy of men lies around 78 and of women around 82 years. Every year the life expectancy will increase by four months, if the trend of the last decades continues in the future. At the same time – and of course related to this – medical technology develops fast and makes many new treatments possible that everyone wants to have access to. Thus is seems safe to expect medical consumption to increase further in the future.

But this problem is – like the pension problem – a problem of demography and of population growth, and not of public sector debt. It – sometimes – only gets disguised as such. Pension and health reforms are necessary, but not with the argument that the public debt has to be paid back. If the public budget is used as a buffer to solve demographic problems, one has to accept high public debt. If reforms are made and society agrees on a different division of tasks, the size of the government can be smaller. But health and pension reforms do not have to be made *because* of the public debt. They have to be made because of the changes on the demand side (ageing) and supply side (new technology) of the health care sector.

4. CAN LEVELLING LEAD TO UNINTENDED AND UNWANTED CONSEQUENCES? THE 'SINT PIETERSBERG PARADOX'

A professed aim of paying back the public debt, and doing so now, is to create more room for manoeuvring future generations. However, under circumstances that are not unlikely, thriftiness could have unintended and unwanted consequences that make it turn into its opposite: instead of lower debt mountains we may find ourselves eventually with even higher piles of debt, reducing rather than increasing the future room to manoeuvre.

Thriftiness may be wise for the individual; for the government it is a risky strategy because the government is a large player. If the state saves today it dampens the economy, reduces income, gets less tax revenues, and has higher expenditures for unemployment and crisis payments. This may result in even higher public debt and less room to manoeuvre. More thriftiness will be necessary in the future and so forth leading to more conflicts, strikes, or even revolutions which are very costly for the economy. However, if the state spends an additional billion of Euros on education today, then additional people get training, find work, acquire income, and are able to pay back part of the state expenditure in the form of taxes. The message being: spend, and thou shalt receive.

Today, the debate whether government expenditures are good and increase employment and output (Keynesians), or dampen the economy because resources get taken away from the more efficient private sector (Neoclassics), seems to favour the latter. Therefore, the unwanted consequences of thrifty governments are not a big issue.

But there is a certain analogy with the Sint Pietersberg. Levelling this mountain might lead to new and perhaps even higher ones popping up elsewhere in the flat Dutch landscape: forests of skyscrapers shaped in concrete, dug out from the St. Pietersberg. Costly unemployment, diseases, strikes, conflict and unforeseen consequences might pop up here and there like rock pieces after the detonation. Not for nothing does the mountain carry the name of St. Pieter, meaning pietro, ‘rock’. Therefore we could call the paradox of levelling mountains leading to yet higher mountains the ‘Sint Pietersberg paradox’.

It is a variation on Keynes’ Savings Paradox which showed that if all people decide to save more, they may end up with saving less, because the aggregate decline in consumption will lower demand and depress the economy, so that finally people cannot realise their planned savings because they have less employment and income. In the end saving declines rather than increases. Similarly public debts will increase, when governments are too thrifty.

5. CONCLUSION

From history and from the fierce economic debate on public debt we can conclude that there is not one best figure or target for the limits of debt but some tolerance room, some room to manoeuvre within which governments can act. Public debt can fluctuate between margins.

Too high debts can create inflation, distrust in the government, and prevent investors from investing in the country, in particular, if these debts are made for wasteful government consumption, as is often the case in third world countries. But the Netherlands would not have to worry about that, given its responsible expenditures and the relative small size of the debt mountain.

However, if the debt is too low, it depresses the economy and does too little for the current or future generation. No debt is nonsense. A government, which wants to repudiate its debt fully is not 'the best boy in school' but rather a boy experimenting with dangerous chemicals which might explode. *Too little debts* mean too little care for the future or too much of a burden for the present generation. In the first case one will get the monkeys that one deserves if one spends only peanuts on education: one will get crime, low skilled labour, unemployment, and low growth. A low debt output ratio means an undersised government. But we need a government to fulfil tasks such as correcting for market failures, providing equity, and guaranteeing long term social well-being. If it does so by levying too high taxes from this generation, it reduces the consumption and saving possibilities of this generation. It, therefore, should pass on the mountain of debt to future generations without too much variation. Economic actors like stability and predictability. One should not frighten citizens time and again by casting doubt on questions like whether they will get their pensions and health care in the future.

In 1995, shortly before the euphoria over the 'poldermodel' started, Frans van Waarden, asked rhetorically: 'Breekt Nederland zijn dijken door?' (Is the Netherlands breaking down its dykes?). With dykes he meant the corporatist institutions that the Dutch developed in the course of history and that reduce risk and uncertainty and increase trust. Behind these institutional dykes it is relatively safe to invest and to engage in transactions, the basic units of employment and economic growth. One could say the same about a stable debt mountain. A mountain that is stable, not too high, and relatively flat on the top, like the Sint Pietersberg, may be hardly noticeable. But it spreads the burden of investments in our society over several generations. It provides stability and predictability, and also facilitates transactions, employment, and growth.

REFERENCES

Allers, M., Haan, J. de, & Kam, F. de (1998). Using survey data to test for Ricardian equivalence. In *Public Finance Review*, *26*, 565-582.

Auerbach, Alan & Feldstein, Martin (1985). *Handbook of Public Economics*, *Vol 1*, Elsevier North Holland.

Bastable, Charles F. (1895). *Public Finance*, *2nd ed.*, London. www.econlib.org/library/Bastable/bastbPFNotes2.html

Barro, Robert (1974). Are government bonds net wealth?, *Journal of Political Economy* , *vol 82, November,* 1095-1117.

Barro, Robert (1979). On the determination of public debt. *Journal of Political Economy*, *87*, 940-971.

Beaulieu, Paul-Leroy (1906). *Traité de la Science des Finances* , *7th ed.*, *Vol II*, Paris.

Becsi, Z. (2000). *The Shifty Laffer Curve*, Federal Reserve Bank of Atlanta Economic Review 85, 53-64.

Blanchard, O. (1981). Current and Anticipated Deficits, Interest Rates and Economic Activity, In *European Economic Review* 25, 7-27.

Blanchard, Olivier J. (1990). Suggestions for a New Set of Fiscal Indicators, *OECD Working Paper No 79*, Paris.

Blinder and Stiglitz (1983) Money, Credit Constraints and Economic Activity. *American Economic Review, Papers and Proceedings*, May.

Buchanan, James M. (1958, 1999). *Public Principles of Public Debt: A Defence and Restatement*, Liberty Fund, US, The Library of Economics and Liberty. www.econlib.org/library/Buchanan/buchCv2c0.html

Buchanan, J.M. (1976). Barro on the Ricardian equivalence theorem. *Journal of Political Economy*, *84*, 337-342.

Buiter, Willem H. (1985). A Guide to Public Sector Debt and Deficits, *Economic Policy*, *Vol 21*, *November,* 14-79.

Buiter, Willem H. (1988). Death, birth, productivity growth and debt neutrality. *The Economic Journal, 98*, 279-293.

Buiter, Willem H. (1990). *Principles of Budgetary and Financial Policy*, Cambridge Mass: MIT Press.

Buiter, Willem H., & Kletzer, K.M. (1992). Government Solvency, Ponzi Finance and the Redundancy and Usefulness of Public Debt, *Working Paper* No. 4076, National Bureau of Economic Research (NBER), Cambridge.

Buiter, Willem H., Corsetti, G. & Roubini, N. (1993). Excessive Deficicits: Sense and Nonsense in the Treaty of Maastricht, *Economic Policy 16*, 57-100. wwlw.uc3m.es/uc3m/gral/TC/ESDO/esdo04macroi.html

Buiter, Willem H. (1999). Notes on 'A Code for Fiscal Stability'. *CEPR Discussion Papers* www.econpapers.hhs.se/scripts/ search.asp?kw=public&pg=7

Buiter, Willem H. & Grafe, Clemens (2003). Patching up the Pact. Some Suggestions for Enhancing Fiscal Sustainability and Macroeconomic Stability in an Enlarged European Union, 13 January www.nber.org/~wbuiter/trans.pdf

Calvo, G. (1988). Servicing the Public Debt: The role of Expectations; *American Economic Review* 78. Reprinted in G. Calvo (1996): *Money, Exchange Rates and Output*; Cambridge Mass: MIT Press.

Cohn, Gustav (1889). *System der Finanzwissenschaft*, Stuttgart.

CPB. (2003). CPB Report 2003/1, *Quarterly Review of CPB Nederlands*, Centraal Plan Bureau, Netherlands' Bureau for Economic Policy Analysis, The Hague.

Croce, Enzo & Ramón, Hugo Juan (2003). Assessing Fiscal Sustainability, A Cross-Country Comparison, *IMF Working Papers* July, WP/03/145.

Detragiache E. & Spilimbergo, A. (2001). Crisis and Liquidity: Evidence and Interpretation, *IMF Working Papers* 01/02.

Di Laurea, Davide & Ricciuti, Roberto (2002). Departures from Ricardian Equivalence: An Experimental Evaluation, Department of Economics, University of Siena, Italy.

Domar, Evsey D. (1944). The Burden of the Debt and the National Income. *American Economic Review 34*, 798-827.

ESB. (2003). Economisch-Statistische Berichten, January.

Feldstein, Martin (1988). The effects of fiscal policy when incomes are uncertain: a contradiction to Ricardian equivalence. *American Economic Review, 78*, 14-23.

Freeman, Richard B. (1999). The New Inequality: Creating Solutions for Poor America. In J. Cohen & J. Rogers (Eds.), *New Democracy Forum Series*. Boston: Beacon Press.

Frenkel, J.A. & Razin, A. (1996). *Fiscal Policies and Growth in the World Economy*. Cambridge: MIT Press.

Frey, Bruno S. (2003). *The Role of Deterrence and Tax Morale in Taxation in the European Union,* Jelle Zijlstra Lecture 1, NIAS, the Netherlands Institute for Advanced Study in the Humanities and Social Sciences, Wassenaar.

Giavazzi, F. & Pagano, M. (1996). Non-Keynesian Effects of Fiscal Policy Changes: International Evidence and the Swedish Experience, *Swedish Economic Policy Review 3*, 69-103.

Groezen, Bas van (2003). *The Wealth of Generations. Ageing, Pensions and Welfare from a Macroeconomic Perspective,* PhD Thesis, Tilburg University.

Hansen, Alvin H. (1941). *Fiscal Policy and Business Cycles*, p. 185, New York.

Harris, Seymour E. (1947). *The National Debt and the New Economics*, New York, McGraw-Hill Book Company, p. 25, p. 55.

Huygevoort, Guus van (2003). Paniek over vergrijzing is misplaatst, *De Volkskrant*, 9.10.2003, p. 7.

Keynes, J.M. (1936). *The General Theory of Employment, Interest and Money*, Vol 7 of the Collected Writings of John Maynard Keynes, Cambridge.

Kleinknecht, A. (2003). *Loonmatiging leidt niet altijd tot economisch herstel*, Vakbondscafe den Haag, Solidariteit, 14.February. http://www.solidariteit.nl/vbcafes/den_haag/2003/feb.html

Lerner, Abba P. (1948). The Burden of the National Debt. In Lloyd A. Metzler, *Income, Employment and Public Policy W,* (pp. 255-275). New York: W. Norton and company.

McCallum , B. (1984). Are Bond-financed Deficits inflationary? A Ricardian Analysis, *Journal of Political Economy, vol. 92, no. II.*

Meade, J.E. (1945). Mr. Lerner on 'The Economics of Control', *Economic Journal, LV, April*, pp. 47-70.

Melon, J.F. (1734). *Essai Politique*, Chapter 23 in: Economistes Financiers du 18me *siecle*, (cited in Bastable, C.F. (1895, p. 613)).

Mongelli, F. (1996). The Effects of European Economic and Monetary Union (EMU) on National Fiscal Sustainability; *IMF Working Paper* WP/96/72, July, Washington.

Morgan, Gareth (1986). *Images of Organizations*, London: Sage.

Musgrave, Richard (1985). A Brief History of Fiscal Doctrine. In: A. Auerbach & M. Feldstein (Eds), *Handbook of Public Economics, Vol 1*, (pp. 1-59, chapter 1), Elsevier, North Holland.

OECD. (1998). *Maintaining Prosperity in an Ageing Socie ty*, Organisation for Economic Development and Cooperation, Paris.

OECD. (2000). *Fiscal Positions and Business Cycles*. Organisation for Economic Development and Cooperation, Paris.

Pattilo, Catherine, Poirson, Helene, & Ricci, Luca (2002). External Debt and Growth, *IMF Working Paper* 02/69.

Pigou, A.C. (1949). *A Study in Public Finance, 3d ed.*, p. 38. London: Macmillan and Co., Ltd.

Ploeg, Frederick van der (2003). Rolling back the Public Sector, Differential Effects on Employment, Investment and Growth, *European University Institute, Florence and CESifo,* September, www.iue.it/Personal/ RickvanderPloeg/ publicemplgrowth.wps.pdf

Radaelli, Claudio (2001). The Code of Conduct against Harmful Tax Competition, Open Coordination Method in Disguise? www.bradford.ac.uk/acad/ssis/staff_contact/ radaelli/code.htm

Ricardo, David (1817). Principles of Political Economy and Taxation. Reprinted in P. Sraffa & M.H. Dobb (Eds.) (1951-1973) *The Works and Correspondence of David Ricardo, Vol 1.* Cambridge: Cambridge University Press, Royal Economic Society.

Ricardo, David (1820). Funding System. Reprinted in P. Sraffa & M.H. Dobb (Eds.) (1951-1973) *The Works and Correspondence of David Ricardo, Vol IV.* Cambridge: Cambridge University Press, Royal Economic Society.

Ricciuti, Roberto (2003). Assessing Ricardian Equivalence, in Journal of Economic Surveys, *Volume 17 Issue 1*, 55-70, February.

Roeper, H. & Weimer, W. (1996). *Die D-Mark. Eine deutsche Wirtschaftsgeschichte*; Societätsverlag, Frankfurt.

Smith, Adam (1776). *An Inquiry into the Wealth of Nations,* In E. Cunnan (1904) (Ed.). New York: Putnam's Sons.

Stein, Lorenz v. (1842). *Der Sozialismus und Kommunismus im heutigen Frankreich*, Leipzig.

Thio, K.B.T. (2002). Aflossen staatsschuld is niet nodig. In ESB, 18 January.

Unger, Brigitte (1987). Die Auswirkungen der Finanzierung von Budgetdefiziten, PhD of the Wirtschaftsuniversitaet Wien, Vienna.

Unger, Brigitte & Heitzmann, Karin (2003). The Austrian Welfare State: Back to Bismarck?, *Journal of European Social Policy,* November.

Van Waarden, Frans (1995). Breekt Nederland zijn dijken door? Shortened version of inaugural lecture, in *Economisch-Statistische Berichten, vol. 80, no. 3993*, 52-57.

Wagner, Adolf (1877). *Finanzwissenschaft Vol. I*, Leipzig.

Wicksell, Knut (1896). *Finanztheoretische Untersuchungen*, Jena.

C.J.M. KOOL

THE GLOBAL MARKET FOR CAPITAL: FRIEND OR FOE

INTRODUCTION

Het Financieële Dagblad of 20th September 2003 reported that Dutch pension funds did much better on their overall stock portfolio in the second quarter of 2003 than did Dutch insurance companies. The reason given is that Dutch pension funds are much better diversified internationally than the insurers. Eighty per cent of the pension funds' stock portfolio consists of foreign stocks against thirty per cent for the insurers. Of course, more diversification does not always provide larger profits. Significant upward swings in Dutch stock prices will benefit insurers more, but large downward swings also hurt them more.

The 2002 annual report of Ericsson, a well-known Swedish-based telecom firm, states that Ericsson conducts business in 140 countries, but reports its results in SEK (Swedish Kroner). Significant revenues, costs, assets and debts are in foreign (non-Swedish) currencies, leading to exposure of the net results to unexpected exchange rate movements. Ericsson uses international financial markets extensively to hedge its exchange rate exposure. In particular, Ericsson funds part of its operations by borrowing US dollars in international debt markets. It uses amongst others both a Medium Term Note programme (for a maximum of US $5 bln, with issuances in Euros, dollars, Swedish Kroners and British pounds) and a Commercial Paper programme (in US dollars, Euros and Swedish Kroner). In addition, Ericsson actively uses international financial markets for derivative products such as forward rate agreements, swaps and futures to limit the currency risk on its operations.

In 2002, the United States obtained over 75 per cent of the excess savings of all capital exporting countries in the world, as shown in figure 1. Most of these excess savings came from Japan (20.9%), Germany (9.2%), China (6.6%), and Switzerland (6.1%).[1] In theory, under perfectly free global capital markets capital flows from countries where it is available in abundance to countries where it is scarce. In particular, it allows capital-poor developing countries to borrow from the rest of the world and to import financial capital to promote investment and growth at a faster rate than would be possible on the basis of its own domestic savings. Mature (capital-rich) economies

1 Source: Global Financial Stability Report, IMF (2003a).

P. de Gijsel and H. Schenk (eds.), Multidisciplinary Economics, 405–424.

with a large working population can save and lend abroad for a while. Subsequently, when this population ages and their own productive capacity declines, such economies can start dissaving and consume the returns on foreign investments.

On a macroeconomic level, international financial markets do indeed facilitate the transfer from countries with excess savings (exporters of financial capital) to countries with a shortage of savings but an excess of investment opportunities (importers of financial capital). As a result financial capital is allocated to where it can be used most profitably, regardless of destination. It does not necessarily imply that capital flows from rich developed countries to poor developing countries, however. Figure 1 provides evidence to the opposite.

Overall, these examples show that the Netherlands and the other industrialised countries are increasingly linked with and dependent on the international financial system. Generally, we hardly realise this to be the case and take its benefits for granted. However, they depend on the almost complete liberalisation of capital flows among the developed countries. It implies that every individual, bank, company, pension fund, and government in these countries can choose without restriction in which country or currency to invest or to borrow. The almost perfect capital mobility, realised through full liberalisation and globalisation of the international financial system has many potential advantages.

Firstly, they help to mobilise global savings and to allocate these efficiently so that profitable investment opportunities can indeed be exploited. Secondly, they facilitate the trading, hedging, diversifying and pooling of risk by individual consumers, corporations, institutional investors, and governments alike. Thirdly, and perhaps most fundamentally, they facilitate international trade in goods and services. Fourthly, they provide information on the performance of the issuers of stocks and bonds by incorporating all available information in market prices efficiently and so contribute to corporate control.[2] In addition, one might argue that opening up one's country for foreign capital not only leads to more discipline on government's macroeconomic policies and contributes to domestic financial development by reducing entry barriers and increasing outside competition but also signals the government's intentions to have more investor-friendly oriented policies in the future, see Prasad et al. (2003).

The above impressive list of advantages laid the foundation for the growing consensus among academics, politicians, and national and supranational policymakers in the late 1980 that a free global capital market should be realised as soon as possible. Therefore, the vanguard of the more advanced developing countries – called emerging market economies – enthusiastically started with domestic and international financial liberalisation.

2 I refer to Obstfeld (1998), Eichengreen et al. (1998) and Prasad et al. (2003) for extensive discussions on the benefits of liberalised international capital markets.

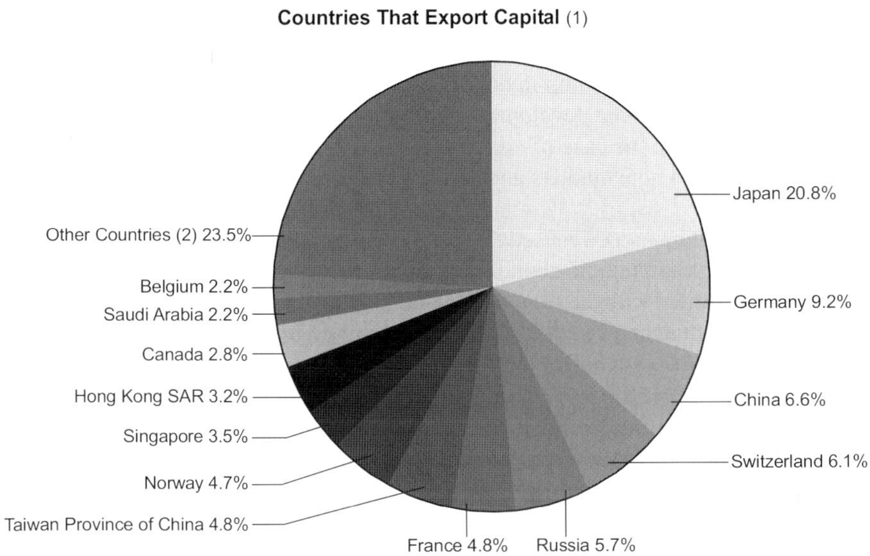

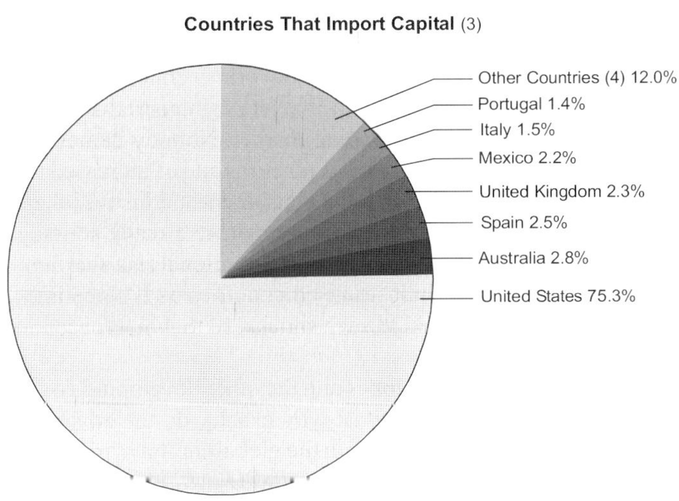

Source: International Monetary Fund, World Economic Outlook database as of August 21, 2003
1) As measured by countries' current (capital) account surplus (deficit).
2) Other countries include all countries with shares of total surplus less than 2.2 per cent.
3) As measured by countries' current (capital) account deficit (surplus).
4) Other countries include all countries with shares of total deficit less than 1.4 per cent.

Figure 1. Global Capital Flows, Sources and Uses of Global Capital in 2002.

Examples of these economies are Chile, Brazil, Russia and Malaysia. Both supranational institutions like the IMF and Western governments, companies and banks strongly stimulated liberalisation in the developing world. Partly from the conviction that it would help economic development and growth in the countries concerned and partly – particularly in the case of multinational banks and companies – because that liberalisation offered new markets and profit opportunities for themselves.

Initially, liberalisation indeed caused fast capital inflows into the emerging economies, leading to high investment and economic growth. However, in the second half of the 1990s, disappointment with the results of financial globalisation policies grew, particularly because a sequence of serious bank and currency crises occurred, which made capital flow out as fast as it had entered in the years before. The crises were characterised by a collapse of the domestic financial system, massive devaluation of the domestic currency, a loss of international reserves, and a domestic recession. Such crises appeared to hit and hurt in a disproportional way exactly those developing countries that had made the largest effort to liberalise their financial markets.[3] Obviously, events in the late 1990s moderated the initial enthusiasm for international financial liberalisation considerably. Some countries instated capital controls again. More generally, a global discussion started on the causes and consequences of financial crises and the costs and benefits of financial globalisation. Even 'The Economist', the British weekly notorious for its principled pro-liberalisation position titled its 2003 annual survey of international finance 'A Cruel Sea of Capital'. Apparently all that glitters is not gold.

It still is as far as the industrialised world is concerned. Multinational corporations and banks as well as governments all over the industrialised world continue to embrace the principles of the global capital market. Nobody denies the benefits of increased hedging and funding opportunities for firms and of increased investment and diversification opportunities for individual consumers and institutional investors. Prasad et al. (2003) show that the advanced economies are already so integrated that they almost fully exploit the potential benefits of international risk sharing. Even when a financial crisis hits one or more industrialised countries as it sometimes does, these countries appear to be quite resilient to such shocks, so that macroeconomic consequences tend to be limited.

For the emerging economies and the other developing countries matters are different. For them, the main issue is: why exactly do the advanced emerging economies appear to be the most vulnerable in the global capital market and to what extent can this vulnerability be reduced by appropriate measures, either by improving market functioning and performance or by limiting use of that market. For the larger group of less financially integrated developing economies the issue may be even more crucial. Should they follow the path of the emerging economies and fully liberalise, and if so along which route, or should they keep their distance from the global capital market for the time being. Perhaps it is good to note that hardly anybody doubts the long-term advantages of financial globalisation. The point is that the fruits of globalisation can

3 See Prasad et al. (2003), and Weller (1999).

apparently be reaped only when the economy has developed and matured sufficiently. Particularly the intermediate transition period seems to bring additional risks.

To illustrate the issue more adequately, let me compare optimal capital mobility with optimal traffic mobility. Take the Dutch highway network. It is the artery network of our traffic infrastructure. Its development over time has increased the set of feasible combinations for living and working enormously, offering more choices both for companies and households. Most people see this as a sign of progress. Even those who don't wouldn't probably fancy a return to the late 19th century when everyday life necessarily took place in a circle with a radius of about 5 miles.

Obviously, not everybody is allowed to drive on the highway; one needs a license and a car that meets a number of basic criteria. Individually, the following order of events can be distinguished in the Netherlands. In his or her early teens, a teenager starts longing to be able to drive, but unfortunately he or she is still too young. At eighteen, he or she can take lessons and drive under the careful supervision of an instructor. At some point, he or she passes the necessary theory and practical exams and finally is allowed to drive independently. With some luck the new driver can sometimes borrow his or her parents' car but in most cases he or she will have to rely on a second- or thirdhand car that has already clocked too many miles. After a number of years, he or she will be able to buy the dream car and use the highway as an experienced and relaxed driver.

This example goes a long way in telling the story about the ups and downs of international capital mobility. The highway system symbolises the global market for capital, where the drivers are participants – individual investors, firms, banks and governments – and the cars represent the stability and institutional quality of the domestic economy in general and of the domestic financial system in particular.

IS FINANCE THE DRIVING FORCE BEHIND GROWTH?

I now turn to the issue of the importance of having a well-developed and stable domestic financial system. Although economists differ in their judgment about how important financial development is for economic growth, the balance has certainly shifted from a definite 'no' in the early 1990s towards a qualified 'yes' today.[4] In the terminology of my previous metaphor, it is important to have a car that is maintained well, checked regularly and equipped with lights, brakes etc. in order to drive safely on the highway.

4 Levine (1997) extensively elaborates on the theoretical foundations of the finance-growth link. The arguments – though in a closed economy setting –are very similar of course to the ones listed above in the case of global markets.

In a recent overview article, Levine (2003) summarises recent empirical evidence on the finance-growth nexus as follows:[5]

- Countries with better-developed financial systems – both financial intermediaries and financial markets – tend to grow faster.
- Simultaneity bias does not seem to be the cause of this result.
- Better-functioning financial systems ease the external financing constraints that impede firm and industrial expansion.

Put differently, according to Levine both the existence of well-developed stock and bond markets and the existence of a well-designed banking system contribute to higher economic growth.[6] In his second point he addresses the possibility of bicausality. In theory, a positive correlation between the level of financial development and the rate of economic growth could result from reverse causation. Higher growth – caused by other exogenous factors – would stimulate the further development of the financial system, according to the saying 'where enterprise leads, finance follows'. Nevertheless, Levine concludes that even accounting for this possibly contaminating effect, the link from finance to growth remains. Thirdly, Levine identifies a specific finance-growth channel by showing that firms are able to exploit existing profit opportunities better when a financial system facilitates their funding. If not, they have to rely mainly on internal funding – withheld profits – which could strongly constrain their operation and future expansion.

Table 1. Selected Indicators on the Size of Capital Markets, 2002[7]

Country	GDP	Equity	Debt	Bank Assets	Total Assets	Asset/GDP (%)
World (bln US $)	32,164	22,077	43,358	85,003	150,438	468
	in % of world:					
US	32,5	50,1	43,8	14,3	35,4	509
EU	26,9	25,0	29,1	40,8	35,1	611
Japan	12,4	9,3	16,2	18,1	16,2	612
Emerging Economies	22,7	8,2	5,8	12,4	9,9	205

5 Rousseau (2003) draws a similar conclusion from four historical case studies from the past 400 years. For a dissenting view on the relevance of financial development, I refer to Favara (2003), who concludes after a reassessment of contemporaneous empirical evidence that the link is weak and unreliable.

6 Standard – admittedly imperfect – empirical proxy variables that are used to measure the depth and liquidity of domestic financial markets are the amount of bank deposits relative to GDP or the stock market capitalisation in terms of GDP and stock market turnover relative to market capitalisation.

7 Source: Global Financial Stability Report, September 2003, IMF.

In table 1 I present a few stylised statistics underscoring Levine's argument. As shown in the table, cross-country differences in domestic financial development are extremely large. Capital market capitalisation in the advanced economies is about 90 per cent of the world's total on average. The emerging market economies only accounted for about 8 per cent of the world's stock markets, 6 per cent of the world's bond markets and 12 per cent of the world's bank assets, whereas they produced 22,7 per cent of the world's GDP in 2002 (measured in current US dollars). The other developing countries lack financial markets of any significance. Also note the cross-country differences in the depth of financial markets as indicated by the ratio of total financial assets to GDP (in percentages). In the EU and Japan this ratio equals about 600, in the US 500 and in the emerging markets on average about 200. For other developing countries, the ratio is much lower still.[8] In general, the stylised facts show that financial development has progressed considerably further in advanced economies than in the rest of the world. Even the most advanced developing countries follow at a big distance only. Summarising, I conclude that substantial support exists for at least a proximate causality link from domestic financial development to economic growth. This suggests that we need strategies for developing countries to improve and expand their financial infrastructures.

Zingales (2003) generally agrees with Levine (2003) but simultaneously points at weaknesses in our understanding of the link between financial development and growth. He stipulates along the lines of La Porta et al. (1999) that

> 'there is a group of countries that seem to be doing the right thing in many dimensions: their legal enforcement is better, their level of generalised trust is higher, their judicial system more efficient and independent; they have less corruption, less regulation, more respect for property rights, and better-developed financial markets.'

Individually, all of the factors probably contribute positively to economic growth. Identifying which factor or which combination of factors is dominant in this respect is quite difficult. Moreover, underlying the presence of these factors may be something called 'social capital'. Guiso, Sapienza and Zingales (2000) show that the presence of social capital is highly correlated with the level of financial development across countries. It takes the analysis just one step further, as we then need to know what contributes to the development of social capital.

COSTS AND BENEFITS OF FINANCIAL GLOBALISATION

To know whether international financial integration is important for countries over and above their indigenous financial development, we need to turn to the theoretical and empirical literature on international financial integration or financial globalisation. In

8 Note these numbers are for the year 2002, after the strong stock market decline in 2000-2001.

this respect, history is quite supportive on the potential contribution of open global capital markets. In the period 1870-1914, the last period of financial globalisation at a level equivalent to today, net capital flows from developed countries like the UK, the Netherlands and France to developing countries like the US, Australia, Canada and Argentina were in the order of magnitude of between 3 and 5 per cent of GDP according to Eichengreen et al. (1998), Obstfeld (1998) and Prasad et al. (2003). The net capital flow stimulated strong investment and economic growth in these capital-poor countries.

Current experience is somewhat different. Firstly, advanced economies have been the prime users and beneficiaries of international capital markets over the past decade, as was clear from figure 1. Secondly, from the early 1990s onward, international capital flows both between developed countries and from developed to developing countries nevertheless surged. For developed countries the upward trend continued up till 2000 when stock markets started to decline globally and the world economy moved into a recession. The observed increase in capital inflows into the developing world – and particularly the group of emerging economies – in the early 1990s corresponded with generally declining capital controls and barriers to financial market access in developing countries, see Prasad et al. (2003). Also, many of these developing countries enjoyed very high rates of economic growth initially. But the increased financial openness of developing countries also facilitated the massive outflow of short-run capital after 1995, typically followed by recession and low economic growth in the countries concerned. Thirdly, huge differences exist in the behaviour of different types of international financial flows. We generally distinguish between foreign direct investment, comprising long-term investment in physical plant and equipment, portfolio investment, consisting of investments in stock markets and different types of debt markets, and other investment, including official capital flows from government and (supra) national financial institutions like the IMF and World Bank, and loans from banks and other private parties. While FDI flows tend to be reasonably stable over time, portfolio investment and bank loans are highly volatile. Table 2 gives an overview of capital inflows and outflows for the US and the emerging market economies for the years 1992, 1999, and 2002. From 1998 onward, emerging economies are confronted with a net outflow of portfolio investment and other investment, leading to a deteriorating economic position.

Prasad et al. (2003) analyse the benefits of financial globalisation for developing countries more systematically. They distinguish between a group of 22 **More Financially Developed** (MFIs) countries – roughly corresponding with the group of emerging market economies introduced before – and a group of 33 **Less Financially Developed** (LFIs) countries. They show that the 22 MFIs receive around 95 per cent of net private capital inflows, leaving 5 per cent for the LFIs.[9] By far the largest category in private capital flows to developing countries consists of Foreign Direct Investment (FDI).

9 In addition, one should note that the IMF in its 2003 World Economic Outlook reports on 125 developing countries and 28 transition countries. Apart from the 22 MFIs and 33 LFIs in Prasad's analysis, over 70 developing countries remain virtually cut off from private international capital flows.

Table 2. Selected Capital Flows (bln of US dollars)[10]

	Inflows			Outflows		
Country	1992	1999	2002	1992	1999	2002
United States						
Direct inv.	19,8	289,4	39,6	48,3	224,9	137,8
Portfolio inv.	72,0	285,6	421,4	49,2	116,2	-15,8
Other inv.	78,9	165,2	245,9	-19,1	288,4	53,3
Total US	170,7	740,2	707,0	78,4	512,4	182,7
Emerging Economies						
Direct inv.	48,7	205,1	165,5	10,0	29,7	22,3
Portfolio inv.	51,7	52,6	-23,3	1,7	39,8	31,9
Other inv.	78,0	-23,0	42,1	19,2	71,1	43,7
Total emerging economies	178,3	234,6	184,4	30,9	140,6	97,9

In addition, MFIs especially received more and more portfolio investments in new emerging market bond and stock markets and bank lending up till 1995-1996. Prasad et al. (2003) fail to find a significant correlation between increasing financial openness and economic growth for their sample of countries between 1982 and 1997.[11] They give an overview of fourteen earlier studies on the issue and find roughly similar conclusions. In addition, Prasad et al. (2003) use a case study approach to give examples of both financially liberalised countries (Peru, South Africa) with slow growth, and non-financially liberalised countries (Botswana, Mauritius) with high growth. Finally, they show that in the 1990s MFIs experienced volatility of both the level of private consumption and the consumption-income ratios. That is, while theory predicts increased financial development results in more income and consumption smoothing, the opposite appears to be true for the MFIs in the 1990. Compared to LFIs their performance deteriorates in this respect. It seems to be the case that exactly those countries that have financially opened up their economies have been affected negatively. Overall, the Prasad et al. (2003) results raise doubts about the urgency and necessity for each and every developing country to start full-fledged liberalisation immediately. Interestingly, they do report evidence that increased FDI flows do have the predicted positive effect on economic growth, particularly when the capital importing countries have a sufficient level and amount of human capital. This suggests the desirability of liberalising different types of capital at different speeds.

10 Source: Global Financial Stability Report, September 2003, IMF

11 Of course, this result may be qualified by noting that all types of methodological problems exist, such as the timing of the liberalisation and the horizon over which any positive effect might be realised, see for instance the discussion in Bekaert et al. (2003).

Of course, all of the above results are affected by the occurrence of a sequence of financial crises in emerging economies in the 1990s. We now turn to a brief analysis of these crises to get a clearer picture of their causes and impact. In particular, we need to address the issue of whether and how financial globalisation influences the probability of a financial crisis.[12]

FINANCIAL CRISES IN DEVELOPING COUNTRIES

In the past decade, major financial crises occurred in Mexico (1994-1995), South-East Asia (1997), Russia (1998), Brazil (1999) and Argentina (2002). Of course, crises occurred before the 1990s as well. Kaminsky and Reinhart (1999) analyse 26 banking crises and 76 currency crises in the period 1970-1995 for a set of 20 small open economies on semi-fixed exchange rates. Fifteen out of these twenty countries are developing countries. Especially in the second half of their sample, twin crises – defined as banking crises followed within two years by a balance of payments crisis – are relatively frequent. According to their analysis, the bail-out costs of a single banking crisis are on average 5.1 per cent of GDP, while they are 13.3 per cent of GDP in the case of a twin crisis. Caprio and Honohan (1999) discuss 59 banking crashes between 1970 and 1997 and arrive at an average bail-out cost of 4 per cent of GDP in industrialised countries and 9 per cent in developing countries. Eichengreen (2002) presents evidence on financial crises from 1880 till 1997 and concludes that 'crises have always been with us and always will be and that they remain a particular problem in developing countries'.

Both Eichengreen (2002), Kaminsky and Reinhart (1999) and Weller (1999) point out that especially the number of banking crises and, correspondingly, twin crises have substantially increased since the late 1970s. They conclude that financial deregulation and liberalisation both internally and externally has often preceded these crises. In many cases, banking and particularly currency crises coincide with severe debt-servicing problems.[13] Again, these are of concern to developing countries mostly. The IMF reports in its September 2003 World Economic Outlook that 48 out of 108 net debt countries – out of 125 developing countries – faced arrears and/or rescheduling problems in the period 1997-2001.

From a slightly different perspective Jeanne and Zettelmeyer (2001) focus on IMF lending programmes, typical of to countries in crisis with debt-servicing problems. They document 165 complete and 88 incomplete debt cycles in the period 1947-2000. Only 31 of the complete debt cycles occurred in advanced economies; the remaining 134 complete and 88 incomplete debt cycles occurred in developing countries. Complete cycles in industrialised countries have an average duration of 4.7 years, in

12 It is not my goal to give an exhaustive evaluation of the literature on financial crises. It is simply too large to do so. For recent overviews, I refer to Efferink et al (2003), Garretsen et al. (1999), and contributions in Glick et al. (2001).

13 For an extensive discussion on the differences between sovereign risk, country risk, and currency risk, see Efferink et al. (2003).

developing countries they take on average 7.1 years. Incomplete cycles last longer, 17.9 years on average. For the group of 27 emerging market economies, Jeanne and Zettelmeyer (2001) report 38 complete debt cycles with an average length of 7.8 years and 15 incomplete debt cycles with an average length of 13.8 years between 1947 and 2000. For this group, 37 out of 38 complete cycles were initiated after 1991. Most incomplete cycles, sometimes reflecting almost indefinite lending programs by the IMF, occur in Africa where most of the HIPC (Highly Indebted Poor Countries) countries are located.

Overall, the above evidence suggests that financial crises are costly and especially hit developing countries after liberalisation. The question then is where these crises come from and whether the global capital market plays a negative role in the run up to and the propagation of a crisis. To answer the question I briefly note a few recurrent characteristics of countries faced with financial crises.

- A fixed or semifixed exchange rate regime
- Internal financial liberalisation in combination with weak regulatory and supervisory institutional frameworks
- External financial liberalisation
- An overvalued real exchange rate in combination with current account deficits
- Large short-run capital inflows
- Extensive build-up of unhedged foreign currency denominated bank loans reflecting extensive domestic borrowing by governments, banks and corporations
- Inappropriate macroeconomic (monetary and fiscal) policies

A combination of a number of these factors, especially, may create so much vulnerability that even small shocks can trigger a crisis. For illustrative purposes, let us consider the following sequence.[14]

Assume that a country liberalises its financial system both internally and externally and simultaneously adopts a fixed exchange rate regime. The rationale for the latter choice is often that it reduces exchange rate uncertainty and thus helps attract more foreign investment (at lower costs). In addition, it disciplines domestic macroeconomic policies: monetary policy must aim at keeping the exchange rate fixed and fiscal deficits cannot be monetised. In short, it is a way of building up credibility in the country's policies, at the expense of flexibility. It ties the government's hands effectively.

However, problems may arise. Firstly, even with reasonably sensible macroeconomic policies, domestic inflation may exceed inflation in the anchor country, leading to an overvaluation of the currency, loss of competitiveness and subsequent current account deficits. That is, the country starts borrowing abroad to pay for spending in excess of production. In itself, that would not be a real problem in the long run, as long as these

14 Inappropriate macroeconomic policies per se can directly trigger a currency crisis. This first generation type crisis has become less frequent in recent years. Therefore, I focus on second and third generation crises. See Copeland (2000) for an overview.

borrowings were used for investment rather than consumption. Clearly, this isn't always the case.

Secondly, borrowing abroad by government, banks or corporations often takes place in foreign currency – for instance US dollars and in the form of short-term bank loans. Moreover, the bank loan contract nowadays regularly contains clauses to allow the lending – multinational – bank to sue the borrower under the jurisdiction of the country in which the bank resides. Finally, most of the debt is short-term.[15] All these elements seemingly reduce the lending bank's risk and lead to borrowing at much lower interest rates than would be the case for loans in domestic currency as well as larger credit volumes. Of course, the risk is not gone but simply reappears in another form, namely that of a higher probability of borrower's default. Nevertheless, the current standard constructions appear to make lending banks easier on credit than they perhaps should be. This is reinforced by the lack of recognition that private foreign debt incurred by banks and corporations in developing countries often is implicitly or explicitly guaranteed by the government. As a result, a country's foreign debt is not in effect a diversified portfolio of loans to different parties with different and uncorrelated credit risk, but more like one undiversified loan to the country, making the debt subject to sovereign country risk. This holds especially if domestic parties taken together do not hedge their foreign currency exposure in the global capital market and jointly face a currency mismatch.

In addition, the moral hazard issue may be relevant in international lending and borrowing decisions. To the extent that supranational institutions like the IMF are expected to bail out developing countries – and indirectly multinational banks – in the case of a crisis, these banks may be willing to lend out more than they would otherwise do, while countries are inclined to borrow more than they would otherwise do. In the popular press, it is often stated that these bail-outs are at the expense of the international taxpayers. Jeanne and Zettelmeyer (2001) however argue that it is the taxpayer in the developing country hit by the crisis that ultimately pays the bill. They document that IMF loans may be channelled through to multinational banks and other private creditors initially to a large extent, but that the borrowing developing countries ultimately repay most of their IMF debt.[16] According to Jeanne and Zettelmeyer, in the end the developing country's government may face a greater moral hazard at the expense of its own citizens. Nevertheless, the experience of the 1990s has started a bout of criticism on the IMF particularly, see for instance Stiglitz (2002), as well as an ongoing discussion on reform of the international financial architecture in general and supranational institutions like the IMF and the World Bank in particular.

Thirdly, it is interesting to note that in principle the fixed exchange rate regime eliminates the threat of direct monetisation of a government deficit, but external

15 Eichengreen (2002) notes that the Basel I requirements lead banks to prefer making short-term loans as these are perceived to be less risky for the bank and thus have lower reserve requirements. From an individual bank point of view this is correct, for the system as a whole however, the effect is perverse leading to more risk due to joint withdrawal of loans when uncertainty increases.

16 Of course, private creditors do bear part of the default costs, but historically they come out positive on average even when incorporating partial default, as stated by Eichengreen (1991).

financial liberalisation in combination with the fixed exchange rate regime immediately opens the door for irresponsible government finances as it facilitates cheap borrowing abroad.[17] So a fixed exchange rate regime does not necessarily discipline a government's policies but – at least temporarily – allows both good and bad policies, as argued by Willett (2000).

Fourthly, weak regulation and supervision of the domestic financial system may result in inappropriate lending by banks to friends and family, resulting in large bad loan portfolios. If domestic banks expect to be bailed out by their government, such lending may be subject to moral hazard again.

A country with a number of the above characteristics finds itself in a fragile equilibrium that can be easily disturbed by even a small shock. Increased investor uncertainty about the political or economic stability of the developing country, a single domestic banking default, or for instance a sudden rise in global interest rates increasing the country's debt-servicing burden can all lead to a loss of confidence and a withdrawal of the short-term capital. Mishkin (1999) shows how incomplete information can contribute to this process and lead to herding and possibly contagion effects in other countries. Contagion may occur both through trade links, because of similarities in economic characteristics and conditions and because of self-fulfilling prophecies and lack of discrimination by irrational investors.[18] According to Willett (2000) this is the 'too much, too late' hypothesis. First, financial markets allow excessive borrowing to go on too long and too much; in the end, the situation is corrected too late, leading to an overshooting reaction.

In the terminology of my highway metaphor, emerging market economies in such a situation can best be compared to the group of young male drivers that recently got their license and still have little driving experience, or in some cases teenagers driving without a license. In the case that such a driver also uses a substandard car, risks are compounded. It is well known that exactly this type of highway user is most likely to be involved in accidents. This may happen either because the car suddenly breaks down with a flat tire or a boiling engine after which the inexperienced driver is unable to get to the side of the road safely, or because the driver takes too much risk – be it on purpose or not – or because he reacts inadequately to dangerous manoeuvres by other more experienced drivers. We all are familiar with big Mercedes driving too fast, forcing other cars to the side. An example of the latter in the global capital market is overlending by multinational banks.

There is an alternative explanation for the high frequency and severity of financial crises in emerging countries. In that explanation, psychological, social and cultural factors primarily determine investors' decisions in a way that turns financial markets into casinos. In that case, irrational speculators are the driving force behind the development of markets for stocks, bonds, and foreign exchange, see for instance Shiller

17 See World Economic Outlook, September 2003, chapter III for an overview of public debt dynamics in emerging countries.

18 Eichengreen (2002) notes that the degree of contagion differs between crises, suggesting it is especially lack of transparency (and differences therein) that determines the extent of contagion.

(1989, 2000). Especially fragile emerging economies may be the victim of such randomness in capital flows. In a situation like this, financial market prices still may satisfy the microefficiency assumption that prices incorporate all available information and are not predictable, but not the macroefficiency assumption reflecting underlying fundamentals. As a result, misallocation of capital may prevail as well as inappropriate restrictions on government policies, leading to important societal losses. If this were the case, many countries should perhaps consider staying away from the highway altogether. More and more often, economists recognise the importance of psychological factors in financial decision making possibly leading to herding phenomena etc. However, concluding that that is the fundamental problem behind most financial crises would be going too far. I am more inclined to agree with Willett (2000) that markets do their job in general, but may do so too much, too late. If market corrections take too long to happen, the ultimate reaction is too large, increasing the damage beyond what is necessary.

POSSIBLE SOLUTIONS

In summary, the foundation for a crisis appears to lie in a combination of insufficient or inappropriate institutional design of domestic and global financial markets, the unhappy combination of fixed exchange rates, low policy credibility and high capital mobility, and mistaken optimism – perhaps caused by unclear or incorrect incentives – from the side of both lenders and borrowers. Or, put differently: bad cars and bad drivers.

There is extensive literature on possible measures to prevent international financial crises and to manage them if prevention fails. Examples are Eichengreen (2002), Fischer (1999), Meltzer (2000), Mishkin (1999), and Rogoff (1999). An exhaustive account of the ideas and suggestions on the issue would extend beyond the scope of this paper. Nevertheless, some discussion is warranted. In principle two directions are possible: one is to think about improving the operation of global financial markets, the other is to constrain global financial markets with the extreme option of closing them completely. I start with discussing possibilities of improving market stability and efficiency.

General agreement exists on the need to improve domestic regulation and supervision of financial institutions and markets in developing countries in general and in partly globalised emerging economies in particular. Eliminating or at least reducing the fragility of the domestic financial system would take away one prime determinant of recent financial crises. Zingales (2003) – drawing on evidence from Guiso, Sapienza and Zingales (2002) – rejects the idea that integration into the global financial market can substitute for the development of domestic financial institutions and markets. He concludes that domestic financial markets will remain an important factor underlying economic growth. To this purpose, developing countries could open up domestic financial markets for foreign competition. In practice, it would imply that foreign banks open up store in emerging markets by establishing new subsidiaries or taking over existing banks. In a recent working paper, Berger et al. (2003) provide additional support for this point. They show empirically that the presence of a healthy system of small private community banks in particular contributes to SME lending and GDP growth. Moreover, they find that the presence of foreign banks on local financial markets in developing countries can play a similar positive role as domestic small private banks. In short, by improving on the quality and maintenance of their car, developing countries can reduce the risks of driving on the highway.

Other suggestions concern increased driving skills, less risky behaviour and better monitoring of actual driving by highway patrols. Some examples are given below.

Theoretical agreement exists with respect to the inconsistency of full global capital mobility, fixed exchange rates and autonomous monetary policy. However, in practice it could and should be more explicitly recognised. In particular, the commitment to full capital mobility in the setting of a fixed exchange rate regime may be hard to keep. It is true that fixing the exchange rate can temporarily help domestic stabilisation in an inflationary environment by building credibility, as argued by Frankel (1999). However, maintaining the peg for longer periods increases the likelihood of speculative pressures. In this respect, Domaç and Peria (2003) document that pegging the exchange rate on average does lead to stabilisation and a lower probability of crisis. But if a crisis nevertheless occurs, the costs are higher. Countries have, therefore, to carefully trade off credibility versus flexibility. Relying on a fixed exchange rate regime too long without appropriate side measures unavoidably leads to overvaluation and current account deficits with corresponding increases in foreign debt. The risk of a sudden withdrawal of capital then increases.[19] Overall, a fixed exchange rate regime may give both borrowers and lenders a false expectation of stability and thus may cause over borrowing and over lending, Flexible exchange rates may be better in making the actual risk transparent to both parties.

The next issue – this time one on which no general agreement exists – is the institutional set-up of international financial markets and the role of supranational organisations like the IMF and World Bank – in other words, the highway patrol system. When and how the IMF should provide emergency lending to countries in crisis and how structural such lending may become remains hotly debated. The same holds for the question of whether the IMF contributes to new crises through the creation of moral hazard by the expectation of bail-outs of countries and multinational banks. More transparency about the nature and degree of risk in international borrowing and lending in general would be a step forward, both to limit over borrowing and over lending and to avoid herding behaviour in the propagation of crises after some negative shock (Mishkin, 1999). The new Basel II agreement on capital adequacy standards provides a modest but promising approach. Hopefully, it will make multinational banks more careful in assessing the risks of foreign lending.

Additional grand ideas for improvement of the international financial system are the creation of a 'deep pocket' International Lender of Last Resort, An International

19 In recent research Kool, Ziesemer, Holle and Haselmann (2002, 2003) show this to be the case both for Latin American and Asian countries.

Financial Crisis Manager, an International Bankruptcy Court and a Global Financial Regulator. All of these suffer from the problem of lack of international enforcement. In the absence of a federal world government, as proposed by Moshirian (2003), it is hard to see how any of these ideas will fly.

Finally, most authors agree that developing countries should rely less on foreign currency debt, in particular bank loans, and more on equity participation and possibly tradable debt claims. That way, risk sharing between developed and developing countries can take place in a better way than has been the case so far. In theory and practice, FDI capital inflows are the best way for emerging economies to attract capital. These are less volatile, less subject to speculative behaviour and lead demonstrably to higher economic growth. Paradoxically, developing countries tend to be reluctant to liberalise FDI flows as they imply a transfer of ownership from domestic residents to foreigners, as reported by Eichengreen et al. (1998).[20] Instead, developing countries should recognise that foreign ownership of domestic firms not only brings in physical capital but also human capital.

Here, I would like to propose an idea coming from history. Nowadays, most FDI originates from multinational companies as part of their global operations. Private investors interested in equity tend to invest in emerging market stock funds. However, in the pre World War I period, the majority of FDI came directly from private investors, as documented by Eichengreen et al. (1998). Freestanding companies in Europe were incorporated with the explicit purpose of investing in mining, agriculture, and transportation in developing countries. This could be an interesting route nowadays as well channelling more long-term and less volatile risk-bearing capital to developing countries. One way to implement such strategy is to create venture capital type funds with the purpose of investing in promising new projects in developing countries. Venture capitalists would bring expertise and monitoring together with financial means into the project. Developing countries' governments would have an incentive to provide a stable and reliable environment for such investors. The country risk involved could be insured. Moreover developed countries' governments might be willing to subsidise this type of investment through the tax system. The Dutch government for example does so for investment in culture (Dutch movies), environmentally sound investment and corporate venture capital under strict conditions. It could do so as well for risk bearing direct investment in developing countries.

Risk sharing is also possible in a different way, using newly developed sophisticated financial derivatives in international financial markets. For a long time, Shiller (1993, 2003) has been an avid supporter of the creation of a global market for trading claims on a country's GDP. In a nutshell, he proposes to sell an asset that entitles the holders to a trivially small part of a specific country's GDP. If GDP turns out to be low, the payment (dividend) is low as well and the country has cheap funding; if GDP (growth) turns out high, the country pays more dividends but can afford to do so

20 Note that such feelings also exist in developed countries. Emotional resistance against the takeover of KLM by Air France is a recent example.

because its wealth is increasing – even though on an absolute level it is still poor. Of course, all sorts of variations can be thought of on the basis of this general principle. In practice, no such markets have developed yet, perhaps due to the lack of reliable GDP data for most developing countries. The complexity of the instrument per se is not larger than that for many popular financial products. One variation that has been tried in a limited way is the issuance of GDP-indexed debt where the level of the interest rate is made dependent on the country's performance in terms of its GDP. In my view, more attention for this type of financial instruments is clearly warranted.

The success of all of the above measures to improve the efficiency and stability of global financial markets in the end depends on the degree to which the incentive structure is appropriate and succeeds in having market participants make the right decisions, by improving the risk-return trade-off and by reducing moral hazard. No guarantees exist, however.

THE CASE FOR CAPITAL CONTROLS

Therefore, it is also useful to consider the alternative option to partly or fully close down external financial markets. In the academic literature, little enthusiasm exists for capital controls in one form or another, although ideas about it have been around for a long time. In practice, some countries like Chile and Malaysia have recently experimented with such controls. Their successfulness is still under discussion. See for instance Edwards (1999) and Willett (2000).

CONCLUSION

Perhaps the most important lesson is that the global capital market by itself is not a good or a bad thing; the same holds for the highway. Financial globalisation in itself is a good thing as it contributes to the expansion of the set of available investment and diversification opportunities. However, its users have more choices, both good ones and bad ones. In that respect financial globalisation is a two-edged sword. It allows risk sharing to minimise income and consumption volatility, but it also allows for risk-seeking behaviour. It facilitates both bad policies and good policies as Willett (2000) argues. In principle, increased financial integration can lead to more volatility in terms of both prices and quantities. If you participate in these markets, you can get hit and hurt. Thus the appropriate advice should be to participate only when everything is in order internally. A stabilised set of macroeconomic conditions and an adequate regulatory and supervisory design of the internal financial system appear to be the prime requirements. Even then, inadvertent events may hit a country. However, its vulnerability will be reduced and its robustness increased.

Even then, emerging economies appear to be extra vulnerable during the transition, as evidenced by both recent and historical evidence, see Eichengreen (2002). In 1989, Eichengreen and Lindert (1989) evaluated the 1980s international debt crisis, which at that time had been more or less resolved. They wrote:

> 'It seems equally clear that soon after debt/GNP and debt/export ratios have finally been reduced, probably by significant write-downs, there will be a new round of enthusiastic lending to developing countries. As we have noted, private creditors do not see any clear signal in the past history of repayment crises, despite the emergence of a problem-debtor tradition in may countries. Starting from low initial debt ratios, the creditors will probably return in a rush...Once the next crisis has hit, its festering will again bring considerable damage to the debtor economies.'

With hindsight, we can conclude they were unfortunately right. Apparently, both creditors and debtors make the same mistakes over and over again. At some point, over optimism prevails and overborrowing and overlending occur. At some point, the market will correct these mistakes, but too late and therefore too much. Overshooting increases costs significantly.

Learning from the past appears not to be easy. Nevertheless, we should try to implement history's lessons. It would be a pity if history were to repeat itself once again in the next decades. The chances are that it will.

In the future new groups of developing countries will want to reap the profits from further financial globalisation and rightfully so as the rewards are high. From the past we know that the transition period is difficult though. Each country should thus be allowed to do so in its own time and with a carefully selected sequence of liberalisation steps. In my speech today, I have indicated some directions.

The ongoing institutional development and design of both the internal and external financial system take a central place. Both will take considerable time. Nationally, economic stabilisation is foremost, followed by improvements in regulation and supervision of the financial sector. More in general, building social capital in its various dimensions should get more attention. Internationally, the global capital market's functioning should be improved through better transparency and information production. This may reduce uncertainty, improve decisions of both debtors and creditors and reduce the possibility of bubbles and runs. Reconsideration of the role played by supranational organisations like the IMF and World Bank is important in this respect. Overall, we should acknowledge that there are no quick solutions.

REFERENCES

Bekaert G., Harvey, C.R., & Lundblad, C.T. (2003). Equity Market Liberalization in Emerging Markets, *Federal Reserve Bank of St. Louis Review, July/August, 85, no. 4*, 53-74.

Berger A. N., Hasan, I., & Klapper, L.F. (2003). Further Evidence on the Link Between Finance and Growth: An International Analysis of Community Banking and Economic Performance. *Finance and Economics Discussion Series 2003-47*, Federal Reserve Board, Washington DC.

Caprio G., & Honohan, P. (1999). Restoring Banking Stability: Beyond Supervised Capital Requirements. *The Journal of Economic Perspectives*, *13 no. 4*, 43-64.

Copeland L.S. (2000), *Exchange Rates and International Finance*, Prentice Hall.

BIS (2002), *Triennial Central Bank Survey: Foreign Exchange and Derivatives Market Activity in 2001*. Basel, Switzerland.

Domaç I. and M.S. Martinez Peria (2003). Banking Crises and Exchange Rate Regimes: Is There a Link?, *Journal of International Economics*, *61*, 41-72.

Edwards S. (1999). How Effective Are Capital Controls? *The Journal of Economic Perspectives, 13 no. 4*, 65-84.

Efferink L., Kool, C., & Veen, T. van, (2003). Country Risk Analysis, *Financiële Monetaire Studies, 21 no. 4,* Amsterdam: NIBE.

Eichengreen B., & Lindert, P. (1989). *The International Debt Crisis in Historical Perspective*. MIT Press.

Eichengreen B., Mussa, M., Dell'Ariccia, G., Detragiache, E., Milesi-Ferreti,G.M., & Tweedie, A. (1998). Capital Account Liberalization: Theoretical and Practical Aspects. *IMF Occasional Paper 172*, Washington DC.

Favara G. (2003), An Empirical Reassessment of the Relationship Between Finance and Growth. *IMF working paper WP/03/123*, Washington DC.

Fischer S. (1999). On the Need for an International Lender of Last Resort, *The Journal of Economic Perspectives*, *13, no. 4*, 85-104.

Frankel J.A. (1999), No Single Currency Regime is Right for All Countries or at All Times. *Essays in International Finance no. 215,* Princeton University Press.

Garretsen H., Ees, H. van, Groeneveld, H.,& Haas, R. de (1999). *Anatomie van Financiële Crises*. Academic Service.

Glick R., Moreno, R., & Spiegel, M.M. (Eds.) (2001). *Financial Crises in Emerging Markets*. Cambridge University Press.

Guiso L., Sapienza, P., & Zingales, L. (2000). The Role of Social Capital in Financial Development. *NBER Working Paper 7563*.

Guiso L., Sapienza, P., & Zingales, L. (2002). Does Local Financial Development Matter? *NBER Working Paper 8923*.

International Monetary Fund (2003a), *Global Financial Stability Report: Market Developments and Issues*, September, Washington DC.

International Monetary Fund (2003b), *World Economic Outlook*, September, Washington DC.

Kool C., Ziesemer, T., Haselmann, R., & Holle, S. (2002). Sovereign Risk and Simple Debt Dynamics: The Case of Brazil and Argentina. *Universiteit Maastricht working paper*.

Kool C., Ziesemer, T., Haselmann, R., & Holle, S. (2003). Sovereign Risk and Simple Debt Dynamics in Asia. *MERIT working paper 2003-02*.

LaPorta R., Lopez de Silanes, F., Schleifer, A., & Vishny, R.W. (1999). The Quality of Government. *Journal of Law, Economics, and Organization*, *March, 15*, 222-279.

Levine R. (1997). Financial Development and Economic Growth: Views and Agenda. *The Journal of Economic Literature*, *35*, 688-726.

Levine R. (2003). More on Finance and Growth: More Finance, More Growth? *Federal Reserve Bank of St. Louis Review*, *July/August, 85, no. 4*, 31-46.

Meltzer A.H. (2000). *Report of the International Financial Institution Advisory Commission* (chairman), Washington DC. Retrieved from (http://phantom-x.gsia.cmu.edu/IFIAC.

Mishkin F.S. (1999). Global Financial Instability: Framework, Events, Issues. *The Journal of Economic Perspectives*, *13, no. 4,* 3-20.

Moshirian F. (2003). Globalization and Financial Market Integration. *Journal of Multinational Financial Management, 13*, 289-302.

Obstfeld M. (1998). The Global Capital Market: Benefactor or Menace? *The Journal of Economic Perspectives, vol 12, no. 4*, 9-30.
Prasad E., Rogoff, K., Wei, S.-J., & Kose, M.A. (2003. Effects of Financial Globalization on Developing Countries: Some Empirical Evidence. *March, working paper IMF.* Washington DC.
Rogoff K. (1999). International Institutions for Reducing Global Financial Instability. *The Journal of Economic Perspectives, 13, no. 4*, 21-42.
Rousseau P.E. (2003). Historical Perspectives on Financial Development and Economic Growth. *Federal Reserve Bank of St. Louis Review, July/August, 85, no. 4*, 81-106.
Shiller R.J. (1989). *Market Volatility.* MIT Press.
Shiller R.J. (1993). *Macro Markets.* Oxford University Press.
Shiller R.J. (2000). *Irrational Exuberance.* Princeton University Press.
Shiller R.J. (2003). *The New Financial Order: Risk in the 21st Century.* Princeton University Press.
Stiglitz J. (2002). *Globalization and Its Discontents.* Norton & Company, New York.
Weller C.E. (1999). Financial Crises After Financial Liberalization: Exceptional Circumstances or Structural Weakness. *ZEI Working Paper B15*, Bonn.
Willett T.D. (2000). International Financial Markets as Sources of Crises or Discipline: The Too Much, Too Late Hypothesis. *Essays in International Finance no. 218,* Princeton University Press.
Zingales L. (2003). Comment on 'More on Finance and Growth: More Finance, More Growth?'. *Federal Reserve Bank of St. Louis Review, July/August, 85, no. 4*, 47-52.

J.H. GARRETSEN[1]

FROM KOOPMANS TO KRUGMAN: INTERNATIONAL ECONOMICS AND GEOGRAPHY

INTRODUCTION

One look out of the window is enough to conclude that economic activities are not neatly distributed over space. Seen from a satellite, the nightly image of our planet shows a concentration of lights across northern America, Europe and parts of Asia, especially Japan, India and China. Assuming that the concentration of lights is indicative of agglomeration or clustering, it is clear that, worldwide, economic activities show an uneven spread. This is also true for the distribution within countries, such as we see, for example, in the US. Based on this fact, one would be inclined to conclude that the question of 'who does what where' occupies a central place in economics. This, however, is not the case. For a long time, the third W, that of 'where', which refers to the importance of location or the geography of economic activities, was hardly ever considered an issue by economists. It is only in the last few years that the relevance of geography for economics has been rediscovered. In this lecture, I hope to explain why the interest in the geographical aspects of economics has to be applauded (certainly in Utrecht), and why it has taken so long for the (re-)discovery of geography to become a fact. I shall answer the second question first, and subsequently try to indicate why economists and also geographers should rejoice in the new developments.[2]

---

1 An abbreviated version of the inaugural lecture was delivered (in Dutch) on 23 October 2003 at Utrecht University. I thank Steven Brakman, Charles van Marrewijk, and Rina de Vries for their comments. I should also like to thank Rina de Vries for her translation of the lecture from Dutch into English. Finally, I should like to express my gratitude to Marius Brülhart, Ron Martin, Marcel Canoy, Albert van der Horst, and other participants for their contributions to the research seminar of 23 October, which preceded this lecture.

2 For obvious reasons, many issues cannot be addressed in this 30-minute speech. I gladly refer to the inaugural lectures of my close colleagues Steven Brakman and Charles van Marrewijk. Fate (or fortune) has caused a spontaneous clustering here, for it must be quite unique that, within the time-span of a mere fortnight, inaugural lectures were being held at three different Dutch universities, on more or less the same theme, all of which were based to a great extent on long-lasting, collaborative research efforts. As regards our (coincidental) division of labour: in my own contribution, the history of the origin and policy implications of geographical economics occupy a central place, whereas in Brakman (2003) and Van Marrewijk (2003) the emphasis lies on, respectively, empirical relevance and dynamic aspects.

P. de Gijsel and H. Schenk (eds.), Multidisciplinary Economics, 425–436 .

KOOPMANS AND INDIVISIBILITIES

The research institute of the Utrecht School of Economics (USE) is named after the winner of the Nobel Prize for economics Tjalling C. Koopmans, who read mathematics and physics here in Utrecht. Koopmans studied many subfields of economics, one of which was location theory. He explained why the attempts of economists to incorporate location or geography into their analyses often bear such a strenuous character. In his well-known publication of 1957, *Three Essays on the State of Economic Science*, Koopmans expressed, amongst others, his view on which requirements an economic theory has to meet if a useful analysis of the spatial distribution of economic activities is to be arrived at. Stated more precisely, he concentrated on the question what is needed to make this spatial distribution, and so economic geography, an endogenous variable. In other words: how can one make the location decisions of economic agents result from the analysis, instead of these being fixed in advance?

Koopmans' answer to this fundamental question was briefly as follows. We can only begin to understand the importance of location or geography for economics if we recognise the fact that economic activities are not infinitely divisible. If economic agents were physically able to divide themselves always and everywhere without costs, location or geography would not matter in the least. Everybody would be indifferent to their choice of location. In a hypothetical world of perfect divisibility, it would be impossible to explain why, as we observe in the real world, a certain amount of clustering or agglomeration of activities occurs at nearly every level of aggregation. For example, the existence and location of the city of Utrecht, the concentration of Utrecht University in certain city areas, yes, even our gathering today in the university hall can only be explained if we presuppose indivisibility. Or, in Koopmans' words, *'Without recognising indivisibilities – in human person, in residences, plants, equipment, and in transportation – ... location patterns, down to those of the smallest village, cannot be understood'*. (Koopmans, 1957, p. 154)

Now some of you no doubt think that one need not be a Nobel Prize winner to arrive at this insight. It goes without saying that if everything and everybody could be partitioned infinitely into identical smaller parts, transport would become redundant and take neither time nor effort. The question *where* something is located would lose its relevance in such a case. Was Koopmans merely stating the obvious, then? As it has turned out, he was not, certainly not when it comes to the development of economic theory. Applied to firms, for instance, Koopmans' 'insight of indivisibility' means that, economically speaking, production takes place with increasing returns of scale. Such scale effects can take many forms, yet the basic idea is always that the average costs decline if the size of the production of a firm or industry increases. If this is true, it follows that firms will not always and everywhere be encountered in space. Quite the reverse: they will only be found in one or several locations, to which they must get the required *inputs* delivered, and from which they themselves must deliver *outputs* to the consumer. Choosing one's location involves striking a balance between the benefits of scale that can be obtained in a certain place, and the costs of transport that are involved in obtaining *inputs* and delivering *outputs*. This means that the location choices of other economic agents are relevant to the assessment of the suitability of a location as well.

Indeed, to explain patterns of agglomeration, it is important to consider transportation costs and increasing returns of scale in *combination* with each other (Fuijta & Thisse, 2002).

BETWEEN KOOPMANS AND KRUGMAN

The consequence of Koopmans' line of reasoning is that the observed uneven spatial spread of economic activities can only be explained if economic theory allows for transportation costs, increasing returns of scale and, in the case of internal scale economies, imperfect competition. However, the problem used to be that the mother of all economic theories, the general equilibrium theory, did not provide for these essential building blocks. The major challenge was, therefore, to formulate a new theory in which the location or geography of economic activities followed from the model, while, at the same time, the core features of equilibrium theory, in particular the requirement that all decisions can be traced back to the behaviour of individual economic agents, were retained.

For a long time, it seemed impossible to meet the challenge such as set by Koopmans in 1957. This was not always perceived as a problem, though. From the 1950s onwards, the need to unite geography with the general equilibrium theory became less and less urgent to economists and, in particular, geographers who thought that equilibrium theory was the wrong starting point for location theory at any rate, no matter which shape such a theory was to take. Up till the present day, the frequent (sometimes heated) discussions that take place, both in Utrecht and elsewhere, between economists and geographers about location issues, boil down in essence to the age-old difference of opinion about the sense and nonsense of the general equilibrium theory, upon which mainstream economics is based (see Brakman, Garretsen & van Marrewijk, 2001, Ch. 11, and Brakman & Garretsen, 2003).

It was only as late as the end of the previous century, in 1991 to be precise, that Koopmans' request for the endogenisation of the role of geography, within the framework of a general equilibrium model, was met. The American economist Paul Krugman (1991a, b, c) was responsible for this breakthrough. In Krugman's model, nothing is imposed in advance upon the geography or spatial distribution of economic activities. The individual location decisions of mobile firms and employees indeed determine the ultimate spatial distribution in this model, as well as the way in which this distribution shifts if economic circumstances change, such as, for instance, in case of a decline in the costs of international trade. The work of Krugman and associates has become known as the *new economic geography*, a somewhat smug label which has vexed many geographers, who are of the opinion that Krugman's model does not contain much that is new, and that he does not practise geography, but at the most bad economics, because his model is based upon the general equilibrium theory (see, for instance, Martin, 1999). Together with my research colleagues, Steven Brakman and Charles van Marrewijk, I therefore suggested replacing the contentious label *new economic geography* with that of *geographical economics*. Not only does this term avoid creating the impression of an imperialistic attempt being made by economists to usurp geography, it also better reflects the central issue at hand, namely, trying to give geography a place in mainstream economics.

Before proceeding with my discussion on the importance of Krugman's model of 1991, which can be designated as the protomodel of geographical economics, I shall first address the following question: did economic science pay no attention at all, then, to the importance of geography between 1957 and 1991? Quite the contrary. For example, in my own research field of international economics, Paul Samuelson (1952) stressed the crucial role of transportation costs as early as in the 1950s. Also, much empirical research has been conducted on the importance of distance for the explanation of (bilateral) trade flows. The gravity equation introduced by, amongst others, Jan Tinbergen (1962) shows that trade flows can be accounted for remarkably well by the GDPs of the countries involved (the more mass, the more mutual trade) and their distance from each other (the greater the distance, the less trade there is). However, this gravity equation was still no more than a (very robust) empirical relationship, which lacked any clear theoretical foundations. Theories of international trade in which geography does play a role, such as the well-known Heckscher-Ohlin theory, have the drawback of geographical characteristics being fixed in the models and treated as exogenous: the focus lies on trade that stems from given relative differences in natural resources, climate, or access to the sea. Such geographical elements are certainly not irrelevant, by the way, and recently much research has been done on the importance of physical geography when explaining differences in economic development: see Mellinger, Sachs & Gallup (2000), Sachs (2003), Easterly & Levine (2002), and Acemoglu et al. (2001). However, in all these analyses the endogenisation of geography does not take place.

Remarkably enough, in 1980 during his stay at Yale University, Krugman developed an innovative model in which many ingredients (but not all!) could be encountered of the analysis of 'indivisibilities' that Koopmans had advocated. In Krugman (1980), we find increasing returns of scale, imperfect competition and transportation costs, which means that many of the elements needed for the analysis of 'indivisibilities' are there. The 1980 model can be considered a real breakthrough, in particular because of its successful attempt to incorporate the market form of imperfect competition in a simple but very manageable way. With respect to the latter, Krugman made grateful use of the analysis of monopolistic competition by Dixit and Stiglitz (1977).

An aside: in 1957, Koopmans worked at the Cowles Foundation of Yale, which is located at 30 Hillhouse Avenue in New Haven. Krugman developed his important model years later, literally across the road from where Koopmans used to sit, at 27 Hillhouse Avenue. Indeed, even economists and their ideas seem to cluster in space. And as a small footnote to this intellectual clustering, Steven Brakman, Charles van Marrewijk and myself first began, without realising the coincidence, our textbook on geographical economics (Brakman, Garretsen & van Marrewijk, 2001) in the very same location, at 56 Hillhouse Avenue. Perhaps the famous (and infamous) geographer Ellsworth Huntington was right, after all, when he named New Haven as the place with the best 'climate' in the world (quoted in Landes, 1998), although it has to be said that Huntington was referring to the physical rather than the mental milieu.[3]

But let me return to the main theme again. Between 1957 and 1991, some advances took place not only in international economics, but in the analysis of the relevance of geography as well. In other fields of economic science, too, theory was on the move. Also, in regional and urban economics progress was being made with the incorporation of elements such as transportation costs and (external) returns of scale. Nevertheless, there was constantly something lacking in these 'pre-1991' theoretical developments. Most analyses were only partial in nature, and too often that which had to be explained, namely, the spatial distribution of economic activities, was still being presupposed. Even in Krugman's forerunner model of 1980 the spatial distribution of the supply and demand for goods was treated as an exogenous entity. All in all, at the beginning of 1991 the state of affairs was such that, despite much ingenious wizardry with alternative models and some genuinely made progress (especially with regard to the analysis of the market form of imperfect competition), the rabbit was still pushed into the hat, instead of being pulled out. The importance of location or geography did not follow from the analysis, but was, at least partly, treated as a given.

KRUGMAN 1991 AND BEYOND

The protomodel of geographical economics which Krugman developed in 1991 strongly resembles his own model of 1980. Nearly all features of the earlier model resurface 11 years later: transportation costs, increasing returns of scale, and the convenient analysis of the market form of imperfect competition (Ottaviano & Thisse, 2003; Head & Mayer, 2003). However, there is one significant difference as compared to 1980: a part of the firms *and* the labour population is now mobile, which means to say that these agents have to make their own location decisions. In particular the mobility of labour is crucial in the 1991 model, for it implies that the spatial distribution of the demand for goods is not a given either – after all, workers also occupy the role of consumers of the goods that firms produce. This crucial element, the *endoge-*

3 Hillhouse Avenue, in particular, has appealed to many people over the years. Rumour has it that after his first visit to the US, Charles Dickens declared Hillhouse Avenue the most beautiful street in New Haven. It is certainly clear from Dickens' *American Notes* that New Haven and, as it was then still called, Yale College pleased him a great deal (contrary to most other places in the US and Canada he saw on his journey) when he visited New Haven in February 1842; see Dickens (1842, p. 125). The vilification of Huntington, and with him of geography, in the US after the Second World War was partly the result of the often-condemned way in which Huntington and others tried to seek an explanation for economic underdevelopment in physical geography and other given (racial) characteristics of certain societies. The cloud of supposed racism surrounding geography in the middle of the 20th century contributed to the removal of geography as a subject from the curriculum of some American universities. Notably, though, in the last few years there has been a revival of interest in the importance of physical geography for economic development. The work of some economists I mentioned earlier, such as Dani Rodrik, Jeffrey Sachs, and Daron Acemoglu, testifies to this.

nous location of demand, distinguishes Krugman 1991 from Krugman 1980. Why did it take no less than 11 years before Krugman apparently became capable of making this addition? It remains guesswork, but it is my surmise that he bought his first PC at the end of the 1980s, or at least a package of simulation software. As it is, Krugman's model of the geographical economy with her mobile firms and production factors cannot be solved analytically. The eventual spatial equilibrium of firms and employees (i.e. who settles where) has to be determined by means of computer simulations.

Afterwards, too, solvable variants of the model have been found, and numerous refinements have been made (see Fuijta, Krugman & Venables, 1999; Fuijta & Thisse, et al., 2002; Baldwin et al., 2003). In the core, though, the main message of all these later models is still the same as in Krugman (1991a), namely, that,

> the spatial distribution of economic activities, and so the underlying location choices of economic agents, results from a strongly nonlinear interplay between forces of agglomeration and spread, whose outcome *cannot* be stated in advance.

What does this mean? Well, first of all, it means that agglomeration or – seen from a dynamic perspective – divergence, as well as an even spread or convergence can be equilibria. What happens exactly depends to a great extent on the initial conditions, and the changes that occur in the economic situation. In the protomodel, for example, a decline in transportation costs below a certain critical threshold leads to a situation where the stable spreading equilibrium (all economic activities are distributed evenly over space) suddenly changes into an unstable equilibrium, as a result of which agglomeration (a very unequal distribution of activities) becomes the new stable equilibrium. I deliberately use the word 'suddenly' here, because the nonlinearity in the world of geographical economics also implies that changes in economic circumstances, whether or not due to policy measures, need not affect the location choices for a long period of time, but can cause an abrupt landslide thereafter. I shall return to this point later.

Let me first try and illustrate the way in which Krugman's model and related models work. I should like to discuss Figure 1 with you.

On the horizontal axis, the degree of economic integration (in model terms, the transportation costs) is indicated, while the vertical axis displays the share of region or country I in the total of all mobile activity. For the sake of convenience, let us assume that there are two regions, with region II being the mirror image of region I. In the case of only a minor degree of economic integration (to the left of point A), the spreading of economic activities will be perfect: region I and region II both contain exactly one half of all activity. Beyond point A, further integration leads to agglomeration (region I 'wins', as it were). If integration increases even further, the point will be reached (B) were spreading gains in importance again. The exact mechanisms behind this 'bell-shaped curve' are not relevant here (for an explanation, see Puga, 1999);[4] what matters

4 The bell-shaped curve does not follow from Krugman (1991), but results if, as has been done in many models since Krugman (1991), one imposes constraints inter alia on the interregional mobility of labour. See Puga (1999).

is that the curve shows that the effect of economic integration on the spatial distribution of activities between the two regions is not linear. Both agglomeration and spreading can continue for a long time, and increasing economic integration has not a smooth, uniform or unequivocal effect. In reference to curves such as the one displayed in Figure 1, Krugman himself, too, speaks of the 'lumpiness' that characterises these models.

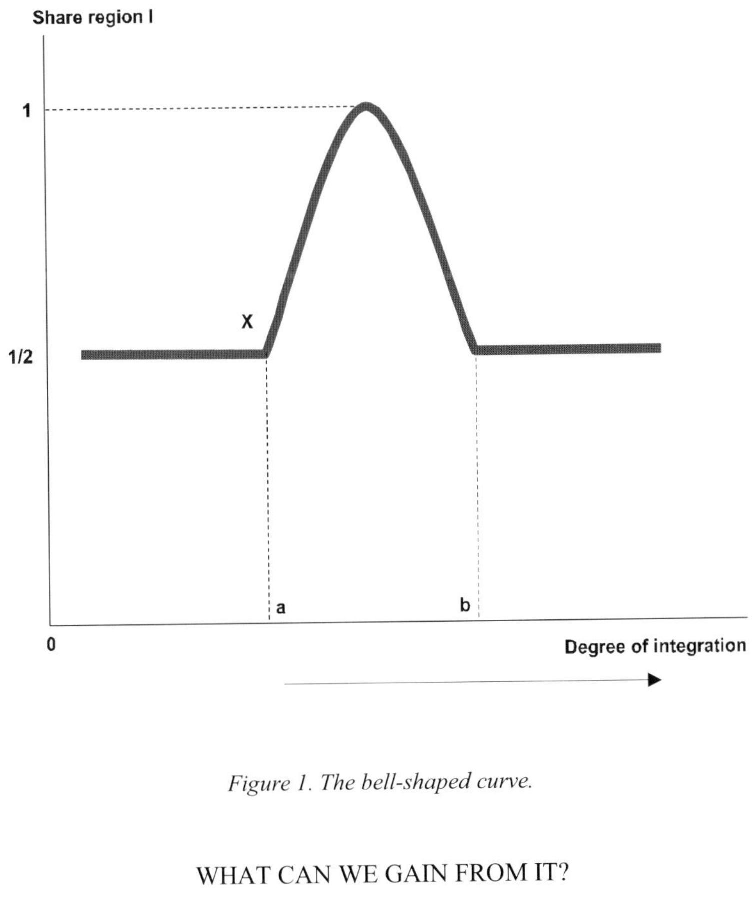

Figure 1. The bell-shaped curve.

WHAT CAN WE GAIN FROM IT?

With their endogenisation of the spatial distribution of economic activities, Krugman and his fellow researchers have successfully met the challenge as set by Koopmans. Yet the question remains whether and how the rest of the world can profit from their achievements. In the final part of my speech, I should therefore like to concentrate on the policy implications and empirical relevance of geographical economics. To start with the former, potentially geographical economics has important implications for policy, which differ in a *qualitative* sense from those offered by current, 'geography-less' economics, on which – either implicitly or explicitly – most economic policy is based. I shall confine myself here to one striking example, which refers back to the curve I have just shown, and which follows directly from the nonlinearity that characterises the underlying models. The same example will also come in handy later as an illustration of the empirical relevance of geographical economics.

The example concerned is the so-called *threshold-effect* (Baldwin et al., 2003, pp. 277 ff.). Policy measures will only have an effect on the spatial distribution of economic activities if these measures reach a certain critical mass. An increase in the degree of economic integration (see Figure 1) can either have no impact or a huge one, depending on the initial economic situation. The possibility of a nonlinear impact of policy measures means that it can be very misleading to take the standard approach to policy analysis, which uses only a marginal model, and base one's expectations of the effects of future policy on linear extrapolation of the past. The reason for the threshold-effect and, basically, for the aforementioned *lumpiness* is that, even though *a priori* there exists a high degree of flexibility of choice of location and the resultant spatial distribution of economic activities, *once* these choices have been made, the spatial pattern turns out to be highly rigid (Ottaviano, 2003). The advantages of a chosen location have a tendency of reinforcing themselves, and the choice of location will only be reconsidered if policy interventions acquire enough mass to outdo (accumulated) benefits. Stated differently, the threshold-effect in the Krugmanian world can be traced back to the 'putty clay' character of geography (Fuijta & Thisse, 2002). (The latter term would probably appeal to my former PhD supervisor, Simon Kuipers: it clearly echoes the 'putty-clay' element in the vintage approach advocated by him for the analysis of changes in the capital stock).

Apart from the threshold-effect, there are at least five other policy implications that present an alternative view on the impact of policy on the economy (see Ottaviano, 2003). Considered separately, these implications are not always unique to geographical economics, but taken together they certainly are. The realisation that the economy and policy operate differently to in the world of the bell-shaped curve, still does not answer the question of the practical or, if you will, empirical relevance of the geographical approach. The short reply to this question is that the actual facts of the spatial distribution and growth of economic activity suggest (!) that, in the real world, *lumpiness* is the rule. As a satellite photo shows, agglomeration can be discerned at several levels (globally, nationally, regionally, or at the level of the city). However, agglomeration is far from complete and, depending on changes in the specific economic situation, it can develop in the course of time, leading to either stronger or weaker patterns of clustering.

Regrettably, a definite answer to the fundamental question of the empirical relevance of geographical economics lies beyond the scope of my speech. However, recent research supports the idea that, potentially, the relevance of geographical economics is very great indeed. First of all, research is being done in which the new models, such as the one on which the bell-shaped curve is based, are being tested *themselves*. One could ask, for instance, whether it is at all possible to make useful estimations of the most important model parameters, such as the 'degree of economic integration' mentioned in Figure 1. The answer to this question is affirmative (I refer the reader to Brakman, 2003; Brakman, Garretsen & Schramm, 2003 a, b; for a very good *survey*, see Head & Mayer, 2003). With this reassurance in mind, we can then proceed to investigate the contribution that the new models can make to the field of international economics. Important recent examples are the application of geographical models to topics such as globalisation, economic (under-)development and – see hereafter – the European integration. Some highly readable and accessible studies on globalisation and economic development are Crafts & Venables (2001), World Bank (2002), Easterly (2001), and van Marrewijk (2003).[5] The shared feature of all these applications is that they show why current economic analyses are (possibly) too simplistic. Most analyses that are being made at present are characterised by an *all or nothing* approach: globalisation is, as if by definition, either good or bad; economic integration always does or does not enhance inequality. The (political) colour of the analysis paints the picture, one could say.

A DIFFERENT VIEW OF EUROPEAN INTEGRATION

Let me now turn to the example of the economic integration of the European Union. Two clear questions involved are the following,

1) In the case of a fully free exchange of labour, and particularly capital, does there remain any scope for national policy?
2) What are the effects of further integration (think of the extension of the EU) on the location choices of the mobile production factors, in particular that of capital?

The standard answer to the first question is that national policy has only little scope left, and national governments are practically forced to dance to the tune of the production factor capital. In this view of the world, if a country's corporate tax rates exceed those of the other EU members by only a minor degree, punishment follows directly: firms will leave for the country with the lowest tax rates. Stated differently, we would be living in a world of policy competition and the notorious *race to the bottom*. The customary answer to the second query, about the effects of further integration, states that the extension of the EU to the east will have a *uniform* and linear impact, with the standard assumption being made that a more equal spatial distribution of economic activities will arise as a result. The European Commission, for one, likes to propagate this idea.

However, if we remember the threshold-effect which we discussed earlier, the answers to both of these questions are rather different (and more in line with reality!). With respect to the supposed annihilation of the scope for national policy, the threshold-effect implies that firms will not leave an agglomeration at the first unpleasant tax difference, but only move out if the economic benefits of being located in the agglomeration are undone by the push of higher taxes and/or the pull of location subsidies in peripheral countries (see, for an argumentation of this point, de Mooij, Gorter &

5 For an extensive theoretical analysis of the effects of globalisation within the framework of geographical economics, see Peeters (2001). A more detailed explanation is given by Peeters and Garretsen (2003).

Nahuis, 2003; and de Mooij, 2003). This insight not only modifies the idea of a reduced scope for national policy, it also explains why the reality of the EU does not show a *race to the bottom* (with respect to, for instance, corporate tax rates). If one realises, moreover, that the net benefit of staying put is also determined by the social and physical infrastructure as created by national policy makers themselves, it becomes clear that geographical economics offers a different view on economic integration and its consequences for national policy (Brakman, Garretsen & van Marrewijk, 2002).

Does this also apply to our second question, about the effects of (further) integration of the EU? The theoretical answer to this has already been given: the bell-shaped curve clearly shows that integration will have no uniform, linear impact. The (initial) level of economic integration determines whether or not an effect will be felt, and also whether the spatial distribution of economic activities will move towards more agglomeration or less (i.e. whether redistribution will take place towards established EU countries or towards the newcomers). Where exactly on the curve the EU must be positioned is an empirical matter. The first estimates, the result of joint research by the Central Planning Bureau (CPB), USE and the University of Groningen, as presented here today by Marcel Canoy and Albert van der Horst, tentatively indicate that in most regions and sectors of the EU the agglomeration regime has yet to begin, or has barely begun.[6] This implies that, ultimately, further economic integration will lead to increasing agglomeration. For example, our preliminary estimates suggest that if the distance between two EU regions is about 600 kilometres, we arrive at point X in Figure 1. For regions that lie further apart, the 'preagglomeration' regime (the horizontal part of the bell curve to the left of A) is relevant and agglomeration has not really started yet. With X as a reference point, an increase in economic integration will stimulate agglomeration or clustering, which means that future satellite photos of Europe will show an even bigger contrast between dark and light zones than they do now. For the methodology of the research results discussed, I refer to Head & Mayer (2003, section 7) and Puga (1999, 2002).

CONCLUSION

As I hope to have shown, the interface between economics and geography is in a state of high and fruitful flux. For the first time in many years, economists are paying serious attention to the geographical aspects of economics. Whether this means that they take geography and geographers seriously enough as well is another question, yet to me, it seems important for both disciplines to continue their collaboration. This collaboration has already become quite successful in Utrecht, in my view. The Utrecht School of Economics (USE) tries to give the trio *space, history, and institutions* a prominent place

6 For a more elaborate discussion of these estimates, as well as of the contributions made by Ron Martin and Marius Brülhart to the seminar 'economic integration of the EU and the empirical relevance of the new economic geography' of 23 October 2003, I refer to the relevant chapters elsewhere in this volume.

in its research and certainly, too, in its tuition. It is clear that the subject of my lecture concurs with this.

How will geographical economics proceed from here? Personally, I think that, 12 years after the publication of Krugman's breakthrough model plus an outpour of (often very abstract) theoretical work, there is first and foremost the need for theory-driven empirical research, and also for models that are better geared to specific (policy) issues (see also Neary, 2001). Hopefully, empirical research will provide more insight into the nature of agglomeration factors. With regard to models aimed at answering certain concrete questions, the inclusion of institutions in these models will be relevant. The big challenge is to continue to combine Krugman's art and courage of making strongly simplified assumptions with Koopmans' theoretical solidity.

REFERENCES

Acemoglu, D., Johnson, S., & Robinson, J.A. (2001). The Colonial Origins of Comparative Development: An Empirical Investigation, *American Economic Review, 91*, 1369-1401.

Baldwin, R., Forslid, R., Martin, Ph., Ottaviano, G., & Robert-Nicoud, F. (2003). *Economic Geography and Public Policy,* Princeton University Press.

Brakman, S., Garretsen, H., & Marrewijk, Ch. van. (2001). *An Introduction to Geographical Economics,* Cambridge University Press.

Brakman, S, Garretsen, H., & Marrewijk, Ch. van. (2002). Locational Competition and Agglomeration: the Role of Government Spending, *CESifo Working Paper,* München.

Brakman, S. (2003). Duitsland op het Grensvlak tussen Economie en Geografie (Germany on the Interface between Economics and Geography), *inaugural lecture, 17 October 2003*, University of Nijmegen.

Brakman, S., & Garretsen, H. (2003). Rethinking the 'New' Geographical Economics. *Regional Studies, 37 (6/7),* 637-649.

Brakman, S., Garretsen, H., & Schramm, M. (2003a). Estimating the Helpman-Hanson Model for Germany, *Journal of Regional Science,* forthcoming, see: http://www.uu.nl/uupublish/tjallingckoopman/publications/discussionpapers/28406main.html

Brakman, S., Garretsen, H., & Schramm, M. (2003b). The Strategic Bombing of German Cities during WWII and its Impact on City Growth. *Journal of Economic Geography,* forthcoming, see: http://www.uu.nl/uupublish/ tjallingckoopman/publications/discussionpapers/28406main.html

Crafts, N., & Venables, A.J. (2001). Globalization in History: A Geographical Perspective, *CEPR Discussion Paper, 3079*, London.

Dickens, Ch. (1842). *American Notes for General Circulation*, London: Penguin.

Dixit, A., & Stiglitz, J. (1977). Monopolistic Competition and Optimal Product Diversity, *American Economic Review, 67,* 297-308.

Easterly, W. (2001). *The Elusive Quest for Growth, Economists Adventures and Misadventures in the Tropics,* MIT Press.

Easterly W., & Levine, R.(2002). Tropics, Germs, and Crops, How Endowments Influence Economic Development, *NBER Working Paper, no. 9106*, Cambridge Mass.

Fujita, M., Krugman, P., & Venables, A.J. (1999). *The Spatial Economy,* MIT Press.

Fujita, M., & Thisse, J-F. (2002). *The Economics of Agglomeration,* Cambridge University Press.

Head, K., & Mayer, Th. (2003). The Empirics of Agglomeration and Trade. In V. Henderson and J-F. Thisse (Eds.), *Handbook of Regional and Urban Economics, vol. IV*, Amsterdam: North-Holland, forthcoming.

Koopmans, Tj.C. (1957). *Three Essays on the State of Economic Science,* New York: McGraw-Hill.

Krugman, P. (1980). Scale economies, product differentiation, and the pattern of trade, *American Economic Review, 70,* 950-959.

Krugman, P. (1991a). Increasing Returns and Economic Geography, *Journal of Political Economy, 99,* 483-499.

Krugman, P. (1991b). History versus Expectations, *Quarterly Journal of Economics, 106,* 651-667.

Krugman, P. (1991c). *Geography and Trade,* Cambridge: MIT Press.
Landes, D. (1998). *The Wealth of Nations,* Londen: Abacus.
Marrewijk, Ch. van, Economische Groei en Agglomeratie (Economic Growth and Agglomeration), *inaugural lecture, 31 October 2003*, Erasmus University Rotterdam.
Martin, R. (1999). The New 'Geographical Turn' in Economics: Some Critical Reflections, *Cambridge Journal of Economics, 23,* 63-91.
Mellinger, A.D., Sachs, J.D., & Gallup, J.L. (2000). Climate, Coastal Proximity and Development. In G.L. Clark, M.P. Feldman and M.S. Gertler (Eds.), *The Oxford Handbook of Economic Geography,* (pp. 169-195). Oxford: Oxford University Press.
Mooij, R. de, Gorter, J., & Nahuis, R. (2003) In de Slag om Bedrijvigheid: Theorie en Praktijk van Vestigingsplaatsconcurrentie. In S. Brakman and H. Garretsen (Eds.), *Locatie en Concurrentie,* (Location and Competition), (pp. 92-123). Preadviezen 2003 Koninklijke Vereniging voor de Staathuishoudkunde.
Mooij, R. de. (2003). Heeft de Vennootschapsbelasting een Toekomst? (Does the Corporate Tax Rate Have a Future?), *inaugural lecture, 21 November 2003*, Erasmus University Rotterdam.
Neary, P. (2001). Of Hype and Hyperbolas: Introducing the New Economic Geography, *Journal of Economic Literature, 39,* 536-561.
Ottaviano, G.I.P. (2003). Regional Policy in the Global Economy: Insights from the New Economic Geography, *Regional Studies, 37(6/7),* 665-675.
Ottaviano, G.I.P., & Thisse, J-F. (2003). On economic geography in economic theory: increasing returns and pecuniary externalities. In V. Henderson and J-F. Thisse (Eds.), *Handbook of Regional and Urban Economics, vol. IV,* North-Holland, forthcoming.
Peeters , J.J.W. (2001). Globalisation, Location, and Labour Markets, *PhD-thesis*, University of Nijmegen.
Peeters, J.J.W., & Garretsen, H. (2003). Globalisation, Wages and Unemployment: An Economic Geography Perspective. In S. Brakman and B. Heijdra (Eds.), *The Monopolistic Competition Revolution in Retrospect,* (pp. 236-261). Cambridge University Press.
Puga, D. (1999). The Rise and Fall of Regional Inequalities, *European Economic Review, 43(2),* 303-335.
Puga, D. (2002). European Regional Policies in the Light of Recent Location Theories, *Journal of Economic Geography, 2,* 372-406.
Sachs, J.D. (2003). Institutions Don't Rule: Direct Effects of Geography on Per Capita Income, *NBER Working Paper, no. 9490*, Cambridge Mass.
Samuelson, P.A. (1952). The Transfer Problem and Transport Costs: the Terms of Trade when Impediments are Absent, *Economic Journal, 62*, 278-304.
Tinbergen, J. (1962) *Shaping the World Economy,* the 20th Century Fund, New York.
World Bank, (2002) *Globalization, Growth and Poverty,* Washington.

INDEX